BLACK THEATER

BLACK THEATER

A 20TH CENTURY COLLECTION OF THE WORK

OF ITS BEST PLAYWRIGHTS

COMPILED WITH AN INTRODUCTION BY Lindsay Patterson

277

DODD, MEAD & COMPANY  NEW YORK

ISBN 0-396-06254-7
Library of Congress Catalog Card Number: 75-135538

Printed in the United States of America
by The Cornwall Press, Inc., Cornwall, N. Y.

St. Louis Woman by Arna Bontemps and Countee Cullen. Text copyright 1944 by Countee Cullen and Arna Bontemps. Reprinted by permission of Arna Bontemps and the Estate of Countee Cullen. Lyrics by Johnny Mercer. Copyright © 1946, 1959 by A-M Music Corporation. Reprinted by permission of Chappell & Co., Inc.

Take a Giant Step by Louis Peterson. Copyright © 1954 by Louis Peterson. Reprinted by permission of International Famous Agency, Inc.

In Splendid Error by William Branch. Copyright © 1953 by William Branch under title of *Frederick Douglass*. Reprinted by permission of William Branch and the Ann Elmo Agency, Inc.

Trouble in Mind by Alice Childress. Copyright © 1970 by Alice Childress. Reprinted by permission of the author and her representative. All inquiries should be addressed to the author's representative: Flora Roberts, Inc., 116 East 59 Street, New York, New York 10022.

Simply Heavenly by Langston Hughes. Based on *Simple Takes a Wife*. Copyright © 1953 by Langston Hughes. *Simply Heavenly,* Copyright © 1956, 1958, 1959, by Langston Hughes and David Martin. Lyrics from *Simply Heavenly* Copyright © 1957 by Bourne, Inc. Reprinted by permission. For rights to the music from *Simply Heavenly* write Bourne Co., 136 West 52 Street, New York, New York 10019.

A Raisin in the Sun by Lorraine Hansberry. Copyright © 1958, 1959, 1966 by Robert Nemiroff as Executor of the Estate of Lorraine Hansberry. Reprinted by permission of Random House, Inc.

Purlie Victorious by Ossie Davis. Copyright © 1961 by Ossie Davis. Reprinted by permission.

Dutchman by LeRoi Jones. Copyright © 1964 by LeRoi Jones. Reprinted by permission of The Sterling Lord Agency.

The Amen Corner by James Baldwin. Copyright © 1968 by James Baldwin. Reprinted by permission of Robert Lantz-Candida Donadio Literary Agency, Incorporated.

In the Wine Time by Ed Bullins. From *Five Plays by Ed Bullins,* Copyright © 1968 by Ed Bullins. Reprinted by permission of the publishers, The Bobbs-Merrill Company, Inc.

No Place to Be Somebody by Charles Gordone. Copyright © 1969 by Charles Gordone. Reprinted by permission of the publishers, The Bobbs-Merrill Company, Inc.

Ceremonies in Dark Old Men by Lonne Elder III. Copyright © 1965, 1969 by Lonne Elder III. Reprinted with the permission of Farrar, Straus & Giroux, Inc.

INTRODUCTION

I was born in a small Louisiana town forty miles from the Arkansas border. Life there was neither sleepy nor slow, but rather zestful since there was light industry, and Saturdays cotton farmers would come from miles around to do their weekly marketing.

The biggest events of the year were the appearances in early and late fall of the *Rabbit Foot* and *Silas Green* minstrel shows, events for which the entire population of six thousand—it seems—turned out. The audiences, of course, were divided into two sections, and everyone, black and white, thoroughly enjoyed the humor, the songs and the dancing.

None of us then thought of the blackfaced comedians as anything more than comic exaggerations, and certainly, we did not dream that blacks anywhere were being judged by or likened to "those showfolk" from the north. To us, their antics were merely daring, risqué and outrageous.

But there comes a time in life when one loses his innocence and is pushed boldly into the real world. For us, it was the day two white policemen pistol whipped a black man who was sitting peacefully on the courthouse square. The man, after being brutally beaten, managed to grab a pistol from one policeman whom he killed, and the other he critically wounded. Whites organized lynching parties, and for several days no blacks were safe on the streets.

The peaceful co-existence ended abruptly, and overnight an ominous change set in. There appeared in all the faces of the black adults a sullen defiance. Now, when someone ventured "uptown" you were not quite certain if he would ever return.

The minstrel shows no longer came in the fall, and people locked their doors at night. Life, of course, did not stop. Business went on as usual, but something was irretrievably lost, and it was only years later that I realized it was a special kind of innocence.

I mean by lost innocence that specific moment when a black discovers he is a "nigger" and his mentality shifts gears and begins that long, uphill climb to bring psychological order out of chaos. It is not a moment, however, easily detected. All of black literature is more or less unconsciously preoccupied with precisely pinpointing and defining it.

It is the theme which dominates all of the plays in this volume, and in *Take a Giant Step, The Amen Corner, A Raisin in the Sun, In the Wine Time, No Place to Be Somebody* and *Ceremonies in Dark Old Men,* it is unwittingly, though more obviously expressed.

It is an elusive, complex moment, with complex reactions and can occur at four or forty, and its pursuit, I believe, will continue to occupy serious black writers for decades to come.

*   *   *

Several years ago I asked a Broadway producer: "Do plays that read well always play well? And do plays that read badly always play badly?" He had not, he said, ever looked at plays in that way, and could not provide an answer.

I have subsequently read a number of scripts and have come to the conclusion that one simply cannot tell how a play will turn out on stage until it is actually staged. But I am inclined to think that most producers—regardless of how well or badly it reads on paper—select a play for production purely because of personal preferences for the subject, or because they believe it will strike a responsive chord in a substantial number of theatergoers.

A preferential subject, however, has not been that of plays dealing with black life, mainly because producers have felt that mass audiences would be uninterested. And though most of the best plays by black writers have been produced (and have been successful), too many were staged long after they ceased to be immediately relevant.

Works of art, especially those dealing with social problems, must appear within a reasonable time-span after their creation; that is, if they are to have the very maximum of impact. *Uncle Tom's Cabin,* certainly would not have significantly aroused this nation's conscience against slavery if it had appeared in 1861 instead of 1851. Nor would James Baldwin's *The Fire Next Time,* exert as much moral force today as it did upon publication in 1962 during the heat of the civil rights demonstrations. At the right place at the right time is not an idle aphorism, and when it happens in art, the work becomes a part of our thinking and language, and we are all irrevocably changed and broadened by it.

Because of this delay, as well as spotty productions, black plays have certainly not had nearly the moral impact upon our nation's mentality (or the theater itself) they could or should have had. In the theater, as in American life generally, blacks have had a "hard row to hoe." Unfortunately, it was not until Federal Theater days in the 1930's that a large number of black playwrights saw their works directed, staged and acted by professionals. But before the program could have any salutary effect, it was terminated by an act of Congress.

Long before the thirties, of course, serious black playwrights and actors had been struggling to establish theater groups and stage plays. In 1821, a group of black actors organized the African Grove Company in Greenwich Village, but the theater was short-lived because white harassment "forced" the authorities of the City of New York to close it.

Today, there still remains a desperate need, not just for more black theaters, but a commitment by other groups as well. Without groups, such as the Greenwich Mews and The New York Shakespeare Festival, that are committed to quality rather than commercialism, *Trouble in Mind, In Splendid Error, Simply Heavenly,* and *No Place to Be Somebody,* might have been lost to us forever.

And without black theater, *The Amen Corner* (Howard University Players), *In the Wine Time* (New Lafayette Theater), and *Ceremonies in Dark Old Men* (Negro Ensemble Company), might, too, have been lost.

To put it mildly, the progressive development of the black playwright since William Wells Brown's *The Escape, or a Leap to Freedom* (the first black play) appeared in 1858, has—in spite of all the odds—been phenomenal. In *Black Theater: A 20th Century Collection of the Work of Its Best Playwrights,* I have tried to amass the best examples of the varying types of plays blacks have written since then. *St. Louis Woman* by Arna Bontemps and Countee Cullen with lyrics by Johnny Mercer and music by Harold Arlen, I felt, offered the best prototype of the musical plays which dominated black theater during the twenties, thirties and early forties. Louis Peterson's *Take a Giant Step* signaled a new epoch in black dramatic theater by dealing with the trauma encountered in growing up far outside and away from the black community. William Branch's *In Splendid Error* is an excellent example of a black historical play; few of which have ever been staged, although a number have been written (mainly one acts) and collected in early anthologies. Alice Childress's *Trouble in Mind* represents a type of play that began to surface after World War II, the challenge to and confrontation with the white establishment in its entrenched racial attitudes. Langston Hughes' *Simply Heavenly,* with music by David Martin, concerns itself entirely with black humor, love and life; a type of play that an increasing number of young black playwrights are using as a model. Lorraine Hansberry's *A Raisin in the Sun,* one of the most perfectly structured plays ever to appear on Broadway, presents among other innovations, the search and acceptance of the African heritage. Ossie Davis' *Purlie Victorious* effectively combines humor with black and white stereotypes to satirize the ridiculousness and danger of formulating racial judgements from archetypes. LeRoi Jones' *Dutchman* broke new ground entirely by departing from strict naturalism and employing an ancient theme (the legend of the Flying Dutchman) as a legato line. James Baldwin's *The Amen Corner* treats movingly and in depth an urban spiritual experience and its concomitant contradictons. Ed Bullins' *In the Wine Time* typifies the use of the black life-style as a subject for broad statements about life—statements, incidentally, which are not necessarily racially restrictive. Charles Gordone's *No Place to Be Somebody,* the most vital play (black or white) to come out of the sixties, scrutinizes the full-scale intercourse and consequences of blacks and whites in a urban setting. And Lonne Elder III's *Ceremonies in Dark Old Men* explores more clearly than any other black play of this or any other century the interior of a black ghetto family.

Black Theater is a collection of plays of which I am intensely proud, for each, in its own probing way, has tried to move us closer to a more intelligent, liberating and human understanding of things.

—LINDSAY PATTERSON
New York City

CONTENTS

Introduction   *vii*

St. Louis Woman *by Arna Bontemps and Countee Cullen*   1

Take a Giant Step *by Louis Peterson*   43

In Splendid Error *by William Branch*   93

Trouble in Mind *by Alice Childress*   135

Simply Heavenly *by Langston Hughes*   175

A Raisin in the Sun *by Lorraine Hansberry*   221

Purlie Victorious *by Ossie Davis*   277

Dutchman *by LeRoi Jones*   319

The Amen Corner *by James Baldwin*   333

In the Wine Time *by Ed Bullins*   379

No Place to Be Somebody *by Charles Gordone*   407

Ceremonies in Dark Old Men *by Lonne Elder III*   451

Arna Bontemps
and Countee Cullen

Lyrics by Johnny Mercer
Music by Harold Arlen

St. Louis Woman

From the Novel G O D S E N D S S U N D A Y

ST. LOUIS WOMAN

St. Louis Woman was first presented at the Martin Beck Theater, New York City, March 30, 1946.

CHARACTERS

BADFOOT
LITTLE AUGIE
BARNEY
LILA
SLIM
BUTTERFLY
DELLA GREEN
BIGLOW BROWN
RAGSDALE
PEMBROCK
JASPER
THE HOSTESS
DRUM MAJOR
MISSISSIPPI
DANDY DAVE
LEAH
JACKIE
CELESTINE
PIGGIE
JOSHUA
MR. HOPKINS
PREACHER
WAITER

ACT ONE

SCENE 1

TIME:
Early afternoon of a day in August 1898.

SCENE:
The stage is in darkness when the Curtain rises. Presently a MAN'S VOICE, *full of a warm folk quality, commences to sing. The singing is accompanied by a guitar. The song is a ballad of the rise and progress of* AUGIE RIVERS, *a wonderful little jockey whose sensational performance on the turf is attributed to the caul with which he has been born, as whatever the secret,* LIL AUGIE *has broken the heart of the opposition on every track. His personality has expanded, too. Dressed in his Sunday best and sauntering down Targee Street in St. Louis, he is a sight to kill and cripple.*

A spot of light picks out BADFOOT, *a trainer, sitting on a stool in the stable of the St. Louis race track. He is a dark, heavy-set Negro.* BADFOOT *is singing the legend of* LIL AUGIE—*"Natural Man."*

BADFOOT. (*Sitting on stool polishing bridle. Sings.*)
They call me Badfoot
'Cause I'm an old stable buck
They call me Badfoot
But I'm ridin' my luck
Yes, I'm ridin' my luck.

(*Music interlude.*)

(*Hangs bridle up. Polishes saddle.*)
Though I never had a education
I'm a-'sociated with a winnin' combination
Come on, you rounders, and hear my
    song.
(*Spoken—coming Down Front Right of Center.*) I wanna tell you 'bout Lil Augie. He's a jockey that's knee-high to a grasshopper, but when he rides—he's as big as all outdoors. . . .
(*Sung—walks to the Right.*)
Since I was a lil boy
I been round the tracks
Seen a lot o' jockeys
Fast as "mountain jacks"
But I know
What I know
Heeeee oooooooo eeeeeeee
Lil Augie is a natural man
He don't need a bridle

(Walks to Center.)
He don't use his hand
Augie talks a language
Hosses understand
An' it's true
That he do
Heeeeeee ooooo eeeeee
Lil Augie is a natural man
I've seen plenty o' back stretch ramblers
(Walks to Left.)
But I'll tell you for fair
Augie sits on a hosses neck
Like most folks sits on a chair
Though he's got a big heart
You can get a bet
He don't weigh a hundred
Even sop and wet
He's as short
(Walks to the Right of stool.)
As his name
Just the same
Augie is the biggest little man.
(Spoken—puts left foot on stool.)
County fairs and small towns wasn't big
enough to hold Lil Augie. Since the day
he was born he was lookin' for he didn't
know what. Maybe I ought to tell you
what he's doin' now. *(Foot off stool, walks
Down Front.)*
(Sung.)
They couldn't hold him in his own back
  yard
He's in St. Louis and he's ridin' hard
And there ain't no tellin' what the end'll
  be—
(Starts off Left.)
We shall see, yes, we shall see
(Stops.)
... what we shall see. ...
(Off Left.)

(Lights down and out.)

ACT ONE

SCENE 2

TIME:
Late afternoon of the same day.

SCENE:
Biglow's Bar, a St. Louis honky-tonk restaurant of the late '90's. At one side is a bar resplendent with glasses, mirrors and bright bottles of fancy wines. On the opposite side are small tables at which are seated a few fancy WOMEN *from St. Louis' darktown with their gaudy masquereaux.*

There is a large door Center back. As the Curtain rises, the COUPLES *at the tables are chatting and indolently sipping their drinks. The young brown girls are pretentiously dressed in the finery of the period; they are heavily jeweled. The "Macks," as in all primitive society, are even more brilliantly attired than the women. They wear gay embroidered skirts and on their fingers, beneath knuckle-length shirts, flash diamonds and polished nails. They wear box-backed coats. Their shoes are the St. Louis "flats," and in the toes tiny mirrors have been set. The cuffs of their coats and trousers are of velvet of a darker shade. High-roller Stetson hats, with nude women or boxers or racing horses worked in small eyelets in the crown are the rule. No costume is without its note of humility, the piece of gold money worn on the watch-chain for luck. A few unattached males are standing at the bar.*

A MUSICAL BRIDGE *has suggested the running and winning of the race on the track, and* BADFOOT's *song continues in the saloon as if it had not been interrupted. The* LIGHT *begins with a spot on him but gradually expands to take in* BARNEY *who stands nearby and* LILA, *a good-looking brown girl who sips her drink in a mood of black dejection, and the rest of the crowd.* BADFOOT *is still singing Lil Augie's praises.*

(Orchestral chord.)

(Freeze.)

(As LIGHTS DIM *in, the* CAST, *as if stopped in their last movements, are*

frozen still. The only movement is the smoke from their cigarettes.)

SLIM. *Pouring a drink at bar.*
A MAN. *Reaching for the drink.*
A MAN. ⎫ *Talking—drinking Down*
A WOMAN. ⎭ *Right of Bar.*

A MAN. *Picking up check from floor.*
A WOMAN. *Seated next to him Right of Down Center table.*
A MAN. *Stands behind table laughing.*

A MAN. ⎫ *Dancing Down Left Cen-*
A WOMAN. ⎭ *ter.*

JOSH. *At piano Right hands raised as if playing.*
BARNEY. *Sitting on piano watching.*

A MAN. *Putting chair in place to sit with* A WOMAN *Down Left table who is fanning herself.*
3 WOMEN. *Sitting Up Left Table. One waving handkerchief, others as if listening to* A MAN *who is against Up Left wall.*
BUTTERFLY. *Down Right by bar calling to* BARNEY.
RAGSDALE. *Up Right foot on platform.*
A MAN. *Entering. Cane raised in greeting to* TWO MEN *at piano.*
LILA. *Leaning against post Up Right of Center with glass looking out of window.*

PASSERSBY:
A MAN. *Wiping brim of his hat.*
A WOMAN. *Looking in window.*
A WOMAN. *Walking by fast.*
A WOMAN. *Strolling by with opened parasol.*

BARNEY *picks up stable stool, takes back to piano.* A WOMAN *comes in looking for her "Jim." General ad libs. As music breaks and the* CAST *finishes out its frozen movements,* A MAN *exits and 2 WOMEN enter.*

(BADFOOT *enters.*)

A MAN. How's Lil Augie doin'?
BADFOOT. *(Proudly.)* Winnin' everythin'. Lil Augie is sure enough lucky.
BARNEY. *(Coming Down Right of* BADFOOT.*)* Hey, Badfoot! Lucky as he is— they's some side bettin' goin' on what says they's one thing his luck won't get him.
BADFOOT. What's that?
BARNEY. Della Green.
LILA. *(Aroused by the mention of* DELLA's *name, crossing Down to Center.)* Who say Lil Augie's aiming at Della?
BARNEY. All Targee Street know Lil Augie is aiming at Della. She's the prettiest gal in town.
LILA. *(Crosses Right of Center.)* But that don't keep her from being the biggest hussy.
BARNEY. *(Actually nudging her on.)* I wouldn't say that, Lila.
LILA. Hell with what you wouldn't say. I ain't asking you that. But do Biglow know about Lil Augie liking Della?
BADFOOT. Lord, I hopes not. Wouldn't like to see Lil Augie get in no trouble with Biglow. *(Crosses to stool by piano.)*
SLIM. *(Remembering. Waving a bar rag and leaning over bar.)* Now, I know why Lil Augie been coming here every day spending his money so free. Just so he can look at Della. Biglow don't know what it's all about. He just glad to see Lil Augie in his saloon spending all that money. Every cent Lil Augie spend mean more for Biglow and more for Biglow mean more for Della.

(ALL *laugh.*)

LILA. More for Biglow mean more for Della, do it? Well, more for Biglow ought to mean more for Lila. Who bought this place and give it to Biglow? Did Della do it? No, she walks in and takes with her little yellow face what I sweated for. God damn her! If ever she cross my path I'll break this glass in her face.
SLIM. *(Coming from behind the bar.)*

You can't carry on like this, Lila. Come on, you got to get out of here now.

LILA. (With dangerous calm.) You know better'n to touch me, Slim. I'm going now, because I got a mind to go, but can't nobody put me out of here, nobody. Not even Biglow. (She goes.)

(MEN whistle. There is general noise.)

WOMAN. He does treat her mean.

BARNEY. (Making a wry face.) Le's have a little sweeten' water, Slim, to wash that taste away.

(SLIM serves the sweeten' water as the MEN sing limericks.)

LIMERICKS:
A MAN.
Sweeten' water's sweet as it can be.
ANOTHER MAN.
Sweeten' water is a sting-a-ree. (Crosses from Down Left to Up of Left table.)
ANOTHER MAN.
You take rock candy an' you pour on gin. (Crosses Down between two tables.)
SLIM.
Give it the la-bel o' sweeten-in water and you bring it in. (Coming from bar with tray of drinks.)
BADFOOT.
Sweeten' water's (ALL.) sweet as rock an' rye. (Rising.)
BARNEY.
Sweeten' water got me Butterfly.

(BUTTERFLY enters, snubs BARNEY.)

BADFOOT.
He bought her Scotch but she was unimpressed.
BARNEY.
So I ordered her sweeten-in' water an' she A-cqui-esced.

(General laughter from the people.)

ALL.
Sweeten' water's sweet as Della Green.

(Ad Libs Off Left.)

A MAN.
Like to put the squeeze on her I mean.
A lady chooses who she's gonna squeeze.
She'll be drinkin' her sweeten' water any place she please.

(Fade-out.)

(DELLA is pushed into the room by BIGLOW. BIGLOW appears.)

DELLA. (Looking at BIGLOW steadily.) You hits me once more and I'm thru.

BIGLOW. (Puzzled.) What's come over you, gal? Used to be you could take a lumping and know it's good for you. A little lumping makes the loving all the sweeter. You know that.

DELLA. Well, I'm taking my sugar without lumps from now on.

BIGLOW. (Sullenly.) Any woman messes wid me gotta take the lumps.

DELLA. Della Green don't gotta take nothin'—lesson she has a mind to.

BIGLOW. (Trying to laugh it off.) You don't know that's good fo' yousef. But I'll learn you. Come on—

DELLA. I'll come when I'm ready.

BIGLOW. All right, spirited Filly, Eh. (Swings around room.) If anyone don't like it . . . try me a barrel. (He exits.)

SLIM. (Coming from behind bar to Down Right.) You better watch yourself, Della. You can't two-time Biglow. He apt to push you face right thru you head, girl.

DELLA. I'll take my chances. (Looks around room.) Cheer up. Ain't no call to go into mourning yet. Bring me a glass a sweeten' water.

(SLIM goes back to bar.)

RAGS. (Coming over to her from Up Right to table Right of Center.) Is that what you want, Della? To be slapped and kicked around? Before God, I don't see how you can take it.

DELLA. (Fixing her garters.) I ain't taking nothing I don't want to take, Rags.

RAGS. (In lighter mood.) Well, I know

self-praise is scandalous. I can't see why you won't take me. Why ain't nothin' I can't give the woman I want . . . clothes, rocks for her fingers, pleanty of good times . . . 'til you can't rest. . . .

DELLA. *(Teasing.)* Go on. You ain't mentioned nothing special yet. I got all those.

RAGS. Yeah. On Targee Street! Honey, you could be living high. This place is just a honky-tonk compared to mine. *(Sighs and DELLA laughs. Suddenly impatient.)* If you knew what was good for you, you'd quit now and come with me.

DELLA. *(Angered.)* Will y'all stop telling what's good for me. I'll stay or I'll go as I please. Ain't no man gonna tell me when or where. I'm here today and gone tomorrow. *(Takes drink.)*

(Music.)

(A GIRL stops to listen who was on her way Left.)

(RAGS sits at table Right of Center.)

(DELLA swings into the song: "Any place I hang my hat is home.")
(First time—piano.)
Free and easy—that's my style
Howdy do me, watch me smile
Fare thee well me, afterwhile
(On vamp walks Right.)
Cause I gotta roam
And any place I hang my hat is home.

ALL.
Sweetnin' water, cherry wine
(To Left Center.)
Thank you kindly, suits me fine
Kansas City, Caroline
(To Left.)
That's my honey comb
'Cause any place I hang my hat is home.
(Chorus.)
(Second time.)
Birds, roostin' in the tree
Pick up and go
And the goin' proves
That's how it oughta be

I pick up too
When the spirit moves me
Cross the river round the bend
Howdy stranger, so-long friend
There's a voice in the lonesome wind that
    keeps whisperin' . . . roam
I'm goin' where a welcome mat is
No matter where that is
'Cause any place I hang my hat is *home.*
(Repeat chorus.)

(At end of number 4 MEN and WOMEN come forward. DELLA finishes Center of stage.)

BARNEY. *(Left of DELLA.)* I be your hatrack any time, baby. You gonna walk for the cake tonight, gal?

DELLA. Oh, I be in it, I reckon.

BARNEY. You oughta let me walk with you, Miss Della.

(BUTTERFLY catches this remark from bar. Crosses from Up Right to Down Left.)

BUTTERFLY. Who you askin' to walk with you, Barney?

BARNEY. *(Caught in the act.)* Oh, nobody, honey, I didn't ask nobody.

BUTTERFLY. You ain't even got a suit of clothes to walk in. *(Pats his face four times and then slaps him.)*

(AUGIE CROWD heard.)

You and your late race horses.

(There's a commotion at the door and LIL AUGIE bursts in. He wears a yellow coat, striped trousers, and gaily flowered satin vest. A small crowd of noisy admirers comes in with him. He is surrounded. DELLA and the OTHERS laugh.)

(DELLA sits Down Left table. RAGS goes Up Right.)

LIL AUGIE. *(At top of his voice.)* Here 'tis!

A WOMAN. Lil Augie!

SLIM. Three winners in one day.

BADFOOT. Three hats full of money!! My boy! My boy!

BARNEY. *(Drawling.)* No flies on Lil Augie.

1ST BYSTANDER. No, sir, Lil Augie's got the world tee-rolled.

SLIM. Name your drink, Lil Augie. The joint is yours. It's a treat to the ridingest lil jockey what ever rid a hoss.

(Piano.)

AUGIE. Can't nobody treat Lil Augie this day. They ain't a bucket-shop in St. Louis big enough to do that. This is Lil Augie what you reads about. *(Shows his roll.)* Looka here! Set up the house, Slim. Set it up on me. And set 'em good.

SLIM. You're the boss, a'right.

BADFOOT. Better go kind of easy son. 'Member tonight's the cakewalk.

AUGIE. Lil Augie'll be ready when the fiddles commence. 'Pend on that, Badfoot.

BADFOOT. Oh, everybody know you can strut; I just say you want to be at your best tonight 'cause we're getting ready to put on the dog. Barney here say he gonna crowd you.

(Piano out.)

AUGIE. *(Laughing.)* Sure enough, Barney? You didn't crowd me much in the race today.

BARNEY. *(Fawning on AUGIE.)* Lord, Augie, that was a pretty race you won. I ain't never seen nobody ride like that.

AUGIE. *(Crosses to Down Left of Center Right in back of BARNEY. Impressed as he looks toward DELLA.)* That so? I thought you was too far behind to see. *(Struts.)*

BARNEY. Well, it'll be a different story at the cakewalk tonight. If you lend me that sky-blue suit of your'n with those big white buttons. I'll walk you from here to N'Awlins and back.

AUGIE. Well I be dog'. Look at this dude, fixin' to outstrut me in my own clothes. Now, ain't that somethin'. Well—

(Music.)

just for develishment, I'm gonna let you borrow that suit, Barney.

BARNEY. *(Surprised.)* No!

(AUGIE starts to strut.)

AUGIE. Yes, I is. I'm gonna let you wear my blue and outwalk you just the same.

(BARNEY sits Right of Center table.)

(AUGIE goes into song and dance: "I feel my luck comin' down.")

(Left of Center.)
> *(Piano.)*

An introduction
Is now in order
And you can call me
    Baby
The ladies love me
(To Center.)
And I don't blame 'em
But do they get me
Maybe
Set em up, boy
(To SLIM.)
Lovin' cup, boy
(To GIRL Right of Center, ROYCE.)
For the ladies and me
Lucky horseshoe
Flew up and hit me
(To Left of Center.)
New suit and dicty lid
Call me the candy kid
I feel my luck comin' down.

(Center.)
A four-leave clover looked me in the eye
And jumped in my label
A lucky seven rolled from out the sky
And rang that joyful bell
(To bar, dances; struts.)
The introductions
Have been accomplished
And you can call me
Honey
(Looking at DELLA.)

My mornin' coffee
Was full of bubbles
You know what that means
Money
Mercenary?
(To Center.)
Not so very
But I won't turn it down
A lucky horseshoe
Flew up and hit me
New suit and dicty lid
Call me the candy kid
I feel my luck comin' down.

(2nd CHORUS danced, last line sung.)

(ANOTHER MAN goes off. A MAN takes a WOMAN off Down Left. The WOMAN has drunk too much.)

BARNEY. Have Mercy!

(BUTTERFLY picks up tray of glasses. BARNEY goes to piano. The drinks have been passed around. AUGIE having finished song, sees that DELLA has not touched hers. He crosses over to her table, RAGS crosses Up Right of piano.)

(Light dims.)

AUGIE. You ain't drinking, Pretty Gal.
DELLA. I had mine.
AUGIE. You ain't had this'n yet.
DELLA. That'n ain't mine.
AUGIE. I bought it for you.
DELLA. You did, huh? Well, you ain't asked me would I *have* a drink.
AUGIE. *(Thinking it a joke.)* Well, I'm asking you now.
DELLA. No, thanks.
AUGIE. *(Taken aback.)* No?
DELLA. Course not. I don't take drinks from stranger.
AUGIE. You St. Louis women is a mess! I ain't strange, gal. I'm Lil Augie. *(He crosses back of table to back of chair.)*
DELLA. Lil Augie what?
AUGIE. Lil Augie what you reads about!
DELLA. Oh! *(Then after a slight pause.)* But I ain't read about no Lil Augie.

AUGIE. You must be can't read. How come you think all this 'miration bust out when I come in?
DELLA. I don't know. You look like any other lil bitty man to me.
AUGIE. Yeah?
DELLA. Sho!
AUGIE. *(Leaning toward her.)* Well, I ain't though. I might be little, but I'm loud. I got greenbacks on me worser'n a dog got fleas. I got money in my shows, money in my hat, money in the lining of my clothes, and money hanging round my neck. And I don't mind spending it neither.
DELLA. *(Unbending.)* Sure enough?

(PIANIST starts playing a very soft, slow-drag tune.)

AUGIE. Sure. Ain't you going to ask me to have some sit down?
DELLA. I'm saving this sit down for somebody else, Lil Augie.
AUGIE. Somebody p'tickla?
DELLA. Kinda . . . kinda p'tickla.
AUGIE. Somebody you're sweet on, huh?
DELLA. Hmm . . . mmm . . . mm.
AUGIE. Oh . . . yet and still, 'tain't no reason why I can't sit down here till he come, is there?
DELLA. Well . . . I reckon . . .

(AUGIE sits. He puts cane and hat on table.)

AUGIE. *(Indicating her drink.)* Go on; be friends.
DELLA. *(She drinks.)*

(AUGIE's eyes brighten as he watches her.)

You look at me so funny, Lil Augie.
AUGIE. You is good for my eyes, gal. That's how come I looks at you.
DELLA. Sure enough?
AUGIE. I been looking all over the country for you.
DELLA. All over what country, Lil Augie?

AUGIE. El Paso, San Antonio, N'Aw-lines, Louisville, Memphis, Alabama . . . everywhere.

DELLA. Ah, Lil Augie is you trying to swell my head?

AUGIE. Swell nothing! I been had my eyes peeled for just such a gal as you.

DELLA. For an old ugly gal like me, Lil Augie?

AUGIE. You wain't what I calls ugly, gal.

DELLA. No?

AUGIE. And I got a good eyes, too. You're pretty as a race hoss. Honey, a race hoss is about the prettiest thing God ever made. Skin smooth like satin, proud head tossing, and dancing feet. Ain't nothin' prettier ceptin' you.

DELLA. (Laughing.) If you rides as fast as you talks, them other riders can't have much of a chance with you.

AUGIE. (Leans back in chair proudly.) All they has a chance at is to see my dust.

DELLA. I think that's what you're trying to do to me, Lil Augie.

AUGIE. What's that?

DELLA. Trying to throw dust in my eyes.

AUGIE. That's the truth, gal, only it ain't just common dirty dust. Know what kinds it is?

DELLA. No. What kind is it?

AUGIE. Lucky dust, the only kind I has anything to do with. I'd like to throw so much of that in your eyes till you couldn't see nobody but me.

DELLA. Lil Augie, I'm half-blinded now.

AUGIE. When I look at you, pretty gal, I think about the sunshine in the clover fields, and dew drops sparkling in the morning.

(BIGLOW enters. Lights come up.)

BIGLOW. (Sees LIL AUGIE.) He-o, Lil Augie.

(Piano arpeggio.)

AUGIE. (Gets up.) He-o, Biglow. Win today?

BIGLOW. None of you damn business.

AUGIE. Oh, guess I wasn't carrying your money! (Crosses Right of DELLA. To DELLA as he leaves.) See yuh, gal. (Taps DELLA on knee with cane, exchanges laugh with BIGLOW and crosses to bar.)

(Piano run.)

(BARNEY and BADFOOT follow AUGIE to bar Down Right corner.)

BIGLOW. (Sitting down Left of table with DELLA.) Lil Augie shining up to you?

DELLA. (Shrugging.) Kinda.

BIGLOW. (Sits.) Ain't he a mighty little excuse for a loving man?

DELLA. He say his pockets is loaded with gold spikes.

BIGLOW. It don't cost nothing to toot your own horn.

DELLA. (Affectionately.) Lil Augie ain't got nothing on you, Biglow. You got money, too.

BIGLOW. Well, I ain't crying.

AUGIE. (At the bar, in a trance.) Before God, I believe that's the most prettiest woman in the world.

BARNEY. (Turning around, steps Down to AUGIE.) You is hard hit, Lil Augie.

AUGIE. I feels my love coming down.

BADFOOT. (Stepping Down to AUGIE's Right.) 'Member, that's Biglow Brown's gal, son.

AUGIE. I'd burn my clothes for a gal like that.

BIGLOW. (Laughs, calling from table.) Sweeten water, Slim.

(TWO COUPLES appear Up Left window.)

AUGIE. (Calling from bar.) This is Lil Augie's day, Biglow. You like champagne?

BIGLOW. I can pick my own drinks, Lil Augie.

AUGIE. Short answer, huh?

DELLA. Why you cut him off like that? Just 'cause he's shining up to me? That ain't even sense. The more he buys means more for you!

BIGLOW. (Condescending.) Well, since you put it that way.

SLIM. (To BIGLOW.) Is you taking the champagne?

BIGLOW. I don't care if I do, Slim.

AUGIE. (Loudly.) Champagne for everybody, Slim. This is Lil Augie's day.

(TWO MEN and slightly drunken WOMAN enter Down Left door. MAN closes door drapes. COUPLES outside window rush in.

THE PIANO PLAYER plunks another blues SONG. SLIM starts opening bottles; they pop and foam gaily as he removes the corks. Glasses are filled and raised. Piano plays. The scene becomes a brown-skinned counterpart of a Parisian Bacchanal of the last century. The carnival spirit prevails; a WOMAN sits on a table, her slippered feet high in the air. One cuts a few pigeon-wings. One of the "macks" stands in his chair. Another drones a song. The ensuing remarks are thrown out above the babble of revelry and laughter.)

BADFOOT. No more cornbread and potatoes.

BARNEY. (Raised glass.) This is righteous.

FIRST BYSTANDER. I mean!

BADFOOT. My boy Augie is money's mammy.

AUGIE. (Beside himself, looking at DELLA.) And all I don't blow in here, I'm going to give to the womens.

A WOMAN. (Puts arms around AUGIE.) That's one more living lil man.

AUGIE. (Spinning around with WOMAN.) Preach it, baby, whilst I shouts: (Handing SLIM a bill.) Here, Slim, throw the change out-doors.

BARNEY. Money ain't no objection to Lil Augie.

AUGIE. Not a bit.

BARNEY. Womens is all what worries you.

AUGIE. (Raising his glass and looking in DELLA's direction.) Pretty womens was made for lucky men.

(Piano stop.)

DELLA. (Hearing the remark.) Biglow is still big with me—lucky or onlucky.

AUGIE. (Still holding his glass high.) Champagne beats sweeten' water, though.

DELLA. (To BIGLOW.) Hear that?

BIGLOW. What he signifying?

(The room quiets down following these words.)

DELLA. He mean you can't set up the house like he done.

BIGLOW. He just blowin' off. He little and biggity. They ain't no call for me to buy drinks in my own saloon.

DELLA. You's obliged to treat the house now.

BIGLOW. I ain't won no race.

DELLA. But you can't let Lil Augie look down on you.

BIGLOW. (With a shrug.) A'righty. Order 'em a round of sweeten' water.

DELLA. (Outraged, gets up.) Sweeten' water!

(BARNEY crosses, sits at table Right of Center.)

BIGLOW. That's what you drinks, ain't it?

DELLA. (Outraged.) Lil Augie ordered champagne.

BIGLOW. That's his little red wagon. I ain't ordering none.

DELLA. He ordered that champagne because of me, Biglow.

BIGLOW. Showing off. That's all . . . biggity.

DELLA. (Insistent.) You going to get the champagne?

BIGLOW. Sweeten' water or nothing. I has champagne to sell, not to give away.

DELLA. *(With device.)* You ain't, huh? *(Crosses to Center. Calling to* SLIM.*)* Slim! Set up the house again.

SLIM. Set it up on Biglow?

DELLA. *(Stepping to Center of stage, melodramatically so that* BIGLOW *is on one side of her and* LIL AUGIE *on the other.)* Set it up on Della Green!

SLIM. What's it going to be?

BIGLOW. Sweeten' water.

DELLA. *(Grimly.)* Champagne!

*(*SLIM *is befuddled by the conflicting orders.)*

BIGLOW. *(Gets up and crosses to* DELLA.*)* Trying to make me 'shamed in front of Lil Augie's crowd, huh?

DELLA. A girl ought to could ask her man for a treat.

BIGLOW. I done said mine. Ain't no woman in this town can put her hand in my pocket. Biglow Brown can spend his own money.

AUGIE. *(Pulling another bill from his roll with a flourish.)* This is Lil Augie's day, Slim. Here, I'm paying the bill. *(He cuts his eyes affectionately at* DELLA.*)*

BIGLOW. *(Crosses Right toward* AUGIE *threateningly.)* Hold on, Slim. Lil Augie can treat the rest of the crowd, but I'm going to buy my woman's drink myself.

*(*LILA *enters.)*

AUGIE. *(Toasting* DELLA.*)* Champagne is better'n sweeten' water. *(Raising his glass to* DELLA.*)*

DELLA. *(Emptying hers defiantly at one tilt.)* Thank you, Lil Augie.

*(*LILA *comes Down through table Down Right.* BIGLOW *takes* DELLA *back to table.)*

BARNEY. You're just in time, Lila. It's champagne.

LILA. Yeah?

BARNEY. I mean!

LILA. Lil Augie celebrating again?

AUGIE. It's Della Green's house. The drinks is all for her.

BARNEY. *(Mischievously.)* Yes, Lil Augie is buying champagne for Biglow Brown's woman.

LILA. *(Winces.)* Biglow's woman?

BARNEY. Everybody know Della's Biglow's woman.

LILA. I don't know it. *(To* SLIM, *coming toward her with glass and bottle and pouring out drink.)* None for me. Not off of Della Green.

*(*SLIM *shrugs. Goes back to bar.)*

BARNEY. *(Crosses to Center. At top of his voice.)* Ha, Ha! I sure like to hear these womens carry on. It do me more good'n a long night's sleep.

(Suddenly he feels awkward and embarrassed, for the OTHERS *do not join his merriment.* BIGLOW *sulks in his chair, gaze averted.* DELLA *looks uncertain and nervous. The rest of the* CROWD *seems to feel something brewing. Presently,* LILA *goes over to* BIGLOW'*s table and explodes.* BARNEY, *taking chair from Right of Center table and turning it around, sits down.)*

LILA. *(Crosses to Down Left table.)* So, Lil Augie is buying drinks for Biglow Brown's woman, is he? In that case he ought to be buying them for me.

BIGLOW. *(Gets up. Goes to* LILA.*)* You . . . I'll be damned. Ain't I had enough worryation for one day?

LILA. *(Grabs him by his lapels.)* But it's true Biglow, I know it's true, I'm your woman.

BIGLOW. *(Shakes her loose.)* You mean, my use to be woman.

LILA. You might regret it, Biglow, mind what I tell you, you might regret it. *(Grabs him by lapels again.)*

BIGLOW. Out of my face woman. *(He pushes* LILA *to the floor.)*

(She falls against stool by piano.)

Let's get out of here. *(Grabs hat and cane from table. Takes* DELLA'*s arm.)*

(At door DELLA stops and BIGLOW continues out.)

DELLA. Thanks for the treat, Lil Augie. Is you coming to the dance tonight?

AUGIE. If I lives. Maybe you and me could walk for that cake.

DELLA. Might could. (Exits.)

RAGS. (Stepping toward AUGIE.) Run along, small change. How do you figure you're gonna beat Biglow Brown's time, when the gal won't even look at me?

AUGIE. It takes small change to break a dollar, big friend. Come on ya'all, a toast before I go. (Crosses to Center.)

BADFOOT. A toast to what?

AUGIE. To my luck, Badfoot. A toast to my luck.

BADFOOT. Sure, a toast to Lil Augie's luck.

AUGIE. To my luck . . . and to Della Green. Come on. Let's all go over to Fannie Brian's.

(They exit noisily.)

(Music introduction on general exit dim.)

SLIM. (Coming over to LILA.) Don't worry, Lila, everything goin' to be all right.

(LILA shakes her head negatively. SLIM crosses back to bar.)

(LILA gets up and leaning on piano sings "Once I had a true love.")

SLIM. Behind bar
MAN. At bar.
JOSH. At piano
MAN. Behind piano
MAN. Right end of large windows
MAN. Left end of large windows
DRUNKEN WOMAN. (At second upstage table.)

I had myself a true love
A true love who was sumpin' to see
I had myself a true love
At least that's what I kept on tellin' me.

The first thing in the mornin'
I still try to think up a way
To be with him some part of the evenin'
And that's the way I live through the day.

(Crosses Down Left, sits on right side of table.)

She had herself a true love
But now he's gone and left her for good.
The Lord knows I done heard those back-
    yard whispers
Going 'round the neighborhood.
There may be a lot of things I miss
A lot of things I don't know
But I do know this
Now I ain't got no love
And once upon a time I had a true love.

In the evenin'
In the doorway
While I stand there and wait for his
    comin'
With the house swept
And the clothes hung
And the pots on the stove there shummin'
Where is he while I watch the risin' moon
With that gal in this damn ol' saloon.
(Walks to Right then Left.)
No—that ain't the way that it used to be
No—and everybody keeps tellin' me
There may be a lot of things I miss
(Sits.)
A lot of things I don' know
But I do know this
Now I ain't got no love
And once upon a time I had a true love.

(DRUNKEN WOMAN's head falls to table. Hand drops off bottle she had used
for headrest.)

(By eighth beat lights down and out.)

CURTAIN

ACT ONE

SCENE 3

TIME:
Twilight of the same day.

SCENE:

A doorstep outside BARNEY's *room. There is some casual coming and going on the street throughout the scene, but this does not interfere with the occasional passing of individuals or couples headed for the cakewalk at the Cotton Flower Ball. These wear capes and hats and carry canes. The occasion is big, and they are on their way. A street lamp bellows out a bright spot in the blue twilight.*

Into it, BUTTERFLY *rushes. She is dressed in her waitress costume, and she carries a man's suit on a hanger. She looks up and down the street to make sure she is not being watched, then turns and raps sharply on* BARNEY's *door. No answer. She raps again. Then again. Finally, someone stirs inside. A light is made behind the window blind. A moment later,* BARNEY *steps out the door. He is wearing a gaudy nightshirt but he still has sleep in his eyes.*

BUTTERFLY. *(Outdoors.)* Well, people . . .

BARNEY. What's the matter, baby? Is it morning?

BUTTERFLY. Nah, it ain't mornin', but you better make haste and get yourself in this here Augie's suit if you aim to take me to the cakewalk.

BARNEY. No need to hurry. They don't never start them things on time.

BUTTERFLY. If you'd hurry up and win a few races, I wouldn't have to be bringin' you this borryed suit of Little Augie's.

BARNEY. *(Grabbing and examining suit.)* Hot tiddy! I'm gonna out-strut Lil Augie in his own clothes.

BUTTERFLY. Here, take these clothes before somebody sees me standin' here holdin' them.

BARNEY. What if they do see you?

BUTTERFLY. I ain't the kind of gal what brings a gentlemen's clothes to a gentlemen's room. Come here and get these things, Barney.

BARNEY. *(Yawning sleepily as he opens the door.)* Come on in, honey.

BUTTERFLY. *(Drawing back suddenly.)* And lose my galhood? Well, I should say not.

BARNEY. *(Giggling.)* What's that you say, sugar lump—lose your galhood?

BUTTERFLY. Young gals don't visit gentlemens in they rooms. It ain't proper. Close that door before the neighbors see you standing there front of me in your night clothes. They might—they might think things.

BARNEY. Everybody thinks things—all the time. You can't stop 'em.

BUTTERFLY. Maybe I can't stop *them,* but I can sure stop *you.* Close that door and put on your clothes.

BARNEY. *(Taking the suit inside as he closes the door.)* If it ain't proper for gals to come in gentlemen's rooms, how about gentlemens coming in gals' rooms?

BUTTERFLY. *(Sweetly.)* Aw, Barney, that's *diffirent.*

(A middle-aged MAN *and* WOMAN *stroll into scene.)*

BARNEY. *(Loudly.)* Where'd you put my silk drawers, baby?

BUTTERFLY. *(Mortified.)* Who you talking to, Barney?

BARNEY. You, honey. Where'd you put them nice new silk drawers you gave . . .

(The COUPLE *pause, bend an ear.)*

BUTTERFLY. *(Trying hard to put them off.)* You right about that, Barney. You got to give your mama a present on her next birthday. What would you like to give her?

BARNEY. I ain't said nothing about my mama, baby. I'm talking about them silk DRAWERS you . . .

BUTTERFLY. Oh, me . . . *(Trying to out-shout him.)* Barney, you can't buy your mama nothing like that.

BARNEY. *(Outdone.)* Not ma mama's, Mine! ! ! ! Where'd—you—put—my . . .

(Their curiosity satisfied, the COUPLE *exit, smiling.)*

BUTTERFLY. *(Killing time till the pair is safely out of hearing.)* A . . . well . . . *(Then angrily.)* Mind how you talk to me out here in public, Barney. I ain't no fancy gal, and I don't do such things.

BARNEY. *(Head out the window. Eyes very big.)* Noooooooo?

BUTTERFLY. Well, you know how I mean. I do but I don't.

*(*BUTTERFLY *sings: "Legalize my name" as* BARNEY *goes into the house and dresses.)*

Will I—won't I—do I—don't I?
All you wanna do is bill and coo.
But you're empty-handed when the bill is due.
If you really love me and you love me true,
LEGALIZE MY NAME.

Will I kiss you—ain't the issue,
You've been sayin' ever since we met
That you—want a sample of the way I pet,
You've had all the samples that you're gonna get
LEGALIZE MY NAME.

'Fore we ever can dwell
Out of one valise
You must learn how to spell
Justice of the peace.
(Spoken.)
And I spell that peace with an E A
My heart's glowin'—sparks are showin'
If you want those little sparks to bust into flame,
You got to . . .
LEGALIZE MY NAME.

Even Adam
Called Eve Madam
And if I have read the good book right,
On the day the serpent made her take that bite

She was heard to murmur as she saw the light,
Come on, Big Boy, let's you and me build a little lean-to where we can raise cane.
Don't eye-ball me
City Hall me
Read your history and you will see
Cleo-patra said the same to Anthony
What was good for her's good enough for me
(Spoken.)
So run up to Tiffany's and get me a silver band for this digit. . . . Oh, honey, it's got such a lonesome look
Wedding licenses cost
Just two dollars—no more
I've seen times when you've tossed
Two away before
(Spoken.)
And that means just what you think it means
To get back to
Ipse factoo
Lawyer I ain't but I know my meaning's the same
You got to . . .
LEGALIZE MY NAME.

Love words—sweet talk
You and me talk
You say just a glimpse of my allure
Is a—glimpse of paradise I may be sure
Brother, if you wanna take the dollar tour
(Spoken.)
I suggest you send out invitations to your nearest and dearest . . . I might even want to come myself.
Sparkin'—spoonin'
Honeymoonin'
That's the kinda talk I get from you
And you often say you wish the whole world knew
Just a pair of witnesses and judge'll do
(Spoken.)
So bring a couple aunts and cousins. Let's change this temporary expedient into a

permanent state of affairs. Kindly affix your signature at the bottom of that document. . . .

Don't care where I live at

Or what I live in

House, apartment or flat

Any place but sin

(Spoken)

And I might even live there—but not alone

If you prize me

(BARNEY comes out dressed.)

Notarize me

Gimme an old piece of parchment that I can frame

You got to . . .

LEGALIZE MY NAME.

CURTAIN

ACT ONE

SCENE 4

TIME:

Evening of the same day.

SCENE:

A ballroom.

At Curtain, DANCERS are on the floor dancing. A HOSTESS, MISSISSIPPI, a MAN and a WOMAN RECEPTIONIST are standing Down Right receiving the guests as they enter. The guests bring their invitation cards, hand them to the MAN and the WOMAN, who place them on a silver tray.

MAN RECEPTIONIST. Good evening. Card, please.

WOMAN RECEPTIONIST. *(As she takes card from entering WOMAN.)* Oh, honey, how gorgeous you look!

A WOMAN. *(As she enters with her escort.)* Have you met my escort, Sadie?

SADIE, THE HOSTESS. No, chile, I ain't had the pleasure.

A WOMAN. Miss Turpin—Mr. Bruce. Mr. Bruce—Miss Turpin.

MR. BRUCE. My regards, Miss Turpin. Hope you're well.

SADIE TURPIN. Pleased to meet you, Mr. Bruce. Hope you the same.

ANOTHER MAN. *(Entering with* MISS CORDELIA.)* What's the good word, Jasper?

JASPER. Save your money, friend.

A WOMAN. *(She and* MR. BRUCE *have worked their way down to table Down Left.)* Good evening, Miss Elvira Hayes.

MR. BRUCE. Good evening, Miss Hayes.

ELVIRA HAYES. *(Introducing* MAN *standing next to her.)* Do you know Mr. Bruce?

THE MAN. No.

ELVIRA HAYES. Mr. Bruce—Mr. Pembrock. Mr. Pembrock—Mr. Bruce.

(ANOTHER MAN works his way with MISS CORDELIA *to Down Left table.)*

MISS CORDELIA. Good evening, Miss Hayes.

ELVIRA HAYES. Why, hello, Miss Cordelia.

MISS CORDELIA. *(To her escort.)* Go 'way, boy. Lemme miss you now.

ANOTHER MAN. *(Leaving* MISS CORDELIA. *Meets* GIRL.)* Will you have a wing, Miss Petunia? *(Offering his arm.)*

(KITTY MAY crosses from Right off Left. Her escort calls her back. She comes back as if to repeat cross. He grabs her and leads her back. Ad libs. SLIM *and* WOMAN *enter. Ad libs becomes louder.* MISSISSIPPI *enters with the cake.)*

MISSISSIPPI. *(Coming to Center stage with cake over his head.)* How this hit you?

(EVERYONE applauds.)

Miss Elvira Hayes baked it!

(EVERYONE applauds. BARNEY *enters on the applause in a hurry.* BADFOOT *catches him as he is about to grab the cake.)*

BARNEY. I'm going to get it.

(Laughter from ALL.)*

Look what's waiting for me.

BADFOOT. I got ten spikes what's crying to say, "Lil Augie gets it."

(Music cue.)

BARNEY. How y'all expect Lil Augie to win when I'm wearing his best suit?

BADFOOT. His used-to-be-best, you mean. Lil Augie gonna be *dressed* this night.

*(*BIGLOW *and* DELLA *enter.)*

BYSTANDER. Look at Papa Biglow.

BADFOOT. He primed all right.

*(*BIGLOW *and* DELLA *seat themselves. Ad libs from crowd.)*

MISSISSIPPI. *(Coming to Center.)* Ladies and Gentlemen. All what's expecting to square off here tonight gotta join up. Gimme your names.

*(*DANCERS *give their names in pantomime.)*

BIGLOW. *(To* DELLA.*)* Come on let's sign up.

DELLA. No, I ain't decided yet.

BIGLOW. You still pouting about this afternoon, huh?

DELLA. I ain't pouting.

BIGLOW. Then how come you don't want to sign up?

DELLA. I just ain't decided yet, I said.

*(*BIGLOW *stands above her as if entreating.)*

MISSISSIPPI. Any more names?

BIGLOW. *(Crossing to him.)* Mississippi, me and Della Green.

*(*AUGIE *enters. General ad libs from* PEOPLE.*)*

BADFOOT. Hello, Son.

MISSISSIPPI. You're just in time. We're fixin' to square off.

DELLA. *(With coquetry as she sees* AUGIE *looking around.)* You looking for somebody, Lil Augie?

AUGIE. *(Going to table, tossing coat and cane to* BADFOOT.*)* I *was.* But I ain't no more.

DELLA. You's a sight to kill and cripple, Lil Augie.

AUGIE. *(Eagerly.)* 'Member what you said today.

DELLA. *Sure* I remember. But you ain't ask me yet.

AUGIE. *(Assured.)* Come on, gal. Le's join up.

DELLA. Can you strut, Lil Augie?

AUGIE. Next to riding hosses, that's my trade.

DELLA. Make me know it.

AUGIE. *(Taking* DELLA *over to* MISSISSIPPI.*)* Lil Augie and Della Green.

(Ad libs from the PEOPLE.*)*

MISSISSIPPI. Hey, ain't you dancing with Biglow?

DELLA. You heard what he said . . .
LIL AUGIE AND DELLA GREEN!

(Ad libs from the PEOPLE.*)*

MISSISSIPPI. Down! All right, folks. Everybody get with me now. Couples will line up out yonder.

*(*QUARTETTE—"CAKEWALK"— *They start and all join in.)*

QUARTETTE. *(Coming down Center stage.)*
(Bow Right.)
Howdy do to you
I has the hon-or to
Start this func-tion
(Bow Left.)
And com-mence the ball.
(Straight Front.)
Grab a la-day fair
Pick out one a-ny where
Better have a partner
When you hear them call
Better have a partner
When you hear them call.

*(*CHORUS *joins in.* QUARTETTE *coming*

front. CHORUS *comes down, semicircle*
across stage behind QUARTETTE.)

Cakewalk your la-day,
Two step your ba-by,
Cakewalk your la-dy left an' right
Trombone is talk-in'
Best get to walk-in'
Don't you miss the boat
Lift your pet-ti-coat
Walk your gent'men for de cake dis night
Mis-sus El-vi-ray Hayes
Who's been cook-in it for days
Won de cake bak-in' prize
At de County seat
An' she whispered to me:
"It's a secret re-ci-pe
A full o' fro-lic, al-co-hol-ic pastry treat,
Choc-lit fil-ler
Pure va-nilla
Big enough to get lost in,
Cakewalk your la-dy
Two step your ba-by
Cakewalk your la-day left to right,
Dress up your proud-est
Sing out your loud-est
It don't have to rhyme
Have your-self a time
Walk your gent'men for de cake dis night,
Walk your gent'men for de cake dis night,
Walk your gent'men for de cake dis night.

(CHORUS *to Left and Right.* QUARTETTE
to Down Left table. SECOND CHORUS *is
sung as* DANCERS *promenade.*)

(*Promenade of dancers. Each couple
does a little specialty. . . .* LIL AUGIE *and*
BARNEY *compete in a Duet Dance. . . .
Finally,* LIL AUGIE *tops* BARNEY *by jumping off the piano into a split. The crowd
cheers and applauds the feat.* MISSISSIPPI
*comes down with the cake and holds it
over* BARNEY'S *head.* EVERYONE *cheers.*
BUTTERFLY *hugs him and then* MISSIS-
SIPPI *holds cake over* AUGIE'S *head and
the crowd cheers again even more and
louder.* AUGIE *is given the cake.* BUTTER-
FLY *beats* MISSISSIPPI *over the head with*

BARNEY'S *hat as he tries to protect himself. Then she goes over to* BARNEY *who
has climbed up on the piano and sits there
dejectedly.* DELLA *gets* AUGIE'S *hat and
puts it on* AUGIE'S *head. She then crosses
to the table Down Left stage to get her
cape.* BIGLOW *comes toward her menacingly.* MISSISSIPPI *tries to stop him.*)

MISSISSIPPI. Hold your hosses, Biglow.
No rough stuff here. This a respectable
dance.

BIGLOW. (*Disregarding* MISSISSIPPI.)
What this mean, Della?

DELLA. It means me and Lil Augie is
eating our cake together . . . from now
on!

ONE OF THE JUDGES. (*Coming forward
near* BIGLOW, *laughing.*) She sure flew
your coop, Biglow.

(BIGLOW *turns and knocks the* MAN *to
the floor. Looks to the Right and upstage menacingly. Then he exits.* LILA
follows.)

SADIE TURPIN. (*To the* MAN *who has
been hit.*) Honey, is you hurt? Get up.

(*General laughter into dance and as*
BIGLOW *starts Off Right . . .*)

CURTAIN

ACT TWO

SCENE 1

TIME:
Late afternoon, the following week.
SCENE:
AUGIE *and* DELLA'S *house. The living
room. There is a door at Left which gives
on to the street. In the back wall is a
window, and a door at Up Right in side
wall leading into the rest of house. The
furnishings of the room are exactly what
you would expect of Lil Augie. On a
small round table near the open window
is a pretentious kerosene lamp with a
painted shade.*

As the Curtain rises, DELLA *is in the house in a lovely white negligee. She is seated on couch with dress in her lap.*

JASPER *comes on with cart from Down Left.)*

JASPER. Jasper's vegetables! Jasper's vegetables!

(WOMAN *crosses Left to Right, appraises vegetables.* MAN *and* WOMAN *cross from Up Right to Down Left.)*

(Greeting AUGIE.*)* Hello, Augie.

AUGIE. *Hello, Jasper. (Entering house and seeing* DELLA.*)* Bring it to me, baby. Lemme taste that sugar.

DELLA. *(Seated on couch with dress in lap.)* How 'bout you comin' to get it?

(AUGIE *comes over to kiss her.)*

AUGIE. *(Catching her to him.)* Pretty gal, I loves you like a hoss loves corn, like a fly do molasses. I love you worser'n a hog loves to waller.

DELLA. Like all that?

AUGIE. *(Takes off coat.)* What you been doin', honey? You ain't fixin to wash that dress yourself, is you? *(Hangs coat over chair.)*

DELLA. Lawd, Lil Augie, I ain't never had my hands in wash suds in all my born days. I just lookin' at this old dress to see if I ought to have it cleaned or throw it away. I done worn it five or six times already. *(Gets up from couch.)*

AUGIE. *(Taking dress and throwing it away.)* Then throw it away, honey. That's four times too many. *(Holding* DELLA'S *hands.)* I can pretty nigh tell a woman what been bendin' over a wash tub too long. Hack hips, piano busts, and skeeter legs. But you is got shape, Della, and it takes me to tell you so.

DELLA. *(Laughs.)* Your eyes is too big, Lil Augie.

AUGIE. Is you happy, Della? *(Sitting down.)*

DELLA. I ain't never been so happy in

all my born days! I got a home and a man. I guess even a woman like me wants that.

AUGIE. Don't say that, honey. It sounds like you're kinda belittlin' yourself. I think 'bout you like somethin' high up and proud, like a pitcher hangin' on a wall.

DELLA. High up and proud. I want you to think of me like that always, Lil Augie. How about some sweeten' water? *(Rising and crossing to table.)*

AUGIE. That's the ticket, baby. Must have our sweeten' water.

DELLA. Ain't this the life, Lil Augie?

AUGIE. Oh, gal, I'se havin' a ball.

(Music cue.)

DELLA. *(Pours one drink.)* You is lucky. *(Crosses with drink to* AUGIE *and stands behind couch.)*

(Lights dim.)

AUGIE. Oh, I was borned lucky. Borned with a veil. That's sure enough lucky. And anybody what takes up with me gets lucky, too. I gonna make you lucky, too, if you loves me hard enough.

DELLA. I'm going to love you hard, Lil Augie. I'm going to love you worser'n I ever did anybody else.

(DELLA *sings "Come rain or come shine."*)

I'm gonna love you like nobody loved you
COME RAIN OR COME SHINE
High as a mountain and deep as a river
COME RAIN OR COME SHINE
I guess when you met me
It was just one of those things
But don't ev-er bet me
Cause I'm gonna be true if you let me.

(AUGIE *holds* DELLA'S *right hand and pulls her around couch.)*

You're gonna love me like nobody's loved me
COME RAIN OR COME SHINE

Happy to-gether, unhappy to-gether
And won't it be fine
Days may be cloudy or sunny
We're in or we're out of the money
But I'm with you Augie
I'm with you rain or shine.

(Orchestra plays first eight bars. AUGIE *gives* DELLA *his glass and crosses to table and makes drink.)*

AUGIE. *(Spoken—as he makes drink.)* You going to love me worse'en you did Biglow?

DELLA. Shucks, Biglow ain't in it. Not the way I'm going to love you.

*(*AUGIE *puts right foot on couch.)*

AUGIE.

(Sings.)

I guess when you met me
It was just one of those things
But don't ever bet me
Cause I'm gonna be true if you let me

You're gonna love me like no-bodys
   loved me
COME RAIN OR COME SHINE
Happy together, unhappy together
And won't it be fine
Days may be cloudy or sunny
We're in or we're out of the money

BOTH.
But I'm with you Della
BOTH.
I'm with you rain or shine.

(Lights dim up.)

AUGIE. That's good, honey *(He kisses her.)*, but this gonna be the law. You got to belong to me entirely. Can't nera 'nother man touch you. Just me. I mean it, and I don't want no two-timin'. No-body but me, understand?

DELLA. Sure, Lil Augie. I promise you that.

AUGIE. *(Boasting. Coming to Down Center.)* You can tell'm all now they got to come by me now.

*(*LEAH *and* BADFOOT *and the* CHILDREN *appear from stage Left ad-libbing. Go up to the door and knock.)*

*(*AUGIE *goes to door. As he opens it, a middle-aged, colored woman enters, followed by* CHILDREN *of varying sizes and behind them shuffles* BADFOOT *with* PIGGY *on his back, who's holding guitar.)*

LEAH. *(Staring at* AUGIE, *then as if recognizing him.)* Well, this *is* Lil Augie. I do declare!

AUGIE. *(Surprised.)* Yeah, this is Lil Augie! But who are you? Badfoot, who is this?

BADFOOT. *(Laughs—to* LEAH.*)* Go on and tell him who you is.

LEAH. *(Tenderly.)* Don't you know me, Lil Augie? I'd a knowed you anywhere, so much I been thinkin' 'bout you and wonderin' 'bout you, and wantin' to see you. This is me. This your big sister Leah!

AUGIE. *(Bowled over.)* No, 't ain't!

LEAH. Yes 't's!

BADFOOT. *(Confirming it.)* Sure is!

CHILDREN. Sure is!

AUGIE. Dog, if it ain't! Ole Leah!

THE CHILDREN. Hello, Uncle Augie. Hello, Uncle.

Hello. *(They tug at his hands but* AUGIE *draws back to inspect them.)*

AUGIE. Wait a minute! Wait a minute! Y'all just hold on there. Who done told you I'se your uncle?

OLDER BOY. Mama showed us your picture in the paper.

GIRL. She told us all about you.

*(*PIGGY *runs up to* AUGIE *and buries his head in* AUGIE's *stomach, trotting.)*

YOUNGEST CHILD. Uncle Augie, I want to ride hosses. I want to be like you.

AUGIE. You Mama die, huh? I ain't so much. You pretty near big as me anyhow, and talkin' 'bout "uncle."

BADFOOT. *(*YOUNGEST CHILD *has run to him, he is sititng on chair and has his arms around* CHILD. *Holds* CHILD *out.)*

This one got Uncle Augie writ all over him. Spittin' image of you, son. Might could make a good jockey outa him some day.

LEAH. (Taking CHILD from BADFOOT.) No thank you, sir. I got plans for my children. They goin' to school. They gonna learn, they gonna be somebody. (Then contritely.) 'Scuse me, Augie. I know you somebody too, a big somebody, but to be the kinda somebody I wants my children to be, they gotta have learnin'. I'm dead set on that. (Fiercely.) They gonna get learnin' if I has to switch 'em to school every day and switch 'em home every night.

AUGIE. Sure, I know what you means, Leah, and you see that these young 'uns gets it the way you wants them to have it. Shucks, I done plumb forgot my manners. Come here, Della. (To DELLA.) This my sister. This the one what raise me. Leah, this Della.

DELLA. My compliments.

(OLDEST BOY gets pictures out of hatrack mirror. BADFOOT and the CHILDREN look at them.)

LEAH. (Warmly.) How do, honey. (She turns to AUGIE.) So you's married, Lil Augie.

AUGIE. Same as married.

LEAH. Same ain't good enough.

(DELLA leaves the room.)

AUGIE. (Angrily.) Same old meddlin' Leah. Look what you done gone and done now.

LEAH. I'm sorry, son, but the truth is the light. If you love her, you ought to be willin' to give her your name.

AUGIE. What do you mean, if I love her? Della the only gal in the world I ever really love. (Crosses Down Right by couch.)

LEAH. That kind of talk don't mean nothin' if you ain't willin' to back it up with a preacher.

AUGIE. (Sits.) Della ain't never say nothin' 'bout gettin' married.

BADFOOT. THAT ain't the gal's business, son.

AUGIE. Lord knows I want to do anythin' I can to make Della happy.

LEAH. That's the way I like to hear you talk, Lil Augie, like a man. (She tries to push him into next room.) Go ahead and ask her now.

AUGIE. (Holding back. Rising, crosses to Center.) Give me time, Leah. Give me time. Let me get 'quainted with these kids. (To CHILDREN now clustered about him.) How would you like some stick candy?

CHILDREN. Yes, Uncle Augie. Please!

AUGIE. (To CHILDREN.) Here y'all, go on out to the store and get about half a peck of jawbreakers and some stick candy. (To LEAH.) How 'bout you, Leah? You still chew Brown Mule?

LEAH. Yeah, tha's my kind. Don't no other 'bacco seem to touch the spot.

AUGIE. (To CHILRDEN.) Tell the man to send four or five plugs of Brown Mule Chewin' 'bacco for Leah. (Peels a bill from his roll and hands it to youngster.)

LEAH. (To CHILDREN as they troop out and exit stage Left.) Now, don't get lost.

AUGIE. (He goes out the door to speak and waves at LITTLE GIRL.) One of these days I'm comin' out to y'all and bring you some presents what's presents.

LEAH. It sure good to see you, son.

AUGIE. Well, I've been aimin' to come back and see you too, Leah. (Reaching for bottle on table.) How 'bout some sweeten' water?

LEAH. Oh no, Lil Augie. I'se a church woman.

BADFOOT. I ain't never knowed that was a hold-back before.

LEAH. I used to keep a lil whiskey in the house in case of sickness, but I found out that as long as the whiskey was there, I was always gettin' sick.

(DELIVERY BOY enters on laugh.)

(Lights dim.)

So I had to give up the whiskey. Now I use rhubarb and soda for my heart-burn.

(There is a knock at the door.)

AUGIE. Come in.

(DELIVERY BOY enters house.)

BOY. For Miss Della Green.
AUGIE. Just leave 'em here. These some new rags for Della. *(Puts boxes on couch. Calls.)* Della! Come here, gal.
DELLA. *(Appearing thru door.)* Oh, they come?
AUGIE. Yeah, they come. *(To DELLA.)* Open 'em up. Let Leah see 'em. Mighty few mens can buy their gals rags like these.

(DELLA opens a box and displays new dress.)

LEAH. Do Jesus!
BADFOOT. Now ain't that the glory!
LEAH. Put this'n on, child. I wants to see you in it.
AUGIE. Sure, Della. Me too. Go put it on.
DELLA. A'right. *(Exits with new dress over arm. AUGIE looking off Right after DELLA.)*
LEAH. That gal sure has a lot of pretty clothes. *(Picks up dress on chair. Her mood is changing.)* Ain't no sense in no one woman havin' all them clothes. It's a sin and a shame before Heaven.
AUGIE. Ain't no sin to look good, is it? Della goin' to look mighty fine in all that silk.
LEAH. Yeah, but God don't like it.
AUGIE. God don't like it?
LEAH. Let me tell you somethin', son. Jesus ain't in this crowd you travels with. He ain't got no time for gamblers and sports and fast women.

(AUGIE puts boxes in upper Right corner.)

BADFOOT. Hush, Leah. There's where you's wrong. This Jesus' crowd. This the crowd what's gettin' most of His attention, else He wouldn't be Jesus. And He ain't forgot Lil Augie neither. Jesus loves him the same way He do you. I'll be damned if He don't!
LEAH. All I got to say, Lil Augie, is this: God done made you lucky, but if you don't pay Him some mind, He goin' to take your luck away. I know you got a pocketful of money, but . . .

(Ad lib till DELLA enters.)

DELLA. *(Entering in new dress.)* How this strike you, Miss Leah?
LEAH. That's pretty, Gal. Sure is. Too pretty.
AUGIE. Too pretty! Come on, Della, sing somethin' for Leah.
LEAH. Oh, she sing too?

(AUGIE crosses to front of couch and sits.)

DELLA. What you like to hear, Miss Leah?
LEAH. *(Primly.)* Does you know "We shall meet to part no never"?
DELLA. *(Apologetically.)* I ain't no church gal, Miss Leah. But I knows a sad tune about a poor gal what's lost her man.
AUGIE. Leah ought to like that.
DELLA. Come on Badfoot.
(DELLA sings. AUGIE gets up.)

Easy rider went and said goodbye
Easy rider left me high and dry
I had some Macks that satisfied my soul
But there ain't nobody else who can rock
  me
With a steady roll.

(While DELLA sings AUGIE smiles proudly. AUGIE falls back on couch from laughter.)

LEAH. *(Forgetting her manners.)* You like that mess?

AUGIE. *(Laughing gleefully.)* It's the most prettiest song that I ever heard. *(Lying back on couch.)*

LEAH. That's an old boogie house song, Lil Augie.

(Meanwhile THE CHILDREN *are playing in the street.)*

AUGIE. Not when Della sings it. It's sweet.

(DELLA exits from the house into alley in hurt. CHILDREN are in alley singing.)

Peekin' around the Chinquapin bush
Peekin' around the Chinquapin bush
Billy-goat came and gimme a push
In Aunt Sally's garden.

(Repeat twice.)

(JASPER enters pushing cart. DELLA gathers CHILDREN around and walks back into house.)

LEAH. *(Indicating children with* DELLA.*)* Look . . . well, Lil Augie, it's gettin' late. Reckon we best be gettin' home.

AUGIE. Awright, Leah. Come back soon.

LEAH. *(To* DELLA.*)* Honey, if I said anythin' to hurt you a while ago, you mustn't hold it against me. I just want to see you and Augie happy. Augie got somethin' to say to you and I want to hear him say it before I go. Go on, Augie.

AUGIE. Shucks, Leah, this a private matter. I don't want no crowd hanging 'round.

LEAH. Go on, Augie.

AUGIE. *(Embarrassed).* Well, Della . . .

DELLA. Yes, Augie?

AUGIE. I been thinkin'—that is, me and Leah been thinkin'—

DELLA. Yes, Lil Augie . . .

AUGIE. *(Blurting it out.)* Della, I wants to get married.

(DELLA runs and throws her arms around him.)

DELLA. Augie, that's what I been wantin' more than anythin' in the world!

(They sit.)

AUGIE. Whyn't you tell me, gal?

DELLA. 'Tain't leap year, Augie.

LEAH. *(Puts hands on* AUGIE's *and* DELLA's *shoulders.)* I'm so happy I could cry. Now you goin' to be like my song says. "We shall meet to part no never." Here, Piggy, sing it for your Uncle Augie and Miss Della.

(YOUNGEST CHILD comes to stage front and sings. BADFOOT gets up, crosses to Left of Center.)

YOUNGEST CHILD.

WE SHALL MEET TO PART NO-NEVER
We shall meet upon the shore
When this veil of tears is over
And they open wide the door
(Flings out arms.)
We shall meet to part no more.
(Arms crossed on chest.)

(Last note—arms out; after last note brushes hair back. Rushes to DELLA *after song and she embraces him.)*

(BADFOOT crosses to Down Left and sits in chair.)

LEAH. *(Intercepting a kiss between* DELLA *and* AUGIE.*)* Now, Augie, come and see me home. And on the way, I want to take you by my preacher's house. I want to get this thing over right away. *(She gets* AUGIE's *coat. Helps him put it on. Gives him his hat.)*

AUGIE. The way you carryin' on, Leah, a person'd think *you* was gettin' married. *(Puts on coat and hat.)*

(CHILDREN go out door and wait.)

I won't be long, Della.

DELLA. All right Augie, I'll be here.

AUGIE. You better come too, Badfoot.

(CHILDREN, AUGIE *and* BADFOOT *exit.* CHILDREN *are singing "Chinquapin Bush" as they turn corner.*)

(Fade-out.)

(LEAH *and* DELLA *embrace.* LEAH *exits.*)

DELLA.
(Sings.)
Peekin around the Chinquapin Bush
(Facing the way they left.)
Peekin around the Chinquapin Bush
(Facing front.)
Billy-Goat came and gimme a push.

(Light dim.)
(Closes door.)
IT SEEMS LIKE YESTERDAY
I heard the grown-up laughter
The clink of dishes
And the sounds I loved the best
And watched the kitchen lamp
Swing gently from the rafter
As I lay half asleep against my mother's breast.
There with my head on her shoulder.

(Second time—Music interlude.)

A million years, a million miles
Have come between us
An yet it seems like only yesterday.

(She sits. Repeat last seven bars.)

(BIGLOW *appears, stops, listens at door then goes around building.* LILA *enters, listens.* BIGLOW *appears at the window.*)

BIGLOW. He-o, Della.

DELLA. Biglow!

BIGLOW. Ain't you gonna ask me to come in and have some sit down?

DELLA. You can't come in here, Biglow. You know Lil Augie ain't got nothin' for you to do.

BIGLOW. He scairt I'll get his gal back, huh! Well he better mind how he leaves you sitting here in the window by yourself because Papa Biglow is first one place and then another. *(He jumps through window.)*

(LILA *exits Down Left.*)

(He crosses to bedroom door.) Where's Lil Augie at?

DELLA. You best go, Biglow. You and me ain't got nothin' more to say to each other.

BIGLOW. *(Crosses Down Right to* DELLA.*)* Oh, yes we do. You got to come back to me, Della. We got to be like we was before Lil Augie came. I can't do without you. I done had to whip three men since the Cotton Flower Ball. Now when I passes down Targee Street, don't none of them say, "There go Biglow Brown what lost his woman to a puny Lil jockey." No they don't say it but they looks it. They laughs behind my back and that hurt worsern' they words do. *(Puts his arms around* DELLA.*)* You got to come back to me, Della. Wasn't I always good to you?

DELLA. *(Breaking away. Crosses to Center.)* You was good enough, Biglow, for you kind. But you was too free with your fists. Lil Augie ain't like that. He likes to see me pretty and satin smooth. He don't like to see no bruises on my arms, nor my eyes swelled up. He's good to me, Biglow. He makes me feel like singing. I loves Lil Augie. We going to be married, Biglow.

BIGLOW. Married! . . . *(Crosses in front of* DELLA *to couch Right. Starts to laugh, then spins around.)* You loves his money that's what.

DELLA. You don't understand. You best go take Lila back. She'd crawl on her hands and knees to you, she loves you.

BIGLOW. You's mighty late pleading for Lila. Once I quits a woman I is through for good.

DELLA. You and me is pretty much the

same. Once I leave a man I don't never come back. You best go now, Biglow.

BIGLOW. Is this final, Della?

DELLA. It's as final as dirt on your grave. (DELLA *retreats as* BIGLOW *slowly walks towards her.*)

BIGLOW. A'right, then, but you listen to me. I'm going, but before I goes I got something to do with Lil Augie. So he likes you pretty and sweet, do he? He don't like to see no bruises on you, and no puffed eyes, do he?

DELLA. If you touches me, Biglow, Lil Augie'll kill you like a snake. You ain't got no right to lay a finger on me.

BIGLOW. Oh, yes I is. (*Puts his arms around her.*) I ain't never give up that right. Every man has the right to beat his own woman. You left me; I ain't left you.

(DELLA *bites* BIGLOW'S *hand, crosses to Right.*)

DELLA. You dassent, Biglow, you dassent.

BIGLOW. When I leave here, Targee Street going to have something else to grin about. They going to talk about how Biglow Brown had to do Lil Augie's manly duties for him, and beat up his woman.

(DELLA *tries to run past* BIGLOW *to Left. He catches her.*)

No you don't.

DELLA. They won't talk about it long. Half hour later, they be putting your body on a cooling board. (*She breaks away. Runs off Right.*)

BIGLOW. Why you . . .

(*He grabs her. She gets away and runs into the bedroom.* BIGLOW *follows her and you hear him hitting* DELLA. DELLA *screams and cries as he beats her.* BIGLOW *appears in doorway.* DELLA *is heard sobbing off in her room.*)

BIGLOW. Tell Lil Augie, I done him that service free of charge. Tell him that's a wedding present. (*He rushes out of the room.* LILA *appears Down Left.* BIGLOW *sees* LILA.) Where you going?

LILA. Della don't love you. I love you. You gotta come back to me. You're lonesome.

BIGLOW. Well if I is lonesome, I ain't looking for your company. You and me is quits months ago.

LILA. I ain't quits with you. Women don't never quit.

BIGLOW. (*Looking toward house.*) They quit sometimes.

LILA. Not my kind. Womens don't never quit when they loves you.

BIGLOW. You might as well make up your mind to get along without me. (*Pushes her aside and goes out of the house.*)

(LILA *follows.*)

You's poison to me, now. Your loving ain't sweet no more.

LILA. You gotta listen to me, Biglow. We gotta be together again.

BIGLOW. (*Spins around with* LILA *as he grabs her.*) Why you . . . I done whipped one woman tonight for worrying my mind, and I'm up to lumping another.

(AUGIE *comes down the alley. Sees and hears this. Rushes into the house followed by* BIGLOW. BIGLOW *leans up against the door laughing.*)

AUGIE. Della . . . Della . . . (*Rushes into room.*) are you hurt?

DELLA. I'm all right, Lil Augie.

AUGIE. You is hurt, Della. And your clothes are all torn. (AUGIE *rushes out of the room.*) You got some 'splaining to do, Biglow.

BIGLOW. I ain't 'splaining nothing.

AUGIE. You better start 'splaining, Biglow.

BIGLOW. (*Taking a step toward* AUGIE.) If you's aiming to make me back water, Lil Augie, you's long gone.

AUGIE. I ain't fattening meat for some mack to slice.

(They spin around each other.)

BIGLOW. Better keep you Chippy under lock and key then.

AUGIE. You got to take that back too, Biglow.

BIGLOW. That's big man talk, son.

AUGIE. Sure it's big man talk.

BIGLOW. *(Slowly reaching in his pocket.)* You's begging for trouble, Lil Augie.

AUGIE. *(Steps to where his gun is in hatstand up Left.)* I's begging for trouble and I's come to get it.

(LILA who has been standing outside the door, shoots BIGLOW just as he and AUGIE are about to draw their guns. LILA rushes off stage. BADFOOT runs on. BIGLOW, as he's hit, looks surprised. As his hand comes out of his pocket, he drops his pistol on the floor.)

BIGLOW. You caught me off my guard, Lil Augie. You little and biggity and you's got all the luck. But your luck is going to change before long. I'm putting a curse on you with my dying breath. *(Sits or falls into chair.)*

AUGIE. I didn't do it, Biglow. I didn't do it.

BIGLOW. GOD damn your soul in hell. You will never win another race. And I hope your luck will fail you at every turn.

(BIGLOW falls to floor dead as DELLA and BADFOOT try to drag AUGIE out.)

AUGIE. I didn't do it, Biglow. Before God I didn't do it. . . . Don't cuss me that way.

BADFOOT. Come, son, we gotta get out of here!

AUGIE. I didn't do it. . . .

DELLA. They ain't goin' to ask you that.

AUGIE. I didn't do it.

BADFOOT. Come on, son. Through the alley, in back of the house.

(They drag AUGIE off. LILA enters, runs into house. Falls to her knees at BIGLOW's body. DELLA sees LILA at BIGLOW's body. LILA looks up, sees DELLA. Their eyes meet for a moment. LILA runs out.)

CURTAIN

ACT TWO

SCENE 2

TIME:
Immediately after.
SCENE:
The alley.
LILA *rushes On. Sees ashcan. Takes revolver out of her bag and wraps a red handkerchief around it and puts it in the can. Walks away toward stage Right. Stops and sings.*

LILA. *(Sings: "Sleep peaceful Mr. Used-to-be.")*

SLEEP PEACEFUL, MISTER USED-TO-BE
I'll see yuh to th' door
Too long you got th' best o' me
But you'll never in dis world
Git th' best of me any more
You'll never find any feather bed as soft
As dat pinewood floor.

I ain'tuh gonna fret my head
I ain'tuh gonna cry
I'm gonna dress myself in red
Gonna walk around da town wid my head in the Good Lord's sky.

Home was a big town hotel
When we was courtin'
You was a money-spendin', true-lovin' mack
And jus' as long as Lila
Did th' supportin'
She was wid yuh when d' train came rollin' down th' track

But you's alone on another train tonight
One dat don't come back.

SLEEP PEACEFUL, MISTER USED-
TO-BE
I'll see you to the door
You never in dis world go'in get the best
of anybody anymore.

(LILA *walks Off Right.*)

CURTAIN

ACT TWO

SCENE 3

SCENE:
*The interior of a small, unpretentious
funeral parlor fitted out with chairs, artificial wreaths, and a few wan palms.*

As the Curtain rises, MISSISSIPPI *and*
HOPKINS, *the undertaker, each with two
bouquets in their hands, are on stage.*
MISSISSIPPI *is dressed as officially as he
was at the cakewalk.* JOSHUA *(the attend-
ant) enters with a wreath.* PEOPLE *continue to come in throughout the scene
until the* PREACHER *begins his talk. This
is unlike any funeral you have ever seen,
for no funeral clothes are worn by anyone; the* WOMEN *wear their usual loud
dresses and the* MEN *wear their equally
loud suits, with here and there a woman
adding the fantastic touch of a long black
veil. The* MEN *wear their hats throughout
the scene.*

HOPKINS. *(Indicating Downstage Center.)* Right there, Mr. Mississippi. *(To
JOSHUA.)* Place that one there, Joshua. I
just love flowers.

JOSHUA. *(A very slow and none too
thorough youth. He pauses in his work of
arranging the chairs.)* You think these
chairs be enough, sir?

HOPKINS. What do you think, Mr. Mississippi?

MISSISSIPPI. *(Gravely considering.)*

Might set out a few mo'. This is going to
be a powerful big funeral, Mr. Hopkins.

HOPKINS. *(Rubbing his hands.)* I'm
sure of it, and I'm greatly appreciative of
your bringing it to the firm of Hopkins
and Hopkins.

MISSISSIPPI. Don't think nothing of it,
Mr. Hopkins. Any time I can throw a
little business your way, I'm bound to do
it.

HOPKINS. And I'll see that you're well
taken care of . . . when your time comes.

MISSISSIPPI. *(First pleased then realizing.)* Huh? . . .

HOPKINS. You know, Mr. Mississippi,
the mortician is man's best friend.

(JOSHUA *comes down.*)

We take you when nobody else wants
you and we serve you when you can't
serve yourself. Ours is a noble and un-
selfish profession. What are your favorite flowers?

MISSISSIPPI. Well, I like yellow . . .

JOSHUA. How tall are you, Mr. Mississippi?

HOPKINS. We can make you very comfortable.

(PEOPLE *start to come in for the funeral.*)

MISSISSIPPI. Don't strain yourself.

JOSHUA. Oh, you won't feel it.

HOPKINS. Do you have the aromatic
spirits of ammonia?

JOSHUA. *(Pulling bottle from his
pocket.)* Yes, sir.

HOPKINS. I'll be very disappointed if a
number of the ladies don't faint. *(Gives
the arrangements a final survey.)*

(BADFOOT *enters. General entrances.*)

SLIM. Sure some pretty flowers, Mississippi. Which ones is our'n?

MISSISSIPPI. That'n. You mighty right
they pretty, and they cost plenty. Everybody ain't paid his portion, though, and

I don't aim to be out nothing. You ready to see me, Barney?

BARNEY. Butterfly's gonna pay for us when she comes.

(BUTTERFLY *enters carrying a small sheaf of flowers.*)

BUTTERFLY. I brung my own, Mississippi.

MISSISSIPPI. So I see.

BARNEY. *(Jumping up.)* What you mean, Butterfly, spending all that money on flowers. *(Looking at tag.)* And what does this mean? "To Biglow! Best wishes wherever you are, love and kisses, from Butterfly."

BUTTERFLY. *(Bursting into tears.)* Don't go fussing with me, Barney. Poor Biglow's dead: the saloon is closed and I ain't got no job, and you ain't never going to have none, and now just because I said love and kisses you want to fuss.

A WOMAN. Don't carry on like that, Butterfly. I needs a girl at my place. You come around right after the funeral and you got a job.

BUTTERFLY. *(Brightening up.)* You hear that, Barney? I got me a job. *(To the* WOMAN.*)* Thank you, ma'am. I sure be there soon as we finished here. *(To* BARNEY.*)* Move over, man, and let me sit down.

MISSISSIPPI. Well, Barney, that puts it up to you. Come on now, where's your contribution to the 'scription?

BARNEY. Well you see it's like this, Mississippi. I was riding a hoss. I was 'specting to come in, and . . .

MISSISSIPPI. *(Angrily.)* Yeah, I know and it didn't come in. And if you don't pay your share you ain't coming in to this funeral neither. Nobody got any business here who ain't put something down on them flowers.

BADFOOT. Hush, you all. This a funeral. Where you think you at? Let Barney alone, Mississippi, and put this here dollar down for him.

(MISSISSIPPI *accepts the money, and* BARNEY *with a sigh sinks back with relief.*)

BARNEY. Thanks, Badfoot, I sure would hate to be put out of this funeral.

(*Enter* RAGSDALE. *Suave and elegant as usual. He goes to* MISSISSIPPI *and hands him a paper.*)

Here it is, Mississippi.

MISSISSIPPI. Did you write it down like I told you?

RAGSDALE. Yes, every lie is in place.

(*General ad libs from the people in the room.*)

(*Dim front rail.*)

MISSISSIPPI. All right folks, Rags done brought the 'bituary.

(PREACHER *enters from Left. Crosses to pulpit.*)

Sh . . . quiet, there comes the preacher. Sh . . . . quiet! (*He hands* PREACHER *the obituary paper.*)

PREACHER. The Shepherd of the sheep has gathered to His bosom another of His lambs.

(MISSISSIPPI *laughs.*)

Our Brother, Biglow Brown, is gone. He was good to his friends and gentle with his enemies. And now in the golden pastures of paradise—(PREACHER *looks at paper more intensely through spectacles.*) this sweet soul looks down upon us with love and forgiveness . . . Who wrote this 'bituary?

MISSISSIPPI. We done it, Preacher.

PREACHER. Well, blessed if I'm gonna preach him up to heaven for you. Death can't change a wolf into a lamb. Tonight Biglow Brown does not look *down* upon us but he looks up from way down below. (PREACHER *points hand down over pulpit.*)

MISSISSIPPI. Hallalulah!

PREACHER. The Devil keeps Hell fires burning for just such rounders as him, so you better mind out how you live cause that's what *counts* when you meet your Maker.

(Music cue.)

A WOMAN. Have mercy!

(A WOMAN's *voice is heard singing, then* ANOTHER *and gradually the* CHORUS *picks it up.)*

A WOMAN.

A baby's born he starts to crawl
He's just like a young saplin' grow'n' tall
  2ND WOMAN.
And just as sure as he must climb
  ALL.
Everybody has his own leavin' time
Everybody has his own leavin' time.
It ain't for you—it ain't for me
One of these days it may have to be
But there's the facts—you can't deny'm
Everybody has his own leavin' time
Everybody has his own leavin' time.
Sinner Sinner
Take a helpin' hand reachin' out to you
Raise up your head and seek the sky

*(*LILA *enters.)*

The sun and moon—both is ridin' high
But just as sure as they must climb
Everybody has his own leavin' time

*(*DELLA *enters Down Left.)*

Everybody has his own leavin' time.
Sinner Sinner
Take the helpin' hand

*(*DELLA *crosses toward* LILA *Down Right.)*

(Dim lights.)

DELLA. *(Facing* LILA.*)* You got no shame, Lila.

LILA. Don't talk to me about shame, Della Green.

DELLA. Lil Augie's in jail for somethin' he didn't do. They're fixin' to try him for murder.

LILA. I ain't his judge.

DELLA. No, you ain't his judge, Lila. You the one that killed Biglow.

LILA. You're out of your head, Della Green.

DELLA. I got a heart, and I know what it tells me.

*(*ENSEMBLE *coming forward singing.)*

ENSEMBLE.
Leav' time—leav' time
Yes, indeed, I hear you
Leav' time—leav' time
Yes indeed I know
Leavin' time—leavin' time
For the highest of the mighty
And for the lowest creature here below.
Yes, yes, you better be ready
Yes, yes, the gospel done said
Yes, yes, you better be ready
When they fits that halo over your head.
A baby's born—he starts to crawl
He's like a young saplin' grow'n' tall
And just as sure as he must climb
Everybody has his own leavin' time
Everybody has his own leavin' time

LILA. *(Surrounded by the* CHORUS, *picks up last phrase.)* Leavin' time! . . . *(Rushes through them to Front Center and falls to her knees.)* Stop! Stop! I did it! I killed Biglow! I had to. Now go 'way death. Take your eyes off me! *(Buries her head in her arms.)*

BADFOOT. Hear that!

DELLA. Lil Augie is free now. *(She and* BADFOOT *embrace and dash out Left.)*

ENSEMBLE. *(Sings.)*
  A MAN.
Brother Biglow Brown gone to meet his Lord
  CHORUS.
Brother Biglow Brown got his just reward
Brother Biglow Brown gone to meet his Lord,

Everybody has his own leavin' time
Leavin' time . . . . Fare—thee—well. . . .

(ENSEMBLE, *in a semi-circle around* LILA, *kneel with heads bowed and rise to standing position with hands raised.* LILA *gets up raising her hands high on last note.*)

CURTAIN

ACT THREE

SCENE 1

TIME:
Early evening.
SCENE:
Augie's and Della's house. DELLA *is sitting at the window, nervously sewing.* CROWD *is heard returning from the races. As they stroll past,* DELLA *goes to Down Left opens it and watches them passing by. Sees* SLIM *and calls to him.* SLIM *enters reluctantly, with bowed head.*

(*Dim lights.*)

DELLA. (*Calling him.*) SLIM! How the race come out, Slim?
SLIM. This was Barney's day, Della. Lil Augie got lost in the dust. His luck is sure gone from him.
DELLA. He ain't won a race in four months. But this one is hardest for us to lose.
SLIM. Did you bet?
DELLA. All we could rake and scrape, all we could borrow and pawn . . . everythin'.
SLIM. That was a heap of weight to put on one hoss.
DELLA. I thought it might help him to break Biglow's cuss. He been feelin' so low-down, Slim, I thought this would make him feel like he just *had* to win.

(RAGS *appears at window.*)

RAGS. Well, Della, it's a sad song when you lose everything on one race.
SLIM. I be seein' you-all sometime. (*He exits.*)
DELLA. 'Bye, Slim.
SLIM. 'Bye, Della.
DELLA. (*To* RAGS.) Lil Augie and me can sing the sad tunes same way we do the sweet ones, Rags.
RAGS. You sure die hard, Della. But I'll wait. (*He turns to go but stops again.*) By the way, I've bought out Biglow's saloon.

(LEAH *and* BADFOOT *enter Up Right.*)

I'm going to make it the finest place in town . . . in honor of you, shall we say? (*He smiles as he goes.*)

(LEAH *and* BADFOOT *knock at door.*)

DELLA. Come in.
LEAH. (*Almost before she gets inside.*) Listen to me, Della Green! Bad luck got hold of Lil Augie soon's he took up with you. You got to leave him, and I'm gonna help him get free.
BADFOOT. Hold on, Leah . . .
DELLA. Augie's his own man. He don't need you.
LEAH. And he sure don't need you. God's got no use for rounders and good-timers. You gotta go, woman.
DELLA. You just a woman like me, Miss Leah. You can't give me no orders.
LEAH. Now I . . .
BADFOOT. (*Stopping* LEAH.) You best go 'long, Leah.
LEAH. (*Leaving. Crosses to Right.*) I'm givin' you God's orders. He told me to keep his temple clean. (*She exits slamming door.*)
BADFOOT. (*Crosses to* DELLA.) Don't pay her no mind, gal. Leah's all worried up. It makes her sick to see Lil Augie havin' things so hard. But she's right you know. All you do is touch a man and his luck goes from him . . . first Biglow and now Lil Augie.

DELLA. (*Sitting on sofa. She turns to him.*) You say it too, Badfoot? But I loves Lil Augie.

BADFOOT. I wouldn't fault you for that. He's easy to love, but you ain't good for him. Winnin' races made him loud and biggity, but 'friendin' the hosses made him sweet and gentle inside, and he ain't never gonna tell you hisself. That's how come I'm tellin' you. I been like his papa to him all these years. We just like this. (*Holds up two fingers close together.*) Yet and still, if ever I thought I was bad for him, I'd leave him like a dream. (*Putting hand on her shoulder.*) It's powerful hard thing to say, Della, but that's what I'm askin' you to do now.

DELLA. I can't quit Lil Augie, Badfoot. I just can't.

BADFOOT. If you love him, you got to get out of his way. He goin' from bad to worse. Before he took up with you he was a natural man. Now . . . he's lost everythin'. You can see that.

DELLA. No, no. Badfoot, I can't leave him! (*Gets up and walks around. Turning to* BADFOOT.) I'll do like you say, Badfoot. I'll go . . . I'll leave him.

BADFOOT. God bless you, gal. Now I know you love him for sure. (*He exits shaking his head.*)

(*REPRISE—DELLA. She sits on couch.*)

(*Lights dim up.*)

"*Come rain or come shine.*"

I'm gonna love you like no—body loved you,
COME RAIN OR COME SHINE
High as a mountain and deep as a riv—er,
COME RAIN OR COME SHINE
I guess when you met me
It was just one of those things
But don't ev-er bet me
Cause I'm gonna be true if you let me.
You're gonna love me like no-body's loved me,

COME RAIN OR COME SHINE
Happy to-gether, unhappy to-gether,
And won't it be fine
Days . . .

(DELLA *is overcome and breaks, sobs, stops singing.* BARNEY *and* BUTTERFLY *enter from Down Left.* DELLA *gets trunk from offstage and drags it to Center. Then gets dresses offstage and packs.*)

(*Lights dim.*)

(BARNEY *and* BUTTERFLY *pause in front of house to argue.*)

BARNEY. (*Stops Down Left.*) I've had my say. Don't bother me no more.

BUTTERFLY. Now there you go on your high hoss again.

BARNEY. I'm gonna be hard to please from now on.

BUTTERFLY. That's what I say about men. Just let 'em win a lil money, and after that can't nobody get along with them.

BARNEY. (*Showing his roll.*) You call this little?

BUTTERFLY. Well, why you don't want to be friends no more?

BARNEY. Yesterday you wouldn't have nothin' to do with me. You quit me clean.

BUTTERFLY. Aw, Barney, you didn't win no race yesterday.

BARNEY. NAW, but I was ridin' po' boy today.

BUTTERFLY. You can say that again. Aw, honey, what makes you so mean?

BARNEY. Look at who's talkin'. Why don't you go on home? (BARNEY *discovers* AUGIE *dragging his feet along in the alley. Stops* AUGIE *as he starts to enter his house.*) Well, Lil Augie, I showed you somethin' today. You'd do better to stop ridin' and just bet on me. If ever you want to borrow a suit to strut in, I'll lend you one.

AUGIE. You talk mighty big, Barney . . . but remember, Lil Augie was born with a veil. You can't get around that.

BARNEY. (Laughs.) Ha . . . ha! ! You wasn't wearin' no veil today. It's bad luck for sure when a dead man cusses you.

BUTTERFLY. Don't talk like that to Augie. It ain't his fault. Besides, seems to me you managed to lose a mighty lot of races without even bein' cussed.

AUGIE. Aw, you ain't no trouble, Barney. (Goes into house.)

BUTTERFLY. (Stepping toward BARNEY.) No trouble to you maybe, but he sure is a headache to me.

BARNEY. Nothin' like I'm gonna be from now on tho.

(They start offstage.)

Keep your distance, woman.

(AUGIE has entered house and sinks into chair, his head down, spirits low.)

(Music.)

AUGIE. We done the best we could, Della. That pony near 'bout bust hisself to pieces tryin'. It wasn't no good.

DELLA. (Crossing to AUGIE. Softly.) I know you done your best, Lil Augie. You the ridinest lil jockey in the whole world!

AUGIE. (Brightening a little.) You still believe that? Even after I loss the race?

DELLA. 'Course, Lil Augie. (Crosses to Cener.)

AUGIE. (Hopefully—taking her hands.) I ain't thru yet, Della. I'll win again for you some time. (He notices trunk.) What's this?

DELLA. Lil Augie, this is the end. I'm goin' to quit you.

AUGIE. No, Della, no!

DELLA. Your luck done change. It's leavin' time.

(Music stop.)

AUGIE. (Bewildered.) I don't understand, Della. I know my luck done change. I know we can't live like we used to, but yesterday you said it didn't make no never-mind to you.

DELLA. (Hysterically.) Don't talk to me 'bout yesterday and what I said then. That's gone. 'Member what you said 'bout you couldn't stand it 'lesson I looked like a picture on the wall? 'Member what you said 'bout the ring of roses 'round the winner's neck?

AUGIE. I guess you's right, Della. Pretty womens like you was made for lucky mens.

DELLA. (Pretending what she does not feel.) It's more'n a notion, Lil Augie. I done got used to havin' things. I got to have them, no matter what I said yesterday. How'd you like to see me washin' clothes and scrubbin' floors? How'd you like to see me sittin' for company like them other gals on Targee Street? That's how come I'm leavin' you. It's leavin' time.

(Music cue.)

AUGIE. Who gonna look after you, Della?

DELLA. (Turning away.) Rags. He's got money. You ain't gonna think hard of me, Lil Augie?

AUGIE. No, gal. All my thoughts of you goin' to be sweet as corn and roses.

DELLA. You is good, Lil Augie.

(AUGIE crosses Center. DELLA grabs hat and parasol and turns to go.)

I'll send a wagon to get the trunk. (She runs out closing door.)

(Music. Dim lights.)

AUGIE pauses a second, goes to window to look after a retreating DELLA. He starts reprise of "Rain or Shine," sinking on trunk.)

Days may be cloudy or sunny
We're in or we're out of the money
But I'm with you DELLA
I'm with you. . . .

(AUGIE breaks as MAN and WOMAN enter from Down Left. They laugh and *exit off Up Right, and he buries his head in his arms.)*

CURTAIN

ACT THREE

SCENE 2

SCENE:

The alley. BARNEY *appears from stage Right with three girls strolling toward stage Left.* BUTTERFLY *appears on scene shortly thereafter from stage Right.*

BUTTERFLY. *(Crosses to Down Left calling.)* Hey, Barney, BARNEY! *(To* WOMEN.*)* Go'way. Stop seducin' around here.

BARNEY. Go 'way, woman.

BUTTERFLY. *(Crosses to Center.)* I'm gonna tell you somethin', Barney. You can't do me like that. Here I done gone and give you some of the best weeks of my life, and now you got yourself a good hoss and won a race for once, you tryin' to play hard to get. You tryin' to high-hat me. I ain't gonna have it!

BARNEY. There you go again.

(Music cue.)

Tryin' to put it on me. You gave me the good-bye yesterday. You told me we was quits. Today you're stuck on me 'cause I'm a hero. That ain't love.

BUTTERFLY. Ha . . . ha . . . Now you listen to me. *(Begins to sing.)* "It's a woman's prerogative."

(Crosses to Down Right.)

I don't know who it was wrote it
Or by whose pen it was signed
Someone once said and I quote it
IT'S A WOMAN'S PREROGATIVE to
    change her mind.
He may have you in a halter
Harnessed before and behind
But till you kneel at that altar

IT'S A WOMAN'S PREROGATIVE to
    change her mind.
Promise anything
Anything at all
Promise everything
Honey, don't swerve
Throw him a curve
String 'em along till they show you what
    they've got in reserve
Though his bank shows a big balance
And he seems heaven-designed
If the boy's short on his talents
IT'S A WOMAN'S PREROGATIVE to
    change her mind.

Any fruit—even a lemon
Should have a beautiful rind
But if that lemon's a lemon
IT'S A WOMAN'S PREROGATIVE to
    change her mind.

If he won't bow from the center
And you're politely inclined
If he won't rise when you enter
IT'S A WOMAN'S PREROGATIVE to
    change her mind.
They say precedent
Makes a thing a law
Hooray precedent
I can say yes
When I mean no
Hard to believe, but they tell me that it's
    legally so.
So don't fret how much you've kissed 'em
If on their couch you've reclined
Don't forget—we've got a system
IT'S A WOMAN'S PREROGATIVE to
    change her mind.

If he's tough or if he's tender
Or just the in—between kind
Long as you're the feminine gender
IT'S A WOMAN'S PREROGATIVE to
    change her mind.
He may be one of those vipers
Who has a cottage all signed
Unless you like to change diapers
I suggest that you oggitate and change
    your mind.

We're the weaker sex
Everybody knows
Stay the weaker sex
Always be pure
Shy and demure
Tell him you don't—but, remember, never
tell him for sure.
He may have horses to curry
Each with a hansom behind
If there's no fringe on his surrey
IT'S A WOMAN'S PREROGATIVE to
change her mind.

CURTAIN

ACT THREE

SCENE 3

SCENE:

The bar. BIGLOW's bar is now owned by RAGSDALE. RAGSDALE is rehearsing three girls in cancan costumes. DELLA is seated on piano watching. RAGSDALE standing nearby Left crosses Up Center. A BARTENDER is behind bar; Two WAITERS Right and Left, one Left takes chairs off table and puts on tablecloths. FOUR MEN are outside window, look in waiting for place to open.

RAGSDALE. *(Calling at intervals.)* Watch
your spaces.
Get together.
Smile, smile.
Get it up.
Watch your spaces.

(At close of number, GIRLS do not finish exiting, but flop in chairs around Down Left table. One GIRL is still munching an apple.)

All right, open up, Jack.

(WAITER is setting chairs down, putting on tablecloths. MEN try to get in. WAITER tells them in pantomime "two minutes." Comes back and chases GIRL Down Left table and puts on cloth.)

(Turning to DELLA, who is sitting on piano.) Sorry I haven't time to get to your songs.

DELLA. *(Gets off piano.)* That's all right. I know them.

SLIM. *(Bursting in the door to Down Right.)* Hey! Everybody! Who you reckon is back in town? Lil Augie and Badfoot.

A MAN. Sure 'nough, Slim?

WAITER. Well, dog my cats!

SLIM. *(Crosses to Left.)* Yes sir, but that ain't all. Augie's ridin' in the Swanee Handicap tomorrow.

SECOND MAN. You must be jokin'.

SLIM. I wouldn't fool you for the world, man. The exercise boy just come back from the track and say Augie's ridin' for Mr. Arthur Weatherby's stable now.

(Ad Lib from CAN-CAN GIRLS.)

It sure do me proud to see Lil Augie in the saddle again.

RAGS. *(To CAN-CAN GIRLS.)* Get out. You got no business here anyway. *(RAGS sits Right Center table.)*

THIRD MAN. Yes, but it's the St. Louis track that's got the jinx on him. *(Exits with GIRL off Left.)*

RAGS. *(Seated Down Right table.)* And that's not the worst of it, Slim. I happen to know that Danny Jenkins is going to be in this race. Do I have to say any more?

MAN. There's not a jockey in the country to touch him.

BARNEY. *(Coming from table.)* Say, I can *touch* him, and I can out *touch* him.

RAGS. Augie never saw the day he could ride with Danny Jenkins.

BARNEY. What about me? I'm winnin' that race.

BUTTERFLY. *(Coming up to him.)* Come on, sweet papa. You gotta ride, not talk!

RAGS. *(Rising.)* Augie would be a long shot in this race even without Biglow's cuss.

SLIM. I reckon he's got his hands full all right, but I wouldn't count Lil Augie out too soon. I'm pullin' for him, me. *(Gives coat to* WAITER *and indicates to take it off Left.)*

*(*RAGS *returns to his seat opposite* DELLA.*)*

RAGS. So are you, aren't you?

DELLA. *(Rises.)* Yes, I am.

RAGS. Can't you get that lil' dude out of your mind? What kind of a spell has he put on you? Look, Della, you've been working here for six months

*(*DELLA *sits.)*

now, when you don't have to. I could give you everything you want. Why won't you marry me?

DELLA. I don't love you, Rags.

RAGS. I'm not asking that yet. You'll change.

DELLA. I'll always love Lil Augie.

RAGS. What are you going to do? When he met you, his pockets were bulging. Two months later they were inside out. Then you quit him, everything changed. He's winning again. It don't take a lawyer to explain that.

DELLA. I know. I can't go back to Augie, that's for sure. And I can't marry you neither.

*(*RAGS *crosses Up Center.* AUGIE *comes down the street with a bunch of admirers and enters the café.)*

BUTTERFLY. Here comes your Easy Rider, Della.

WOMAN. What'd I tell you 'bout Augie?

SLIM. Come on home, boy.

AUGIE. *(Shaking hands with all his old friends.)* Well, here I am. *(Sees* DELLA. *Crosses to her.)* Hello, gal.

DELLA. Hello, Lil Augie.

AUGIE. I done beat it, Della. I done beat Biglow's cuss to a fare—thee—well. I whipped him from Dallas to Havannah.

DELLA. I knowed you would.

AUGIE. I been lookin' all over the country for you, gal—El Paso, San An-

tonia, N'Awlines, Memphis, Alabama—everywhere. I been thinkin' bout you every day, and here I is now to get you back. *(Opens up his arms.)*

DELLA. *(Rises, steps Down Right.* RAGS *comes forward.)* I can't come with you, Lil Augie.

AUGIE. You can't.

DELLA. *(Reaching for a reason to tell him—seeing* RAGS.*)* You—see—Rags—I'm with Rags now, and we gonna get married. *(Hangs onto* RAGS.*)*

*(*RAGS *starts in surprise.)*

AUGIE. *(After a startled pause.)* That how it is? I should of knowed.

(Crowd turns away.)

But I reckon I loved you too hard. I had dust in my eyes. Not lucky dust, Della. Jus' plain old dirty race track dust. All I could see when I was ridin' through them clouds was you. I thought you was more than a picture, but you ain't. You ain't made for nothin' but proud clothes and rings. You got diamonds in your ears and pearls round your neck, and a great big lump of gold where your heart oughta be.

RAGS. *(Going to* DELLA *who is sobbing with her head on Down Right table.)* Della . . . hell, it's about time you knew the truth, Lil Augie.

*(*ENSEMBLE *turns back to listen.)*

This gal loves you. She ain't with me—never has been. She's just working here. For months I've wanted to marry her, but she wouldn't. The reason she left you was because she thought she brought you trouble. What she did, she did for you. She's your "ring of roses." *(*RAGS *exits Off Left.)*

AUGIE. Well, how come you didn't tell me, gal? *(Puts his arms out.)* Bring it to me, baby. Lemme taste that sugar.

DELLA. No, Lil Augie. What Rags said is for real. I brung you bad luck once, and I ain't aimin' to start you down the hill again.

AUGIE. Don't say nothin' to me 'bout luck. I been round a heap these last six months, and can't nobody talk to me 'bout luck now. I've growed up, Della. I know can't no one jockey win all the races. We up today and we down tomorrow, and that's how it goes all the time with everything.

(Music starts.)

But you, gal, you and me . . . that was somethin' better than luck. That was love.

(AUGIE sings: "Riding on the moon." Leans over table on right arm.)

High luck or low luck or no luck at all,
I'll never care if I rise or I fall,
I learned a lesson since we've been apart
I'll do all right if I follow my heart.
(Gets up, goes to Center.)
I walk under ladders
Number thirteen doesn't scare me
Cause I'm dressed up in a rainbow
And I'm ridin' on the moon.
Old Jinx had me cornered
But I found out how to shake it
And my true love helped me break it,
Now I'M RIDIN' ON THE MOON
Ah, yes, you can preach it, sister,
While I shout for joy
Ah, yes, say hello to Lady Love's baby boy.
You're my ring o' roses
So I can't be heavy hearted
Cause I'm right back where I started
And I'm RIDIN' ON THE MOON

ALL.
He walks under ladders
Number thirteen doesn't scare him,

(AUGIE appeals to DELLA.)

'Cause he's dressed up in a rainbow
And he's RIDIN' ON THE MOON.

AUGIE.
You're my ring o' roses

So I can't be heavy hearted.

ALL.
'Cause he's right back where he started
And he's ridin' . . .

AUGIE.
Yes, I'm RI . . . DIN' ON THE MOON!

DELLA. No, Lil Augie, you can't sing bad luck away.

AUGIE. I'm here to show you what I mean, Della. Tomorrow I'm riding against the jinx. It's gonna be me and Old Biglow on that track, gal. I whipped him every other place, and I'm equal to whipping him here, too.

DELLA. I hope you are, Lil Augie, I'll be the proudest one of all if you do.

AUGIE. But will you come back then? That's what I want to know.

DELLA. *(Rises.)* If yo can win right here in St. Louis, I'll come back, Lil Augie, . . . I'll come back *forever.*

AUGIE. Slim, champagne for everybody! Here! *(Tossing a roll of bills to Slim.)* And throw the change out the door. Come on, everybody! *(Lifting his glass.)* A toast . . . to my luck!

DELLA. What's that you say 'bout luck, Lil Augie?

AUGIE. 'Scuse me, gal. To tomorrow! *(Starts out, turns back to DELLA.)* I'll be seein' you, gal.

(Orchestra.)

(AUGIE and BADFOOT exit out door.)

(General ad libs.)

CURTAIN

ACT THREE

SCENE 4

SCENE:
The stable.
TIME:
Before the race. At the rise of the Curtain 4 stable boys are seen lazily

dancing to the music. One is sweeping dirt into a dust pan and handing it to AN-OTHER who passes it to still ANOTHER who throws it out the stable door. Then throws the dust pan back to the first BOY.

BARNEY *appears at stable door on 16th bar of music.*

2ND BOY. You're the best, Barney.

BARNEY. *(Entering.)* You said it. *(He starts to dance.)* Just keep your eyes on me today.

3RD BOY. *(Opening door as AUGIE appears.)* Here comes my ticket. Lil Augie!

(AUGIE coming down to BARNEY.)

AUGIE. *(As he and BARNEY start dancing.)* The track is like a silver dollar.

BARNEY. Watch me shine it.

(AUGIE and BARNEY do their dance on an orchestral tasset. BADFOOT enters at stable door. JOSHUA, MR. HOPKINS and SLIM appear at door. After the dance BARNEY starts fixing his shoe.)

BADFOOT. Lucky day son?

AUGIE. I'm gonna make it lucky, BAD-FOOT.

BARNEY. Well, Lil Augie, you ready to take your medicine?

AUGIE. Not from nobody like you, Barney.

BARNEY. Ha, ha . . . You and Biglow on one hoss. How do you expect to win? *(He exits laughing.)*

BADFOOT. That Barney's like a devilish gnat fly, son. Don't pay him no mind.

AUGIE. Everything ridin' on this race. I've gotta win, I just gotta win.

BADFOOT. Why, with me singing for you, and you standing in them stirrups ridin' like a home-sick angel, you're just bound to win.

AUGIE. Is that your opinion?

(BADFOOT sings: "That's my opinion.")

I say this and with impunity
If you seize your opportunity
You will thrive in your community
Least THAT'S MY OPINION
I will bet you if you're bettable
Idle hands are most regrettable
Honest effort unforgettable
Least THAT'S MY OPINION

JOSH, SLIM, HOPKINS *sing.*
Oh yes, oh, ain't it a shame
The hare could go
And the tortoise was slow
But he got there just the same.

(HOPKINS and SLIM enter.)

In conclusion, I reiterate
Educated or illiterate
Work is what you can't obliterate
Rent is high

HOPKINS.
And time do fly
At least THAT'S MY OPINION.

(JOSH kneels.)

SLIM.
I'll try anything that's tryable
But my rules the old reliable
Elbow grease is still appliable
Least THAT'S MY OPINION

JOSH. *(Changing knees.)*
Birds who start their day out merrily
Get the worm—but necessarily
I say yes—and I say verily
Merely an opinion.

ALL.
Oh yes, oh, ain't it the truth

BADFOOT.
You can't collect
Till you learn to correct
The mistakes you make in youth
Take a philosophic attitude
And allow your smile some latitude
Folks will smile right back in gratitude
Ask me why
ALL.

And we'll reply
At least THAT'S MY OPINION.

CURTAIN

ACT THREE

SCENE 5

SCENE:

A street corner close to the race track, a square with a cigar store.

LEAH *is singing and selling racing forms.* BADFOOT *is standing on a chair looking over a fence at stage Right, shielding his eyes with his hand. A* LOAFER *is asleep on the cigar store steps.* TWO MEN *enter shortly, together, and buy racing forms from* LEAH. MR. PEMBROCK *and a* LADY *walk on.*

LEAH. *(Selling the forms, walking back and forth as people enter.)*
Racin' forms
Sister Leah
Picks them all.
(Crossing to the LOAFER, *holding out a racing form.)*
Get you green sheet . . .

*(*TWO MEN *enter.)*

LOAFER. *(Annoyed at being awakened.)* Go way, woman, let me alone.

MR. PEMBROCK. *(To* BADFOOT.*)* How the track look?

BADFOOT. The grandstand is packed full! I'd rather watch the race from here though. See the finish a whole lot better. *(Sees* LEAH *and gets off the chair.)* Hello, Leah, what you doin' sellin' racin' forms?

LEAH. Hello, Badfoot. Well, you see, I got my children to support.

BADFOOT. I thought you was a church woman.

LEAH. I is. I works outside the track, not inside.

*(*BADFOOT *shakes his head, amused.* LEAH *continues with her song where she left off.)*

LEAH.
Seven winners
Yesterday
Every day
Racin' forms
Racin' forms.
Got everything a poor man needs but money.

(Ad lib)

Sister Leah's
Crystal ball
One thin dime
Buys it all.
Seven winners
Yesterday
Everyday
Racin' forms
Racin' forms

WOMAN. *(Down Left.)* Hey, Charlie, lend me twenty dollars.

MAN. I haven't got twenty dollars. But I got ten.

WOMAN. Well, lend me ten, and you'll owe me ten. *(Grabs money and runs in store.)*

(Ad lib from the CROWD. *The phone in the cigar store rings.* BADFOOT *answers it, hangs up and runs out of the store.)*

BADFOOT. Hey, everybody! The race will start soon. You better get your seats.

*(*ALL *begin to exit.)*

LEAH. *Racin' forms. (Bumps into* DELLA *who enters Down Left.)* Here you come—still taggin' after Lil Augie. Now I know my lil brother's gonna start losin' again.

DELLA. Augie's gonna win this time, Miss Leah. I'm prayin' for him.

LEAH. Huh! God's particular 'bout whose prayers he hears.

*(*BADFOOT *enters.)*

DELLA. We'll see.

LEAH. *(Turning to* BADFOOT.*)* Here,

Badfoot, I'm puttin' all this on Danny Jenkins. *(Hands him coins.)*

BADFOOT. *(Surprised.)* You bettin' against Lil Augie?

LEAH. I'm bettin' to win, man. Lil Augie can't do no good with *her* followin' him around, and I got a family to think about.

*(*TWO MEN *enter.)*

PEMBROCK. *(Handing roll of bills to* BADFOOT.*)* On Danny Jenkins.

BADFOOT. I'm not gettin' any money for Augie.

DELLA. *(To* BADFOOT.*)* Here's some Augie money, Badfoot. *(Hands him bills.)*

PEMBROCK. You gonna lose it, Della.

(RACE NUMBER begins . . . Scene leading into "Come on Lil Augie.")

*(*JASPER *comes out of the cigar store with two chairs.)*

PEMBROCK. *(Calling.)* Jasper, have you my box?

JASPER. *(Goes into cigar store and brings out a wooden box.)* Yes, sir.

PEMBROCK. *(To his lady friend.)* I have a box reserved for the whole season.

*(*JOSH *and* MISSISSIPPI *enter.* JOSH *carries a newspaper in which is wrapped a brace and bit.)*

JOSH. Come on, man. We can see the race great from right here. *(Indicating the fence.)*

MISSISSIPPI. Man that's too high. I can't see a thing.

JOSH. Silly boy. Ha, ha . . . I can fix that. *(He takes out the brace and bit, drills a hole in fence.)*

*(*MISSISSIPPI *pushes him away to take a look.)*

Hey, that's my seat.

ELVIRA HAYES. *(Running in with a chair.)* Move over, man. That's my place.

JOSH. Oh, Elvira, why don't you stay home and take care of your babies?

MISSISSIPPI. Let me see. *(Tries to get on chair.)*

*(*ELVIRA HAYES *pushes him away and* JOSH *helps her up.)*

WOMAN (OLLIE). *(Runs in with a stool and umbrella, also a hot dog, starts climbing on stool.)* Come, Josh, help me up.

(He helps her and as he turns away.) Open this umbrella, come on, boy. The sun isn't good for my face.

*(*MR. HOPKINS *strolls on with a chair, has a high hat and cane. He very nonchalantly picks out a spot and gets on chair.)*

ELVIRA HAYES. *(Gushing.)* Why, there's Mr. Hopkins. How-do, Mr. Hopkins.

WOMAN (OLLIE.) How-do-you-do, Mr. Hopkins. Nice day.

MR. HOPKINS. *(Gallantly tipping his hat.)* Hello, ladies, beautiful day for the races.

WOMAN (OLLIE). And where's your wife?

MR. HOPKINS. She's . . . oh . . . indisposed.

WOMAN (OLLIE). As usual.

*(*MR. HOPKINS *takes out a telescope and unfolds it. A* WOMAN *tries to get on his chair as he is looking over fence through telescope.)*

HOPKINS. Sorry, Madame, there's no room.

ELVIRA HAYES. *(As* MAN *and* KITTY MAY *come in with chair.)* There's Kitty May. Hello, Kitty May.

*(*MAN *sits in chair he has brought.* KITTY MAY, *annoyed by this, climbs on his shoulders.)*

JASPER. *(Standing by the two chairs he brought out.* TWO LADIES *come up and try to take chairs.)* Hey! Pay me first.

(General entrances start. First a group with a straight ladder from Down Left to

Upstage, then ladder against the building. Then, other ladders appear. Everyone climbs into position. Ad libs.)

MISSISSIPPI. The race is on. . . . *(Falls off ladder.)*

(They begin the song "Come on Lil Augie.")

ENSEMBLE.
There they go. There they go. Like a thunder crack
There they go. There they go. Burnin' up the track
Every son-of-a-gun runnin' in a row,
No two ways about it, there they go!

(Ad libs and repeat.)

FIRST ONLOOKER.
Hey, man, look at number seventeen
That boy carryin' the red and green
SECOND ONLOOKER.
He's some streak o' lightning,
What I mean!
ENSEMBLE. He's fast.
BUTTERFLY.
There's old Barney goin' to the rail.
FIRST ONLOOKER.
And there's Augie sittin' on his tail.
ALL ONLOOKERS.
And now where is number seventeen?
ENSEMBLE.
He's last.

(Ad libs.)

DELLA. *(Praying.)*
Come on, Lil Augie.
Throw dust in their eyes.
Come on, Lil Augie.
And cut 'em down to your size.
AUGIE GROUP.
Throw lucky dust in their eyes
And cut 'em down to your size.
Come on, Lil Augie,
Ain't no time to fail.
We're all bettin' on you
Come on and carry that mail
And keep us all out of jail,

Come on and carry that mail.
BARNEY GROUP.
Hey, Augie, whatcha doin' now?
Hey, Augie, whatcha doin' now?
Hey, Augie, whatcha doin' now?
BUTTERFLY.
He must have found that horse behind a plow.
BARNEY GROUP.
Hey, Augie, whatcha doin' now?
Hey, Augie, whatcha doin' now?
Hey, Augie, whatcha doin' now?
BUTTERFLY.
That thoroughbred appears to be a cow.
ONE GROUP.
Here they come, here they come, in a cloud of dust
Here they come, here they come, and it's win or bust
If you can't hear the noise, then you're deaf and dumb
No two ways about, here they come!
OTHER GROUP.
They're all comin' in a cloud of dust
They're all comin' and it's win or bust
There ain't any doubt about it
Here they come!
PIGGY. *(Running over and climbing up on BADFOOT's shoulders.)*
Come on, Uncle Augie, today is the day
My heart's ridin' with you,
I'm with you all of the way.
ENSEMBLE.
We're with you all of the way
We're with you all of the way.
Come on—come on—come on—come on—come on—come on—come on!

He walks under ladders
Number thirteen doesn't scare him
Cause he's dressed up in a rainbow
And he's *ridin' on the moon.*
He's our ring o' roses,
And we can't be heavy hearted
Cause he's right back where he started,
And he's ridin'
Yes, he's ridin'.

Come on, Lil Augie! !

COME ON, DANNY
(Alternating.)
COME ON, AUGIE
COME ON, DANNY
COME ON, AUGIE
DANNY
AUGIE
DANNY
AUGIE

SLIM. (Spoken.) Augie's in the lead!

(Ensemble ad lib.)

ENSEMBLE. THERE'S THE FINISH AND AUGIE WINS!

FINALE

(After CHORUS cheers and ad libs.)

SLIM. (Watching from the ladder.)
What a race!
He's slowin' down now.
He's turnin' the horse around.
Now they're leading the hoss over to the paddock.
Yes, there he is. Look at him. The horse is shyin'.
They're puttin' flowers around the horse.
They're takin' pictures.

What's he doin' now? He's jumped off the hoss.
He's headin' this way!
BADFOOT. Look at the crowd around him.

(Crowd cheers.)

SLIM. Yeah, here he comes this way.
BADFOOT. Look at him run!
SLIM. There he is. There he is.

(AUGIE jumps over the fence. DELLA comes up to him. A wreath of flowers is tossed over the fence. BADFOOT and SLIM hold it over AUGIE's head. Everyone cheers. MR. HOPKINS appears with a camera. His assistant, JOSH, is helping him. The crowd rushes into position to take picture.)

MR. HOPKINS. (With head covered by black cloth of the camera. Counting.) 1, 2, 3, 4, 5, 6, 7 . . .

CURTAIN DOWN

CURTAIN UP

28, 29, 30! NOW!

(JOSH looks into camera and squeezes bulb.)

JOSH and MR. HOPKINS have business of realizing picture has not been taken because cover was not removed from lense of camera. They silently steal off with camera.

(Group, released from picture, starts to sing "Ridin' on the moon.")

CURTAIN

THE END

Louis Peterson

Take a Giant Step

A DRAMA IN TWO ACTS

TAKE A GIANT STEP

Take a Giant Step was first presented at the Lyceum Theater, New York City, September 24, 1953.

STORY OF THE PLAY
(9 males; 7 females)

His hero is a high school lad who has been suspended for a week because he resented something his history teacher said about Negroes in the Civil War. He talked to her and retired to the boys' room and smoked a cigar. This is regarded by his father, a respected bank employee, as a heinous offense, and his mother agrees that he must always remain in his place and never speak up to white people. But his old grandmother, a semi-invalid, comes to his defense. She maintains that the kid must have pride, that his parents should support him in his lonely pursuit of it. There is a poignant scene in which the old man recants and makes every effort to win back his son's affection. And another when the boy opens his heart to the family maid and finds her singularly receptive. In the end, after the death of his grandmother, the lad finally comes of age. He has resolved his problems; he doesn't need the companionship of the white boys in the neighborhood; he's going on with his music and his studies and he's going to college.

CHARACTERS:

SPENCER SCOTT
GRANDMOTHER
TONY
IGGIE
FRANK
MAN
VIOLET
POPPY
ROSE
CAROL
LEM SCOTT
MAY SCOTT
CHRISTINE
GUSSIE
JOHNNY REYNOLDS
BOBBY REYNOLDS

SYNOPSIS OF SCENES

ACT ONE

SCENE 1: *The home of the Scotts. Late afternoon.*
SCENE 2: *A bar in the Negro section. A few hours later.*
SCENE 3: *Violet's room. Immediately following.*

ACT TWO

SCENE 1: *Same as Act I, Scene 1. Later the same evening.*
SCENE 2: *Spencer's bedroom. Two weeks later—early afternoon.*
SCENE 3: *Same as Act I, Scene 1. The following day.*

NOTE: *It is essential to the mood of the play that the settings be simple and suggestive rather than elaborately realistic.*

ACT ONE

SCENE 1

If you walked down a rather shady, middle-class street in a New England town, you would probably find a house very similar to the one in which the Scotts live. It was a rather ordinary house when it was built and it is a rather ordinary house now, but it has been well cared for, devotedly watched and cared for, and it gives off an aura of good health and happiness if houses can ever know such things. The house has been cut away to expose to view to the audience the back entrance hall, a kitchen up Left, a dining room Left, a living room and a hall Right in which there is a front door and a staircase leading to the upstairs. At the very top of the stairs, there is a little chair almost like a child's chair. If the house has any character at all it should resemble a fat old lady who has all the necessary equipment of living about her person.

If you walked down a rather shady, middle-class street in a New England town you would probably hear the same sounds that you are hearing when the Curtain rises. The sounds of boys playing baseball in the lot across the street. Spencer Scott *enters from Right into his own yard. He is a Negro boy of seventeen years. He has a croquet stake in one hand that he has pulled up out of the ground, and books in his other hand. He is hitting the side of his leg with the stake. The time is the present—fall—late October. It is a fine day—a golden warm day which is typical of New England at this time of year. After a moment* Spence, *still carrying the stake, walks into the hall. He slams the front door. On the door slam offstage noises stop.* Grandma *immediately calls offstage:*

Grandma. *(In bedroom upstairs.)* Spence. Spence. Is that you?

Spence. Yes, it's me, Gram. Who the hell does she think it is—Moses? *(Jacket and books on sofa.)*

Grandma. Where have you been?

Spence. No place.

Grandma. Well, why are you so late coming home?

Spence. No reason in particular, Gram. I just took my time. You know how that is—don't you, Gram—when you just want to take your time coming home? *(Sits on sofa. Takes off shoes.)*

Grandma. Just a minute—I can't hear you. I'll be right down.

Spence. If you do—I'll tell Mom that you've been horsing around again today.

Grandma. Just you be quiet and come up and help me.

Spence. *(Gets up, goes upstairs.)* You know you haven't got any business coming downstairs. Mom told you to stay up. Not only am I going to tell Mom, but when the doctor comes, I'm going to tell him too.

Grandma. *(Appears at door.)* Tell him. You think I care. Now come up and help me.

Spence. *(Goes all the way upstairs and helps her.)* Just lean on me, and hold tight to the railing, and I think we'll make it.

Grandma. *(Comes downstairs.)* I don't know why I can't come downstairs if I want to. *(Pauses as she labors down the stairs.)* And you keep your mouth shut about it, too.

Spence. *(Coming downstairs.)* I've already told you what I'm going to do. I'm going to spill the beans all over the house.

Grandma. You do and I'll tell your mother you were late coming home from school and that you haven't practiced yet.

Spence. You'd better put all your concentration on getting down the steps, Gram, or you're gonna fall and break your behind.

Grandma. Now you stop that kind of talk—you hear me?

Spence. Now be careful, Gram—and don't get excited.

Grandma. Well then—you stop it—you hear me?

Spence. All right, Gram. All right. Just stop hopping around like a sparrow.

Grandma. I never thought I'd live to

see the day when my own daughter's child was cursing like a trooper.

SPENCE. Haven't said anything yet, Gram. All I said was if you weren't careful you'd fall down and break your behind. And you will, too.

GRANDMA. Take your hands off me. I can do the rest myself. (*Crosses downstage toward kitchen. She notices the stake.*) What are you doing with that dirty thing in the house?

SPENCE. I wanted it. Something to bang around.

GRANDMA. You're banging dirt all over the rug. (*She is going into the kitchen.*)

(SPENCE *is going toward the living room.*)

Where are you going?

SPENCE. I'm going in and practice. (*Crosses to piano.*)

GRANDMA. Wouldn't you like something to eat first?

SPENCE. No, I wouldn't. You think you can trick me—don't you? (*Crosses Down Center to* GRANDMA. *Crosses to piano.*) I'm going in and practice and then you won't have a thing to tell Mom when she gets home.

GRANDMA. Suit yourself. (*She sits on sofa.*)

(*He sits down and begins practicing scales. There is a pause.*)

Spencer, would you get me a glass of water? I'm so out of breath.

SPENCE. (*Still practicing.*) You mooched down all those stairs without batting an eye. You can get your own water.

(*Piano starts.*)

GRANDMA. You're a mean little beggar.

SPENCE. I know it.

GRANDMA. Well, come out and talk to me. I won't tell her.

SPENCE. You're sure?

GRANDMA. You don't take my word?

SPENCE. I took your word the day be-

fore yesterday, and as a result I had to practice two hours in the morning.

GRANDMA. Well go get it and stop that racket.

SPENCE. (*Gets up, crosses to bookcase for book.*) You know, sometimes Gram, I think that you're uncultured and have no respect for art. (*Crosses to sofa with book.*) Put your right hand on this. Now repeat after me.

GRANDMA. I'll do no such thing.

SPENCE. (*Taking the book.*) O.K. then —don't. (*Moves Right.*)

GRANDMA. What do you want me to say?

SPENCE. (*Coming back, sits on sofa.*) I swear and promise that—no matter what happens—I will not tell anybody that Spencer Scott did not practice this afternoon—and if asked I will lie and say that he did.

GRANDMA. I swear and promise that —no matter what happens—I will not tell anybody that Spencer Scott did not practice this afternoon—and if asked I will lie and say that he did.

SPENCE. Telling also includes writing notes to said parties.

GRANDMA. Telling also includes writing notes to said parties.

SPENCE. I swear and promise under fear of death.

GRANDMA. I swear and promise under fear of death.

SPENCE. Amen.

GRANDMA. (*Starts to answer, changes her mind.*) No—I'm not—

(*He puts her hand on book.*)

Amen.

SPENCE. Kiss the book.

GRANDMA. I'll do not such thing. It's dirty.

SPENCE. Just one more time, Gram. Kiss the book.

GRANDMA. (*She kisses and notices.*) This isn't the Bible.

SPENCE. (*Gets up. Puts book on TV.*)

It's *Crime and Punishment*. Don't try welching. *(Crosses toward kitchen.)* What do you want to eat?

GRANDMA. Anything will do.

SPENCE. We'll have some crackers and cheese. *(Gets cheese out of refrigerator.)* Gram—now there's just one more thing. I won't tell Mom about your coming downstairs if you'll—

GRANDMA. *(Crossing for shoes at window Right.)* No—I'm not going to do it. I'll be a party to no such thing.

SPENCE. O.K., Gram. It's your funeral. You don't even know what kind of a bargain I was going to strike up with you.

GRANDMA. Yes, I do. You want a bottle of your father's beer.

SPENCE. *(Closes refrigerator.)* All right, Gram. Fine. When you're taking twice as many of those ugly, nasty tasting pills—don't say I didn't try to be a good sport.

GRANDMA. *(Gets shoes at window.)* One glass.

SPENCE. *(Opens refrigerator.)* It's a deal. One glass. *(To kitchen.)* What shall I do with the rest of the bottle?

(GRANDMA crosses Left.)

If he sees half a bottle he'll know right away.

GRANDMA. Pour it down the sink. *(Crosses to Right of table.)*

SPENCE. Good idea. *(He opens the bottle and pours a glass.)*

GRANDMA. *(As he starts to pour the rest out.)* How much is left?

SPENCE. Not much.

GRANDMA. Well bring it here. Shame to let it go to waste.

SPENCE. *(As he brings another glass over to the table.)* You know, Gram, you ought to be in politics. You sure strike a hard bargain. *(Sits Left of table.)*

GRANDMA. *(Sits Right of table.)* If I didn't you'd walk all over me. *(Pouring beer.)* This is nice—isn't it?

SPENCE. Sure is. *(He picks up the stake again and starts hitting his leg.)*

GRANDMA. Put that dirty thing down. Stop hitting yourself with it. Where have you been?

SPENCE. *(Still hitting himself.)* Well I suppose I might as well tell you. Mom's probably going to hear it coming up the street.

GRANDMA. Well—what is it?

SPENCE. What could you possibly imagine as being just about the worst thing that could happen to me?

GRANDMA. You haven't gotten any little girls in trouble—have you?

SPENCE. Nothing like that, Gram. Worse.

GRANDMA. What have you done? Will you stop hitting yourself with that thing.

SPENCE. Well, Gram, I just went and got my ass kicked out of school today.

GRANDMA. Spencer Scott! What were you doing?

SPENCE. Nothing much. Just smoking in the john.

GRANDMA. Smoking! Where?

SPENCE. In the john—the can, Gram. The Men's Room.

GRANDMA. Well that's a pretty nasty place to be smoking if you ask me. What were you smoking?

SPENCE. A cigar.

GRANDMA. A cigar. Cigarettes are not dirty enough, I suppose. You have to start smoking cigars.

SPENCE. What are you getting so excited for? I took one of Pop's.

GRANDMA. Well you ought to be ashamed of yourself. Disgracing yourself in school.

SPENCE. *(Gets up, crossing Right.)* Well I sure loused myself up proper this time.

GRANDMA. Where are you going?

SPENCE. To see if there's any mail. *(At piano. Takes mail.)*

GRANDMA. There's none for you.

SPENCE. Well you don't mind my looking anyhow, do you? *(He goes through the mail.)*

GRANDMA. You come right back here. I want to know more about this.

SPENCE. Just a second, Gram. Be patient—will you? *(Pause.)* I sure think that's a crummy way to behave. *(Crosses down.)* I've written him three letters now—the least he could do is answer one of them. *(Puts letters on TV.)*

GRANDMA. Who are you talking about now?

SPENCE. Mack—I'm talking about Mack.

GRANDMA. Your brother's probably busy with his lessons. You know what college is like.

SPENCE. No, I don't know what college is like. He's probably busy with the broads. The last letter I wrote him was about some damn important problems I got. He'll answer soon enough when he finds out they've shoved me into some loony bin. *(Crosses back to Left of table, hitting himself with stake.)*

GRANDMA. What's the matter with you, Spence?

SPENCE. Aw! I don't know, Gram.

GRANDMA. Stop hitting yourself with that thing.

SPENCE. Will you leave me alone? Don't you understand that when a guy's upset he's got to hit himself with something? You gotta do something like that.

GRANDMA. *(Softly.)* What's the matter, Spence?

SPENCE. Aw, Gram. Cut out the sympathy please. Go on and finish your beer and get back upstairs before Mom catches you.

GRANDMA. Tell me about it, Spence?

SPENCE. *(Pause.)* There's nothing to tell. What's there to it? *(Pause.)* If you're gonna sit there and look at me that way I'm gonna start feeling sorry for myself and then I'm gonna start bawling—and then you'll start bawling and we won't get anywhere.

GRANDMA. What do you want me to do?

SPENCE. Keep eating.

GRANDMA. All right. I'm eating.

SPENCE. *(Pause.)* Well—from the very beginning of school I could've told you that Miss Crowley and I weren't going to see eye to eye.

GRANDMA. Who's Miss Crowley?

SPENCE. The history teacher, Gram. The one that thinks she's cute. She's always giving the guys a preview of the latest fashions in underwear.

GRANDMA. Nasty little hussy.

SPENCE. That's the one. Well, today they started talking about the Civil War and one of the smart little skirts at the back of the room wanted to know why the Negroes in the South didn't rebel against slavery. Why did they wait for the Northerners to come down and help them? And this Miss Crowley went on to explain how they were stupid and didn't have sense enough to help themselves. *(Crosses chair Left of table; sits.)* Well, anyway, Gram, when she got through talking they sounded like the worst morons that ever lived and I began to wonder how they'd managed to live a few thousand years all by themselves in Africa with nobody's help. I would have let it pass—see—except that the whole class was whispering and giggling and turning around and looking at me—so I got up and just stood next to my desk looking at her. She looked at me for a couple of minutes and asked me if perhaps I had something to say in the discussion. I said I might have a lot of things to say if I didn't have to say them in the company of such dumb jerks. Then I asked her frankly what college she went to.

GRANDMA. What did she say?

SPENCE. She told me I was being impudent. I told her it was not my intention to be impudent but I would honestly like to know. So she puts one hand on her hip —kinda throwing the other hip out of joint at the same time—and like she wants to spit on me she says "Scoville." Then I says, "And they didn't teach you nothing about the *uprising* of the slaves during the Civil War—or Frederick Douglass?" She says, "No—they didn't." "In that case," I said, "I don't want to be in your crummy history class." And I walk out of the room. When I get out in the hall, Gram, I'm shaking, I'm so mad —and I had this cigar I was going to sell for a sundae. I knew I couldn't eat a sundae now 'cause it would just make me sick so—I just had to do something so I went into the Men's Room and smoked the cigar. I just had about two drags on the thing when in comes the janitor and hauls me down to old Hasbrook's office —and when I get down there—there's Miss Crowley and old Hasbrook talking me over in low tones—and in five short minutes he'd thrown me out of school.

GRANDMA. I should've thought he would've given you another chance.

SPENCE. He's given me many other chances, Gram. I guess I'm just a chronic offender.

GRANDMA. How long are you out for?

SPENCE. It would've been one week, but since we have a week's vacation next week, he made it two weeks. Then I'm supposed to come back dragging Pop behind me like a tail. Is he going to be burned! *(Pause.)* Do you suppose Mom will go for the story, Gram?

GRANDMA. I'm not sure.

SPENCE. You mean she's not going to go for it at all.

GRANDMA. I'm afraid that you're going to get what you rightfully deserve.

SPENCE. That's a nasty thing to say— considering the fact that I was justified.

GRANDMA. There are ways and ways of being justified.

SPENCE. You mean that I shouldn't have gotten sassy with the fruit cake.

GRANDMA. Spencer, I'm not going to say one more word to you if you don't stop using language like that—and put that stick down.

SPENCE. *(Gets up, throwing the stake on the floor.)* God—you're getting to be a crumb—just like the rest of the whole crummy world.

GRANDMA. Where are you going?

SPENCE. No place. Where in hell is there to go?

GRANDMA. You ought to be thrashed with a stick for using that kind of language to me.

SPENCE. Listen—are you my friend or not? *(Crosses back to GRANDMA.)*

GRANDMA. No—I'm not—when you talk like that.

SPENCE. *(Closer to GRANDMA.)* Well— thanks for that. Thanks. You're a real good Joe. You're a psalm singer—just like the rest of them, Gram. Love me when I'm good—hate me when I'm bad. Thanks. *(Crosses Right.)*

GRANDMA. Don't mention it.

SPENCE. You're welcome. *(Sits in armchair Right.)*

GRANDMA. The pleasure was all mine.

SPENCE. For an old lady—you can sure be plenty sarcastic when you want to be.

(Pause.)

GRANDMA. These will be exactly the last words I will say to you today, Master Scott.

(From outside a VOICE begins calling SPENCE. Softly at first, and then more loudly.)

TONY. Spence.

GRANDMA. Who's that calling you?

SPENCE. Tony.

TONY. Hey—Spence!

GRANDMA. Well—what does he want?

SPENCE. I don't know, Gram. I haven't asked him yet.

TONY. Spencer!

GRANDMA. Well, why don't you answer him?

SPENCE. Let him wait—let him wait—it won't hurt him. He likes to holler like that anyway—he has to use his voice some place. No one could ever accuse him of speaking up while he's in school. *(Rises.)*

TONY. Spencer!

GRANDMA. *(Gets up.)* Spencer Scott—if you don't answer him—I will.

SPENCE. All right, all right. *(He starts for the door and opens it.)* What're you doing there?

(TONY bounces in. He is a young Italian boy.)

Rehearsing for the Metropolitan or something? Come on in. *(Crosses to GRANDMA Left.)*

TONY. *(Crosses to Center.)* Hi, Spence. Hello, Mrs. Scott.

GRANDMA. Tony—since the first day you could talk— *(Sits.)* I've told you that I'm not Mrs. Scott. I'm Mrs. Martin. How long are you going to keep doing that?

TONY. I forget, Mrs. Martin. *(Front of sofa)*

SPENCE. You forget lots of things—don't you, pal. *(Pause. Back of chair)* Well—you got a week's vacation so it certainly can't be because you want me to help you with your algebra—besides I won't be doing algebra for a while. I got the heave-ho as you well know.

TONY. Thrown out?

SPENCE. Yep.

TONY. For how long? *(Crosses to Right.)*

SPENCE. Not counting vacation—for a week.

TONY. Gee!

SPENCE. You can say that again. *(Crosses to below table Left).*

TONY. Gee!

SPENCE. Well—you said it. Thanks, pal. *(Pause. Sits Left of table.)* Well, Tony—what little favor can I do you?

TONY. Gee, Spence. I'm sure sorry. All the guys were talking about it on the way home from school.

SPENCE. Yeh! Yeh! I know. I caught their sympathy when Miss Crowley was bitching me out.

GRANDMA. I'm going to tell your mother.

SPENCE. *(Looking at GRANDMA.)* Gram.

TONY. That's not the way it was at all. *(Pause.)* What could we say?

SPENCE. Exactly what you did. It was fine. What'd I call you when you came in —a pal? That's what you all were.

(GRANDMA goes into kitchen.)

Two hundred carat, solid gold plate pals. *(To piano. Sits.)*

TONY. *(Crosses Right.)* Geez—Spence —I'm sorry you feel that way about it.

SPENCE. *(Gets up.)* Ah! You're scratching my back with a rake, Tony. Remember the time the cop had you for stealing apples down at Markman's?

TONY. Sure I remember.

SPENCE. Did I or did I not shoot him with my slingshot? Remember the time Mrs. Donahue comes out of her house and calls you a dirty wop?

TONY. Well, hell, this was in school.

(GRANDMA crosses to sink with glass.)

SPENCE. Did I stand there and let her get away with it? I did not. That night, as nice as you please, I throw a nest of caterpillars through her window.

TONY. *(To Center.)* Yeah! And when she found out who did it—I cut your telephone wires for three nights running so she couldn't get to your mother.

GRANDMA. *(Enters room.)* I think I should warn you both now—that everything you're saying is going to be used against you—because I'm going to tell all of it.

SPENCE. *(Crossing to GRANDMA.)* Oh! No, you won't. If you so much as open your craw, Gram, I'll spill everything—

and I'll really spill. I'm desperate. *(Crosses to* TONY.*)* So there's a big difference about whether it's in school or not. Has that ever made any difference to me?

TONY. Naw!

SPENCE. Naw! Is that all you've got to say?

TONY. No—it isn't.

SPENCE. You're a crumb, Tony—just like the rest of them. *(Crosses to Right.)* And another thing—I dunno—maybe I'm getting deaf and need a hearing aid or something, but I don't hear you guys calling me for school any more in the morning.

TONY. *(Crosses to* SPENCE.*)* Ah, Spence—how many times do I have to tell you. I'm taking Marguerite to school in the morning.

SPENCE. And where are you taking her at night when you mozey past the house with her curled around your arm like a snake?

TONY. We're doing our home work together.

SPENCE. It's a little dark up in the park for home work.

TONY. Spence—cut it out—your grandmother.

SPENCE. My grandmother knows what the score is. She's been knowing it an awful long time now. She's going on eighty-three years old. You can talk freely in front of her.

TONY. Lay off—will you?

SPENCE. I'll lay off, Tony. I'll lay off plenty. You and that Marguerite Wandalowski. Two crumbs together. That don't even make a damn saltine.

TONY. *(Close to* SPENCE.*)* It's not her fault. I told you before.

(SPENCE crosses to Center.)

She likes you. She thinks you're a nice kid. *(Crosses; sits on ottoman.)* It's her father—he—well he just doesn't like colored people. I'm sorry, Mrs. Martin. But

that's the damn truth, Spence—he just doesn't like them.

(SPENCE goes to piano.)

GRANDMA. Well, I don't like Polish people either. Never have—never will. They come over here—haven't been over, mind you, long enough to know "and" from "but"—and that's the first thing they learn. Sometimes I think Hitler was right—

SPENCE. *(Down two steps.)* You're talking off the top of your head, Gram. You know he wasn't right. What've you got to say that for?

GRANDMA. I don't care—I don't like them. Never have—never will.

SPENCE. *(Crosses to* GRANDMA.*)* You say "them" as though it was some kind of bug or something. *Will* you do me a favor like a real pal, Gram? Quit trying to mix in things that you don't understand. *(To* TONY.*)* O.K., Friend—you've said your piece—what did you come over for? *(Crosses down to* TONY.*)*

TONY. Nothing—I didn't want nothing.

SPENCE. Aw—cut the bull, Tony. You must've come over here for something. You just don't come here for nothing any more. What do you *want?*

(TONY crosses to TV set.)

(SPENCE crosses to above chair Right.) You feel uncultured—you want to hear a little Bach or something? You want to see a little television—borrow a book? I just read a good one—all about the causes and preventions of syphilis.

GRANDMA. Spencer Scott!

SPENCE. *(Turns to* GRANDMA.*)* That's what the book said, Gram. Bring it out in the open—so I'm bringing it out.

GRANDMA. I'm going to tell your mother about that.

SPENCE. *(Crosses Left.)* I'll betcha I'll tell her about it before you do. *(To* TONY.*)* So what'd you come over for?

(No answer.)

Maybe I can guess. You're playing baseball over in the lot. You haven't got enough equipment. You thought maybe I'd be willing to lend some of mine. Right, Tony?

TONY. The guys asked me. I didn't want to.

SPENCE. Aw!—why didn't you want to? You're my friend, aren't you? Just because I'm sore at you? Damn sore at you?

TONY. Cut it out now, Spence. I did the best I could.

SPENCE. There's no doubt—and I'm a bum to be mad at you— (Crosses to kitchen.) So I'll tell you what I'm going to do. (He goes out into the back hall off kitchen and comes back with a baseball glove.) Who's the pitcher?

TONY. Gussie.

SPENCE. (Back to TONY. Throws glove.) Give this to Gussie with my regards. (Crosses to kitchen.)

TONY. Give it to him?

SPENCE. (Crossing back to living room with mask and mitts.) As a gift—you know what I mean—like Christmas— give it to him. And here's a catcher's mitt and mask for you. (Crosses to kitchen.)

GRANDMA. What on earth are you doing? Are you drunk, Spencer?

SPENCE. They're mine—aren't they— well, I don't want them any more. (Crosses to TONY.) And here's a bat I'm contributing to the game. I think that's just about everything.

TONY. (Picks up stuff.) You're sure you won't be wanting these back?

SPENCE. Geez—the things you can't understand. I'm giving them to you because you've been such good friends to me—one and all.

TONY. (Starts to pick up equipment. Starting to go.) Well thanks, Spence— thanks.

SPENCE. Think nothing of it. But there's just one more thing I want you to know. If I couldn't do any better than Marguerite Wandalowski and her old man

I'd cram my head into a bucket of horse manure.

GRANDMA. Now see here—

TONY. (Crosses to SPENCE.) See—that's the way you are. You can't do one nice thing without a dirty dig at the end. I ought to throw these things in your puss—

SPENCE. You won't though—will you?

GRANDMA. (Gets up.) Take 'em back, Spence. Take them right back.

TONY. Somebody—some day is going to take a poke at you.

GRANDMA. (Takes swing.) If he hits you, Spence—hit him right back.

SPENCE. (Crosses Up.) He's not going to hit anyone, Gram. He's just talking to be sure he hasn't lost his mouth some damned place. (Throws TONY to door.) Now scram the hell out of my house before I beat you and your whole team over the head. Get out!

(TONY exits quickly.)

Well I sure went and milked myself in public that time. (Sits on chair Right.)

GRANDMA. What are you talking about now?

SPENCE. Aw, Gram—I just went and did it again. You think I wanted that crumb to know how he hurt me?

GRANDMA. (Crosses to SPENCE.) Come on, Spence, let's you and I go watch television.

SPENCE. Sometimes, Gram—you get the most disgusting ideas.

GRANDMA. Well, then I'm going back upstairs. I don't understand what's wrong with you. You're just no fun to be with any more—cussing and ripping and tearing. Won't even watch a little television with me.

SPENCE. (Gets up, crosses to ottoman.) Go on in and watch it by yourself then— go on. Spend the rest of life with your head stuck in front of an old light bulb. (Sits.)

GRANDMA. What on earth is wrong with you, Spencer?

SPENCE. (Rises.) Gram—you've been sitting down here listening all afternoon. Don't you see that I'm an outcast? (Sits ottoman.)

GRANDMA. How?

SPENCE. They don't want me around any more, Gram. I cramp their style with the broads.

GRANDMA. Why?

SPENCE. Why! That's a stupid question. Because I'm black—that's why.

GRANDMA. Well, it's a good thing if they don't want you around. (Turns Right to window.) I told your mother years and years ago. "May—stay out of the South End, cause mark my words there's nothing down there, nothing—

(SPENCE crosses to kitchen.)

but Wops and Germans and Lord knows what else they'll get in the future." And what did they get—more Wops and Germans and a few Polacks thrown in for good measure and not one self-respecting colored family in the whole lot.

SPENCE. (Crosses to sofa.) Cut out that kind of talk. Sometimes, Gram—you're no help at all. I tell you my troubles and you tell me how we shouldn't have moved here in the first place. (Sits sofa.) But we're here, Gram—right here—and I was born here—and they're all the friends I've got—and it makes me damned unhappy, Gram.

GRANDMA. (Crosses close to SPENCE.) Now—now—don't cry. Don't cry, Spencer. Everything's going to be all right.

SPENCE. I had it all planned how I was going to make Tony feel like two cents the next time I saw him—and I had to go and get mad.

GRANDMA. Your father is going to get you a new bicycle.

SPENCE. Shove the bicycle.

GRANDMA. Now why would you want to do that? The best thing to do, I should think, would be to get on it and ride it. (Crosses to ottoman with pillow.) Go and get the hairbrush, Spencer. Your hair's a mess.

SPENCE. I don't want you messing around with my hair. That's sissy.

GRANDMA. Suit yourself. (Sits ottoman.)

SPENCE. (Rises, crosses to kitchen.) If I get the hairbrush you've got to promise to help me.

GRANDMA. All right. (He exits Left in kitchen for the hairbrush.) Spence, you don't suppose you could go back up to school and tell them you were eating one of those chocolate cigars, could you?

SPENCE. (Returns, sits down at GRANDMA's feet, gives her brush.) I got a feeling that those things don't light too well, Gram. (Pause.) What am I going to do, Gram?

GRANDMA. (Brushing his hair.) Well, now—I'm not sure—but one thing I am sure of. I don't know why you gave that boy all of your things. I think that's silly —damn silly if I might say so.

SPENCE. Do you suppose this happens to everyone, Gram?

GRANDMA. I suppose so. (Pause.) We haven't done this in a long time—have we?

SPENCE. What?

GRANDMA. Don't you remember when you were a little boy I used to do this every day. You'd stand—you were much shorter than you are now—and I'd brush and comb your haiir. I used to do that for all my boys. They'd sit and tell me all their troubles while I combed and brushed their hair.

SPENCE. One dumb crummy girl at school the other day asked me if we had to comb and brush our hair.

GRANDMA. What did you tell her?

SPENCE. I told her we very seldom bothered until the bugs got so fierce they started falling into food and things like that—then it was an absolute necessity.

GRANDMA. Spencer—you didn't?

SPENCE. I would've if I'd thought of it

in time. *(Pause.)* Gram—if you take the bus down at the corner and stay on it when it gets to Main Street—it will take you right out to the colored section, won't it?

GRANDMA. Well, it used to. I don't know if it still does or not. Why?

SPENCE. I was just wondering. It's getting late, Gram. Mom will be home in about a half hour. You'd better get back upstairs.

GRANDMA. *(Putting down the brush.)* Yes—hurry—come on and help me. *(Gets up, crosses to stairs.)*

SPENCE. *(Stays seated.)* Gram—I don't suppose you could lend me five dollars, could you?

GRANDMA. *(At foot of stairs.)* What on earth do you need that much money for?

SPENCE. Well, Gram—you and I know that an hour from now I'm going to be about the smallest thing crawling on two legs. The Old Lady is sure going to give me hell.

GRANDMA. You shouldn't talk about your mother that way.

SPENCE. *(Rises, crosses to stairs.)* I know, Gram—I know. It's easy for you to say—but it's true. And then I'm going to get cussed out. Pop is going to say that I'm no good and I'm no son of his. In short—he's going to call me a bastard.

GRANDMA. That isn't what he means.

SPENCE. *(Helping* GRANDMA *upstairs.)* It's sure the hell what it sounds like. In other words, Gram—if you'd lend me five dollars—I could go out and get some flowers for Mom and some cigars for Pop and begin by telling them how sorry I am, and it might take the edge off what is going to be at best a hell of an evening.

*(*GRANDMA *on landing.)*

What do you say, Gram?

GRANDMA. Well—all right. You go back downstairs and I'll get it for you.

*(*SPENCE *helps her off. Pause. Then he*

runs to kitchen, gets suitcase and clothes. *DOORBELL rings.)*

SPENCE. Dear, dear God—if that's my mother, just kill me as I open the door. *(Crosses to door. He hides suitcase Left of piano. Opens door.)* Hi! Iggie—did you give me a scare!

IGGIE. Hiya, Spence.

SPENCE. I'm in a terrible hurry, Iggie. What do you want?

IGGIE. I just came over to see if you have any stamps to trade.

SPENCE. *(Crosses Left, gets shoes.)* I haven't got much time. Come on in—but you can't stay long. I've got to go somewhere.

IGGIE. *(Comes in.)* Where are you going?

SPENCE. No place. *(Pause.)* You sure you came over to trade stamps?

IGGIE. *(At sofa.)* Sure—that's what I came over for. I finished my home work early—and so I thought I might—

SPENCE. *(Sits in chair Left of table.)* You know, Iggie—you're going to be out of school for a week. You didn't have to get your home work done so soon. That's the most disgusting thing I ever heard.

IGGIE. *(Crosses to table.)* Now look, if I want to get my home work done—that's my business. I don't tell you it's disgusting when you don't get yours done at all, do I?

SPENCE. *(Crosses back to sofa.)* O.K., O.K., Iggie. I only thought you came over because you heard I got kicked out of school.

IGGIE. No, Spence—I hadn't heard.

SPENCE. You're sure?

IGGIE. I told you I hadn't heard, didn't I? *(Sits Right of table.)*

SPENCE. *(Crosses Right to close door.)* That kind of news has a way of getting around. *(Looking at him.)* Well, what are you thinking about? *(Crosses back to sofa.)*

IGGIE. Nothing. I was just thinking that

if I got kicked out of school, I guess I'd just as soon I dropped dead right there on the floor in the principal's office.

SPENCE. O.K., Iggie. You don't need to rub it in. I get the picture. *(Looks upstairs.)*

IGGIE. I'm sorry, Spence. Is there anything I can do?

SPENCE. Now, Iggie—pardon me for being so damn polite—but what in the hell could you do about it?

IGGIE. I only want to help, Spence.

SPENCE. *(Crosses Left to below table.)* Well, you can't—so let's drop it, shall we?

IGGIE. I didn't mean that business about dropping dead. I probably wouldn't drop dead anyway. There's nothing wrong with my heart.

SPENCE. *(Sits sofa.)* Iggie—will you please cut it out.

IGGIE. Anything you say. I didn't mean to offend you.

SPENCE. You didn't offend me, Iggie. You just talk too much—that's all.

IGGIE. I'll try to do better in the future.

SPENCE. Look, Iggie—I've gone and hurt your feelings—haven't I? Hell—I'm sorry. I've always liked you, Iggie. You're a good kid. I'm apologizing, Iggie.

IGGIE. It's O.K., Spence. I know you're upset.

SPENCE. *(Crosses Down Left.)* I know how sensitive you are and all that and I just mow into you like crazy. I wish someone would tell me to shut my mouth. *(He walks to the stairs.)* Gram—hurry up with that dough, will you. Iggie—look—I'll tell you what I'm going to do for you. *(He goes over to the piano and comes back with his stamp album.)* Here—Iggie—it's yours. I want you to have it—because you're my friend.

IGGIE. Your album! But don't you want it, Spence?

SPENCE. No, Iggie. I don't want it.

IGGIE. But why? I think you must be crazy. *(Stands.)*

SPENCE. Hell, Iggie—because I'm growing up. I'm becoming a man, Iggie. And since I'm going out in just a few minutes with my girl friend—you know it's time for me to quit fooling around with stuff like that.

IGGIE. Have you got a girl friend?

SPENCE. Yeh! Yes—I have—as a matter of fact I might get married soon. Forget all about school and all.

IGGIE. Really. Who is the girl, Spence?

SPENCE. Just a girl—that's all. And if everything works out O.K., I won't be coming back. You know, I'll have to get a job and stuff like that. Now you've got to go, Iggie, 'cause I've got to finish packing and get dressed. *(Leads IGGIE Center.)*

IGGIE. Where are you going, Spence?

SPENCE. I can't tell you, Iggie.

IGGIE. Are you sure you're feeling all right?

SPENCE. Yes, Iggie, I'm feeling all right.

IGGIE. *(Crossing to door.)* Thank you for the gift. I appreciate it.

SPENCE. Forget it.

IGGIE. It's a beautiful album.

SPENCE. It certainly is.

IGGIE. *(Crosses to Center.)* Hey, I was just thinking—maybe I could go up and talk to old Hasbrook. It might do some good.

SPENCE. *(Crosses to door.)* I don't care about that any more, Iggie. I'm pretty sure I won't be coming back to school.

IGGIE. Are you sure you want me to have this, Spence?

SPENCE. Yes, Iggie, I want you to have it.

IGGIE. *(Crossing to door.)* Well—I hope I'll see you soon. *(He is opening the door.)*

SPENCE. *(At door.)* Hey, Iggie! You won't mind if just once in a while—I come over and see how you're doing with it?

IGGIE. I hope you will. Goodbye. *(Exits.)*

SPENCE. Geez—I don't know what's

wrong with me. I think maybe my brains are molding or something. (*Gets suitcase, shoves clothes inside and runs upstairs.*) Hey, Gram—will you hurry up with that five bucks so I can get the hell out of here before I really do something desperate!

CURTAIN

ACT ONE

SCENE 2

The Curtain rises on a bar and restaurant. It is a very small bar with very few bottles. The bottles that are there are mostly of blended whiskey and rum. A WOMAN stands at the telephone which is on the Right wall. There is one table and a booth at Left; a table and chairs Down Center, table Up Center; juke box Left. The bartender, FRANK, stands behind the bar, getting it ready for the evening. ROSE and POPPY are seated at the Center table, and CAROL sits at the table in the Left corner. VIOLET, the woman at the telephone, is speaking. FRANK and a MAN are arguing loudly at the bar.

VIOLET. (*At phone.*) Hello. Hello. Is Lonny there? What's that you say? Hey, Frank, I can't hear a god damned thing.

FRANK. Aw, shut up.

VIOLET. What's that you said to me?

FRANK. I said "Aw, shut up." Now shut up.

VIOLET. Listen, Frank, don't you be jumping salty with me.

POPPY. (*At Center table.*) Hey Violet— cut the crap, will you, and get back on the phone.

FRANK. Comes in here, spends the whole damn afternoon, and buys two bottles of ginger ale. Cheap—(*He smothers the last word under his breath.*)

ROSE. (*Gets up.*) What's that you called us?

FRANK. You didn't hear it, did you?

ROSE. It's just as well I didn't—cause if I'd heard it—(*Sits.*)

VIOLET. Hey! All of you—shut up. I can't hear a word. (*Returns to the phone.*) I said is Lonny there? He's not. Well, Sugar, could you tell me when you expect him? What? Would you mind telling me for how long? What in hell did he do? Lonny did that? Well, ain't that something. Well, if you happen to see him on visiting days—just tell him Violet called. Violet—roses are red—you know. That's right—thank you. (*Hangs up.*) Well, Poppy, you can scratch Lonny's name out of the book. (*Sits stool, faces Right.*)

POPPY. Hell, Violet—by the time we're through today—you're going to have more scratched-out names than anything else in this book. What happened to him?

VIOLET. (*Faces Center.*) You remember reading in the paper about that girl— in the three paper bags at the railroad station—in the locker?

POPPY. (*Nods.*) Yeh.

VIOLET. Lonny!

ROSE. Girl—are you kidding?

VIOLET. (*Crosses to table, sits back of it.*) Frank, bring us another bottle of ginger ale.

FRANK. What do you want in it?

VIOLET. We still have whiskey of our own—thank you.

FRANK. Then it'll be fifteen cents a bottle.

(*MAN crosses to Right of juke box. SPENCE enters down Right. He is carrying some books. He stands by the door looking Left at CAROL at the corner table.*)

ROSE. Fifteen cents?

FRANK. Either put your money where your mouth is or shut up.

VIOLET. Well—give us the bottle and some ice.

FRANK. The ice will cost you a dime. (*Crosses to CAROL with drink.*)

POPPY. Damn—let's get the hell out of here before he begins charging for sitting down.

VIOLET. It's all right, Poppy. Pay the man.

POPPY. (To FRANK.) Well, bring it on over—you chinchy skunk.

FRANK. Call me names like that—you can come over and get it yourselves. (FRANK notices SPENCE at bar.) Can I help you pal?

(SPENCE doesn't hear at first. EVERYONE turns around.)

Hey! You—over there.

SPENCE. You talking to me?

FRANK. Yeh. What do you want?

SPENCE. Nothing. It's kind of warm outside—and I kind of came in here to get cool.

FRANK. Out.

SPENCE. (With great discomfort.) I'm cool now. So—I'll be going. (Looks at CAROL. He hovers about door back of bar and finally exits.)

(FRANK crosses back to bar.)

POPPY. (After a pause.) Well—do we get our stuff or don't we?

FRANK. I told you—get it yourselves.

ROSE. (Rising.) Let's get the hell out of this dump.

VIOLET. It's all right—I'll get it. (Goes to bar and picks up the bottle of ginger ale and the ice.) And here's a quarter tip for you, Frank, for being so gracious.

POPPY. All right, Violet—don't be going crazy over there now. Every little bit helps, and if we don't raise the money for the rent, we'll be out in the street tomorrow.

VIOLET. (Ignoring her.) Thank you, Frank. You're a real gentleman. I'm going to tell all my friends to come over and trade with you. (Crosses to table with glasses and ice.)

FRANK. You can tell those whores that I don't want them in my place.

POPPY. Aw man—shut up.—Who else is left in that book of yours, Violet?

VIOLET. I don't know—let me see. Well, there's Sidney. We haven't called Sidney.

POPPY. What's his number? (Gets up.)

VIOLET. Two—eight nine two seven. Whose turn is it?

POPPY. (Crosses to phone.) Mine. Why in hell you think I'm getting up?

FRANK. And don't be coming in here with food. This ain't no lousy picnic grove.

VIOLET. Well, it's lousy.

POPPY. Shh.

FRANK. (Throws rag at her.) You heard what I said. Just be sure you clean up that mess before you leave.

VIOLET. (Throws rag back.) I ain't no janitor.

POPPY. (On phone.) Hello, Sidney. This is Poppy. One and the same. Haven't seen you lately. Well that's too bad. (Pause.) Sugar, we're in a bad spot 'cause tomorrow the rent man is coming around, an—

(VIOLET crosses to phone.)

Well now, Sugar, Violet is sitting right here and she's upset about the rent too. Do you remember the time you took Violet down to New York and registered in that hotel as Mr. and Mrs.?

(ROSE crosses to bar above POPPY.)

Well now—Honey—to get down to New York, you had to cross a state line. Now have you ever heard of the Mann Act? Well, Violet has. Well—I don't know all the details of it, but it seems you can get into about ten or fifteen years worth of trouble for carrying girls over state lines for the kind of purposes you had in mind.

(MAN crosses to bar.)

Now all Violet is asking for is about ten dollars—that roughly comes out to seventy-five cents a year, and she wants it tonight—at Carter's drug store—or else the F.B.I. Now have you got all that, Sugar? Fine—we'll be looking for you, hear? *(She hangs up, crosses back to her chair.)* Well, Sidney suddenly decided he had ten loose dollars around some place. We're supposed to meet him in Carter's in fifteen minutes. *(Sits in her chair.)*

(VIOLET follows, sits above table.)

ROSE. *(Crosses back to her chair, sits.)* Girl! I ain't never seen anything like you in my whole life.

POPPY. How much more we got to raise, Violet?

VIOLET. Let's see—that's Sidney—ten dollars! *(Gets up, crosses Up to rear table.)* All we need is fifteen more.

FRANK. Coming in here—blackmailing people on my telephone.

POPPY. We ain't blackmailing anybody. We're just keeping ourselves available. There's no telling—next week sometime —one of those boys might be glad that we're still here.

MAN. *(At the bar.)* I can't see why.

ROSE. Why don't you shut up?

MAN. This is a place of business. Man comes in here to have a quiet drink. If it ain't a bunch of whores, it's a television set.

POPPY. Mister—don't you be calling us whores, hear—or I'm liable to come over there and knock you breathless.

ROSE. Come on, Poppy. Don't pay no attention to him.

VIOLET. Coming in here for a quiet drink—he calls it. I seen you lamping the little girl over in the corner. You ought to be ashamed of yourself. *(Crosses to CAROL.)* Baby, if he bothers you—just come over and tell me and I'l knock his brains out. Hear?

(CAROL says nothing. VIOLET returns to Center table. SPENCE appears down Right, outside door; carries books.)

ROSE. Violet—come on and get your book out. We ain't got all night.

POPPY. I don't know why in hell we ain't got all night. We haven't got anything else to do.

(They look at her.)

Well—have we?

VIOLET. No—we haven't, stupid.

(SPENCE enters, sits stool below bar, puts books on bar.)

But you don't have to say it in here—do you? Hell—you have to keep up some pretenses, Poppy. *(Crosses up stage, sits in chair.)*

SPENCE. *(Knocking on the bar.)* How about a little service here—sport?

(ROSE crosses to VIOLET.)

FRANK. *(Eyeing him.)* What do you want now?

SPENCE. A glass of beer.

(FRANK laughs, still eyes him.)

I said a glass of beer.

FRANK. How old are you?

SPENCE. *(Pointing at the MAN.)* Did you ask him how old he was?

FRANK. No—I didn't.

SPENCE. Then why in hell are you asking me?

FRANK. I know him. He comes in here all the time.

(MAN crosses Left to juke box.)

SPENCE. Well, my name is Spencer Scott—so now you know me. Give me a glass of beer.

FRANK. What're you—just coming from school with all those books? The teacher didn't keep you after school all this time, did she? *(He laughs. He reaches for a book.)* What's this? *(Reading the title.)* The Interpretation of Dreams by Sigmund—

(SPENCE gets up, grabs book.)

You don't believe in that stuff, do you?

SPENCE. Hey—do you run a quiz show or something? You know there are other joints on this street that probably got colder beer than you got anyway. *(Pause.)* I've been to the library, see. And inside this book is my library card. They have pink cards for children and yellow cards for adults. This is a yellow card. Now as to more personal things— I've been walking a hell of a long way and I've got a headache—now will you please give me a glass of beer. I've got money for it—see—I can pay for it. I'm not drunk already. What do you say?

FRANK. How old are you?

SPENCE. Twenty-one.

FRANK. When were you born?

SPENCE. *(Without batting an eye.)* January 20, 1932.

FRANK. *(Getting a piece of paper.)* Let's see. Yep. *(Figuring it out.)* That makes you—twenty-one.

SPENCE. That's what I said.

FRANK. You look mighty young to be twenty-one.

SPENCE. Beer—Hah? A nice tall one.

FRANK. We got a special on whiskey today.

SPENCE. You know—hot shot—you got remarkable powers of persuasion there. But I asked you for a beer.

POPPY. That's right, Sugar—don't drink none of that man's whiskey. He ferments it himself.

VIOLET. You sure are right, Frank— that whiskey is special. Specially awful.

(THREE FLOWERS laugh uproariously.)

FRANK. Quiet over there. I'm minding my business.

POPPY. Say, Sugar—did I hear you say something about a dream book?

SPENCE. Yeh—I found it in the library.

(MAN blows smoke at CAROL.)

It's supposed to be pretty sexy.

VIOLET. Come on over and sit down with us.

SPENCE. Sure. *(Crosses to Center table.)*

POPPY. Does that book say anything about umbrellas? I keep having the damnedest dreams with umbrellas in them.

SPENCE. I don't know. I've just glanced through it. *(Sits Left chair.)*

POPPY. Do you mind if I take a look?

(ROSE crosses Down, sits Center.)

SPENCE. Help yourself. *(Looks at CAROL.)* You girls hang around here a lot?

ROSE. No, this isn't one of our usual hangouts. We come here about once a month to take care of a financial transaction. Do you live around here?

SPENCE. Yeh—around here. *(Pause.)* Say—do any of you know the girl over in the corner?

(MAN crosses to bar.)

ROSE. No—we don't know her at all. Mousey little thing—ain't she?

SPENCE. No, I don't think she's mousey at all.

POPPY. Hell, I can't find a thing about umbrellas in this book. This is the damnedest dream book I ever saw.

SPENCE. Give it to me—Here, I'll find it for you. *(He takes the book.)*

VIOLET. *(Gets up, crosses to ROSE. Looking at her book.)* Whose turn is it next?

ROSE. Mine. *(Gets up, starts for phone.)*

VIOLET. You call Homer. The number is two—five eight seven six.

ROSE. Two—five eight—

VIOLET. Seven six—and here's the dime.

(BOTH cross to phone. ROSE dials. VIOLET at bar.)

SPENCE. Did you say a cane or an umbrella?

POPPY. An umbrella, Sugar. (*Moves to Center chair.*) Hell—there ain't much difference between canes and umbrellas, is there? What does it say about canes?

(VIOLET *turns to Center.*)

SPENCE. It doesn't say much. It just says that a woman dreams about a man carrying a cane. It must mean you're plenty batty because they've got her whole case history written up here.

POPPY. Well, I didn't say I dreamed of canes, did I? Don't be trying to push her dreams off on me. Look for umbrellas—and don't be looking in those crazy people's dreams either. Look for some nice person that dreams of umbrellas.

ROSE. Nobody answers.

VIOLET. Well, keep ringing—his mother is always home.

ROSE. Well, what will I say if his mother answers?

VIOLET. Just ask for Homer, stupid.

ROSE. (*At phone.*) Hello, Homer? This is Rose. Well, I know an awful lot of Homers, too, and I know which one you are. Rose Thompson. How you been? Haven't seen you in a month of Sundays.

SPENCE. Wouldn't that be a hell of a thing—a month with only Sundays in it? You'd spend your whole life in church.

VIOLET. Ssh.

POPPY. Shut up.

ROSE. (*At phone.*) Well, Sugar, I was calling you because we are kind of in a jam. Violet—Poppy and me. That's right —the three flowers. We need money for the rent. I don't know—I guess everyone is trying to save money what with Christmas coming and all and they must be cutting down on the little luxuries. Oh! Homer—you say the most terrible things. (*Putting her hand over the mouthpiece.*) The son of a bitch. (*She takes her hand off.*) Well, how about it? Well, I guess we'll just have to talk to your wife, Sugar. No, I don't think I want to talk to her tonight. You'd never. Well just thanks for nothing, Homer. The same to you quartetted. (*Hangs up and sits on stool.*) Can you beat that? He said he didn't give a damn whether his wife knew or not. There's something terrible immoral about that.

POPPY. You're damn right. It's getting to the point where no one has any respect for marriage these days. I just wish somebody would ask me to marry them. I'd split their heads wide open.

SPENCE. (*Putting down the book.*) Hey! Pardon me, are you girls prostitutes or something?

(ALL *turn to him.*)

POPPY. Honey—we try to be.

SPENCE. You know—I've never met any real prostitutes before. You wouldn't mind if I asked you a couple of questions —would you?

VIOLET. Well, Honey—right now we're in a little hot water—and we also got to go out and pick up a little something down at Carter's drug store. (*At table Down Center.*) But as soon as we come back we'll answer all your questions. Why don't you go over and talk to the little girl over there until we come back? (*Crosses back to table Up Center.*)

SPENCE. Are you sure she wouldn't mind my bargin' over there like that?

POPPY. What if she does? You can sit anywhere you want in this place. Go over there and sit down. (*Gets up.*)

VIOLET. (*Crossing Down to table.*) Let's go, girls.

ROSE. I don't see why all of us have to go to get a little ten dollars from Sidney.

POPPY. Because in union there is strength. (*Crosses to* ROSE.) Now get the hell off that stool and let's go. I assume that none of us have any more names in our books? (*Exits Up Right.*)

VIOLET. Your assumption is absolutely correct.

(VIOLET *and* ROSE *exit Up Right.*

FRANK *crosses table Center, gets bottles, cleans table, returns to bar.)*

SPENCE. *(Who has been going over to the Left table very slowly—has just arrived—and is standing undecided Right of booth.)* Do you mind if I sit down?

*(*CAROL *shakes her head.)*

*(*SPENCE *sits down. He sits looking at her for a time.)* You're sure I'm not bothering you or anything, 'cause if I am, I can get the hell up and go someplace else.

CAROL. These tables aren't reserved. You can sit anywhere you please. If you bother me I can get up and get the hell out of here, that's all.

SPENCE. *(Rises, crosses Right.)* I'm sorry.

CAROL. Where are you going?

SPENCE. I guess—

CAROL. Sit down, kid. I didn't mean to scare you away.

SPENCE. *(Looks at* MAN.*)* I suppose a nice girl does have to be careful about who she talks to in a joint like this. *(Crosses back to booth.)* You don't need to be afraid of me, though.

CAROL. What makes you think that I'm such a nice girl?

SPENCE. *(Sits Right in booth.)* You can just tell—that's all.

CAROL. What makes you think that I'm not like Violet, Rose, and Poppy?

SPENCE. Aw! Quit your kidding.

CAROL. Well, thanks for thinking that I'm different from Violet, Rose, and Poppy.

SPENCE. Well, you are—aren't you?

CAROL. Yeh—in one or two respects I guess I am.

SPENCE. *(Relieved.)* I thought you were. *(Pause. Gets closer—hand out.)* My name's Spencer Scott. Everybody calls me Spence.

CAROL. *(Takes hand.)* I know. I heard you when you came in.

SPENCE. Yeh. That's because I've got such a damn big mouth. I've got a theory as to why I talk so loud. I think it's because of my youth. I guess as I get older like Mack maybe—I won't talk so loud. *(Pause.)* Mack is my brother. *(Pause.)* He used to talk loud when he was a kid.

CAROL. You're not really twenty-one, are you?

SPENCE. I was lying then. See, I've got to lie about my age until I get to be twenty-one. Since I lie about that, as you can guess, I lie about other things too. But as soon as I get to be twenty-one not another goddamn lie is going to pass my lips.

CAROL. That's very sweet.

SPENCE. I really honestly mean it.

CAROL. I really honestly believe you. *(She takes a sip of her drink and then nervously bangs the drink down on the table. Looks at* MAN.*)* Damn it. Who in hell does he think he's looking at?

SPENCE. Who?

CAROL. That guy over there. He keeps staring at me.

SPENCE. You want me to go over and speak to him?

CAROL. *(Restraining him.)* No! No! Don't bother.

(Pause. MAN *sits at chair upstage, reads paper.* FRANK *has fallen asleep, his head on the bar.)*

SPENCE. Well, now that we know each other—would you mind telling me your name?

CAROL. My name's Carol—Carol Pearson.

SPENCE. Is that Carol spelt with an "e" or with the "e" left off?

CAROL. That's Carol with the "e" left off.

SPENCE. I never knew a Carol with the "e" left off before except in a book I used to read as a kid. It was called *The Birds' Christmas Carol.* Did you ever read it?

CAROL. No, I don't think I ever did.

SPENCE. I know you'd never believe it

to look at me—but I read that book around ninety times I guess. That book used to make me cry like a baby. It was about a little girl named Carol who was doomed to die—and finally at the end, she dies—on the same day she was born —Christmas Day. Well, the last time I read that book I expected to cry again. I grabbed the old box of Kleenex and opened the book, and as I was reading, it was like me and the author had a big fight. She was trying to make me cry and I was damned if I was going to do her the favor. The whole book, believe it or not, was set up to make you cry. I gave the book to Iggie the next day.

CAROL. (After a pause.) So—what about it?

SPENCE. Iggie's a friend of mine. He's kind of hard to talk to because he's real shy. You know what I mean? But he knows I like him and I think he's getting a lot better. I got a theory about that. Would you like to hear it?

CAROL. I can hardly wait.

SPENCE. Well—it's this. My theory is that everybody needs somebody else. What do you think about that?

CAROL. I think you've got something.

SPENCE. I kind of thought that you'd think so. (Pause.) I need somebody too, I guess. I know you wouldn't believe it to look at me but you're looking at one of the most friendless persons in the whole United States.

CAROL. Aw! Come on—

SPENCE. Well, I guess that that wasn't exactly the truth—because you see there's my Gram. She's the only pal I got left— I guess.

CAROL. (Pulling out a cigarette.) Have you got a match, kid?

(SPENCE pulls out matches. CAROL takes them.)

Thanks. So your mom and pop don't trust you, is that it?

SPENCE. They'd like to—but I sure as

hell think they're not so sure that I'm not going to turn out the family skeleton.

CAROL. So what makes you think that you're so friendless? (Crosses to juke box.)

SPENCE. Well, that's a story and a half. You see I live—I mean used to live down at the South End. (Turns Right.) There aren't many colored families down there; in fact, there are about two. So Mack and I grew up with the white kids who lived on our street. We had lots of good times together—and it wasn't until the kids started getting interested in sex that my troubles began.

CAROL. How do you mean?

SPENCE. Well, actually it started happening last summer. For weeks they wouldn't call me. To be frank with you— I thought it was because my personality wasn't so hot maybe. You see—I'm a real guy.

(CAROL has put a nickel in juke box which doesn't work. She gives up and returns to booth. Sits.)

I play the piano—but not enough for the guys to think I'm a sissy. I'm a little thin but I got a build that would knock you out to be perfectly honest with you—but I still thought that something was wrong with me—

CAROL. That's an old, old story, kid.

SPENCE. What do you mean?

CAROL. I can finish it for you. You're pretty fed up with the whole business, aren't you? You don't know what the hell to do because you're lonely. It's a hell of a feeling. So you start smoking, drinking beer. You want to be a real grown up guy before your time. The only thing you know is that this kid stuff is for the birds —so you're going to run away from it— get to be an adult because maybe being an adult will bring a couple of things with it. Happiness—a nice girl—maybe—

SPENCE. Yes, I guess that's it. But all the kids my age are interested in the broads now. So I was passing by here—saw you in the window—and decided to give it a whirl.

CAROL. *(Laughs.)* Thanks—for seeing me in the window.

SPENCE. I know you think it sounds pretty silly because I know how girls are about going around with boys that are younger than they are—but have you ever gotten a really good look at the Kinsey report?

CAROL. No, I'm afraid I don't read much.

SPENCE. Well—I'm honestly not one to boast—but it says in that book that boys my age are usually pretty sexy. In fact, they're sexier at my age than they ever will be again in their whole goddamn lives. And what with my other qualifications that I told you about, I should be a pretty good boy friend to have.

CAROL. You know—I'd almost bet that that was the truth.

SPENCE. Well, what do you say? I know I started off all wrong. I should have started off by shooting you the old bull about how lovely you are and all that stuff, but I figured that if I asked you to be my girl friend you'd know that I thought you were pretty and all that because I really couldn't be interested in a lemon. I also want you to know that if everything goes right between me and you and we decide that we love each other, I'm perfectly willing to get married.

(CAROL moves downstage on bench.)

My father wants me to go to college but I'd be perfectly willing to forego that if everything works out okay. How about it?

CAROL. Spence, youre a sweet kid and that was about the sweetest proposal I've ever had. *(She watches SPENCE who has pressed glass to forehead.)* Is there something wrong?

SPENCE. Naw—just a headache. Too much beer, I guess.

CAROL. *(Taking glass from him.)* You know what you ought to do? Go on home and let your grandmother give you a great big kiss and tuck you in.

SPENCE. Don't you understand? I won't be going home. I've got to look for a job. What do you say?

CAROL. I've already told you what I say. Go on home. I don't want to hear any more of your troubles. I've got troubles of my own. You talk about getting a job. What in hell could you do? You couldn't do any better than my husband.

SPENCE. Your husband?

CAROL. Yes. He works all day and he works all night and we've still got nothing. He's what is commonly known as unskilled labor. I guess you know what that means. *(Pause.)* I'm sorry, kid.

SPENCE. You should have told me you were married in the first place. I feel like a great big can of garbage. *(Turns away.)*

CAROL. You didn't hear a word I said, did you, kid? *(Gathers her purse.)*

(MAN crosses bar.)

I've got to go now.

SPENCE. Where are you going?

CAROL. You see that guy in the corner of the bar? Well, he's been staring at me all night. I hope he has some money. I hope he has a car—a nice car with a top that goes down. I can go for a drive in the country and for maybe two hours I can have some fun.

SPENCE. I think that's terrible.

CAROL. So do I—so there's two of us. *(Finishes drink.)* And if my husband ever finds out, he'd kill me, so I guess there's three of us. But I'm going anyway because I've got to. I can't go home to that lousy one-room flat and wait all night. It's too quiet there. There's nobody to talk to. It's just no fun—that's all.

SPENCE. *(Pause.)* If you're going—why don't you go?

CAROL. It's funny how when you're young you can be so selfish about your

feelings, isn't it? Thank you for the pro-posal. *(Rises, crosses Right of table.)* Please don't be sore. I tried to help you, Spence. There's a nursery rhyme I used to know. It goes,
"Merry have we met, and merry have we been,
Merry let us part, and merry meet again."
Let's not part angrily.

(He doesn't answer.)

Spence! *(She walks over and kisses him squarely on the mouth.)* Good luck, kid.

(She walks over to the MAN *at the bar. He pays for her, and they leave together Up Right. The* THREE FLOWERS *re-enter Up Right.* VIOLET *enters first.)*

VIOLET. *(Offstage.)* I don't care what you say, it's a stinking way to behave. *(Sees money* MAN *has left on bar, picks it up, crosses to Center table, sits.)* Stand-ing us up like that.

POPPY. Every little bit helps.

ROSE. *(Crosses to juke box, puts nickel in.)* And then not answering the phone is the rudest thing I ever heard of.

POPPY. *(Crosses to Right of table, sits.)* I told you to stop worrying about it. To-morrow morning, on his way to work, I'll get him. And he'll either cough up that ten bucks or I'l snatch him baldheaded. That ten-spot is as good as got—so stop worrying about it.

(JUKE BOX starts playing.)

VIOLET. Hey! Spence. We're through with our business. You can come over now if you want to.

(SPENCE doesn't move.)

ROSE. *(Crossing to Center table, sits Left.)* Well as far as I can see we might just as well be dead. We might just as well amble on over to the graveyard and lie down.

(SPENCE sits for one more moment, with his head hidden from them, and then he rises, crosses in.)

SPENCE. Hey! Violet—is there any lip-stick on my mouth to speak of?

VIOLET. There sure is, Honey.

POPPY. What're you doing smearing lipstick all over your mouth like that? You queer or something?

SPENCE. Cut the comedy. Did you see that girl over there in the corner?

ROSE. You mean she kissed you?

SPENCE. Yeh. I guess I'm what you call a pretty fast worker, huh?

VIOLET. How would you like to come with me? *(Gets up.)*

SPENCE. Where are we going?

VIOLET. You said you wanted to talk to me, didn't you? I just thought we could go someplace where we could be alone—a quieter place.

SPENCE. Sure—that's okay with me.

VIOLET. Let's go, Sugar—I know just the place.

(SPENCE leans against booth.)

What's the matter, Honey?

SPENCE. Nothing. Been drinking too much, I guess.

VIOLET. Well, come on, Sugar—You got enough money to buy me a sandwich or something?

SPENCE. *(As he exits Up Right,* VIOLET *following.)* Sure—I got two dollars and thirty-nine cents.

VIOLET. *(Coming back to table Down Center.)* That sounds like the price of something in a fire sale—doesn't it? Well, Hell— *(Exits Up Right.)*

CURTAIN

ACT ONE

SCENE 3

Violet's room. VIOLET *is turning the key in the lock as the Curtain rises.*

SPENCE *is behind her. When they enter there is the distinct sound of muffled VOICES.*

SPENCE. What's that?

VIOLET. *(Sits chair Right, takes off shoes.)* The two men next door. Don't worry about them—they're deaf.

SPENCE. *(Standing Center.)* It sounded like they were in the next room.

VIOLET. They are. The walls here are very thin.

SPENCE. Thin is hardly the word. You might say they were put together with spitballs. You been away or something?

VIOLET. *(Crossing Left to drapes.)* No, why?

SPENCE. Nothing except that it looks like you've put everything to bed for the night.

VIOLET. *(Crosses to bed, takes off cover, folds it, puts it behind curtain.)* Oh. Those are my covers. It keeps things neat and clean.

SPENCE. Say, I thought you wanted to go to another restaurant where we could talk?

VIOLET. It's much more comfy to talk here. We can have something sent in if we want it. Don't you want to take your jacket off? It's pretty warm in here. *(Turns on light above bureau.)*

SPENCE. *(Crossing chair Right.)* Thanks —I guess I will. You wouldn't happen to have something to eat hanging around, would you?

(VIOLET crosses behind drapes.)

I'm feeling pretty groggy. I think perhaps it's because I haven't had any supper.

VIOLET. There's some crackers up there. *(She points to the bureau. Crosses to bureau—then behind drapes.)*

SPENCE. Thanks. *(Crosses to bureau, gets them and starts eating them.)* What kind of radio is this?

VIOLET. It's a short wave radio. It gets the police calls. *(Takes clothes off line, crosses behind drapes.)*

SPENCE. Why would anyone want the crumby police calls?

VIOLET. For a number of reasons.

SPENCE. What ever happens in this crumby town that should interest anybody?

VIOLET. *(Crossing to him.)* Sugar—that radio is like a husband to me. Now why don't you stop worrying about the radio and take off your tie and get comfortable so we can talk.

SPENCE. *(At bureau.)* I can talk with my tie on. That's never been one of my difficulties.

VIOLET. Would you like to hear a little music?

SPENCE. That would be nice.

VIOLET. *(Turns on the RADIO. Crosses back of drapes.)* You wouldn't mind if I changed into something a little more comfortable, would you?

SPENCE. Not at all.

VIOLET. I won't be a minute.

SPENCE. You wouldn't have a little cheese to go with these crackers, would you?

(RADIO plays Chopin Sonata in B flat minor, Opus 35, Funeral March.)

VIOLET. Look around and see.

SPENCE. Any place in particular? *(Looks in sink.)*

VIOLET. Just look around. I seem to remember seeing some cheese around here a couple of days ago. What's that they're playing?

SPENCE. It's Chopin.

VIOLET. Is he playing or being played?

SPENCE. He's being played. Chopin's dead.

VIOLET. Recently?

SPENCE. *(Crossing Right.)* Not too recently. Over a hundred years ago.

VIOLET. Isn't that sad?

SPENCE. *(Looking on bed table and under bed.)* I guess it was when it happened. Well—I don't seem to find any cheese around here at all.

VIOLET. I guess Poppy must've taken it for the trap. *(Re-enters.)* Now—how do I look? *(She has emerged in a bronze satin negligee with maribou around the collar and down the front.)*

SPENCE. Do you honestly feel more comfortable in that?

VIOLET. Oh! Much much more. *(She moves over to bed, sits.)* Now come on and let's sit down over here so we can talk.

SPENCE. *(Sits in chair Right.)* I should think that it would tickle the back of your neck something awful. What shall we talk about?

VIOLET. Why I thought you wanted to talk to me. *(Pause.)* Do you have to listen to that?

SPENCE. Not necessarily. *(Rises and switches RADIO off.)* These crackers don't seem to be doing a damn bit of good.

VIOLET. Come on back.

SPENCE. Sure. *(He sits back down on the chair Right.)*

VIOLET. Come on closer.

SPENCE. What for? I can hear you from here.

VIOLET. *(Crawling over bed.)* Aw! Come on, Sugar. Stop being so bashful.

SPENCE. I'm not being bashful.

(She pulls SPENCE by the hand.)

All right, I'll come. You don't have to pull me. *(He sits on bed.)*

VIOLET. *(Puts her arms around his neck.)* Now tell Violet all about it.

SPENCE. All about what?

VIOLET. What's troubling you.

SPENCE. Nothing's troubling me.

VIOLET. Supposing you give Violet a little kiss. That might make you feel better.

SPENCE. I honestly don't see how a kiss is going to do anything for my hunger.

VIOLET. Well, try it, baby, and see.

(SPENCE gives her an experimental peck on the cheek.)

Oh! Come on, Sugar. You can do better than that. *(She grabs SPENCE, pulls him back on the bed and kisses him.)*

SPENCE. *(After some time breaks away, crosses Right.)* God damn it.

VIOLET. What's the matter?

SPENCE. *(Gets jacket from chair and starts to put it on.)* I left my books over in the bar.

VIOLET. Well—what about it?

SPENCE. They're library books. If they were my books I wouldn't care.

VIOLET. *(Gets up, stands Left of bed.)* Say—what's the matter with you anyway?

SPENCE. I told you. My books are over there.

VIOLET. So let them stay there. No one's going to run away with them.

SPENCE. How can you be so sure of that?

VIOLET. Listen, Sugar—no one that ever goes in Frank's ever reads nothing. Take my word for it.

SPENCE. I'd better go.

VIOLET. *(Jumps onto bed, runs over it, and holds door.)* Hey! Are you trying to run out on me?

SPENCE. Why would I do a thing like that?

VIOLET. *(Still standing on bed.)* Well that's sure as hell what it looks like. *(Pause).* What happened to all those questions you had to ask me? What happened to all that big talk you were throwing around in the bar?

SPENCE. Nothing happened to it. I got a headache and I'm hungry—at least I think I'm hungry.

VIOLET. I think you're just plain scared.

SPENCE. Scared of who?

VIOLET. Scared of me—that's who. *(A thought dawning on her, gets down from bed.)* Hey! How old are you anyway?

SPENCE. I told you—twenty-one.

VIOLET. *(Sits on bed.)* If you're twenty-one, I'm sweet sixteen. Come over here.

(SPENCE sits in chair.)

You've never been in a place like this before—have you? You're kind of scared, aren't you?

SPENCE. Well—to be perfectly honest with you, I guess I am kind of scared. I guess I just want to go and get my books —if you don't mind. *(Crosses to door.)*

VIOLET. *(Crossing to door.)* Look, kid —I most certainly do mind.

(SPENCE sits chair.)

Let me tell you how this mess works. You've taken me out of circulation for roughly fifteen minutes now—fifteen minutes in which anything could happen— and if you think that you're just going to put your coat on and walk out of here— you've got another thought coming. I want my two dollars and thirty-nine cents.

SPENCE. But that's all the money I have.

VIOLET. I know it's all the money you have. You think if you had more I'd be asking for two dollars and thirty-nine cents? What do you take me for anyway? It ain't that I don't understand, Sugar, it's just that business is business.

SPENCE. *(Reaching into his pocket.)* Is it all right if I keep a half a dollar for supper?

VIOLET. You can take the crackers as you leave. I want my two thirty-nine. *(Taking it, crossing to bureau, puts money away.)* Thank you. And another thing— if you ever tell anybody that all you paid me was two thirty-nine I'll have your head on a platter. You hear me? *(Sits on bed, leans back.)*

SPENCE. I understand. Is it all right if I go now?

VIOLET. Suit yourself. *(Puts key on bed table.)*

(SPENCE starts to go, then stops.)

What's the matter—did you lose something?

SPENCE. I was just thinking.

VIOLET. Thinking what?

SPENCE. Well—if I go back to that bar —Poppy and Rose are still there—aren't they?

VIOLET. They'd better be.

SPENCE. Well—I was just thinking— if I go back over there in such a short time, they'll know that—

VIOLET. You was a bust? They sure will.

SPENCE. I was just wondering—if you'd mind terribly if I stayed about fifteen minutes more.

VIOLET. Help yourself.

SPENCE. *(Goes over and sits stiffly in Down Right chair.)* You wouldn't tell them—would you?

VIOLET. Tell them what?

SPENCE. That I was such a—bust?

VIOLET. If you can keep my secret I can keep yours.

(They sit in silence for some time.)

You know—if you're going to sit there— I'm afraid that you're going to have to say something. If there's one thing I can't stand it's silence.

SPENCE. What do you want me to say?

VIOLET. I don't want you to say anything that you don't want to say. Just talk. *(Gets pillows and doll from behind drapes.)*

SPENCE. What time is it?

VIOLET. The fifteen minutes ain't passed yet. You know the old saying about a watched pot never boiling. *(Sits back on bed, arranges doll's dress.)*

SPENCE. Would you like me to read to you for a while?

VIOLET. Do I look like an old lady to you?

SPENCE. No.

VIOLET. Well I can see to read to myself, thank you very much.

SPENCE. I'm sorry. I'm—

VIOLET. Forget it. Just forget it.

SPENCE. I wonder—if you'd do me a favor?

VIOLET. As long as there's no money involved—yes.

SPENCE. Well—there is. I was wondering if you'd loan me a dime for bus fare. I want to go home.

VIOLET. Well, can't you walk?

SPENCE. It's down at the South End.

VIOLET. Well that's what I get for playing around with kids. Just reach in and take a dime—and only a dime.

(SPENCE walks over to the bureau and opens it and takes a dime. VIOLET watches carefully, lying on her stomach, head downstage. He closes it and then stops and leans on it.)

What's the matter with you, anyway?

SPENCE. Nothing—I just don't feel good. (Starts for the door.) Thanks for the dime.

VIOLET. Don't bother thanking me. It hurts me to give it to you.

SPENCE. (At door.) Well—thanks anyway. But there's one thing I want you to know.

VIOLET. What's that?

SPENCE. I think that's one of the ugliest bath robes I've ever seen in my life! (He walks out the door as—)

CURTAIN

ACT TWO

SCENE 1

As the Curtain rises on Spence's home —there is one light on—the light over LEM SCOTT's chair. He is in it. He is asleep with a newspaper in his lap. The rest of the house is quiet—superficially at least. It is later the same evening. Someone passes in the street outside— they are whistling. It wakes LEM.

LEM. (Half-asleep.) May—we got to— (Rises, crosses to Center below stairs.) Well, I'll be damned. May! May!

MAY. (Upstairs.) What do you want?

LEM. What time is it?

MAY. Five minutes have passed since you asked me that the last time. It's ten minutes after ten.

LEM. (Yawns.) Well—where the hell is he?

MAY. Daddy—I don't know. I've told you that over and over again. I haven't one idea left.

LEM. Well, how can you be up there asleep—when for all you know he could be dead some place? (Crosses down Right.)

MAY. If he's dead, Daddy—there's nothing we can do about it until we know. I'm not asleep.

LEM. Is that mother of yours asleep?

MAY. I don't see how she could be.

LEM. (Picks up more newspapers.) I think she knows more than she's letting on.

MAY. Well, there's a five hundred watt light downstairs in the pantry. Why don't you bring it up along with your rubber hose and give her the third degree?

LEM. Why don't you cut out being so smart? That's the trouble with your whole family—they think they're smart. (Kicks stool.)

MAY. (Appears at head of stairs.) Why don't you just go back to your paper, Daddy—or watch the television for a while?

LEM. When I get my hands on that little bastard I'll break every bone in his body.

MAY. (Coming down the stairs to Left side of sofa, sits.) Now that's no way to talk, Daddy.

GRANDMA. (Offstage.) It most certainly is not. It's disgraceful.

MAY. Mama—will you please keep out of it? (Turns on lamp by sofa.)

GRANDMA. The truth is the truth and should be spoken at all times.

MAY. Mother, please!

GRANDMA. (Enters, sits landing.) Don't please Mother me. The truth is the truth.

It's disgraceful. If there are any bastards around—it's you who've sired them. My May is a good girl.

LEM. Would you please tell her to stay out of it?

MAY. Mother, please.

GRANDMA. Well, speak up to him. Don't let him get away with talk like that. Just speak up.

MAY. I'd speak up, Mama, if you'd give me half a chance.

GRANDMA. Calling your husband "Daddy" all the time. If that isn't the silliest thing I ever heard.

MAY. Mother, if you don't keep out of this, I'll come upstairs and give you a pill and shut your door.

GRANDMA. And I'll spit out the pill and open the door. So there.

LEM. *(Gets up—crosses to foot of stairs.)* Will you two stop that bickering and let's get down to the point at hand. *(Calling up to* GRANDMA.*)* Do you know where he is?

(No answer.)

Hey! Old lady—I'm talking to you.

GRANDMA. If you're talking to me—my name is Mrs. Martin, and I'd thank you to remember that. No—I don't know where he is, and if I did I wouldn't tell you.

(LEM turns away.)

MAY. Would you tell me, Mama?

GRANDMA. Tell you?—after your telling me to shut up? I wouldn't tell you a thing.

MAY. I didn't tell you to shut up, Mama.

GRANDMA. Well, you said "Mother please," which is the same thing.

LEM. There's no use talking to her. *(Sits in his chair, takes up paper.)*

GRANDMA. Calling your son a bastard—the very idea. No wonder he uses such terrible language. No wonder he's in trouble down there at—*(She stops.)*

LEM. Where is he in trouble?

(No answer.)

MAY. Mama—what trouble is Spence in?

GRANDMA. *(Rising.)* I'm a little tired. If you don't mind I think I'll go to bed now. *(From arch.)* Good night.

LEM. *(Rises, crosses to stairs. On stairs.)* I'm gonna—

MAY. It's no use, Lem. She won't tell you. She's as stubborn as an old mule.

GRANDMA. I heard that—and I'll remember it.

LEM. *(From stairs.)* What are we going to do?

MAY. We'll sit here and wait for him—that's all.

(LEM crosses Right to chair.)

I'm a little worried now, Lem.

LEM. It's about time.

MAY. Oh, don't be silly. I was worried before. You don't suppose we should call the police, Lem?

LEM. What for? We haven't done anything—have we?

MAY. They'd help us find him.

LEM. There'll be no police in this house —ever—for any reason.

MAY. Now you're being silly.

LEM. You heard what I said. I don't want any police in this.

MAY. *(Rises; crosses Right to window.)* Ssh! He's coming up the steps—and he's carrying a bag, Lem.

LEM. *(Crosses to Center.)* A bag? Well, I'll be damned!

MAY. Now don't holler at him until we find out what's wrong.

LEM. Don't worry. I'll handle this. You just stay out of it.

(SPENCE enters Right. LEM lights cigar.)

GRANDMA. *(As SPENCE shuts front door.)* Spence—is that you?

SPENCE. *(Takes off coat; crosses to foot of stairs.)* Yes, it's me, Gram.

GRANDMA. Would you come right upstairs, please. I've dropped my glasses and can't seem to find them.

SPENCE. I'll be right up, Gram.

LEM. You'll come in this house and sit down, young man. I want to talk to you.

SPENCE. It'll just take a second, Pop.

LEM. A second too long. Sit down now. The traitor upstairs can wait for her glasses. She can't read in the dark, anyhow.

(SPENCE sits on stool.)

MAY. *(Crosses to Left of SPENCE.)* Spence—you don't look well. Where have you been?

SPENCE. To the library.

GRANDMA. Spence—I haven't told them a thing. If they say I have they're lying.

LEM. *(Crossing down to SPENCE.)* Will you shut her up?

MAY. *(To Center.)* Mother, please.

GRANDMA. Oh! Shut up yourself. Mother please—Mother please. Why don't you tell me to shut up and be done with it?

LEM. *(Over GRANDMA's last sentence.)* I can't even think with her carrying on up there. So—you were at the library and you brought a suitcase to carry home a couple of books.

(MAY crosses to SPENCE.)

SPENCE. Well—I had a tough time finding the books.

LEM. I get it. You knew you were going to have a tough time finding the books so you just packed an overnight bag in case you had to spend the night.

MAY. Have you had anything to eat, Spence?

SPENCE. As a matter of fact I haven't.

LEM. Will you please stop interrupting?

MAY. I'll go and heat up something.

(Goes into the kitchen, turns on kitchen light.)

LEM. Do you think I'm crazy, Spence?

SPENCE. I honestly don't think you're crazy, Pop.

LEM. Well, you must think something like that. Don't you think I know what time the library closes?

SPENCE. What time does the library close, Pop?

LEM. *(A pause.)* May! *(Crosses to arch Up Left Center.)*

MAY. Yes?

LEM. You'd better come in here and talk to this little bastard before I break his neck.

GRANDMA. There he goes again. It's disgraceful.

(MAY comes in with saucepan and ladle. LEM crosses up Right.)

MAY. *(To GRAM.)* All right now. Spence, where have you been?

SPENCE. I told you—to the library. I got the books to prove it.

MAY. I think it's been pretty well settled, Spence—that you did go to the library. The point is, where did you go after that?

(He doesn't answer.)

It isn't like you, Spence, not to answer.

(They wait.)

(MAY puts pan on dining table, crosses to SPENCE.) Very well, Spence. When you came in I smelled beer on your breath. Have you been drinking beer?

SPENCE. Yes.

LEM. Well, I'll be damned.

MAY. Daddy—please.

GRANDMA. Don't be calling that man "Daddy." He's no husband of mine.

MAY. Who have you been drinking beer with, Spence?

SPENCE. I'd rather not say.

MAY. Why not, Spence?

SPENCE. *(Gets up, crosses to TV.)*

Well, Mom, to be frank with you, I don't honestly think that you'd know any of them.

MAY. I'd still like to know.

SPENCE. Mom, I'm trying to be honest with you. If you keep asking me I'm going to lie about it—and I'd rather not lie about it, Mom.

MAY. *(Crosses to* SPENCE.) Very well, Spence—we'll let that pass for now. A few minutes ago your grandmother said that you were in some kind of trouble.

GRANDMA. I didn't quite hear that. What's that you said I said?

MAY. Are you in trouble, Spence?

SPENCE. I sure am.

MAY. What happened?

SPENCE. I—got kicked out of school.

LEM. *(Crosses to Left.)* Well, I'll be good and goddamned.

MAY. Do you know what you did that was wrong?

LEM. *(Crossing to Right.)* The little genius gets kicked out of school.

SPENCE. I don't think that I honestly did anything that was wrong.

LEM. That cinches it. He gets kicked out of school for doing nothing.

SPENCE. I didn't mean that, Pop. I didn't mean that I didn't do anything. I just felt that I was justified.

MAY. What happened, Spence?

SPENCE. Look, Mom—I don't want to go through all that again. I don't feel like it. *(Crosses to ottoman downstage of* MAY.) The teacher, Miss Crowley, that is, said something about Negroes. I was sitting there. I told her she was wrong. She got mad—I got mad. I walked out of her room and went into the Men's Room. I was mad so I smoked a cigar. *(Sits ottoman.)* They caught me and brought me down to the principal. They threw me out of school for a week. That's all there was to it.

LEM. *(Moves to* SPENCE.) What are you talking about—that's all there was to it? We got a genius on our hands, May. He

knows more than the teacher. What do you think of that? *(Turning on* SPENCE.) Where did you get that cigar?

SPENCE. Out of your box.

LEM. *(To* MAY.) There you are!

MAY. In other words you stole cigars from your father?

SPENCE. I wouldn't exactly call it that.

LEM. Well, that's damn well what I'd call it. *(Crosses to above chair Right.)*

MAY. You and I will go back to school Monday, Spence, and you will apologize to Miss Crowley and be reinstated in school.

SPENCE. There's a week's vacation.

MAY. Then we will go up on the following Monday.

SPENCE. I don't think I can see my way clear to doing that, Mom.

MAY. *(Crosses sofa table for knitting.)* There will be no more discussion about it, Spence. A week from Monday—and it's settled.

SPENCE. I'm not going up to school with you, Mom. I'm going to stay out for the week. I won't go back to school and apologize to anyone.

MAY. You want to disobey both your father and me?

SPENCE. I don't want to disobey either of you. I kind of felt that you'd be on my side.

LEM. You'll do what you're told. *(Comes downstage.)*

SPENCE. I suppose you can make me go up there with you—but I won't apologize to anyone.

LEM. Stop talking back to your mother.

SPENCE. I'm not talking back to her. I just want her to understand how I feel.

(MAY is above Spence.)

LEM. *(Crossing to* SPENCE.) We don't care how you feel. Now, what do you think of that? You talk about what you'll do and what you won't do. We do things we don't like to do every day of our lives. I hear those crumbs at the bank talking about niggers and making jokes about niggers every day—and I stay on—because I need the job—so that you can have the things that you need. And what do you do? You get your silly little behind kicked out of school. And now you're too proud to go back. *(Crosses Up Right.)*

GRANDMA. Will you listen to him running his big mouth.

MAY. *(Crossing Down.)* Mama. We've given you boys everything that you could possibly want. You've never been deprived of anything, Spence. I don't need to tell you how hard we both work, and the fact that I'm in pain now doesn't seem to make any difference to you. I have arthritis in my wrist now, so badly that I can barely stand it, and it certainly doesn't help it any to hear you talk like this.

SPENCE. I'm sorry your wrist hurts, Mom.

(LEM is at piano.)

MAY. *(Crosses Right.)* You're not sorry at all. If you were, you'd do something about it. We've bent every effort to see that you were raised in a decent neighborhood and wouldn't have to live in slums because we always wanted the best for you. But now I'm not so sure we haven't made a terrible mistake—because you seem not to realize what you are. You're a little colored boy—that's what you are—and you have no business talking back to white women, no matter what they say or what they do. If you were in the South you could be lynched for that and your father and I couldn't do anything about it. So from now on my advice to you is to try and remember your place.

SPENCE. You'll pardon me for saying so—but that's the biggest hunk of bull I've ever heard in my whole life.

LEM. *(Crossing Down to him.)* What's that you said?

SPENCE. *(Rises.)* You both ought to be ashamed to talk to me that way.

LEM. *(Walks over and slaps him full across the face.)* Now go upstairs and don't come down until you can apologize to both of us. Go on.

SPENCE. *(Crosses to foot of stairs, stops second step.)*

(MAY crosses Down Right.)

I'll go upstairs, Pop, because you're my father and I still have to do what you tell me. But I'm still ashamed of you and I want you both to know it. *(He is walking upstairs.)*

LEM. *(Crossing to foot of stairs.)* That smart mouth of yours is going to get you into more trouble if you don't watch out.

(SPENCE has disappeared.)

(LEM crosses Down Right.) It's those damn books you've been reading—that's the trouble with you.

MAY. I don't think you should have slapped him, Lem.

LEM. What was I supposed to do? Let the little skunk stand there and cuss us both out? *(Going over to the stairs.)* And be sure you go straight upstairs. Don't be stopping in the traitor's room.

GRANDMA. He can stop in my room if he wants to. Who's to stop him, I'd like to know?

LEM. *(Starts upstairs, holding paper.)* I will.

GRANDMA. If you come into my room with your nasty mouth I'll bat you on the head with my cane.

LEM. *(Returns to room, waves paper.)* It's a fine thing when a man can't get a little respect in his own house.

GRANDMA. What have either of you done to get respect, I'd like to know? Nothing but bully the boy.

MAY. All right, Mother—now you keep out of it.

GRANDMA. *(On stairs.)* I'll not keep out of it. When I've got something to say, I say it, and you know it, so don't try to hush me up.

MAY. (Crossing to foot of stairs.) Mother, if you come down those stairs I'm going to tell the doctor.

GRANDMA. (Comes downstairs.) Oh! Tell him, smell him, knock him down and sell him. What you think I care? All this slapping and going on.

LEM. Where did Spence go? (Sits on his chair.)

GRANDMA. (At banister, crossing to sofa.) He went to his room. Where do you suppose he would go? He still does what you tell him, though why I'll never know.

MAY. Mother—please.

LEM. Oh! Let her go ahead and run herself down. It won't take long.

GRANDMA. That's where you're wrong. I have no intention of running down. I've got a few things to say and I'm going to say them. (Picks papers off sofa, throws them at LEM.)

LEM. Well, hurry up and say them and let's get it over with.

GRANDMA. I will. Don't you worry your head about that. I'm going to sit down first. (GRANDMA sits sofa.)

(MAY crosses to piano.)

Now in the first place—that nasty little hussy that's teaching history in that school deserves exactly what she got—and the only thing that I think is that Spence didn't tell her enough.

MAY. He can't go around talking to people like that.

GRANDMA. That's a lot of twaddle and you know it.

(MAY crosses Left to kitchen arch.)

Now, in the second place—when you moved down here, did you ever stop to take into consideration that something like this was bound to happen sooner or later, and that the most important thing might be just having your love and company? You did not. You kept right on working —and instead of your company, they got a book or a bicycle or an electric train. Mercy—the stuff that came in this house was ridiculous.

LEM. (Gets up, crosses to piano.) That's none of your—

GRANDMA. Will you let me finish? Well, I don't agree with that kind of raising one bit—and allow me to be the first to tell you both. You got away with it with Mack because Mack had Spence. But do you know that that boy is absolutely alone? He hasn't a friend in the world. You didn't know, did you, that all his little pals around here have taken to the girls and the little girls' mothers don't want their little daughters going around with a colored boy. Did you know that there was a dance up at school last week and Spence couldn't go because he didn't have anybody to take? Well, whether you know it or not, he's alone. And now you want to desert him completely by not backing him up. You moved him out of a slum and taught him to think of himself as something to be respected—and now you get mad when he does the things that you made it possible for him to do. That bull—as he called it about staying in his place. I'm ashamed of you both and I want you to know it. I've said what I came down here to say—now help me out of this sofa. Well, don't just stand there like a dumb ox—help me up.

(LEM moves over, helps her.)

MAY. You hadn't ought to come downstairs, Mother. You know that.

GRANDMA. I'll come downstairs when I want to. Now—what do you think of that? (Shoves LEM away.) The trouble with you two is that you're too careful. I'm an old lady and I haven't got much longer to live one way or the other. I'll come downstairs when I want to. (Crosses to stairs.)

MAY. Did Spence tell you all this? *(Crosses Right.)*

GRANDMA. Well, I certainly didn't find it out by talking to the neighbors.

LEM. *(Crosses to sofa, sits.)* Well—why in hell didn't he say so when we were talking to him?

GRANDMA. How could he? You attacked him like a rattlesnake the minute he came in the door.

LEM. I did not.

GRANDMA. You laid in wait and attacked him just like a rattlesnake. I heard you. *(She is starting up the stairs.)* I'm going to send him downstairs. *(She is slowly mounting the stairs.)* Talk to him. Be nice to him. *(On landing.)* Don't be crumbs all your lives. *(She disappears.)*

MAY. *(Starting to go to kitchen.)* I'd better go and put the food on again.

LEM. *(Gets up, follows her.)* You'll stay right here.

MAY. He's hungry, Lem.

LEM. You can do all of that when we're through. You're not going to leave me here by myself. What will I say to him?

MAY. I don't know.

LEM. Why didn't you tell me all this was going on anyway?

MAY. Because I didn't know, Daddy.

LEM. It's a mother's place to know what's happening to her son—isn't it?

MAY. *(Crossing to LEM.)* You know— I didn't know how it was going to take place, but somehow I knew it would turn out to be my fault.

LEM. *(Moves Right.)* I didn't say—

MAY. Oh! Shut up.

LEM. *(Turns to her.)* What did you say to me?

MAY. *(Moves Right.)* I said "Shut up." I told you not to hop on him the minute he came into the house. Maybe if you'd asked him questions instead of calling him names you would've found all this out and you wouldn't have to stand here looking so foolish now.

LEM. You were just as bad as I was.

MAY. I'm going out in the kitchen. You can talk to him by yourself.

(She starts to exit as SPENCE starts down the stairs.)

LEM. *(Sotto voce.)* You stay in here.

MAY. I will not. So there. *(She exits into kitchen.)*

LEM. *(His back to stairway, pretends not to notice SPENCE, gets up his nerve and then)* Come on down, Spence.

(SPENCE starts down again.)

(LEM crosses Right.) We're going to have a little talk.

(SPENCE comes into the room.)

Sit down—Son.

SPENCE. *(Walking over to the chair Right.)* Thanks, Pop. *(Sits on stool.)*

LEM. Are you comfortable?

SPENCE. Yes, Pop.

LEM. *(At Right of SPENCE.)* How do you feel?

SPENCE. I feel all right, Pop. I'm a little groggy, but I guess that's from the— *(He pauses.)* stuff I've been drinking.

LEM. *(Moves close to SPENCE.)* Serves you right. Now you gotta stop going around doing things like that. You hear? And another thing—You've got to stop talkin' back to me. If there's one thing that makes me good and damned mad it's talking back. I can't stand it and I won't stand it. *(Crossing Left.)* It don't show the proper respect. You got that?

SPENCE. Yes, Pop.

LEM. *(After a glance into the kitchen.)* You heard from Mack lately?

SPENCE. No I haven't, Pop.

LEM. *(Crossing Right.)* Well, I guess he's busy. You know how it is when you go to college.

SPENCE. Yes, I guess he is busy.

LEM. And that's what you've got to start thinking about—because you'll be busy, too, when you get to college. And you're going to college—you know that, don't you?

SPENCE. Yes, Pop—I do.

LEM. Well—just be sure. Now you go on and forget these little bastards around here. Don't pay any attention to them. *(Crosses chair Right.)* You've got bigger things to think about—and if they won't play with you—you just tell them to go to hell—because you're better than any ten of them put together. All right. Now —you got your books and you've got your music—and if there's anything you want—you just tell me about it and I'll get it for you. Understand? *(LEM sits.)*

SPENCE. Yes, Pop.

LEM. *(Rises, crosses Up.)* And don't mind what those lousy teachers say either. The big thing is for you to graduate and get the hell out of that lousy school. And if they say anything you don't like —just forget it—'cause you're going to college—and you can't afford to get your butt thrown out of school too often. You understand?

SPENCE. Yes, Pop.

LEM. All right then. *(Crosses to his chair, sits.)* It's all settled. Now you just forget the whole business. And if anything else happens—you just come to us and we'll take care of it. Understand?

SPENCE. Yes, Pop.

LEM. All right then. *(LEM returns to paper. Pause.)* Your mother's fixing you something to eat. You'd better go out and get it.

SPENCE. If you don't mind, Pop, I don't feel like eating. I think I'll just go to bed now.

LEM. Now—that's what I'm talking about. It's silly to go around moping.

SPENCE. *(Rises, crosses to stairs.)* I know it's silly, Pop. I know that. I'm going to try to do what you told me, but I want to go to bed now—that's all. *(He is on the stairs.)* Goodnight, Pop. *(He turns.)* And thanks for helping me, Pop. *(Starts up.)*

LEM. It's all right. *(He is sitting down with the paper.)*

(From upstairs a voice—muffled and rather terrified, cries.)

GRANDMA. Spence! Spence!

(SPENCE pauses for a moment and then rushes upstairs.)

LEM. *(Jumping from the chair and running upstairs.)* May! Come up here.

MAY. *(From the kitchen.)* What? What's the matter? *(She comes out.)* Where are you?

LEM. Up here—come up here quickly.

(MAY runs up the stairs. There is the sound of LEM's voice.)

Now that's right—up here on the bed. There. Go down and call the doctor; tell him to get here as soon as he can. The number is on the pad.

MAY. Mama! Mama!

LEM. Get out of the way, May.

SPENCE. *(Rushes downstairs, goes to the telephone and dials the number. He waits.)* Hello! Is Doctor Sloane there? This is Doctor Sloane? This is Spencer Scott. You've got to come over as soon as you can. It's my grandmother. I don't know what's the matter with her. You've got to come—

MAY. *(Enters from the top of the stairs).* Spence!

(SPENCE puts his hand over the mouthpiece and waits.)

Tell him he doesn't have to hurry. She's dead.

(SPENCE hangs up the phone without telling him.)

(MAY keeps coming down the stairs and Down Right; sits in chair.) She didn't have to suffer, Spence, and she died quickly. We can thank God for that.

(SPENCE starts for the stairs as LEM

starts down. He meets his father, who holds him.)

LEM. Where are you going?

SPENCE. Let me go—Pop, I said let me go. Damn it, Pop—take your hands off me.

MAY. *(Rising.)* Let him go, Lem.

(LEM releases him. SPENCE goes off as LEM comes down the stairs. MAY sits down and LEM stands silent, above her. SPENCE comes down the stairs again and goes into the kitchen. He doesn't notice his father or mother and goes quickly to get his coat, off Left in kitchen.)

LEM. Where are you going, Spence?

SPENCE. *(Putting on coat.)* Out—outside for a while.

LEM. *(Crosses to Center.)* I think you'd better stay here with your mother, Spence. She needs you.

SPENCE. I can't. She's got you anyway.

LEM. I don't think you'd better go out now.

SPENCE. Leave me alone! Will you?

LEM. How can you be so selfish? Your mother needs you.

(He starts Right. LEM holds him.)

LEM. What's the matter with you anyway? You've got a fever. You'd better go to bed.

SPENCE. I'm not going to bed. I want to go out for a few minutes. That's all. I want to be by myself for a few minutes.

MAY. You don't have to go outside to cry, Spence. You don't have to be ashamed before us.

(SPENCE begins to sob incoherently, his head on LEM's shoulder; breaks away from his father and runs out of the house. LEM starts after him.)

MAY. Let him go, Lem.

LEM. *(Stopping at front door.)* But he's got a fever. He can't—

MAY. Let him alone, Lem.

LEM. *(Crosses Down Right to her.)* I'll call the doctor. You go and rest. He can have a look at Spence while he's here.

MAY. You'd better call Mack too, Lem. He's so far away. I don't think he'll be able to come home.

LEM. I'll call him.

MAY. What's Spence doing, Lem?

LEM. He's standing over in the lot—that's all.

CURTAIN

ACT TWO

SCENE 2

At the Curtain's rise, Spence's room is in semi-darkness because the shades are drawn. The door is shut. On the chair by Spence's bed stands a tray of food. On the bureau is a decanter of water, a bottle of pills and medicine. SPENCE is in bed—asleep to all obvious intents. A WOMAN appears climbing the stairs outside of the room and enters. She is carrying a clean pillow slip, which she places on the chair Right. She glances over at the bed and then begins to pull the shades. SUN springs into the room as she does so. She is a woman perhaps in her late twenties, good-looking and trim. It is two weeks later—early afternoon.

CHRISTINE. You know, I've met many a mulish critter in my day, but you're the worst mule I've ever met. Now you ain't asleep because I heard you tipping around up here not ten minutes ago. Now open your eyes and eat your lunch.

SPENCE. I don't want it.

CHRISTINE. *(Crosses with tray to bureau.)* You know you don't have to eat it? You know that, don't you? But don't blame anyone but yourself when your bones are rattling around inside of your skin like two castanets hit together—you understand? I suppose you don't want your medicine either. *(Crosses Up of bed.)*

Boy, you sure do beat all. You're the stubbornest cuss I ever met. I'll ask you one more time. Are you going to take this medicine or aren't you? Speak up, cause I don't have all day.

SPENCE. No.

CHRISTINE. I didn't quite catch that. Don't be mumbling at me, boy. Was it "Yes" or "No" that you said?

SPENCE. I said "No."

CHRISTINE. Boy, you know you're going to make some girl a pretty miserable husband one of these days. Course, you know, I don't believe you're not eating. *(Crosses to bureau.)* I think you sneak downstairs after I leave and eat everything in sight. *(Pause.)* Did you hear me?

(No answer.)

(Crosses to bed.) Spence, won't you please sit up and eat something? Anything? Crust of bread? You know it kills me when folks don't eat.

(No answer.)

I never knew anybody who could pick out just the right way to worry somebody. Won't you eat just a little bit?

SPENCE. *(Head up in bed.)* I said "No."

CHRISTINE. *(Crosses to chair for pillow slip, returns.)* Well, I guess that settles it—don't it? Then you can get out of bed so I can make it.

SPENCE. You don't need to make it today.

CHRISTINE. The devil you say. I've taken enough from you today already. Now just get out of that bed before I pick you up and throw you out of it. You're not supposed to stay in bed all day anyway. The doctor said to get up and walk around and to get some air if you felt like it.

SPENCE. Don't you get sick of repeating yourself?

CHRISTINE. *(Crosses to bureau, returns with decanter.)* You've got 'til I

count three. One—two—three—*(Throws water.)*

SPENCE. *(Throwing the covers off and laughing in spite of himself.)* All right—all right. I'm getting up now. *(He goes Right and sits in chair.)* You make me sick.

CHRISTINE. The feeling is oh so mutual. *(She begins to make the bed—stands above it.)* I've seen a mess of mourning in my day, but if the mourning you do don't beat anything I've ever seen yet, I don't want a nickel. But at the rate you're going you're not going to have much longer to mourn. You're going to be joining them that you're mournin' for if you don't watch your step.

SPENCE. What do you say to my making a little bargain with you?

CHRISTINE. What is it?

SPENCE. I'll eat that slop that you brought up here if as soon as that bed is made you get the hell out of here and leave me alone.

CHRISTINE. *(Takes food tray from chair to bureau.)* There ain't no call to be rude and nasty. All I'm saying is that you look like a bag of bones and you do.

SPENCE. I've always been skinny.

CHRISTINE. *(Pours medicine in soup.)* It's humanly impossible for somebody to be as skinny as you are and live. Consumption is chasing you in one direction and pneumonia is chasing you in the other—and when they meet with you in the middle, it's sure going to be a mess.

SPENCE. Why don't you shut up?

CHRISTINE. *(Moves to above bed, continues making it.)* Why don't you eat your lunch instead of sitting up there looking like death warmed over?

SPENCE. *(Gets out of the chair and viciously picks up the tray from the bureau; brings it back, sits down with it and begins to eat.)* Now will you let me alone?

CHRISTINE. *(Crosses to bureau, gets out socks.)* Who's bothering you?

SPENCE. You are.

CHRISTINE. *(Crosses to him, puts wrapper around shoulders.)* Aw! Go on, boy. You know you love it.

SPENCE. *(Tasting the soup.)* What kind of soup is this?

CHRISTINE. *(Putting on left sock.)* What'd you say?

SPENCE. I said, "What kind of soup is this?"

CHRISTINE. Chicken.

SPENCE. Well, it tastes damn peculiar. *(Tasting it again.)* What's in it?

CHRISTINE. Nothing.

SPENCE. What's in this soup? *(Pause.)* You put the medicine in the soup.

CHRISTINE. Does it taste awful?

SPENCE. It tastes like hell. You sure are a lousy cook. No wonder you can't keep a husband.

CHRISTINE. I'll have you know that I've only had one husband—and he died.

SPENCE. I'm not surprised.

CHRISTINE. *(Throws socks down, rises, crosses to bed, works on sheets.)* I'm not speaking to you again today. And that's final.

SPENCE. You're not really mad are you, Christine? *(Pause.)* Christine, I was just kidding. *(Pause.)* Aw! Come on, Christine. You know I don't really think that you killed your husband.

CHRISTINE. *(Laughing. Crosses to SPENCE.)* Boy, you sure are a mess.

(They look at one another.)

You feel better now—don't you?

SPENCE. I guess so.

CHRISTINE. *(Puts on right sock.)* You're getting some color in your cheeks.

SPENCE. Don't you think that you're hurrying things a little, Christine? I haven't finished eating yet.

CHRISTINE. If there's one thing I can't stand it's skinny men around me. Never could stand skinny men since I can first remember. You wouldn't be a bad-looking boy if you just weren't so skinny.

SPENCE. Thanks, Christine. Thanks. You're a real tin pitcher full of complaints today. You're as generous with the old complaints as Gram. *(He stops eating.)*

CHRISTINE. *(Rises, stands over SPENCE Left of him.)* Now what's the matter? What've you stopped eating for?

SPENCE. You know what's the matter.

CHRISTINE. *(Fixes something on tray.)* Now there isn't any point in thinking about that now.

SPENCE. I know there isn't, but I can't help it.

CHRISTINE. Just don't think about it.

SPENCE. That's a very stupid thing to say. You can't just stop thinking about someone because they're dead, can you?

CHRISTINE. Yes, yes you can if you want to. You just don't open the door and let yourself in, that's all.

SPENCE. What are you talking about?

CHRISTINE. Nothing. Now eat your lunch. *(To above bed.)*

SPENCE. *(Begins eating again.)* You know, it's funny. I got expelled from school—Gram died—and I got sick—and so I couldn't go to school anyway—even if they hadn't kicked me out. Funny the way things turn out.

CHRISTINE. Yes, it is—isn't it? *(She stops work, listens.)*

SPENCE. You know, Christine, I was just thinking. Course last week was the funeral and I figure maybe the guys didn't want to come and see me then. But I've been home all this week.

(CHRISTINE crosses to him, gets tray.)

Wouldn't you have thought that one of them would have come over to see me by now?

CHRISTINE. *(Putting tray on bureau.)* Nothing surprises me any more.

SPENCE. What do you mean by that?

CHRISTINE. Nothing. *(Feels his head.)* I don't think you have any more fever. You want to take your temperature?

SPENCE. Naw! (Pause.) Your hands are very warm, Christine.

CHRISTINE. Warm hands—warm heart.

SPENCE. That would be fine except that that's not the way it goes.

CHRISTINE. (Crossing to bed.) It goes that way for me, and that's what matters.

SPENCE. (Rises, crosses to Right of bureau.) Were you born here, Christine?

CHRISTINE. No. I was born in Alabama. Birmingham, Alabama, in Ensley, near the steel mills.

SPENCE. I'll bet you didn't like it much down there, did you?

CHRISTINE. No, I didn't like it much down there.

SPENCE. Is your family still there?

CHRISTINE. (Crosses Down to front of bed. Changes pillow slip.) My father was killed in the mills when I was a little girl. My Ma died a couple of years ago. I had two brothers and two sisters. I don't know where they are now.

SPENCE. (Crosses to bed, sits.) What made you come way the hell up here by yourself?

CHRISTINE. (Laughing.) I wanted something better, I guess. I decided I was coming up North to try my luck. I worked for a whole year before I'd saved the money, and the day I had what I thought was enough, I went down to the railroad station. (Stops work.) Boy, that was some day! The sun was shining and I felt real good like you feel maybe once or twice in your whole life. When I got to the ticket window, the man had a calendar, and it had an advertisement for a big insurance company on it. So I looked at the name of the town and then I told him that that's where I wanted my ticket to take me. Then I went home and packed my mama's cardboard suitcase, and that same night I caught the train. And that's the last I ever saw of my mother and my brothers and sisters and Rusty.

SPENCE. Who the hell was Rusty?

CHRISTINE. (Sits at head of bed.)

(SPENCE sits in middle.)

Rusty was my dog. Well, I didn't go to work for the insurance company. I went into service for a while and then I got married. And that's what I meant when I was telling you about the doors. See, my husband died about two years after that and about two months after he died, I had a baby and he was born dead.

SPENCE. Christine!

CHRISTINE. Well, I tell you for a while I felt like all I wanted to do was die myself. Then I realized that you just can't go on like that. It's like your mind is divided into little rooms and each time you go back into one of those rooms your heart likes to break in two. So all you do is shut the doors—and lock them—to those little rooms in your mind and never let yourself in them again. So I've got two little locked rooms in my mind. One for Bert, my husband, and one for my baby that never had a name. Do you want some more to eat?

SPENCE. No, Christine, I don't think so. You sure do make me feel crumby, Christine.

CHRISTINE. Why?

SPENCE. Well, I've been giving you a pretty hard time about what's been happening to me. (Pause.) I'm sorry, Christine.

CHRISTINE. That's all right, boy. You're just unhappy—that's all. But you'll get used to that. Pretty soon you'll be able to laugh a little bit and make jokes, even while you're unhappy. It won't be this bad forever. (Rises.) Well, the bed's made, the house is clean, and you've had your lunch. So—

SPENCE. Don't go, Christine. Stay with me.

CHRISTINE. (Crossing to bureau for tray.) I've got another cleaning job, boy.

SPENCE. Just for a little while longer. (Pause.) If you have to go, well then I guess you have to, but if you could stay just a little while longer it would mean a lot to me. It isn't that I'm afraid of anything, but I get to thinking about all the things I've got to do.

CHRISTINE. What have you got to do?

SPENCE. Well, I've got to really get well—first of all. I'll take the medicine and I'll take a hell of a lot of vitamins and I figure that'll fix me up all right.

CHRISTINE. (Crossing to him with pills.) There's no time like the present to begin.

SPENCE. Honest, Christine.

CHRISTINE. A little water? (She gets water glass from tray.)

SPENCE. (Takes the pill.) I know what you're going to say. "You're beginning to look fatter already."

(She laughs merrily and hugs him.)

You're going to make me spill the water.

CHRISTINE. (Releases him. Takes glass and puts it on tray.) What else?

SPENCE. Well, I'm going to cut out the damn smoking and drinking and that ought to fix up the old body. (Rises, crosses Right.) Then I've got to go up to school and make peace with old Hasbrook and Crowley. But the other things are going to be a hell of a lot harder to do.

CHRISTINE. What are they?

SPENCE. (Sits chair Right.) I've got to do something about the guys and my Gram, Christine. I'm going to be honest with you about Gram—it's going to be hard. I miss her a hell of a lot. But she's dead, Christine. She's dead—and you can tell yourself that and you can accept it, and maybe I'm a little selfish about it, but you know that no other living soul is talking with her or having fun with her. She didn't ditch you. She died. But the guys are different, Christine. They're not dead. They're over in the lot playing baseball. They're still horsing around up in the park. I don't suppose they can really help what's happened because that's the way

it is. I've said some pretty lousy things to them, Christine, and I don't want it to be that way. (He pauses. He is near tears.) God damn it—I hate being black, Christine. I hate it. I hate it. I hate the hell out of it.

CHRISTINE. (Crosses to him, holds him.) Ssh!

SPENCE. I'm sorry I said that, Christine.

CHRISTINE. It's all right, Spence. You don't have to explain to me. (She releases him, but still holds his hand.)

SPENCE. And I've got to cut out this goddamn crying. Everything makes me cry. I don't understand it. I was watching television the other day—a damn soap opera—and started crying like a baby. That's damn peculiar.

CHRISTINE. It's not so peculiar as you think.

SPENCE. There's just one more thing, Christine.

CHRISTINE. What is it?

SPENCE. I don't know whether I should tell you or not.

CHRISTINE. Sure you can tell me.

SPENCE. How are you so sure? You don't even know what it is yet.

CHRISTINE. I'll take the risk.

SPENCE. You promise you won't say anything about it to anybody?

CHRISTINE. I won't mention it to a soul.

SPENCE. No matter what it is?

CHRISTINE. I've already said I won't tell it, haven't I?

SPENCE. Well, I want to sleep with a girl, Christine.

(CHRISTINE turns away laughing.)

What's the matter with you?

CHRISTINE. Nothing. I just swallowed wrong.

SPENCE. Yeh!

CHRISTINE. (Turns to him.) Yeh! And many more of them right back at you. Who's the lucky girl?

SPENCE. Aw! Christine. You know I haven't got any girl in mind. I think about it quite often, but I can't think of anybody. I suppose you think that sounds pretty horny to be thinking of it all the time?

CHRISTINE. *(Turns away.)* No, I wouldn't say that.

SPENCE. You wouldn't?

CHRISTINE. No, I wouldn't.

SPENCE. You know, Christine. You're a funny Joe. To look at you no one would think that somebody could talk to you like this.

CHRISTINE. *(Quite dryly, turns to him.)* Thanks.

SPENCE. Have you had much experience, Christine?

CHRISTINE. Enough.

SPENCE. Offhand—how much experience would you say you've had?

CHRISTINE. Now that's the kind of question it's every woman's right to leave unanswered.

SPENCE. You think that's a pretty nosey question?

CHRISTINE. I not only think it's a nosey question. I know it is.

SPENCE. O.K. *(Rises. Crosses to below bed.)*

*(*CHRISTINE *sits chair Right. Pause.)*

Would you say, offhand, that I was trying to rush things, Christine?

CHRISTINE. How do you mean?

SPENCE. *(Crossing Down Right.)* You'd just as soon we talked about something else, wouldn't you?

CHRISTINE. I just didn't understand what you meant, that's all.

SPENCE. *(Crossing to Center.)* Well, I mean about my age and all. Do you realize that I'm going on eighteen and have never slept with a girl?

CHRISTINE. That's terrible—isn't it? *(Turns away.)*

SPENCE. It sure as hell is. Hell, I'm practically a virgin. And you know I was thinking when I was sick, supposing I died. Supposing I just passed out now and died. *(Indicates imaginary body on floor.)* Why, I'd regret that I hadn't slept with anybody for the rest of my life practically.

CHRISTINE. I guess that would be pretty terrible—wouldn't it?

SPENCE. I think that you're having a hell of a good time laughing at me.

CHRISTINE. I most certainly am not.

SPENCE. You sure as hell are. You've got a sneaky laugh line around your whole mouth.

CHRISTINE. *(Turns to him.)* Spence— I'm not laughing. I wouldn't laugh at you when you're telling me things like this. If I'm doing anything I'm remembering, and I might be just smiling a little bit at the memory, but I'm not laughing at you.

SPENCE. You really honestly don't think that it's peculiar or anything?

CHRISTINE. How could anything so natural be peculiar?

SPENCE. That's a funny thing for you to say.

CHRISTINE. Why is it so funny, might I ask?

SPENCE. *(Sits on foot of bed.)* Well, I'm pretty sure, although I've never asked her, that Mom would give me a swat for my pains if—

CHRISTINE. *(Rises, crosses to him.)* And what makes you think that your mother and I should have the same ideas?

SPENCE. Well—you're both older than I am.

CHRISTINE. Well, I'm not anywhere near as old as your mother. I might be a widow, but I'm a young widow, and I'm not through yet by a long shot.

SPENCE. I didn't mean—

CHRISTINE. I know exactly what you meant. Just remember you're no Tiny Tim yourself.

SPENCE. I didn't mean what you thought I meant at all. I just meant that you seem to understand a lot of things. Aw! Hell—I don't mean that. I mean you seem to understand me—and I'm grateful. That's all.

CHRISTINE. (*Crosses to chair Left. After a pause.*) Well, we've done enough talking for one afternoon. I've got to go.

SPENCE. Christine!

CHRISTINE. (*Turning around.*) What is it now?

SPENCE. (*Pause.*) Nothing.

CHRISTINE. (*Crossing to Center.*) Nothing is what you ask for, nothing is what you'll get.

SPENCE. (*Rises.*) Christine!--

(*She stops.*)

I'd appreciate it if you didn't turn around.

CHRISTINE. Why?

SPENCE. (*Standing behind her.*) Because I'm going to ask you something and if you're going to laugh at me I'd just as soon you weren't laughing in my face.

CHRISTINE. I won't laugh.

SPENCE. Well, would you mind not turning around just the same?

CHRISTINE. All right.

SPENCE. Well—I don't know quite how to say it. (*Pause.*) Do you like me, Christine?

CHRISTINE. I certainly do.

SPENCE. No kidding?

CHRISTINE. No kidding.

SPENCE. I was sure hoping you weren't. Because I like you too, Christine.

CHRISTINE. Thank you.

SPENCE. Well, I know that liking doesn't mean loving—but I kind of thought—that since—well—you're lonely, aren't you, Christine?

CHRISTINE. I've been lonely for a long time now, boy.

SPENCE. Well—in case you didn't know, I'm lonely too, Christine—and I know that you're older than I am and I know it makes a lot of difference.

CHRISTINE. I have to go, Spence.

SPENCE. But what I'm lacking in age,

Christine, I sure make up for in loneliness, and so we do have that much in common. Don't we, Christine?

CHRISTINE. Yes.

SPENCE. So maybe—if you stayed, Christine—since things are like I said they were—we might find a little happiness together. I don't mean for forever or anything like that—but could you call and say that you couldn't make it?

CHRISTINE. You know you're very young, Spence, and you could be very foolish too. You know that—don't you?

SPENCE. Yes, Christine. I know.

CHRISTINE. And I could be very foolish to listen to you.

SPENCE. I know, Christine.

CHRISTINE. (*Turns to him.*) It's funny. I have to look at you, because I can't believe that you said what you just said. You said, that since we were both lonely maybe—just for an afternoon—we could find happiness together. You know that so soon?

SPENCE. Yes, Christine.

CHRISTINE. You see, I didn't laugh. I ain't laughing at all. I'll try to come back. I'll try. (*She gets the tray from the bureau and goes to the door.*)

SPENCE. You know where the phone is. If you can't come back, Christine, you don't need to come up and tell me. Just go. But if you can, there's a bell downstairs on the table that Mother uses to call us to meals. Would you ring it—if you can?

CHRISTINE. I'll try. (*She exits.*)

SPENCE. (*Crossing Down Right, then to door; listens.*) Why in hell is she taking so long?

(*Sound of hand BELL off Right. SPENCE crosses slowly to window, pulls shade down as LIGHTS fade.*)

CURTAIN

ACT TWO

SCENE 3

The scene is the same as Scene 1. As the Curtain rises, MAY is coming out of the kitchen. She walks over to the piano and rings the bell. It is the following afternoon—Saturday.

MAY. Spence! Spence! Are you asleep?

SPENCE. *(Upstairs.)* No.

MAY. Well, suppose you come downstairs and get lunch. Hurry up now. I have a lot of work to do, and you're holding me up.

SPENCE. What's the big hurry?

MAY. *(Crosses to dining room, gets fruit salad and milk from refrigerator.)* Never mind. Just come downstairs and don't ask so many silly questions.

SPENCE. *(Appears at head of stairs.)* O.K. So I'm coming. You sure do get yourself upset about nothing at all. Why don't you take it easy? *(Makes basketball throw with sweater from stairs onto armchair Right.)*

MAY. Have you gotten your clothes together yet?

SPENCE. *(Coming downstairs, crossing to dining table.)* What clothes?

MAY. *(Counting groceries on shelf.)* Your school clothes. I told you to get them ready and I'd have them pressed this afternoon.

SPENCE. *(Sits Right of table, starts eating.)* They're all right.

MAY. I'm not going to have you going to school looking like a tramp.

SPENCE. You sure got peculiar notions of what a tramp looks like.

MAY. Never mind the sass. Did you get them ready?

SPENCE. They're hanging up in the closet—just waiting to be taken off the hangers and brought down to the tailor's. How much more ready could they be?

MAY. I told you to bring them down. You know you could cooperate a little bit more. Now I suppose I'm going to have to climb upstairs and bring them down. I told you my knee—

SPENCE. All right. All right. I'll get them—*(Gets up, crosses to stairs.)*

MAY. You're hollering at me, Spencer. *(Pause.)* You can't get them now. Just sit down and eat your lunch.

SPENCE. *(Crosses back to chair.)* You know, Mom, I got to give it to you. You sure do know how to fix a guy's stomach for this lunch. *(Pause as he sits again.)* You know, I could wear my Sunday suit to school Monday and Chris could take these clothes. I don't want you to strain your knee any more than you have to. Or I could take them down myself?

MAY. *(Turns to shelf.)* Chris? Christine won't be back Monday or any other day.

SPENCE. *(Pushes chair back.)* What are you talking about?

MAY. Christine will not be back. You're no longer ill. There's no need for Christine any longer.

SPENCE. *(Rises, crosses to MAY.)* But I thought you said—

MAY. I changed my mind. I called her and told her this morning.

SPENCE. What did you tell her?

MAY. I told her that her services were no longer needed by me. I decided that there was no need to spend that money since I could do the things myself. I've been doing them myself anyway.

SPENCE. But you said you were too tired when you got home.

MAY. Well, I've changed my mind. Why all this interest in Christine?

SPENCE. *(Crossing back to table.)* Nothing. I just thought—

MAY. I know what you just thought, young man, and don't think I don't.

SPENCE. Now what are you talking about?

MAY. You know my eyes weren't put on—

SPENCE. The way they were put on for nothing. I know.

MAY. All that pampering and coddling she did with you makes me sick to my stomach.

SPENCE. *(Crossing to her.)* Will you please explain what you mean by that?

MAY. I don't know. What should I mean by that? Maybe you can tell me. Well, I've heard those stories about maids being left alone in houses with boys before. I'm not saying it's gone that far yet. But an ounce of prevention is worth a pound of anybody's cure.

SPENCE. *(Crossing Down.)* You know, you sure have got a dirty mind.

MAY. Don't be so sure that it's I that have a dirty mind. And if you say that to me again you'll get a good slap for your pains.

SPENCE. How in hell—

MAY. Don't use that kind of language before me.

SPENCE. All I did was come down to eat lunch and then you start on me about a suit of clothes. *(Crosses Right.)* I'll take the suit down to the tailor myself. I wouldn't have you strain yourself. As far as Christine is concerned, if she pampered and coddled me—then I'm grateful to her. And you promised her a job after I was sick and I think you're damned dirty—

MAY. Spencer!

SPENCE. *(Crossing to table.)* Yes, I think you're damned dirty to get rid of her. Now—that's all I've got to say and you can take this food away now because I can't eat it. *(Crosses Right.)*

MAY. *(Taking glass away.)* Suit yourself. No one is going to beg you to eat, young man.

SPENCE. Mom—no one had to beg me to eat. All I wanted was a little peace to eat. I was perfectly willing to eat. *(Crosses to stairs.)*

MAY. Where are you going?

SPENCE. *(Climbing stairs.)* To the tailor. Where did you think I was going?

MAY. You haven't got time.

SPENCE. What do you mean I haven't got time? All in hell—

MAY. *(Crosses to living room.)* Be careful.

SPENCE. All in hell I got left in the world is time—time for everything. If there's any little thing you want done from now on—just let me know.

MAY. *(Crosses to table, takes plate away.)* You haven't got time to go to the tailor's now.

SPENCE. *(On landing.)* Why not?

MAY. Because I asked some of your friends over this afternoon.

SPENCE. You did what?

MAY. *(Turning to shelf.)* I asked some of your friends over for ice cream and cake this afternoon.

SPENCE. *(Coming downstairs.)* Are you kidding?

MAY. I'm perfectly serious.

SPENCE. *(In Center.)* Why didn't you make a little pink punch to go with it?

MAY. I did.

SPENCE. Well, you can call them the hell back up and tell them to stay home.

MAY. *(Turns, crosses to him.)* Spence— don't you dare.

SPENCE. You heard what I said. You can call them up and tell them to stay home.

(MAY crosses Left.)

(SPENCE follows her.) What right did you have to do that? It's none of your business. It's my business and you stay out of it. I'm not bribing those kids with ice cream, cake or pink punch. I'm never going to bribe anyone to be my friend.

MAY. You'll do what you're told and you'll stop being so fresh. Do you understand that?

(SPENCE crosses to below table.)

And I don't want to hear another word out of you about what you'll do and what you won't do. When you start talking like that it's about time you went out and got a job of your own and bought a house of your own—

(SPENCE *tucks in shirt-tails*.)

but as long as you're under this roof, you will do what you're told.

(SPENCE *turns to go to front door*.)

Where are you going?

SPENCE. I'm going to get the hell out of here. That's where I'm going.

MAY. (*Following him.*) Go ahead—and see how far you get acting the way you act.

(BOTH *at front door*.)

Your father's right about you. You're too proud. You think you can go through life being proud, don't you? Well, you're wrong. You're a little black boy—and you don't seem to understand it. But that's what you are. You think this is bad; well, it'll be worse. You'll serve them pink punch and ice cream—and you'll do a lot worse. You'll smile when you feel like crying. (*She begins to cry.*) You'll laugh at them when you could put knives right into their backs without giving it a second thought—and you'll never do what you've done and let them know that they've hurt you. They never forgive you for that. So go on out and learn the lesson. Now get out of here. Get out of here and don't ever come back. (MAY *crosses to sofa, sits. Pause.*) You think it's easy for me to tell my son to crawl when I know he can walk and walk well? I'm sorry I ever had children. I'm sorry you didn't die when you were a baby. Do you hear that? I'm sorry you didn't die. (*She is completely overcome.*)

SPENCE. (*Crossing Down.*) Don't cry, Mom. I'm sorry. I'm sorry I've made it so difficult. I didn't mean to hurt you, Mom. (*Pause.*) What time did you tell them to be here?

MAY. Around one.

SPENCE. Well, they'll be here any minute. Is everything ready?

MAY. It's in the pantry. The ice cream is in the refrigerator.

(TONY *and* GUSSIE *enter outside the door*.)

SPENCE. Don't cry, Mom. I'm sorry. It seems to me that for the past two weeks all I've done is apologize to people. I seem to be apologizing for trying to be a human being.

(*The BELL rings.*)

That must be some of them now.

MAY. Do you want me to stay.

SPENCE. No. You can go out if you want to.

MAY. (*Crosses to stairs, starts up.*) I have some shopping to do. (*Stops on landing, turns.*) Spence, don't be rude to them.

(SPENCE *opens the door*.)

GUSSIE. Hi, Spence!

SPENCE. Hi, Gussie! Hi, Tony!

(TONY *and* GUSSIE *enter.* GUSSIE *first. He crosses to Right of sofa.*)

What's the matter, Tony? You're not speaking or something?

TONY. Hi, Spence! I'm sorry about your grandmother. (*Crosses to below armchair Right.*)

SPENCE. Thanks. Where are the rest of the guys?

GUSSIE. They'll be around. (*Pause.*) You going back to school Monday?

SPENCE. Yeh! I'm going back Monday. It's kind of creepy having a party for no reason—isn't it? See—I've been sick— you probably didn't know—my Mom thought it would be a big surprise if the gang came in today. That's all. Sit down.

TONY. (*Sits on stool.*) We didn't see you around. We wondered what was wrong.

GUSSIE. (*Sits right arm of sofa.*) You're better now—ain't you?

SPENCE. Yeh! I'm better now. *(Pause.)* What you guys been doing?

GUSSIE. Knocking around. That's all. *(Pause.)*

SPENCE. You been playing baseball lately?

TONY. Not much—no. We've had too much home work lately.

SPENCE. *(Crosses Left.)* Oh! I thought I heard you guys a couple of times but it was probably somebody else.

GUSSIE. Yeh! It must've been somebody else.

SPENCE. Would you like some ice cream or anything?

(MAY appears at head of stairs. They rise.)

MAY. *(Coming downstairs.)* Don't get up. It's nice seeing all of you again.

TONY and GUSSIE. How do you do, Mrs. Scott!

MAY. Just stay where you are. I'm going down to the grocer's. Haven't seen you in a long time, Tony.

TONY. I've been pretty busy lately.

MAY. Well, don't be such a stranger. We miss you.

SPENCE. *(Crosses to kitchen.)* I'll get the ice cream.

GUSSIE. Yeah. We've been pretty busy.

(IGGIE enters Right, crosses to door, followed by JOHNNY and BOBBY REYNOLDS.)

MAY. Well, any time you want to come over and watch television—come. Spence will be very glad to see you.

(BELL rings.)

I'll get it.

SPENCE. *(Puts ice cream, plates and spoons on table as MAY opens door.)* Well, here you are. Help yourselves.

(TONY crosses to table, sits Left of it. GUSSIE crosses to Left of table.)

MAY. Hello, boys. Come on in.

IGGIE. Hello, Mrs. Scott. *(Crosses Left.)*

JOHNNY. Hello, Mrs. Scott.

(MAY is at door. IGGIE crosses Left to table.)

(JOHNNY is Right of BOBBY.) My brother and I were very sad to hear of your recent—

BOBBY. death in your family.

MAY. Thank you, boys. I have to go now. Spence will entertain you. I'll be back in a little while. *(Exits.)*

(BOBBY and JOHNNY cross Left.)

SPENCE. *(Crosses to them.)* Well, if it isn't the Reynolds boys. Come on in.

IGGIE. *(Above table, his rear in TONY's ice cream.)* Hey, Spence. I didn't come to see you, because I thought maybe you wouldn't want any visitors, but I kept asking your mother about you.

SPENCE. *(Crossing to IGGIE.)* Well—thanks, Iggie. Thanks.

TONY. Hey, Iggie, will you get your ass out of my ice cream?

IGGIE. I'm sorry. *(Crosses to ottoman, sits.)*

(SPENCE is just about to tell TONY off.)

TONY. Nothing to be sorry about. Just get out of it is all.

GUSSIE. *(Interrupting impending fight between TONY and SPENCE, crosses in. Nervously.)* This is fun—ain't it, Spence?

SPENCE. Yeah! *(Crosses REYNOLDS Boys in living room.)* Come on, you guys. Get yours while the getting is good.

(BOBBY and JOHNNY cross to table. GUSSIE crosses Right.)

GUSSIE. Hey! Spence. This is fun. We ain't had so much fun since we made that party that time—stealing off Mr. Markman. Remember that?

(IGGIE rises, crosses to dining room shelf for cake.)

SPENCE. I sure do. I was responsible for getting the dill pickles. What did you have to get?

GUSSIE. The ice cream. I had to get the ice cream.

JOHNNY (Crosses to ottoman, sits.) How did you do it?

GUSSIE. (To Center.) Gee, you guys are new around here. Well, Tony here— was the onliest one of us that had any money. He had a lousy dime—a lousy dime—so we all goes into Sam Markman's store big as you please and tells him we want a ten-cent guinea grinder. (Puts icecream on sofa.) Can you imagine—that fat Jew bastard—with a damn Jew store making guinea grinders.

TONY. (Crosses Right to GUSSIE, then to stool, sits.) For Christ sake. Will you cut it out? Iggie's here.

GUSSIE. (Turns Left.) Who? Oh! Iggie —I didn't even see you, Iggie. Geez—I'm sorry. No offense meant, Iggie.

IGGIE. (By refrigerator.) It's all right.

GUSSIE. (With rising intensity.) Yeh! Well, there we all were. So while he's cutting the damn bread in two, I'm practically falling into his ice cream freezer. I'm pulling the pints of ice cream out as fast as a son-of-a-bitch and throwing them out the door. Tony is behind the candy counter stuffing his pocket with chocolate bars.

(IGGIE crosses to Center.)

And old Spence is in the barrel with the pickles. They're way down at the bottom, see, and he can't reach them—so there he is practically swimming in the pickle juice when Old Markman turns around and sees him. So he pulls his arm out, and he's got a pickle in his hand, and he says without blinking an eyelash, "Looks like you'd better be ordering some more pickles, Mr. Markman. They're getting pretty damn hard to reach." Remember that, Spence? (Sits right end of sofa.)

SPENCE. Sure—I remember. You want some more cake, Iggie?

IGGIE. No thanks, Spencer. (Sits left end of sofa.)

SPENCE. Well, if you want more just reach for it. (Sits piano chair.)

BOBBY. What happened after that, Gussie?

GUSSIE. (Rises, crosses Down.) What do you mean what happened? We goes up to the park with a guinea grinder, six quarts of ice cream, twelve chocolate bars, and a big loaf of cake that Spence finally got under his sweater. Geez—did he look funny. He looked like he had eight babies in there. (Sits sofa.) Boy, did we have fun.

(JOHNNY crosses to table.)

Got any more of the cake, Spence? Goddamn it, your mother sure does make good cake.

SPENCE. Sure! (He takes the plate. Crosses to shelf for cake.)

GUSSIE. Gee, I don't know why we been staying away from here so long. I've been missing that good stuff your Mom dishes out.

(Pause.)

SPENCE. (At shelf.) That was the day Tony broke his arm, remember?

GUSSIE. (Taking the cake.) Geez, that's right.

JOHNNY. (Crosses to ottoman, sits.) How did that happen?

GUSSIE. Geez, you guys are new around here, ain't you? (Rises, crosses to JOHNNY.) Well, after we'd stuffed with all that food, we decided to play Tarzan. So, you know that big oak tree over near the golf course? We decides to play in that. We're all leaping for the branches and making the ape call—(He imitates it.) then it gets to be Tony's turn—so Tony makes with the ape call and jumps for the branch, and the next thing you know he's falling right through the goddamn tree, hitting his head on one branch, his can on the next, and finally *VOOM* he hits the ground with the damndest noise I've ever heard. I'm convinced that he's dead. We're both honestly convinced that he's dead, he's so still. We're both scared to go near him so we keep calling from a distance—*(Calling to* TONY *who sits on stool Right.)* "Tony! Tony!" Finally we notice his stomach moving, so we goes over, and son of a bitch if there ain't a big piece of bone sticking right through his damn shirt. What the hell did they call that, Tony?

TONY. A compound fracture.

GUSSIE. Yeh! That's right. We sure did have fun that summer. *(Sits sofa.)* Remember, Spence?

*(*TONY *crosses to table, sits.)*

SPENCE. Yeh! I remember.

GUSSIE. Those sure were the good old days. *(Pause.)* Hey! As a matter of fact we're going up to the park tonight. We're going on a hay ride. You're all better, ain't you, Spence?

SPENCE. Yes.

GUSSIE. Well, why in hell don't you come along?

TONY. *(Puts down his plate sharply on the table, rises.)*

*(*EVERYBODY *reacts to the slip.)*

You did say you were coming back to school Monday, didn't you, Spence?

SPENCE. Yes, Tony. Monday I'm coming back to school.

TONY. *(Crosses to living room.)* Well, I guess we gotta be going.

*(*BOBBY *rises.)*

Why don't we call you for school on Monday?

SPENCE. *(Rises.)* Well, as a matter of fact my father is going to be driving me up to school on Monday. He's got to come with me—so we'll go up together.

TONY. Yeh! Well, Gus and me gotta be going.

*(*GUSSIE *rises.)*

SPENCE. *(Crosses Down Right.)* As a matter of fact, you know, I said when you first came in there was no damn reason for this party. Well, actually this is.

TONY. *(Crosses Down Right to* SPENCE.*)* Yeh! What? It ain't your birthday. I know when your birthday is.

SPENCE. Well, you know, I've been doing a hell of a lot of fooling around and I've been neglecting my lessons, not practicing, and all manner of things like that. And if you're going to college you got to be a little more serious about things than I've been. So from now on I've got to buckle down to the old books and concentrate on things of the mind.

GUSSIE. Yeh! I guess you're right.

SPENCE. So I've got a little schedule made out for myself. In the morning before school I've got to practice. And in the afternoon after school I've got my homework to do. So you see I'm going to be pretty busy.

GUSSIE. Geez, Spence. You sure do play the piano damn good. You know that? Are you going to be a musician or something?

SPENCE. I don't know. Maybe. I haven't given it too much thought. So I had all you guys over to kind of say goodbye and all 'cause I don't think I'm going to have much time for playing around. Course, it's going to be a little hard at first 'cause I'm not used to it, so all you guys could help me if you just kind of let me alone and let me get my work done.

TONY. Sure, we'll do that, Spence.

GUSSIE. Sure. Sure, Spence.

*(*GUSSIE *crosses to Left of piano.)*

SPENCE. Thanks—you're real pals.

TONY. Thanks for the icecream. *(He exits front door.)*

SPENCE. It's O.K. It was fun.

JOHNNY. *(On exit.)* Sure. Geez, you guys sound like you must've been pretty crazy in those days. See you, Spence.

(IGGIE rises also.)

SPENCE. Stay a second, Iggie. I want to talk to you.

BOBBY. *(On exit.)* Thanks for the party, Spence.

GUSSIE. *(Crosses down to SPENCE.)* Hey, Spence! Geez, I can't get over that summer. We really did have a hell of a lot of fun, didn't we?

SPENCE. *(With a hand on GUSSIE's shoulder.)* Yeh! We sure did. It was the best summer I ever had.

GUSSIE. Goodbye, Spence.

(They shake hands. General ad libs from BOYS Off Right.)

SPENCE. *(Crosses Left to IGGIE.)* Hey! Iggie, I'm sorry for what happened—I mean Gussie's talking that way. He's just dumb and he needs a good paste in the jaw for his pains, but I couldn't do it. I'm sorry, Iggie.

IGGIE. I understand.

SPENCE. Then O.K., Iggie. That's all I wanted to talk to you about. Thanks for coming to my party. *(Crosses to ottoman, sits.)*

IGGIE. Sure. *(Starts to go, stops.)* Did you really mean it, Spencer, about going to college?

SPENCE. Yeh! Yeh, I did. That is something, isn't it?

(Live ad libs blend into recorded baseball game.)

IGGIE. You don't know which one?
SPENCE. No, no, not yet.

IGGIE. Well. *(Pause.)* I'd better be going. *(He starts for the door.)*
SPENCE. Iggie!

(IGGIE turns.)

Look, I know you're busy and all that but would you mind if I came over and looked at the old stamp collection?

IGGIE. Do you want it back, Spencer?
SPENCE. No, I don't want it back. I'd just like to see what you've added to it— that's all.

IGGIE. Come over any time.
SPENCE. Thanks, Iggie. Thanks.
IGGIE. *(On exit.)* Goodbye, Spence.

(Pause. IGGIE has exited, leaving front door open.)

SPENCE. Goodbye, Iggie.

(SPENCE rises, crosses to table to get plates as MAY enters Up Left, crosses to kitchen door and enters. She carries a full shopping bag.)

MAY. Where is everyone?
SPENCE. Gone.
MAY. They didn't stay long.
SPENCE. No, they didn't.
MAY. *(Puts bag on dining table.)* What happened?
SPENCE. *(Center. Stopping.)* Nothing— nothing. I just told them that I didn't want to see them anymore. That's all. I just said it to them before they said it to me.
MAY. You'll never learn, will you?
SPENCE. Mom, you've just got to believe that I'm trying to learn. I'm trying as hard as I know how. I might be wrong, but if I am, I think I'd like to find that out for myself.
MAY. What are you going to do?
SPENCE. I don't know, Mom. I don't know.
MAY. *(Crosses in.)* Spence, look at me —you're not running away, are you?
SPENCE. No, Mom, I'm not running away—and if you don't mind, Mom, let's not talk about it any more—I did the right thing. So let's just both try to forget it happened and go on to something else. Okay? *(He walks to piano, starts to sit, then walks to front door and*

closes it, shutting out the baseball sounds. He sits at piano and starts to play "Praeludium.")

MAY. (After a few bars.) Spence—I love you very much.

(MAY picks up bag, crosses to kitchen.

SPENCE watches her, surprised, then turns back to the piano. As he resumes playing, MAY crosses to dining table and starts collecting dishes.)

SLOW CURTAIN

William Branch

In Splendid Error

A PLAY IN THREE ACTS

IN SPLENDID ERROR

In Splendid Error was first presented at the Greenwich Mews Theater, New York City, October 26, 1954.

CHARACTERS

THE REVEREND LOGUEN
JOSHUA
ANNA DOUGLASS
LEWIS DOUGLASS
GEORGE CHATHAM
THEODORE TILTON
FREDERICK DOUGLASS
JOHN BROWN
ANNIE DOUGLASS
SHEILDS GREEN
COLONEL HUGH FORBES
SANBORN

SCENES:

The entire action takes place in the parlor of Frederick Douglass's residence in Rochester, New York, in 1859–60.

ACT ONE

A late afternoon in the spring of 1859.

ACT TWO

SCENE 1. *Several months later.*
Noon.
SCENE 2. *A few nights later.*
SCENE 3. *A few weeks later.*
Early morning.

ACT THREE

Six months later. Early evening.

ACT ONE

SCENE:
The parlor of Frederick Douglass's house in Rochester, New York.

TIME:
A late afternoon in the spring of 1859, two years before the Civil War.

The parlor is a large, "company" room on the first floor of the Douglasses' modest residence. Furnished in a manner far from lavish—or even necessarily stylish for the period—it nevertheless suffices as a comfortable sitting room for the Douglass family and an orderly, dignified reception room for their guests.

In the Center of the Left wall is the customary fireplace. Up Left, at an angle, are large French doors leading into the dining room, and through the curtained glass may be seen the end of the dining table, a few chairs, sideboard, etc. A low settee squats against the wall Up Center, to the right of which is a large archway opening onto the front hall. The "front door" of the house is off Right of the hallway, while a flight of stairs can be plainly seen rising to the Left. There is a window in the hallway wall, and Down Right is a door opening onto a small library or study.

Left Center is a horsehair sofa. To right and left of the sofa are partly upholstered parlor chairs. At far Left is another, next to a small table.

At Rise, the REVEREND LOGUEN and JOSHUA are discovered. The REVEREND, who sits at the table far Right, is dressed soberly in dark suit with clerical collar. He is a Negro, slight of frame and advanced in years. Yet there is perennial youth about him in his sharp, distinct speech and quick, virile mind. His hat is on the table beside him, and with spectacles on he is making entries in a small notebook as he questions JOSHUA, who sits to his left.

JOSHUA is a young Negro dressed in ill-fitting but clean clothes. He is obviously a little out of place in these surroundings, but endeavors to respond with dignity to LOGUEN's queries.

LOGUEN. (Writing.) Haynes . . . Point, . . . Maryland . . . Tell me, where is that near?

JOSHUA. Uh, it's near Washington Town, suh. 'Bout five mile down the 'Tomac River, on the east'n sho'.

LOGUEN. I see. And are all three of you from there?

JOSHUA. Uh, yes suh. We all belongs to d' same massuh.

LOGUEN. (Chiding gently.) That's true, very true, Joshua, but a different master than you refer to. Now that you've made your escape you must realize that you never belonged to the man who held you in bondage. Regardless of what they taught you to think, we are all the children of God the father, and equal in His sight. Now . . . you and your companions escaped from Haynes Point, and hiding by day, picked your way to New York where you contacted our agents, is that right?

JOSHUA. Uh, yes suh. Ol' Miz Oss'ning, white lady who talk real funny, she giv' us dese clothes and gits us a ride on a big ol' furniture wagon comin' up dis way, an' she tell d' man to put us off in Rochester. Den we s'pose to ax 'round fo' a man name a Douglass. Frederick Douglass.

LOGUEN. I see. And when did you arrive?

JOSHUA. Jus' now, suh. Little befo' you come.

(ANNA DOUGLASS enters from the dining room. She is a Negro woman of forty, of medium height and build, and though not handsome, she nevertheless radiates the beauty of warmth of heart. Overshadowed outwardly by her husband's fame, she concentrates on being a good wife and mother and manages the household and occasional business with assurance and dispatch. ANNA has an apron on over her print dress and holds a cooking spoon in her hand.)

ANNA. My goodness, Rev'n Loguen, you two still in here talkin'? Let the poor man eat—the other two's nearly finished and the food's gettin' cold!

LOGUEN. Eh? Oh, I've about got it all now, it's all right, Mrs. Douglass. Uh— one thing, Joshua, before you join the others. Joshua, from now on, no matter what happens, you are never to reveal to anyone again the names of the people who helped you get away. I want you to explain that to the others, do you understand?

JOSHUA. Uh, yes suh, I unnerstan's. I tell 'em.

LOGUEN. All right. Now there's a man standing by over at the blacksmith's shop with a rig, ready to take you on to where you'll catch a boat for Canada. You'll be safe there. You'll be among friends, men and women like yourselves who've made their way to freedom, following the northern star. I congratulate you, Joshua, and welcome you to the fraternity of free men.

JOSHUA. (Nodding.) Yes suh. Thank you, suh.

LOGUEN. (Starting again.) And when you get to the settlement in Canada, Joshua, I want you to—

ANNA. (Impatiently.) Rev'n Loguen, if you don't shut your mouth and let this poor man come on in here an' get his supper, you better!

LOGUEN. Oh—I'm sorry, Anna. It was just that—

ANNA. Come on, Joshua. Your plate's all ready for you. If you need anything, you jus' call me, now, hear?

JOSHUA. Yes ma'am. Thank you, ma'am. (He goes out Left.)

ANNA. (*Turns to* LOGUEN.) I declare, Rev'n Loguen, I don't know what in the world I'm gonna do with you. You know them poor boys is got to get to the boat landin' by six o'clock. Fred's gone down there hisself to make the arrangements and he says have 'em there on time, 'cause the boat don't wait!

LOGUEN. I know, I know, Anna. (*Proudly.*) Do you know how many we've taken care of already this year, Anna? Thirty-three! Thirty-three free souls passing through our little station on the Underground Railroad.

ANNA. Yes, but if you keep on holdin' 'em up to pass the time of day, there's gonna be somebody up here lookin' for 'em 'fore they *gets* their souls free.

(JOSHUA *reappears at the door Up Left.*)

Why, Joshua. You want me for something?

JOSHUA. (*Somewhat sheepish.*) Uh, no ma'am. It's jus' dat I—I forgit somethin'.

LOGUEN. Yes? What is it, son?

JOSHUA. Well . . . dis Miz Oss—I mean, dis ol' white lady, she . . . she gimme what y' call a message. I'se s'pose to tell Mr. Douglass, but I—I forgit.

ANNA. Well, that's not so terrible, Joshua, you can tell us. It'll be all right.

JOSHUA. (*Considers, then.*) Yes, ma'am. Thank you, ma'am. Well, . . . dis lady, she say for to tell Mr. Douglass dat dere's a new shipment comin' through mos' any day now. One what's wuth a lots a money. She say for to be on the lookout for it, an' to han'le with care. Dat's it. Dem's d' words she spoke to me, tol' me to use 'em too. "A new shipment . . . handle with care."

LOGUEN. (*Echoes.*) Handle with care . . .

JOSHUA. An' now—now kin I go an' eat, ma'am? I feels a whole lots better, now dat I 'members!

ANNA. Yes, Joshua, you go right ahead. You did a fine job.

JOSHUA. (*Grins.*) Thank you, ma'am. Thank you. (*He exits.*)

ANNA. (*Soberly.*) What you make of it, Rev'n?

LOGUEN. I don't know . . . I don't know.

ANNA. Sounds to me like somebody awful important. Somebody we have to be extra careful to keep secret about.

LOGUEN. Yes, that's logical. But who?

ANNA. I may be wrong, but seems to me, couldn't be nobody else . . . but him! (*Her eyes shine strangely.*)

LOGUEN. Who? (*Looks at her, then comprehends.*) But—it's too dangerous! He'll never make it. Why, they'd pick him off in an instant—you know what a price there is on his head!

ANNA. I know, I know. But he'll get through. Don't know how he does it, but he'll get through.

LOGUEN. God help him . . . ! Well, I suppose I'd better go back and get these boys started if they're going to make that boat. (*Starts for the dining room.*)

ANNA. (*Heading him off.*) Hmmph! *Now* you're hurryin', jus' when Joshua's settin' down to eat. I declare, Rev'n, sometimes I think if you wasn't a man of the cloth—

LOGUEN. (*Laughs.*) Now, now, Anna. Give me another sixty years and I promise you, I'll reform! Well, I'll go down to the corner and signal Jim to bring up the rig so we won't lose any time. As soon as Joshua's finished, have them come right out and join me.

ANNA. All right, Rev'n. I'll do that.

(REVEREND LOGUEN *goes up to the hallway as* ANNA *sighs, smoothes her apron and starts for the kitchen. As* LOGUEN *passes the window he halts, glances out and whirls around.*)

LOGUEN. Quick! Anna! Tell them out the back way!

ANNA. What is it, Rev'n—?

LOGUEN. Somebody's coming up the

walk! Lewis and two white men—quickly, now! We've got to get them out. Here, Joshua—! *(He and* ANNA *hurry Off Left.)*

ANNA. *(Off.)* Wait, I'll get that door for you . . . !

(From Off Left comes the sound of the front door opening and closing. Then LEWIS *is heard calling.)*

LEWIS. *(Off.)* Mother! Oh, Mother!

*(*LEWIS *enters, a tall, pleasant-faced Negro youth, ushering in two distinguished-looking white gentlemen:* GEORGE CHATHAM *and* THEODORE TILTON.*)*

LEWIS. Come right in, please. Let me take your hats. *(He does so and places them upon the clothes tree as the gentlemen stand poised in the archway, glancing over the room.)*

*(*CHATHAM *is the larger and older of the two. With balding head and large, graying sideburns, his stout form suggests a successful, comfortable businessman just past middle age.* TILTON *is small, wiry, with sharp quick eyes behind his spectacles, and is perhaps in his middle forties. Both are well dressed and obviously men of importance in their fields.)*

LEWIS. *(Joining them.)* Won't you both be seated? I hope it will not be long before my father arrives.

CHATHAM. Thank you, thank you very much, Lewis. We'll be quite comfortable, I'm sure.

LEWIS. *(Bows and goes out through the dining-room, calling.)* Mother! Oh, Mother! I've brought guests. . . .

CHATHAM. *(Sitting.)* Well-mannered lad, isn't he?

TILTON. *(Has been absorbed in gazing around.)* What? Oh—oh, yes. Very.

CHATHAM. Cigar?

TILTON. Well, if you think it . . .

CHATHAM. Of course, of course. I've been here many times before, the lady of the house won't mind in the least. Here,

try this if you will. Havana. Deluxe. Imported, mind you, none of these homegrown imitations.

TILTON. Why, thank you.

CHATHAM. *(Smiling.)* Of course, it is still probably not so fancy as those you're accustomed to in your editorial board sessions in New York, but . . . *(He breaks off in a little light laughter.)*

TILTON. Oh, come now, come now, Mr. Chatham. Despite the fact that you practically dragged me here by the scruff of my neck, you don't have to flatter me.

CHATHAM. *(Smiling, as he extends a match.)* And if I had to I would have gotten ten strong men to help me, too! Ah—here.

TILTON. Thank you. *(He draws upon the cigar, considering.)* Ah . . . excellent. I must be sure to recommend these to my editors.

*(*CHATHAM *nods in deference.* TILTON *again appraises his surroundings.)*

So this is his house . . . I've never been in the home of a . . . *(Choosing his words carefully.)* . . . of a man of color before. I must say I'm impressed.

CHATHAM. *(Nods.)* And a warmer and more friendly household you'll not find in all of Rochester.

TILTON. Yes, I gather you're all rather proud of him here.

CHATHAM. But of course! Any city would do well to have a man of such prominence as Frederick Douglass choose to live within its bounds. And to think of it, Mr. Tilton. A scant twenty years ago this man was a slave—a chattel, a "thing." A piece of property forced with lash and chain to grovel under the tyranny of his "masters"! Oh, it just goes to show you, sir, that—

TILTON. *(Smiling.)* I take it also, Mr. Chatham, that you are an abolitionist.

CHATHAM. *(Emphatically.)* That I am, sir, and proud of it!

TILTON. *(Calmly.)* Well spoken, sir. I

like a man who speaks the courage of his convictions. It makes it so much easier to classify him, then.

CHATHAM. *(Alert.)* Why, sir, what do you mean by that?

TILTON. *(Urbanely.)* Oh, don't misunderstand me, my dear Chatham, I have nothing against the abolitionists. Quite the contrary, I am opposed to slavery, in principle. What I mean is that in New York, a man who declares himself an abolitionist *per se* is sure not to be a very popular figure.

CHATHAM. Popular?

TILTON. Why, yes. There have been cases where men have been stoned in the streets if they so much as spoke a disparaging word over a glass of beer in the corner saloon against the slave system. Why I believe William Lloyd Garrison himself, the "High Priest of Abolition" as it were, has sometimes been forced to close his meetings and flee for his very life before the onslaught of armed ruffians.

CHATHAM. Yes, that is true. I have heard many such accounts, of *New York* and other places.

TILTON. Well, practically each time your own Douglass speaks, outside of a few chosen localities that know him well, he does so at constant risk of personal assault.

CHATHAM. That cannot be denied. It is one of the reasons we admire him so. He has been shot at, stabbed and bludgeoned half to death, but he goes on.

TILTON. Well, you can hardly blame one then, can you, for being rather wary of . . .

CHATHAM. *(Frowns.)* Mr. Tilton, since when have we become so debased, so unmanly that we allowed fear of a little retribution to abridge our sacred right of free speech and conviction?

TILTON. Well, now, I—

CHATHAM. And especially, sir, if you will permit me, in terms of the press, with its responsibility for fearless . . .

TILTON. *(Hastily.)* Yes, yes—let me hasten to apologize, my dear Mr. Chatham, if I have offended through the slightest reflection upon the abolitionists. It merely seems to me at this time rather more *wise* to devote oneself a little less obtrusively to one's ideals. After all, you must admit there are great numbers of good people who intensely hate slavery who are not numbered among the ranks of the abolitionists *per se*.

CHATHAM. True, still—

TILTON. Well, in any event, it should be interesting after all to meet the celebrated Frederick Douglass: escaped slave, abolitionist orator, and self-made genius. *(This last with a trace of amused scorn.)*

CHATHAM. *(Retaliates.)* Yes, it should be. It isn't every day I'd go out of my way to bring even the noted editor of one of New York's most influential newspapers to meet a man like Douglass.

TILTON. *(Smiles icily.)* Again, you do me more than honor.

CHATHAM. It's a pity you must rush on so. On Friday nights, you see, we have a series of public lectures in Corinthian Hall. Douglass is a frequent figure on that rostrum and he is scheduled again for tomorrow. Couldn't you possibly—?

TILTON. You tempt me, my dear Chatham, really you do. But I have pressing appointments in the City, and by the way, what time is it getting to be? *(He reaches for his watch.)*

CHATHAM. Oh, never fear, Mr. Tilton, there is ample time, ample. *(Starts for the window.)* I'm sure if Mr. Douglass knew we were coming he . . . *(He breaks off as* ANNA *enters from the dining room.)* Well, Mrs. Douglass!

ANNA. How d' do, Mr. Chatham! It's so nice to see you again. *(She curtsies.)*

CHATHAM. *(With a little bow.)* The pleasure is all mine, Mrs. Douglass. I have the honor to present Mr. Theodore

Tilton of New York City, editor and publisher of the *New York Independent.* Mr. Tilton, Mrs. Douglass.

TILTON. It is my very great pleasure. *(He bows stiffly in reply to her curtsey.)*

ANNA. We're happy to have you, Mr. Tilton. Are you enjoyin' our little city?

TILTON. Oh, very much, very much indeed! It's always a pleasure to visit Rochester. And this time I told my friend Mr. Chatham here I should never forgive him if he didn't bring me around to meet your husband.

ANNA. That's very kind of you. Gentlemen . . . ? *(She motions and they sit, after her.)* I understand you went by the office?

CHATHAM. Yes. Young Lewis told us Mr. Douglass had gone to the Post Office. I should have remembered that Thursday is publication day. . . .

ANNA. Oh, that's all right. I guess you supply paper to so many big publications you just couldn't expect to remember 'bout all the little ones like us.

CHATHAM. Oh, quite the contrary, Mrs. Douglass. I have no client I think more highly of than *The North Star.*

ANNA. Now, just for that you'll have to stop and have supper with us. Both of you.

(TILTON looks distressed.)

CHATHAM. Thank you so much, Mrs. Douglass, but I'm afraid my Ellen has already prepared. Else we surely would take you up on your generosity. *(To TILTON.)* Mrs. Douglass has the reputation of spreading one of the finest tables in Rochester.

TILTON. *(Weakly.)* Yes, I'm sure.

ANNA. *(Flattered.)* Well, at least let me get you a cup of tea while you're waitin'. No, now you just make yourself 't home.

CHATHAM. All right, Mrs. Douglass. I know there's no use trying to get around you.

(From off in the hallway a door opens and closes. ANNA, *who has started for the kitchen, stops and turns.)*

ANNA. Why, I b'lieve that's Mr. Douglass now. *(Calls.)* Fred? That you, Fred?

DOUGLASS. *(Off.)* Yes, Anna.

ANNA. *(Coming to the archway.)* You got company . . .

DOUGLASS. Well, now.

*(*FREDERICK DOUGLASS *enters, a bundle of papers under his arm. He is a tall, broad, compelling figure of a man, forty-two years of age. His face, of magnificent bone structure, would be a sculptor's delight with the high cheekbones, the strong broad nose, the proud flare of the nostrils. His eyes, brown, deepset, peer intently from beneath the ridge of his prominent brow, and the straight grim line of the mouth seems on the verge at any moment of an awesome pronouncement. A long mane of crinkly black hair sweeps back from his stern forehead, and, together with heavy moustache and beard, lends a strikingly distinguished, leonine air. His large frame, bolt erect, is dressed conservatively in a suit of black broadcloth, with embroidered waistcoat and gold watch fob. His is an impression of challenge, achievement, dignity, together with strength, quiet but omnipresent.*

DOUGLASS *pauses in the archway, then depositing his bundle on the small table nearby, he strides forward to* CHATHAM, *hand extended.)*

DOUGLASS. George Chatham! Well, this is quite an unexpected pleasure.

CHATHAM. *(Beaming.)* So it is, so it is!

DOUGLASS. *(His voice is sonorous; he speaks with cultured ease.)* And is this a business visit? Am I more than two years behind in my account?

CHATHAM. Well, if that were so, I should hardly have come myself. I should rather have had my creditors, to collect *my* debts from *you!*

(They both laugh heartily.)

Frederick—Frederick, I wish to present Mr. Theodore Tilton of New York City. Mr. Tilton is the editor and publisher of the *New York Independent,* and I wanted him to make your acquaintance while he is in the city. Mr. Tilton, Mr. Douglass.

TILTON. *(Again bowing stiffly.)* It is my very great pleasure . . .

DOUGLASS. Not at all, the honor is mine, Mr. Tilton. *(He goes to* TILTON *hand extended.)*

*(*TILTON *shakes hands uncomfortably.)*

Will you be long in Rochester?

TILTON. No, I'm afraid I must return to the City tonight.

DOUGLASS. That's too bad. Anna, have you asked our guests to stay for supper?

CHATHAM. Yes, she has, Frederick, but I'm afraid Mrs. Chatham has already prepared.

ANNA. I was just goin' to make some tea—

TILTON. Pray don't, Mrs. Douglass. You see, we really don't have much more time to stay, I'm afraid.

DOUGLASS. Oh? Well, another time perhaps. Meantime, please be seated again. I refuse to let you leave at once.

ANNA. Oh, uh—Fred . . . ? 'Scuse me, but did you get them letters off in the mail while you was out? Three letters, goin' to Canada . . . ? *(She looks at him with meaning.)*

DOUGLASS. Oh . . . ! Yes, my dear. They're safely in the mail and on the way.

ANNA. *(Smiles.)* I'm glad. 'Scuse me. *(She gives a little curtsey and goes out via the dining room.)*

DOUGLASS. *(Turns back to his guests.)* Now, then . . .

CHATHAM. Oh, er—will you have a cigar, Frederick? I have some special—

DOUGLASS. No thank you, George. I've never been able to develop the habit personally, but by all means . . . *(Indicates*

for them to continue. They settle themselves.)*

(After a pause.)

Tell me, Mr. Tilton. What is the talk in New York these days?

TILTON. Oh, the same as here, I would suppose. Stocks and bonds . . . the railroads . . . migration west . . . Kansas . . . the Indians . . .

DOUGLASS. Ah, Kansas! So they speak of Kansas, do they?

TILTON. Oh, yes. It is much in the conversation round about.

DOUGLASS. And what do they say of Kansas, Mr. Tilton?

TILTON. Well, they discuss its impending admission into the Union. It seems certain by now that it comes as a free State, though there is much bitterness on both sides. And there's a great deal of pro and con about this fellow Brown. . . .

CHATHAM. You mean Captain John Brown?

TILTON. Yes, yes, I do believe he calls himself by some military title or other. Personally, I will be very happy to see Kansas enter *our* fold, so to speak, instead of the South's. But I can't very well agree with the way in which it was won.

DOUGLASS. Oh? And why?

TILTON. Well, I'm thoroughly against slavery, *per se,* you understand—you'll find our paper has stood out staunchly on that matter. But I think old Brown has done more to hinder the cause of the slaves, with his self-appointed crusade to keep Kansas free, than all the splendid work of the past several decades by persons like yourself to advance things.

DOUGLASS. Has he now?

TILTON. Why, of course! Good God, for him and his lawless band to call men out from their cabins in the dead of night, and without note or warning, judge or jury, run them through with sabres! Why, it's ghastly even to contemplate.

CHATHAM. But, sir, you overlook that

it was the partisans of slavery that first made war in Kansas, burning farmhouses and towns, assassinating and driving out those who dared voice opinion that Kansas should be kept free. It was these murderers—known to all—that Captain Brown avenged himself upon.

TILTON. Yes, but—

CHATHAM. And then, when the slave state of Missouri sent an armed militia across the border into Kansas, who but old Ossawatomie Brown, with a comparative handful of men—

TILTON. Oh, there is no doubt as to their bravery—or even foolhardiness, if you will allow—but to seize the lawful prerogative of the federal government, whose authority it is to protect these territories, is a very dangerous and outlandish course of action!

DOUGLASS. (Has picked up a copy of his paper, reads.) ". . . still today, and with no help from the federal government, Kansas stands at the gateway to statehood as a free territory. Is there any denying it would not have been so except for old John Brown?"

TILTON. Then you give your endorsement to such guerrilla tactics?

DOUGLASS. I have never particularly enjoyed the prospect of human beings wantonly killing one another. But from what I have gathered, there was left no choice in Kansas. It was either be driven out at gunpoint, or face those guns and fight. And that I think John Brown has done most admirably.

TILTON. (Frowns—considering.) Hmm . . . well, actually, Mr. Douglass, the conflict in Kansas has proved little point with respect to abolishing slavery. Rather, keeping the system from spreading—Free Soil, as they call it—was the actual issue there. For all his reckless bravado, old Brown liberated not a single slave.

CHATHAM. Ah, but to prevent the spread of the system across a single mile of border is a noble service indeed!

DOUGLASS. Quite so, George, but more than that: Free Soil and freedom for slaves must be regarded as coats of the same cloth. The one will never be secure without the other.

TILTON. Why, how do you mean?

DOUGLASS. (Smiles—pointedly.) I mean, sir, that those who seek only to exclude slavery from the territories—for their own political or business interests—without concerning themselves about abolishing the system altogether, are merely evading the ultimate issues. Slavery is like a spawning cancer; unless it is cured at its core, then despite all precaution it will eventually infect the whole organism. It must be stamped out entirely, not merely prevented from reaching other parts of the body.

TILTON. Ah—but we are dealing here with semi-sovereign States, not hospital patients. Unlike a physician, we have no license to delve into the internal affairs of the South.

DOUGLASS. Human slavery cannot be considered a purely internal affair of the South, Mr. Tilton. Especially when it seeks with guns and powder to extend the system further.

TILTON. I feel quite confident the federal government is capable of preserving law and order in any such eventuality.

CHATHAM. The government! A government rife from top to bottom with Southerners?

TILTON. (Protests.) President Buchanan is not a Southerner—

CHATHAM. Buchanan—hah! A Northern man without Southern principles who bends over backwards to concede every fantastic demand of the hotheads from Dixie! Or take Congress—frightened into hasty compromise every time the "Gentleman" from Carolina or Georgia or Mississippi bellows threats and abuse at his Northern colleagues! Or must I even mention the Supreme Court, it's blasphemous Dred Scott decision still fresh upon the page? And you speak to me of the government, sir! Why, if I had my way, I'd line 'em all up at my sawmill, start up that blade and hold a Bastille Day such as the French never dreamed of . . . !

DOUGLASS. (Amused.) Careful, now, George. You'll have poor Mr. Tilton thinking Rochester's a nest of fiery revolutionists.

TILTON. Well, at least there's an election next year. You may then express your opinions of your government under the protective mantle of party politics—without being liable to arrest for sedition.

CHATHAM. Hah—if I did adequately express my opinions I should still be arrested. For use in public of profane and obscene language!

TILTON. (Wryly.) A great loss to the cause of abolition that would be. (Turning to DOUGLASS.) Seriously, though, I do believe the continued existence of slavery is fast becoming the prime political issue of the day.

DOUGLASS. Quite so, quite so! Why, take even last year's Senatorial campaign, the widespread debates out in Illinois between Senator Stephen Douglas and this other fellow, Lincoln—

CHATHAM. (Interrupts.) But Lincoln was defeated!—a paltry, small-town, hayseed lawyer with more audacity than ability. Think no more of him. He's politically, uh—passé.

DOUGLASS. Nonetheless, George, the issue there was plain: the enslavement of human beings and all the evils it gives rise to must either be sanctioned nationally, or it must be abolished. Try as it may, the nation cannot much longer avoid decision on the matter. I believe the outcome of the election will depend upon this one issue.

TILTON. (Craftily.) And perhaps the outcome of the nation too, eh? However, I can only reiterate that drastic measures —such as old Brown's—can at best only aggravate the situation.

CHATHAM. (Protesting.) But slavery, sir, is an outrageously drastic condition. And when other means have failed, drastic conditions call for drastic measures!

TILTON. (Tolerantly.) Now, my dear Chatham, I have heard of many instances where masters are voluntarily freeing their Negroes. And of others who provide in their wills for manumission upon their deaths.

CHATHAM. Whose deaths? The master's?—or the slave's! Ha!

DOUGLASS. (Calmly.) May I point out to you, sir, that my own freedom was not given to me: I had to take it. And if you were a slave, Mr. Tilton, knowing full well that you of right ought to be free, would you be content to wait until your master died to walk on your own two feet?

CHATHAM. Ha! I for one would help him along a little.

TILTON. (Ignoring this—to DOUGLASS.) But can you not see that to press for all-out abolition at a time like this can but only further alienate the South? Why already they have threatened an ultimatum in the elections next year: unless a man friendly to them and their policies continues to sit in the White House they may bolt the Union! And you know we can never permit such a split.

CHATHAM. Quite so, but—

TILTON. (Exasperated.) Well, think of it, man! It would mean war, actual all-out fighting, one section of the citizenry against another, with muskets and sabres and cannon. Why it would be disastrous, catastrophic!

CHATHAM. Certainly—disastrous to the slaveholders, catastrophic to slavery!

TILTON. (Turning to DOUGLASS.) Surely, Mr. Douglass—notwithstanding the great multitude of wrongs committed against your enslaved people, the cardinal crime of bondage itself—still, surely you must see that if war comes between the States, not only will your people not benefit, but the nation as a whole stands in imminent peril of perishing!

DOUGLASS. (Quietly.) Mr. Tilton, if I spoke to you as a slave, I would say: "No matter, let it perish." As a being denied of all human dignity, reduced to the level of the beasts of the field, it would be of no consequence to me whether this ethereal idea known as a government survived or disintegrated. I would have nothing to lose, quite possibly everything to gain. If I spoke to you as a free man and a citizen, I would say: "War is destructive, cruel, barbaric. It must be avoided—if possible." But wrongs will have their righting, debts will have their due. And if in the last resort it should come to war, then we must make intelligent use of it, once involved, to destroy the malignant growths, to set right the festering wrongs, and to eliminate for all time this present grounds for complaint.

CHATHAM. Hear, hear! (He thumps the arm of his chair vigorously.)

TILTON. (With a smile.) I see you drive a hard bargain.

DOUGLASS. No more than the slaveholders, sir.

TILTON. (Slowly.) Mr. Douglass . . . though I cannot say that I altogether agree with you, nonetheless I can recognize a forceful sincerity when I see one. Will you permit me, sir, to make a note or two of this for publication? (He takes out pad and pencil.)

DOUGLASS. (Spreading his hands.) If my humble words—

TILTON. Oh no, no modesty here. I am sure our readers will be as interested as I in giving your arguments careful thought. (He busies himself with making notes.)

(CHATHAM flashes a congratulatory smile at DOUGLASS and is about to speak when from Off in the hallway the front door KNOCKER is heard.)

DOUGLASS. (Starting for the door.) Will you excuse me . . .

LEWIS. (Appears, coming from the rear of the house.) I'll get it!

DOUGLASS. All right, Lewis.

CHATHAM. I've tried to interest Mr. Tilton in hearing you speak sometime, Frederick. But unfortunately, he's a rather busy man, and . . .

TILTON. (Looks up.) I mean to correct that fault, Mr. Chatham, as soon as possible. When will you be in our city again, Mr. Douglass?

DOUGLASS. New York? Oh, I couldn't say. I've been trying to confine myself as much as possible to the paper lately, and I—

TILTON. (Reaching inside his coat.) If you will permit me, here is my card. Please do me the honor of stopping with me when next you're in the City.

DOUGLASS. (Taking the card.) Why, that's kind of you, Mr. Tilton.

(LEWIS appears at the archway.)

LEWIS. Excuse me, father. There's a Mr. Nelson Hawkins here to see you.

DOUGLASS. (Puzzled.) Hawkins? Nelson Hawkins?

LEWIS. Yes sir—he . . . well, I mean— (He seems to be suppressing some excitement.)—he just got in from out of town, and he—shall I ask him to wait in your study?

CHATHAM. (Rising.) Oh, by no means, Frederick, please don't neglect your guest on our account. We have to get going now, anyway. That is, if Mr. Tilton—

TILTON. (Still writing.) Yes, yes. I'm nearly ready. Just one minute . . .

DOUGLASS. (To LEWIS.) Ask him to step into the study for a moment, Lewis. I'll be right with him.

LEWIS. Yes sir! (He goes off.)

CHATHAM. Well, Frederick, it's been much too long since I've seen you.

DOUGLASS. Yes, it has. You must have dinner with us again very soon, George. We've missed you.

CHATHAM. I mean to take you up on

that. In the meantime, the wife and I will be at the lecture tomorrow night, as usual.

DOUGLASS. Good. I'll be looking for you. *(To* TILTON, *who has put away his notebook and risen.)* And so you're leaving us tonight, Mr. Tilton?

TILTON. Yes, I must. Though I'd very much like to be at the Hall tomorrow. What is your subject?

DOUGLASS. I'm speaking on "The Philosophy of Reforms."

TILTON. Oh, I would mightily like to hear that!

DOUGLASS. Then perhaps you would care to take along a copy of *The North Star* to glance at in your free time. *(He secures a copy.)* My remarks will be merely an expansion of this week's editorial.

TILTON. *(Accepting it.)* Thank you, sir, you are most kind. Our office subscribes to your paper, but it is not every week that I get to read it first hand.

DOUGLASS. Well, I shall have to remedy that by placing you personally on our subscription lists.

TILTON. Excellent! But you must bill me for it.

DOUGLASS. *(Nods in deference.)* You may send us your check if you wish.

CHATHAM. And now, we really must be going, or my Ellen will be furious.

(They go out via the hallway, ad libbing amenities, the murmur of their voices continuing in the background. After a pause, the door Down Right opens and LEWIS *appears. Making sure the others are out of sight, he turns smiling and holds open the door.)*

LEWIS. Please step in here now, Mr. Hawkins. Oh, let me get your bag.

*(*HAWKINS *enters. He is a lean sinewy man of over fifty. His flowing hair and ragged beard are streaked with gray, and his steel-gray eyes bore with deep, lively penetration. Dressed in plain woolen, cowhide boots, and carrying a well-worn leather strap bag, he presents a figure of indomitable energy and determination.)*

HAWKINS. *(Crossing to a chair.)* Oh, no thank you, Lewis. I can manage all right for an old man, don't you think? *(He grins at* LEWIS *with a twinkle in his eye and lays down his bag by the chair.)* Well, Lewis, you've grown—haven't you? —since I was here last. Getting to be quite a young man. How old are you now?

LEWIS. Seventeen, sir.

HAWKINS. Seventeen! Why, that's hard to believe. *(His eyes twinkle.)* And I suppose you cut quite a figure with the young ladies now, do you?

LEWIS. *(Blushes.)* Why, no sir, I—

HAWKINS. Oh, come now! I'll wager you've already picked out your young lady-fair.

LEWIS. Well, not exactly, sir.

HAWKINS. Not exactly? Ha, then *she* has picked *you* out!

LEWIS. Well—I do like a certain girl, but . . . it's just that—well, girls can act pretty silly sometimes. You just don't know what they're thinking or what they're going to do next. Sometimes they say no when they mean yes and yes when they mean no. I can't understand them at all!

HAWKINS. Well, well. This sounds pretty serious, Lewis. Tell me. Is she pretty?

LEWIS. Oh, yes! She's very pretty, I think.

(Pause.)

She's . . . she's the minister's daughter.

HAWKINS. I see. And is she religious?

LEWIS. Well, rather, I suppose. *(An afterthought.)* She's the minister's *daughter,* you understand.

HAWKINS. Ah, yes! That does make a difference.

LEWIS. I walked home with her from church last Sunday. I couldn't think of anything much to say, so we started out talking about the weather. And when we got to her house we were still talking about the weather. Six blocks about the weather!

HAWKINS. My, that certainly is a lot of weather!

LEWIS. (Miserably.) I just don't understand them, that's all.

HAWKINS. Well, Lewis, if you ever arrive at the point where you think you do, come and tell me, will you? I've had two wives and eleven children, and if God has ever seen fit to distribute understanding of women, then I must have been behind the barn door when He passed it out!

LEWIS. (Grins.) Yes sir.

(DOUGLASS re-enters from the front, glancing hastily at his watch.)

DOUGLASS. And now, Mr. Hawkins . . .

(Pause. HAWKINS turns toward him expectantly, but does not speak.)

Mr. Hawkins? . . . (He stares questioningly at HAWKINS while LEWIS watches eagerly.)

HAWKINS. (An amused twinkle in his eye.) Hello, Frederick Douglass!

DOUGLASS. (Slowly recognition—and joy—come into DOUGLASS's face.) Why . . . bless my soul, it's Captain Brown! (He rushes to him.) John! John!

(BROWN laughs and they embrace warmly. LEWIS grins in delight and exits toward the kitchen.)

DOUGLASS. But that beard!—You were always clean-shaven. And these clothes! Why, if it hadn't been for your voice I never would have—!

BROWN. (Laughs loudly.) You're looking well, Frederick!

DOUGLASS. Why, so are you, only— well, come and sit down, John. How did you ever manage to get through? Why,

there's an alarm out for you in seven States!

BROWN. (Laughs.) Oh, I have means, Frederick. I have means.

DOUGLASS. Oh, I must tell Anna. (Calls.) Anna! Anna, guess who's here!

(ANNA rushes in from the kitchen followed by LEWIS.)

ANNA. Lewis just told me! Welcome, Captain Brown! Welcome!

BROWN. Thank you, thank you, Anna. My, but you're the picture of health and brightness! You've got a wonderful wife here, Frederick. A fine woman!

ANNA. Oh, go on with that kind of foolishness, John Brown!

BROWN. Oh, yes, yes! God has been bountiful to you both. How are all the children?

ANNA. They're all very well, thank you.

BROWN. Good, good.

DOUGLASS. And how's your family, John?

BROWN. (His smile fading.) Oh . . . well. Well. For the most part, that is. These past few years have been hard on us, Frederick. Kansas . . . the price was very dear.

DOUGLASS. (Concerned.) Sit down, John. Tell us about it.

BROWN. (Sitting.) Thank you. I am a little tired.

ANNA. And you must be hungry too, poor man. Supper's nearly ready, but now that you're here I'll have to get up somethin' special for dessert. A pie, maybe. Sweet potato still your favorite?

BROWN. It certainly is.

ANNA. All right. Now you just make yourself 't home. Lewis! Come on and set the table for me, son.

LEWIS. (Reluctantly.) Aw . . . (Glances at his father, then rises quickly and follows Anna out.)

DOUGLASS. John, we've had no word of you for months. We didn't know if you were alive or dead.

BROWN. *(Smiling.)* Oh, I'm still above ground, Douglass. It will take more than a few cowardly ruffians in the Territories to put John Brown in his grave. And a lot more to keep him there! *(Sobers.)* They did get one of my sons, though. My Frederick.

DOUGLASS. Oh, no . . . !

BROWN. Yes. They shot him down one night, not far from Ossawatomie. Owen, too—the big one. But Owen still lives. Back on the farm at North Elba, Mary's nursing him back to health. He's . . . paralyzed. The waist down.

DOUGLASS. *(Softly.)* My God! And you, John, are you well?

BROWN. Oh, yes. I've been a little tired, but I'm gathering strength to go on with the work.

DOUGLASS. To go on? But John, Kansas is won! Surely now you can rest. You've done what no other man has been able to do: you've stopped the slave power dead in its tracks!

BROWN. Not quite, Douglass, not quite. Try as we might, the Free Soil constitution adopted in Kansas says nothing about the emancipation of slaves. It offers sanctuary to not a blessed black soul. I must get back to my true work: to free enslaved black folk, and not further waste my energies and resources on political partridges like Kansas. That is why I am here.

DOUGLASS. Yes?

BROWN. I shall want you to put me up for a time, Frederick. Several weeks, a month perhaps.

DOUGLASS. You know, John, that my house is always yours.

BROWN. Good. I knew I could count on you. I will pay for my accommodations. Oh no—no, I insist! I will not stay with you unless I can contribute my share to the household expenses. What shall it be?

DOUGLASS. Now, now, John—

BROWN. Come, come, Douglass! You must be practical.

DOUGLASS. Well, all right. Shall we say —three dollars a week for room and board? No, not a penny more! You are my guest.

BROWN. All right, settled then. *(He withdraws a purse and hands to DOUGLASS three dollars in silver coin.)* For the first week.

DOUGLASS. You are now a member of the Douglass household, in good financial standing.

BROWN. Fine! And one other thing, Frederick. While I am here I wish to be known in public only as "Nelson Hawkins." I want John Brown to be thought still in the Territories. Though Kansas is won, still there's a price on my head some enterprising young scamp might be ambitious to collect.

DOUGLASS. Ha! I shall turn you in at once!

(They laugh.)

As you wish, John. I shall inform the entire household at supper.

(The outside door opens and a child's voice cries, "Momma! Momma! We're back!" DOUGLASS smiles and looks up expectantly. In runs ANNIE DOUGLASS, a vivacious little six-year-old, followed by SHEILDS GREEN, a stockily built Negro with a bundle of papers under his arm.)

ANNIE. *(Sees her father and runs to him.)* Oh, Poppa! Guess what I've been doing! Me and Sheilds. I helped Sheilds take out the papers!

DOUGLASS. *(Lifts her in his arms.)* You did? Well now, aren't you Poppa's big, big girl!

ANNIE. Yes, I am! *(She gives him a hug, then giggles.)* Oh, Poppa, your whiskers. They tickle! *(She squirms around in his arms and for the first time sees BROWN across from them. She abruptly stops her laughter and her eyes grow big with wonder.)*

DOUGLASS. *(Setting her down.)* John, this is the light of my life, my little Annie.

BROWN. Well, she's quite a young lady now, isn't she!

DOUGLASS. Annie, this is Mr.— Mr. Hawkins. Say how-do-you-do like Poppa's big girl.

ANNIE. *(Steps forward timidly and gives a little curtsey.)* How de do? *(Then rushes back into her father's arms.)*

BROWN. And how-do-you-do to you, little lady!

DOUGLASS. Mr. Hawkins is going to stay with us for a while, Annie. Is that all right with you?

ANNIE. *(Considers—suspiciously.)* Doesn't he have a house of his own?

BROWN. Yes, I have, Annie. But it's a long way off.

ANNIE. *(Bolder now.)* Do you have a little girl?

BROWN. Why, yes—in fact one of my girls has the same name as you, Annie. Only she's a big girl now.

ANNIE. Bigger than me?

BROWN. *(Smiles.)* Yes, a little. But you'll soon be grown up and married too. You just wait and see!

DOUGLASS. Hold on there! Don't go marrying off my baby so soon.

ANNIE. *(Her timidity dispelling, she leaves her father's arms and moves toward the stranger.)* You got whiskers, just like my Poppa. Do they tickle too?

(DOUGLASS laughs and winks at SHEILDS, who stands in the background, watching the proceedings with a wide grin.)

BROWN. Well, I don't know. Do they? *(He bends down and juts out his chin.)*

(ANNIE reaches out and tugs gently at his beard.)

Uh-uh, careful!

(They laugh as ANNIE jumps back, startled.)

DOUGLASS. Well, how about it, Annie? Has he passed the test? May he stay, or shall we turn him out?

ANNIE. *(Considers this idea for a moment—then joyously.)* No, no! He can stay! He can stay!

DOUGLASS. Good! It's all settled.

BROWN. *(With a little bow.)* Much obliged to you, ma'am!

(ANNA enters from Off Left.)

ANNA. I thought I heard another woman in here!

ANNIE. *(Running to her.)* Oh, Momma, Momma! I helped Sheilds with the papers! I helped with the papers!

ANNA. You did, sweetie? Well, that's nice. And did you meet our guest?

ANNIE. Oh, yes! He's got a little girl too, with the same name as me, and his whiskers tickle just like Poppa's.

DOUGLASS. A dubious compliment!

ANNA. All right, dear. Suppose you run on upstairs now and get yourself ready for supper? Make sure you hang up your coat.

ANNIE. All right, Momma. *(She curtsies to BROWN.)* 'Scuse me, please. I have to go now. *(She runs over to SHEILDS.)* Can I help you again sometime, Sheilds?

SHEILDS. Yes, honey. Anytime you want.

ANNIE. *(As she runs off and up the stairs.)* Gee, Momma, I'm so hungry I could eat a whole hippopotamus!

DOUGLASS. *(To BROWN.)* Now you see where all our money goes. To buy her hippopotamuses!

(BROWN laughs. ANNA returns to her kitchen, and SHEILDS GREEN starts to follow.)

DOUGLASS. Oh, Sheilds! Come, I want you to meet our guest, er—Nelson Hawkins. *(To BROWN.)* This is Sheilds Green, sometimes known as "the Emperor"!

BROWN. *(Extending his hand.)* The Emperor? Am I in the presence of royalty here? Glad to know you, Mr. Green. *(He shakes hands vigorously.)*

SHEILDS. Glad to know you, suh.

DOUGLASS. Royalty in a sense. Because of his great strength, Sheilds's master nicknamed him "The Emperor"—used to point him out to his guests, laugh and make fun of him. Now it's Sheilds's turn to laugh. Not agreeing to be whipped one day, he left his master with a wrenched arm, three loose teeth and a dislocated collar bone.

BROWN. Well, well! Now that's an odd going-away present. And you reside here in Rochester now, I take it?

SHEILDS. Yes suh.

DOUGLASS. Sheilds has made his home with us since his escape.

BROWN. Good! We'll be seeing a lot of each other then, Mr. Green. I have an idea you may fit into our scheme quite handily, too, if you've a mind to. I shall need a number of men like you—strong, courageous, unafraid.

DOUGLASS. Tell us, what is this scheme of yours? *(He motions them toward seats.)*

BROWN. All right, Now is as good a time as any. *(He reaches for his bag, and withdraws a large rolled parchment.)* All the while I was in Kansas, Douglass, I have been thinking, planning, praying over this thing. Kansas was but an interlude, an opening skirmish. It has given me a hard core of trusted men, baptized in fire and blood, who will follow me anywhere. And now . . . now the time has come to carry the war into Africa itself, into the very heart of the Southland. *(Unrolling the parchment, he lays it over the table Down Right.)* Here. Will you be so good as to hold one edge for me, Mr. Green?

SHEILDS. Yes suh. I got it, suh.

BROWN. Now. If you will look carefully, Douglass—and you too, Mr. Green —here we have a map of the States from New Hampshire to Florida, and Maryland to Missouri. Now: here are the Allegheny Mountains sweeping from the North clear through to Alabama. Do they portend anything to you, eh?

DOUGLASS. I don't quite know what you mean. They form more or less a natural chain from North to South, but—

BROWN. Exactly! These mountains are the basis of my plan, Douglass. I believe these ranges to be God-given, placed there from the beginning of time by some divine pre-arrangement for but a single purpose . . . the emancipation of the slaves. *(He pauses, eyes shining.)*

DOUGLASS. Go on. Explain.

BROWN. Look here, at the Blue Ridge Mountains of Virginia. These ranges are full of natural forts, where one man for defense would be the equal to a hundred for attack. Now, I know these mountains well. My plan, then, is to take a force of men into the Virginia hills. There I will post them in squads of fives along a line of twenty-five miles. Now, when these are properly schooled and drilled in the arts of mountain warfare, it will then be possible to steal down to the plantations and run off slaves in large numbers. Think of it, Douglass! Think of the consternation among the Virginia slavemasters when they see their slaves disappearing into the hills!

DOUGLASS. *(Weighing it all.)* Yes . . . yes, I can imagine.

BROWN. Not only for the good of delivering these people from their bondage, you understand—though that is of course the paramount end. But the prospect of valuable property which is disappearing in the middle of the night—ah! Here Douglass, we attack the slave system at its core, and that is its pocketbook. *(Springing up.)* Oh, Douglass, you and I know that eloquent appeals to men's emotions, their reasons, their sense of justness and fair play have little effect if the evil you would have them discard is the means of their bread and syrup. They may turn a deaf ear to God himself, but once you remove the monetary profit from their vices, take away the means by which they gain their filthy dollars, they will desert it as if in fear of plague and seek other means more economically secure to furnish their tables.

DOUGLASS. *(Has been listening carefully.)* Yes . . . yes, there is much truth in what you say. But—suppose you succeed in running off a few slaves. What is to prevent them from merely selling their slaves further South?

BROWN. Ah! That in itself would be a show of weakness. Besides, we would follow them up. Virginia would be only the beginning.

DOUGLASS. But they would employ bloodhounds to hunt you out in the mountains.

BROWN. That they might attempt, but we would whip them—and when we have whipped one squad, they would be careful how they pursued again.

DOUGLASS. And the slaves themselves? What would become of them once you had liberated them from their bonds?

BROWN. We would retain the brave and the strong in the mountains, and send the rest north into Canada by way of the Underground Railroad. You're a part of that operation, Douglass, and I'm counting on you for suggestions along that line.

DOUGLASS. I see. But won't it take years to free any appreciable number of slaves this way?

BROWN. Indeed not! Each month our line of fortresses will extend further South—Tennessee, Georgia, Alabama, Mississippi . . . to the Delta itself. *(He points them out on the map, which SHEILDS now holds, gazing in wonder.)* The slaves will free themselves!

DOUGLASS. And those you retain in the mountains. How do you propose to support this growing band of troops?

BROWN. We shall subsist upon the enemy, of course! Slavery is a state of war, Douglass, and I believe the slave has a right to anything necessary to obtain his freedom.

DOUGLASS. *(Thoughtfully.)* Now, if you were surrounded, cut off . . . if it's war, then you must not underestimate the enemy.

BROWN. True, that's true, but I doubt that we could ever be surprised in the mountains so that we would not be able to cut our way out.

DOUGLASS. Perhaps . . . still, if the worst were to come?

BROWN. *(Impatiently.)* Then let it come! At least we will have been doing something. Action . . . action is the basis of reform, and long ago, Douglass, I promised my God I had no better use for the means, the energies and the life He gave me than to lay them down in the cause of the slaves. *(Turns to SHEILDS.)* Mr. Green. You've been silent. Let us hear from you.

SHEILDS. *(Admiration in his voice.)* You're Cap'n John Brown, ain't you?

BROWN. *(With an amused glance at DOUGLASS.)* Why, yes—yes I am, Mr. Green.

SHEILDS. Jus' call me Sheilds.

BROWN. All right. Sheilds.

SHEILDS. I'm not a what-you-call eddicated man, suh. Mr. Douglass here's jus' now learnin' me readin' and writin'. I ain't much to offer, I knows, but when you gits ready to send them mens into the mountains, please let me know. I'd powerful like to be one of 'em, Cap'n Brown.

BROWN. And so you shall, Sheilds, so you shall! *(He strides to SHEILDS and shakes hands vigorously. To DOUGLASS.)* There, you see? My first recruit! I'll have to write Forbes about this. Oh, I haven't told you about Forbes, have I?

DOUGLASS. Forbes?

BROWN. Yes. Colonel Hugh Forbes. By an extraordinary stroke of good fortune, Douglass, I've met a certain Englishman, a military man who has engaged in several of the revolutionary movements of Europe. I've verified that he fought with old Garibaldi himself. I've engaged this man as drillmaster for my troops.

DOUGLASS. Drillmaster?

BROWN. Yes. I have induced Colonel Forbes to join me and supervise the proper training of a fighting force. I consider it very fortunate that I could persuade him.

DOUGLASS. Where is he now?

BROWN. In New York, writing a military manual for the use of our troops.

DOUGLASS. Why, it all sounds so incredible! An English drillmaster and a military manual . . . ! I know your accomplishments, John. You were successful in Kansas by personally leading a small band of men. But now all this talk of a drillmaster and a special manual—

BROWN. But you fail to realize the scope of the mission, Douglass! This is to be no minor skirmish, this is war and war demands extensive preparation. You can see how important it is to make allowances now for whatever might arise in the future. Douglass . . . (intensely) Douglass, I've spent years perfecting this plan in detail. I've tested my methods under fire. Believe me, I know whereof I speak!

DOUGLASS. (Slowly.) Yes, in the past you've proved that beyond all question, John.

BROWN. Then you're with me, Douglass?

DOUGLASS. (Turns away—thoughtfully.) Your plan at best is risky, very risky. If it fails it may undo a great deal of work that's been built up over the years . . . even set off a spark that might destroy us all. But there is one thing that cannot be denied: you have not just talked about slavery, you are doing something about it. And against such odds. . . . We

cannot rely upon time and the kindness of men's hearts to free our people, John. You have proved your worth as a fighter, and you have my support.

BROWN. (Goes to him—in emotion.) Oh, Douglass . . . Douglass!

DOUGLASS. What can I do to help you?

BROWN. All right. I shall need men to add to my force, brave men and strong —like Sheilds here. I need your aid in assembling them.

DOUGLASS. John, do you know Harriet Tubman?

BROWN. No, but I've heard of her. The "Conductor" of the Underground Railroad.

DOUGLASS. She is now in Canada, resting at a settlement of fugitive slaves. I will take you to her. She will find you all the men you can use.

BROWN. Good.

DOUGLASS. And what of money and supplies?

BROWN. Yes—though I do not grudge the sums I spent in Kansas, now my funds are nearly gone. I intend to solicit contributions from antislavery men of means.

DOUGLASS. Tomorrow you shall meet another, a wealthy millowner who often has aided in the operation of the "Railroad." He will be most anxious to help.

BROWN. Splendid! I shall write to others in Boston, Philadelphia, and New York. I'll have them communicate with me here, as "Nelson Hawkins."

DOUGLASS. And I can reach leaders among the slaves from Virginia to Mississippi. When you are ready to move, they will know you are coming.

BROWN. Oh, Douglass! Douglass! (He grasps DOUGLASS by the shoulders.) I knew I could count on you! It's coming . . . I can feel that it's coming! As Moses led the children of Israel from Egyptian bondage to the land of Canaan, so shall we lead the children of Africa from Southern bondage to the land of Canada. It is God's will! Together—together we will free the slaves! (*He stands with arms outstretched toward* DOUGLASS *and* SHEILDS *as—*

CURTAIN

ACT TWO

SCENE 1

TIME:

Several months later. Noon.

At Rise, ANNA DOUGLASS *is discovered tidying up in the hallway. She comes down into the parlor for a quick look around, then starts to leave, when she spies a hat resting on a chair. She picks it up and examines it; it is of curious military design. She glances ominously toward the closed study door then drops the hat back onto the chair in disgust. Off Right the front door opens and* LEWIS *enters, whistling gaily.*

LEWIS. Hello, Mother.

ANNA. Oh, that you, son? You're home early. I ain't fixed dinner yet.

LEWIS. Oh, that's all right. There was nothing going on at the office anyway. Where's Dad?

ANNA. (*Indicates the study.*) In there. That man is here again.

LEWIS. What man?

ANNA. That soldier man. You know, Captain Brown's friend. Colonel somebody.

LEWIS. Oh, you mean Colonel Forbes.

ANNA. That's the one. He's in there with Fred.

LEWIS. What's he want this time?

ANNA. I don't know, but I'll bet it's money. Fred's keepin' the old man's funds for him and he has to handle his business when he's gone.

LEWIS. But Captain Brown's not ready to move yet. He's still out raising funds. Doesn't seem right to be paying Colonel Forbes for doing nothing.

ANNA. That's what I been tellin' Fred! But he says the old man insists. Says he'll need Forbes and he'll be ready pretty soon now.

LEWIS. I hope he knows what he's doing.

ANNA. So do I, Lewis. Every time Fred talks to him he just says, "God'll take care of everything." 'S if God ain't got enough to do already.

(*The front door slams and* ANNIE *runs in, shrieking.*)

ANNIE. Momma! Momma!

ANNA. My gracious! What's the matter, baby?

ANNIE. Quick, Momma, I have to hide!

ANNA. Hide from what, Annie?

ANNIE. From Bobby and Henry. They're after me!

ANNA. Bobby and Henry? What are they after you about?

ANNIE. We was playin' slavery, an' I'm the slave. Only I ran away!

(LEWIS *grins and shakes his head, exiting toward the kitchen.*)

ANNA. Oh . . . well, you better get away quick then, 'fore you get caught. That'd be just terrible, wouldn't it?

ANNIE. No, it won't be so bad. Jackie's playin' Mr. Hawkins and he always helps me get free again.

ANNA. Oh, I see. Well, your poppa's got company in the liberry and I hate to turn you out. But you better go back outside and play. (*She guides* ANNIE *toward the hallway.*)

ANNIE. All right, Momma. But if they catch me, they're gonna sell me off to the highest bidder!

ANNA. Oh? Well, if that happens, I'll come out an' see if I can't buy you back with some gingerbread and cookies. Run on, now.

(ANNIE *starts out but then, glancing out the hallway window, she squeals and comes running back.*)

ANNIE. Momma, Momma! They saw me! I have to get away! I have to get away! *(She dashes off toward the kitchen.)*

ANNA. *(Following.)* Lawd-a-mussy! I don't know what I'm gonna do with you. . . .

(As they leave the study door opens and DOUGLASS *enters, followed by* COL- ONEL HUGH FORBES. FORBES *is a tall, once-handsome man in his thirties with a harried, hungry look about his eyes.)*

DOUGLASS. *(Is frowning.)* I'm very sorry, Mr. Forbes, but that is the state of affairs and I don't see that there's any- thing more to say. Now, if you'll excuse me, I have quite a bit of work to do.

FORBES. Now, just a minute, just a minute here! Am I to understand, then, that you refuse to discharge these obliga- tions?

DOUGLASS. *(Displeased.)* I am under no obligation to you whatsoever, sir.

FORBES. Well, perhaps not you per- sonally, Mr. Douglass, but you *are* acting for Brown. And I tell you that he is be- hind on my salary. Again! Now really, old chap, just how much do you fellows expect me to put up with? I have tried to be patient, man, but even my endurance has its obvious limitations. Why, so far I think I have been rather agreeable about this whole thing, and—

DOUGLASS. *(Smoldering.)* Oh, you have, have you? And I suppose you were just being agreeable when you wrote this letter to George Chatham demanding by return mail a check for fifty dollars! Mr. Chatham is not responsible for your sal- ary, Mr. Forbes. Nor am I. From here on you will have to make your arrange- ments personally through Captain Brown, or not at all. Now again, I am asking that you excuse me. I have more important matters to attend to.

(LEWIS appears at the dining room door and stands listening.)

FORBES. Important matters! What is more important than my salary? Really, Mr. Douglass, I am amazed at your ap- parent lack of understanding. Can you possibly fail to appreciate that I am in a rather unique position here? That a word from me in the proper ears would spell the end of this whole scheme? The end of Brown and you and all the rest?

DOUGLASS. So now it's out! At last!

FORBES. *(Daring.)* Yes, at last, if you couldn't get it before! Where do you think you'd be, any of you, if it weren't for me? Why, this whole thing constitutes in essence a conspiracy—a conspiracy against the peace of Virginia and a plot against the government. All I'd have to do would be go to Washington and seek the proper authorities, and it would be a bad day for you, sir!

DOUGLASS. *(Flaring.)* Bad day for me indeed! Mr. Forbes, if you think you're going to blackmail me—or John Brown either, for that matter—you've got quite a surprise coming. I'll not give you an- other cent of his money. You may go where you like and tell whom you please, but you'll not intimidate me one whit! Now, I'll thank you to leave my house.

FORBES. *(Placatingly.)* Now, now— there's no need for haste. You needn't upset yourself so, Mr. Douglass. I—

DOUGLASS. We will speak no more about it, sir!

FORBES. Take until tomorrow to think it over. After all, only two hundred dol- lars.

DOUGLASS. Take your hat and get out. Before I feel compelled to assist you!

FORBES. *(Indignant.)* Now, really, I—! *(He draws himself up with arrogant dig- nity.)* Very well. You force me to take action. I have tried to reason with you, I should have known that that is impos- sible. And I am not in the habit of being insulted by . . . by . . .

*(*DOUGLASS *removes his spectacles,*

calmly. FOBRES *turns and beats a hasty exit.)*

LEWIS. *(Steps into the room.)* We can stop him! I'l catch him before he gets around the corner—!

DOUGLASS. No, Lewis, let him go! I must reach the old man at once—I want you to go to the telegraph office and get off a message. Here, take this down. *(He looks around for paper and pencil, but* LEWIS *withdraws his own.)* To Nelson Hawkins, Esquire. Care of Gerrit Smith, 17 East Locust Street, Peterboro, New York. . . .

LEWIS. I've got it. Go on.

DOUGLASS. "Return at once. A wolf has upset the pail."

CURTAIN

ACT TWO

SCENE 2

A few nights later.

Gathered in the room are DOUGLASS, BROWN, CHATHAM, LOGUEN, SHEILDS *and another gentlemen to be identified as* SANBORN. *They appear to have been having a conference, but now they have paused and are finishing up refreshments of cake and coffee.* LEWIS *is circulating with a plate of cake slices, but everyone seems to have had enough.* ANNA *has the coffee service and pours another cup for one or two of the guests. Several light up cigars or pipes, and the room begins to take on the air of a political caucus. At length,* SANBORN *puts down his cup and calls the meeting to order. He is a mild, cultured gentleman with a Boston accent.*

SANBORN. Gentlemen. Gentlemen. It's getting very late. Shall we get on with our business?

(There are ad libs of "Yes. Quite so. By all means.")

All right. *(He turns to* BROWN *who sits near the fireplace facing the others, as if in a witness chair.)* Captain Brown, we have all listened earnestly to your arguments in favor of continuing with your plan. I think I can speak for all of us here when I say that we greatly admire your spirit and have implicit faith in your capability. We have supported you before, and are most anxious to do so again, in order to advance the day of freedom for our enslaved brethren.

However—and here I speak not only for himself but also the committee I represent—however, we cannot afford to ignore this new and most distressing development. A trust *was* misplaced. The man *has* gone to the authorities—Senator Seward himself telegraphed me in Boston and asked me to get to you right away. He is trying to keep it quiet, but still for all we know, right now we may be under the watchful eye of federal agents merely awaiting the opportune moment to pounce!

Under these circumstances it seems that your plan is doomed to failure if you insist upon pursuing it now. You have convinced us in the past that you are worth supporting. We have subscribed funds and promised supplies and arms and ammunition. We do not withdraw them now!

(There are ad libs of disagreement from the others.)

BROWN. Mr. Sanborn, I do not concede that now is a less favorable time than in some distant future. We can do it still! We must not be made timid by the first dark shadow that falls across our path. A swift blow, a swift blow now, gentlemen, before they get a chance to believe the scoundrel—!

*(*SANBORN *frowns and shakes his head firmly.)*

CHATHAM. But why not, Sanborn, why

not? If we could get things rolling now, catch them off their guard—!

SANBORN. You mean let them catch us off our guard! And remember—they've got Forbes with them, now. He knows the whole plan in detail.

BROWN. If you will only leave that matter to me—I have those who can be put on his trail. Forbes will get what traitors deserve!

(There is a disapproving murmur.)

SANBORN. That is simply impossible, Brown. In the face of what has happened, it's sheer madness!

LOGUEN. Careful . . . careful, Captain.

CHATHAM. Well, John, I'm not so sure that that's at all advisable. . . .

SANBORN. You should never have taken the man into your confidence.

DOUGLASS. Well, I think we've *all* been fools not to have seen through his game from the very first. But still, Frank, it seems so . . . tragic to have to postpone the entire operation now.

CHATHAM. Of course! What's the matter with Gerrit and Higginson and the others on the committee, Sanborn? Are they getting cold feet because of a handful of stupid men in Washington, or have they been this timid from the very first—!

SANBORN. Now, now, Chatham, there's no need to go too far over the matter. From the first we've had to consider that we could all be prosecuted for conspiring to violate the Fugitive Slave Law and a score of other such measures. But we all take our chances in this work and regard it as our Christian duty, and I'm sure none of us regrets a single action or dollar spent up to now.

CHATHAM. Well, good. Who was it said: "We must all hang together, or most assuredly we shall all hang separately."

(There is a little light laughter.)

LOGUEN. *(With a frown.)* Well, gentlemen, it is all very well to joke about it, but I for one am behind Captain Brown one hundred per cent. I protest against any postponement. If the thing is postponed now, it is postponed forever—because Forbes can do as much evil next year as this. I believe we have gone too far to turn back now!

BROWN. *(Encouraged.)* Aye, Reverend Loguen! And I tell you, sirs, that I can do it. I have the means and I will not lose a single day now. I tell you we can be freeing slaves a week from tonight in Virginia.

CHATHAM. What? So soon?

BROWN. Absolutely, sir! *(Rises.)* There is no need for delay. I would have been in Virginia now were not Harriet Tubman lying ill in Canada. But she can send me others who know the "Railroad's" route as well as she. I and my men will free the slaves, and hers will lead them out.

CHATHAM. But with so small a band? I thought you needed scores—

BROWN. General Tubman will dispatch a good-sized force to me as soon as I have need of them. And when the first blow is struck the slaves will rise throughout the countryside. Men from the free States will come down and join. An army will form, consolidate and march southward. Oh, I tell you, sir, it can be done and I can do it now! *(He pauses, trembling with the emotion of it.)*

(And all eyes turn toward SANBORN. SANBORN meets BROWN's gaze gravely, then slowly and firmly shakes his head. There is a pause as the others register their disappointment.)

But my men will fall away . . . everything that I have been building in my lifetime will come down to nothing, nothing. . . . *(He sinks to his chair.)* You don't know what you're doing . . . you just don't know. . . .

SANBORN. We know how disappointed you are, Captain Brown, and we regret it exceedingly, believe me. But we cannot listen further. Our hearts are still with you, but I believe it is pretty well decided. *(Turns toward* DOUGLASS.*)* Frederick . . . ?

DOUGLASS. I . . . no. No, Frank, I have nothing further to add to what I've already said.

SANBORN. All right. Captain Brown, this is what you must do. You must stay low, let time pass. The alarm will die down, the suspicions. Then you will return and strike, and we shall be behind you. In the meantime, tell us no more of your plans. We will trust you with our money, but we can aid you no further for now. Go back to Kansas and wait. Time must pass.

(There is silence. BROWN'*s eyes are smoldering but he does not speak.* SANBORN *rises, signifying that the conference is at an end, and the others follow suit.* SANBORN *turns to* DOUGLASS.*)*

We must thank you, Frederick, for receiving us so graciously on such short notice.

DOUGLASS. That's quite all right, Frank. I'm only sorry that I can't put you all up for the night.

CHATHAM. Oh, we have plenty of room at our place. I'll take good care of him.

SANBORN. That's very kind of you, George.

DOUGLASS. *(One last try.)* Stop by tomorrow, unless you have to hurry back.

SANBORN. *(Smiles and shakes his head.)* I'm afraid I'm catching the early Boston train. So I'll say goodbye now. Until the next time. *(He grasps* DOUGLASS'*s hand, then turns to leave.)*

(He stops, seeing BROWN *still sitting brooding by the fireplace, but* BROWN *abruptly turns away, refusing to say goodbye, and* SANBORN *continues out via the hallway.* CHATHAM *follows.* LOGUEN *puts a sympathetic hand on* BROWN'*s shoulder before passing on.* DOUGLASS *accompanies them all to the door as* SHEILDS *stands looking after, flashing hostile eyes at the departing guests.*

ANNA *and* LEWIS *reappear and gather up the cups and saucers. They exit. Sheilds seats himself dejectedly by the table and gazes with sympathy at* BROWN, *who continues to sit in defeated silence, solemnly regarding the fire.*

Presently DOUGLASS *returns. He pauses near the archway, then comes slowly Down and sits, drawing his chair nearer the fire. For a moment he does not speak.)*

DOUGLASS. *(Quietly.)* I'm sorry, John.

BROWN. *(Stirs and smiles weakly.)* It's all right, Frederick. You told me how it would be.

DOUGLASS. Perhaps it *is* better to wait.

BROWN. *(Sighs.)*
"There is a tide in the affairs of men,
Which, taken at the flood, leads on . . ."
I am at my tide, Frederick. Despite what they say, I cannot turn back now.

DOUGLASS. You don't mean that. Another year, a few months perhaps—

BROWN. *(Shakes his head.)* I cannot delay further.

DOUGLASS. Surely you can't mean that you're going on with it now.

BROWN. It will be now or never.

DOUGLASS. *(Alarmed.)* Has all this tonight meant nothing to you?

BROWN. Oh yes, yes. It has meant a great deal. They have failed me at the first small sign of difficulty. I cannot afford to leave them that opportunity again —I will proceed without them. It means altering my plans somewhat, but I have already prepared for that. You see, Frederick, I leave nothing to chance.

DOUGLASS. *(Sympathetically.)* You're tired, disappointed. . . .

BROWN. For twenty years this plan to free slaves has held me like a passion. It will be desperate, perhaps, but it will be holy. For I was created to be the deliverer of slaves, and the time is now.

DOUGLASS. *(Goes to him.)* Come up to bed, and we will speak more of it tomorrow.

BROWN. No, my friend. There is no time to waste in sleeping now.

DOUGLASS. Now, really, John, you're taking this too far. After a good night's rest things will look different in the morning.

BROWN. Morning must find me on my way. I am leaving tonight.

(SHEILDS, sitting silently on the other side of the room, sits up at this, and listens intently.)

DOUGLASS. Leaving? But what can you do now, alone?

BROWN. I still have my band, Frederick. I must get them word immediately— listen to this. *(He takes out a telegraph sheet and reads.)* "The coal banks are open. Old miners will come at once." Ha! They'll know what I mean. And where.

DOUGLASS. But what about arms, supplies—?

BROWN. I already have enough cached away in a warehouse in Pennsylvania with which to begin. Once we reach Virginia, we'll live off the land. As for arms, there will be all we can use just waiting for us at Harpers Ferry. Once there, we can begin our operatiions without want of—

DOUGLASS. Just a minute! Did you say . . . Harpers Ferry?

BROWN. Yes.

DOUGLASS. There is a United States Government Arsenal at Harpers Ferry.

BROWN. Of course! That is what I mean. We shall seize it first. With its store of weapons and supplies we can arm our forces as they expand, equip Harriet Tubman's men as they come, supply the slaves for miles around.

DOUGLASS. Brown! What are you thinking of?

BROWN. *(Speaking fervently now.)* Can't you see it, Frederick? The word traveling from lip to lip . . . the slaves rallying to the call . . . the mountain passes sealed with bullets . . . liberty spreading southward like a trail of fire! . . .

DOUGLASS. John!

BROWN. The nation roused—

DOUGLASS. Do you know what you're saying?

BROWN. The chains dropping—

DOUGLASS. It's mad. It's madness, I tell you!

BROWN. Free men rising from the muck of enslavement!—

DOUGLASS. *(Shouts.)* John! ! Listen to me. You cannot do it!

BROWN. *(Slowly realizing what DOUGLASS is saying.)* What? . . .

DOUGLASS. It is impossible, insane! You must not even think of it.

BROWN. You're . . . going to fail me, then? You too, Douglass? I'm counting on you to help me, Frederick, are you going back on me too?

DOUGLASS. *(Taking him by the arm.)* Sit down. Sit down, John.

(They sit.)

Do you believe I'm your friend? That I want to do what's right?

BROWN. I believe you, Frederick.

DOUGLASS. Then listen to me. I have helped you as much as I could. I intend to help you further, when the right time comes, in your great slave-freeing raids. But what you are saying now is wholly different.

BROWN. Wherein is it different? This is greater, that's all, greater. We shall free more slaves and free them faster.

DOUGLASS. But don't you realize what you'd be doing? You can't attack Harpers Ferry. You'd be attacking the United States Government. It would be treason!

BROWN. *(Eyes flashing.)* Treason! Government! Laws! Blast them all to hell! I answer you back, Douglass. I answer you back with humans and right! I answer you back there is a higher law than all!

DOUGLASS. John, you're living on earth —you're dealing with men.

BROWN. *(Defiantly.)* I deal with God!

DOUGLASS. Oh, I see! You deal with God. And is it God who counsels you to rash, inopportune action? Is it God who calls you to dash away your talents and your usefulness in a single ill-considered stroke? And what of the slaves themselves —you want to help them, you say. Why then do you think of doing the very thing that will harm them most? Why bring the nation's anger on them? *You* may defy the federal government, but they cannot.

BROWN. But we will rouse the nation behind them! It needs rousing. It's cursed. It's dying. It needs to be startled into action.

DOUGLASS. Oh, can't you see, John? By running off slaves from southern plantations, you attack the slave system without endangering retaliation by the whole nation. Aye! There will be many who will approve and come rallying to your support. But if you start by attacking Harpers Ferry your blow is not at slavery itself. Your blow is against the whole nation, and will bring down on your head— and the slaves—the panic and condemnation of thousands whose sentiment would otherwise be with you.

BROWN. I cannot concern myself with public opinion just now. Action! Action is the only means to reform. You know that, Douglass . . . you've said it yourself.

DOUGLASS. Yes, John, yes—but must we have action, any action, at so great a price? Tell me. Tell me, John: is there ever any justification for such unprovoked violence, even in pursuit of a righteous cause?

BROWN. Yes! Yes, by God, I believe there is. If we cannot persuade the nation with words to purge itself of this curse, then we must do so with weapons.

This is war, I tell you, and in war there must often be sacrifices made to expediency.

DOUGLASS. Be careful, John! Think now of what you say. Some day *you* may be sacrificed to *their* expediency.

BROWN. I am thinking. And I am unafraid. In God's good time, as we sweep southward, those of good faith will see their trust was not misplaced.

DOUGLASS. You'll never get South, John! Not if you insist upon starting at Harpers Ferry. I know the area—it's like a steel trap. Once in you'll never get out alive. They'll surround you, hem you in!

BROWN. *(Defiantly.)* They surrounded me in Kansas! They never took me there!

DOUGLASS. They'll hurl all their military might against you!

BROWN. We'll cut our way through! We'll take prisoners and hold them as hostages.

DOUGLASS. Virginia will blow you and your hostages to hell rather than let you hold the arsenal for an hour!

BROWN. I'm not afraid of death! Is that why it's insane, Frederick? Because we may spill a little blood?

DOUGLASS. We're talking about freeing slaves, John! Not throwing lives away in a hopeless insurrection—!

BROWN. But this is the way to free slaves—all of them, not just a few! *(Intensely, with great passion.)* It must be by blood! The moral suasion of Moses and Aaron was in vain, even with the abetment of the locusts and the boils. Not till the shedding of the blood of the first born of Egypt was there release for Israel. Through blood out of bondage, Douglass! Without the shedding of blood there is no remission of sins—

DOUGLASS. John! Do you think you are God?

BROWN. *(Stops, momentarily stunned.)* God? . . . God is different things to different men, Frederick. To some He is a separate entity, dispensing wrath or reward from philanthropic heights. To some He is watchdog conscience, knawing at the marrow. To me . . . God is simply the perception and the performance of right. And so I am a little bit of God. Or trying to be.

DOUGLASS. (Starts to speak, then sighs.) I cannot argue with you further, John Brown. I see I cannot hope to change your mind.

BROWN. Then you're coming with me, Frederick?

DOUGLASS. I cannot.

SHEILDS. (Interrupting from the background.) Wait for me, Cap'n Brown! I'm goin' up to get a few things.

DOUGLASS. (Turning.) What? Sheilds . . . ?

SHEILDS. Yes, Mistuh Douglass. I believe I'll go wid de ole man. (He turns and goes upstairs.)

BROWN. Come with us, Frederick. I need you.

DOUGLASS. I cannot.

BROWN. Douglass! I will defend you with my life.

DOUGLASS. John—

BROWN. I want you for a special purpose. When I strike the bees will begin to swarm and I shall need you to help me hive them.

DOUGLASS. You have changed your plan. I cannot go with you now.

BROWN. Will you fail me then? Will you fail your people? (Suddenly smoldering.) Or are you so far removed from slavery that you no longer care!

DOUGLASS. (Taken by surprise.) What—?

BROWN. (Tauntingly.) Have you carried the scars upon your back into high places so long that you have forgotten the sting of the whip and the lash?

DOUGLASS. John, that's not being fair! Don't—

BROWN. (Like a whip.) Or are you afraid to face a gun?

(DOUGLASS gasps as if struck. Then, catching himself, he grasps the back of a chair for support.)

DOUGLASS. (Slowly.) I have never really questioned it before, John. If it would do good . . . if it would do good, this moment I would die, I swear it, John! But I cannot cast away that which I know I can do for that which I know I cannot do. I have no right to do that. I should rather fail you, John, than feel within myself that I have failed my people. For them . . . I believe it is my duty to live, and to fight in ways that I know can succeed.

(BROWN stares at DOUGLASS for a moment, then turns and starts for the stairway. Reaching it, he pauses and turns to DOUGLASS.)

BROWN. I shall miss you, Frederick. . . .

CURTAIN

ACT TWO

SCENE 3

A few weeks later. Early morning.

Except for a faint GLOW from the fireplace, the room is in darkness. Breaking the stillness rudely is the SOUND OF SOMEONE KNOCKING at the door, excitedly. There is a pause, and the KNOCKING resumes, louder than before. A pause, then again. This time a light appears from the top of the stairway, and ANNA's voice is heard calling: "Yes, just a minute! Just a minute!" Then LEWIS is heard saying, "I'll go down, Mother, you stay up here."

LEWIS *appears descending the stairway with a candle, a pair of trousers pulled on hastily over the bottom of his nightshirt. He goes Off to the door.)*

LEWIS. (As he unbolts the door.) All right, just a minute.

(The door opens.)

Yes?

VOICE. *(Off.)* Are you Lewis Douglass?

LEWIS. Yes.

VOICE. Fred Douglass's boy?

LEWIS. Yes, I am.

VOICE. Then this here telegram must be for you.

LEWIS. Telegram? For me?

(ANNA appears on the stairway with a light. She descends halfway, peering toward the door. She is in a nightgown with a shawl thrown over her shoulders, and her hair hangs down in a braid.)

VOICE. That's right. Telegraph operator asked me to drop it by to you right away. Urgent.

LEWIS. Why, thanks. Thanks very much, Mister—?

VOICE. Oh, that's all right. You don't need to know my name, it's better that way. You just get to what that wire says.

LEWIS. Hey, wait! Wait a minute, mister.

VOICE. *(Farther away.)* Good night!

ANNA. Lewis! What is it, son?

LEWIS. *(Closes the door and returns.)* It's a wire, Mother. It's addressed to "B. F. Blackall, Esq."

ANNA. That's Mister Blackall, the telegraph operator.

LEWIS. *(Opens it hastily and reads.)* "Tell Lewis, my oldest son, to secure all important papers in my high desk at once." That's all it says. Not even signed.

ANNA. It doesn't have to be, you know it's from Fred.

LEWIS. Gee, Mother, do you think he's in trouble?

ANNA. I don't know, son. But I been on pins and needles for the past two days now. The high desk, did he say?

LEWIS. Yes, Mother.

ANNA. Then he must mean those letters and papers he been keepin' for Captain Brown. Come on, son. *(She heads for the study.)*

LEWIS. Oh!—but the high desk is locked. And Poppa always keeps the key with him.

ANNA. *(Turning.)* Then look in the kitchen and get a knife or something. Lewis, hurry!

LEWIS. All right. *(He goes.)*

(From the stairway comes a small voice crying, "Mom-ma . . . ?" ANNA looks up and sees little ANNIE's face peering from between the banisters.)

ANNA. Annie! What you doin' out of bed?

ANNIE. *(Affecting baby talk.)* Big noise wake me up. Peoples talkin' and bangin' on doors.

ANNA. Now you know you ain't supposed to be gettin' out of your bed in the middle of the night, even if the Walls of Jericho is tumblin' down! And you with such a cold.

ANNIE. But I'm scared, Mom-ma. . . .

ANNA. Not half as scared as you're gonna be if you don't put your little behin' back in that bed!

(ANNIE begins to cry. ANNA goes to her.)

Now, now there, baby. That's no way to do. There ain't nothin' to be afraid of. *(Takes her in her arms.)* Hush, now, everything's gonna be all right.

LEWIS. *(Re-enters with a chisel.)* This ought to get it open, Mother!

ANNA. All right, Lewis. You go ahead. You know what to take out?

LEWIS. Yes. Yes, I know. *(He goes into the study.)*

ANNIE. Mom-ma, where's Poppa?

ANNA. Poppa's in Pennsylvania, honey, tendin' to some business.

ANNIE. When's he comin' home? I miss him.

ANNA. I know you do, darlin'. So do I. He'll be home soon, though. Maybe tomorrow or the next day.

ANNIE. Is Sheilds comin' back with him?

ANNA. (Quietly.) I don't know, honey.

ANNIE. Mr. Hawkins?

ANNA. No . . . no, I don't think so, baby. You come on here, now, 'n let me tuck you back in like a nice little lady, 'fore you catch your death of—

(ANNIE sneezes.)

There! You see? (She rises and starts upstairs with ANNIE in her arms.) Now you just come on and go right back to sleep. There's nothin' for you to be afraid of, an' nobody's gonna wake you up again. . . . (Her voice trails off as they move from sight.)

(KNOCKING begins at the door again. LEWIS comes out of the study, startled, a bunch of papers in his hands. The KNOCKING repeats. After a hasty look around, LEWIS stuffs the papers into his waist, arranges his nightshirt over them, and starts for the hallway. Remembering the library door, he dashes back to close it, then on to the Front.)

LEWIS. (Breathlessly.) Who is it?

CHATHAM. (Off.) It's George Chatham, Lewis.

LEWIS. (Relieved.) Oh! (He opens the door.) Come in, Mr. Chatham, you gave me quite a start.

CHATHAM. (Enters, removing his hat.) Thank you, my boy. Now, where's Frederick?

LEWIS. Oh, he's not here. He's away on a trip to Pennsylvania.

CHATHAM. I know, Lewis, but he's due back tonight, isn't he? Have you had no word from him?

LEWIS. Well, yes. But he didn't say when he was coming. Just told me to take care of a little business for him, that's all.

CHATHAM. But I just left Reverend Loguen. He said he was looking for Frederick tonight. I even went down to meet the train, but he wasn't on it.

LEWIS. Well, I'm sorry, sir. Is something the matter?

CHATHAM. Yes, by God, there's a great deal the matter! This attack on Harpers Ferry has stirred up a regular hornet's nest. I've got to see your father to find out what's going on.

ANNA. (Appears at the head of the stairs.) Lewis? Who is it?

CHATHAM. (Turns.) It's George Chatham, Mrs. Douglass.

ANNA. (Descending quickly.) Oh, Mr. Chatham. What is it?

CHATHAM. Oh no, don't become unduly alarmed. I bear no bad tidings. I just came here looking for Frederick.

ANNA. He's on his way home?

CHATHAM. Why, yes, didn't you know? Loguen had a telegram from Philadelphia. He should have arrived on the twelve-forty. Perhaps he'll be in on the three-oh-two.

ANNA. Oh, Well, I'm so glad. I been near 'bout worried to death, wonderin' where he was and what's goin' on.

CHATHAM. You're not the only one, Mrs. Douglass. This thing has set everybody back on their heels.

LEWIS. Uh—'scuse me. (He heads for the study.)

ANNA. Go 'head, son. . . . Well, what do you think, Mr. Chatham. Have they got much of a chance?

CHATHAM. I'm afraid it looks bad, pretty bad right now, Mrs. Douglass. So far the Captain's still managed to hold the Arsenal with his little band. But Buchanan's ordered in government troops, you know.

ANNA. Aw-aww . . . !

CHATHAM. They've got the place surrounded. It'll take a miracle to get them out now. (Shakes his head in grudging admiration.) Oh, that Brown, that Captain Brown! Even if he fails, you've got to give it to him. We told him no, but he went right ahead anyhow. And the sheer nerve of it all—Harpers Ferry! Well, God help him.

(LEWIS *returns from the library with a sheaf of letters and papers.*)

LEWIS. Here, Mother. What shall I . . . (*Conscious of Chatham's presence.*)

ANNA. (*Distressed.*) Oh, I don't know, Lewis, I—out in the woodshed! Hide them under the eaves!

LEWIS. Good! (*He dashes out.*)

ANNA. (*Impatient for something to do.*) I . . . I think I'll go on back and fix up a little somethin' to eat. I know Fred'll be near 'bout starved when he gets off the train. Sit down, Mr. Chatham, and make yourself 't home.

CHATHAM. No, thank you, Mrs. Douglass. I'm going to run on back to the telegraph office to catch the latest news. Then I'll meet the train and look for Frederick.

ANNA. All right, but at least you ought to stop and take a cup of tea. It's gettin' pretty chilly out, and you know you're gettin' too old to be chasin' aroun' in the middle of the night like some young buck.

CHATHAM. Thank you, Mrs. Douglass. But if I were a young buck I'd be out chasing around for different reasons than I am now!

(*From Off Right the front door is heard to open.* CHATHAM *and* ANNA *move to the archway.*)

ANNA. Fred!

(DOUGLASS *enters, carrying a traveling bag. He removes his hat as* ANNA *runs to greet him.*)

DOUGLASS. (*Surprised.*) Anna, my dear. What are you doing up so late? And George!

CHATHAM. Hello, Frederick, I'm so glad you're back. What happened?—I met the train, you weren't on it.

DOUGLASS. No, I got off in the freight yard and walked home, as I often do.

CHATHAM. No matter, as long as you're here. Frederick—this Harpers Ferry business. Did you know about this?

DOUGLASS. Yes. Yes, I knew.

CHATHAM. But Frederick! This wasn't the plan. And even if it were, I thought we'd decided—

DOUGLASS. You're perfectly right, George. I tried to talk him out of it, but to no avail. I even went down to Pennsylvania, caught up with John in an abandoned stone quarry near Chambersburg. We argued on and on. But the old man was like steel . . . !

CHATHAM. So you couldn't stop him, eh? Oh, that's just like him—stubborn as an old mule. A magnificent old mule! Tell me, Frederick. How much longer do you think he can hold out?

DOUGLASS. (*Looks at them both quickly—they haven't heard.*) The arsenal fell an hour ago. It's all over now.

CHATHAM. What!

DOUGLASS. Yes. The Army troops, under a Colonel Robert E. Lee, they stormed the place. John and his men fought bravely, but it fell.

CHATHAM. Frederick! And the Captain?

DOUGLASS. They took John alive, though they say he's badly wounded. One or two escaped but the others are all killed or captured.

ANNA. Have mercy . . . ! And Sheilds? How 'bout Sheilds, did you hear—?

DOUGLASS. Yes, Anna, they have him too. According to reports, Sheilds was on the outside when they surrounded the place. He could have gotten away! Instead he slipped back in, said he had to go back to the old man.

ANNA. (*Turns away.*) Poor Sheilds . . .

CHATHAM. Well, that's that. So it's all over.

ANNA. Oh, Fred—what will they do with them now?

DOUGLASS. It doesn't take much to imagine. If they're lucky, they'll get a trial first. And that's where you can help, George, if you will.

CHATHAM. (*Eagerly.*) Yes?

DOUGLASS. We may have a slight chance of saving them if we act right away.

CHATHAM. All right, Frederick. You just point the way.

DOUGLASS. Good. Now first we have to contact Sanborn and Gerrit Smith and Higginson and the others. We'll have to hire a lawyer, the most brilliant legal mind we can obtain.

CHATHAM. (Beginning to make notes.) All right. Just give me a list and I'll get off wires at once.

(From Off in the hallway comes a BANGING at the door and a VOICE crying: "Douglass! Douglass!")

DOUGLASS. (Looking up.) What's that?

(ANNA scurries to the door and opens it.)

ANNA. (Off.) Why, Rev'n Loguen!

DOUGLASS. (As LOGUEN enters.) Loguen! What's all the excitement?

LOGUEN. (Breathing heavily.) I've . . . I've just heard—

DOUGLASS. About John and the arsenal? Yes. We're just mapping plans for their defense. In the next few days we have to rally support from all quarters, perhaps even go to Virginia ourselves, and—

LOGUEN. Virginia! In the next few days you'll be as far away from Virginia or Rochester as the fastest ship can sail!

ANNA. What!

DOUGLASS. What does this mean?

LOGUEN. It means you've got to get away, Douglass. At once! They're after you.

DOUGLASS. Who?

LOGUEN. Federal agents!

CHATHAM. But what for?

LOGUEN. They found papers in Brown's knapsack, some of them letters from Douglass. They've issued a warrant for his arrest!

CHATHAM. But Frederick wasn't there! They can't—

LOGUEN. They have, I tell you. Listen, Douglass. I've just come from Selden's house, the Lieutenant Governor of the State.

DOUGLASS. Yes?

LOGUEN. Selden summoned me half an hour ago to tell me the governor's office had just received requisition from the governor of Virginia for "the deliverance up of one Frederick Douglass," charging him with "murder, robbery, and inciting servile insurrection." And two United States marshals—with no less than President Buchanan's authorization—have been secretly dispatched from Buffalo and should arrive here before dawn.

ANNA. Tonight! !

LOGUEN. That's right!

DOUGLASS. Well, I expected they might send someone here. But so soon! (To ANNA.) Did you get my message? Did you see to the papers?

ANNA. Lewis is takin' care of them right now.

DOUGLASS. Good. Well, let them come. (He turns back to Chatham and his notebook.)

ANNA. (Goes to him.) Fred. Fred, listen. If they're after you you've got to get away!

LOGUEN. Don't you understand, Douglass? You can't stay here.

DOUGLASS. (Smiles.) But I wasn't at Harpers Ferry. And now that my papers are secure—

LOGUEN. And you actually think they'll stop to consider that? Listen—Selden has instructions from Albany. He will have to surrender you if they find you here.

DOUGLASS. But we must help John and Sheilds and the others—

LOGUEN. Right now you have to help yourself! Or you'll be in the same jailhouse they're in.

CHATHAM. But Frederick wasn't involved in this thing, Loguen. Why should he—

LOGUEN. (Exasperated.) That's not the

point, George! Just once let them get their hands on him. Just once let them get him down to Virginia—

CHATHAM. (To DOUGLASS.) But you can prove, can't you, that—

LOGUEN. What do you think he can prove at the end of a rope!

(CHATHAM halts.)

Listen now. I have Jim Mason standing by down at the smithy's shop with his team and rig. With a little luck he can get you over the border by sunrise. You'll be safe in Canada for a few days, and by then we can arrange for your passage to England.

DOUGLASS. To England!

LOGUEN. Yes, Douglass, yes! Once they find out you're in Canada, don't think for one minute they won't try to bring you back.

DOUGLASS. You're right, of course, Loguen. But . . . (He looks with concern towards Anna.)

ANNA. You go 'head, Fred, don't you worry none about us.

CHATHAM. I'll look out for them, Frederick. They'll be safe, believe me.

(LEWIS has returned quietly and stands in the background, his joy at seeing his father back giving way to bewilderment as he catches on to what is being said.)

DOUGLASS. (With a wry smile.) And so this time you've come for me, eh Loguen? . . . And Jim, Jim Mason's standing by again with his rig, for me. . . . Well, I've been a fugitive before . . . hunted, running like a beast . . . pursued by human hounds.

LOGUEN. (Nods.) I know the feeling well, Douglass. Now—(Indicates that it is time to go.)

DOUGLASS. (Shrugging him off—bitterly.) Then tell me, Loguen—how long this night? How long this dark, dark night when no man walks in freedom, without fear, in this cradle of democracy, no man

who's black? How will it happen, what will we have to do? Nat Turner tried it with guns, and he failed. Dred Scott went to the high courts, and they hurled him back into slavery. Old John said it must be by blood, and tonight he lies wounded in a Virginia prison. When will it end, Loguen—how long this night?

LOGUEN. (Slowly.) Douglass, this I believe as surely as God gives me breath to speak it: no man lives in safety so long as his brother is in fear. Once arouse consciousness of that, and there will be those living and those dead, there will be guns and blood and the high courts too. . . . But it will come. I may not be here to see it, Douglass, but it will come.

DOUGLASS. How often do I wonder. (He turns to go, sees Lewis.)

LEWIS. Poppa! . . .

DOUGLASS. (Reaching toward him.) Hello, son.

LEWIS. You're going away?

DOUGLASS. You'll have to take care of the family for me, Lewis. You're the man of the house, now.

LEWIS. (Choking up.) Poppa, I—!

DOUGLASS. Now, now, son. In front of your mother?

LOGUEN. I hate to rush you, Douglass, but—

(From the stairway comes ANNIE's voice, asking, "Poppa?")

DOUGLASS. (Looking up.) Yes, Annie, darling!

(ANNIE races down the stairs and leaps into DOUGLASS's arms.)

ANNIE. Oh, Poppa! You're back, you're back.

ANNA. (Aware of the time.) All right, now, baby. It's back to bed for you, before you catch any more cold.

DOUGLASS. (Concerned.) What? Has she been sick?

ANNA. Only a little cold, Fred. Here, Annie. Let's go back upstairs.

ANNIE. (*Hugging* DOUGLASS *more tightly.*) I don't wanna! I wanna see Poppa some more!

ANNA. Now, Annie. That's no way for a little lady to act. You'll see Poppa again —(*She stops.*) Again . . . Come on, honey. Kiss Poppa goodnight.

ANNIE. (*Kissing him.*) Goodnight, Poppa. See you in the morning.

DOUGLASS. Yes . . . yes, dear. In the morning. (*He lets her down.*)

LEWIS. (*Sensing the situation.*) Here, Mother, I'll take her up.

ANNA. Thank you, Lewis.

(ANNIE *sneezes.*)

Be sure and tuck her in tight, now.

LEWIS. I will. (*He turns to his father.*) Poppa, I—

(DOUGLASS *indicates for him not to say any more in front of* ANNIE. LEWIS *turns and goes upstairs with* ANNIE.)

ANNIE. (*As she goes Off.*) Goodnight, Poppa. Goodnight, Momma.

DOUGLASS. (*Watching her.*) Goodnight, dear . . . !

ANNA. (*Goes to him.*) Fred—

DOUGLASS. Now I'll be all right, Anna. Take care of yourself.

ANNA. (*Her arms around him.*) Oh, Fred! Be careful!

DOUGLASS. I'll send you word as soon as I can. Maybe I won't have to go very far or stay very long. Maybe—

LOGUEN. (*He and* CHATHAM *are in the hallway.*) Douglass—! Time grows short.

DOUGLASS. Yes, Loguen, I'm ready. (*He starts for the door.*)

(ANNA *runs to him again and they embrace. He breaks away quickly and goes out, giving a last glance up the stairway.* CHATHAM *precedes him, carrying* DOUGLASS's *bag.*)

LOGUEN. (*To* ANNA *as he follows.*) If anyone comes . . .

ANNA. (*Nods her head.*) I know. I know what to say.

(*He exits, and the door is heard to close.*

ANNA *stands at the window for a moment, fighting back the tears. Then she comes slowly back into the room. She goes quickly to the lamps and blows them out, leaving herself just a candle. Then she pauses, looking in the fireplace. Taking up a poker, she stirs the dying embers and sings softly to herself:*)

"Didn't it rain, children . . .
    Rain, oh my Lord . . .
        Didn't it . . . ?
        Didn't it . . . ?
        Didn't it—
    Oh, my Lord, didn't it rain . . ."

There is a sharp RAP at the door. ANNA *looks up, frightened. The KNOCK sounds again, crisply.* ANNA *goes to the archway and looks toward the front door. The KNOCKING sounds again, louder and more insistent.* ANNA *lifts her head, draws her shawl about her shoulders, and strides bravely toward the door with her candle, as—*

CURTAIN

ACT THREE

TIME:
Six months later. Early evening.

LEWIS *is seated at the table at Right, going over a ledger book with pen and ink. There is a stack of* North Star's *on a chair nearby. From Off Right, at the front door,* ANNA *is heard talking with a caller.*

ANNA. (*Off.*) All right. Thank you, thank you very much. I hope you enjoy it. Goodbye. . . .

(*The door closes and* ANNA *enters. She sighs happily.*)

Well, that's another one. Here Lewis, put this with the rest. *(She gives him a bill and some change.)*

LEWIS. Fine! Say, we could use you at the office. You're getting to be our star salesman.

ANNA. *(Smiles.)* My, the word certainly got around in a hurry. I don't know how many times today I've answered that door to folks wantin' their copy.

LEWIS. Same way at the office. Guess they really missed it while Pa was gone.

ANNA. That's what everybody says. But there's a lot of people comin' by who never took it before. *(Proudly.)* I sold nine new subscriptions today.

LEWIS. That's fine! Well, I'm certainly glad we're back in business again. Though I still can't get over them calling off that investigation all of a sudden.

ANNA. Well, what with the election campaign comin' up, there wasn't much else they could do. By the way, them folks out in Chicago. Them Republicans. Have they nominated anybody yet?

LEWIS. Last I heard this afternoon, Senator Seward of Massachusetts was still leading on the second ballot. But Abraham Lincoln of Illinois was coming up strong.

ANNA. *(Frowns.)* Poor Mr. Seward certainly has worked hard for it. Well, soon's you find out you better go in there and tell your father. That's all he's been studyin' 'bout all day.

LEWIS. But isn't that newspaper man still in there?

ANNA. Mr. Tilton? Yes, son. Seems he came all the way up here from New York to get Fred to write some articles for his paper.

LEWIS. Oh?

ANNA. Yes, and then—*(She breaks off as the study door opens and* DOUGLASS *enters, frowning.)*

DOUGLASS. *(Searching about among papers, books, etc.)* Anna, what did you do with that little book I use for keeping names and addresses in? I can't find it anywhere.

ANNA. Well, I don't know, Fred. I haven't bothered it. Lewis, you know what he's talkin' about?

LEWIS. Why, no. No, Pa, I haven't seen it.

DOUGLASS. *(Annoyed.)* Well, somebody must have moved it! I always keep it in the lower right hand drawer of my high desk, and now it's not there. Anna, are you sure . . . ?

ANNA. *(Calmly.)* Now, Fred, you don't have to holler like that at me!

DOUGLASS. What? Oh—oh, I'm sorry, I . . .

ANNA. When did you have it last, do you remember? Have you looked in all the drawers? Try all your pockets? How 'bout upstairs? Here, let me go see—*(She starts for the stairway, but halts as* DOUGLASS *feels his pockets and withdraws a small book.)*

DOUGLASS. *(Slowly raising his eyes.)* I'm . . . sorry, Anna.

ANNA. That's all right, Fred.

(Pause.)

Now don't stay 'way from your guest.

DOUGLASS. Huh? Oh, yes. Yes . . . *(He goes back into the study, closing the door.)*

ANNA. *(Shakes hear head.)* Lawd-a-mussy!

LEWIS. Mother, what's wrong? Do you think he's sick?

ANNA. Well, Fred ain't really sick, not like you usually think of somebody being sick.

LEWIS. Then what is it?

ANNA. I don't know just how to explain it, son. But there's somethin' pressin' on his mind. Somethin' heavy. Yes, I guess Fred is sick, Lewis. Sick somewhere in his soul. He's not the same since he's been back.

LEWIS. Mother, do you think maybe it's because . . . because of Annie?

ANNA. *(Softly.)* That may be part of it,

son. Fred loved that child more than anything else in the world, and when she died —especially with him away in Europe—I . . . I guess a part of him died, too. I know it's the same way with me.

LEWIS. (*Comfortingly.*) Mother . . . do you think maybe if *I* talked to him . . .

ANNA. No, Lewis. Leave him alone. When he's ready to talk about it, he will.

(*The door knocker sounds.*)

Lord-a-mussy! I been answerin' that door all day.

LEWIS. You sit right down now, I'll get it. Probably another one of those subscribers. (*He goes to the door.*)

ANNA. All right, Lewis. If you need me I'll be back in the kitchen. (*She straightens up the newspapers and goes out Left.*)

(*The study door opens and* DOUGLASS *appears, ushering out* THEODORE TILTON.)

DOUGLASS. . . . And believe me, Mr. Tilton, it is with great reluctance that I must turn you down.

TILTON. (*Somewhat in annoyance.*) Yes, and it is with great reluctance that I must leave without getting what I came for. (*Stops and turns.*) You know, Douglass, the first time we met I was impressed, greatly impressed. Completely aside from considerations of race, I thought: "Here is a man of whom the whole nation should be proud!" And now I find you here, twiddling your thumbs, as it were, sulking in the wake of your exile because of this Harpers Ferry business—

DOUGLASS. Mr. Tilton, it is well known that I was not present at Harpers Ferry. Perhaps I should have been, but the fact of it is I had no part in the matter.

TILTON. But do you deny you had dealings with John Brown? I was at the trial, I saw the letters and documents, I—

DOUGLASS. (*Electrified.*) You were at the trial? ! !

TILTON. Why, yes. I covered the sessions personally for my paper. . . .

DOUGLASS. Then you saw John Brown before—before . . .

TILTON. Yes, Mr. Douglass. I was there.

DOUGLASS. Tell me . . . tell me, Mr. Tilton. I . . . (*He indicates a chair.*)

(TILTON *sits.*)

TILTON. (*Solemnly.*) The old man was quite a brave soul. . . . His conduct and deportment during the trial were commendable—even the prosecution had the greatest respect for him, you could tell. . . . Of course, they did rush things a bit. Brown's wounds hadn't healed before they dragged him into court. . . . But his mind was clear and his tongue quite sharp. When the counsel they appointed to him tried to introduce a plea of insanity, he rejected it himself, told the court in booming tones that he considered it a "miserable artifice and pretext," and he viewed such a motion with contempt. . . . And then, after the verdict, when they asked him if he had anything to say . . . he rose erect, though it must have pained him terribly to do so . . . and he said—

DOUGLASS. (*Staring into space.*) ". . . Had I so interfered in behalf of the rich, the powerful, the so-called great . . . every man in this Court would have deemed it an act worthy of reward. To have interfered in behalf of His despised poor, I did no wrong, but right."

TILTON. (*Nods his head.*) It was . . . well, little short of magnificent.

DOUGLASS. (*Whispers.*) John! . . .

TILTON. I tried to get to see him afterwards. But they kept him under heavy guard, barred all visitors except his wife. . . .

DOUGLASS. Mary . . . Poor Mary.

TILTON. President Buchanan ordered a detachment of federal troops in to guard the town, three hundred strong, under Colonel Robert E. Lee—he's quite famous now, you know, they say he'll be made a general for sure. All Charlestown became an armed camp . . . the army troops, State Militia with cannon, volunteers, even fresh-faced cadets from Virginia Military Institute. Ha!—every so often some young fool would cry out, shoot at a branch in the dark, and the whole lot of them would scurry around in the night like terrified idiots!

DOUGLASS. And . . . then?

TILTON. *(Starts to speak, then rises, shaking his head.)* I cannot talk about it. I'd never seen a hanging before, and I hope to God I shall never see one again. *(Turns.)* But you, Douglass . . .

DOUGLASS. Don't . . . don't. *(To himself.)* I know the old man was wrong, but I should have gone with him anyway. . . . Sheilds! Did you see Sheilds Green? The Negro they called the Emperor?

TILTON. No. I did not stay for the other trials. But, of course, you know . . .

DOUGLASS. *(Turns away.)* Yes, I know.

TILTON. When I learned that you were back from England, it excited me! Here is a man so brave, that even with the shadow of a congressional investigation stalking him, he comes home to continue the fight—I must have articles, a whole series of writings from this man for my paper, I said! And then your letter, turning me down . . .

DOUGLASS. You give me more credit than I am due, Mr. Tilton. I came home at this time only because of death in the family.

TILTON. Oh, I'm sorry to hear that. But still, why not back to the struggle?

DOUGLASS. *(Evasively.)* I . . . need time to think, I—if I could have brought my family to England, I might have stayed there. . . . Slavery . . . this whole situation, Mr. Tilton! Frankly, I'm beginning to think it's . . . hopeless.

TILTON. *(Stunned.)* Hopeless . . . ? Hopeless . . . ? *(Begins with sadness and builds toward anger.)* So . . . the great Frederick Douglass creeps home, tail between his legs. The man who argued so

bravely that the philosophy of reforms lies in earnest struggle is tired of struggling himself. "If there is no struggle, there is no progress," he says. "Those who profess to favor freedom, and yet depreciate agitation, are men who want crops without plowing up the ground. They want rain without thunder and lightning . . . the ocean without the roar of its many waters." And now this sterling writer, this august philosopher declares the situation hopeless. He writes words of fiery revolution to others, and after he persuades them *he* sinks to the ground, exhausted and faint!

DOUGLASS. *(Stiffly.)* So . . . you read my paper?

TILTON. Every issue you sent me! And I must say I was taken in like a perfect fool. Even started echoing your sentiments on the editorial pages of my own paper, causing me to lose circulation by the thousand and forciing me into debt to raise funds for its continued existence. Hah! And now I find my inspiration, my dauntless messiah has lost his faith. Behold . . . ! He heals the blind, and when they see enough to follow him, lo! the man is blind himself!

DOUGLASS. *(Calling a halt.)* Mr. Tilton! *(Turns away.)*

TILTON. *(Emotion subsiding.)* No matter, no matter! . . . The newly enlightened will carry aloft the brazier even if it does burn the hands a bit. As a matter of fact, I shall be surprised when I reach New York if my plant is still standing.

DOUGLASS. Why so?

TILTON. Oh, I'm quite the radical abolitionist these days, you should see! I've passionately eulogized John Brown, attacked the federal government as a proslavery bunch of horse thieves, and called President Buchanan a pig-headed ass in inch-high headlines on the front page! Oh, you should just see the stack of lawsuits filed again me.

DOUGLASS. You are either very brave or very foolish.

TILTON. Who cares—I've been having fun! (*Impishly.*) And besides, I'm right. Why, have you ever taken a close look at a picture of Buchanan's face? . . . But I see you are in no mood for jest. Well, can't say I haven't tried. No harsh feelings, I hope?

DOUGLASS. No. No, of course not.

(*There is a KNOCK at the door. Presently* ANNA *appears, going to answer it.*)

TILTON. I'll be going now. Got to get back down and start beating the drums for the election campaign. If you should change your mind, and decide to help me make a little music, don't hesitate to join the band, eh?

DOUGLASS. If I should, I'll let you know—

TILTON. No—no, no promises now one way or the other. If you come to the point where you must, you will.

(ANNA *comes on with* GEORGE CHATHAM.)

Well . . . Chatham!

CHATHAM. (*Carries an odd-shaped bundle which he leaves in the hallway.*) Mr. Tilton! Why, I didn't know you were in town. Hello, Frederick.

DOUGLASS. Hello, George.

TILTON. I didn't expect to be, but I ran up on a little editorial business. How's Ellen and the girls?

CHATHAM. Oh, fine, just fine. You're not leaving, are you? I just—

TILTON. Yes, I'm afraid I must. My mission was fruitless and I must go on back. What's the latest on the convention, have you heard?

CHATHAM. Yes, they've just finished the second ballot and are getting ready for a third. Our man Seward's still leading. Perhaps he'll take it on the next ballot.

ANNA. And how about Lincoln? I thought he was pressin' pretty hard.

CHATHAM. Oh, I wouldn't give him a second thought. He's gained a few votes, true, but they'd never be so stupid as to nominate such an idiot!

TILTON. Well, Lincoln might not be as bad as we expect. He has already distinguished himself in debate with Stephen Douglas, and as for the "rump" candidate, Breckinridge, I don't think we'll have to worry much about him. So pluck up, George!

CHATHAM. Well, if they do nominate Lincoln, I shall have the greatest difficulty in resigning myself to the necessity of supporting him, hayseeds and all. Why the man's simply impossible! "Honest Abe" they call him. Sounds like a used-carriage dealer.

TILTON. Now, now, George. Just because the man is not of solid New England abolitionist stock is no reason to give him up for lost. He may prove his worth, in time.

CHATHAM. (*Hands together.*) Let us pray . . .

TILTON. (*Laughs.*) On that, I'll take my leave! Goodbye, Chatham. (*Bows.*) Mrs. Douglass. (*To* DOUGLASS, *who starts to see him out.*) No, that's all right, I can find my way to the door. And Douglass! . . . (*Extends his hand—sincerely.*) I'm leaving my first drummer's chair open. Just in case . . . (*With a wave of the hand he is off, escorted to the door by* ANNA.)

CHATHAM. (*Smiling.*) What's all this, Frederick? Are you going in for musicianship these days?

DOUGLASS. No . . . no, George. I'm afraid I'd play out of tune. Now, what have you come to see me about?

CHATHAM. Well, two things, really. The first I think you already have some idea of.

DOUGLASS. (*Turning away.*) Yes. Yes, I know.

CHATHAM. Then what is it, Frederick? Yesterday at your office I asked you to join with us in our rally tonight at Corinthian Hall. But tonight I hear you have tendered your regrets. Is this true, Frederick?

DOUGLASS. Yes. It's true.

CHATHAM. But Frederick! Why are you refusing us now, when we need you most? We haven't had so good a chance in years to upset the slave-holders' stranglehold on the Presidency. We have to stir up all the support we can get.

DOUGLASS. I know all that, George, you don't have to—

CHATHAM. Then you'll do it, Frederick? The whole town will be so glad to see you. You know, you've become quite a celebrity since you've been gone.

DOUGLASS. Oh. And why?

CHATHAM. Why, why, you ask! Why, because *l'affaire* John Brown has captured the hearts and imaginations of the whole North! It's fired the flame of liberty and turned many a pussyfooting ne'er-do-well into an ardent Abolitionist! John Brown's gallows has become a cross. And all Rochester is proud to know that you helped him, that you believed in him when other less hardy souls failed him. That you had to flee the screaming, anguished wrath of the Virginia slavers because of your part in the undertaking.

DOUGLASS. *(Stricken.)* Is that what people think? ! !

CHATHAM. Why, you're a hero, man! Rochester's own representative in John Brown's great venture.

DOUGLASS. George . . . ! George . . . *(Suddenly.)* I cannot speak for you tonight. That's all.

CHATHAM. But Frederick. I told the Rally Committee I'd come here personally, and—

DOUGLASS. *(Curtly.)* You should have consulted me before making any such promise.

CHATHAM. *(At first, taken aback. Then, challenging.)* Frederick . . . what's wrong?

DOUGLASS. Wrong? Why—I'm tired . . .

I haven't been feeling too well, lately. Yes, I've been ill.

CHATHAM. Frederick . . . we've been friends for a long time. Ever since you first came to Rochester and started your paper.

DOUGLASS. Please! Please, George, I'd be the first to admit that I owe you a great deal, but don't try to use that to force me to do something I am not agreed to doing.

CHATHAM. That's not it at all, Frederick! I meant that I had come to believe the two of us could sit down and talk openly and fairly with each other. But it is hardly honorable of you, is it, to hide behind such a paltry excuse? You, who have braved storms and mobs and defied death itself in bringing your message to the people?

DOUGLASS. *(Turns to him.)* George, I cannot speak for you. I can no longer stand upon a platform and address an audience as I have in the past.

CHATHAM. Why, Douglass, you're one of the ablest public speakers I've ever known.

DOUGLASS. Able or not, I am not worthy.

CHATHAM. Not worthy? Why, who—if not you, of all people—who can lay claim to greater right?

DOUGLASS. I have forfeited my right! I have failed to live up to the confidence placed in me.

CHATHAM. Douglass! . . . You're talking riddles!

(DOUGLASS turns despairingly, and starts into his study. His hand freezes on the doorknob, then, resignedly, he closes the door and turns again to face CHATHAM.)

DOUGLASS. George . . . you mentioned that the people of Rochester think of me as a hero, their own representative in John's great venture. You know as well as I do that it isn't true.

CHATHAM. Frederick, I have always known you to be a man of the highest dedication to the cause of liberty, and—

DOUGLASS. We're not talking about past reputation, George, and we cannot base supposed fact upon such schoolboy idealism as dedication to a cause! The question is: was I or was I not an accomplice of John Brown in his raid on Harpers Ferry on October 16, 1859?

CHATHAM. Listen, Frederick, I—

DOUGLASS. Why, you have me sailing under false colors, cloaked by the public imagination in a role of glory that is as false to me as if I played Romeo upon the stage. *(Turns.)* Shall I tell you the truth of the matter? Shall I—

CHATHAM. But Frederick, I don't see—

DOUGLASS. Well, I'll tell you whether you want to hear it or not! *(He wheels about and paces, the Prosecuting Attorney, his own conscience on trial.)* George, that night after you and Sanborn and the others left, John told me he was going on with it, that he was going to start at Harpers Ferry. I argued against it, but in vain. When he implored me to go with him, I told him I thought it was more important for me to speak and to write, to stay alive for my people, than to take the chance of dying with him at Harpers Ferry. And so I let him go, alone—except for Sheilds Green. . . . But George . . . I have discovered that it is possible for a man to make a right decision, and then be tormented in spirit the rest of his life because he did not make the wrong one. There are times when the soul's need to unite with men in splendid error tangles agonizingly with cold wisdom and judgement. . . .

Then in London, when the news came . . . how brave the old man was . . . how steadfastly he refused to name or implicate anyone . . . how he died upon the gallows, it came to me in a rush that John, in his way, had succeeded! In splendid error he had startled the sleeping conscience of the nation and struck a blow for freedom that proves stronger every hour.

And now you come to me and ask me to play the hero. To accept the plaudits of the crowd for my "gallant alliance" with a man who was wrong in life, but in death has scored a victory—a victory you propose me to take the bows for.

CHATHAM. Frederick, you must hear me—

DOUGLASS. Don't you see, George, that I cannot do it! John believed in his mission and however wrong he was he gave his life for it. But what have I done, except talk about it—I who have *been* a slave!

CHATHAM. *(Rising.)* Frederick, you're torturing yourself! Don't—

DOUGLASS. I will not go on masquerading as a crusader, a leader of my people, a brave warrior for human rights!

CHATHAM. Will you stop a moment and listen!

DOUGLASS. You are in the presence of a fraud! I resumed publishing my paper because I must feed my family, but do not believe that I can stand on a platform and look an audience in the eyes with this burning inside me: *"Are you afraid to face a gun? ! !"*

CHATHAM. *(Takes* DOUGLASS *forcibly by the arm—shouts.)* Frederick, I demand that you be quiet!

*(*DOUGLASS *grasps the back of a chair, his energy spent.)*

*(*CHATHAM *speaks gently.)* That's it. Listen. There is a second reason I came to see you tonight, Frederick. It is to fulfil a request.

DOUGLASS. *(Wearily, as in delirium.)* Request . . . request . . . what kind of request?

CHATHAM. *(As he secures his package from the hallway.)* Early this winter I made a trip to North Elba. There, by a great boulder in which he himself once carved the letters "J. B." is where they buried Captain Brown. I talked to his widow, Mary, a proud, fierce-eyed woman whose composure made me half ashamed of my tears. When she learned I was from Rochester, she gave me something to give to you, Frederick. *(He takes the package to the sofa.)* I told her you were in England, but she smiled and said you would be back. You had a job to do, she said, and she knew you would be back to finish it. *(He undoes the canvas and withdraws a tarnished old musket and a torn, bespattered American flag.)* She asked me to give these to you personally, Frederick. That John wanted you to have them. *(He carries the musket to* DOUGLASS, *who slowly reaches out for it, then suddenly cringes, folding his hands.)*

DOUGLASS. His . . . musket?

CHATHAM. Yes. *(He takes the musket back to the sofa and lays it down, carefully. Then picks up the flag and drapes it over the musket.)* And the flag he carried with him to Harpers Ferry . . . *(Fumbles in his waistcoat.)* He gave her a message for you, there in the prison, while he was waiting. *(Withdraws a folded piece of paper.)* Here . . .

DOUGLASS. *(Takes it slowly, and reads; barely audible.)* "Tell Douglass I know I have not failed because he lives. Follow your own star, and someday unfurl my flag in the land of the free." *(He bows his head, his shoulders shaking silently. Then slowly, haltingly, he makes his way toward the sofa.)*

(Dimly, from a distance, comes the sound of the booming of a DRUM. CHATHAM *goes to the balcony window and looks out. He turns and watches* DOUGLASS, *who, having reached the sofa, bends over to touch the flag and musket.)*

CHATHAM. *(Softly.)* It's nearly time for the rally, Frederick. They are marching from the square. *(Comes to him.)* Come, Frederick. Will you join us?

DOUGLASS. *(Quiet now. When he speaks his voice is steady.)* You go on ahead, George. I'll be along in a moment.

CHATHAM. *(Understandingly.)* All right. All right.

DOUGLASS. But . . . I must tell them the truth. I did not go with John.

CHATHAM. *(Nods admiringly.)* You tell them, Frederick. You tell them what you must.

(He goes to the hallway just as LEWIS *comes rushing in from outside, where there is excitement in the air. The DRUMBEATS are nearer and there are VOICES.)*

LEWIS. *(Joyously.)* They're coming! They're coming! It's a torchlight parade!

CHATHAM. Well, let's see it, son! Let's see it!

LEWIS. And the convention's decided. The candidate is chosen!

CHATHAM. *(Stops.)* What! Who is it, Lewis?

LEWIS. Lincoln!

CHATHAM. *(Astonished—roars like a wounded bull.)* Lincoln? ! ! We cry out for a leader, a saviour, a knight in shining armor! And who do they offer us? Barabbas!

(ANNA comes quickly down the stairs.)

ANNA. Lord-a-mussy! What's goin' on out here!

CHATHAM. It's a torchlight parade, Mrs. Douglass. Come! *(He guides* ANNA *and* LEWIS *out, then stops and turns for a moment, puffing his cheeks indignantly.)* Lincoln! *(He stomps out.)*

*(*DOUGLASS *stands gazing down at the flag and musket.*

Outside the excitement has increased, and now a bright flicker of orange and yellow LIGHT dances in from the street, bathing the hallway with bobbing shafts of LIGHT. The booming DRUM is very near now, and amid the accompanying babble a VOICE cries, "There's Fred Douglass's house!" ANOTHER takes it up: "Yeah, where is he?" And ANOTHER: "We want Douglass!" And now the others join in, shouting: "We want Douglass! We want Douglass!"

DOUGLASS stirs and turns his head to listen. ANNA rushes back into the room excitedly.)

ANNA. Fred! Where are you, Fred! They callin' for you! For you, Fred! (She pauses Upstage, arm extended.) Well, come on! They callin' for you!

DOUGLASS. (Lifts his hand.) I'm coming, Anna.

(ANNA goes back off.

A fife and drum corps has approached and now swings into Battle Hymn of the Republic, and the voices take it up, singing:

"John Brown's body lies a-mould'ring in the grave . . ."

DOUGLASS picks up the flag. He folds it. He holds it against his breast for a moment. Then laying it over his arm, he draws himself to full height and strides manfully off to the door, as)

CURTAIN

Alice Childress

Trouble in Mind

A COMEDY-DRAMA IN TWO ACTS

TROUBLE IN MIND

Trouble in Mind was first presented at the Greenwich Mews Theater, New York City, November 4, 1955.

CHARACTERS:

WILETTA MAYER
HENRY
JOHN NEVINS
MILLIE DAVIS
SHELDON FORRESTER
JUDY SEARS
AL MANNERS
EDDIE FENTON
BILL O'WRAY

ACT ONE

TIME:
Ten o'clock Monday morning, fall, 1957.
PLACE:
A Broadway theater in New York City. BLUES MUSIC in—out after LIGHTS UP.
SCENE:
The stage of the theater. Stage Left leads to the outside entrance, Stage Right to upstairs dressing rooms. There are many props and leftovers from the last show: a plaster fountain with a cupid perched atop, garden furniture, tables, benches, a trellis, two white armchairs trimmed with gold gilt. Before the Curtain rises we hear BANGING SOUNDS from offstage Left, the banging grows louder and louder. CURTAIN RISES. WILETTA MAYER, a middle-aged actress, appears. She is attractive and expansive in personality. She carries a purse and a script. At the moment, she is in quite a huff.

WILETTA. My Lord, I like to have wore my arm off bangin' on that door! What you got it locked for?

(LIGHTS up brighter.)

Had me standin' out there in the cold, catchin' my death of pneumonia!

(HENRY, the elderly doorman, enters.)

HENRY. I didn't hear a thing . . . I didn't know . . .
WILETTA. *(Is suddenly moved by the sight of the theater. She holds up her hand for silence, looks out and up at the balcony. She loves the theater. She turns back to HENRY.)* A theater always makes me feel that way . . . gotta get still for a second.
HENRY. *(Welcomes an old memory.)* You . . . you are Wiletta Mayer . . . more than twenty years ago, in the old Galy Theater. . . .

(Is pleased to be remembered.)

You was singin' a number, with the lights changin' color all around you. . . . What was the name of that show?
WILETTA. *Brownskin Melody.*
HENRY. That's it . . . and the lights . . .
WILETTA. Was a doggone rainbow.
HENRY. And you looked so pretty and sounded so fine, there's no denyin' it.
WILETTA. Thank you, but I . . . I . . . *(Hates to admit she doesn't remember him.)*
HENRY. I'm Henry.
WILETTA. Mmmmm, you don't say.
HENRY. I was the electrician. Rigged up all those lights and never missed a cue. I'm the doorman here now. I've been in show business over fifty years. I'm the doorman . . . Henry.

WILETTA. That's a nice name. I . . . I sure remember those lights.

HENRY. Bet you can't guess how old I am, I'll betcha.

WILETTA. (Would rather not guess.) Well . . . you're sure lookin' good.

HENRY. Go ahead, take a guess.

WILETTA. (Being very kind.) Ohhhhh, I'd say you're in your . . . late fifties.

HENRY. (Laughs proudly.) I fool 'em all! I'm seventy-eight years old! How's that?

WILETTA. Ohhhh, don't be tellin' it. (She places her script and purse on the table, removes her coat.)

(HENRY takes coat and hangs it on a rack.)

HENRY. You singin' in this new show?

WILETTA. No, I'm actin'. I play the mother.

HENRY. (Is hard of hearing.) How's that?

WILETTA. I'm the mother!

HENRY. Could I run next door and get you some coffee? I'm goin' anyway, no bother.

WILETTA. No, thank you just the same.

HENRY. If you open here, don't let 'em give you dressin' room "C." It's small and it's got no "john" in it . . . excuse me, I mean . . . no commode . . . Miss Mayer.

WILETTA. (Feeling like the star he's made her.) Thank you, I'll watch out for that.

HENRY. (Reaches for a small chair, changes his mind and draws the gilt arm-chair to the table.) Make yourself comfortable. The old Galy. Yessir, I'm seventy-eight years old.

WILETTA. Well, I'm not gonna tell you my age. A woman that'll tell her age will tell anything.

HENRY. (Laughs.) Oh, that's a good one! I'll remember that! A woman that'll tell her age . . . what else?

WILETTA. Will tell anything.

HENRY. Will tell. Well, I'll see you a little later. (He exits stage Left.)

WILETTA. (Saying goodbye to the kind of gentle treatment she seldom receives.) So long. (Rises and walks downstage, strikes a pose from the "old Galy" and sings a snatch of an old song.)

Oh, honey babe
Oh, honey baby . . .

(She pushes the memory aside.) Yes indeed!

(JOHN NEVINS, a young Negro actor, enters. He tries to look self-assured but it's obvious that he is new to the theater and fighting hard to control his enthusiasm.)

Good morning. Another early bird! I'm glad they hired you, you read so nice er . . . ah . . .

JOHN. John, John Nevins.

WILETTA. This is new for you, ain't it?

JOHN. Yes, ma'am.

WILETTA. Yes, ma'am? I know you're not a New Yorker, where's your home?

JOHN. Newport News, that's in Virginia.

WILETTA. HOT DOG, I shoulda known anyone as handsome and mannerly as you had to come from my home. Newport News! Think of that! Last name?

JOHN. Nevins, John Nevins.

WILETTA. Wait a minute . . . do you know Estelle Nevins, used to live out on Prairie Road . . . fine built woman?

JOHN. Guess I do, that's my mother.

WILETTA. (Very touched.) No, she ain't!

JOHN. (Afraid of oncoming sentiment.) Yes . . . ah . . . yes she is.

WILETTA. What a day! I went to school with Estelle! She married a fella named Clarence! Used to play baseball. Last time I hit home she had a little baby in the carriage. How many children she got?

JOHN. I'm the only one.

WILETTA. You can't be that little baby in the carriage! Stand up, let me look at you! Brings all of yesterday back to my mind! Tell me, John, is the drugstore still on the corner? Used to be run by a tall, strappin' fella . . . got wavy, black hair . . . and, well, he's kind of devilish . . . Eddie Bentley!

JOHN. Oh, yes, Mr. Bentley is still there . . .

WILETTA. Fresh and sassy and . . .

JOHN. But he's gray-haired and very stern and businesslike.

WILETTA. *(Very conscious of her age.)* You don't say. Why you want to act? Why don't you make somethin' outta yourself?

JOHN. *(Is amazed at this.)* What? Well, I . . .

WILETTA. You look bright enough to be a doctor or even a lawyer maybe. . . . You don't have to take what I've been through . . . don't have to take it off 'em.

JOHN. I think the theater is the grandest place in the world, and I plan to go right to the top.

WILETTA. *(With good humor.)* Uh-huh, and where do you think I was plannin' to go?

JOHN. *(Feeling slightly superior because he thinks he knows more about the craft than WILETTA.)* Ohhhh, well . . .

WILETTA. *(Quick to sense his feeling.)* Oh, well, what?

JOHN. *(Feels a bit chastised.)* Nothing. I know what I want to do, I'm set, decided, and that's that. You're in it, aren't you proud to be a part of it all?

WILETTA. Of what all?

JOHN. Theater.

WILETTA. *Show business*, it's just a business. Colored folks ain't in no theater. You ever do a professional show before?

JOHN. Yes, some off-Broadway . . . and I've taken classes.

WILETTA. Don't let the man know that. They don't like us to go to school.

JOHN. Oh, now.

WILETTA. They want us to be naturals . . . you know, just born with the gift. 'Course they want you to be experienced too. Tell em' you was in the last revival of *Porgy and Bess.*

JOHN. I'm a little young for that.

WILETTA. They don't know the difference. You were one of the children.

JOHN. I need this job but . . . must I lie?

WILETTA. Yes. Management hates folks who *need* jobs. They get the least money, the least respect, and most times they don't get the job.

JOHN. *(Laughs.)* Got it. I'm always doing great.

WILETTA. But don't get too cocky. They don't like that either. You have to cater to these fools too. . . .

JOHN. I'm afraid I don't know how to do that.

WILETTA. Laugh! Laugh at everything they say, makes 'em feel superior.

JOHN. Why do they have to feel superior?

WILETTA. You gonna sit there and pretend you don't know why?

JOHN. I . . . I'd feel silly laughing at everything.

WILETTA. You don't. Sometimes they laugh, you're supposed to look serious, other times they serious, you supposed to laugh.

JOHN. *(In polite disagreement.)* Sounds too complicated.

WILETTA. *(Warming to her subject.)* Nothin' to it. Suppose the director walks in, looks around and says . . . *(She mimics MANNERS.)* "Well, if the dust around here doesn't choke us to death, we'll be able to freeze in comfort."

JOHN. Yes?

WILETTA. We laugh and dispute him. *(She illustrates.)* "Oh, now, Mr. Manners, it ain't that bad!" . . . White folks can't stand unhappy Negroes . . . so laugh, laugh when it ain't funny at all.

JOHN. Sounds kind of Uncle Tommish.

WILETTA. You callin' me a "Tom"?

JOHN. No, ma'am.

WILETTA. Stop sayin' ma'am, it sounds countrified.

JOHN. Yes.

WILETTA. It is Tommish . . . but they do it more than we do. They call it bein' a "yes man." You either do it and stay or don't do it and get out. I can let you in on things that school never heard of . . . 'cause I know what's out here and they don't.

JOHN. Thank you. I guess I'll learn the ropes as I go along.

WILETTA. I'm tellin' you, now! Oh, you so lucky! Nobody told me, had to learn it for myself.

(JOHN *is trying to hide the fact that he does not relish her instructions.*)

Another thing, he's gonna ask your honest opinion about the play. Don't tell him, he don't mean it . . . just say you're crazy about it . . . butter him up.

JOHN. (*This remark really bothers him.*) What *do* you think of our play?

WILETTA. Oh, honey, it stinks, ain't nothin' atall. Course, if I hear that again, I'll swear you lyin'.

JOHN. Why are you doing it? A flop can't make you but so rich.

WILETTA. Who said it's gonna flop? I said it ain't nothin', but things that aggravate me always *run* for a long time . . . cause what bugs me is what sends somebody else, if you know what I mean.

JOHN. (*Defensively.*) I studied it thoroughly and . . .

WILETTA. Honey, don't study it, just learn it.

JOHN. I wouldn't, couldn't play anything I didn't believe in . . . I couldn't.

WILETTA. (*Understands he's a bit upstage now.*) Oh, well, you just a lost ball in the high grass.

(MILLIE DAVIS, *an actress about thirty-five years old, enters. She breezes in, beautifully dressed in a mink coat, pastel wool dress and hat, suede shoes and bag.*)

MILLIE. Hi!

WILETTA. Walk, girl! Don't she look good?

MILLIE. Don't look to hard, it's not paid for. (*Models the coat for* WILETTA *as she talks to* JOHN.) You got the job! Good for you.

(WILETTA *picks up* MILLIE's *newspaper.*)

JOHN. And congratulations to you.

MILLIE. (*Taking off her coat and hanging it up.*) I don't care one way or the other 'cause my husband doesn't want me workin' anyway.

WILETTA. Is he still a dining-car waiter?

MILLIE. I wanted to read for your part but Mr. Manners said I was too young. They always say too young . . . too young.

WILETTA. Hear they're lookin' for a little girl to play Goldilocks, maybe you should try for that.

MILLIE. Oh, funny.

WILETTA. (*Commenting on the headlines.*) Look at 'em! Throwin' stones at little children, got to call out the militia to go to school.

JOHN. That's terrible.

MILLIE. (*Quite proud of her contribution to Little Rock.*) A woman pushed me on the subway this mornin' and I was ready for her! Called her everything but a child of God. She turned purple! Oh, I fixed her!

(JUDITH SEARS, *a young actress, is heard offstage with* SHELDON FORRESTER, *an elderly character man.*)

JUDY. This way. . . .

SHELDON. Yes, ma'am. Don't hurt yourself.

(SHELDON *and* JUDY *enter,* JUDY *first.*)

JUDY. Good morning.

(*Others respond in unison.*)

JOHN. Hello again, glad you made it.

MILLIE. Hi! I'm Millie, that's John, Wiletta, and you're?

JUDY. Judith, just call me Judy.

SHELDON. *(Bundled in heavy overcoat, two scarves, one outer, one inner.)* And call me Shel!

WILETTA. Sheldon Forrester! So glad to see you! Heard you was sick.

MILLIE. I heard he was dead.

SHELDON. Yeah! Some fool wrote a piece in that *Medium Brown Magazine* 'bout me bein' dead. You can see he was lyin'. Bet I lost a lotta work on accounta that. Doctor says that with plenty of rest and fresh air, I oughta outlive him.

WILETTA. Bet you will, too.

SHELDON. Mr. Manners was lookin' all over for me, said nobody could play this part but me.

MILLIE. Not another soul can do what you're gonna do to it.

SHELDON. Thank you.

(JOHN starts over to JUDY but SHELDON stops him.)

Didn't you play in er . . . ah . . . er . . .

WILETTA. He was in the last revival of *Porgy and Bess.* Was one of the children. *(She watches JOHN's reaction to this.)*

SHELDON. Yeah, I know I remembered you. He ain't changed much, just bigger. Nice little actor.

JOHN. *(Embarrassed.)* Thank you, sir.

WILETTA. Sheldon got a good memory.

MILLIE. *(To JUDY.)* What're you doing?

SHELDON. She's *Miss* Renard, the Southerner's daughter. Fights her father 'bout the way he's treatin' us.

MILLIE. What I want is a part where I get to fight him.

WILETTA. Ha! That'll be the day!

SHELDON. Bill O'Wray is the father, he's awful nice.

MILLIE. Also wish I'd get to wear some decent clothes sometime. Only chance I get to dress up is offstage. I'll wear them baggy cotton dresses but damn if I'll wear another bandanna.

SHELDON. That's how country people do! But go on the beach today, what do you see? Bandannas. White folks wear 'em! They stylish!

MILLIE. That's a lot of crap!

SHELDON. There you go! You holler when there's no work, when the man give you some, you holler just as loud. Ain't no pleasin' you!

(JOHN starts toward JUDY again, this time MILLIE stops him.)

MILLIE. Last show I was in, I wouldn't even tell my relatives. All I did was shout "Lord, have mercy!" for almost two hours every night.

WILETTA. Yes, but you did it, so hush! She's played every flower in the garden. Let's see, what was your name in that T.V. mess?

MILLIE. Never mind.

WILETTA. Gardenia! She was Gardenia! 'Nother thing . . . she was Magnolia, Chrysanthemum was another. . . .

MILLIE. And you've done the jewels . . . Crystal, Pearl, Opal! *(MILLIE laughs.)*

JOHN. *(Weak, self-conscious laughter.)* Oh, now . . .

(JUDY has retreated to one side, is trying to hide herself behind a book.)

SHELDON. Do, Lord, let's keep peace. Last thing I was in, the folks fought and argued so, the man said he'd never do a colored show again . . . and he didn't!

WILETTA. I always say it's the man's play, the man's money and the man's theater, so what you gonna do? *(To MILLIE.)* You ain't got a pot nor a window. Now, when you get your own . . .

(SHELDON clears his throat to remind them that JUDY is listening.)

Honey, er . . . what you say your name was?

JUDY. Judy.

WILETTA. *(Sweeps over to JUDY and tries to cover the past argument.)* I know

I've seen you in pictures, didn't you make some pictures?

JUDY. No, this is my first job.

JOHN. (Joshing WILETTA.) Oh, you mustn't tell that because . . .

WILETTA. (Cutting him off.) You're just as cute as a new penny.

SHELDON. Sure is.

(A brief moment of silence while they wait for JUDY to say something.)

JUDY. (Starts hesitantly but picks up momentum as she goes along.) Thank you, and er . . . er . . . I hope I can do a good job and that people learn something from this play.

MILLIE. Like what?

JUDY. That people are the same, that people are . . . are . . . well, you know . . . that people are people.

SHELDON. There you go . . . brotherhood of man stuff! Sure!

WILETTA. Yes, indeed. I don't like to think of theater as just a business. Oh, it's the art . . . ain't art a wonderful thing?

MILLIE. (Bald, flat statement to no one in particular.) People aren't the same.

JUDY. I read twice for the part and there were so many others before me and after me . . . and I was so scared that my voice came out all funny. . . . I stumbled on the rug when I went in . . . everything was terrible.

MILLIE. (Another bald, flat statement.) But you got the job.

JUDY. (Uneasy about MILLIE's attitude.) Yes.

JOHN. (To the rescue.) And all the proud relatives will cheer you on opening night!

JUDY. (Nothing can drown her spirits for long.) Yes! My mother and father . . . they live in Bridgeport . . . they really don't want me here at all. They keep expecting something terrible to happen to me . . . like being murdered or something! But they're awfully sweet and

they'll be so happy. (Abrupt change of subject.) What do you think of the play?

WILETTA. Oh, I never had anything affect me so much in all my life. It's so sad, ain't it sad?

JUDY. Oh, there's some humor.

WILETTA. I'm tellin' you, I almost busted my sides laughin'.

(SHELDON is busy looking in the script.)

JOHN. It has a social theme and something to say.

JUDY. Yes.

WILETTA. Art! Art is a great thing!

MILLIE. It's all right except for a few words here and there . . . and those Gawd-awful clothes. . . .

JOHN. Words, clothes. What about the very meaning?

SHELDON. (Startles everyone by reading out loud. His finger runs down the page, he skips his cues and reads his lines.) Mr. Renard, sir, everything is just fine. . . . Yes, sir. . . . Thank you, sir. . . . Yes, sirreee, I sure will . . . I know. . . . Yes, sir. . . . But iffen, iffen . . . (He pauses to question the word.) Iffen? (Now he understands.) Iffen you don't mind, we'd like to use the barn.

MILLIE. Iffen.

SHELDON. Hush, Millie, so I can get these lines, I'm not a good reader, you know.

MILLIE. Iffen you forget one, just keep shakin' your head.

(Offstage we hear a door slam. AL MANNERS, the director (white) is giving EDDIE FENTON, the stage manager (white) a friendly chastising.)

MANNERS. (Offstage.) Eddie, why? Why do you do it?

EDDIE. (Offstage.) I didn't know.

SHELDON. (Assumes a very studious air and begins to study his script earnestly.) Mr. Manners.

(EDDIE and MANNERS enter, followed by HENRY. EDDIE is eager and quick. He *carries a portfolio and a stack of scripts.* MANNERS *is in his early forties, hatless, well-tweeded product of Hollywood. He is a bundle of energy, considerate and understanding after his own fashion; selfish and tactless after ours.* HENRY *is following him around, ready to write out a coffee order.)*

EDDIE. *(With a smile.)* You asked my opinion.

MANNERS. That, my friend, was a mistake.

EDDIE. *(Laughing while cast smiles in anticipaion of* MANNERS' *words.)* Okay, I admit you were right, you were.

MANNERS. *(Enjoying himself.)* Of course I was. *(To company.)* All of his taste is in his mouth!

(Burst of company laughter, especially from SHELDON *and* WILETTA.*)*

EDDIE. *(Playfully correcting* MANNERS.*)* All right, Al, play fair . . . uncle . . . a truce.

MANNERS. *(To company.)* Greetings to New York's finest.

ALL. Good morning. . . . Flatterer. . . . Hello. . . . Good Morning

MANNERS. *(To* HENRY.*)* Coffee all around the room and count yourself in. *(Hands him a bill.)* Rolls? Cake? No . . . how about Danish . . . all right?

ALL. Yes. . . . Sure. . . . Anything. . . . O.K.

SHELDON. I like doughnuts, those jelly doughnuts.

MANNERS. Jelly doughnuts! What a horrible thought. Get Danish . . . all right?

ALL. Sure. . . . Anything. . . . That's fine.

MANNERS. *(After* HENRY *exits.)* If you were looking for that type, you could never find it! A real character.

JOHN. One of the old forty-niners.

MANNERS. No, no . . . not quite that. . . . *(Turns off that faucet and quickly switches to another.)* Everyone on speaking terms?

ALL. Of course. . . . Old friends. . . . Oh, yes. . . . Sure

MANNERS. *(Opens the portfolio with a flourish.)* Best scenic design you've ever laid eyes on.

(ALL gasp and sigh as they gather around him. They are quite impressed with the sketch. JUDY *is very close and* MANNERS *looks down at her hair and neck which is perched right under his nostrils.* JUDY *can feel his breath on her neck. She turns suddenly and* MANNERS *backs away a trifle.)*

You er . . . wear a beautiful dress in the third act and I wanted to see if you have nice shoulders.

(JUDY backs away slightly.)

I wasn't planning to attack you.

(Cast laughs.)

MILLIE. I got nice shoulders. You got one of those dresses for me?

SHELDON. *(Determined to enjoy everything.)* Ha! He wasn't gonna attack her!

MANNERS. *(Suddenly changes faucets again.)* Oh, I'm so weary.

EDDIE. *(Running interference.)* He was with Melton on this sketch until four a.m.

MANNERS. Four thirty.

EDDIE. Four thirty.

MANNERS. *(Swoops down on* WILETTA.*)* Ahhhhh, this is my sweetheart!

WILETTA. *(With mock severity.)* Go on! Go 'way! Ain't speakin' to you! He won't eat, he won't sleep, he's just terrible! I'm mad with you.

SHELDON. Gonna ruin your health like that!

WILETTA. Gonna kill himself!

MANNERS. Bawl me out, I deserve it.

EDDIE. Melton is so stubborn, won't change a line.

MANNERS. But he did.

EDDIE. Yes, but so stubborn.

MANNERS. A genius should be stubborn. *(Points index finger at* SHELDON.*)* Right?

SHELDON. *(Snaps his finger and points back.)* There you go!

(Cast laughs.)

MANNERS. *(To* WILETTA.*)* You'd better speak to me. This is my girl, we did a picture together.

CAST. *(Ad lib.)* Really? How nice. She sure did. That's right.

MANNERS. *(As though it's been centuries.)* Ohhhhhh, years and years ago. She and I worked together, too.

MILLIE. *(To* WILETTA.*)* Remember that?

SHELDON. *(Proudly.)* I was helpin' the Confederate Army.

MANNERS. And what a chestnut, guns, cannons, drums, Indians, slaves, hearts and flowers, sex and Civil War . . . on wide screen!

JUDY. Oh, just horrible.

MANNERS. *(Touchy about outside criticism.)* But it had something, wasn't the worst. . . . I twisted myself out of shape to build this guy's part. It was really a sympathetic character.

SHELDON. Sure, everybody was sorry for me.

MANNERS. *(To* JOHN.*)* Hear you went to college. You're so modest you need a press agent.

SHELDON. He was one of the children in the last revival of *Porgy and Bess.*

MANNERS. Ohhhh, yes . . . nice clean job.

JUDY. I'm not modest. I finished the Yale drama course. Girls . . . girls . . . can go to the Yale drama. . . .

MANNERS. Yale. I'm impressed.

JUDY. You're teasing.

MANNERS. No, you are. Well, where are we? Bill O'Wray is out until tomorrow, he's in a rehearsal for a TV show tonight.

(Proper sighs of regret from the cast.)

WILETTA. Oh, I was lookin' forward to seein' him today.

SHELDON. Yeah, yeah, nice fella.

MANNERS. Works all the time.

(Now some attention for MILLIE.*)*

You look gorgeous. This gal has such a flair for clothes. How do you do it?

*(*MILLIE *is pleased.* MANNERS *changes the subject.)*

Ted Bronson is one of our finest writers.

WILETTA. Knows art, knows it.

EDDIE. He was up for an award.

MANNERS. Really, Eddie, I wish you'd let me tell it.

EDDIE. I'm sorry.

MANNERS. Ted's been out on the coast batting out commercial stuff . . . meat grinder . . . he's in Europe now . . . Italy . . . about a week before he can get back . . . he did this "Chaos in Belleville" a while back. Producers gave him nothing but howls. . . . "It's ahead of the times!" "Why stick your neck out?" "Why You?"

SHELDON. *(Raises his hand, speaks after* MANNERS *gives him a nod.)* Who is chaos?

EDDIE. Oh, no.

JOHN. *Who?*

MANNERS. *(Holds up his hand for silence.)* Chaos means er . . . ah, confusion. Confusion in Belleville, confusion in a small town.

SHELDON. Ohhhhhh.

MANNERS. I was casually talking to Ted about the er . . . er, race situation, kicking a few things around . . . dynamic subject, hard to come to grips with on the screen, TV, anywhere . . . explosive subject. Suddenly he reaches to the bottom shelf and comes up with "Chaos." I flipped a few pages . . . when I read it bells rang. This is *now*, we're living this, who's in the headlines these days?

(Eloquent pause.)

SHELDON. How 'bout that Montgomery, Alabama? Made the bus company lose one, cold, cash, billion dollars!

JOHN. Not a billion.

MANNERS. Here was a contribution to the elimination of . . .

SHELDON. I know what I read!

MANNERS. A story of Negro rights that . . .

SHELDON. How 'bout them busses!

JUDY. And they're absolutely right.

MILLIE. Who's right?

MANNERS. A contribution that really . . .

JUDY. The colored people.

MANNERS. Leads to a clearer understanding . . .

MILLIE. Oh. I thought you meant the other people.

MANNERS. A clearer understanding.

JUDY. I didn't mean that.

MANNERS. Yale, please!

(All silent.)

I placed an option on this script so fast. . . .

(SHELDON raises his hand.)

I tied it up, Sheldon, so that no one else could get hold of it. When I showed it to Hoskins . . .

WILETTA. *(To SHELDON.)* The producer. Another nice man.

MANNERS. Well, the rest is history. This is my first Broadway show. . . .

(Applause from cast.)

But I definitely know what I want and however unorthodox my methods, I promise never to bore you.

SHELDON. *(Popping his fingers rapidly.)* He's like that.

MANNERS. I bring to this a burning desire above and beyond anything I've . . . well, I'm ready to sweat blood. I want to see you kids drawing pay envelopes for a long time to come and . . .

(SHELDON applauds, the others join him. SHELDON aims his remark at MILLIE.)

SHELDON. Listen to the man! Listen.

MANNERS. *(Holds up his hand for silence.)* At ease. *(Mainly for JOHN and JUDY.)* I ask this, please forget your old methods of work and go along with me. I'll probably confuse the hell out of you for the first few days but after that . . . well, I hope we'll be swingin'. Now, you're all familiar with the story. . . .

WILETTA. Oh, I never had anything affect me so much in all my life.

ALL. *(Ad lib.)* There was one part. . . . I have a question. . . . Uh-huh. . . . A question. . . .

MANNERS. We will *not* discuss the parts.

(JOHN groans in mock agony.)

JUDY. One little thing.

MANNERS. We will not discuss the parts.

(EDDIE smiles knowingly.)

We will not read the play down from beginning to end.

SHELDON. *(Popping his fingers.)* There he goes!

MANNERS. We will *not* delve into character backgrounds . . . not now. Turn to act one, scene two, page fifteen.

(Actors scramble madly for places in scripts.)

Top of the page. Eddie, you read for O'Wray. Judy! Stand up!

(JUDY stands hesitantly while MANNERS toys with a sheet of paper.)

Walk downstage!

(JUDY is startled and nervous, she walks upstage. The others are eager to correct her but MANNERS will not tolerate cast interference. He crumbles the paper, throws it to the floor, takes JUDY by the shoulders and speedily leads her around the stage.)

Downstage! Center stage! Left Center! Right Center! Up Right! Up Left, Down Center, Down Right, Down Left, Upstage . . . DOWNSTAGE!

JUDY. I know, I forgot. . . .

MANNERS. Don't forget again. Take downstage. (*Notices the paper he threw on the floor.*) A trashy stage is most distracting.

(*JUDY starts to pick up the paper.*)

Hold your position! Wiletta, pick up the paper!

(*JOHN and SHELDON start for the paper.*)

I asked Wiletta! (*Catches WILETTA's eye.*) Well?

WILETTA. (*Shocked into a quick flare of temper.*) Well, hell! I ain't the damn janitor! (*Trying to check her temper.*) I . . . well, I . . . shucks . . . I . . . damn.

MANNERS. (*Even though he was trying to catch them off-guard, he didn't expect this.*) Cut! Cut! It's all over.

(*Everyone is surprised again.*)

What you have just seen is . . . is . . . is fine acting. (*He is quite shaken and embarrassed from WILETTA's action.*) Actors struggle for weeks to do what you have done perfectly . . . the first time. You gave me anger, frustration, movement, er . . . excitement. Your faces were alive! Why? You did what came naturally, you believed. . . . That is the quality I want in your work . . . the firm texture of truth.

JUDY. Oh, you tricked us.

MILLIE. I didn't know what to think.

JOHN. Tension all over the place.

WILETTA. (*Still having a hard time getting herself under control. She fans herself with a pocket handkerchief and tries to muster a weak laugh.*) Yes indeed.

MANNERS. (*Gingerly touches WILETTA and shivers in mock fear.*) She plays rough. "Well, hell!" Honey, I love you, believe me.

SHELDON. Oh, she cut up!

WILETTA. (*Tries to laugh along with them but it's hard going. From this point on, she watches MANNERS with a sharp eye, always cautious and on the look-out.*) Yes . . . well, let's don't play that no more.

MANNERS. Top of the page. Judy, you're appealing to your father to allow some of his tenant farmers . . . (*He glances at script to find the next direction. SHELDON leans over and whispers to WILETTA.*)

WILETTA. Sharecroppers.

SHELDON. Oh.

MANNERS. . . . hold a barn dance. Now! Some of them have been talking about voting.

SHELDON. Trouble.

MANNERS. (*Points first to MILLIE, then WILETTA.*) Petunia and Ruby are in your father's study . . . er . . . er . . . (*Consults script again.*)

SHELDON. (*Without consulting script.*) Cleanin' up. Sure, that's what they're doin'.

MANNERS. Tidying up. Your father is going over his account books, you're there . . .

SHELDON. (*With admiration.*) Lookin' pretty.

MANNERS. There's an awful echo coming from our assistant director.

SHELDON. (*Laughs.*) 'Sistant director! This man breaks me up all the time!

MANNERS. (*Liking the salve.*) What, what did you say?

SHELDON. Say you tickle me to death.

WILETTA. Tickles me too.

MANNERS. Take it!

JUDY. (*Reading.*) Papa, it's a good year, isn't it?

EDDIE. (*With a too-broad Southern accent.*) I'd say fair, fair to middlin'.

(*Cast snickers.*)

MANNERS. All right, Barrymore, just read it.

JUDY. Papa, it's Petunia's birthday today.

EDDIE. That so? Happy birthday, Petunia.

MILLIE. *(Wearily.)* Thank you, sir.

MANNERS. *(Correcting the reading.)* You feel good, full of ginger . . . your birthday!

MILLIE. *(Remembers the old, standard formula. Gives the line with a chuckle and extra warmth.)* Thank you, sir.

JUDY. It would be nice if they could have a stomp in the barn.

MILLIE. *(Her attitude suggests that JUDY thought up the line.)* Hmmph.

EDDIE. No need to have any barn stomp until this election business is over.

MILLIE. What the hell is a stomp?

JUDY. I can't see why.

MANNERS. A barn dance. You know that, Millie.

EDDIE. Ruby, you think y'all oughta use the barn?

WILETTA. *(Pleasantly.)* Lord, have mercy, Mr. Renard, don't ask me 'cause I don't know nothin'.

EDDIE. Well, better forget about it.

JUDY. Oh, papa, let the . . . let the . . .

MILLIE. *(For JUDY's benefit.)* Mmmmmmmmmmph. Why didn't they *call* it a barn dance?

JUDY. . . . let the . . . *(Stops reading.)* Oh, must I say that word?

MANNERS. What word?

MILLIE. *Darkies.* That's the word. It says, "Papa, let the darkies have their fun."

MANNERS. *What* do you want to say?

MILLIE. She could say . . . "Let *them* have their fun."

MANNERS. But that's Carrie. *(To SHELDON.)* Do you object?

SHELDON. Well, no, not if that's how they spoke in them days.

MANNERS. The time is now, down south in some remote little county, they say those things . . . now. Can you object in an artistic sense?

SHELDON. No, but you better ask him, he's more artistic than I am.

JOHN. No, I don't object. I don't like the word but it is used, it's a slice of life. Let's face it, Judy wouldn't use it, Mr. Manners wouldn't . . .

MANNERS. *(Very pleased with JOHN's answer.)* Call me Al, everybody. Al's good enough, Johnny.

JOHN. Al wouldn't say it but Carrie would.

(MANNERS gives WILETTA an inquiring look.)

WILETTA. Lord, have mercy, don't ask me 'cause I don't know. . . . *(She stops short as she realizes she is repeating words from the script. She's disturbed that she's repeating the exact line the author indicated.)*

MANNERS. *(Gives JUDY a light tap on the head.)* Yale! Proceed.

EDDIE. *(Reads.)* Ruby and Petunia leave the room and wait on the porch.

JUDY. Please, papa, I gave my word. I ask one little thing and . . .

EDDIE. All right! Before you know it, them niggers will be runnin' me!

JUDY. Please, don't use that word!

MANNERS. Oh, stop it!

WILETTA. That's her line in the play, Mr. Manners, Carrie says . . .

ALL. Please, don't use that word.

(MANNERS signals EDDIE to carry on.)

EDDIE. *(Reads.)* Carrie runs out to the porch.

JUDY. You can use the barn!

MILLIE. Lord, have mercy . . .

EDDIE. *(Intones.)* Wrong line.

MILLIE. *(Quickly corrects line.)* Er . . . er, somethin' seems to trouble my spirit, a troublous feelin' is in old Petunia's breast. *(Stops reading.)* Old Petunia?

WILETTA. Yes, *old* Petunia!

JUDY. *(Reads.)* I'm going upstairs to lay out my white organdy dress.

WILETTA. No, you ain't, I'm gonna do that for you.

JUDY. Then I'll take a nap.

MILLIE. No, you ain't, I'm gonna do that for you.

EDDIE. Wrong line.

MILLIE. Sorry. *(Corrects line.)* Yes, child, you rest yourself, you had a terrible, hard day. Bless your soul, you just one of God's golden-haired angels.

MANNERS. *(Frantically searching for that certain quality. He thinks everything will open once they hit the right chord.)* Cut! Top of page three, act one, as it's written. Ruby is shelling beans on the back porch as her son Job approaches.

JOHN. If I can read over . . .

MANNERS. Do as I ask, do it. Take it, Wiletta.

SHELDON. *(Popping his fingers.)* He's just like that.

WILETTA. *(Reads.)* Boy, where you goin'?

JOHN. Down to Turner's Corner.

WILETTA. You ain't lost nothin' down there. Turner and his brother is talkin' 'bout votin', I know.

JOHN. They only talkin', I'm goin'.

SHELDON. Mr. Renard say to stay outta that.

JOHN. I got a letter from the President 'bout goin' in the army, Turner says when that happen's, a man's sposed to vote and things.

(MILLIE and JUDY are very pleased about this line.)

SHELDON. Letter ain't from no President, it come from the crackers on the draft board.

JOHN. It *say* from the President.

WILETTA. Pa say you don't go.

(MANNERS is jotting down a flood of notes.)

JOHN. Sorry, but I say I'd be there.

SHELDON. I don't know who that boy take after.

EDDIE. Ruby dashes from the porch and Sam follows her. Carrie comes outside and Renard follows her. *(EDDIE reads RENARD.)* You pamper them rascals too much, see how they do? None of 'em's worth their weight in salt, that boy would steal the egg out of a cake.

JUDY. *(Tries to laugh while MILLIE watches coldly. MANNERS is amazed at the facial distortion.)* It says laugh.

MANNERS. Well?

JUDY. *(Laughs and continues reading.)* But I can't help feeling sorry for them, they didn't ask to be born.

MILLIE. *(Just loud enough for JUDY's ears.)* Hmmmmmph.

JUDY. I keep thinking, there but for the grace of God go I. If we're superior we should prove it by our actions.

SHELDON. *(Commenting on the line.)* There you go, prove it!

(MANNERS is taking more notes. JUDY is disturbed by the reactions to her reading. She hesitates, MANNERS looks up. The PHONE RINGS. EDDIE goes off to answer.)

JUDY. She *is* their friend, right? It's just that I feel reactions and . . .

MANNERS. What reactions?

MILLIE. I was reacting.

MANNERS. Ohhhhh, who pays Millie any attention, that's her way.

MILLIE. There you go.

SHELDON. Sure is.

JUDY. *(Tries again but she's very uncomfortable.)* I . . . I keep thinking . . . there but for the grace of God . . .

MANNERS. Are you planning to cry?

JUDY. No, but . . . no. *(She's fighting to hold back the tears.)*

SHELDON. Millie is pickin' on her.

MANNERS. Utter nonsense!

JUDY. My part seems . . . she seems so smug.

MILLIE. *(To SHELDON.)* Keep my name out of your mouth.

WILETTA. (To SHELDON.) Mind your business, your own affairs.

MANNERS. This is fantastic. What in the hell is smug?

(HENRY enters with a cardboard box full of coffee containers and a large paper bag.)

Cut! Coffee break! (To JUDY.) Especially you.

HENRY. Told the waiter feller to fix up everything nice.

MANNERS. (Looks in bag.) What's this?

HENRY. That's what you said. I heard you. "Jelly doughnuts!" you said.

(SHELDON gets a container of coffee for JUDY and one for himself.)

MANNERS. I won't eat it!

HENRY. But I heard you.

MANNERS. Take your coffee and leave.

(HENRY starts to leave without the coffee.)

Don't play games, take it with you.

(HENRY snatches a container and leaves in a quiet huff. SHELDON hands coffee to JUDY but MILLIE snatches it from his hand.)

MILLIE. I know you brought that for me.

MANNERS. Where do they find these characters? All right, he's old but it's an imposition . . . he's probably ninety, you know.

WILETTA. (Laughs and then suddenly stops.) We all get old sometimes.

EDDIE. (Hurries onstage. Looks worried.) It's Mrs. Manners . . . she . . . she says it's urgent. She has to talk to you now . . . immediatly.

MANNERS. Oh, you stupid jerk. Why did you say I was here? You and your big, stupid mouth. Couldn't you say "He isn't here now, I'll give him your message"?

EDDIE. I'm sorry. She was so . . .

so. . . . Well, she said right off "I know he's there." If I had any idea that she would . . .

MANNERS. I don't expect you to have ideas! Only common sense, just a little common sense. Where do you find a stage manager these days?

EDDIE. I can tell her you can't be disturbed now.

MANNERS. No, numbskull, don't do another thing, you've done enough. (With wry humor.) Alimony is not enough, every time I make three extra dollars she takes me to court to get two-thirds of it. If I don't talk to her I'll have a subpoena. You're stupid. (He exits to the telephone. During the brief silence which follows, EDDIE is miserably self-conscious.)

WILETTA. (Tries to save the day.) Well, . . . I'm glad it's getting a little like winter now. We sure had a hot summer. Did you have a nice summer?

EDDIE. (Choking back his suppressed anger.) I worked in stock . . . summer theater. It was O. K.

WILETTA. That's nice. What did you do?

EDDIE. (Relaxing more.) Kind of Jack of all trades . . . understudied some, stage managed, made sets. . . .

MILLIE. And did three people out of a job.

JUDY. I spent the summer with my folks. Soon as we open, I want everyone to come up to Bridgeport and have a glorious day!

(MANNERS returns, looks up briefly.)

Daddy makes the yummiest barbecue, you'll love it.

WILETTA. You better discuss it with your folks first.

JUDY. Why?

MILLIE. 'Cause we wouldn't want it discussed after we got there.

SHELDON. No, thank you, ma'am. I'm plannin' to be busy all winter lookin' for an apartment, I sure hate roomin'.

EDDIE. I have my own apartment. It's only a cold-water walk-up but I have it fixed real nice like the magazines show you . . . whitewashed brick and mobiles hanging in the kitchen and living room. I painted the floors black and spattered them with red and white paint . . . I learned that in stock . . . then I shellacked over it and waxed it . . . and I scraped all of the furniture down to the natural wood. . . .

MILLIE. Oh, hush, you're making me tired. Cold-water flat!

EDDIE. It gives a cheery effect. . . .

MILLIE. And it'll give you double pneumonia.

SHELDON. Yeah, that's the stuff you got to watch.

EDDIE. Well, it's only thirty dollars a month.

SHELDON. They got any colored livin' in that buildin'?

EDDIE. I . . . I . . . I don't know. I haven't seen any.

SHELDON. Well, there's none there then.

EDDIE. (Slightly ill at ease.) Sheldon, I'll gladly ask.

SHELDON. (In great alarm.) Oh, no, no, no! I don't want to be the first.

MILLIE. Damn cold-water flats! I like ease, comfort, furs, cars, big, thick steaks. I want everything.

EDDIE. (Trying to change the subject.) Aren't there a lot of new shows this season?

JUDY. My mother says . . . gosh, every time I open my mouth it's something about my parents. It's not stylish to love your parents . . . you either have a mother-complex or a father-fixation!

(She laughs and MANNERS looks up again. He doesn't care for her remarks.)

But I'm crazy about my parents, but then maybe that's abnormal. I probably have a mother-father-fixation.

WILETTA. What did your mother say?

JUDY. "Never have limitations on your horizon, reach for infinity!" She also feels that everyone has a right to an equal education and not separate either.

JOHN. She sounds like a wonderful woman who . . .

JUDY. (Raising her voice.) Oh, I get so mad about this prejudice nonsense! It's a wonder colored people don't go out and kill somebody, I mean actually, really do it . . . bloody murder, you know?

SHELDON. There's lotsa folks worse off than we are, Millie.

MILLIE. Well, all I hope is that they don't like it, dontcha know.

MANNERS. (Boastful about his trials and troubles.) The seven-year-old kid, the seven-year-old kid . . . to hear her tell it, our son is ragged, barefoot, hungry . . . and his teeth are lousy. The orthodontist says he needs braces . . . they wanta remake his mouth. The kid is falling to pieces. When I go for visitation . . . he looks in my pockets before he says hello. Can you imagine? Seven years old. The orthodontist and the psychiatrist . . . the story of my life. But he's a bright kid . . . smart as a whip . . . you can't fool him. (A big sigh.) Oh, well, let's go. Suppose you were all strangers, had never heard anything about this story except the snatches you heard today. What would you know?

MILLIE. It's my birthday.

(WILETTA is following him closely; she doesn't care to be caught off-guard again.)

JOHN. Carrie's father has tenant farmers working for him.

MANNERS. Yes and . . .

JUDY. They want to hold a barn dance and he's against it because . . .

JOHN. Some of the Negroes are planning to vote for the first time and there's opposition . . .

SHELDON. His ma and pa don't want him mixed in it 'cause they smell trouble.

JUDY. And my father overheard that John is in it.

SHELDON. And *he don't like it,* that's another thing.

WILETTA. *(Amazed that they have learned so much.)* Mmmmmm, all of that.

JOHN. But Job is determined.

JUDY. And he's been notified by the draft board.

SHELDON. And the paper, the paper!

MANNERS. Paper?

WILETTA. You know, upstage, downstage and doin' what comes natural.

MANNERS. Not bad for an hour's work.

EDDIE. Amazing.

SHELDON. *(Popping his fingers.)* Man is on the ball. Fast.

MANNERS. Now we can see how we're heading for the lynching.

SHELDON. *(Starts to peep at back page of script.)* Lynchin'?

MANNERS. We're dealing with an anti-lynch theme. I want it uncluttered, clear in your mind, you must see the skeleton framework within which we're working. Wiletta, turn to the last page of act one.

EDDIE. Fifty.

MANNERS. Wiletta, dear heart . . . the end of the act finds you alone on the porch, worried, heartsick . . .

WILETTA. And singin' a song, sittin', worryin', and singin'.

MANNERS. It's not simply a song, it's a summing up. You're thinking of Renard, the threats, the people and your son. . . .

(WILETTA is tensely listening, trying to follow him. MANNERS stands behind her and gently shakes her shoulders.)

Loosen up, let the thoughts flood over you. I know you have to read. . . .

WILETTA. Oh, I know the song, learned it when I was a child.

MANNERS. Hold a thought, close your eyes and think aloud . . . get a good start and then sing . . . speak your mind and then sing.

WILETTA. *(Not for thinking out loud.)* I know exactly what you want.

MANNERS. Blurt out the first thing that enters your mind.

WILETTA. *(Sings a mournful dirge of despair.)* Come and go with me to that land, come and go with me to that land . . .

MANNERS. Gosh, that guy can write.

WILETTA.
Come and go with me to that land where I'm bound
No confusion in that land, no confusion in that land
No confusion in that land where I'm bound . . .

MILLIE. *(Wipes her eyes.)* A heartbreaker.

EDDIE. Oh, Wiletta, it's so . . . so . . . gosh.

JOHN. Leaves you weak.

MANNERS. Beautiful. What were you thinking?

WILETTA. *(Ready to move on to something else.)* Thank you.

MANNERS. What were you thinking?

WILETTA. I thought . . . I . . . er, er . . . I don't know, whatever you said.

MANNERS. Tell me. You're not a vacuum, you thought something.

JOHN. Your motivation. What motivated . . .

MANNERS. *(Waving JOHN out of it.)* You thought *something,* right?

WILETTA. Uh-huh.

MANNERS. And out of the thought came song.

WILETTA. Yeah.

MANNERS. What did you thiink?

WILETTA. I thought that's what you wanted. *(She realizes she is the center of attention and finds it uncomfortable.)*

MANNERS. It won't do. You must know why you do a thing, that way you're true to me, to the part and yourself. . . .

WILETTA. Didn't you like it?

MANNERS. Very much but . . . I'm sure you've never worked this way before, but you're not carrying a tray or answering doorbells, this is substance, meat. I demand that you *know* what you're doing and *why,* at all times. I will accept nothing less.

WILETTA. *(To* JOHN *and* JUDY.*)* I know, you have to justify.

SHELDON. *(Worried and trying to help* WILETTA.*)* You was thinkin' how sad it was, wasn't you?

WILETTA. Uh-huh.

MANNERS. It's new to you but it must be done. Let go, think aloud and when you are moved to do so . . . sing.

*(*WILETTA *looks blank.)*

Start anywhere.

WILETTA. Ah, er . . . it's so sad that folks can't vote . . . it's also sad that er, er . . .

MANNERS. No. *(Picks up newspaper.)* We'll try word association. I'll give you a word, then you say what comes to your mind and keep on going . . . one word brings on another. . . . Montgomery!

WILETTA. Alabama.

MANNERS. Montgomery!

WILETTA. Alabama.

MANNERS. Montgomery! !

WILETTA. Reverend King is speakin' on Sunday.

MANNERS. Colored.

WILETTA. Lights changin' colors all around me.

MANNERS. Colored.

WILETTA. They . . . they . . .

MANNERS. Colored.

WILETTA. "They got any colored in that buildin'?"

MANNERS. Children, little children.

WILETTA. Children . . . children. . . . "Pick up that paper!' Oh, my . . .

MANNERS. Lynching.

WILETTA. Killin'! Killin'!

MANNERS. Killing.

WILETTA. It's the man's theater, the man's money, so what you gonna do?

MANNERS. Oh, Wiletta . . . I don't know! *Darkness!*

WILETTA. A star! Oh, I can't, I don't like it. . . .

MANNERS. Sing.

WILETTA. *(Sings a song of strength and anger.)*
Come and go with me to that land

(The song is overpowering, we see a woman who could fight the world.)

Come and go with me to that land
Come and go with me to that land—
where I'm bound.

JUDY. Bravo! Magnificent!

MANNERS. Wiletta, if you dare! You will undo us! Are you out of your senses? When you didn't know what you were doing . . . perfection on the nose. I'll grant you the first interpretation was right, without motivating. All right, I'll settle for that.

WILETTA. *(Feeling very lost.)* I said I *knew* what you wanted.

MANNERS. Judy! I . . . I want to talk to you about . . . about Carrie. *(He rises and starts for the dressing room.)* Eddie, will you dash out and get me a piece of Danish? Okay, at ease.

*(*EDDIE *quickly exits.* MANNERS *and* JUDY *exit Stage Right toward dressing rooms.)*

MILLIE. *(To* JOHN.*)* Look, don't get too close to her.

SHELDON. Mind your own business.

JOHN. What have I done?

MILLIE. You're too friendly with her.

WILETTA. Justify. Ain't enough to do it, you got to justify.

JOHN. I've only been civil.

MILLIE. That's too friendly.

WILETTA. Got a splittin' headache.

SHELDON. *(To* WILETTA.*)* I wish I had a aspirin for you.

MILLIE. *(To* JOHN.*)* All set to run up and see her folks. Didn't you hear her say they expect something terrible to happen to her? Well, you're one of the terrible things they have in mind!

SHELDON. Mind your business.

MILLIE. It is my business. When they start raisin' a fund for his defense, they're gonna come and ask me for money and I'll have to be writin' the President and signin' petitions . . . so it's my business.

SHELDON. I tell you, son, I'm friendly with white folks in a distant sorta way but I don't get too close. Take Egypt, Russia, all these countries, why they kickin' up their heels? 'Cause of white folks. I wouldn't trust one of 'em sittin' in front of me on a merry-go-round, wouldn't trust 'em if they was laid up in bed with lockjaw and the mumps both at the same time.

JOHN. Last time I heard from you, you said it was the colored who made all the trouble.

SHELDON. They do, they're the worst ones. There's two kinda people that's got the world messed up for good, that's the colored and the white, and I got no use for either one of 'em.

MILLIE. I'm going to stop trying to help people.

JOHN. Hell, I'm through with it. Oh, I'm learning the ropes!

SHELDON. *That's* why they don't do more colored shows . . . trouble makers, pot boilers, spoon stirrers . . . and sharper than a serpent's tooth! Colored women wake up in the mornin' with their fists ball up . . . ready to fight.

WILETTA. What in the devil is all this justifyin'? Ain't necessary.

MILLIE. *(To* SHELDON.*)* And you crawlin' all over me to hand her coffee! Damn "Tom."

SHELDON. You talkin' 'bout your relatives, ain't talkin' 'bout me, if I'm a "Tom," you a "Jemima."

JOHN. I need out, I need air. *(He exits Stage Left.)*

SHELDON. White folks is stickin' together, stickin' together, stickin' together . . . we fightin'.

WILETTA. Hush, I got a headache.

MILLIE. I need a breath of air, too, before I slap the taste out of somebody's mouth. *(*MILLIE *grabs her coat and exits Stage Left.)*

SHELDON. I hope the wind blows her away. They gonna kick us until we all out in the street . . . unemployed . . . get all the air you want then. Sometimes I take low, yes, gotta take low. Man say somethin' to me, I say . . . "Yes, sure, certainly." You 'n' me know how to do. That ain't *tommin'*, that's common sense. You and me . . . we don't mind takin' low because we tryin' to accomplish somethin'. . . .

WILETTA. I mind . . . I do mind . . . I mind . . . I mind. . . .

SHELDON. Well, yeah, we all mind . . . but you got to swaller what you mind. What you mind won't buy beans. I mean you gotta take what you mind to survive . . . to eat to breathe. . . .

WILETTA. *(Tensely.) I mind.* Leave me alone.

*(*SHELDON *exits with a sigh.)*

HENRY. *(Enters carrying a lunch box.* WILETTA *turns, she looks so distressed.)* They've all flown the coop?

WILETTA. Yes.

HENRY. What's the matter? Somebody hurt your feelin's?

WILETTA. Yes.

HENRY. Don't fret, it's too nice a day. I believe in treatin' folks right. When you're just about through with this life, that's the time when you know how to live. Seems like yesterday I was forty years old and the day before that I wasn't but nineteen. . . . Think of it.

WILETTA. I don't like to think . . . makes me fightin' mad.

HENRY. *(Giving vent to his pent-up feelings.)* Don't I know it? When he yelled about jelly doughnuts, I started to land one on him! Oh, I almost did it!

WILETTA. I know it!

HENRY. But . . . "Hold your temper!"

I says. I have a most ferocious temper.

WILETTA. Me too. I take and take, then watch out!

HENRY. Have to hold my temper, I don't want to kill the man.

WILETTA. Yeah, makes you feel like fightin'.

HENRY. (Joining in the spirit of the discussion.) Sure I'm a fighter and I come from a fightin' people.

WILETTA. You from Ireland?

HENRY. A fightin' people! Didn't we fight for the home rule?

WILETTA. Uh-huh, now you see there.

(WILETTA doesn't worry about making sense out of Henry's speech on Ireland, it's the feeling behind it that counts.)

HENRY. O, a history of great men, fightin' men!

WILETTA. (Rallying to the call, she answers as though sitting on an amen bench at a revival meeting.) Yes, carry on.

HENRY. Ah, yes, we was fighttin' for the home rule! Ah, there was some great men!

WILETTA. I know it.

HENRY. There was Parnell! Charles Stewart Parnell!

WILETTA. All right!

HENRY. A figure of a man! The highest! Fightin' hard for the home rule! A parlimentarian! And they clapped him in the blasted jailhouse for six months!

WILETT. Yes, my Lord!

HENRY. And Gladstone introduced the bill . . . and later on you had Dillon and John Redmond . . . and then when the home rule was amost put through, what do you think happened? World War One! That killed the whole business!

WILETTA. (Very indignant.) Oh, if it ain't one thing, it's another!

HENRY. I'm descended from a great line! And then the likes of him with his jelly doughnuts! Jelly doughnuts, indeed, is it? What does he know? Tramplin' upon a man's dignity! Me father was the greatest, most dignified man you've ever seen . . . and he played vaudeville! Oh, the bearin' of him! (Angrily demonstrating his father's dignity.) Doin' the little soft-shoe step . . . and it's take your hat off to the ladies . . . and step along there. . . .

WILETTA. Henry, I want to be an actress, I've always wanted to be an actress and they ain't gonna do me the way they did the home rule! I want to be an actress 'cause one day you're nineteen and then forty and so on . . . I want to be an actress! Henry, they stone us when we try to go to school, the world's crazy.

HENRY. It's a shame, a shame. . . .

WILETTA. Where the hell do I come in? Every damn body pushin' me off the face of the earth! I want to be an actress . . . hell, I'm gonna be one, you hear me? (She pounds the table.)

HENRY. Sure, and why not, I'd like to know!

WILETTA. (Quietly.) Yes, dammit . . . and why not? Why in the hell not?

(BLUES RECORD in. Woman singer.)

CURTAIN

ACT TWO

TIME:

Ten o'clock Thursday morning.

PLACE:

Same as Act I.

(BLUES MUSIC—in—up and out.)

SCENE:

Same as Act One, except furniture has been changed around; some of the old set removed. BILL O'WRAY, a character actor (white) stands upstage on a makeshift platform. He radiates strength and power as he addresses an imaginary audience. MANNERS stands stage Left, tie loosened, hair ruffled. He is hepped up with nervous energy, can barely stand still. EDDIE is stage Right, in charge of the script and a tape recorder; he follows the script and turns up the tape recorder on cue from MANNERS. O'WRAY *is delivering a "masterful" rendition of Renard's speech on "tolerance."* MANNERS *is elated one moment, deflated the next.* EDDIE *is obviously nervous, drawn and lacking the easy-going attitude of Act One.*

BILL. *(Intones speech with vigor and heartfelt passion.)* My friends, if all the world were just, there would be no need for valor. . . . And those of us who are of a moderate mind . . . I would say the majority . . .

(Light applause from tape recorder.)

. . . we are anything but light-hearted. But the moving finger writes and having writ moves *on.* No, you can't wash out a word of it. Heretofore we've gotten along with our Nigra population . . . but times change.

(Applause from tape recorder.)

I do not argue with any man who believes in segregation. I, of all people, will not, cannot question that belief. We all believe in the words of Henry Clay—"Sir, I would rather be right than be president."

(EDDIE sleeps his cue.)

MANNERS. Dammit! Eddie!

(EDDIE suddenly switches to loud applause.)

BILL. But difficulties are things that show what men are, and necessity is still the mother of invention. As Emerson so aptly pointed out—"The true test of civilization is not the—census, nor the size of cities, nor the crops—but the kind of man the country turns out." Oh, my friends, let every man look before he leaps, let us consider submitting to the present evil lest a greater one befall us—say to yourself, my honor is dearer to me than my life.

(Very light applause.)

I say moderation—for these are the times that try men's souls! In these terrible days we must realize—how oft the darkest hour of ill breaks brightest into dawn. Moderation, yes.

(Very light applause.)

Even the misguided, infamous Adolph Hitler said—"One should guard against believing the great masses to be more stupid than they actually are!"

(Applause.)

Oh, friends, moderation. Let us weigh our answer very carefully when the dark-skinned Oliver Twist approaches our common pot and says: "Please, sir, I want some more." When we say "no," remember that a soft answer turneth away wrath. Ohhh, we shall come out of the darkness, and sweet is pleasure after pain. If we are superior, let us show our superiority!

(MANNERS directs EDDIE to take applause up high and then out.)

Moderation. With wisdom and moderation, these terrible days will pass. I am reminded of the immortal words of Longfellow. "And the night shall be filled with music and the cares that infest the day shall fold their tents like the Arabs and silently steal away."

(Terrific applause.)

MANNERS. *(Slaps BILL on back. Dashes to EDDIE and turns the applause up and down.)* Is this such a Herculean task? All you have to do is listen! Inattention—aggravates the hell out of me!

BILL. *(When BILL drops out of character we see that he is very different from the strong RENARD. He appears to be worried at all times. He has a habit of negatively shaking his head even though nothing is wrong. BILL O'WRAY is but a shadow of a man—but by some miracle he turns into a dynamic figure as RENARD.*

As BILL—*he sees dragons in every corner and worries about each one.*) I don't know, I don't know. . . .

MANNERS. *(Fears the worst for the show as he watches* BILL.) What? What is it?

BILL. *(Half dismissing the thought.)* Oh, well . . . I guess. . . .

(EDDIE is toying with the machine and turns the applause up by accident.)

MANNERS. Hell, Eddie, a little consideration! Why do you do it? Damned childish!

(EDDIE turns off machine.)

What's bothering you?

BILL. Well, you never can tell . . . but I don't know. . . .

MANNERS. Bill, cut it out, come on.

BILL. That *Arab* stuff . . . you know, quietly folding his tent . . . you're gonna get a laugh . . . and then on the other hand you might offend somebody . . . well, we'll see. . . .

MANNERS. Eddie, make a note of that. Arab folding his tent. I'll take it up with Bronson.

(EDDIE is making notes.)

BILL. I'm tellin' you, you don't need it . . . wouldn't lose a thing . . . the Longfellow quote . . . I don't know, maybe I'm wrong but . . .

MANNERS. You act like you've lost your last friend! I'm the one holding the blasted bag.

BILL. *(Taking "Show Business" out of his coat pocket.)* Well, maybe I shouldn't have said . . .

MANNERS. I'm out of my mind! When I think of the money borrowed, and for what! Oh, I'm just talking. This always happens when the ship leaves port. The union's making me take three extra stage hands. *(Laughs.)* . . . they hate us! *Co-produce,* filthy word! You know who I had to put the bite on for an extra ten

thousand? My ex-wife's present boyfriend. Enough to emasculate a man for the rest of his life!

BILL. How is Fay? Sweet kid. I was sure surprised when you two broke it off. Oh, well, that's the way. . . .

MANNERS. She's fine and we're good friends. Thank God for civilization.

BILL. That's nice. Ten thousand? She must have connected up with a big wheel, huh?

MANNERS. I've known you long enough to ask a favor.

BILL. All depends.

MANNERS. Will you stop running off at lunch hour? It looks bad.

BILL. Now, wait a minute. . . .

EDDIE. I eat with them all the time.

MANNERS. Drop it, Eddie. Unity in *this* company is very important. Hell, I don't care, but it looks like you don't want to eat with the colored members of the cast.

BILL. I don't.

EDDIE. I guess you heard him.

MANNERS. Bill, this is fantastic. I never credited you with this kind of . . . silly, childlike . . .

BILL. There's not a prejudiced bone in my body. It is important that I eat my lunch. I used to have an ulcer. I have nothing against anybody but I can't eat my damn lunch . . . people *stare.* They sit there glaring and staring.

MANNERS. Nonsense.

BILL. Tuesday I lunched with Millie because I bumped into her on the street. That restaurant . . . people straining and looking at me as if I were an old lecher! God knows what they're thinking. I've got to eat my lunch. After all . . . I can't stand that . . .

MANNERS. *(Laughs.)* All right but mix a little . . . it's the show . . . do it for the show.

BILL. Every time I open my mouth somebody is telling me don't say this or that . . . Millie doesn't want to be called "gal" . . . I call *all* women "gal" . . . I don't know . . . I'm not going into analysis about this . . . I'm not. How do you think my character is shaping up?

MANNERS. Great, no complaints . . . fine.

(WILETTA *drags in, tired and worn.*)

'Morning, sweetie.

EDDIE. Good morning.

WILETTA. (*Indicating script.*) I been readin' this back and forth and over again.

MANNERS. (*Automatic sympathy.*) Honey, don't . . .

WILETTA. My neighbor, Miss Green, she come up and held the book and I sat there justifyin' like you said. . . .

MANNERS. Darling, don't think. You're great until you start thinking. I don't expect you to. . . .

WILETTA. (*Weak laugh.*) I've been in this business a long time, more than twenty-five years and . . .

MANNERS. Don't tell it, you're beautiful.

WILETTA. Guess I can do like the others. We was jutsifyin' and Miss Green says to me . . .

BILL. (*Gets in his good deed.*) Wiletta, you look wonderful, you really do.

WILETTA. Huh?

BILL. You . . . you're looking well.

WILETTA. Thank you, Miss Green says . . .

MANNERS. (*Wearily.*) Oh, a plague on Miss Green. Darling, it's too early to listen to outside criticism, it can be dangerous if the person doesn't understand . . .

WILETTA. Miss Green puts on shows at the church . . . and she had an uncle that was a sharecropper, so she says the first act . . .

MANNERS. (*Flips the script to Act Three.*) We're hitting the third today.

WILETTA. Miss Green also conducts the church choir . . .

MANNERS. Wiletta, don't complicate my life. (*To* BILL *and* EDDIE.) Isn't she

wonderful? (*To* WILETTA.) Dear heart, I adore you.

WILETTA. (*Feels like a fool as she limply trails on.*) She . . . she did the Messiah . . . *Handel's* Messiah . . . last Easter . . . and folks come from downtown to hear it . . . all kinds of folks . . . white folks too.

MANNERS. Eddie! Did I leave the schedule at home?

EDDIE. (*Hands him the schedule.*) I have a copy.

WILETTA. Miss Green says, now . . . she said it . . . she says the third act doesn't justify with the first . . . no, wait . . . her exact words was, "The third act is not the natural outcome of the first." I thought, I thought she might be right.

MANNERS. (*Teasing.*) Make me a solemn promise, don't start thinking.

SHELDON. (*Enters in a rush and hastily begins to remove scarves, coat etc.*) Good mornin', there ain't no justice.

(BILL O'WRAY *glances at "Show Business" from time to time.*)

EDDIE. What a greeting.

SHELDON. I dreamed six, twelve, six, one, two . . . just like that. You know what come out yesterday? Six, one, three. What you gonna do?

MANNERS. Save your money.

BILL. Hey, what do you know?

MANNERS. Did we make the press?

SHELDON. (*To* WILETTA.) Friend of mine died yesterday, went to see about his apartment . . . gone! Just like that!

BILL. Gary Brewer's going into rehearsal on *Lost and Lonely.*

MANNERS. Been a long time.

BILL. He was in that Hollywood investigation some years ago.

SHELDON. (*To* EDDIE.) They musta applied whilst the man was dyin'.

MANNERS. He wasn't really in it, someone named him I think.

BILL. You knew him well, didn't you?

MANNERS. Me? I don't know him. I've

worked with him a couple of times but I don't really know him.

BILL. A very strange story reached me once, some fellow was planning to name me, can you imagine?

(MILLIE *enters wearing a breathtaking black suit. She is radiant.*)

EDDIE. That's ridiculous.

BILL. Nothing ever happened, but that's the story. Naming *me.*

MANNERS. *(As he studies schedule.)* Talking about the coast, I could be out there now on a honey of a deal . . . but this I had to do, that's all.

SHELDON. Y'all ever hear any stories 'bout people namin' me?

MANNERS. What?

BILL. Oh, Shel!

SHELDON. *(This is a burden he has carried for quite some time.)* I sang on a program once with Millie, to help some boy that was in trouble . . . but later on I heard they was tryin' to overthrow the gov'ment.

(MANNERS, EDDIE *and* BILL *are embarrassed by this.*)

MILLIE. Oh, hush! Your mouth runs like a race horse!

SHELDON. Well, ain't nothin' wrong with singin' is there? We just sang.

MILLIE. *(As she removes her hat.)* A big fool.

MANNERS. *(Making peace.)* Oh, now. . . . we're all good Americans.

BILL. *(To ease the tension.)* I . . . I . . . er, didn't know you went in for singing, Sheldon.

SHELDON. Sure, I even wrote me a coupla tunes. Can make a lotta money like that but you gotta know somebody, I ain't got no pull.

WILETTA. *(To* MILLIE.*)* He talks too much, talks too much.

MANNERS. Ah, we have a composer, popular stuff?

SHELDON. *(Stands and mechanically rocks to and fro in a rock and roll beat as he sings.)*
You-oo-hoo-oo are my hon-honey
Ooo-oo-ooo-oo, you smile is su-hu-hunny
My hu-hu-hunny, Bay-hay-hay-bee-e-e-e
. . . and it goes like that.

MANNERS. Well!

SHELDON. Thank you.

BILL. I don't know why you haven't sold it, that's all you hear.

(SHELDON *is pleased with* BILL's *compliment but also a little worried.*)

MILLIE. Hmmmmmph.

EDDIE. Really a tune.

SHELDON. *(To* BILL.*)* My song . . . it . . . it's copyrighted.

BILL. Oh?

SHELDON. I got papers.

MILLIE. *(Extends her wrist to* WILETTA.*)* Look. My husband is in off the road.

WILETTA. What's the matter?

MILLIE. A new watch, and I got my suit out . . . brought me this watch. We looked at a freezer this morning . . . food freezer . . . what's best, a chest freezer or an upright? I don't know.

JUDY. *(She enters dressed a little older than Act One, her hair is set with more precision. She is reaching for a sophistication that can never go deeper than the surface. She often makes graceful, studied postures and tries new attitudes, but very often she forgets.)* Greetings and salutations. Sheldon, how are you dear?

SHELDON. Thank you.

JUDY. *(As* MILLIE *displays her wrist for inspection.)* Millie, darling, how lovely, ohhhhh, exquisite . . .

WILETTA. *(Really trying to join in.)* Mmmm, ain't it divine.

(HENRY *and* JOHN *enter together.* HENRY *carries a container of coffee and a piece of Danish for* MANNERS. HENRY *is exact, precise, all business. He carries the container to* MANNERS' *table, places* pastry, taps EDDIE on the shoulder, points to MANNERS, points to container, nods to MANNERS and company, turns and leaves, all while dialogue continues.)

JOHN. (Enters on a cloud. He is drifting more and more toward the heady heights of opportunism. He sees himself on the brink of escaping WILETTA, MILLIE and SHELDON. It's becoming very easy to conform to MANNERS' pattern.) I'm walking in my sleep. I was up all hours last night.

MANNERS. At Sardi's no doubt.

JOHN. No!

JUDY. Exposed! We've found you out.

(General laughter from MILLIE, JUDY, BILL, EDDIE and MANNERS. JUDY is enjoying the intangible joke to the utmost but as she turns to WILETTA her laughter dies . . . but WILETTA quickly picks it up.)

WILETTA. Oh, my, yes indeed!

JOHN. I struggled with the third act. I think I won.

(MILLIE sticks out her wrist for JOHN's inspection.)

Exquisite, Millie, beautiful. You deserve it.

(During the following the conversation tumbles criss-cross in all directions and the only clear things are underscored.)

MANNERS. Tell him what I told you this morning.

BILL. Why should I swell his head?

MANNERS. (Arm around JOHN's shoulder.) Hollywood's going to grab you so fast! I won't drop names but our opening night is going to be the end.

MILLIE. (To WILETTA.) Barbara died!

JUDY. (To MANNERS.) Oh, you terrify me!

MILLIE. Died alone in her apartment. Sudden-like!

JOHN. I've got to catch Katherine's performance, I hear it's terrific!

BILL. She's great, only great.

MILLIE. I wouldn't live alone!

MANNERS. She's going to get the award, no doubt about it!

JUDY. Marion Hatterly is good.

MANNERS. Marion is as old as the hills! I mean, she's so old it's embarrassing.

JOHN. But she has a quality.

SHELDON. (To MILLIE and WILETTA.) People dyin' like they got nothin' else to do!

JUDY. She has, John, a real quality.

SHELDON. I ain't gonna die, can't afford to do it.

MANNERS. You have to respect her.

EDDIE. Can name her own ticket.

JOHN. Imperishable talent.

MILLIE. Funeral is Monday.

WILETTA. (Weakly, to no one in particular.) Mmmmm, fascinatin'. . . .

MANNERS. Picnic is over! Third Act!

SHELDON. I know my lines.

BILL. Don't worry about lines yet.

MANNERS. No, let him worry . . . I mean it's okay. Beginning of third!

WILETTA. (Feels dizzy from past conversation. She rises and walks in a half-circle, then half-circles back again. She is suddenly the center of attraction.) It . . . it's night time and I'm ironin' clothes.

MANNERS. Right. We wander through it. Here's the ironing board, door, window . . . you iron. Carrie is over there crying.

JUDY. Oh, poor, dear, Carrie, crying again.

MANNERS. Petunia is near the window, looking out for Job. Everyone is worried, worried, worried like crazy. Have the lynchers caught Job? Sam is seated in the corner, whittling a stick.

SHELDON. (Flat statement.) Whittlin' a stick.

MANNERS. Excitement. Everyone knows that a mob is gathering.

SHELDON. (Seated and busy running one

index finger over the other.) I'm whittlin' a stick.

MANNERS. *(Drumming up excitement.)* The hounds can be heard baying in the distance.

(SHELDON bays to fill in the dog bit. MANNERS silences him with a gesture.)

Everyone *listens!* They are thinking—has Job been killed? Ruby begins to sing.

WILETTA. *(Begins to sing with a little too much power but MANNERS directs her down.)* Lord, have mercy, Lord have mercy . . . *(Hums.)*

MILLIE. *(In abject, big-eyed fear.)* Listen to them dogs in the night.

(MANNERS warns SHELDON not to provide sound effects.)

WILETTA. *(Trying to lose herself in the part.)* Child, you better go now.

(BILL whispers to EDDIE.)

EDDIE. *Line.* Miss Carrie, you better go now.

MANNERS. Oh, bother! Don't do that!

(EDDIE feels resentful toward BILL as BILL acts as though he had nothing to do with the correction.)

WILETTA. This ain't no place for you to be.

JUDY. *(Now plays CARRIE in a different way from Act One. There is a reserved kindliness, rather than real involvement.)* I don't want to leave you alone, Ruby.

SHELDON. Thassa mistake, Mr. Manners. She can't be alone if me and Millie is there with her.

MANNERS. Don't interrupt!

SHELDON. Sorry.

(BILL shakes his fist at SHELDON in playful pantomime.)

WILETTA. Man that is born of woman is but a few days and full of trouble.

JUDY. I'm going to drive over to the next county and get my father and Judge Willis.

MILLIE. No, you ain't. Mr. Renard would never forgive me if somethin' was to happen to you.

(SHELDON is very touched and sorry for all concerned as he whittles his stick.)

JUDY. I feel so helpless.

SHELDON. *(Interrupts out of sheer frustration.)* Am I still whittlin' the stick?

WILETTA. Dammit, yes.

MANNERS. *(Paces to control his annoyance.)* Shel.

SHELDON. I thought I lost my place.

WILETTA. *(Picks up MANNERS' signal.)* Nothin' to do now but pray!

SHELDON. *(Recognizes his cue.)* Oh, yeah, that's me. *(Knows his lines almost perfectly.)* Lord, once and again and one more time . . .

(MILLIE moans in the background. WILETTA's mind seems a thousand miles away. MANNERS snaps his fingers and she begins to moan background for SHELDON's prayer.)

Your humble servant calls on your everlastin' mercy . . .

MILLIE. Yes, Lord!

SHELDON. . . . to beseech, to beseech thy help for all your children this evenin'. . . .

MILLIE. This evenin', Lord.

(MANNERS is busy talking to JOHN.)

SHELDON. But most of all we ask, we pray . . . that you help your son and servant Job. . . .

WILETTA. Help him, Lord!

SHELDON. *(Doing a grand job of the prayer.)* Walk with Job! Talk with Job! Ohhhhh, be with Job!

JUDY. Yes!

(MANNERS and BILL give JUDY disapproving looks and she clasps her hand over her mouth.)

TROUBLE IN MIND : 161

WILETTA. *(Starts to sing and is joined by* SHELDON *and* MILLIE.*)*
Death ain't nothin' but a robber, cantcha see, cantcha see . . .
MANNERS. *(Is in a real tizzy, watching to catch* BILL's *reaction to the scene, and trying with his whole body to keep the scene up and going.)* Eddie! Direction!
EDDIE. The door opens and Job enters!
WILETTA. Job, why you come here?

*(*MANNERS *doesn't like her reading. It is too direct and thoughtful.)*

MILLIE. *(Lashing out.)* They after you! They told you 'bout mixin' in with Turner and that votin'!
MANNERS. Oh, good girl!
WILETTA. I'm the one to talk to my boy!
JOHN. *(A frightened, shivering figure.)* If somebody could get me a wagon, I'll take the low road around Simpkin's Hollow and catch a train goin' away from here.
WILETTA. Shoulda gone 'fore you started this misery.

*(*MANNERS *indicates that she should get rougher, she tries.)*

Screamin' 'bout your rights! You got none! You got none!
JOHN. I'm askin' for help, I gotta leave!
MANNERS. *(To* JOHN.) Appeal, remember it's an appeal.
JOHN. *(As though a light has dawned.)* Ah, you're so right. *(Reads with tender appeal.)* I gotta leave.
MANNERS. Right.
WILETTA. You tryin' to tell me that you runnin' away?
SHELDON. *(Worried about* JOB's *escape and getting caught up outside of the scene.)* Sure! That's what he said in the line right there!

*(*MANNERS *silences* SHELDON *with a gesture.)*

WILETTA. You say you ain't done nothin' wrong?

*(*MANNERS *looks at* EDDIE *and* BILL *with despjair.)*

JOHN. I ain't lyin' . . .
WILETTA. Then there's no need to be runnin'. Ain't you got no faith?
SHELDON. *(Sings in a shaky voice as he raps out time.)*
Oh, wella, time of trouble is a lonesome time
Time of trouble is a lonesome time . . .

(Joined by MILLIE.)

Feel like I could die, feel like I could die . . .
WILETTA. Tell 'em you sorry, tell 'em you done wrong!
MANNERS. Relate, Wiletta. Relate to what's going on around you!

(To JOHN.)

Go on.
JOHN. I wasn't even votin' for a black man, votin' for somebody white same as they. *(Aside to* MANNERS.) Too much? Too little? I fell off.

*(*MANNERS *indicates that he's on the beam.)*

WILETTA. I ain't never voted!
SHELDON. No, Lord!
WILETTA. I don't care who get in! Don't make no nevermind to us!
MILLIE. The truth!
JOHN. *(All afire.)* When a man got a decent word to say for us down here, I gonna vote for him.
WILETTA. A decent word! And that's all you ever gonna get outta him. Dammit! He ain't gonna win nohow! They done said he ain't and they gonna see to it! And you gonna be dead . . . for a decent word!
JOHN. I ain't gonna wait to be killed.
WILETTA. There's only one right thing to do!

(Everyone turns page in unison.)

You got to go and give yourself up.

JOHN. But I ain't done nothin'.

SHELDON. *(Starts to sing again.)*
Wella, trouble is a lonesome thing . . . lonesome . . . lonesome . . .

MANNERS. *(The song even grates on him.)* Cut it, it's too much.

JUDY. My father will have you put in the county jail where you'll be safe.

JOHN. But I ain't done nothin'!

JUDY. I'm thinking of Ruby and the others, even if you aren't. I don't want murder in this community.

WILETTA. *(Screams.)* Boy, get down on your knees.

MANNERS. *(To EDDIE.)* Muscular tension.

(EDDIE makes a note.)

WILETTA. Oh, Lord, touch this boy's heart!

SHELDON. Mmmmmm, Hmmmmmmmm. Hmmmmmmm . . .

WILETTA. Reach him tonight! Take the fear and hatred out of his soul!

MILLIE. Mercy, Lord!

JOHN. Stop, I can't stand no more. Whatever you say, anything you say.

SHELDON. Praise the Lord!

EDDIE. Renard enters.

BILL. Carrie, you shouldn't be here.

WILETTA. I told her. I'm beggin' you to help my boy, sir. . . . *(She drops script and picks it up.)*

JOHN. Ohhh, I can't sustain.

MANNERS. Don't try. We're breaking everything down to the simplest components . . . I want simple reactions to given circumstances in order to highlight the outstanding phases.

(WILETTA finds her place.)

Okay, let it roll.

WILETTA. I'm beggin' you to help my boy.

BILL. Boy, you're amighty little fella to fly in the face of things people live by

'round here. I'll do what I can, what little I can.

WILETTA. Thank you, sir.

JUDY. Have Judge Willis put him in jail where he'll be safe.

BILL. Guess it wasn't his fault.

WILETTA. He don' know nothin'.

BILL. There are all kinds of white men in the world.

SHELDON. The truth.

BILL. This bird Akins got to sayin' the kind of things that was bound to stir you folks up.

MILLIE. I ain't paid him no mind myself.

BILL. Well, anything you want to take to the jailhouse with you? Like a washcloth and . . . well, whatever you might need.

JOHN. I don't know, don't know what I'm doin'.

BILL. Think you learned a lesson from all this?

MILLIE. You hear Mr. Renard?

SHELDON. He wanna know if you learned your lesson.

JOHN. I believed I was right.

SHELDON. Now you know you wasn't.

BILL. If anything happens, you tell the men Mr. Akins put notions in your head, understand?

SHELDON. He wanna know if you understand.

BILL. Come along, we'll put you in the jailhouse. Reckon I owe your ma and pa that much.

JOHN. I'm afraid, I so afraid. . . .

MILLIE. Just go, 'fore they get here.

EDDIE. Job turns and looks at his father.

(SHELDON places one finger to his lips and throws up his arms to show that he has no line.)

Finally he looks to his mother, she goes back to her ironing.

BILL. Petunia, see that Miss Carrie gets home safe.

MILLIE. Yes sir.

EDDIE. Job follows Renard out into the night as Ruby starts to sing.

WILETTA. *(Sings.)*
Keep me from sinkin' down
O, Lord, O, my Lord
Keep me from sinkin' down. . . .

MANNERS. Cut, relax, at ease!

MILLIE. *(Brushes lint from her skirt.)* I'll have to bring work clothes.

SHELDON. *(To* MILLIE.*)* I almost hit the number yesterday.

MILLIE. I'm glad you didn't.

*(*BILL *crosses to* MANNERS, *we hear snatches of their conversation as the others cross-talk.)*

JUDY. *(To* JOHN.*)* Did you finish my book?

*(*JOHN *claps his hand to his forehead in a typical* MANNERS *gesture.)*

BILL. *(A light conference on* WILETTA.*)* A line of physical action might . . .

SHELDON. *(To* MILLIE.*)* I almost got an apartment.

MANNERS. Limited emotional capacity.

MILLIE. *(To* SHELDON.*)* Almost don't mean a thing.

MANNERS. Well, it's coming. Sheldon, I like what's happening.

SHELDON. Thank you, does he give himself up to Judge Willis and get saved?

MANNERS. *(Flabbergasted, as are* JOHN, JUDY, BILL *and* EDDIE.*)* Shel, haven't you read it? Haven't you heard us read it?

SHELDON. No, I just go over and over my own lines, I ain't in the last of the third act.

JUDY. Are my motivations coming through?

MANNERS. Yeah, forget it. Sit down, Sheldon . . . just for you . . . Renard drives him toward jail, deputies stop them on the way, someone shoots and kills Job as he tries to escape, afterward they find out he was innocent, Renard makes everyone feel like a dog . . . they realize they were wrong and so forth.

SHELDON. And so forth.

MANNERS. He makes them realize that lynching is wrong. *(He refers to his notes.)*

SHELDON. *(To* WILETTA.*)* What was he innocent of?

WILETTA. I don't know.

JOHN. About the voting.

SHELDON. Uh-uh, he was guilty of that 'cause he done confessed.

MANNERS. Innocent of wrong-doing, Sheldon.

SHELDON. Uh-huh, oh, yeah.

MANNERS. Yale, you're on the right track. John, what can I say? You're great. Millie, you're growing, gaining command . . . I begin to feel an inner as well as the outer rendering.

JOHN. If we could run the sequence without interruption.

SHELDON. Yeah, then we could motor-ate and all that.

MANNERS. *(To* WILETTA.*)* Dear heart, I've got to tell you . . .

WILETTA. I ain't so hot.

MANNERS. Don't be sensitive, let me help you, will you?

WILETTA. *(Trying to handle matters in the same way as* JOHN *and* JUDY.*)* I know my relations and motivation may not be just so . . .

SHELDON. *(Wisely.)* Uh-huh, *motivation,* that's the thing.

WILETTA. They not right and I think I know why . . .

MANNERS. Darling, that's my department, will you listen?

*(*JOHN *is self-conscious about* WILETTA *and* SHELDON. *He is ashamed of them and has reached the point where he exchanges knowing looks with* BILL, EDDIE *and* MANNERS.*)*

WILETTA. You don't ever listen to me. You hear the others but not me. And it's 'cause of the school. 'Cause they know 'bout justifyin' and the . . . antagonist . . . I never studied that, so you don't want to hear me, that's all right.

JUDY. (*Stricken to the heart.*) Oh, don't say that.

SHELDON. He listen to me, and I ain't had it.

JOHN. (*Starts to put his arm around* WILETTA.) Oh, Wiletta . . .

WILETTA. (*Moving away from him.*) Oh, go on.

MANNERS. Wiletta, dear, I'm sorry if I've complicated things. I'll make it as clear as I can. You are pretending to act and I can see through your pretense. I want truth. What is truth? Truth is simply whatever you can bring yourself to believe, that is all. You must have integrity about your work . . . a sense of . . . well, sense.

WILETTA. I'm tryin' to lose myself like you say but . . .

JOHN. (*Wants to help but afraid to interrupt.*) Oh, no . . .

MANNERS. (*Sternly.*) You can't lose yourself, you are you . . . and you can't get away. You, Wiletta, must relate.

SHELDON. That's what I do.

WILETTA. I don't see why the boy couldn't get away . . . it's the killin' that . . . something's wrong. I may be in fast company but I got as much integrity as any. I didn't start workin' no yesterday.

MANNERS. No, Wiletta, no self-pity. Look, he can't escape this death. We want audience sympathy. We have a very subtle point to make, very subtle. . . .

BILL. I hate the kind of play that bangs you over the head with the message. Keep it subtle.

MANNERS. (*Getting very basic.*) We don't want to antagonize the audience.

WILETTA. It'll make 'em mad if he gets away?

MANNERS. This is a simple, sweet, lovable guy. Sheldon, does it offend you that he gives himself up to Judge Willis?

SHELDON. No, not if that's how they do.

MANNERS. We're making one beautiful, clear point . . . violence is wrong.

WILETTA. My friend, Miss Green, say she don't see why they act like this.

JOHN. (*Thinks he knows how to handle* WILETTA. *He is about to burst with an idea.* MANNERS *decides to let* JOHN *wade in.*) Look, think of the intellectual level here . . . they're under-privileged, uneducated. . . .

WILETTA. (*Letting* JOHN *know he's treading on thin ice.*) Look out, you ain't so smart.

JOHN. (*Showing so much of* MANNERS.) They've probably never seen a movie or television . . . never used a telephone. They . . . they're not like us. They're good, kind, folksy people . . . but they're ignorant, they just don't know.

WILETTA. You ain't the director.

SHELDON. (*To* JOHN.) You better hush.

MANNERS. We're dealing with simple, backward people but they're human beings.

WILETTA. 'Cause they colored, you tellin' me they're human bein's. . . . I *know* I'm a human bein'. . . . Listen here . . .

MANNERS. I will not listen! It does not matter to me that they're Negroes. Black, white, green or purple, I maintain there is only one race . . . the human race.

(SHELDON *bursts into applause.*)

MILLIE. That's true.

MANNERS. Don't think "Negro," think "people."

SHELDON. Let's stop segregatin' ourselves.

JOHN. (*To* WILETTA.) I didn't mean any harm, you don't understand. . . .

BILL. (*To* MILLIE *as he looks heavenward and acts out his weariness.*) Oh, honey child!

MILLIE. Don't call me no damn honey child!

BILL. Well, is my face red.

MILLIE. Yeah, and on you it looks good.

MANNERS. What's going on?

MILLIE. Honey child.

WILETTA. *(Mumbling as all dialogue falls pell-mell.)* Justify.

BILL. *(With great resignation.)* Trying to be friendly.

WILETTA. Justify.

MILLIE. Get friendly with someone else.

MANNERS. May we have order!

SHELDON. *(In a terrible flash of temper.)* That's why they don't do more colored shows! Always fightin'! Everybody hush, let this man direct! He don't even have to be here! Right now he could be out in Hollywood in the middle of a big investigation!

EDDIE. The word is production!

SHELDON. That's what I said, production.

EDDIE. No, you didn't.

SHELDON. What'd I say?

MANNERS. *(Bangs table.)* I will not countenance another outbreak of this nature. I say to each and everyone of you . . . I am in charge and I'll thank you to remember it. I've been much too lax, too informal. Well, it doesn't work. There's going to be order.

WILETTA. I was only sayin' . . .

MANNERS. I said *everyone!* My patience is at an end. I demand your concentrated attention. It's as simple as A, B, C, if you will apply yourselves. The threat of this horrible violence throws you into cold, stark fear. It's a perfectly human emotion, anyone would feel it. I'm not asking you to dream up some fantastic horror . . . it's a lynching. We've never actually seen such a thing, thank God . . . but allow your imagination to soar, to take hold of it . . . think.

SHELDON. I seen one.

MANNERS. *(Can't believe he heard right.)* What?

BILL. What did you see?

SHELDON. A lynchin', when I was a little boy 'bout nine years old.

JUDY. Oh, no.

WILETTA. How did it happen? Tell me, Sheldon did you really?

MANNERS. Would it help you to know, Wiletta?

WILETTA. I . . . guess . . . I don't know.

BILL. *(Not eager to hear about it.)* Will it bother you, Sheldon? It could be wrong for him . . . I don't know. . . .

(EDDIE gives MANNERS a doubtful look.)

MILLIE. That must be something to see.

MANNERS. *(With a sigh.)* Go on, Sheldon.

(MANNERS watches cast reactions.)

SHELDON. I think it was on a Saturday, yeah, it had to be or elsewise I woulda been in the field with my ma and pa.

WILETTA. What field?

SHELDON. The cotton field. My ma said I was too little to go every day but some of 'em younger'n me was out there all the time. My grandma was home with me. . . . *(Thinks of grandma and almost forgets his story.)*

WILETTA. What about the lynchin'?

SHELDON. It was Saturday and rainin' a sort of sifty rain. I was standin' at the window watchin' the lilac bush wavin' in the wind. A sound come to my ears like bees hummin' . . . was voices comin' closer and closer, screamin' and cursin'. My granny tried to pull me from the window. "Come on, chile." She said, "They gonna kill us all . . . hide!" But I was fightin' to keep from goin' with her, scared to go in the dark closet.

(JUDY places her hands over her ears and bows her head.)

The screamin' comin' closer and closer . . . and the screamin' was laughin'. . . . Lord, how they was laughin' . . . louder and louder. *(SHELDON rises and puts in his best performance to date. He raises one hand and creates a stillness . . . ev-*

eryone is spellbound.) Hush! Then I hear wagon wheels bumpin' over the wet, stony road, chains clankin'. Man drivin' the wagon, beatin' the horse . . . Ahhhhhhhh! Ahhhhhhhh! Horse just pullin' along . . . and then I saw it! Chained to the back of the wagon, draggin' and bumpin' along. . . . *(He opens his arms wide.)* The arms of it stretched out . . . a burnt, naked thing . . . a burnt, naked thing that once was a man . . . and I started to scream but no sound come out . . . just a screamin' but no sound. . . . *(He lowers his arms and brings the company back to the present.)* That was Mr. Morris that they killed. Mr. Morris. I remember one time he come to our house and was laughin' and talkin' and everything . . . and he give us a fruit cake that his wife made. Folks said he was crazy . . . you know, 'bout talkin' back . . . quick to speak his mind. I left there when I was seventeen. I don't want to live in no place like that.

MANNERS. When I hear of barbarism . . . I feel so wretched, so guilty.

SHELDON. Don't feel that way. You wouldn't kill nobody and do 'em like that . . . would you?

MANNERS. *(Hurt by the question.)* No, Sheldon.

SHELDON. That's what I know.

(BILL crosses and rests his hand on SHELDON's shoulder. SHELDON flinches because he hadn't noticed BILL's approach.)

Oh! I didn't see you. Did I help y'all by tellin' that story?

MANNERS. It was quite an experience. I'm shot. Break for lunch, we'll pick up in an hour, have a good afternoon session.

MILLIE. Makes me feel like goin' out in the street and crackin' heads.

JUDY. *(Shocked.)* Oh!

EDDIE. Makes my blood boil . . . but what can you do?

MANNERS. We're doing a play.

MILLIE. *(To JUDY.)* I'm starved. You promised to show us that Italian place.

JUDY. *(Surprised that MILLIE no longer feels violent.)* Why . . . sure, I'd love to. Let's have a festive lunch, with wine!

SHELDON. Yeah, that wine that comes in a straw bottle.

JUDY. Imported wine.

MILLIE. And chicken cacciatore . . . let's live!

WILETTA. *(Crosses to MANNERS while others are getting coats. She has hit on a scheme to make MANNERS see her point.)* Look here, I ain't gonna let you get mad with me. You supposed to be my buddy.

JOHN. Let's go!

MANNERS. *(Opens his arms to WILETTA.)* I'm glad you said that. You're my sweetheart.

MILLIE. Bill, how about you?

BILL. *(Places his hand on his stomach.)* The Italian place. Okay, count me in.

EDDIE. *(Stacking scripts.)* I want a king-size dish of clams . . . raw ones.

WILETTA. Wouldn't it be nice if the mother could say, "Son, you right! I don't want to send you outta here but I don't know what to do. . . ."

MANNERS. Darling, darling . . . no.

MILLIE. Wiletta, get a move on.

WILETTA. Or else she says "Run for it, Job!", and then they catch him like that . . . he's dead *anyway*, see?

MANNERS. *(Trying to cover his annoyance.)* It's not the script, it's *you*. Bronson does the writing, you do the acting, it's that simple.

SHELDON. One race, the human race. I like that.

JUDY. Veal Parmesan with oodles and oodles of cheese!

WILETTA. I was just thinkin' if I could . . .

MANNERS. *(Indicating script.)* Address yourself to this.

JUDY. *(To JOHN.)* Bring my book tomorrow.

JOHN. Cross my heart.

WILETTA. I just wanted to talk about . . .

MANNERS. You are going to get a spanking. *(He leaves with* EDDIE *and others.)*

MILLIE. Wiletta, come on!

WILETTA. *(Abruptly.)* I . . . I'll be there later.

MILLIE. *(Miffed by the short answer.)* Suit yourself.

JUDY. *(To* WILETTA.*)* It's on the corner of Sixth Avenue on this side of the street.

JOHN. Correction. Correction, Avenue of the Americas.

(Laughter from MANNERS, MILLIE, SHELDON *and* BILL *offstage.)*

JUDY. *(Posturing in her best theatrical style.)* But no one, absolutely no one, ever says it. He's impossible, absolutely impossible!

WILETTA. Oh, ain't he though.

JOHN. *(Bows to* JUDY *and indicates that she goes first.)* Dear Gaston, Alphonse will follow.

WILETTA. John, I told you everything wrong 'cause I didn't know better, that's the size of it. No fool like a old fool. You right, don't make sense to be bowin' and scrapin' and tommin'. . . . No, don't pay no attention to what I said.

JOHN. *(Completely* MANNERS.*)* Wiletta, my dear, you're my sweetheart, I love you madly and I think you're wonderfully magnificent!

JUDY. *(*JUDY *suddenly notices his posturing and hers, she feels silly. She laughs, laughter bordering on tears.)* John, you're a puppet with strings attached and so am I. Everyone's a stranger and I'm the strangest of all. *(She quickly leaves.)*

JOHN. Wiletta, don't forget to come over! *(He follows* JUDY.*)*

WILETTA. *(Paces up and down, tries doing her lines aloud.)* Only one thing to do, give yourself up! Give yourself up . . . give up . . . give up . . . give up . . . give up . . . give up.

(LIGHTS WHIRL AND FLICKER. BLUES RECORD comes in loud—then down—LIGHTS FLICKER to indicate passage of time. WILETTA *is gone. Stage is empty.)*

BILL *enters, removing his coat. He has a slight attack of indigestion and belches his disapproval of pizza pie. Others can be heard laughing and talking offstage.*

BILL. Ohhhhhh, Ahhhhh. . . .

MANNERS. *(Enters with* EDDIE. EDDIE *proceeds to the table and script.* MAN-NERS *is just getting over the effects of a good laugh . . . but his mirth suddenly fades as he crosses to* BILL.*)* I am sorry you felt compelled to tell that joke about the colored minister and the stolen chicken.

BILL. Trying to be friendly . . . I don't know . . . I even ate pizza.

EDDIE. I always *think* . . . think first, is this the right thing to say, would I want anyone to say this to me?

(Burst of laughter from offstage.)

BILL. Oh, you're so noble, you give me a pain in the ass. Love thy neighbor as thyself, now I ask you, is that a reasonable request?

MANNERS. *(For fear the others will hear.)* All right. Knock it off.

BILL. Okay, I said I was sorry, but for what . . . I'll never know.

*(*SHELDON, MILLIE, JUDY *and* JOHN *enter in a hilarious mood.* JUDY *is definitely feeling the wine.* SHELDON *is supplying the fun.)*

SHELDON. Sure, I was workin' my hind parts off . . . Superintendent of the buildin' . . .

JOHN. But the tenants, Shel! That's a riot!

SHELDON. One day a man came along and offered me fifty dollars a week just to walk across the stage real slow. *(Mimics his acting role.)* Sure, I took it! Hard as I worked I was glad to slow down!

(Others laugh.)

JUDY. *(Holds her head.)* Ohhhhhh, that wine.

MILLIE. Wasn't it good? I wanna get a whole *case* of it for the holidays. All that I have to do! My liquors, wreathes, presents, cards . . . I'm gonna buy my husband a tape recorder.

JUDY. *(To JOHN.)* I'm sorry I hurt your feelings but you are a little puppet, and I'm a little puppet, and all the world. . . . *(She impresses the lesson by tapping JOHN on his chest.)*

MANNERS. Judy, I want to go over something with you. . . .

JUDY. No, you don't . . . you're afraid I'm going to . . . hic. 'Fraid I'll go overboard on the friendship deal and *complicate* matters . . . complications. . . .

MANNERS. Two or three glasses of wine, she's delirious. Do you want some black coffee?

JUDY. No, no, I only have hiccups.

MILLIE. *(To JOHN.)* Which would you rather have, a tape recorder or a camera?

JOHN. I don't know.

SHELDON. I'd rather have some money, make mine cash.

MANNERS. *(To JUDY.)* Why don't you sit down and get yourself together? *(She sits.)*

JOHN. *(To MANNERS.)* I . . . I think I have some questions about Wiletta and the third act.

MANNERS. It's settled, don't worry, John, she's got it straight.

JOHN. I know but it seems . . .

MANNERS. Hoskins sat out front yesterday afternoon. He's mad about you. First thing he says, "Somebody's going to try and steal that boy from us."

JOHN. *(Very pleased.)* I'm glad I didn't know he was there.

MANNERS. Eddie, call it, will you? Okay, attention!

EDDIE. Beginning of the third.

(Company quiets down, opens scripts. WILETTA enters.)

MANNERS. You're late.

WILETTA. I know it. *(To MILLIE.)* I had a bowl of soup and was able to relate to it and justify, no trouble at all. *(To MANNERS.)* I'm not gonna take up your time now but I wanta see you at the end of the afternoon.

MANNERS. Well . . . I . . . I'll let you know . . . we'll see.

WILETTA. It's important.

MANNERS. *(Ignoring her and addressing entire company.)* Attention, I want to touch on a corner of what we did this morning and then we'll highlight the rest of three!

(Actors rise and start for places.)

John, top of page four.

JOHN. When a man has a decent word to say for us down here, I gonna vote for him.

WILETTA. *(With real force. She is lecturing him rather than scolding.)* A decent word? And that's all you ever gonna get out of him. Dammit, he ain't gonna win nohow. They done said he ain't and they gonna see to it! And you gonna be dead for a decent word.

MANNERS. *(To EDDIE.)* This is deliberate.

JOHN. I gotta go, I ain't gonna wait to be killed.

WILETTA. There's only one right thing to do. You got to go and give yourself up.

JOHN. I ain't done nothin'.

JUDY. My father will have Judge Willis put you in the County Jail where you'll be safe.

(MANNERS is quite disheartened.)

WILETTA. Job, she's tryin' to help us.

JUDY. I'm thinking of the others even if you aren't. I don't want murder in this community.

WILETTA. Boy, get down on your knees.

(JOHN *falls to his knees.*)

Oh, Lord, touch this boy's heart. Reach him tonight, take the fear and hatred out of his soul!

SHELDON. Hmmmmmmm, mmmmmmmm, mmmmmmmmm. . . .

MILLIE. Mercy, Lord.

JOHN. Stop, I can't stand anymore. . . .

(WILETTA *tries to raise* JOHN.)

MANNERS. No, keep him on his knees.

JOHN. I can't stand anymore . . . whatever you say. . . .

(*Again* WILETTA *tries to raise him.*)

SHELDON. (*To* WILETTA.) He say keep him on his knees.

WILETTA. Aw, get up off the floor, wallowin' around like that.

(*Everyone is shocked.*)

MANNERS. Wiletta, this is not the time or place to . . .

WILETTA. All that crawlin' and goin' on before me . . . hell, I ain't the one tryin' to lynch him. This ain't sayin' nothin', don't make sense. Talkin' 'bout the truth is anything I can believe . . . well, I don't believe this.

MANNERS. I will not allow you to interrupt in this disorganized manner.

WILETTA. You been askin' me what I think and where things come from and how come I thought it and all that. Where is this comin' from?

(*Company murmuring in the background.*)

Tell me, why this boy's people turned against him? Why we sendin' him out into the teeth of a lynch mob? I'm his mother and I'm sendin' him to his death. This is a lie.

JOHN. But his mother doesn't understand . . .

WILETTA. Everything people do is counta their mother . . . well, maybe so.

JOHN. There have been cases of men dragged from their homes . . . for voting and asking others to vote.

WILETTA. But they was *dragged* . . . they come with guns and dragged 'em out. They weren't sent to be killed by their mama. The writer wants the damn white man to be the hero—and I'm the villain.

MILLIE. I think we're all tired.

SHELDON. Outta order, outta order, you outta order. This ain't the time.

MANNERS. Quiet please. She's confused and I'd just as soon have everything made clear.

WILETTA. Would you do this to a son of yours?

MANNERS. She places him in the hands of Judge Willis and . . .

WILETTA. And I tell you she knows better.

BILL. It's only because she trusts and believes. Couldn't you trust and believe in Al?

MANNERS. Bill, please.

WILETTA. No, I wouldn't trust him with my son's life.

MANNERS. Thank you.

SHELDON. She don't mean it.

WILETTA. Judge Willis! Why don't his people help him?

MANNERS. The story goes a certain way and . . .

WILETTA. It oughta go another way.

ENTIRE COMPANY. (*In unison.*) Talk about it later. We're all tired. Yes. We need a rest. Sometime your own won't help you.

MANNERS. Leave her alone! (MANNERS *is on fire now. He loves the challenge of this conflict and is determined to win the battle. He must win.*) Why this great fear of death? Christ died for something and . . .

WILETTA. Sure, they came and got him and hauled him off to jail. His mother didn't turn him in, in fact, the one who did it was one of them so-called friends.

MANNERS. His death proved something. Job's death brings him the lesson.

WILETTA. That they should stop lynchin' *innocent* men! Fine thing! Lynch the guilty, is that the idea? The dark-skinned Oliver Twist. *(Points to* JOHN.*)* That's you. Yeah, I mean, you got to go to school to justify this!

MANNERS. Wiletta, I've listened, I've heard you out . . .

WILETTA. *(To* SHELDON.*)* And you echoin' every damn word he says—"Keep him on his knees."

MANNERS. I've heard you out and even though you think you know more than the author . . .

WILETTA. You don't want to hear. You are a prejudiced man, a prejudiced racist.

(Gasp from company.)

MANNERS. *(Caught off-guard.)* I will not accept that from you or anyone else.

WILETTA. I told this boy to laugh and grin at everything you said, well . . . I ain't laughin'.

MANNERS. While you give me hell-up-the-river, I'm supposed to stand here and take it with a tolerance beyond human endurance. I'm white! You think it's so wonderful to be white? I've got troubles up to here! But I don't expect anyone to hand me anything and it's high time you got rid of that notion. No, I never worked in a cotton field, I didn't. I was raised in a nice, comfortable, nine-room house in the mid-West . . . and I learned to say nigger, kike, sheeny, spick, dago, wop and chink . . . I heard 'em plenty! I was raised by a sweet, dear, kind old aunt, who spent her time gathering funds for missionaries . . . but she almost turned our town upside down when Mexicans moved in on our block. I know about

troubles . . . my own! I've never been *handed* any gifts. Oh, it's so grand to be white! I had to crawl and knuckle under step by step. What I want and what I believe, indeed! I directed blood, guts, fist-fights, bedroom farces and the lowest kind of dirtied-up sex until I earned the respect of this business.

WILETTA. But would you send your son out to . . .

MANNERS. I proclaim this National Truth Week! Whites! You think we belong to one great, grand fraternity? They stole and snatched from me for years, and I'm a club member! Ever hear of an idea man? They picked my brains! They stripped me! They threw me cash and I let the credit go! My brains milked, while somebody else climbed on my back to take bows. But I didn't beg for mercy . . . why waste your breath? I learned one thing that's the only damned truth worth knowing . . . you get nothin' for nothin', but nothin'! No favors, no dreams served up on silver platters. Now . . . finally I get something for all of us . . . but it's not enough for you! I'm prejudiced! Get wise, there's damned few of us interested in putting on a colored show at all, much less one that's going to say anything. It's rough out here, it's a hard world! Do you think I can stick my neck out by telling the truth about you? There are billions of things that *can't be said* . . . do you follow me, billions! Where the hell do you think I can raise a hundred thousand dollars to tell the unvarnished truth? *(Picks up the script and waves it.)* So, maybe it's a lie . . . but it's one of the finest lies you'll come across for a damned long time! Here's bitter news, since you're livin' off truth. . . . The American public is not ready to see you the way you want to be seen because, one, they don't believe it, two, they don't want to believe it, and three, they're convinced they're superior—and that, my friend, is why Carrie and Renard have to carry the ball!

Get it? Now you wise up and aim for the soft spot in that American heart, let 'em pity you, make 'em weep buckets, be helpless, make 'em feel so damned sorry for you that they'll lend a hand in easing up the pressure. You've got a free ride. Coast, baby, coast.

WILETTA. Would you send your son out to be murdered?

MANNERS. (So wound up, he answers without thinking.) Don't compare yourself to me! What goes for my son doesn't necessarily go for yours! Don't compare him (Points to JOHN.) . . . with three strikes against him, don't compare him with my son, they've got nothing in common . . . not a Goddam thing! (He realizes what he has said, also that he has lost company sympathy. He is utterly confused and embarrassed by his own statement.) I tried to make it clear.

JOHN. It is clear.

(MANNERS quickly exits to dressing room. EDDIE follows him. JUDY has an impulse to follow.)

BILL. No, leave him alone.

JOHN. (To WILETTA.) I feel like a fool. . . . Hmmph, "Don't think Negro, think people."

SHELDON. (To BILL.) You think he means we're fired?

BILL. I don't know . . . I don't know. . . .

MILLIE. Wiletta, this should have been discussed with everyone first.

SHELDON. Done talked yourself out of a job.

BILL. Shel, you don't know that.

SHELDON. (During the following scene, SHELDON is more active and dynamic than ever before.) Well, he didn't go out there to bake her no birthday cake.

(JUDY is quietly crying.)

MILLIE. We got all the truth we bargained for and then some.

WILETTA. Yes, I spoke my mind and he spoke his.

BILL. We have a company representative, Sheldon is the deputy. Any complaints we have should be handled in an orderly manner. Equity has rules, the rule book says . . .

SHELDON. I left my rule book home. Furthermore, I don't think I want to be the deputy.

MILLIE. He was dead right about some things but I didn't appreciate that last remark.

SHELDON. (To WILETTA.) You can't spit in somebody's eye and tell 'em you was washin' it out.

BILL. Sheldon, now is not the time to resign.

SHELDON. (Taking charge.) All right, I'm tryin' to lead 'em, tryin' to play peace-maker. Shame on y'all! Look at the U.N.!

MILLIE. The U.N.?

SHELDON. Yes, the United Nations. You think they run their business by blabbin' everything they think? No! They talk sweet and polite 'til they can outslick the next feller. Wisdom! The greatest gift in the world, they got it! (To WILETTA.) Way you talked, I thought you had the 'tomic bomb.

WILETTA. I'm sick of people signifyin' we got no sense.

SHELDON. I know. I'm the only man in the house and what am I doin'? Whittlin' a doggone stick. But I whittled it, didn't I? I can't write a play and I got no money to put one on. . . . Yes! I'm gonna whittle my stick! (Stamps his foot to emphasize the point.)

JOHN. (Very noble and very worried.) How do you go about putting in a notice?

SHELDON. (To JOHN.) Hold on 'til I get to you. (To WILETTA.) Now, when he gets back here, you be sure and tell him.

WILETTA. Tell him what?

SHELDON. Damn, tell him you sorry.

BILL. Oh, he doesn't want that.

WILETTA. Shame on him if he does.

MILLIE. I don't want to spend the rest of the day wondering why he walked out.

WILETTA. I'm playin' a leadin' part and I want this script changed or else.

SHELDON. Hush up, before the man hears you.

MILLIE. Just make sure you're not the one to tell him. You're a great one for runnin' to management and telling your guts.

SHELDON. I never told management nothin', anybody say I did is lyin'.

JUDY. Let's ask for a *quiet* talk to straighten things out.

BILL. No. This is between Wiletta and Manners and I'm sure they can . . .

JOHN. We all ought to show some integrity.

SHELDON. Integrity . . . got us in a big mess.

MILLIE. (To JOHN.) You can't put in your notice until after opening night. You've got to follow Equity rules. . . .

SHELDON. Yeah, he's trying to defy the union.

WILETTA. (Thumping the script.) This is a damn lie.

MILLIE. But you can't tell people what to write, that's censorship.

SHELDON. (To WILETTA.) And that's another point in your disfavor.

JOHN. They can write what they want but we don't have to do it.

SHELDON. You outta order!

BILL. (To JOHN.) Oh, don't keep stirring it up, heaping on coals . . .

JUDY. Wiletta, maybe if we appeal to Mr. Hoskins or Mr. Bronson . . .

SHELDON. The producer and the author ain't gonna listen to her, after all . . . they white same as Manners.

JUDY. I resent that!

BILL. I do too, Shel.

JUDY. I've had an awful lot of digs thrown at me . . . remarks about white, white . . . and I do resent it.

JOHN. (To JUDY. *He means what can you expect from* SHELDON.) Sheldon.

BILL. (To JUDY.) I'm glad you said that.

SHELDON. I'm sorry, I won't say nothin' 'bout white. (To WILETTA.) Look here, Hoskins, Manners, and Bronson . . . they got things in . . . er . . . common, you know what I mean?

WILETTA. Leave me alone . . . and suit yourselves.

MILLIE. I know what's right but I need this job.

SHELDON. There you go . . . talk.

WILETTA. Thought your husband doesn't want you to work.

MILLIE. He doesn't but I have to anyway.

JUDY. But you'll still be in New York. If this falls through I'll have to go back to Bridgeport . . . before I even get started.

JOHN. Maybe I'll never get another job.

MILLIE. Like Al Manners says, there's more to this life than the truth. (To JUDY.) You'll have to go to Bridgeport. Oh, how I wish I had a Bridgeport.

BILL. Okay, enough, *I'm* the villain. I get plenty of work, forgive me.

JUDY. Life scares me, honestly it does.

SHELDON. When you kick up a disturbance, the man's in his rights to call the cops . . . police car will come rollin' up here, next thing you know . . . you'll be servin' time.

MILLIE. Don't threaten her!

JOHN. Why don't you call a cop *for* him . . . try it.

(HENRY *enters carrying a paper bag.*)

HENRY. I got Mr. Manners some nice Danish, cheese and prune.

MILLIE. He can't eat it right now . . . leave it there.

(EDDIE *enters with a shaken but stern attitude.*)

EDDIE. Attention company. You are

all dismissed for the day. I'll telephone you about tomorrow's rehearsal.

SHELDON. Tell Mr. Manners I'm gonna memorize my first act.

(EDDIE *exits and* SHELDON *talks to company.*)

I still owe the doctor money . . . and I can't lift no heavy boxes or be scrubbin' no floors. If I was a drinkin' man I'd get drunk.

MILLIE. Tomorrow is another day. Maybe everybody will be in better condition to . . . talk . . . just talk it all out. Let's go to the corner for coffee and a calm chat. (*Suddenly solicitous with* JUDY.) How about you, honey, wouldn't you like to relax and look over the situation? Bill?

BILL. I have to study for my soap opera . . . but thanks.

JUDY. Yes, let's go talk.

MILLIE. John? Wiletta, honey, let's go for coffee.

WILETTA. I'll be there after a while. Go on.

JOHN. We couldn't go without you.

SHELDON. We don't want to leave you by yourself in this old theater.

WILETTA. There are times when you got to be alone. *This is mine.*

(JOHN *indicates they should leave.* MILLIE, SHELDON, JUDY, JOHN *and* BILL *exit.*)

HENRY. Are you cryin'?

WILETTA. Yes.

HENRY. Ah, don't do that, It's too nice a day. (*Sits near tape recorder.*) I started to throw coffee at him that time when he kicked up a fuss, but you got to take a lotta things in this life.

WILETTA. Divide and conquer . . . that's the way they get the upper hand. A telephone call for tomorrow's rehearsal . . . they won't call me. . . . But I'm gonna show up any damn way. The next move is his. He'll have to fire me.

HENRY. Whatcha say?

WILETTA. We have to go further and do better.

HENRY. That's a good one. I'll remember that. What's on this, music?

WILETTA. (*Turns the machine on and down. The applause plays.*) Canned applause. When you need a bit of instant praise . . . you turn it on . . . and there you are.

(*He tries it.*)

HENRY. Canned applause. They got everything these days. Time flies. I bet you can't guess how old I am.

WILETTA. Not more than sixty.

HENRY. I'm seventy-eight.

WILETTA. Imagine that. A fine-lookin' man like you.

(*Sound of police siren in street.*)

HENRY. What's that?

WILETTA. Police siren.

HENRY. They got a fire engine house next to where I live. God-in-heaven, you never heard such a noise . . . and I'm kinda deaf. . . . Didn't know that, did you?

WILETTA. No, I didn't. Some live by what they call great truths. Henry, I've always wanted to do somethin' real grand . . . in the theater . . . to stand forth at my best . . . to stand up here and do anything I want. . . .

HENRY. Like my father . . . he was in vaudeville . . . doin' the softshoe and tippin' his hat to the ladies. . . .

WILETTA. Yes, somethin' grand.

HENRY. (*Adjusting the tape recorder to play applause.*) Do it . . . do it. I'm the audience.

WILETTA. I don't remember anything grand . . . I can't recall.

HENRY. Say somethin' from the Bible . . . like the twenty-third psalm.

WILETTA. Oh, I know. (*She comes downstage and recites beautifully from Psalm 133.*)

Behold how good and how pleasant it is

for brethren to dwell together in unity. It is like the precious ointment upon the head, that ran down upon the beard, even Aaron's beard; that went down to the skirts of his garment; as the dew of Hermon, and as the dew that descended upon the mountains of Zion; for there the Lord commanded the blessing, even life forevermore.

(HENRY turns on applause as WILETTA stands tall for the CURTAIN.)

CURTAIN

Langston Hughes

Music by David Martin

Simply Heavenly

A   COMEDY   WITH   MUSIC

SIMPLY HEAVENLY

Simply Heavenly was first presented at the 85th Street Playhouse, New York City, May 21, 1957.

CHARACTER NOTES FOR *SIMPLY HEAVENLY*

GENERAL: The characters in *Simply Heavenly* are, on the whole, ordinary, hard-working lower-income bracket Harlemites. Paddy's Bar is like a neighborhood club, and most of its patrons are not drunkards or bums. Their small kitchenette rooms or overcrowded apartments cause them to seek the space and company of the bar. Just as others seek the church as a social center, or the poolhall, or dancehall, these talkative ones seek the bar.

SIMPLE: Simple is a Chaplinesque character, slight of build, awkwardly graceful, given to flights of fancy, and positive statements of opinion—stemming from a not so positive soul. He is dark with a likable smile, ordinarily dressed, except for rather flamboyant summer sport shirts. Simple tries hard to succeed, but the chips seldom fall just right. Yet he bounces like a rubber ball. He may go down, but he always bounds back up.

JOYCE: Joyce is a quiet girl more inclined toward club work than bars, toward "culture" rather than good-timing. But she is not snobbish or cold. She is tall, brownskin, given to longish earrings, beads, scarfs, and dangling things, very feminine, and cries easily. Her charm is her sincerity.

BOYD: Boyd has probably been halfway through college before his army service in Europe. Serious-minded, pleasant-looking, trying to be a writer, perhaps taking English courses at New York University on the last of his G. I. money. Almost every Harlem bar has such a fellow among its regular customers, who acts sometimes as a kind of arbiter when "intellectual" discussions come up.

ZARITA. Zarita is a lively bar-stool girl wearing life like a loose garment, but she is *not* a prostitute. Brassy-voiced, good-hearted, good-looking, playing the field for fun and drinks, she lives a come-day-go-day existence, generous in accepting or giving love, money, or drinks. A good dancer.

MISS MAMIE: Mamie is a hard-working domestic, using biting words to protect a soft heart and a need for love too often betrayed.

GITFIDDLE: Gitfiddle is a folk artist going to seed, unable to compete with the jukebox, TV, and the radio, having only his guitar and his undisciplined talents. He furnishes all the music, with the Barfly pianist, for the songs and interludes.

MADAM BUTLER: Madam Butler has a bark that is worse than her bite—but her bark is bad enough. Large, fat, comical and terrible, she runs her rooming house as Hitler ran Germany.

CHARACTERS

JESSE B. SEMPLE
MADAM BUTLER
ANANIAS BOYD
MRS. CADDY

JOYCE LANE
HOPKINS
PIANIST
MISS MAMIE
BODIDDLY
CHARACTER

MELON
GITFIDDLE
ZARITA
ARCIE
JOHN JASPER
ALI BABA
A POLICEMAN
A NURSE

TIME: *The present.*
PLACE: *Harlem, U. S. A.*
MOOD: *Of the moment.*

SYNOPSIS OF SCENES

ACT ONE

SCENE   1: *Simple's room.*
SCENE   2: *Joyce's room.*
SCENE   3: *Paddy's bar.*
SCENE   4: *Hospital room.*
SCENE   5: *Paddy's bar.*
SCENE   6: *Joyce's room.*
SCENE   7: *Simple's room.*

ACT TWO

SCENE   1: *Paddy's bar.*
SCENE   2: *Joyce's room.*
SCENE   3: *Simple's room.*
SCENE   4: *Paddy's bar.*
SCENE   5: *Simple's room.*
SCENE   6: *Lenox Avenue.*
SCENE   7: *Joyce's room.*
SCENE   8: *Simple's room.*
SCENE   9: *Paddy's bar.*
SCENE 10: *A phone booth.*
SCENE 11: *Simple's room.*

MUSICAL NUMBERS

ACT ONE

SCENE   2: *"Simply Heavenly."* Joyce and Simple.
SCENE   5: *"Did You Ever Hear the Blues?"* Mamie and Melon.
SCENE   6: *"Deep in Love With You."* Simple.

SCENE   7: *"I'm Gonna Be John Henry."* Simple.

ACT TWO

SCENE   1: *"When I'm in a Quiet Mood."* Mamie and Melon.
"Look for the Morning Star." Pianist and Joyce.
SCENE   2: *Look for the Morning Star."* Joyce and Simple.
"I Want Somebody to Come Home To." Joyce.
SCENE   3: *"Let's Ball Awhile."* Zarita and Guests.
SCENE   9: *"A Good Old Girl."* Mamie.
SCENE 11: *"Look for the Morning Star."* Ensemble.

GUITAR MUSIC

The guitar music is all live, provided for interludes between scenes by Gitfiddle offstage in wings, with amplifier if needed on guitar. This music may be variations on "Did You Ever Hear the Blues?" or improvised blues chords. The interlude music is not published. If guitarist is a good folk musician, he can easily improvise it. If not, use sufficient portions of "Did You Ever Hear the Blues?" to cover the stage waits between scenes; or any traditional folk blues.

The set is divided into three sections: Down Right, Simple's room; Down Left, Joyce's room; and Up Center, Paddy's Bar. A traveler, or a scrim of Lenox Avenue shops and bars, can be used to block off the bar during the scenes in Joyce's and Simple's rooms. Scenes on the street are played Down Center, in front of Paddy's Bar. The traveler can be closed during these scenes also. The entrance to Simple's room is downstage in the Right wall. There is a bed against the upstage wall of the room, and a dresser marks the Left wall of his room. The entrance to Joyce's room is downstage in the Left wall, with the bed against the upstage wall of the room and the dresser marking the Right wall. Joyce's room also has a screen or a closet up Left. A chair in each bedroom.

In Paddy's Bar, the entrance is upstage in the Right wall. The bar runs parallel to the rear wall. The piano is against the Right wall, below the entrance door. A stool Left of the piano and another stool just below it. Three tables with chairs are scattered around the bar. All furniture in the bar section is located upstage of the traveler.

ACT ONE

SCENE 1

A lonely guitar is playing in the darkness—it's the Blues . . .

Simple's room. Early spring evening. SIMPLE, *just coming home from work, removes his jacket as he enters, but before he can hang it up, the voice of* MADAM BUTLER, *his landlady, is heard calling up the stairs, through the half-open door.*

LANDLADY. Mr. Semple! Oh, Mr. Semple!

SIMPLE. Yes'm?

LANDLADY. I heard you come in! Mr. Semple, would you mind taking Trixie out for a walk? My arthritis is bothering me.

SIMPLE. Madam Butler, please! I've got no time to walk no dog tonight. Joyce is waiting for me.

LANDLADY. From all I've heard, that girl's been waiting for you to marry her for years! A few minutes of waiting for you to show up tonight won't hurt.

SIMPLE. Madam, my private affairs ain't none of your business.

LANDLADY. Um-hum! Well, you don't need to take Trixie to no tree—just the nearest fireplug.

(BOYD, *a fellow-roomer, peers in.*)

SIMPLE. Aw, I ain't hardly got home from work good, yet. . . . Hello, Boyd. Come on in. Landladies is a bodiddling! How come she never make none of the other roomers—or you—to walk her dog?

BOYD. She knows I won't do it, that's why?

SIMPLE. Don't you ever get behind in your rent?

BOYD. Not to the point of walking dogs. But you seem to walk Trixie pretty often.

SIMPLE. Mostly always.

LANDLADY. Did you say you would take the dog?

SIMPLE. Oh, hell, lemme go walk the bitch.

LANDLADY. No profanity in my house.

SIMPLE. Madam, that's a perfectly good word meaning a fine girl dog—bitch —for female dog.

LANDLADY. There'll be no bitches in my house—and that goes for your girl friend, Zarita, too.

SIMPLE. I'll thank you to leave my friends out of this.

LANDLADY. I'll thank you to keep your profanity to yourself. This is a decent house. Now, come on and walk my dog —else pay me my rent.

SIMPLE. I'll walk your dog—because I love Trixie, though, that's what! If I had a dog, I wouldn't keep it penned up in the house all day neither. Poor old thing, airless as she is.

LANDLADY. She's not hairless.

SIMPLE. I said *airless*, Madam! Shut up airtight, wonder Trixie don't get arthritis, too. Dogs and womens, dogs and womens! Damn! What am I gonna do?

BOYD. Good luck, pal.

(SIMPLE *and* BOYD *exit. BLACKOUT. In the darkness, Trixie's bark is heard. Auto HORNS, street NOISES.* SIMPLE's *voice addresses the barking dog.*)

SIMPLE. Now, Trixie, come on now. Come on, Trixie, do your duty. Leave that other dog alone, Trixie! Hound, get away from here! O.K., O.K., let's head on in the house. *(Bark.)* Now, go on to your madam. I guess you love her. Well, I love somebody, too! My choice, Joyce! She's the one I found—and that's where I'm bound. Trixie, that's where I am bound.

(The music of "Simply Heavenly" rises happily as the LIGHTS come up to reveal JOYCE's room.)

ACT ONE

SCENE 2

Joyce's room a bit later. JOYCE is singing as, in a frilly dressing gown, she is putting her clothes away.

JOYCE.

> Love is simply heavenly!
> What else could it be?
> When love's made in heaven
> And you are made for me.
> Love is simply heavenly!
> What else can I say?
> When love sends an angel
> To hold me close this way.
> Love is like a dream
> That's too good to be true,
> But when your lips kiss mine
> The dream turns into you.
> Yes, it's simply heavenly!
> Our love's just divine—
> For love is made in heaven
> And you, my love, are mine!

> Love is simply heavenly—

(VOICE of her LANDLADY calls from below stairs.)

MRS. CADDY. Oo-oo-oo-oo! Miss Lane!
JOYCE. Yes?
MRS. CADDY. I'm letting Mr. Semple come up. OK?
JOYCE. Yes, indeed, Mrs. Caddy, I'm expecting him.

(SIMPLE knocks lightly and enters grinning.)

SIMPLE. Hey, Baby! *(He closes the door, to which JOYCE objects.)*
JOYCE. Jess! No! Just a crack. . . .
SIMPLE. Aw, your old landlady's worse than mine. At least I can shut my door when I got company.
JOYCE. You're a man, I'm a—

(SIMPLE hugs JOYCE.)

SIMPLE. Lady! Which is what I like about you. Joyce, morals is your middle name. But you can still be a lady behind closed doors.
JOYCE. I know, Jess, those are the landlady's rules. Besides, I respect Mrs. Caddy.
SIMPLE. She don't respect you if she thinks soon as the door is shut—
JOYCE. Sshhss! Come on, rest your jacket, honey. It's warm.
SIMPLE. I knowed there was something! I forgot to bring your ice cream! I passed right by the place, too!
JOYCE. We can walk out for a soda.
SIMPLE. Or a beer?
JOYCE. Tomorrow's communion Sunday, and I do not drink beer before communion.
SIMPLE. You just don't drink beer, period! Gimme a little sugar and we'll skip the beer.
JOYCE. Don't think I'll skip the ice cream.
SIMPLE. Let's set on the— *(He dances toward the studio bed.)*
JOYCE. There's a chair.
SIMPLE. Baby, what's the matter? Don't you trust me yet?
JOYCE. I don't mind you being close to me. But when you get close to a bed, too—
SIMPLE. Then you don't trust yourself.
JOYCE. Have you ever known me to—
SIMPLE. That's the trouble . . .
JOYCE. That goes with marriage, not

courtship. And if you don't move on from courtship to engagement soon, Jess Semple, and do something about that woman in Baltimore.

SIMPLE. My wife! Isabel—she run me out—but she could claim I left her. She could find some grounds to get a divorce.

JOYCE. Since you're not together, why don't you get one?

SIMPLE. Joyce, I don't want to pay for no woman's divorce I don't love. And I do not love Isabel. Also, I ain't got the money.

JOYCE. I would help you pay for it.

SIMPLE. One thing I would not let you do, Joyce, is pay for no other woman's divorce. No!

JOYCE. Well, if you and I just paid for half of it, you'd only be paying for your part of the divorce.

SIMPLE. That woman wants me to pay for it all. And, Joyce, I don't love her. I love you. Joyce, do you want me to commit bigamy?

JOYCE. Five years you've been away from your wife—three years since you met me! In all that time you haven't reached a point yet where you can ask for my hand without committing bigamy. I don't know how my love holds out so long on promises. But now my friends are all asking when I'm going to get married. Even my landlady's saying it's a mighty long time for a man to just be "coming around calling," just sitting doing nothing.

SIMPLE. I agree, baby—when there ain't no action, I get kinder drowsy.

JOYCE. Well, to me, a nice conversation is action.

SIMPLE. Conversationing makes me sleepy.

JOYCE. Then you ought to go to bed early instead of hanging over Paddy's Bar until all hours. You have got to go to work just like I do.

SIMPLE. When I sleep, I sleep fast.

Anyhow, I can't go to bed early just because you do, Joyce, until—unless—

JOYCE. Until what?

SIMPLE. Until we're married.

JOYCE. Simple!

SIMPLE. But, listen! It's Saturday night, fine outside. Spring in Harlem! Come on, let's us get some ice cream.

JOYCE. OK, but, Jess, are you coming to church in the morning to see me take communion?

SIMPLE. You know I'll be there. We'll just take a little stroll down Seventh Avenue now and catch some air, heh?

JOYCE. And you'll bring me home early, so we can both get our rest.

SIMPLE. In a jiffy, then I'll turn in, too.

JOYCE. You don't mean into a bar?

SIMPLE. Baby, one thing I *bar* is bars.

JOYCE. Turn your back so I can dress.

SIMPLE. Don't stand over there. Anybody could be looking in.

JOYCE. There are no peeping-toms in this house.

(SIMPLE *turns his back as she dresses, but drops his pack of cigarettes on the floor, bends down to get it, then remains that way, looking at Joyce from between his legs.*)

Baby, is your back turned?

SIMPLE. Yes'm.

(JOYCE *glances his way, clutches her dress to her bosom and screams.*)

JOYCE. Oh, Simple!

SIMPLE. I love it when you call me Simple. (*Head still down, he proceeds to turn a somersault, coming up seated on the floor with his back toward her.*) Now say my back ain't turned.

JOYCE. I didn't mean you had to turn inside out.

SIMPLE. That's the way you've got my heart—turned in. . . . (*He turns his eyes to look at her.*)

JOYCE. Then turn your head so I can dress.

SIMPLE. O.K., Joyce. Now, is everything all right?

JOYCE. Everything is all right.

SIMPLE. So you feel O.K.?

JOYCE. Simply heavenly! Oh, Jess, it's wonderful to be in love.

SIMPLE. Just wonderful—wonderful—wonderful—

(As JOYCE dresses, they sing.)

BOTH.
> Love is simply heavenly!
> What else could it be?
> When love's made in heaven
> And you are made for me.
> Love is simply heavenly!
> What else can I say?
> When love sends an angel
> To hold me close this way.
> Love is like a dream
> That's too good to be true,
> But when your lips kiss mine
> The dream turns into you.
> Yes, it's simply heavenly!
> Our love's just divine—
> For love is made in heaven
> And you, my love, are mine!

SIMPLE.
> Love is simply heavenly!
> What else could it be?
> When love is made in heaven
> And you are made for me.

JOYCE.
> Love is simply heavenly!
> What else can I say?
> When love sends me an angel
> To hold me close this way.

SIMPLE.
> Love is like a dream
> That's too good to be true,

(Dressed now, JOYCE emerges and SIMPLE rises to embrace her.)

JOYCE.
> But when your lips kiss mine
> The dream turns into you.

BOTH.
> Yes, it's simply heavenly!

> Our love's just divine—
> For love is made in heaven
> And you, my love, are mine!

BLACKOUT

ACT ONE

SCENE 3

Paddy's Bar. Midnight.

At a battered old piano in the corner a roustabout pianist is playing a syncopated melody while HOPKINS, the bartender, beats lightly on the bar with a couple of stirrers as if playing drums. The music ceases as MISS MAMIE, a large but shapely domestic servant, enters and sits at her usual table.

HOPKINS. Good evening, Miss Mamie. How's tricks?

MAMIE. Hopkins, them white folks over in Long Island done like to worked me to death. I'm just getting back to town.

PIANIST. You ought to have a good man to take care of you, Miss Mamie— like me.

MAMIE. Huh! Bill, from what I see of you, you can hardly take care of yourself. I got a mighty lot of flesh here to nourish.

PIANIST. Big woman, big appetite.

MAMIE. Right—which is why I like to work for rich folks. Poor folks ain't got enough to feed me.

PIANIST. I never eat much. But I sure am thirsty.

MAMIE. Stay that way! Hopkins, gimme a gin.

(BODIDDLY, a dock worker, leaps in shouting.)

BODIDDLY. Hey, now, anyhow!

MAMIE. Anyhow, what?

BODIDDLY. Anyhow, we're here! Who's setting up tonight?

(Dead silence. No one answers.)

Well, Hop, I'l take a short beer.

MAMIE. It ain't nobody's payday in the middle of the week, Bodiddly. And the only man in this bar who manages to keep a little change in his pocket is Mr. Boyd here, drawing his G. I. pension.

(BODIDDLY *points at* BOYD *proudly*.)

BODIDDLY. My boy!

BOYD. Hi, Bo!

MAMIE. Huh! There's as much difference between you and Ananias Boyd as between night and day.

BODIDDLY. Yeah, I know! His predilect's toward intellect—and mine's toward womens.

HOPKINS. And beer.

BODIDDLY. Boyd's the only man around here who's colleged.

BOYD. For all the good it does me. You dock workers make more a week than I ever see writing these stories.

BODIDDLY. But none of us gets pensions.

MAMIE. None of you-all in the war and got wounded neither. But if I was a man, I would have gone to war so I could get me a pension.

PIANIST. They had lady soldiers.

BODIDDLY. Whacks and Wavers.

MAMIE. By that time I were too big.

(A LITTLE MAN *in nose glasses, carrying an umbrella, enters with an armful of highbrow papers and magazines. Noticing no one, he takes a table and begins to remove his gloves.*)

There comes that character trying to make people think he's educated. One thing I like about Boyd here, even if he is a writer, he ain't always trying to impress folks. Also he speaks when he comes in a public place.

(*The* LITTLE MAN *sits at an empty table.*)

CHARACTER. A thimble of Scotch, please.

BODIDDLY. A *thimble* of Scawtch!

(*All laugh but* BOYD.)

CHARACTER. And a tumbler of plain water, no ice.

HOPKINS. Right, sir! Like the English.

(*As if to show her derision,* MAMIE *orders loudly.*)

MAMIE. Hopkins, gimme some more gin.

HOPKINS. Coming up, Miss Mamie!

(*A VENDOR'S CRY is heard outside. Carrying a watermelon, a jovial fellow, Watermelon Joe, enters.*)

MELON.

> Watermelons! Juicy sweet!
> Watermelons! Good to eat!
> Ripe and red—
> That's what I said—
> Watermelons!

MAMIE. Joe, you better shut up all that catterwalling! You ain't working this time o' night?

MELON. Yes I is. I done sold all but one watermelon. Who wants it? Sweet as pie! No lie! My, my, my!

(MAMIE *inspects the melon.*)

MAMIE. Hmmm! It do look good. Thumps good, too. Leave it for me behind the bar. I'll take it.

MELON. Thank you, Miss Mamie.

BODIDDLY. Better tie your pushcart to the curb 'fore somebody steals it.

MELON. I'm ahead of you, Diddly—got it locked to the lamp post. Boy, when I cry "Watermelons!" do you-all know what happens to womens?

BODIDDLY. What?

MELON. Their blood turns to water and their knees start to shake—'cause they know I'm a man, and no mistake! Why, I sold a woman a watermelon one day and moved in and stayed three years.

BODIDDLY. That's nothing. I just spoke to a strange lady once setting on a stoop —and went upstairs and ain't come down yet. That was in 1936.

MELON. Diddly, you lying. Your wife done run you out twice with a kitchen knife.

BODIDDLY. I mean, excusing temporary exits.

MAMIE. Well, I been buying watermelons, Joe, for two summers, and I finds your fruits sweeter than you.

MELON. That's because you don't know me well, baby. Besides, I do not use my professional voice in your personal presence:

Wa-ter—melons!
Melons! Melons! Melons!
Sweet as they can be!
Sweet, good Lord!
But they ain't as sweet as me!
Watermelon Joe has got your
Wa-ter—melons!

(He eases up to her cheek.)

Me-lawns. . . . Me-loans! . . . Me-loons!

MAMIE. Man, you better get away from me! You know I got a husband, Watermelon Joe.

MELON. Where's he at?

MAMIE. I don't know where he's at, but I got one. And if I ain't, I don't want you.

(He croons in her ear.)

MELON. Watermelons. Wa-ter-melons. . . .

MAMIE. I sure do like your watermelons, though.

MELON. Nice red melons . . .

(The LITTLE MAN *rises indignantly.)*

CHARACTER. Stereotypes! That's all both of you are. Disgraceful stereotypes!

*(*MAMIE *turns on him furiously.)*

MAMIE. Mister, you better remove yourself from my presence before I stereo your type! I like watermelons, and I don't care who knows it. That's nothing to be ashamed of, like some other colored folks are. Why, I knowed a woman once was so ashamed of liking watermelons that she'd make the clerk wrap the melon up before she'd carry it out of the store. I ain't no pretender, myself, neither no passer.

BODIDDLY. What do you mean, passer?

MAMIE. Chitterling passer—passing up chitterlings and pretending I don't like 'em when I do. I like watermelon and chitterlings both, and I don't care who knows it.

CHARACTER. Just stereotypes, that's all. *(He shakes his head.)*

MAMIE. Man, get out of my face!

CHARACTER. Stereotypes . . . stereotypes . . . stereo . . . *(He retreats muttering.)*

MAMIE. Why, it's getting so colored folks can't do nothing no more without some other Negro calling you a stereotype. Stereotype, hah! If you like a little gin, you're a stereotype. You got to drink Scotch. If you wear a red dress, you're a stereotype. You got to wear beige or chartreuse. Lord have mercy, honey, do-don't like no blackeyed peas and rice! Then you're a down-home Negro for true —which I is—and proud of it! *(*MAMIE *glares around as if daring somebody to dispute her. Nobody does.)* I didn't come here to Harlem to get away from my people. I come here because there's more of 'em. I loves my race. I loves my people. Stereotype!

CHARACTER. That's what I said, stereotypes!

MAMIE. You better remove yourself from my presence, calling me a stereotype.

CHARACTER. Tch-tch-tch! *(Clicking his tongue in disgust, the* LITTLE MAN *leaves the bar as* MAMIE *rises and threatens him with her purse.)*

(The PIANIST *rushes over to congratulate her.)*

PIANIST. Gimme five, Miss Mamie, gimme five! *(They shake hands.)*

MAMIE. Solid!

PIANIST. You and me agreed! I could drink on that.

MAMIE. You go right back where you was and set down.

BODIDDLY. Who agrees is me! Bartender, set up the bar—this far—from Mamie to me. What'll you have, Cleopatra, a beer?

MAMIE. You know I drinks gin, Bodiddly. And I needs another one. That character done got me all upset. Where's all the decent peoples tonight? Where's Jess Simple?

BODIDDLY. I seen old Simp a couple of hours ago walking down Lenox Avenue with his girl. But Joyce turns in early. And when she turns in, she turns him out.

MAMIE. That's what I call a decent woman.

MELON. Damn if I do.

MAMIE. And that Simple is a good man. He needs himself a decent woman —instead of gallivanting around with chippies like Zarita that keeps a bar door flapping all night long. I never seen a woman could run in and out of a bar so much and so fast.

BODIDDLY. Ah, but that Zarita, she's sure a fine-looking chick.

MAMIE. She wears her morals like a loose garment. Ain't no woman's man safe with her around.

MELON. She sure will drink a body up. Zarita damn near drunk me out of a whole carload of melons one night.

MAMIE. You sure is weak for young womens.

MELON. Miss Mamie, I could be weak for you.

MAMIE. Melon, scat! I done told you, get from over me! Scat!

GITFIDDLE. Hey, Hop!

(The door flies open and a seedy-looking fellow rushes in calling to the bartender.)

Hey, Hop! Lend me my guitar from behind the bar there, please. Hurry up, man! I'll bring it back.

HOPKINS. What's the hurry?

GITFIDDLE. There's a big party of folks in the Wonder Bar down the street spending money like water.

HOPKINS. Here you are, Git.

GITFIDDLE. Thank you, man! *(He takes guitar and exits.)*

HOPKINS. I sure hope he can play up a few dollars—that man has been broke so long, it just ain't fair.

MAMIE. A good musicianer—doing nothing but playing for quarters folks throw him!

MELON. They say a woman brought old Gitfiddle low.

MAMIE. Getting high brought him low! Womens helps more mens than they don't.

MELON. I sure wish you'd help me.

MAMIE. Wish again, honey, because I ain't coming. I likes a man who works in one place, with one job, not all up and down the streets where he's subject to temptation. And as for me, I don't need nobody to help me.

(MELON shrugs.)

MELON. Well, so that's that!

(SIMPLE enters.)

SIMPLE. Good evening!

MAMIE. We been missing you. Excusing Boyd there, this bar's full of nothing but characters.

BOYD. Thank you, Miss Mamie.

MAMIE. Where you been, Simple?

SIMPLE. Eating ice cream.

CROWD. What?

SIMPLE. And I had my picture took.

BODIDDLY. With your lady fair.

SIMPLE. For my lady lair. All posed like this. *(SIMPLE assumes an attitude.)*

HOPKINS. She must've fell out laughing at that pose.

SIMPLE. She did not. That's one thing about Joyce. She never laughs at nothing about me, never does, which is why I loves that girl.

BOYD. You can find more reasons for liking a woman, Jess. Every time, a different woman, it's a different reason.

HOPKINS. Pay him no mind, Mr. Boyd. Zarita laughs with him and at him.

SIMPLE. Zarita's different. I do not, never will, can't—won't, and don't love no jumping jack of a Zarita. A man can't hardly keep Zarita in his arms, let alone in his heart.

HOPKINS. So we know, Jess Simple!

SIMPLE. But I have kept Joyce in my heart ever since I met her—and she is there to stay. Dog-gone it, I wish I had my divorce from Isabel. But at last, it looks like I am making some headway. They say a man's life changes every seven years. I sure hope I am going through the change.

HOPKINS. Mr. Change, what are you drinking?

(SIMPLE *takes the envelope from his pocket.*)

SIMPLE. Give me and Boyd a couple of beers. Then I want you to read something. Didn't even show it to Joyce yet—not to get her hopes up too high. It's from my wife.

BOYD. I don't want to read your personal letters, Jess.

SIMPLE. Here, pal, read it—because I can't believe my eyes.

BOYD. Um-mmmm! Well, here goes: "Dear Mr. Semple: Jess, at last I have found a man who loves me enough to pay for my divorce. This new man is a mail clerk, his first wife being dead, so he wants me for his second."

SIMPLE. Thank you, Father!

BOYD. "He knows I been married and am still married in name only to you, as you have not been willing to pay for the legal paper which grants freedom from our entanglement. This man is willing to pay for it. He says he will get a lawyer

to furnish me grounds unless you want to contest. I do not want no contest, you hear me! All I want is my divorce. I am writing to find out if you will please not make no contest out of this. Let me hear from you tonight as my husband-to-be has already passed the point where he could wait. Once sincerely yours, but not now, Isabel."

SIMPLE. Sounds just like my wife!

HOPKINS. I suppose you've no intention of cross-filing.

SIMPLE. I would not cross that wife of mine no kind of way. My last contest with that woman was such that the police had to protect me. So that man can have her. I do not even want a copy of the diploma. I told Isabel when we busted up that she had shared my bed, my board, my licker, and my hair oil, but that I did not want to share another thing with her from that day to this, not even a divorce. Let that other man pay for it—they can share it together. Me, I'll be married again before the gold seal's hardly out from under the stamper.

HOPKINS. Good! Perhaps you'll settle down, stop running around, and stay home nights with Joyce.

SIMPLE. Married, I'll get somewhere in the world, too. Let's drink to it. And that man in Baltimore better pay for my wife's divorce! If he don't, I'll fix him. Here's my toast. (*He lifts his glass of beer.*)

In a horserace, Daddy-o,
One thing you will find—
There ain't NO way to be out in front
Without showing your tail
To the horse behind. . . .

(ZARITA *enters glittering.*)

ZARITA. Hey now! Hi, all and sundry!

SIMPLE. Zarita!

ZARITA. Excuse me, folks, for being in a hurry.

MAMIE. I told you so!

ZARITA. Jess, I'm going to Jersey! Come on! Coleman and his girl've got their car outside.

SIMPLE. The one with the top down?

ZARITA. That's the chariot—and I got nobody to ride back there with me.

MAMIE. Don't that child just bring you to tears?

SIMPLE. Is Coleman sober?

ZARITA. Just feeling a little groovy that's all! Come on!

BODIDDLY. Woman, shut that outside door! It's chilly. You know it ain't official summer yet.

ZARITA. Your blood's thin. My, it's hot in here! Come on, Jess. The motor's running.

SIMPLE. The motor might be running, but I ain't. Come here, girl, I got somethings to say to you. Zarita, you know I'm almost engaged to be married. I can't be running around with you.

ZARITA. You really got yourself tangled up. Well, anyhow, we'll just ride over the bridge to a little after-hours spot in New Jersey for a few drinks, and come right back. There's no harm in that.

SIMPLE. You sure you coming right back? And Coleman is gonna drive me right to my door?

ZARITA. Or mine! Your room is kinder little and small and cold. Sugar, is you is, or is you ain't? (She moves toward the door.)

SIMPLE. Zarita, it's chilly out there and I ain't got my top coat.

ZARITA. Oh, Knuckle-Nose, we got a fifth of licker in the car to keep us warm. And there's some fine bars just across the George Washington bridge. You does or you don't?

SIMPLE. Aw, Zarita!

ZARITA. Old Simple Square, do I have to beg and plead with you? Listen! I've got my own money. I'll even treat you to a couple of drinks. Come on! Aw, come on! (She entices him with a caress and they exit.)

MAMIE. There goes a lamb to slaughter again. Ain't it a shame the kind of a deal a good woman gets when she goes to bed early!

BODIDDLY. Huh?

MAMIE. I ain't talking about a man like you with 17 children. I'm talking about Joyce.

BODIDDLY. Oh!

MAMIE. She goes to bed early, leaving Simple to yield to temptation.

MELON. I'd never yield, Miss Mamie. But if I did, I'd yield with you.

MAMIE. Melon, I say, get out of my face. It's mighty near midnight. Lemme go home.

MELON. If I didn't have my pushcart to wheel, I would 'scort you, Miss Mamie.

MAMIE. Watermelon Joe, with you at the handle, I might have to jump out and walk—or roll out, one—wild as you is with womens. Hopkins, hand me my watermelon and let me go to my virtuous couch. Good night, all, good night! (MAMIE exits with her watermelon under her arm.)

MELON. Huh, so she don't trust me to 'scort her home. Anyhow, I think I'll truck along after her and see can't I tote her melon to a taxi. Watermelons! Nice red ones! (MELON exits.)

BODIDDLY. Gimme a sherry, man. What'll you have, Boyd?

BOYD. Nothing, thanks.

(ARCIE enters bustling.)

BODIDDLY. Arcie, my love, what you doing out this time of night?

ARCIE. I came out looking for you—and done looked in seven bars.

(HOPKINS automatically pours ARCIE some sherry.)

BODIDDLY. And had a drink in each and every one!

ARCIE. Naturally! A lady don't go in a bar and not buy nothing. Diddly, lover, listen, there ain't but five of our children home—which means an even dozen is still out in the streets.

BODIDDLY. The children's big enough to take care of themselves.

ARCIE. If you was any kind of a father —if you was any kind of . . .

BODIDDLY. Woman, hush! And put that sherry wine down—before you be walking sidewise to keep from flying. Let's be getting upstairs—before some more of our children don't get home. Be seeing you, folks!

ARCIE. That man!

(ARCIE and BODIDDLY exeunt. The bar is empty except for BOYD who rises to leave.)

HOPKINS. Say, Boyd, as a writer, would you say them folks are stereotypes?

BOYD. In the book I'm writing they're just folks. Good night, Hop.

(GITFIDDLE comes reeling into the bar as BOYD exits.)

GITFIDDLE. Got-dog it! I done broke another string!

HOPKINS. Well, did you make any money?

GITFIDDLE. They paid me off in drinks. I had nothing to eat all day. Here, Hop, lend me another half for a sandwich— and keep this for security. (GITFIDDLE offers his guitar to HOPKINS.)

HOPKINS. You must think Paddy's Bar is a bank. I lent you two dollars and a quarter already this week. Here's fifty cents more.

GITFIDDLE. Thanks, Hop! But wait a minute, Hop—lemme play you just one more blues. (The woebegone GITFIDDLE strums a lonesome blues on his guitar as the lights fade to darkness.)

BLACKOUT

ACT ONE

SCENE 4

Hospital room. Next day. During Blackout *a bed backed by a white screen already attached is wheeled Downstage Center with* SIMPLE *already propped up in bed, very quiet. Both his legs are up in traction. Near the head of his bed is a single white chair. A* NURSE *all in white tiptoes in and calls softly. He answers with a groan.*

NURSE. Mr. Semple.

SIMPLE. Aw-um-mmm-mm-m!

NURSE. Such groaning! You aren't that bad off.

SIMPLE. When I suffers, Nurse, I like to suffer loud.

NURSE. There's a gentleman to see you. (She beckons the caller.) Here he is, sir.

MELON. Thank you, Nurse. (MELON enters.)

(NURSE exits.)

Oh, man! You're all packed for shipping!

SIMPLE. Strung, hung, and slung's what I am. Melon, this is the most! Um-mmm-mm-m!

MELON. All I heard was, you was in an accident.

SIMPLE. It were an accident, all right. Got-dog that Zarita! My mind told me—

MELON. Never mind what your mind told you, Daddy-o, just gimme the details. Here.

SIMPLE. What's that?

MELON. I brought you some books.

SIMPLE. I wish you'd of brought me a quart of beer and some pigs' feet. I ain't much on books.

MELON. Comic books, man.

SIMPLE. Oh! *Horror in Hackensack. Terror in Trenton.*

MELON. Man, that's the crazy history of New Jersey.

SIMPLE. This makes me feel better already. Thanks, Melon.

MELON. Now, tell me what happened.

SIMPLE. The car tried to climb the George Washington Bridge, instead of going *across* it—turned half over—Coleman, his girl, and Zarita and me. But I was the *only* one that got throwed out, and on my—bohunkus. Melon, I'm all bruised up on my sit-downer.

MELON. I told you, you should stop balling, and take care of yourself.

SIMPLE. If I had took care of myself, I would not have these pretty nurses taking care of me now.

MELON. But look at the big hospital bill when you get out.

SIMPLE. Lemme hit one number, I'll settle it. But what worries me is when I'm going to get out.

MELON. You will never get out if you don't observe the rules and stop telling folks to bring you beer and pigs feet and things you are not supposed to have.

SIMPLE. But alcohol had nothing to do with it.

MELON. Oh, no?

SIMPLE. Womens aggravate a man, drunk or sober. Melon, I hope Joyce knows Zarita ain't nothing to me, even if I do accidentally go riding with her. But I don't want to discuss how come I'm in this hospital. You know, no matter what a man does, sick or well, something is always liable to happen—especially if he's colored. In this world, Melon, it's hard for a man to live until he dies.

(The NURSE enters.)

MELON. I think you'll make it.

NURSE. There's a Miss Joyce Lane to see you.

(A look of great helplessness comes over SIMPLE. He appeals to his friend.)

SIMPLE. Melon.

MELON. It's Joyce.

SIMPLE. Just like a man has to face his Maker alone, the same goes for facing a woman.

MELON. You want to see her, don't you?

SIMPLE. Worse than anything, I want to see Joyce, Melon. Also, I—I—I—

MELON. Also, you don't want to see her. I know. Good luck, old man.

(The NURSE shows MELON out. As they exit, JOYCE enters.)

JOYCE. Jess! *(Tears come, and she takes out her handkerchief.)*

SIMPLE. Baby, please don't cry. I'm all right.

JOYCE. But your legs! Are they broken?

SIMPLE. Doc says they ain't. But they sure are bent.

JOYCE. Then why are they all trussed up that way?

SIMPLE. Because I can't lay on my hine, that's why.

JOYCE. Your what?

SIMPLE. My hindparts is all skint up, Joyce. I hope that's a polite word for saying it.

JOYCE. But aren't you hurt badly?

SIMPLE. No.

JOYCE. I am.

SIMPLE. Baby, don't you want to set down? Here on the bed. Then pull your chair up close, please.

JOYCE. Oh, Jess!

SIMPLE. I know, Joyce, I know. I hadn't ought to done it.

JOYCE. With a drunken driver, too—and Zarita.

SIMPLE. You know I love you.

JOYCE. And that's the way you show it? With your legs tied up in the air—on account of a—

SIMPLE. Auto wreck—

JOYCE. Woman.

SIMPLE. Just a little old innocent joy ride.

JOYCE. Oh, stop it!

SIMPLE. Baby, did you take communion this morning?

JOYCE. Yes, Jess, I did. I was almost late. I waited for you to go with me.

SIMPLE. Did they sing, "Jesus Knows Just How Much I Can Bear"?

JOYCE. Not today.

SIMPLE. I used to like that song. You know how I feel now? Just like I felt the last time Aunt Lucy whipped me. Did I ever tell you about that, Joyce?

JOYCE. No.

SIMPLE. It were a girl caused that whipping.

JOYCE. I'm not surprised, Jess.

SIMPLE. Aunt Lucy is dead and gone to glory, Joyce. But it were Aunt Lucy taught me right from wrong. When I were a little young child, I didn't have much raising. I knocked around every-which-where, pillar to post. But when Aunt Lucy took me, she did her best to whip me and *raise* me, too—'cause Aunt Lucy really believed in her Bible. "Spare the rod and spoil the child." I were *not* spoiled. But that last whipping is what did it—made me the man I am today. . . . I could see that whipping coming, Joyce, when I sneaked out of the henhouse one of Aunt Lucy's best hens and give it to that girl to roast for her Sunday School picnic, because that old girl said she was aiming to picnic *me*—except that she didn't have nothing much to put in her basket. I was trying to jive that girl, you know. Anyhow, Aunt Lucy found out about it and woke me up the next morning with a switch in her hand. . . . But I got all mannish that morning, Joyce. I said, "Aunt Lucy, you ain't gonna whip me no more. I'se a man now—and you ain't gonna whip me." Aunt Lucy said, "You know you had no business snatching my best laying hen right off her nest." Aunt Lucy was angry. And big as I was, I was scared. . . . Yet I was meaning not to let her whip me, Joyce. But, just when I was aiming to snatch that switch out of her hand, I seed Aunt Lucy was crying. I said, "What you crying for?" She said, "I'm crying 'cause here you is a man and don't know how to act right *yet*, and I

done did my best to raise you so you'll grow up to be a good man. I wore out so many switches on your back—still you tries my soul. But it *ain't* my soul I'm thinking of, son, it's you. Jess, I wants you to carry yourself right. You understand me? I'm getting too old to be using my strength up like this. Here!" Aunt Lucy hollered, "Bend over and lemme whip you one more time!" . . . Big as I was, Joyce, you know I bended. When I seen her crying, I would have let Aunt Lucy kill me before I raised a hand. When she got through, I said, "Aunt Lucy, you ain't gonna have to whip me no more— I'm going to do my best to do right from now on, and not try your soul. And I am sorry about that hen. . . ." Joyce, from that day to this, I have tried to behave myself. Aunt Lucy is gone to Glory, now, but if she's looking down, she knows that's true. That was my last whipping. But it wasn't the whipping that taught me what I needed to know. It was because she cried and cried. When peoples care for you and cry for you—and *love* you—Joyce, they can straighten out your soul. (SIMPLE, *lost in his story, had not been looking at* JOYCE. *Instead, as he finishes, he is looking at the ceiling. Suddenly* JOYCE *turns to bury her head on the back of her chair, sobbing aloud.* SIMPLE, *forgetting that his legs are tied and that he cannot get out of bed, tries to rise.*) Joyce! . . . Joyce! . . . Joyce! (*If he could, he would go to her and take her in his arms.*) Joyce, you're crying for me!

JOYCE. I'm not! I'm crying for your grandmother.

SIMPLE. It wasn't my grandmother I was telling you about, Joyce, it were my Aunt Lucy.

JOYCE. Well, whoever it was, she had her hands full with you.

SIMPLE. She loved me, Joyce, just like I love you. . . . Come here, feel my heart—it's beating just for you. . . . Joyce, please come here. (SIMPLE *reaches out his hand and* JOYCE *comes. She takes it, and he pulls her toward him.*) Feel my heart. (*He puts her hand on his heart. But suddenly* JOYCE *buries her head on his chest and sobs violently.* SIMPLE *puts an arm about her and smiles, quietly happy.*)

BLACKOUT

ACT ONE

SCENE 5

Paddy's bar. Saturday night. The joint is jumping. GITFIDDLE *is plunking his guitar.* BODIDDLY *is at the bar,* HOPKINS *behind it.* ARCIE *is in the middle of the floor, cutting up as if she were a young woman.* MAMIE *and* MELON *sit at a table.* JOHN JASPER, *one of her teenage jitterbug sons, comes in, hits a few steps himself, whirls around, then taps her on the shoulder.*

JOHN JASPER. Mama! Hey, Mama!

(ARCIE *stops dancing.*)

ARCIE. Get away from me, son! Can't you see your mama is having a good time and don't want to be bothered with no children? Stop that dancing! Where's all my children? Arcilee and Melinda and Mabel and Johnny and Little Bits and Cora? Also Lilac? Huh?

JOHN JASPER. They all in the street, gone to Saturday night parties and things. Mama, lend me a quarter. I want to take the bus down to 96th Street to the Swords and Sabres dance.

ARCIE. Ask your daddy. He ain't paid me off yet. Got his pockets just full of wages—I hope. Hey! Hey! Hey! (ARCIE *again continues dancing as the boy approaches* BODIDDLY *at the bar.*)

JOHN JASPER. Hey, Daddddy, gimme a quarter.

BODIDDLY. Scram! You too young to be in this bar, John Jasper. Here take this quarter, boy, and scram! Children all under a man's feet!

JOHN JASPER. Thanks, Dad. (*He skips off.*)

(MISS MAMIE *and* MELON *do a slow Lindy hop to the music.*)

ARCIE. Bartender, another sherry—on my husband there.

BODIDDLY. Woman, you better stop spending my money before you get it. Is you done your Saturday night shopping yet?

ARCIE. Can I do it on credit? Hand it over, Diddly, lover!

BODIDDLY. Many mouths as you got to feed, you better get to the stores before they close.

ARCIE. Them's your children, too. Ain't you gonna help me carry the grits?

BODIDDLY. Woman, you know I'm tired. Go do your shopping.

ARCIE. Treat me first.

BODIDDLY. Hop, give this woman a glass of Domesticated Sherry.

(HOPKINS *laughs and pours her another glass of sherry before she exits.* ZARITA *enters.* MELON *and* MAMIE *stop dancing.*)

ZARITA. Simple hasn't been in yet tonight, has he, Hop?

HOPKINS. Not yet.

BODIDDLY. But if he's able to walk, he'll be here before it's over.

ZARITA. He's been back at work three or four days, and I haven't seen him. You know, Hop, when I went by Harlem Hospital, he acted like he was mad at me.

HOPKINS. No wonder—you took him riding and got him all banged up.

ZARITA. He didn't have to go. Nobody forced him. I just said, "Come on." Say, Hop, what you doing this morning when you get off from work?

HOPKINS. I'm going home, Zarita.

ZARITA. There's a nice new after-hours spot opened down on Seventh Avenue.

HOPKINS. I said, I am going home.

ZARITA. You didn't always go home so early after work. Mr. Hopkins.

HOPKINS. Do you call three o'clock in the morning early?

ZARITA. Real early! Don't you remember that night you drove me over to Newark?

HOPKINS. I remember.

ZARITA. And we didn't get back early either.

HOPKINS. Zarita, this is one morning I'm turning in. Maybe Simple'll take you to this new Bottle Club.

ZARITA. Maybe he will—if he ain't still mad. Anyhow, if you see him, tell him I'll be back. I will be back.

HOPKINS. Cool, Zarita, cool.

(ZARITA *exits in rhythm to* GITFIDDLE'*s guitar.*)

MELON. Hey, Git, you sounds mighty good plunking over there in the corner. C'mon, Miss Mamie, let's dance some more.

MAMIE. Yes, you ought to be on the juke box.

GITFIDDLE. Juke boxes is the trouble now, Miss Mamie. Used to be, folks liked to hear a sure-enough live guitar player. Now, I start playing, somebody puts a nickel in the piccolo, drowns me out. No good for musicianers any more, but I got to make the rounds, try to hustle. See you later, Miss Mamie.

MAMIE. Git, I'd rather hear you than records any day. When you come back, I'm gonna throw you a dollar just to pick a blues for me.

GITFIDDLE. I won't be long, Miss Mamie, won't be long. (GITFIDDLE *exits as* JOHN JASPER *runs in. At the piano the* BARFLY *continues to jazz.*)

JOHN JASPER. Papa!

BODIDDLY. John Jasper, now what you want? A man can't . . .

JOHN JASPER. Ronnie Belle . . .

BODIDDLY. A man can't enjoy his self . . .

JOHN JASPER. Ronnie Belle . . .

BODIDDLY. . . . without some child stuck up in his face.

(JOHN JASPER *dances as he talks.*)

JOHN JASPER. Ronnie Belle says she won't stay home and mind the babies, and it's my turn to go out this Saturday night. She says if I go, she's going.

BODIDDLY. You tell Ronnie Belle I'll come up there and fan her good, if she don't do what she's supposed to. I declare to goodness, these young folks nowadays! You get upstairs, John Jasper, and tell your sister what I said.

JOHN JASPER. Yes, sir, Papa! (JOHN JASPER *exits.*)

MAMIE. Diddly, you sure got some fine children.

BODIDDLY. And every one of them born in New York City, Harlem. When I left the South, I never did go back.

(JOHN JASPER *returns, dancing to the piano.*)

JOHN JASPER. I forgot.

BODIDDLY. Lord, that boy's back again. John Jasper, now what do you want?

JOHN JASPER. Mama says for you to come on upstairs and bring her a pint of cooking sherry.

BODIDDLY. You know your mama ain't gonna do no cooking this time of the night! Tell Arcie to come down here and get her own wine. Scat, boy, scat!

(JOHN JASPER *dances out.*)

MAMIE. Diddly, that's the cutest one of your children. I'll give him a dime myself.

BODIDDLY. Lemme get way back in the corner so's no more of my kin folks can find me—not even my wife. (*He goes into a corner as* SIMPLE *enters.*)

MAMIE. Look who's coming there!

PIANIST. Hey, Jess!

MELON. Jess Semple!

HOPKINS. (THE BARTENDER *lifts a bottle of beer.*) It's on the house!

MAMIE. Welcome home!

BODIDDLY. To the land of the living!

MAMIE. Amen! Bless Jess!

HOPKINS. Zarita was just looking for you.

(Happily the customers retire to tables with the drinks as SIMPLE *remains leaning stiffly on the bar.)*

SIMPLE. Don't mention Zarita, please, Hop! She's near about ruint me. Joyce is treating me cool, cool, cool, since I come out the hospital and I explained to her over and over I was just out riding. Hop, oh, Hop! Oh, man, have I got a worried mind! You know when I reached home my old landlady come handing me a Special Delivery from my wife which stated that the Negro in Baltimore has only made one payment on our divorce, leaving two payments to go. Hop, you're educated. How much is one payment on $400, leaving two payments to go?

HOPKINS. $133.33 and one-third cents.

SIMPLE. Now I could just about pay one-third cents.

HOPKINS. I thought you said that man in Baltimore loved your wife so much he was willing to pay for the whole divorce.

SIMPLE. Inflation's got him—so he just made one down payment. Isabel writ that if I would make one payment now, she would make one, then everybody could marry right away. But I cannot meet a payment now—with the hospital bill, rent up, food up, phones up, cigarettes up—everything up—but my salary. Divorces are liable to go up, too, if I don't hurry up and pay up. Lord! Women, women, women. (*He paces the floor.*)

MELON. Don't let women get you excited, man! Set down and take it easy.

(Offered a seat, SIMPLE *protects his haunches with his palms.)*

SIMPLE. The last thing I want to do is set down!

MAMIE. Then stand up to it like a man! You made your own bed hard. What you drinking?

SIMPLE. Whiskey.

VOICES. Whiskey?

MELON. And you're usually a beer man!

SIMPLE. Tonight I want whiskey. Hop, I said, whiskey! I'm broke, busted, and disgusted. And just spent mighty near my last nickel for a paper—and there ain't no news in it about colored folks. Unless we commit murder, robbery or rape, or are being chased by a mob, do we get on the front page, or hardly on the back. Take flying saucers. For instance according to the *Daily News*, everybody has seen flying saucers in the sky. Everybody but a Negro. They probably won't even let flying saucers fly over Harlem, just to keep us from seeing one. Not long ago, I read where some Karl Krubelowski had seen a flying saucer, also Giovanni Battini saw one. And way out in Pennsylvania mountains some Dutchman named Heinrich Armpriester seen one. But did you read about Roosevelt Johnson or Ralph Butler or Henry Washington or anybody that sounded like a Negro seeing one? I did not. Has a flying saucer ever passed over Lenox Avenue yet? Nary one! Not even Daddy Grace has glimpsed one, nor Ralph Bunche. Negroes can't even get into the front page news no kind of way. I can't even see a flying saucer. When I do, that will be a great day.

HOPKINS. It would probably scare you to death—so you wouldn't live to see your name in the papers.

SIMPLE. Well, then—I could read about it in the other world then—and be just as proud—me, Jess Semple, kilt by a flying saucer.

(ARCIE enters yelling tipsily.)

ARCIE. Bodiddly! Bodiddly! Why don't you come on upstairs?

BODIDDLY. Aw, woman, hush! Every time I turn around there's families under my feet. Set down and leave me be.

ARCIE. I did not come to set down. It's past midnight. I come to get you to go to bed.

BODIDDLY. I know when to go to bed my own self.

ARCIE. Then come on, you great big no-good old bull-necked son-of-a-biscuit eater!

BODIDDLY. Sit down, I'll buy you a sherry wine. Hop!

(ZARITA enters with ALI BABA, an enormous well-dressed fellow in a turban.)

ZARITA. Hello, you-all! Hey, Jess Semple! Folks, dig this champion roots-herbs —and numbers-seller from south of the border. I just come by to show you my new man I met at the Baby Grand. Don't he look like a sultan? But we got business. Come on! We're gonna do the town, ain't we, Ali Baba?

MAMIE. Ali Baba?

ZARITA. Sugar Hill, Smalls, and every place! Come on, Texas Tarzan, come on! Jess, I'm glad you came out of that little accident O.K. 'Bye, all! (ZARITA kisses ALI BABA.)

(He sneezes. MELON ducks. As ZARITA and her new man exit, SIMPLE looks sheepish.)

BODIDDLY. She don't need us tonight.

HOPKINS. She's got her a two-ton Sugar Daddy.

MELON. She's got her a human shower.

MAMIE. Paddy's Bar is small-time to Zarita this evening. She'll be in here Monday all beat out, though—and looking for Jess Semple.

SIMPLE. Or somebody else simple— but it won't be me.

MELON. Where have I heard that before?

SIMPLE. Where have I heard that before? (They glare at each other.)

MELON. Where have I heard that before?

(SIMPLE's feelings are hurt.)

SIMPLE. I'm going and see Joyce. I need to see somebody that loves me.

(A POLICEMAN'S VOICE is heard in the street.)

POLICEMAN. Hey, you! Stay off the street with that noise box. Don't you know it's against the law, out here hustling for dimes? Next time I hear that racket, I'll run you in.

GITFIDDLE. Yes, sir, Officer! (GITFIDDLE enters crestfallen.) A man can't play music nowhere no more. Juke box drowns him out in the bars, cops run him off the street, landlady won't let you play in your own room. I might as well break this damn box up!

MAMIE. Gitfiddle, I told you, you can play for me.

BODIDDLY. Me too.

ARCIE. Sure, Git.

MELON. And me, Git.

MAMIE. Come on, now! Let's have some music like you feels it, Gitfiddle.

MELON.
Did you ever hear the Blues
On a battered old guitar?
Did you ever hear the Blues
Over yonder, Lord, how far?
Did you ever hear the Blues
On a Saturday night?
Did you ever hear the Blues
About some chick ain't done you right?
Baby, did you ever hear the Blues?

MAMIE.
Did you ever hear the Blues
On an old house-rent piano?
Did you ever hear the Blues
Like they play 'em in Savannah?
Did you ever hear the Blues
In the early, early morn?

Wondering, wondering, wondering
Why you was ever born?
Baby, did you ever hear the Blues?

MELON.
When the bar is quiet
And the night is almost done,
Them old Blues overtake you
At the bottom of your fun.
Oh, Lord, them Blues!
Echo . . . echo . . . echo . . . of the Blues!

MAMIE.
Good morning, Blues! Good morning!
Good morning, Blues, I say!
Good morning, Blues, good morning!
You done come back to stay?
You come back to bug me
Like you drug me yesterday?

MELON.
Blues, I heard you knock last night,
But I would not let you in.
Knock, knock, knock, last night
But I would not let you in.
I tried to make believe
It weren't nothing but the wind.

ALL.
Blues, Blues, Blues!
It were the Blues!
Maybe to some people
What the Blueses say is news
But to me it's an old, old story.

MAMIE.
Did you ever hear the Blues
On a battered old guitar?
Did you ever hear the Blues
Over yonder, Lord, how far?
Did you ever hear the Blues
On a Saturday night?

BOTH.
Did you ever hear the Blues
About some chick ain't done you right?
ALL.
Baby, did you ever hear the Blues?

BLACKOUT

ACT ONE

SCENE 6

JOYCE's *room. Sunday evening.*
JOYCE *is sewing. The bell rings seven
times. The* LANDLADY *calls from offstage.*

MRS. CADDY. I'll answer it, Miss Lane.
I'm right here in the hall.
JOYCE. Oh, thank you, Mrs. Caddy.
You're about the nicest landlady I know.
MRS. CADDY. Are you decent? Do you
want to see Mr. Semple? He's kinda crip-
ple—so down here or up there?
JOYCE. I'm sewing, so let him come
up here, please—if he can make it.

(SIMPLE *enters and closes the door.*)

SIMPLE. I've made it. Well, I'm back on
my feet, up, out, and almost at it.
JOYCE. I see. You may come in. Remember the door—Mrs. Caddy's rules.

(*He opens the door a crack.*)

SIMPLE. Dog-gone old landlady! Joyce,
I know I'm a black sheep. But I explained
it all to you the last time you come by
the hospital.
JOYCE. I accepted your explanation.
SIMPLE. But you don't seem like you're
glad to see me, now I'm out—the way
you didn't say almost nothing when I
come by Friday.
JOYCE. I'm glad to see you.
SIMPLE. Then lemme kiss you. Ouch!
My back! (*He yells in pain as he bends
over.*)
JOYCE. Oh!
SIMPLE. I think my veterbrays is dis-
connected.
JOYCE. What did the X-rays show?
SIMPLE. Nothing but a black mark.
The doctor says I'm O.K. Just can't set
down too suddenly for a while.
JOYCE. Then have a slow seat.
SIMPLE. Joyce, is you my enemy? You
sound so cool. Am I intruding?
JOYCE. Oh, no. I'm just having a nice

peaceful Sunday evening at home—which I must say, I haven't had too often since I've been knowing you.

SIMPLE. Baby darling, I'm sorry if I'm disturbing you, but I hope you're glad to see me. What you making?

JOYCE. Just lingerie for a girl friend who's getting married.

SIMPLE. Step-ins or step-outs?

JOYCE. Slips, Jess, slips. Jess Semple, stop breathing down my neck. The way you say things sometimes, you think I'm going to melt again, don't you? Well, instead you might get stuck with this needle. Listen, hand me that pattern book over there. Let me see how I should insert this lace.

SIMPLE. What're you doing with all those timetables and travel books, baby?

JOYCE. Just in case we ever should get married, maybe I'm picking out a place to spend our honeymoon—Niagara Falls, the Grand Canyon, Plymouth Rock . . .

SIMPLE. I don't want to spend no honeymoon on no rock. These books is pretty, but, baby, we ain't ready to travel yet.

JOYCE. We can dream, can't we?

SIMPLE. Niagara Falls makes a mighty lot of noise falling down. I likes to sleep on holidays.

JOYCE. Oh, Jess! Then how about the Far West? Were you ever at the Grand Canyon?

SIMPLE. I were. Facts, I was also at Niagara Falls, after I were at Grand Canyon.

JOYCE. I do not wish to criticize your grammar, Mr. Semple, but as long as you have been around New York, I wonder why you continue to say, I were, and at other times, I was?

SIMPLE. Because sometimes I were, and sometimes I was, baby. I was at Niagara Falls and I were at the Grand Canyon—since that were in the far distant past when I were a coachboy on the

Santa Fe. I was more recently at Niagara Falls.

JOYCE. I see. But you never were "I were"! There is no "I were." In the past tense, there is only "I was." The verb *to be* is declined, "I am, I was, I have been."

SIMPLE. Joyce, baby, don't be so touchous about it. Do you want me to talk like Edward R. Murrow?

JOYCE. No! But when we go to formals I hate to hear you saying for example "I taken" instead of "I took." Why do colored people say, "I taken," so much?

SIMPLE. Because we are taken—taken until we are undertaken, and, Joyce, baby, funerals is high!

JOYCE. Funerals are high.

SIMPLE. Joyce, what difference do it make?

JOYCE. Jess! What difference does it make? Does is correct English.

SIMPLE. And do ain't?

JOYCE. Isn't—not ain't.

SIMPLE. Woman, don't tell me *ain't* ain't in the dictionary.

JOYCE. But it ain't—I mean—it isn't correct.

SIMPLE. Joyce, I gives less than a small damn! What if it aren't? (*In his excitement he attempts to sit down, but leaps up as soon as his seat touches the chair.*)

JOYCE. You say what if things aren't. You give less than a damn. Well, I'm tired of a man who gives less than a damn about "What if things aren't." I'm tired! Tired! You hear me? Tired! I have never known any one man so long without having some kind of action out of him. You have not even formally proposed to me, let alone writing my father for my hand.

SIMPLE. I did not know I had to write your old man for your hand.

JOYCE. My father, Jess, not my old man. And don't let it be too long. After all, I might meet some other man.

SIMPLE. You better not meet no other man. You better not! Do and I will marry you right now this June in spite of my first wife, bigamy, your old man—I mean your father. Joyce, don't you know I am not to be trifled with? I'm Jesse B. Semple.

JOYCE. I know who you are. Now, just sit down and let's spend a nice Sunday evening conversing, heh?

(SIMPLE *sits down, but it hurts him.*)

SIMPLE. Ouch!
JOYCE. Oh, Sweety! Let me make you a nice cool drink. Lemonade?
SIMPLE. Yes, Joyce, lemonade.

(JOYCE *exits.*)

(*Suddenly* SIMPLE *realizes what he has agreed to drink and cries in despair.*) Lemonade! (*He sits dejected until* JOYCE *returns.*) Baby, you ain't mad with me, is you?

(JOYCE *smiles and shakes her head, no.*)

Because I know you know what I mean when I say, "I is"—or "I are" or "was" or whatever it be. Listen, Joyce, honey, please. (*He sings.*)
When I say "I were" believe me.
When I say "I was" believe me, too—
Because I were, and was, and I *am*
Deep in love with you.

If I say "You took" or "taken"
Just believe I have been taken, too,
Because I were, and am, and I *is*
Taken in by you.

If it *is* or it *ain't* well stated,
And it *ain't* or it *aren't* said right,
My love still must be rated
A love that don't fade over night.

When I say "I am" believe me.
When I say "I is" believe me, too—
Because I were, and was, and I *is,*
Deep in love with you.

Damn if I ain't!

JOYCE. A small damn? (*He grabs her.*)

(JOYCE *screams.*)

BLACKOUT

ACT ONE

SCENE 7

SIMPLE'*s room. A month later.*
MR. BOYD *comes down the hall and sees* SIMPLE'*s door ajar. He looks in.*

BOYD. Hey, fellow, what you doing home on Saturday night?
SIMPLE. Boyd, man, come on in. Joyce is gone to some gal's wedding shower—and damn if I'm going out to any bar. Still and yet, Boyd, I'm in a good mind to take that money I been saving and blow it all in, every damn penny, because man, it looks hopeless. Push done come to shove on that divorce, I got to pay for my part of it. So last month I started saving. But, damn, I got so far to go!
BOYD. How much do you have to save in all?
SIMPLE. One hundred thirty-three dollars and thirty-three cents. I'm as far as Leviticus.
BOYD. What do you mean, Leviticus?
SIMPLE. Aunt Lucy always said, "The Bible is the Rock: Put your trust therein." So that's where I'm putting my money. I got to save $133.33. If I put a ten dollar bill in each chapter every week from Genesis on, in eighteen and a half weeks I will have it—and I'll only have to go as far as Nahum.
BOYD. Nahum?
SIMPLE. That's a book in the Bible, somewhere down behind Ezekiel. If I ever get to Nahum that's it. I done put ten in Genesis, ten in Exodus, and five in Levi.
BOYD. I thought you said *ten* every week.

SIMPLE. I were a little short this week. Anyhow, I got twenty-five.

BOYD. Come on, let's go around to Paddy's.

SIMPLE. Thanks, Daddy-o! I will not yield to temptation! No! Not especially since I done got another letter from that used-to-be wife of mine, Isabel. Sit down, Boyd. Listen. "Jesse B. Semple, you are less than a man. You marry a girl, neglect her, ignore her, and won't help her divorce herself, not even when your part ain't only but one-third of the payment. You can go to hell! You do not deserve no gold seal on your decree, because you have not put a cent into it. Therefore, since I am going to pay for this divorce myself, your paper may not be legal. From now on, you kiss my foot! Isabel Estherlee Jones. P.S. I have taken back my maiden name, as I wants no part of you attached to me any longer. MISS JONES."

BOYD. She's angry.

SIMPLE. Seems like it. Boyd, I will not let Isabel get the last word on me. I'll send that lawyer my part of the money next week, even if I have to put my whole paycheck in to do it. Right now I got twenty-five in the Bible. When I add my old check, that won't leave but about ah—er—a sixty to go. I can pawn a suit, one overcoat, and my radio—which might still leave about fifty. Boyd, can you lend me fifty?

BOYD. Fellow, are you out of your mind?

SIMPLE. This is an emergency. I need a gold seal on my divorce, too—so I got to pay for it. I got to have that gold seal, Boyd! I got to have it! It's got to be legal for Joyce. But then it's up to me to get that money, ain't it, Boyd? It ain't up to you nor nobody else—it's just up to me.

BOYD. Yes, Simple, I'm afraid it is. Get hold of yourself, make a man out of yourself. You got to live up to your obligations.

SIMPLE. You done said a big word, Boyd.

BOYD. And it's a big thing you've got to do, fellow, facing up to yourself. You're not the first man in the world to have problems. You've got to learn how to swim, Jess, in this great big ocean called the world.

SIMPLE. This great big old white ocean —and me a colored swimmer.

BOYD. Aw, stop feeling sorry for yourself just because you're colored. You can't use race as an excuse forever. All men have problems. And even if you are colored, you've got to swim beyond color, and get to that island that is you—the human you, the man you. You've got to face your obligations, and stand up on that island of *you,* and be a man.

SIMPLE. Obligations! That's a word for you, Boyd! Seems like to me obligations is just a big old rock standing in a man's way.

BOYD. Then you've got to break that rock, fellow. Or, maybe I should say rocks.

SIMPLE. I know what you mean—like the beer rock, huh, Boyd?

BOYD. Um-hum!

SIMPLE. And the licker-rock—only I don't drink much whiskey.

BOYD. Well, say the bar-rock in general.

SIMPLE. That night-owl rock.

BOYD. Out until four A.M.

SIMPLE. Yes, the chick-chasing rock.

BOYD. Zarita!

SIMPLE. Not mentioning no names! But, man, I done shook that chick. But then there's always that old trying-to-save-money rock.

BOYD. You mean putting-it-off-until-tomorrow rock.

SIMPLE. Which has really been my stumbling rock.

BOYD. You got to bust it, man. You know about John Henry, don't you?

SIMPLE. Sure I do.

BOYD. He was the champion rock-buster of them all.

SIMPLE. My Uncle Tige used to sing about him. Boyd, I been making up my mind to break through my rocks, too.

(BOYD *smiles.*)

Yes, I is, Boyd, I is.

BOYD. You just got to bust 'em, fellow, that's all. (BOYD *exits.*)

(SIMPLE *takes off his shirt and changes into a ragged pajama top.*)

SIMPLE. Bust 'em! I got to bust 'em. Like that song of Uncle Tige's. That old man sure could sing—made up songs, too. (SIMPLE *sits on bed to take off his shoes.*) Made his own about John Henry which went—lemme see. (*He tries to remember.*) How did it go? Something about—
They say John Henry was a man.
And they say he took a hammer in his hand—

(*He uses one shoe as a hammer.*)

That's it!

And busted a rock
So hard he gave the world a shock!
Yes, they say John Henry was a man.

(SIMPLE *rises.*)

They say John Henry won a prize,
And they say he gave his life to win that prize.

(*He comes forward.*)

Yes, they say he hammered on
Until his breath was gone!

(*As if speaking to himself.*)

They say John Henry won a prize.

(*He reaches toward his back pocket.*)

Well, there's a prize I'm gonna win,
And the time's long gone I should begin.

(*From his wallet he shakes his last five*

dollar bill, opens the Bible, and puts it in between the pages.)

But it's better late than never,
And no time ain't forever.

(*He clasps the Bible to his chest.*)

So right now, I'm gonna start to win.

(*He turns forward resolutely, putting Bible down.*)

It takes a long haul to get there, so they say,
And there's great big mountains in the way.
But I'm gonna make it through
It it's the last damn thing I do.

(*He bangs his hand on the Bible.*)

I'm gonna be John Henry, be John Henry,
I'm gonna be John Henry, too.

BLACKOUT

END OF ACT ONE

ACT TWO

SCENE 1

The music of the Blues on the guitar, slow, haunting, syncopated, precedes the rise of the curtain.
Paddy's Bar. A week later. Evening.
ARCIE *is sitting alone at a table drinking sherry wine and working a crossword puzzle in the paper.* BOYD *is writing in a notebook at another table. The* PIANIST *lazily runs his fingers over the keys as* HOPKINS, *behind the bar, stifles a yawn.*

HOPKINS. Blue Monday night, no money, and I feel like hell. What you writing, Boyd?

BOYD. Just making some notes for a story I might write—after observing life in Harlem over the weekend.

HOPKINS. You didn't go to Philly Sunday to see that young lady?

BOYD. She's vacationing in Paris, which is O.K. by me, because when we get ready to honeymoon, I won't have to take her to Europe.

HOPKINS. Far as I could take a chick on a honeymoon would be the Theresa Hotel.

BOYD. That's about as far as I *could* take one, unless I sell some of this stuff I've been writing.

(MAMIE enters, panting.)

HOPKINS. Hey, Mamie! What's the matter?

MAMIE. I'm seeking escape—that Melon—

(MELON enters with a hangdog-air.)

Man, if you would just stop following me! Now that you're so bold to call at my house every night, at least let me have a little peace when I take a walk, without you at my heels.

MELON. Aw, Miss Mamie, you know I'm drawn to you.

MAMIE. When I get home from work, man, *I am tired*. I just want to set down, and rest, and read my paper. But Tang-a-lang-lang! You ring the bell! It looks like here lately, at home, in the bar, any-where, every time—

When I'm in a quiet mood, here you come.

When I'm deep in solitude, here you come.

When I feel like settling down—
MELON.
There I are!
MAMIE.
When I'm gazing at the moon—
MELON.
In falls your star!
MAMIE.
My dial is set, the tone is low,
There's nice sweet music on my radio.
I take a book, the story's fun—
But when you ring my bell I never get
my reading done.

When I'm in a quiet mood, up you pop.
When I'm playing solitaire, in you drop.
MELON.
The way you upset me makes my heart-strings hum—
MAMIE.
When I'm in a quiet mood—
BOTH.
Here you (I) come!
MAMIE.
It's raining outside. It's nice in the house.
Everything is cool—quiet as a mouse.
The doorbell rings. Who can it be?
My solitude is ended, Lord, you're look-ing for me!
Slippers on my feet, in my boudoir chair,
F-M on the dial, "The Londonderry Air."
The telephone rings, you say you're com-ing by.
When you get to my door—
BOTH.
My! Oh, my!

(MAMIE walks away, MELON follows.)

MELON.
Oh, you act so cute and you switch so coy—
Mamie, I was meant to be your playboy.
I dial your phone, hear you yell, "Damn Sam!"
Which means that you know I'm your honey lamb.
With hankering heart, I just follow you.
Your kisses are as sweet as sweet moun-tain dew.
I ring your bell, it's just old me.—
I come around to try to keep you com-pany.
I've sampled lots of melons whose flavor's fine,
But you are the sweetest melon on my vine.
I know that you love me by the look in your eye.
When I knock at your door—
BOTH.
My! Oh, my!
MAMIE.

When I'm in a quiet mood, up you pop.
When I'm playing solitaire, in you drop.
MELON.
The way you upset me makes my heart-
strings hum.
MAMIE.
When I'm in a quiet mood—
BOTH.
Here you (I) come!
MAMIE.
When the night is free to get my beauty
sleep,
I cannot sleep, so I'm counting sheep.
The doorbell rings—I shoot the sheep—
Bam! Bam!
'Cause there in the door stands some old
moth-eaten lamb.
I could scream! It's not a dream—
Here you come—to upset me! . . . And,
honey, I'm leaving.
Here I go! . . . And I mean it!

MELON. Well, I guess this time she
really means it.
MAMIE. Well, if you're coming, come
on!
MELON. I'm going to follow—here I
come!

(MAMIE and MELON exeunt. SIMPLE
bursts in exuberantly.)

SIMPLE. Hey, now, moo-cow! Gimme
a little milk. Barman, untap your keg.
Suds us up! Let's drink to it, even if it
is my last dollar.
HOPKINS. Your last dollar, didn't you
get paid this week?
SIMPLE. I did, but I took that money
—all of it—and added it to what was in
the Bible and sent it off to Baltitmore—
$133.34. Being last on payments, I had
to pay that extra penny to change Divorce Pending to Divorce Ending!
HOPKINS. Congratulations!
SIMPLE. Joyce knows I love her. But
to get a woman to make his bed down, a
man has to make his mind up. Joyce is

sweet, I mean! My queen—my desire, my
fire, my honey—the only woman who
ever made me save my money!
ARCIE. Simple.
SIMPLE. Yes, ma'am?
ARCIE. What's a four-letter word for
damn?
SIMPLE. Arcie, do you see that sign?
(He points to: "NO PROFANITY IN
HERE.") Well, I do not repeat no four-
letter words in public.
ARCIE. Damn!

(ZARITA enters, briskly switching.)

ZARITA. Hi, folks! I thought I'd stop by
and have a quick one. Mr. Semple, how
do you do? Set me up, Hop. (She approaches SIMPLE.) How are you, Sugar?
SIMPLE. Zarita, could I have a word
with you, private?
ZARITA. Of course! It won't be the first
time.
ARCIE. Hummmmm-mm-m! I thought
so. That girl is like a magnet to that man.

(HOPKINS pours ARCIE a drink as
SIMPLE and ZARITA go outside.)

HOPKINS. Stay out of other people's
business, Arcie.
ARCIE. O.K.! O.K.!
ZARITA. So you're not even going to
speak to me again?
SIMPLE. What I do say is, I ain't gonna
talk to you. Good evening—and good-
bye! Excuse me.
ZARITA. Aw, not like that, Jess, listen
. . . (ZARITA puts an arm around SIMPLE.)
ARCIE. Hey there, you writer, Boyd.
What is the path in the field which a plow
makes called?
BOYD. Furrow.
ARCIE. Six letters, just right. Now, wait
a minute. Tell me, what is a hole with
just one opening?
BOYD. How many letters?
ARCIE. Six, starts with D.
HOPKINS. Dugout?

ARCIE. Just fits. A dead general. A Goddamn dead general!

(SIMPLE *pulls away from* ZARITA.)

ZARITA. But, Jess, you know you and me together always has fun.

SIMPLE. Zarita, I'm the same as about to get married. I got responsibilities.

ZARITA. I am a lady, Jess Semple. Don't worry, I'll stay out of your life. I'm tired of paying you a sometime call when I'm feeling lonely. Anyhow, I always did bring my own licker. You never had none.

SIMPLE. But I always treat you when I meet you—when I can. Zarita, you know I'd give you the shirt off my back.

ZARITA. And I'd gladly give you mine. Go on and get your rest, Jess. You never turned in this early before.

SIMPLE. I still got to make a week's work before that lay-off comes.

ZARITA. I guess you'll say good night, even if you wouldn't say hello.

SIMPLE. Good night.

ZARITA. Good night.

(SIMPLE *expects* ZARITA *to leave. Instead she stands there and smiles at him her sweetest smile.* SIMPLE *looks at the bar as if he wants to sit down on the stool again, then looks at* ZARITA. *Finally he decides to leave.*)

SIMPLE. Going my way, Boyd?

BOYD. I might as well, it's getting late. So long, folks.

ARCIE. And I ain't finished this puzzle.

BOYD. Hop'll help you. Good night.

(SIMPLE *and* BOYD *exit, as the* PIANIST *ripples the keys.*)

ARCIE. It ain't but a quarter to twelve. What's happening to Simple?

ZARITA. He's getting domesticated. You know, Arcie, I wish someone would feel about me the way Simple feels about Joyce, and she about him, even if they do have their ups and downs. I guess a little trouble now and then just helps to draw people together. But you got to have somebody to come together with.

(*The notes on the piano rise hauntingly.*)

Gee, Bill, you play pretty sometimes.

PIANIST. I studied to be a concert pianist, but the concert never did come off.

ZARITA. What's that you're playing now? Sounds familiar. (ZARITA *leans on the piano.*)

PIANIST. Some new piece a colored boy wrote, I heard it on the radio. Let me croon it to you:
Just a little shade and shadow
Mixed in with the light
Helps to make the sunshine brighter
When things turn out right.

ZARITA.
Just a little pain and trouble
Mixed in with the fair
Helps to make your joys seem double
When clouds are not there.

Look for the morning star
Shining in the dawn?
Look for the rainbow's arch
When the rain is gone!

Don't forget there're bluebirds
Somewhere in the blue.
Love will send a little bluebird
Flying straight to you.

(*The light fades as* JOYCE *is heard singing.*)

Look for the morning star
Shine, shine, shining in the dawn!
Rainbow, rainbow, rainbow's arch
When the rain is gone.

Don't forget you'll find bluebirds
Somewhere in the blue.
Love will send a little bluebird
Flying straight to you. . . .

(BLACKOUT *as the melody continues into the next scene.*)

ACT TWO

SCENE 2

JOYCE's *room. Two weeks later.*
JOYCE *is serving* SIMPLE *some sand-wiches as she continues to sing.* SIMPLE *looks very serious.*

JOYCE.
. . . Love will send a little bluebird
Flying straight to you . . .
Just a little shade and shadow . . .

SIMPLE. . . . Shades and shadows, just like the song says. Listen, Joyce, you know when I first met you on that boat-ride, I said to myself, "That girl's too good for me. I can't make no headway with that kind of woman." Yes, I did! To tell the truth, Joyce, you gave me a kinder hard road to go—you know, with your morals and—

JOYCE. And you already married.

SIMPLE. Yes, but not wedlocked. . . .

JOYCE. Still and yet there was a shadow between us. . . .

SIMPLE. Of bigamy,

JOYCE. And gossip,

SIMPLE. Old landladies,

JOYCE. Friends,

SIMPLE. And I run around a lot in them days, too. . . .

JOYCE. In shady places—speakeasies, and things, so you said . . .

SIMPLE. Shady nothing! Them places was really dark—after-hours spots, Joyce. Now I know better. I'm older! And when I look at you, oh, I can see the sun, Joyce! It was dark, but now the clouds are rolling by.

JOYCE.
Just a little shade and shadow
Mixed in with the light
Helps to make the sunshine brighter
When things turn out right.

SIMPLE. True, so true!

JOYCE.
Just a little pain and trouble
Mixed in with the fair

Helps to make your joys double
When clouds are not there.

SIMPLE.
Wonderful the morning star
Shining in the dawn!

JOYCE.
Wonderful the rainbow's arch

BOTH.
When the rain is gone!

JOYCE.
Don't forget you'll find bluebirds
Somewhere in the blue.
Love will send a little bluebird
Flying straight to you.

SIMPLE.
Sing about the morning star
Shine-shine-shining in the dawn!
Rainbow, rainbow, rainbow's arch

BOTH.
When the rain is gone.

JOYCE.
I am sure we'll find bluebirds
Right here in the blue.

BOTH.
Love has sent a singing bluebird
Straight to me and you.

(*They kiss as the music rises lyrically.*)

JOYCE. Oh, Jess! Life is really wonderful!

SIMPLE. I wouldn't be caught dead without it. But—er—a—

JOYCE. But what, Jess?

SIMPLE. It's wonderful. But, Joyce, baby, something is always happening to a Negro—just when everything is going right. Listen—I'm sorry, but there's something I got to tell you, much as I don't want to.

JOYCE. About your divorce?

SIMPLE. No, sugar, that's all filed, paid for, ought to be ready for the seal soon. Something else has come up. It's that—it's that—well, the notice come last week that it was coming. I just didn't tell you—I'm being laid off my job.

JOYCE. Oh, Jess! Not fired?

SIMPLE. No, not fired, just temporary, three or four months till after New Year's while they converts. Converting! And us planning to get married. Every time a Negro plans something—

JOYCE. Aw, come now! We'll get married, Jess.

SIMPLE. I can't even get my laundry out—let alone put my dirty shirts in.

JOYCE. Jess, I'll do your laundry. Bring me a bundle tomorrow and I'll bring them back to you—rub-a-dub-dub—white as snow.

SIMPLE. You're a doll, Joyce, you almost never come to my room.

JOYCE. Well, this'll give me a chance to see the curtains I made for you.

SIMPLE. Come see.

JOYCE. I will—when I bring this laundry, and if you need it, Jess, I can let you have a little money.

SIMPLE. I couldn't take no money from you.

JOYCE. But you can have it.

SIMPLE. I'd be embarrassed.

JOYCE. Have you got enough to eat?

SIMPLE. Oh, sure, I'll make out.

JOYCE. Well, on the weekend, Mr. Semple, you're going to dine with me. Make up your mind to that. And don't say one word about being embarrassed. Everything is going to be all right, I know. I talk to the Lord every night on my knees and I know.

SIMPLE. How long exactly it'll be before that job opens up again, to tell the truth, I don't know. Joyce, what are we going to do? We wants to get married, and all these years I have not saved a thing. Baby, have you figured up how much our wedding is going to cost?

JOYCE. There's no need to worry about that now. You've got enough on your mind tonight, darling. I just want you to know that I'm behind you.

SIMPLE. But, Joyce, baby, look! I ain't got nothing put away. I don't know if our plans are gonna go through or not.

JOYCE. Look, Jess, don't worry. If you ain't got the money to buy no license, well, when we get ready to get married we gonna get that license.

SIMPLE. But, Joyce, honey, I don't want you to be building no castles in the sand.

JOYCE. Jess, I have built my castles in my heart. They're not in no sand. No waves is gonna beat them down. No wind is gonna blow them apart. Nothing can scatter my castles. I tell you, nothing! Their bricks are made out of love and their foundations are strong. And you, Jess Semple, you are the gate-keeper of my castle—which is in my heart. You are the gate-keeper of my castle. *(JOYCE sits on the floor at SIMPLE's feet and lays her head in his lap.)* Oh, Jess, we'll have our own little place, our own little house, and at night we'll both be there after jobs are done. Oh, Jess, baby, you don't know how much—

I want somebody to come home to
When I come home at night.
I want someone to depend upon
I know will do right.

I want somebody to come home to
I'm sure will be at home.
I want someone who is sweet and kind
I know will not roam.

I'm a homebody—and this homebody
Wants somebody to share my share
For each homebody needs somebody
Who will always be right there.

I want somebody to come home to
Who'll make my dreams come true
A nice someone who'll be the one
I know will be you.

(Repeat from release closing with this.)

A nice homebody who's just somebody
Lovely to come home to.

BLACKOUT

ACT TWO

SCENE 3

SIMPLE's *room. Early evening.*

SIMPLE *is lying on his bed, shoes off and shirttail out, dozing. A DOORBELL is heard ringing madly. Commotion downstairs and in the hallway.* ZARITA *busts in on a startled* SIMPLE. *A large red pocketbook swings from one of her arms.*

ZARITA. It's my birthday, Jess! And I brought my friends around to celebrate —since you're broke these days and don't come out no more.

(SIMPLE *leaps up and begins to tuck his shirt in and put on a shoe. VOICES are heard on the stairs.*)

BODIDDLY. What floor is it on?
HOPKINS. You're sure he's expecting us?
MAMIE. We rung the bell.
MELON. I been here before.
ARCIE. I'm having trouble with these steps.

(BOYD *is seen outside* SIMPLE's *door.*)

BOYD. Shsss-ss-sss! Be quiet. What the hell is going on? You want to get us in trouble with the landlady?

(By now the crowd—which includes all the bar customers and as many strangers as desired to make the staging lively—has pushed BOYD into the room.)

ZARITA. I tell you, it's my birthday, Jess! Come on in, everybody.
MELON. Happy birthday!
PIANIST. Happy birthday, Zarita!

(GITFIDDLE *begins to play.*)

SIMPLE. Zarita, your birthday ain't mine. And I don't want—
ZARITA. But I want to share it with you, Daddy! We brought our own liquor. When it runs out, we'll send and get some more. Won't we, Melon?

MELON. Liquor's about gone now, Whoopee-ee-ee!
ARCIE. Have some o' my sherry, Simple. I got my own bottle.
ZARITA. Jess, honey, I forgot to tell you I'd be twenty-some odd years old today. We started celebrating this morning and we're still going strong.
BODIDDLY. The ball is on!
ZARITA. Let the good times roll!
BODIDDLY. Let the good times roll in "D"!
MELON. Whoopee!

(ZARITA *begins to sing.*)

ZARITA.
If you ain't got nothing
And there's nothing to get,
Who cares long as you're doing it?
If you ain't got anything
Better to do,
Why not do what's good to do?

MELON. What's that?
ZARITA.
Ball, ball, let's ball awhile!
Ball, ball, honey chile!
Sing! Shout! Beat it out!

ALL.
Dance! Prance! Take a chance!
Grab the blues and get them told—
When you're happy in your soul.

ZARITA.
Start the music playing
Let the good times roll.

ALL.
Wail! Sail! Let it fly!

ZARITA.
Cool fool: we're riding high!

ALL.
Ball, ball, let's ball awhile!

(Everybody dances wildly with a dazed SIMPLE in their midst, one shoe still off.)

ZARITA.
Ball, ball, let's ball awhile!
Ball, ball, honey chile!
Sing! Shout! Beat it out!
Dance! Prance! Take a chance!
Grab the blues and get them told—
When you're happy in your soul.
Start the music playing,
Let the good times roll.
Wail! Sail! Let it fly!
Cool fool: We're riding high!
Ball, ball, let's ball awhile!

(ZARITA forces SIMPLE to dance.)

ALL.
Ball, ball, let's ball awhile!
Ball, ball, honey chile!
Sing! Shout! Beat it out!
Dance! Prance! Take a chance!
Grab the blues and get them told—
When you're happy in your soul.

ZARITA.
Start the music playing
Let the good times roll!

(The whole room starts rocking.)

ALL.
Wail! Sail! Let it fly!
Cool fool! We're riding high!
Ball! Ball! Let's ball awhile!

BODIDDLY. Hey, now!
ZARITA. Ow! It's my birthday! We're balling!
HOPKINS. Happy birthday, Zarita!
MELON. Dog-gone it! This bottle is empty.
ARCIE. Mine, too. Diddly, go get some more.
BODIDDLY. Send Melon. Here's fifty cents. (He tosses MELON a coin.)
ZARITA. Play that again, Git, "Let's Ball Awhile."
MAMIE.
Ball! Ball! Honey chile!
Ball! Ball! Let's ball awhile!

ARCIE. Yippeee-ee-ee-e! Diddly, shake yourself!
(ZARITA's big red pocketbook is swinging wildly on her arms as the crowd stops dancing and moves back to let her and SIMPLE cavort madly together in a fast and furious jitterbug, each trying to outdo the other in cutting capers.)

Aw, do it, Zarita!

(ZARITA spins around and around with her purse in her hand swirling high above her head. Suddenly the clasp comes open —the innumerable and varietd contents of her enormous pocketbook fly all over the room, cascading everywhere: compact, lipstick, handkerchief, pocket mirror, key ring with seven keys, scattered deck of cards, black lace gloves, bottle opener, cigarette case, chewing gum, bromo quinine box, small change, fountain pen, sun glasses, address books, finger-nail file, blue poker chips, matches, flask and a shoe horn.)

ZARITA. Oh, ooo-oo-o! My bag! Stop the music! Stop, Git, stop!
ARCIE. Girl, your perfume done broke!
ZARITA. My Night in Egypt!
BODIDDLY. If you broke your mirror, it's seven years bad luck.
PIANIST. Help her pick her things up, man.
BODIDDLY. I'm helping. But what's this? (Holding up a red brassiere.)
BOYD. Lord, women sure can have a lot of stuff in their pocketbooks!
MAMIE. She's even got poker chips!
ZARITA. Jess, you help me, baby. The rest of you-all stay where you are. I don't know some of you folks, and I don't want to lose nothing valuable.
ARCIE. You ain't got nothing I want, child.
ZARITA. Where's my China Girl lipstick in the jade-studded holder? I don't want to lose that lipstick! Jess, you reckon it rolled outside?

SIMPLE. Might could be. Lemme look.

(Just then the DOORBELL rings nine times.)

My ring!

ZARITA. My lipstick! Where's my lipstick? Help me, sugar. *(ZARITA pulls SIMPLE down with her on the floor to search for the lipstick in the doorway as the bell continues to ring.)*

ARCIE. Somebody let Melon in with that licker.

BODIDDLY. Let that man in.

HOPKINS. The door's still open. He ought to have sense enough to come in.

BODIDDLY. I say to hell with the bell, and help Zarita find her stuff. Whee! Smell that "Night in Egypt"!

(SIMPLE finds the lipstick and ZARITA kisses him.)

SIMPLE. Here it is!

ZARITA. Aw, goody!

(GITFIDDLE starts the music again and all dance.)

Aw, Simple, just because we're dancing, you don't have to keep on kissing me.

SIMPLE. Who's kissing who, Zarita? *You're* kissing me.

BODIDDLY. Come up for air, you two! Come up for air! Aw, play it, Git.

(The music soars. But suddenly the room becomes dead silent as everyone stops still, except SIMPLE and ZARITA who are embracing. JOYCE is standing in the doorway. Drunkenly ARCIE speaks.)

ARCIE. Come on in, girl, and join the fun!

PIANIST. Slappy Slirthday!

(JOYCE can hardly believe her eyes.)

JOYCE. This is Mr. Semple's room, isn't it?

PIANIST. Sure is. We're having a ball.

(Her back to the door, ZARITA hollers.)

ZARITA. Play it again, Git! Come on—"Let's Ball a While!" Where's Melon with the licker? . . . Oh!

(Suddenly both she and SIMPLE see JOYCE. SIMPLE is astounded.)

SIMPLE. Joyce!

JOYCE. Jess, I brought your laundry I washed for you. I thought you might want to wear one of the shirts Sunday.

ZARITA. Tip on in, Joyce, and enjoin my birthday. We don't mind. I'm Zarita. Just excuse my stuff all over the place. We been having a ball, Simp and me and—

JOYCE. I did not know you had company, Jess.

(WATERMELON JOY arrives with his arms full of bottles and pushes past JOYCE.)

MELON. Gangway! The stuff is here and it's mellowed! Get out of the door, woman! Make room for Watermelon Joe —and the juice with the flow.

(JOYCE hands SIMPLE his bundle as MELON distributes bottles.)

JOYCE. Excuse me for being in your guests' way. Here, please take your laundry.

(The loud VOICE of SIMPLE's LAND-LADY is heard calling angrily as she enters in kimono and curlers.)

LANDLADY. Wait a minute! I'm the landlady here, and what I want to know is, who is this strange man walking in my house with his arms full of bottles? And *who* left my front door open? Who? I want to know who? Did you, Jess Semple? This is a respectable house. What's going on here? Do you hear me, Mr. Semple?

(Meekly SIMPLE answers.)

SIMPLE. Yes'm. These is just some guestests, that's all.

LANDLADY. Well, get 'em out of here—raising sand in my house! Get 'em out I say. *(She exits in a huff.)*

JOYCE. I'm going—as quick as I can. *(JOYCE starts to pass SIMPLE.)*

SIMPLE. Joyce! . . . Joyce! You know she don't mean you. I wants a word with you, Joyce.

(JOYCE turns on him furiously, fighting back her tears.)

JOYCE. With me? You don't need to explain to me, Jess Semple. Now I have seen that Zarita woman with my own eyes in your bedroom. No wonder you're giving a birthday party to which I am not invited. I won't be in your way tonight, Jess—nor ever—any more. *(She looks back into the room as she leaves.)* Enjoy yourselves. Good night! *(JOYCE rushes down the hall and out of the house.)*

SIMPLE. Joyce! . . . Joyce! . . . Joyce! . . .

ZARITA. Huh! Who does that old landlady think she is? You pay your rent, don't you, Simple? Come on, folks, let's ball awhile.

PIANIST. Happy slirthday!

(SIMPLE stands holding his parcel of laundry.)

SIMPLE. I'm sorry, Miss Arcie, Boyd, Diddly! . . . *To hell with your birthday,* Zarita! . . . Folks, I'm sorry. Will you all go?

(ARCIE scurries out. The others follow. MELON retrieves several of the bottles and takes them with him. ZARITA picks up her red bag and swaggers out with MAMIE behind her.)

ZARITA. I know where we can ball, folks—at my house! Come on!

MAMIE. I been throwed out of better places than this.

(GITFIDDLE turns at the door and looks

at SIMPLE *as if to say he's sorry, but* SIMPLE *does not look up.* BOYD, *the last to go, closes the door.* ALL *exit down the stairs leaving* SIMPLE *in the middle of the floor. He feels his cheek, looks in the mirror, then takes his handkerchief and violently tries to wipe Zarita's lipstick from his jaw. He throws the handkerchief on the dresser and sinks down on the bed, his head in his hands.)*

SIMPLE. Oh, my God!

(GITFIDDLE's guitar is heard going down the stairs.)

Oh, my God! . . . My God! . . . Oh, God!

(THE LIGHTS DIM TO A SINGLE SPOT on the forlorn figure. There is the snapping of a broken string on the distant guitar.)

CURTAIN

ACT TWO

SCENE 4

Paddy's bar. A quiet Sunday evening.
SIMPLE *enters and gloomily begins taking articles from his pockets and putting them on the bar.*

SIMPLE. Hop, is you seen Zarita?

HOPKINS. Nope. Guess she's still recovering from her birthday.

SIMPLE. If you do see her, give her this junk.

HOPKINS. Looks like to me you've snatched her purse.

SIMPLE. I'd snatch her head if I could! That woman has ruint me now—Joyce is out of my life.

HOPKINS. Have a drink, fellow, on me.

SIMPLE. This is one time I do not want a drink, Hop. I feel too bad. I have phoned her seventeen times, and Joyce will not answer the phone. I rung her bell four nights straight. Nobody would let me in. I sent Joyce eight telegrams, which she do not answer.

HOPKINS. And Zarita?

SIMPLE. I don't never want to see Zarita no more. The smell of that "Night in Egypt" is still in my room.

HOPKINS. A man should not fool around with a bad woman when he's got a good woman to love.

SIMPLE. Don't I know that now!

HOPKINS. Have you tried to see Joyce today? Sunday, she might be home.

SIMPLE. Tried? Are you kidding? That's all I've done. These is my bitter days! Hop, what shall I do?

HOPKINS. I don't know, Jess.

SIMPLE. Negroes never know anything important when they need to. I'm going to walk by her house again now. I just want to know if Joyce got home safe from church.

HOPKINS. She's been getting home safe all these years.

SIMPLE. Hop, I'm nearly out of my head. I got to talk to her. I'll stand in front of her house all night if I have to.

(ZARITA enters, cool, frisky, and pretty as ever.)

HOPKINS. Uh-oh!

ZARITA. Hel-lo! Jess, I'm glad I caught you. I was a little shy about coming around to your place for my things.

SIMPLE. I brought your things here, Zarita.

(HOPKINS puts them on the bar.)

ZARITA. I thought you might, you're so sweet, sugar. Lemme treat you to a drink, and you, too, Hop.

SIMPLE. No thank you.

ZARITA. Don't be that way. Set us up, here, Hopkins.

SIMPLE. I'm not drinking no more myself.

ZARITA. What? Just because you're out of work, you don't have to put down all the pleasures. Say, listen, Jess, if you're broke, I can let you have a little money.

HOPKINS. Zarita!

ZARITA. But no jive, Jess. Because you're wifeless and workless, a nice little old guy like you don't have to go hungry, never. I cook stringbeans and ham almost every day.

SIMPLE. I don't like stringbeans.

ZARITA. I'll fry you some chicken, then.

SIMPLE. Forget it, please!

ZARITA. O.K. If you're that proud. *(ZARITA opens her purse.)* Anyhow, here honey-boy, take this ten—in case you need it.

SIMPLE. Um-um! NO! Thanks, Zarita, no! *(SIMPLE backs away.)*

ZARITA. I meant no harm. I'm just trying to cheer you up. Like that party which I brought around to your house. Knowing you wasn't working, thinking maybe you'd be kinder embarrassed to come to my place for my birthday and not bring a present, I brought the party to you. Meant no harm—just to cheer you up.

SIMPLE. Please don't try to cheer me up no more, Zarita. Hop, I'm cutting out. I'm going by—you know where I told you, one more time. *(SIMPLE starts out.)*

HOPKINS. Don't try to break her door down.

SIMPLE. I'm just gonna stand on the sidewalk and look up at her window.

HOPKINS. I hope you see a light, pal.

(SIMPLE exits as the PIANIST begins to play softly, "Look for the Morning Star." He sings, starting with the release.)

PIANIST.
Look for the morning star
Shining in the dawn.
Look for the rainbow's arch
When the rain is gone.

(The remainder of the song he hums. ZARITA, lonely, looks around at the quiet bar, then cries in desperation.)

ZARITA. I'm lonesome, Hop! I'm lonesome! I'm lonesome! (ZARITA *buries her head on the bar and weeps as the piano continues.*) I'm lonesome. . . .

BLACKOUT

ACT TWO

SCENE 5

SIMPLE's *room. Late evening.*

SIMPLE *is lighting a cone of incense in a saucer on his dresser as* BOYD *pokes his head in the door, sniffs, and enters.*

BOYD. Hy, fellow! What's that burning on the dresser?

SIMPLE. Incense. I lit it to keep warm. I really hates winter.

BOYD. Oh, man, cold weather makes you get up and go, gives you vim, vigor, vitality!

SIMPLE. It does not give me anything but a cold—and all that snow outside!

BOYD. Perhaps you are just not the right color for winter, being dark. In nature you know, animals have protective coloration to go with their environment. Desert toads are sand-colored. Tree lizards are green. Ermine, for example, is the color of the snow country in which it originates.

SIMPLE. Which accounts for me not having no business wading around in snow, then. It and my color do not match. But, please, let's stop talking about snow, Boyd.

BOYD. Agreed—as cold as it is in this icebox!

SIMPLE. Landladies has no respect for roomers a-tall, Boyd. In fact, ours cares less for her roomers than she does for her dog. She will put a roomer out—dead out in the street—when he does not pay his rent, but she does not put out that dog. Trixie is her heart! She keeps Trixie warm. But me, I has nothing to keep

warm by, but incense. I'm sick of this kind of living, Boyd. Maybe if I just had a little something, a place to live, some money, I could win Joyce back. If I don't get her back, Boyd, I don't know! I just don't know!

BOYD. I can lend you a small amount, Jess, if you need it—you know, five or ten.

SIMPLE. But I borrows only when I *hope* I can pay back, Boyd.

(*A creaking sound is heard on the steps. The* LANDLADY's VOICE *is heard outside.*)

LANDLADY. I do believes somebody's smoking marijuana in my house.

SIMPLE. Listen! Don't I hear a elephant walking?

(*She knocks loudly on* SIMPLE's *door.*)

Come in!

LANDLADY. Mr. Semple, I am forced to inform you that I allows no reefer smoking in my home.

SIMPLE. I allows none in my room, neither.

LANDLADY. Then what do I smell?

SIMPLE. Chinese incense from Japan.

LANDLADY. Is you running a fast house?

SIMPLE. Madam, you have give me a idea!

LANDLADY. I am not joking, Jess Semple. Tell me, how come you burning that stuff in my house? Is it for bad luck or good?

SIMPLE. I don't believe in no lucky scents. I am just burning this for fun. It also gives out heat. Here, I will give you a stick to perfume up your part of the house.

LANDLADY. Thank you, I'll take it, even if it do smell like a good-time house to me. And that nude naked calendar you got hanging on your wall ain't exactly what I'd call decent. Don't your licker store give out no respectable girls on their calendars?

SIMPLE. They do, but they got clothes on.

LANDLADY. Naturally! Never would I pose in a meadow without my clothes on.

SIMPLE. I hope not, Madam.

LANDLADY. Meaning by that . . . ?

SIMPLE. Meaning you have such a beautiful character you do not have to show your figure. There is sweetness in your face.

LANDLADY. I appreciates that, Mr. Semple. (She shivers.) Whee! It is right chilly up here.

SIMPLE. It's a deep freeze.

LANDLADY. If you roomers would go to bed on time—and your guests would go home—including Mr. Boyd—I would not have to keep heat up until all hours of the night.

SIMPLE. Has the heat been up tonight?

LANDLADY. You know it were warm as toast in this house at seven P.M. Funny where *your* heat disappears to. Downstairs I fails to notice any change myself.

SIMPLE. Madam, science states that heat is tied in with fat.

LANDLADY. Meaning . . . ?

SIMPLE. You're protected.

LANDLADY. I don't study ways of insulting roomers, Jess Semple, and that is the second sly remark you made about me tonight. I'll thank you to regret it.

SIMPLE. Madam, I does regret it!

LANDLADY. To my face—fat! Huh! You heard him, Mr. Boyd. (She exits muttering.) Elephant, huh? Behind in your rent, huh!

BOYD. Now our landlady's angry.

SIMPLE. I tell you, something's always happening to a colored man! Stormy weather! Boyd, I been caught in some kind of riffle ever since I been black. All my life, if it ain't raining, it's blowing. If it ain't sleeting, it's snowing. Man, you try to be good, and what happens? You just don't be good. You try to live right. What happens? You look back and find out you didn't live right. Even when

you're working, and you try to save money, what happens? Can't do it. Your shoes is wore out. Or the dentist has got you. You try to save again. What happens? You drunk it up. Try to save another time. Some relative gets sick and needs it. What happens to money, Boyd? What happens?

BOYD. Come on, man, snap out of it! Let's go down to Paddy's and have a drink. At least we can sit up in the bar and get warm—and not think about what happens.

SIMPLE. You go, Boyd. What happens has done already happened to me.

(Slowly BOYD leaves. Half through the door suddenly a bright thought comes to him. He smiles and snaps his fingers, then exits closing the door, leaving SIMPLE alone as the LIGHT FADES SLOWLY TO DARKNESS.)

BLACKOUT

ACT TWO

SCENE 6

Sidewalk on Lenox Avenue, downstage apron, with a sign LENOX AVENUE, a let-down flap at Left. Early evening. BOYD walks briskly down the street as if on a mission, entering Right. Exits Left. Following him, JOHN JASPER comes dancing along the sidewalk Right selling papers and stopping to hit a step now and then.

JOHN JASPER. Paper! . . . Amsterdam News! . . . Reall all about it! Get your paper! (He dances off Left.)

(BODIDDLY enters Right followed by ARCIE hobbling along behind him. BODIDDLY turns, stops.)

BODIDDLY. Woman, you better stop tagging *behind* me on the street, and walk *beside* me, like a wife should—before I lose my impatience.

ARCIE. Diddly, these new shoes hurt my feet.

BODIDDLY. I paid $20 for them shoes for you! Arcie, ain't you read in the Bible where Moses walked for forty years in the wilderness *barefooted?* Now, here you can't walk a block without complaining!

ARCIE. But, Diddly, lover, I ain't Moses.

BODIDDLY. Aw, come on, woman! *(Exeunt.)*

(Enter MAMIE, trailed by MELON Right.)

MAMIE. Melon, you got more nerve than Liberace's got sequins. You ain't gonna get nowhere, so there's no need of you trailing me through the streets like this.

MELON. I can't help it, Miss Mamie. I'm marked by a liking for you! *(He addresses her in a rhymed jive, spoken.)*
You're my sugar,
You're my spice,
You're my everything
That's nice.

MAMIE. Melon, I done told you—
You *ain't* my sugar
You *ain't* my spice.
If you was a piece of cheese
I'd throw you to the mice.

(She moves on with MELON in pursuit.)

MELON. Miss Mamie—
Your words are bitter
But your lips are sweet.
Lemme kiss you, baby—
And give you a treat.

MAMIE. Melon—
When cows start playing numbers
And canary birds sing bass,
That is when you'll stick your
Big mouth in my face.

(MAMIE exits indignantly with MELON pleading as he follows.)

MELON. Aw, Miss Mamie, listen!
Wait a minute now!
I ain't no canary bird,
And you sure ain't no cow.
But . . .

(Exit MELON.)

BLACKOUT

ACT TWO

SCENE 7

JOYCE's *room. Same evening.*

BOYD *stands at the door as* JOYCE *opens it.*

BOYD. I hope you'll pardon me, Miss Lane—and maybe it's none of my business at all—but I was just walking down Lenox Avenue when the idea came to me and I felt like I ought to come and talk to you. *(He stands awkwardly.)*

JOYCE. You may sit, Mr. Boyd. *(She takes his hat.)*

BOYD. Thank you. I—I—

JOYCE. Yes?

BOYD. Well, it's about Simple. You know, I mean Jess Semple. He didn't ask me to come to see you. In fact he doesn't know I'm here at all. But he's been rooming right next to me quite a while now, and I—well—well, I never saw him like he is before.

(JOYCE begins to freeze.)

JOYCE. You know him well?

BOYD. Very well.

JOYCE. Are you one of his drinking buddies of the Paddy's Bar set?

BOYD. I'm not much of a drinking man, Miss Lane. I'm a writer.

JOYCE. A writer! What do you write?

BOYD. Books.

JOYCE. Books!

BOYD. About Harlem.

JOYCE. Harlem! I wish I could get away from Harlem.

BOYD. Miss Lane, I'm worried about Simple.

JOYCE. You're worried about Simple. He never seems to worry about himself.

BOYD. I think maybe you really don't know about that birthday party.

JOYCE. There's really nothing I want to learn.

BOYD. Except that it wasn't Simple's party. He didn't plan it, and didn't know anything about it until it descended on him.

JOYCE. Huh! Just like that—from above.

BOYD. They came to surprise us.

JOYCE. You too? You don't look like the type of man to attract that conglomeration of assorted humans. If you're going to tell me something, Mr. Boyd, tell me the truth.

BOYD. Well, everybody just likes Simple. That's his trouble. He likes people, so they like him. But he's not going with all those women. He wasn't even going with Zarita.

(JOYCE does not believe him.)

JOYCE. You can have your hat, Mr. Boyd, if you will.

(As he takes his hat he continues talking.)

BOYD. I mean, not lately, not for two or three years, since he's met you—why, he doesn't talk about anybody but you, hasn't for a long time.—Joyce, Joyce, Joyce! Now, he's even talking to himself in the night, trying to explain to you. I room next door, and sometimes I can hear him crying late in the night. Nobody likes to hear a grown man crying, Miss Lane.

(Sternly she dismisses him.)

JOYCE. Thank you very much, Mr. Boyd.

BOYD. Miss Lane!

(She closes the door as he backs out. JOYCE comes toward the center of the room, stops, thinks, then rushes to the closet and begins to put on her coat.)

BLACKOUT

ACT TWO

SCENE 8

SIMPLE'*s room. Same evening.*

SIMPLE *is alone, standing beside his dresser turning the pages of the Bible.*

SIMPLE. My old Aunt Lucy always said, "The Bible is the Rock, and the Rock is the Truth, and Truth is the Light." Lemme see. *(He reads from Job.)* It says here, "Let thy day be darkness. Let no God regard it from above, neither let the light shine upon it. . . . Man is born unto trouble." Lemme turn over! *(He tries the next page.)* Uh-huh! This is just as bad. "They meet with darkness in the daytime and grope in the noonday like as in the night." Great Gordon Gin! What part of the Bible am I reading out of? *Job!* No wonder! He's the one what suffered everything from boils to blindness. But it says here the Lord answered Job. Looks like don't nobody answer me. Nobody! *(He shuts the Bible and goes to the window.)*

(JOYCE comes up the stairs and down the hall. Outside his door she calls.)

JOYCE. Jess!

(His body stiffens.)

SIMPLE. Am I hearing things?

JOYCE. Jess!

SIMPLE. I must be going crazy! Can't be that voice.

(She knocks softly and enters.)

JOYCE. Jess!

SIMPLE. Joyce! Why are you here?

JOYCE. To see you, Jess. There's something maybe I ought to tell you.

SIMPLE. There's nothing for you to tell me, Joyce.

JOYCE. But, Jess—

(After a long silence he speaks.)

SIMPLE. You've come to *me*, Joyce.

JOYCE. Yes, Jess.

SIMPLE. Every time something's happened between us, in the end you come to me. It's my turn to come to you now.

JOYCE. You tried. I wouldn't let you in. I got those messages. I heard you ringing my bell. It's my fault, Jess.

SIMPLE. It's not your fault, Joyce. I had no business trying to see you *then*. But I wasn't man enough not to try.

JOYCE. Jess, you were at my door and I wouldn't let you in.

SIMPLE. All my life I been looking for a door that will be just mine—and the one I love. Joyce, I been looking for *your* door. But sometimes you let the wrong *me* in, not the me I want to be. This time, when I come through your door again, it's gonna be the *me* I ought to be.

JOYCE. I know, Jess—we've had problems to solve. But—

SIMPLE. The problem to solve is me, Joyce—and can't no one solve that problem but me. Until I get out of this mud and muck and mire I been dancing in half my life, don't you open your door to the *wrong* me no more. *Don't open your door.* And don't say nothing good to me, Joyce. Don't tell me nothing a-tall. *(He has already risen. Now she rises, embracing him, but he pushes her away.)* Joyce, baby, darling, no. . . . *(He wants to call her all the sweet names he knows, to take her in his arms, to keep her then and there and always. But instead he speaks almost harshly.)* No! Don't say nothing—to me—Joyce. *(He opens the door.)*

(As JOYCE turns to go, she looks at

JESS, *lifts her head, and smiles the most beautiful smile a man has ever seen—a smile serene and calm and full of faith. THE LIGHTS DIM TO A SPOT on her face as she turns and leaves without a word. Suddenly there is a great burst of music, wild, triumphant, wonderful and happy.)*

BLACKOUT

ACT TWO

SCENE 9

Paddy's Bar on a winter night.

BODIDDLY, BOYD, GITFIDDLE, *and the* PIANIST *are scattered about.* MELON *leans over* MISS MAMIE's *table and emits a playful howl.*

MELON. Ow-ooo-oo-o! Miss Mamie, you're a killer, that you is! Sweet my lands! You-oo-O!

MAMIE. Melon, I don't want no wolf-howling compliments. I just come here to set in peace. I don't want to be bothered with you drunken Negroes.

MELON. Who is drunk?

MAMIE. You!

BODIDDLY. She's right, you is.

MELON. Listen here! Diddly and Mamie, both you-all belong to my church—the Upstairs Baptist—yet you go around talking about me like a dirty dog.

MAMIE. Well, you do drink—guzzle, guzzle, guzzle!

MELON. I don't get drunk!

MAMIE. I say you do!

MELON. Woman, listen! Miss Mamie, I respects you too much to dispute your word. If you say I do, I does.

MAMIE. Now that that's settled, come and have a drink on me. A little eye-opener in the morning, a bracer at noon, and a nightcap at night, never hurt nobody.

MELON. Mamie, you got money?

MAMIE. I always got me some money,

been had money, and always will have money. And one reason I do is, I'm a lone wolf, I runs with no pack.

MELON. I would pack you on my back if you would let me.

MAMIE. I don't intend to let you. To tell the truth, I doubt your intentions. And, Melon, I wants you to know: *(She sings.)*

I been making my way for a long, long time,
I been making my way through this world.
I keep on trying to be good
'Cause I'm a good old girl.
I been making my way with a boot and a shoe.
In no oyster have I found a pearl.
I trust myself—so I've got luck
'Cause I'm a good old girl.
Sometimes the devil beckons
I look at the devil and say,

(MELON touches her hand.)

Stop that!
Devil, devil, devil—
Devil, be on your way!
I been making my way through thick and thin
'Spite o' devilish men in this world.
There ain't no man can get me down
Not even Harry Belafonte,
'Cause I'm a good old girl.

(MAMIE rises and addresses the entire bar.)

I make five or ten dollars, sometimes more a day.
You men what ain't working know that that ain't hay.
Don't let no strange man get his hands on you—
There's no telling, baby, what a strange cat will do.
It takes all kinds of folks to spin this globe around,
But *one* bad actor tears your playhouse down.

Don't ever let no bad actor come around—
There's no telling, Baby, what that cat's trying to lay down!
Sometimes the devil beckons.
I look at the devil and say,

(MELON approaches.)

Ain't you got enough trouble?
Devil, devil, devil—
Devil, be on your way!
I been making my way through thick and thin
'Spite o' devilish men in this world.
There's no man can get me down
'Cause I'm a good old girl.
My name is Mamie—
I'm a good old girl!
Like Mamie Eisenhower,
I'm a good old gal!

(To shouts of approval from the bar crowd, she continues.)

I been making my way for a long, long time!
Now listen, Punchy: I've been making my way:
I've been making my very own way for a long, long time.
I don't need you, Melon.
I've been making my way through this world.
Who needs that face?
I keep on trying to be good.
You think I'm a doll?
I'm a good old girl—
Might be a human doll! Anyhow—
I been making my way through thick and thin
'Spite o' devilish men in this world,

(MELON grins.)

You always been this ugly, Melon?
There ain't no man can get me down—
'Cause I'm a good old girl!
I keep repeating—I'm a good old girl!
Now what's the sense of going on with this?

BODIDDLY. Melon, I guess you realize there's nothing more independent than an independent woman. You'd better stop worrying Miss Mamie or she'll floor you and stomp on your carcass.

MELON. Diddly, if you don't have some respect for my personal conversation, I'm going to bust a watermelon over your head.

BODIDDLY. Take it easy, man. See you later. Hi, Simp.

(SIMPLE enters shivering, passing BO-DIDDLY as he exits.)

SIMPLE. Hi, Bo! Hop! Man, this bar is the warmest place I know in winter. At least you keep steam up here.

HOPKINS. Cold as it is, do you mean to tell me you haven't got any steam in your room?

SIMPLE. I done beated on my radiator pipe six times today to let my old landlady know I was home—freezing.

HOPKINS. And what happened?

SIMPLE. Nothing—she just beat back on the pipes at me. Which is why I come down here, to get warm, just like Boyd.

HOPKINS. Want a drink?

SIMPLE. I sure could use one.

HOPKINS. Coming up.

SIMPLE. Hey, Boyd! I got something to tell you. I'm working part-time, back down at the plant as a helper—helping reconvert.

BOYD. That's wonderful!

SIMPLE. With a good job and a good wife, man, it'll be like Joyce used to say when I kissed her—"Simply Heavenly." And when we get married, Boyd, you're gonna be standing there beside me at my wedding. You're gonna hand me the ring. Ain't that what the best man does?

MAMIE. Yeah, that's right.

(MELON approaches.)

Melon, ain't you got no home?

BOYD. Hey, this is the first time you've sprung this on me, about being your best man. After all we've only known each other for a few years. A best man is usually somebody you grew up with, or something.

SIMPLE. I didn't grow up with nobody, Boyd. So I don't know anybody very well. So, will you please be my best man?

BOYD. Best man, eh? Then I'll have to start buying me a brand new suit. And a best man is due to give a bachelor's party for the groom a night or two before the ceremony. Your wedding's going to cost me a lot of dough, Jess.

SIMPLE. Just a keg of beer. I mean a private one—with my name on it.

BOYD. You got it, lad. I live to see the day! (BOYD rises.)

SIMPLE. Where you going, Boyd?

BOYD. Listen, Jess! Hot or cold, I've got to bust that book-writing rock and I've got to get home to my typewriter. Good night, all.

SIMPLE. Well, that's settled. Thank God, I don't have to worry about Zarita. I ain't seen her for months.

HOPKINS. Zarita's getting ready to fly to Arizona for Christmas. That Big Boy, Ali Baba, sent her a ticket. She's all set to go. I think they're going to get married.

SIMPLE. I wishes her all the luck in the world. But I sure wish I could understand a woman.

HOPKINS. Socrates tried, he couldn't. What makes you hold such hopes?

SIMPLE. Long as I live, Hop, I lives in hopes.

(Loud weeping is heard outside.)

Damn, there's some woman hollering now.

HOPKINS. I wonder what's wrong.

(ARCIE enters crying and sinks at a table.)

What's wrong, Arcie?

ARCIE. Gimme a sherry, Hopkins, quick! Gimme a sherry.

HOPKINS. What's the matter, Arcie?

ARCIE. Abe Lincoln is going to the army.

SIMPLE. The army?

ARCIE. My oldest son, Abraham Lincoln Jones.

SIMPLE. Well, why didn't you say so?

ARCIE. I'm trying to! Abe got his draft call.

SIMPLE. Don't cry, Arcie. The army'll do the boy no harm. He'll get to travel, see the world.

ARCIE. The first one of my children to leave home!

SIMPLE. As many as you got, you shouldn't mind *one* going somewhere.

ARCIE. I does mind. Abe is my oldest, and I does mind. Fill it up again, Hop.

SIMPLE. That boy Abe is smart, Arcie. You'll be proud of him. He's liable to get to be an officer.

HOPKINS. At least a sergeant—and come back here with stripes on his sleeve.

SIMPLE. Else medals on his chest. Now, me, if I was to go in the army today— now that we's integrated—I would come back a general.

HOPKINS. Quit your kidding.

SIMPLE. I would rise right to the top today and be a general—and be in charge of white troops.

MELON. Colored generals never command white troops.

SIMPLE. The next war will be integrated. In fact, I'd like to command a regiment from Mississippi.

HOPKINS. Are you drunk?

SIMPLE. No, sir.

MELON. Then why on earth would you want to be in charge of a white regiment from Mississippi?

SIMPLE. In the last war, they had white officers in charge of Negroes. So why shouldn't I be in charge of whites? Huh? General Simple! I would really make 'em toe the line. I know some of them Dixiecrats would rather die than left face for a colored man, but they would left face for me.

MELON. Man, you got a great imagination.

SIMPLE. I can see myself now, in World War III, leading white Mississippi troops into action. Hop, I would do like all the other generals do, and stand way back on a hill somewhere and look through my spy-glasses and say, "Charge on! Mens, charge on!" Then I would watch them Dixiecrats boys go—like true sons of the Old South, mowing down the enemy. When my young white lieutenants from Vicksburg jeeped back to headquarters to deliver their reports in person to me, they would say, "Captain General, sir, we have taken two more enemy positions." I would say, "Mens, return to your companies—and tell 'em to keep on charging on!" Next day, when I caught up to 'em, I would pin medals on their chest for bravery. Then I would have my picture taken in front of all my fine white troops—me—the first *black* American general to pin medals on white soldiers from Mississippi. Then, Hop—man, oh, man—then when the war be's over, I would line my companies up for the last time and I would say, "Mens, at ease. Gentlemen of the Old South, relax. Put down your fighting arms and lend me your ears—because I am one of you, too, borned and bred in Dixie.

(GITFIDDLE *begins to play a syncopated march—a blend of "Dixie," "Swanee River," and "Yankee Doodle."*)

And I'm willing to let bygones be bygones, and forget how you failed to obey my orders in the old days and right faceted when I said "Left," because you thought I was colored. Well, I is colored. I'll forget that. You are me—and I am you—and we are one. And now that our fighting is done, let's be Americans for once, for fun. Colonels, captains, majors, lieutenants, sergeants, and, Hopkins, open up a keg of nails for the men—let's all drink to you, brave sons of the South! Drink, mens, drink! And when we all stagger back to peace together, let there be peace—between you, Mississippi, and me! Company—'tention! Right shoulder arms! . . . Forward, march! . . . Come on, boys, I'm leading you! Come on! By the left flank march!" (SIMPLE *proudly inspects his troops as they pass in review.*)

(*Others in the bar, except* MISS MAMIE, *applaud and cheer.*)

HOPKINS. March, fellows, march!
SIMPLE. By the right flank, march!
HOPKINS. March, fellows, march!
ARCIE. Ain't that fine!
HOPKINS. March, march, march!
SIMPLE. Forward! March!
HOPKINS. March! March! March!

(SIMPLE *exits as if leading an army with banners. The music rises to a climax, then suddenly ends. In the silence* MISS MAMIE *speaks.*)

MAMIE. You know something—that boy is sick!

BLACKOUT

ACT TWO

SCENE 10

A phone booth. Christmas Eve.
Chimes are softly tolling "Jingle Bells"
as SIMPLE *speaks excitedly into the phone.*

SIMPLE. Joyce? . . . Joyce? . . . Is this Joyce? . . . Yes, it's Jesse B. . . . It's Simple, honey! . . . What? You say I sound like a new man! I *am* a new man! And I got something for you, Joyce. It's Christmas Eve and, you know, well—like it says in the Bible, "Wise men came bringing gifts." . . . Joyce, I got a few little gifts for you on my Christmas tree.

. . . Sure, I got a tree! What's on it for you? . . . I don't want to tell you, Joyce. I want to show you. You say you're coming right over? . . . Oh, baby! (*With the receiver still in his hand, he rises excitedly and starts out, but is jerked back by the cord. Quickly he hangs up and leaves as the music of "Jingle Bells" fillls the air.*)

BLACKOUT

ACT TWO

SCENE 11

SCENE:
 SIMPLE'*s room.*
TIME:
 Christmas Eve.
AT RISE:
 A star shines in the darkness. The lights come up revealing SIMPLE *and* JOYCE *standing before a tiny Christmas tree. The star glows atop this tree hung with tinsel and little balls of colored glass. On the tree there are four gifts tied with ribbons: one is a letter, one a roll of paper, one a long parchment, and one is a tiny box.* JOYCE *has just entered the room.*

JOYCE. Jess!
SIMPLE. Look. (*He shows her the tree.*)
JOYCE. Oh! It's beautiful!
SIMPLE. May I take your coat? Won't you sit down? (*He hands her the parchment as* JOYCE *perches on the edge of a chair.*)
JOYCE. Jess, what is it? A picture of some kind? Maybe a map? Why, it's all in Roman letters. It's a divorce!
SIMPLE. With a gold seal on it, too.
JOYCE. Free! Jess, you're free! Like in Uncle Tom's Cabin!
SIMPLE. Yes, baby, I'm free. That's the paper.
JOYCE. It's dated a whole month ago. Jess, why didn't you tell me you had your divorce?

SIMPLE. I was waiting for something else to go with it. Here, this is for you, too. *(He hands her an envelope.)*

JOYCE. My father's writing!

SIMPLE. Read it. You see, your ole— your father—gimme your hand. *(While she reads the letter, SIMPLE opens the little box on the tree and polishes a ring on his coat lapel.)* Now, can I take your hand? *(He slips the ring on her finger.)* For you—if you'll wear it?

JOYCE. Forever! *(She starts to rise, but gently he pushes her down and returns to the tree.)*

SIMPLE. This is something only married people can have. And it's not ready, yet, either. They just about now digging the first hole in the ground—busting that first rock. We both got to sign our names —if you're willing.

JOYCE. An apartment! Oh, Jess! A place to live! An apartment!

SIMPLE. Can we both sign our names, Joyce?

JOYCE. Yes, Jess! *(JOYCE rises, scattering papers, and flings her arms about him.)*

SIMPLE. Now we can get ready for that wedding in June.

JOYCE. Oh, Jess! Jess, baby! Jess!

(Singing, they embrace.)

SIMPLE.
Just for you these Christmas tokens
On our Christmas tree—

JOYCE.
Help to make me know that you are
Santa Clause to me.

SIMPLE.
Just a little pain and trouble
Mixed in with the past

BOTH.
Help to make our joys double
When we're sure they'll last.

JOYCE.
Wonderful the morning star
Shining in the dawn!

BOTH.
Wonderful the rainbow's arch
When the rain is gone.

(The bar is revealed as the entire company enters singing and form tableaux, some around the paino, MAMIE at her table with MELON, BODIDDLY, ARCIE, and JOHN JASPER making a family group at another table. The entire chorus of "Look for the Morning Star" is repeated as all come forward for bows.)

ALL.
Don't forget there's bluebirds
Somewhere in the blue.
Love will send a little bluebird
Flying straight to you.

(Repeat chorus on bows.)

END OF PLAY

Lorraine Hansberry

A Raisin in the Sun

To Mama:

in gratitude for the dream

What happens to a dream deferred?
Does it dry up
Like a raisin in the sun?
Or fester like a sore—
And then run?
Does it stink like rotten meat?
Or crust and sugar over—
Like a syrupy sweet?

Maybe it just sags
Like a heavy load.

Or does it explode?

—Langston Hughes

A RAISIN IN THE SUN

A Raisin in the Sun was first presented by Philip Rose and David J. Cogan at the Ethel Barrymore Theater, New York City, March 11, 1959.

CHARACTERS:

RUTH YOUNGER
TRAVIS YOUNGER
WALTER LEE YOUNGER (BROTHER)
BENEATHA YOUNGER
LENA YOUNGER (MAMA)
JOSEPH ASAGAI
GEORGE MURCHISON
KARL LINDNER
BOBO
MOVING MEN

The action of the play is set in Chicago's Southside sometime between World War II and the present.

ACT ONE

SCENE 1: *Friday morning.*
SCENE 2: *The following morning.*

ACT TWO

SCENE 1: *Later, the same day.*
SCENE 2: *Friday night, a few weeks later.*
SCENE 3: *Moving day, one week later.*

ACT THREE

An hour later.

ACT ONE

SCENE 1

The YOUNGER *living room would be a comfortable and well-ordered room if it were not for a number of indestructible contradictions to this state of being. It's furnishings are typical and undistin-guished and their primary feature now is that they have clearly had to accommodate the living of too many people for too many years—and they are tired. Still, we can see that at some time, a time probably no longer remembered by the family (except perhaps for MAMA), the furnishings of this room were actually selected with care and love and even hope and brought to this apartment and arranged with taste and pride.*

That was a long time ago. Now the once loved pattern of the couch upholstery has to fight to show itself from under acres of crocheted doilies and couch covers which have themselves finally come to be more important than the upholstery. And here a table or a chair has been moved to disguise the worn places in the carpet; but the carpet has fought back by showing its weariness, with depressing uniformity, elsewhere on its surface.

Weariness has, in fact, won in this room. Everything has been polished, washed, sat on, used, scrubbed too often. All pretenses but living itself have long since vanished from the very atmosphere of this room.

Moreover, a section of this room, for it is not really a room unto itself, though the landlord's lease would make it seem so, slopes backward to provide a small kitchen area, where the family prepares the meals that are eaten in the living room proper, which must also serve as dining room. The single window that has been provided for these "two" rooms is located in this kitchen area. The sole natural light the family may enjoy in the course of a day is only that which fights its way through this little window.

At Left, a door leads to a bedroom which is shared by MAMA *and her daughter,* BENEATHA. *At Right, opposite, is a second room (which in the beginning of the life of this apartment was probably a breakfast room) which serves as a bedroom for* WALTER *and his wife,* RUTH.

TIME:
Sometime between World War II and the present.
PLACE:
Chicago's Southside.
AT RISE:
It is morning dark in the living room. TRAVIS *is asleep on the make-down bed at Center. An ALARM CLOCK sounds from within the bedroom at Right, and presently* RUTH *enters from that room and closes the door behind her. She crosses sleepily toward the window. As she passes her sleeping son she reaches down and shakes him a little. At the window she raises the shade and a dusky Southside morning light comes in feebly. She fills a pot with water and puts it on to boil. She calls to the boy, between yawns, in a slightly muffled voice.*

RUTH *is about thirty. We can see that she was a pretty girl, even exceptionally so, but now it is apparent that life has been little that she expected, and disappointment has already begun to hang in her face. In a few years, before thirty-five even, she will be known among her people as a "settled woman."*

She crosses to her son and gives him a good, final, rousing shake.

RUTH. Come on now, boy, it's seven thirty!

(Her son sits up at last, in a stupor of sleepiness.)

I say hurry up, Travis! You ain't the only person in the world got to use a bathroom.

(The child, a sturdy, handsome little boy of ten or eleven, drags himself out of the bed and almost blindly takes his towels and "today's clothes" from drawers and a closet and goes out to the bathroom, which is in an outside hall and which is shared by another family or families on the same floor.)

*(*RUTH *crosses to the bedroom door at Right and opens it and calls in to her husband.)* Walter Lee! . . . It's after seven thirty! Lemme see you do some waking up in there now! *(She waits.)* You better get up from there, man! It's after seven thirty I tell you. *(She waits again.)* All right, you just go ahead and lay there and next thing you know Travis be finished and Mr. Johnson'll be in there and you'll be fussing and cussing round here like a mad man! And be late too! *(She waits, at the end of patience.)* Walter Lee —it's time for you to get up! *(She waits another second and then starts to go into the bedroom, but is apparently satisfied that her husband has begun to get up. She stops, pulls the door to, and returns to the kitchen area. She wipes her face with a moist cloth and runs her fingers through her sleep-disheveled hair in a vain effort and ties an apron around her housecoat.)*

(The bedroom door at Right opens and her husband stands in the doorway in his pajamas, which are rumpled and mismated. He is a lean, intense young man in his middle thirties, inclined to quick nervous movements and erratic speech habits—and always in his voice there is a quality of indictment.)

WALTER. Is he out yet?
RUTH. What do you mean *out?* He ain't hardly got in there good yet.
WALTER. *(Wandering in, still more oriented to sleep than to a new day.)* Well, what was you doing all that yelling for if I can't even get in there yet? *(Stop-*

ping and thinking.) Check coming today?

RUTH. They *said* Saturday and this is just Friday and I hopes to God you ain't going to get up here first thing this morning and start talking to me 'bout no money—'cause I 'bout don't want to hear it.

WALTER. Something the matter with you this morning?

RUTH. No—I'm just sleepy as the devil. What kind of eggs you want?

WALTER. Not scrambled.

(RUTH starts to scramble eggs.)

Paper come?

(RUTH points impatiently to the rolled-up Tribune on the table, and he gets it and spreads it out and vaguely reads the front page.)

Set off another bomb yesterday.

RUTH. *(Maximum indifference.)* Did they?

WALTER. *(Looking up.)* What's the matter with you?

RUTH. Ain't nothing the matter with me. And don't keep asking me that this morning.

WALTER. Ain't nobody bothering you. *(Reading the news of the day absently again.)* Say Colonel McCormick is sick.

RUTH. *(Affecting tea-party interest.)* Is he now? Poor thing.

WALTER. *(Sighing and looking at his watch.)* Oh, me. *(He waits.)* Now what is that boy doing in that bathroom all this time? He just going to have to start getting up earlier. I can't be being late to work on account of him fooling around in there.

RUTH. *(Turning on him.)* Oh, no he ain't going to be getting up no earlier no such thing! It ain't his fault that he can't get to bed no earlier nights 'cause he got a bunch of crazy good-for-nothing clowns sitting up running their mouths in what is supposed to be his bedroom after ten o'clock at night. . . .

WALTER. That's what you mad about, ain't it? The things I want to talk about with my friends just couldn't be important in your mind, could they? *(He rises and finds a cigarette in her handbag on the table and crosses to the little window and looks out, smoking and deeply enjoying this first one.)*

RUTH. *(Almost matter of factly, a complaint too automatic to deserve emphasis.)* Why you always got to smoke before you eat in the morning?

WALTER. *(At the window.)* Just look at 'em down there . . . running and racing to work . . . *(He turns and faces his wife and watches her a moment at the stove, and then, suddenly.)* You look young this morning, baby.

RUTH. *(Indifferently.)* Yeah?

WALTER. Just for a second—stirring them eggs. It's gone now—just for a second it was—you looked real young again. *(Then, drily.)* It's gone now—you look like yourself again.

RUTH. Man, if you don't shut up and leave me alone.

WALTER. *(Looking out to the street again.)* First thing a man ought to learn in life is not to make love to no colored woman first thing in the morning. You all some evil people at eight o'clock in the morning.

(TRAVIS appears in the hall doorway, almost fully dressed and quite wide awake now, his towels and pajamas across his shoulders. He opens the door and signals for his father to make the bathroom in a hurry.)

TRAVIS. *(Watching the bathroom.)* Daddy, come on!

(WALTER gets his bathroom utensils and flies out to the bathroom.)

RUTH. Sit down and have your breakfast, Travis.

TRAVIS. Mama, this is Friday. *(Gleefully.)* Check coming tomorrow, huh?

RUTH. You get your mind off money and eat your breakfast.

TRAVIS. (Eating.) This is the morning we supposed to bring the fifty cents to school.

RUTH. Well, I ain't got no fifty cents this morning.

TRAVIS. Teacher say we have to.

RUTH. I don't care what teacher say. I ain't got it. Eat your breakfast, Travis.

TRAVIS. I *am* eating.

RUTH. Hush up now and just eat!

(The boy gives her an exasperated look for her lack of understanding, and eats grudgingly.)

TRAVIS You think Grandmama would have it?

RUTH. No! And I want you to stop asking your grandmother for money, you hear me?

TRAVIS. (Outraged.) Gaaaleee! I don't ask her, she just gimme it sometimes!

RUTH. Travis Willard Younger—I got too much on me this morning to be—

TRAVIS. Maybe Daddy—

RUTH. TRAVIS!

(The boy hushes abruptly. They are both quiet and tense for several seconds.)

TRAVIS. (Presently.) Could I maybe go carry some groceries in front of the supermarket for a little while after school then?

RUTH. Just hush, I said.

(TRAVIS jabs his spoon into his cereal bowl viciously, and rests his head in anger upon his fists.)

If you through eating, you can get over there and make up your bed.

(The boy obeys stiffly and crosses the room, almost mechanically, to the bed and more or less carefully folds the covering. He carries the bedding into his mother's room and returns with his books and cap.)

TRAVIS. (Sulking and standing apart from her unnaturally.) I'm gone.

RUTH. (Looking up from the stove to inspect him automatically.) Come here. (He crosses to her and she studies his head.) If you don't take this comb and fix this here head, you better!

(TRAVIS puts down his books with a great sigh of oppression, and crosses to the mirror. His mother mutters under her breath about his "slubbornness.")

'Bout to march out of here with that head looking just like chickens slept in it! I just don't know where you get your slubborn ways. . . . And get your jacket, too. Looks chilly out this morning.

TRAVIS. (With conspicuously brushed hair and jacket.) I'm gone.

RUTH. Get carfare and milk money— (Waving one finger.)—and not a single penny for no caps, you hear me?

TRAVIS. (With sullen politeness.) Yes'm. (He turns in outrage to leave.)

(His mother watches after him as in his frustration he approaches the door almost comically. When she speaks to him, her voice has become a very gentle tease.)

RUTH. (Mocking; as she thinks he would say it.) Oh, Mama makes me so mad sometimes, I don't know what to do! (She waits and continues to his back as he stands stock still in front of the door.) I wouldn't kiss that woman goodbye for nothing in this world this morning!

(The boy finally turns around and rolls his eyes at her, knowing the mood has changed and he is vindicated; he does not, however, move toward her yet.)

Not for nothing in this world! (She finally laughs aloud at him and holds out her arms to him and we see that it is a *way between them, very old and practiced.)*

(He crosses to her and allows her to embrace him warmly but keeps his face fixed with masculine rigidity. She holds him back from her presently and looks at him and runs her fingers over the features of his face.)

(With utter gentleness.) Now—whose little old angry man are you?

TRAVIS. *(The masculinity and gruffness start to fade at last.)* Aw gaalee—Mama . . .

RUTH. *(Mimicking.)* Aw—gaaaaallee-eee, Mama! *(She pushes him, with rough playfulness and finality, toward the door.)* Get on out of here or you going to be late.

TRAVIS. *(In the face of love, new aggressiveness.)* Mama, could I *please* go carry groceries?

RUTH. Honey, it's starting to get so cold evenings.

WALTER. *(Coming in from the bathroom and drawing a make-believe gun from a make-believe holster and shooting at his son.)* What is it he wants to do?

RUTH. Go carry groceries after school at the supermarket.

WALTER. Well, let him go. . . .

TRAVIS. *(Quickly, to the ally.)* I *have* to—she won't gimme the fifty cents. . . .

WALTER. *(To his wife only.)* Why not?

RUTH. *(Simply, and with flavor.)* 'Cause we don't have it.

WALTER. *(To* RUTH *only.)* What you tell the boy things like that for? *(Reaching down into his pants with a rather important gesture.)* Here, son—*(He hands the boy the coin, but his eyes are directed to his wife's.)*

(TRAVIS takes the money happily.)

TRAVIS. Thanks, Daddy. *(He starts out.)*

(RUTH watches both of them with murder in her eyes. WALTER stands and stares back at her with defiance, and suddenly reaches into his pocket again on an afterthought.)

WALTER. *(Without even looking at his son, still staring hard at his wife.)* In fact, here's another fifty cents. . . . Buy yourself some fruit today—or take a taxicab to school or something!

TRAVIS. Whoopee—*(He leaps up and clasps his father around the middle with his legs, and they face each other in mutual appreciation.)*

(Slowly WALTER LEE *peaks around the boy to catch the violent rays from his wife's eyes and draws his head back as if shot.)*

WALTER. You better get down now—and get to school, man.

TRAVIS. *(At the door.)* O.K. Good-bye. *(He exits.)*

WALTER. *(After him, pointing with pride.)* That's *my* boy.

(She looks at him in disgust and turns back to her work.)

You know what I was thinking 'bout in the bathroom this morning?

RUTH. No.

WALTER. How come you always try to be so pleasant!

RUTH. What is there to be pleasant 'bout!

WALTER. You want to know what I was thinking 'bout in the bathroom or not!

RUTH. I know what you thinking 'bout.

WALTER. *(Ignoring her.)* 'Bout what me and Willy Harris was talking about last night.

RUTH. *(Immediately—a refrain.)* Willy Harris is a good-for-nothing loud mouth.

WALTER. Anybody who talks to me has got to be a good-for-nothing loud mouth, ain't he? And what you know about who is just a good-for-nothing loud mouth? Charlie Atkins was just a "good-for-nothing" loud mouth too, wasn't he! When he wanted me to go in the dry-cleaning business with him. And now—he's grossing a hundred thousand a year. A hundred thousand dollars a year! You still call *him* a loud mouth!

RUTH. (*Bitterly.*) Oh, Walter Lee. . . . (*She folds her head on her arms over the table.*)

WALTER. (*Rising and coming to her and standing over her.*) You tired, ain't you? Tired of everything. Me, the boy, the way we live—this beat-up hole—everything. Ain't you?

(*She doesn't look up, doesn't answer.*)

So tired—moaning and groaning all the time, but you wouldn't do nothing to help, would you? You couldn't be on my side that long for nothing, could you?

RUTH. Walter, please leave me alone.

WALTER. A man needs for a woman to back him up . . .

RUTH. Walter—

WALTER. Mama would listen to you. You know she listen to you more than she do me and Bennie. She think more of you. All you have to do is just sit down with her when you drinking your coffee one morning and talking 'bout things like you do and—(*He sits down beside her and demonstrates graphically what he thinks her methods and tone should be.*) —you just sip your coffee, see, and say easy like that you been thinking 'bout that deal Walter Lee is so interested in, 'bout the store and all, and sip some more coffee, like what you saying ain't really that important to you—and the next thing you know, she be listening good and asking you questions and when I come home—I can tell her the details. This ain't no fly-by-night proposition, baby. I mean we figured it out, me and Willy and Bobo.

RUTH. (*With a frown.*) Bobo?

WALTER. Yeah. You see, this little liquor store we got in mind cost seventy-five thousand and we figured the initial investment on the place be 'bout thirty thousand, see. That be ten thousand each. Course, there's a couple of hundred you got to pay so's you don't spend your life just waiting for them clowns to let your license get approved—

RUTH. You mean graft?

WALTER. (*Frowning impatiently.*) Don't call it that, See there, that just goes to show you what women understand about the world. Baby, don't *nothing* happen for you in this world 'less you pay *somebody* off!

RUTH. Walter, leave me alone! (*She raises her head and stares at him vigorously—then says, more quietly.*) *Eat your eggs, they gonna be cold.*

WALTER. (*Straightening up from her and looking off.*) That's it. There you are. Man say to his woman: I got me a dream. His woman say: Eat your eggs. (*Sadly, but gaining in power.*) Man say: I got to take hold of this here world, baby! And a woman will say: Eat your eggs and go to work. (*Passionately now.*) Man say: I got to change my life, I'm choking to death, baby! And his woman say—(*In utter anguish as he brings his fists down on his thighs.*)—Your eggs is getting cold!

RUTH. (*Softly.*) Walter, that ain't none of our money.

WALTER. (*Not listening at all or even looking at her.*) This morning, I was lookin' in the mirror and thinking about it . . . I'm thirty-five years old; I been married eleven years and I got a boy who sleeps in the living room—(*Very, very quietly.*)—and all I got to give him is stories about how rich white people live. . . .

RUTH. Eat your eggs, Walter.

WALTER. DAMN MY EGGS . . . DAMN ALL THE EGGS THAT EVER WAS!

RUTH. Then go to work.

WALTER. (Looking up at her.) See— I'm trying to talk to you 'bout myself— (Shaking his head with the repetition.) —and all you can say is eat them eggs and go to work.

RUTH. (Wearily.) Honey, you never say nothing new. I listen to you every day, every night and every morning, and you never say nothing new. (Shrugging.) So you would rather be Mr. Arnold than be his chauffeur. So—I would rather be living in Buckingham Palace.

WALTER. That is just what is wrong with the colored woman in this world . . . don't understand about building their men up and making 'em feel like they somebody. Like they can do something.

RUTH. (Drily, but to hurt.) There are colored men who do things.

WALTER. No thanks to the colored woman.

RUTH. Well, being a colored woman, I guess I can't help myself none. (She rises and gets the ironing board and sets it up and attacks a huge pile of rough-dried clothes, sprinkling them in preparation for the ironing and then rolling them into tight fat balls.)

WALTER. (Mumbling.) We one group of men tied to a race of women with small minds.

(His sister BENEATHA enters. She is about twenty, as slim and intense as her brother. She is not as pretty as her sister-in-law, but her lean, almost intellectual face has a handsomeness of its own. She wears a bright-red flannel nightie, and her thick hair stands wildly about her head. Her speech is a mixture of many things; it is different from the rest of the family's in so far as education has permeated her sense of English—and perhaps the Midwest rather than the South has finally—at last—won out in her inflection; but not altogether, because over all of it is a soft slurring and transformed use of vowels which is the decided influence of the Southside. She passes through the room without looking at either RUTH or WALTER and goes to the outside door and looks, a little blindly, out to the bathroom. She sees that it has been lost to the Johnsons. She closes the door with a sleepy vengeance and crosses to the table and sits down a little defeated.)

BENEATHA. I am going to start timing those people.

WALTER. You should get up earlier.

BENEATHA. (Her face in her hands. She is still fighting the urge to go back to bed.) Really—would you suggest dawn? Where's the paper?

WALTER. (Pushing the paper across the table to her as he studies her almost clinically, as though he has never seen her before.) You a horrible-looking chick at this hour.

BENEATHA. (Drily.) Good morning, everybody.

WALTER. (Senselessly.) How is school coming?

BENEATHA. (In the same spirit.) Lovely. Lovely. And you know, biology is the greatest. (Looking up at him.) I dissected something that looked just like you yesterday.

WALTER. I just wondered if you've made up your mind and everything.

BENEATHA. (Gaining in sharpness and impatience.) And what did I answer yesterday morning—and the day before that?

RUTH. (From the ironing board, like someone disinterested and old.) Don't be so nasty, Bennie.

BENEATHA. (Still to her brother.) And the day before that and the day before that!

WALTER. (Defensively.) I'm interested in you. Something wrong with that? Ain't many girls who decide—

WALTER and BENEATHA. (In unison.) —To be a doctor.

(Silence.)

WALTER. Have we figured out yet just exactly how much medical school is going to cost?

RUTH. Walter Lee, why don't you leave that girl alone and get out of here to work?

BENEATHA. (Exits to the bathroom and bangs on the door.) Come on out of there, please! (She comes back into the room.)

WALTER. (Looking at his sister intently.) You know the check is coming tomorrow.

BENEATHA. (Turning on him with a sharpness all her own.) That money belongs to Mama, Walter, and it's for her to decide how she wants to use it. I don't care if she wants to buy a house or a rocket ship or just nail it up somewhere and look at it. It's hers. Not ours—hers.

WALTER. (Bitterly.) Now ain't that fine! You just got your mother's interest at heart, ain't you, girl? You such a nice girl—but if Mama got that money she can always take a few thousand and help you through school too—can't she?

BENEATHA. I have never asked anyone around here to do anything for me!

WALTER. No! And the line between asking and just accepting when the time comes is big and wide—ain't it!

BENEATHA. (With fury.) What do you want from me, Brother—that I quit school or just drop dead, which!

WALTER. I don't want nothing but for you to stop acting holy 'round here. Me and Ruthie done made some sacrifices for you—why can't you do something for the family?

RUTH. Walter, don't be dragging me in it.

WALTER. You are in it—don't you get up and go to work in somebody's kitchen for the last three years to help put clothes on her back?

RUTH. Oh, Walter—that's not fair. . . .

WALTER. It ain't that nobody expects you to get on your knees and say thank you, Brother; thank you, Ruth; thank you, Mama—and thank you, Travis, for wearing the same pair of shoes for two semesters—

BENEATHA. (Dropping to her knees.) Well—I do—all right?—thank everybody . . . and forgive me for ever wanting to be anything at all . . . forgive me, forgive me!

RUTH. Please stop it! Your mama'll hear you.

WALTER. Who the hell told you you had to be a doctor? If you so crazy 'bout messing 'round with sick people—then go be a nurse like other women—or just get married and be quiet. . . .

BENEATHA. Well—you finally got it said. . . . It took you three years but you finally got it said. Walter, give up; leave me alone—it's Mama's money.

WALTER. HE WAS MY FATHER, TOO!

BENEATHA. So what? He was mine, too —and Travis' grandfather—but the insurance money belongs to Mama. Picking on me is not going to make her give it to you to invest in any liquor stores—(Underbreath, dropping into a chair.)—and I for one say, God bless Mama for that!

WALTER. (To RUTH.) See—did you hear? Did you hear!

RUTH. Honey, please go to work.

WALTER. Nobody in this house is ever going to understand me.

BENEATHA. Because you're a nut.

WALTER. Who's a nut?

BENEATHA. You—you are a nut. Thee is mad, boy.

WALTER. (Looking at his wife and sister from the door, very sadly.) The world's most backward race of people, and that's a fact.

BENEATHA. (Turning slowly in her chair.) And then there are all those prophets who would lead us out of the wilderness—(WALTER slams out of the house.)—into the swamps!

RUTH. Bennie, why you always gotta

be pickin' on your brother? Can't you be a little sweeter sometimes?

(Door opens. WALTER walks in.)

WALTER. *(To RUTH.)* I need some money for carfare.

RUTH. *(Looks at him, then warms; teasing, but tenderly.)* Fifty cents? *(She goes to her bag and gets money.)* Here, take a taxi.

(WALTER exits. MAMA enters. She is a woman in her early sixties, full-bodied and strong. She is one of those women of a certain grace and beauty who wear it so unobtrusively that it takes a while to notice. Her dark-brown face is surrounded by the total whiteness of her hair, and, being a woman who has adjusted to many things in life and overcome many more, her face is full of strength. She has, we can see, wit and faith of a kind that keep her eyes lit and full of interest and expectancy. She is, in a word, a beautiful woman. Her bearing is perhaps most like the noble bearing of the women of the Hereros of Southwest Africa—rather as if she imagines that as she walks she still bears a basket or a vessel upon her head. Her speech, on the other hand, is as careless as her carriage is precise—she is inclined to slur everything—but her voice is perhaps not so much quiet as simply soft.)

MAMA. Who that 'round here slamming doors at this hour? *(She crosses through the room, goes to the window, opens it, and brings in a feeble little plant growing doggedly in a small pot on the window sill. She feels the dirt and puts it back out.)*

RUTH. That was Walter Lee. He and Bennie was at it again.

MAMA. My children and they tempers. Lord, if this little old plant don't get more sun than it's been getting it ain't never going to see spring again. *(She turns from the window.)* What's the matter with you this morning, Ruth? You looks right peaked. You aiming to iron all them things? Leave some for me. I'll get to 'em this afternoon. Bennie honey, it's too drafty for you to be sitting 'round half dressed. Where's your robe?

BENEATHA. In the cleaners.

MAMA. Well, go get mine and put it on.

BENEATHA. I'm not cold, Mama, honest.

MAMA. I know—but you so thin. . . .

BENEATHA. *(Irritably.)* Mama, I'm not cold.

MAMA. *(Seeing the make-down bed as TRAVIS has left it.)* Lord have mercy, look at that poor bed. Bless his heart—he tries, don't he? *(She moves to the bed TRAVIS has sloppily made up.)*

RUTH. No—he don't half try at all 'cause he knows you going to come along behind him and fix everything. That's just how come he don't know how to do nothing right now—you done spoiled that boy so.

MAMA. Well—he's a little boy. Ain't supposed to know 'bout housekeeping. My baby, that's what he is. What you fix for his breakfast this morning?

RUTH. *(Angrily.)* I feed my son, Lena!

MAMA. I ain't meddling—*(Under breath; busy-bodyish.)* I just noticed all last week he had cold cereal, and when it starts getting this chilly in the fall a child ought to have some hot grits or something when he goes out in the cold—

RUTH. *(Furious.)* I gave him hot oats—is that all right!

MAMA. I ain't meddling. *(Pause.)* Put a lot of nice butter on it?

(RUTH shoots her an angry look and does not reply.)

He likes lots of butter.

RUTH. *(Exasperated.)* Lena—

MAMA. *(To BENEATHA. MAMA is inclined to wander conversationally sometimes.)* What was you and your brother fussing 'bout this morning?

BENEATHA. It's not important, Mama. *(She gets up and goes to look out at the bathroom, which is apparently free, and she picks up her towels and rushes out.)*

MAMA. What was they fighting about?

RUTH. Now you know as well as I do.

MAMA. *(Shaking her head.)* Brother still worrying hisself sick about that money?

RUTH. You know he is.

MAMA. You had breakfast?

RUTH. Some coffee.

MAMA. Girl, you better start eating and looking after yourself better. You almost thin as Travis.

RUTH. Lena—

MAMA. Un-hunh?

RUTH. What are you going to do with it?

MAMA. Now don't you start, child. It's too early in the morning to be talking about money. It ain't Christian.

RUTH. It's just that he got his heart set on that store—

MAMA. You mean that liquor store that Willy Harris want him to invest in?

RUTH. Yes—

MAMA. We ain't no business people, Ruth. We just plain working folks.

RUTH. Ain't nobody business people till they go into business. Walter Lee say colored people ain't never going to start getting ahead till they start gambling on some different kinds of things in the world—investments and things.

MAMA. What done got into you, girl? Walter Lee done finally sold you on investing.

RUTH. No. Mama, something is happening between Walter and me. I don't know what it is—but he needs something—something I can't give him any more. He needs this chance, Lena.

MAMA. *(Frowning deeply.)* But liquor, honey—

RUTH. Well—like Walter say—I 'spec' people going to always be drinking themselves some liquor.

MAMA. Well—whether they drinks it or not ain't none of my business. But whether I go into business selling it to 'em is, and I don't want that on my ledger this late in life. *(Stopping suddenly and studying her daughter-in-law.)* Ruth Younger, what's the matter with you today? You look like you could fall over right there.

RUTH. I'm tired.

MAMA. Then you better stay home from work today.

RUTH. I can't stay home. She'd be calling up the agency and screaming at them, "My girl didn't come in today—send me somebody! My girl didn't come in!" Oh, she just have a fit. . . .

MAMA. Well, let her have it. I'll just call her up and say you got the flu—

RUTH. *(Laughing.)* Why the flu?

MAMA. 'Cause it sounds respectable to 'em. Something white people get, too. They know 'bout the flu. Otherwise they think you been cut up or something when you tell 'em you sick.

RUTH. I got to go in. We need the money.

MAMA. Somebody would of thought my children done all but starved to death the way they talk about money here late. Child, we got a great big old check coming tomorrow.

RUTH. *(Sincerely, but also self-righteously.)* Now that's your money. It ain't got nothing to do with me. We all feel like that—Walter and Bennie and me—even Travis.

MAMA. *(Thoughtfully, and suddenly very far away.)* Ten thousand dollars—

RUTH. Sure is wonderful.

MAMA. Ten thousand dollars.

RUTH. You know what you should do, Miss Lena? You should take yourself a trip somewhere. To Europe or South America or someplace—

MAMA. *(Throwing up her hands at the thought.)* Oh, child!

RUTH. I'm serious. Just pack up and

leave! Go on away and enjoy yourself some. Forget about the family and have yourself a ball for once in your life—

MAMA. *(Drily.)* You sound like I'm just about ready to die. Who'd go with me? What I look like wandering 'round Europe by myself?

RUTH. Shoot—these here rich white women do it all the time. They don't think nothing of packing up they suitcases and piling on one of them big steamships and—swoosh!—they gone, child.

MAMA. Something always told me I wasn't no rich white woman.

RUTH. Well—what are you going to do with it then?

MAMA. I ain't rightly decided. *(Thinking. She speaks now with emphasis.)* Some of it got to be put away for Beneatha and her schoolin'—and ain't nothing going to touch that part of it. Nothing. *(She waits several seconds, trying to make up her mind about something, and looks at RUTH a little tentatively before going on.)* Been thinking that we maybe could meet the notes on a little old two-story somewhere, with a yard where Travis could play in the summertime, if we use part of the insurance for a down payment and everybody kind of pitch in. I could maybe take on a little day work again, few days a week—

RUTH. *(Studying her mother-in-law furtively and concentrating on her ironing, anxious to encourage without seeming to.)* Well, Lord knows, we've put enough rent into this here rat trap to pay for four houses by now. . . .

MAMA. *(Looking up at the words "rat trap" and then looking around and leaning back and sighing, in a suddenly reflective mood.)* "Rat trap"—yes, that's all it is. *(Smiling.)* I remember just as well the day me and Big Walter moved in here. Hadn't been married but two weeks and wasn't planning on living here no more than a year. *(She shakes her head at the dissolved dream.)* We was going to set away, little by little, don't you know, and buy a little place out in Morgan Park. We had even picked out the house. *(Chuckling a little.)* Looks right dumpy today. But Lord, child, you should know all the dreams I had 'bout buying that house and fixing it up and making me a little garden in the back—*(She waits and stops smiling.)* And didn't none of it happen. *(Dropping her hands in a futile gesture.)*

RUTH. *(Keeps her head down, ironing.)* Yes, life can be a barrel of disappointments, sometimes.

MAMA. Honey, Big Walter would come in here some nights back then and slump down on that couch there and just look at the rug, and look at me and look at the rug and then back at me—and I'd know he was down then . . . really down. *(After a second very long and thoughtful pause; she is seeing back to times that only she can see.)* And then, Lord, when I lost that baby—little Claude—I almost thought I was giong to lose Big Walter too. Oh, that man grieved hisself! He was one man to love his children.

RUTH. Ain't nothin' can tear at you like losin' your baby.

MAMA. I guess that's how come that man finally worked hisself to death like he done. Like he was fighting his own war with this here world that took his baby from him.

RUTH. He sure was a fine man, all right. I always liked Mr. Younger.

MAMA. Crazy 'bout his children! God knows there was plenty wrong with Walter Younger—hard-headed, mean, kind of wild with women—plenty wrong with him. But he sure loved his children. Always wanted them to have something—be something. That's where Brother gets all these notions, I reckon. Big Walter used to say, he'd get right wet in the eyes sometimes, lean his head back with the water standing in his eyes and say, "Seem like God don't see fit to give the black man nothing but dreams—but He did give us children to make them dreams seem worthwhile." (She smiles.) He could talk like that, don't you know.

RUTH. Yes, he sure could. He was a good man, Mr. Younger.

MAMA. Yes, a fine man—just couldn't never catch up with his dreams, that's all.

(BENEATHA comes in, brushing her hair and looking up at the ceiling, where the sound of a vacuum cleaner has started up.)

BENEATHA. What could be so dirty on that woman's rugs that she has to vacuum them every single day?

RUTH. I wish certain young women 'round here who I could name would take inspiration about certain rugs in a certain apartment I could also mention.

BENEATHA. (Shrugging.) How much cleaning can a house need, for Christ's sakes.

MAMA. (Not liking the Lord's name used thus.) Bennie!

RUTH. Just listen to her—just listen!

BENEATHA. Oh, God!

MAMA. If you use the Lord's name just one more time—

BENEATHA. (A bit of a whine.) Oh, Mama—

RUTH. Fresh—just fresh as salt, this girl!

BENEATHA. (Drily.) Well—if the salt loses its savor—

MAMA. Now that will do. I just ain't going to have you 'round here reciting the scriptures in vain—you hear me?

BENEATHA. How did I manage to get on everybody's wrong side by just walking into a room?

RUTH. If you weren't so fresh—

BENEATHA. Ruth, I'm twenty years old.

MAMA. What time you be home from school today?

BENEATHA. Kind of late. (With enthusiasm.) Madeline is going to start my guitar lessons today.

(MAMA and RUTH look up with the same expression.)

MAMA. Your what kind of lessons?

BENEATHA. Guitar.

RUTH. Oh, Father!

MAMA. How come you done taken it in your mind to learn to play the guitar?

BENEATHA. I just want to, that's all.

MAMA. (Smiling.) Lord, child, don't you know what to do with yourself? How long it going to be before you get tired of this now—like you got tired of that little play-acting group you joined last year? (Looking at RUTH.) And what was it the year before that?

RUTH. The horseback-riding club for which she bought that fifty-five-dollar riding habit that's been hanging in the closet ever since!

MAMA. (To BENEATHA.) Why you got to flit so from one thing to another, baby?

BENEATHA. (Sharply.) I just want to learn to play the guitar. Is there anything wrong with that?

MAMA. Ain't nobody trying to stop you. I just wonders sometimes why you has to flit so from one thing to another all the time. You ain't never done nothing with all that camera equipment you brought home—

BENEATHA. I don't flit! I—I experiment with different forms of expression—

RUTH. Like riding a horse?

BENEATHA. People have to express themselves one way or another.

MAMA. What is it you want to express?

BENEATHA. (Angrily.) Me!

(MAMA and RUTH look at each other and burst into raucous laughter.)

Don't worry—I don't expect you to understand.

MAMA. (To change the subject.) Who you going out with tomorrow night?

BENEATHA. *(With displeasure.)* George Murchison again.

MAMA. *(Pleased.)* Oh—you getting a little sweet on him?

RUTH. You ask me, this child ain't sweet on nobody but herself. *(Under-breath.)* Express herself!

(They laugh.)

BENEATHA. Oh—I like George all right, Mama. I mean I like him enough to go out with him and stuff, but—

RUTH. *(For devilment.)* What does *and stuff* mean?

BENEATHA. Mind your own business.

MAMA. Stop picking at her now, Ruth. *(A thoughtful pause, and then a suspicious sudden look at her daughter as she turns in her chair for emphasis.)* What *does* it mean?

BENEATHA. *(Wearily.)* Oh, I just mean I couldn't ever really be serious about George. He's—he's so shallow.

RUTH. Shallow—what do you mean he's shallow? He's RICH!

MAMA. Hush, Ruth.

BENEATHA. I know he's rich. He knows he's rich, too.

RUTH. Well—what other qualities a man got to have to satisfy you, little girl?

BENEATHA. You wouldn't even begin to understand. Anybody who married Walter could not possibly understand.

MAMA. *(Outraged.)* What kind of way is that to talk about your brother?

BENEATHA. Brother is a flip—let's face it.

MAMA. *(To RUTH, helplessly.)* What's a flip?

RUTH. *(Glad to add kindling.)* She's saying he's crazy.

BENEATHA. Not crazy. Brother isn't really crazy yet—he—he's an elaborate neurotic.

MAMA. Hush your mouth!

BENEATHA. As for George. Well. George looks good—he's got a beautiful car and he takes me to nice places and, as my sister-in-law says, he is probably the richest boy I will ever get to know and I even like him sometimes—but if the Youngers are sitting around waiting to see if their little Bennie is going to tie up the family with the Murchisons, they are wasting their time.

RUTH. You mean you wouldn't marry George Murchison if he asked you someday? That pretty, rich thing? Honey, I knew you was odd—

BENEATHA. No I would not marry him if all I felt for him was what I feel now. Besides, George's family wouldn't really like it.

MAMA. Why not?

BENEATHA. Oh, Mama—the Murchisons are honest-to-God-real-*live*-rich colored people, and the only people in the world who are more snobbish than rich white people are rich colored people. I thought everybody knew that. I've met Mrs. Murchison. She's a scene!

MAMA. You must not dislike people 'cause they well off, honey.

BENEATHA. Why not? It makes just as much sense as disliking people 'cause they are poor, and lots of people do that.

RUTH. *(A wisdom-of-the-ages manner. To MAMA.)* Well, she'll get over some of this—

BENEATHA. Get over it? What are you talking about, Ruth? Listen, I'm going to be a doctor. I'm not worried about who I'm going to marry yet—if I ever get married.

MAMA *and* RUTH. IF!

MAMA. Now, Bennie—

BENEATHA. Oh, I probably will . . . but first I'm going to be a doctor, and George, for one, still thinks that's pretty funny. I couldn't be bothered with that. I am going to be a doctor and everybody around here better understand that!

MAMA. *(Kindly.)* 'Course you going to be a doctor, honey, God willing.

BENEATHA. *(Drily.)* God hasn't got a thing to do with it.

MAMA. Beneatha—that just wasn't necessary.

BENEATHA. Well—neither is God. I get sick of hearing about God.

MAMA. Beneatha!

BENEATHA. I mean it! I'm just tired of hearing about God all the time. What has He got to do with anything? Does he pay tuition?

MAMA. You 'bout to get your fresh little jaw slapped!

RUTH. That's just what she needs, all right!

BENEATHA. Why? Why can't I say what I want to around here, like everybody else?

MAMA. It don't sound nice for a young girl to say things like that—you wasn't brought up that way. Me and your father went to trouble to get you and Brother to church every Sunday.

BENEATHA. Mama, you don't understand. It's all a matter of ideas, and God is just one idea I don't accept. It's not important. I am not going out and be immoral or commit crimes because I don't believe in God. I don't even think about it. It's just that I get tired of Him getting credit for all the things the human race achieves through its own stubborn effort. There simply is no blasted God—there is only man and it is he who makes miracles!

(MAMA absorbs this speech, studies her daughter and rises slowly and crosses to BENEATHA and slaps her powerfully across the face. After, there is only silence and the daughter drops her eyes from her mother's face, and MAMA is very tall before her.)

MAMA. Now—you say after me, in my mother's house there is still God.

(There is a long pause and BENEATHA stares at the floor wordlessly. MAMA repeats the phrase with precision and cool emotion.)

In my mother's house there is still God.

BENEATHA. In my mother's house there is still God.

(A long pause.)

MAMA. *(Walking away from BENEATHA, too disturbed for triumphant posture. Stopping and turning back to her daughter.)* There are some ideas we ain't going to have in this house. Not long as I am at the head of this family.

BENEATHA. Yes, ma'am.

(MAMA walks out of the room.)

RUTH. *(Almost gently, with profound understanding.)* You think you a woman, Bennie—but you still a little girl. What you did was childish—so you got treated like a child.

BENEATHA. I see. *(Quietly.)* I also see that everybody thinks it's all right for Mama to be a tyrant. But all the tyranny in the world will never put a God in the heavens! *(She picks up her books and goes out.)*

RUTH. *(Goes to MAMA's door.)* She said she was sorry.

MAMA. *(Coming out, going to her plant.)* They frightens me, Ruth. My children.

RUTH. You got good children, Lena. They just a little off sometimes—but they're good.

MAMA. No—there's something come down between me and them that don't let us understand each other and I don't know what it is. One done almost lost his mind thinking 'bout money all the time and the other done commence to talk about things I can't seem to understand in no form or fashion. What is it that's changing, Ruth?

RUTH. *(Soothingly, older than her years.)* Now . . . you taking it all too seriously. You just got strong-willed children and it takes a strong woman like you to keep 'em in hand.

MAMA. *(Looking at her plant and*

sprinkling a little water on it.) They spirited all right, my children. Got to admit they got spirit—Bennie and Walter. Like this little old plant that ain't never had enough sunshine or nothing—and look at it. . . .

(She has her back to RUTH, *who has had to stop ironing and lean against something and put the back of her hand to her forehead.)*

RUTH. *(Trying to keep* MAMA *from noticing.)* You . . . sure . . . loves that little old thing, don't you? . . .

MAMA. Well, I always wanted me a garden like I used to see sometimes at the back of the houses down home. This plant is close as I ever got to having one. *(She looks out of the window as she replaces the plant.)* Lord, ain't nothing as dreary as the view from this window on a dreary day, is there? Why ain't you singing this morning, Ruth? Sing that "No Ways Tired." That song always lifts me up so—*(She turns at last to see that* RUTH *has slipped quietly into a chair, in a state of semiconsciousness.)* Ruth! Ruth honey—what's the matter with you . . . Ruth!

CURTAIN

ACT ONE

SCENE 2

It is the following morning; a Saturday morning, and house cleaning is in progress at the YOUNGERS. *Furniture has been shoved hither and yon and* MAMA *is giving the kitchen-area walls a washing down.* BENEATHA, *in dungarees, with a handkerchief tied around her face, is spraying insecticide into the cracks in the walls. As they work, the RADIO is on and a Southside disc-jockey program is inappropriately filling the house with a rather exotic saxophone blues.* TRAVIS,

the sole idle one, is leaning on his arms, looking out of the window.

TRAVIS. Grandmama, that stuff Bennie is using smells awful. Can I go downstairs, please?

MAMA. Did you get all them chores done already? I ain't seen you doing much.

TRAVIS. Yes'm—finished early. Where did Mama go this morning?

MAMA. *(Looking at* BENEATHA.*)* She had to go on a little errand.

TRAVIS. Where?

MAMA. To tend to her business.

TRAVIS. Can I go outside then?

MAMA. Oh, I guess so. You better stay right in front of the house, though . . . and keep a good lookout for the postman.

TRAVIS. Yes'm. *(He starts out and decides to give his* AUNT BENEATHA *a good swat on the legs as he passes her.)* Leave them poor little old cockroaches alone, they ain't bothering you none. *(He runs as she swings the spray gun at him both viciously and playfully.)*

*(*WALTER *enters from the bedroom and goes to the phone.)*

MAMA. Look out there, girl, before you be spilling some of that stuff on that child!

TRAVIS. *(Teasing.)* That's right—look out now! *(He exits.)*

BENEATHA. *(Drily.)* I can't imagine that it would hurt him—it has never hurt the roaches.

MAMA. Well, little boys' hides ain't as tough as Southside roaches.

WALTER. *(Into phone.)* Hello—Let me talk to Willy Harris.

MAMA. You better get over there behind the bureau. I seen one marching out of there like Napoleon yesterday.

WALTER. Hello, Willy? It ain't come yet. It'll be here in a few minutes. Did the lawyer give you the papers?

BENEATHA. There's really only one way to get rid of them, Mama—

MAMA. How?

BENEATHA. Set fire to this building.

WALTER. Good. Good. I'll be right over.

BENEATHA. Where did Ruth go, Walter?

WALTER. I don't know. *(He exits abruptly.)*

BENEATHA. Mama, where did Ruth go?

MAMA. *(Looking at her with meaning.)* To the doctor, I think.

BENEATHA. The doctor? What's the matter? *(They exchange glances.)* You don't think—

MAMA. *(With her sense of drama.)* Now I ain't saying what I think. But I ain't never been wrong 'bout a woman neither.

(The phone rings.)

BENEATHA. *(At the phone.)* Hay-lo. . . . *(Pause, and a moment of recognition.)* Well—when did you get back! . . . And how was it? . . . Of course I've missed you—in my way. . . . This morning? No . . . house cleaning and all that and Mama hates it if I let people come over when the house is like this. . . . You *have?* Well, that's different . . . What is it—oh, what the hell, come on over. . . . Right, see you then. *(She hangs up.)*

MAMA. *(Who has listened vigorously, as is her habit.)* Who is that you inviting over here with this house looking like this? You ain't got the pride you was born with!

BENEATHA. Asagai doesn't care how houses look, Mama—he's an intellectual.

MAMA. WHO?

BENEATHA. Asagai—Joseph Asagai. He's an African boy I met on campus. He's been studying in Canada all summer.

MAMA. What's his name?

BENEATHA. Asagai, Joseph. Ah-sah-guy. . . . He's from Nigeria.

MAMA. Oh, that's the little country that was founded by slaves way back. . . .

BENEATHA. No, Mama—that's Liberia.

MAMA. I don't think I never met no African before.

BENEATHA. Well, do me a favor and don't ask him a whole lot of ignorant questions about Africans. I mean, do they wear clothes and all that—

MAMA. Well, now, I guess if you think we so ignorant 'round here maybe you shouldn't bring your friends here—

BENEATHA. It's just that people ask such crazy things. All anyone seems to know about when it comes to Africa is Tarzan—

MAMA. *(Indignantly.)* Why should I know anything about Africa?

BENEATHA. Why do you give money at church for the missionary work?

MAMA. Well, that's to help save people.

BENEATHA. You mean save them from heathenism—

MAMA. *(Innocently.)* Yes.

BENEATHA. I'm afraid they need more salvation from the British and the French.

(RUTH comes in forlornly and pulls off her coat with dejection. They both turn to look at her.)

RUTH. *(Dispiritedly.)* Well, I guess from all the happy faces—everybody knows.

BENEATHA. You pregnant?

MAMA. Lord have mercy, I sure hope it's a little old girl. Travis ought to have a sister.

(BENEATHA and RUTH give her a hopeless look for this grandmotherly enthusiasm.)

BENEATHA. How far along are you?

RUTH. Two months.

BENEATHA. Did you mean to? I mean did you plan it or was it an accident?

MAMA. What do you know about planning or not planning?

BENEATHA. Oh, Mama.

RUTH. *(Wearily.)* She's twenty years old, Lena.

BENEATHA. Did you plan it, Ruth?

RUTH. Mind your own business.

BENEATHA. It is my business—where is he going to live, on the *roof*?

(There is silence following the remark as the three women react to the sense of it.)

Gee—I didn't mean that, Ruth, honest. Gee, I don't feel like that at all. I—I think it is wonderful.

RUTH. *(Dully.)* Wonderful.

BENEATHA. Yes—really.

MAMA. *(Looking at RUTH, worried.)* Doctor say everything going to be all right?

RUTH. *(Far away.)* Yes—she says everything is going to be fine. . . .

MAMA. *(Immediately suspicious.)* "She"? What doctor you went to?

(RUTH folds over, near hysteria.)

MAMA. *(Worriedly hovering over RUTH.)* Ruth honey—what's the matter with you—you sick?

(RUTH has her fists clenched on her thighs and is fighting hard to suppress a scream that seems to be rising in her.)

BENEATHA. What's the matter with her, Mama?

MAMA. *(Working her fingers in RUTH's shoulder to relax her.)* She be all right. Women gets right depressed sometimes when they get her way. *(Speaking softly, expertly, rapidly.)* Now you just relax. That's right . . . just lean back, don't think 'bout nothing at all . . . nothing at all—

RUTH. I'm all right. *(The glassy-eyed look melts and then she collapses into a fit of heavy sobbing.)*

(The BELL rings.)

BENEATHA. Oh, my God—that must be Asagai.

MAMA. *(To RUTH.)* Come on now,

honey. You need to lie down and rest awhile . . . then have some nice hot food.

(They exit, RUTH's weight on her mother-in-law. BENEATHA, herself profoundly disturbed, opens the door to admit a rather dramatic-looking young man with a large package.)

ASAGAI. Hello, Alaiyo—

BENEATHA. *(Holding the door open and regarding him with pleasure.)* Hello. . . . *(Long pause.)* Well—come in. And please excuse everything. My mother was very upset about my letting anyone come here with the place like this.

ASAGAI. *(Coming into the room.)* You look disturbed too. . . . Is something wrong?

BENEATHA. *(Still at the door, absently.)* Yes . . . we've all got acute ghetto-itus. *(She smiles and comes toward him, finding a cigarette and sitting.)* So—sit down! How was Canada?

ASAGAI. *(A sophisticate.)* Canadian.

BENEATHA. *(Looking at him.)* I'm very glad you are back.

ASAGAI. *(Looking back at her in turn.)* Are you really?

BENEATHA. Yes—very.

ASAGAI. Why—you were quite glad when I went away. What happened?

BENEATHA. You went away.

ASAGAI. Ahhhhhhhh.

BENEATHA. Before—you wanted to be so serious before there was time.

ASAGAI. How much time must there be before one knows what one feels?

BENEATHA. *(Stalling this particular conversation. Her hands pressed together, in a deliberately childish gesture.)* What did you bring me?

ASAGAI. *(Handing her the package.)* Open it and see.

BENEATHA. *(Eagerly opening the package and drawing out some records and the colorful robes of a Nigerian woman.)* Oh, Asagai! . . . You got them for me! . . . How beautiful . . . and the records too! *(She lifts out the robes and runs to the mirror with them and holds the drapery up in front of herself.)*

ASAGAI. *(Coming to her at the mirror.)* I shall have to teach you how to drape it properly. *(He flings the material about her for the moment and stands back to look at her.)* Ah—Oh-pay-gay-day, oh-gbah-mu-shay. *(A Yoruba exclamation for admiration.)* You wear it well . . . very well . . . mutilated hair and all.

BENEATHA. *(Turning suddenly.)* My hair—what's wrong with my hair?

ASAGAI. *(Shrugging.)* Were you born with it like that?

BENEATHA. *(Reaching up to touch it.)* No . . . of course not. *(She looks back to the mirror, disturbed.)*

ASAGAI. *(Smiling.)* How then?

BENEATHA. You know perfectly well how . . . as crinkly as yours . . . that's how.

ASAGAI. And it is ugly to you that way?

BENEATHA. *(Quickly.)* Oh, no—not ugly . . . *(More slowly, apologetically.)* but it's so hard to manage when it's, well —raw.

ASAGAI. And so to accommodate that —you mutilate it every week?

BENEATHA. It's not mutilation!

ASAGAI. *(Laughing aloud at her seriousness.)* Oh . . . please! I am only teasing you because you are so very serious about these things. *(He stands back from her and folds his arms across his chest as he watches her pulling at her hair and frowning in the mirror.)* Do you remember the first time you met me at school? . . . *(He laughs.)* You came up to me and you said—and I thought you were the most serious little thing I had ever seen— you said: *(He imitates her.)* "Mr. Asagai —I want very much to talk with you. About Africa. You see, Mr. Asagai, I am looking for my *identity!*" *(He laughs.)*

BENEATHA. *(Turning to him, not laughing.)* Yes—*(Her face is quizzical, profoundly disturbed.)*

ASAGAI. *(Still teasing and reaching out and taking her face in his hands and turning her profile to him.)* Well . . . it is true that this is not so much a profile of a Hollywood queen as perhaps a queen of the Nile—*(A mock dismissal of the importance of the question.)*—but what does it matter? Assimilationism is so popular in your country.

BENEATHA. *(Wheeling, passionately, sharply.)* I am not an assimilationist!

ASAGAI. *(The protest hangs in the room for a moment and* ASAGAI *studies her, his laughter fading.)* Such a serious one. *(There is a pause.)* So—you like the robes? You must take excellent care of them—they are from my sister's personal wardrobe.

BENEATHA. *(With incredulity.)* You— you sent all the way home—for me?

ASAGAI. *(With charm.)* For you—I would do much more. . . . Well, that is what I came for. I must go.

BENEATHA. Will you call me Monday?

ASAGAI. Yes . . . we have a great deal to talk about. I mean about identity and time and all that.

BENEATHA. Time?

ASAGAI. Yes. About how much time one needs to know what one feels.

BENEATHA. You never understood that there is more than one kind of feeling which can exist between a man and a woman—or, at least, there should be.

ASAGAI. *(Shaking his head negatively but gently.)* No. Between a man and a woman there need be only one kind of feeling. I have that for you . . . now even . . . right this moment . . .

BENEATHA. I know—and by itself—it won't do. I can find that anywhere.

ASAGAI. For a woman it should be enough.

BENEATHA. I know—because that's what it says in all the novels that men write. But it isn't. Go ahead and laugh— but I'm not interested in being someone's little episode in America or—(*With feminine vengeance.*)—one of them!

(ASAGAI *has burst into laughter again.*)

That's funny as hell, huh!

ASAGAI. It's just that every American girl I have known has said that to me. White—black—in this you are all the same. And the same speech, too!

BENEATHA. (*Angrily.*) Yuk, yuk, yuk!

ASAGAI. It's how you can be sure that the world's most liberated women are not liberated at all. You all talk about it too much!

(MAMA *enters and is immediately all social charm because of the presence of a guest.*)

BENEATHA. Oh—Mama—this is Mr. Asagai.

MAMA. How do you do?

ASAGAI. (*Total politeness to an elder.*) How do you do, Mrs. Younger. Please forgive me for coming at such an outrageous hour on a Saturday.

MAMA. Well, you are quite welcome. I just hope you understand that our house don't always look like this. (*Chatterish.*) You must come again. I would love to hear all about—(*Not sure of the name.*) —your country. I think it's so sad the way our American Negroes don't know nothing about Africa 'cept Tarzan and all that. And all that money they pour into these churches when they ought to be helping you people over there drive out them French and Englishmen done taken away your land. (*The mother flashes a slightly superior look at her daughter upon completion of the recitation.*)

ASAGAI. (*Taken aback by this sudden and acutely unrelated expression of sympathy.*) Yes . . . yes. . . .

MAMA. (*Smiling at him suddenly and relaxing and looking him over.*) How many miles is it from here to where you come from?

ASAGAI. Many thousands.

MAMA. (*Looking at him as she would* WALTER.) I bet you don't half look after yourself, being away from your mama either. I 'spec' you better come 'round here from time to time and get yourself some decent home-cooked meals. . . .

ASAGAI. (*Moved.*) Thank you. Thank you very much. (*They are all quiet, then—*) Well . . . I must go. I will call you Monday, Alaiyo.

MAMA. What's that he call you?

ASAGAI. Oh—"Alaiyo." I hope you don't mind. It is what you would call a nickname, I think. It is a Yoruba word. I am a Yoruba.

MAMA. (*Looking at* BENEATHA.) I—I thought he was from—

ASAGAI. (*Understanding.*) Nigeria is my country. Yoruba is my tribal origin—

BENEATHA. You didn't tell us what Alaiyo means . . . for all I know, you might be calling me Little Idiot or something. . . .

ASAGAI. Well . . . let me see . . . I do not know how just to explain it. . . . The sense of a thing can be so different when it changes languages.

BENEATHA. You're evading.

ASAGAI. No—really it is difficult. . . . (*Thinking.*) It means . . . it means One for Whom Bread—Food—Is Not Enough. (*He looks at her.*) Is that all right?

BENEATHA. (*Understanding, softly.*) Thank you.

MAMA. (*Looking from one to the other and not understanding any of it.*) Well . . . that's nice. . . . You must come see us again—Mr.—

ASAGAI. Ah-sah-guy.

MAMA. Yes . . . do come again.

ASAGAI. Good-bye. (*He exits.*)

MAMA. (*After him.*) Lord, that's a pretty thing just went out here! (*Insinuatingly, to her daughter.*) Yes, I guess I see why we done commence to get so interested in Africa 'round here. Missionaries my aunt Jenny! *(She exits.)*

BENEATHA. Oh, Mama! . . . *(She picks up the Nigerian dress and holds it up to her in front of the mirror again. She sets the headdress on haphazardly and then notices her hair again and clutches at it and then replaces the headdress and frowns at herself. Then she starts to wriggle in front of the mirror as she thinks a Nigerian woman might.)*

(TRAVIS enters and regards her.)

TRAVIS. You cracking up?

BENEATHA. Shut up. *(She pulls the headdress off and looks at herself in the mirror and clutches at her hair again and squinches her eyes as if trying to imagine something. Then, suddenly, she gets her raincoat and kerchief and hurriedly prepares for going out.)*

MAMA. *(Coming back into the room.)* She's resting now. Travis, baby, run next door and ask Miss Johnson to please let me have a little kitchen cleanser. This here can is empty as Jacob's kettle.

TRAVIS. I just came in.

MAMA. Do as you told. *(He exits and she looks at her daughter.)* Where are you going?

BENEATHA. *(Halting at the door.)* To become a queen of the Nile! *(She exits in a breathless blaze of glory.)*

(RUTH appears in the bedroom doorway.)

MAMA. Who told you to get up?

RUTH. Ain't nothing wrong with me to be lying in no bed for. Where did Bennie go?

MAMA. *(Drumming her fingers.)* Far as I could make out—to Egypt.

(RUTH just looks at her.)

What time is it getting to?

RUTH. Ten twenty. And the mailman going to ring that bell this morning just like he done every morning for the last umpteen years.

(TRAVIS comes in with the cleanser can.)

TRAVIS. She say to tell you that she don't have much.

MAMA. *(Angrily.)* Lord, some people I could name sure is tight-fisted! *(Directing her grandson.)* Mark two cans of cleanser down on the list there. If she that hard up for kitchen cleanser, I sure don't want to forget to get her none!

RUTH. Lena—maybe the woman is just short on cleanser—

MAMA. *(Not listening.)* Much baking powder as she done borrowed from me all these years, she could of done gone into the baking business!

(The BELL sounds suddenly and sharply and all three are stunned—serious and silent—mid-speech. In spite of all the other conversations and distractions of the morning, this is what they have been waiting for, even TRAVIS, who looks helplessly from his mother to his grandmother. RUTH is the first to come to life again.)

RUTH. *(To TRAVIS.)* GET DOWN THEM STEPS, BOY!

(TRAVIS snaps to life and flies out to get the mail.)

MAMA. *(Her eyes wide, her hand to her breast.)* You mean it done really come?

RUTH. *(Excited.)* Oh, Miss Lena!

MAMA. *(Collecting herself.)* Well . . . I don't know what we all so excited about 'round here. We known it was coming for months.

RUTH. That's a whole lot different from having it come and being able to hold it in your hands . . . a piece of paper worth ten thousand dollars. . . .

(TRAVIS *bursts back into the room. He holds the envelope high above his head, like a little dancer, his face is radiant and he is breathless. He moves to his grandmother with sudden slow ceremony and puts the envelope into her hands. She accepts it, and then merely holds it and looks at it.*)

Come on! Open it . . . Lord have mercy, I wish Walter Lee was here!

TRAVIS. Open it, Grandmama!

MAMA. (*Staring at it.*) Now you all be quiet. It's just a check.

RUTH. Open it. . . .

MAMA. (*Still staring at it.*) Now don't act silly. . . . We ain't never been no people to act silly 'bout no money—

RUTH. (*Swiftly.*) We ain't never had none before—OPEN IT!

(MAMA *finally makes a good strong tear and pulls out the thin blue slice of paper and inspects it closely. The boy and his mother study it raptly over* MAMA's *shoulders.*)

MAMA. TRAVIS! (*She is counting off with doubt.*) Is that the right number of zeros?

TRAVIS. Yes'm . . . ten thousand dollars. Gaalee, Grandmama, you rich.

MAMA. (*She holds the check away from her, still looking at it. Slowly her face sobers into a mask of unhappiness.*) Ten thousand dollars. (*She hands it to* RUTH.) Put it away somewhere, Ruth. (*She does not look at* RUTH; *her eyes seem to be seeing something somewhere very far off.*) Ten thousand dollars they give you. Ten thousand dollars.

TRAVIS. (*To his mother, sincerely.*) What's the matter with Grandmama—don't she want to be rich?

RUTH. (*Distractedly.*) You go on out and play now, baby.

(TRAVIS *exits.* MAMA *starts wiping dishes absently, humming intently to herself.*)

(RUTH *turns to her, with kind exasperation.*) You've gone and got yourself upset.

MAMA. (*Not looking at her.*) I 'spec' if it wasn't for you all . . . I would just put that money away or give it to the church or something.

RUTH. Now what kind of talk is that. Mr. Younger would just be plain mad if he could hear you talking foolish like that.

MAMA. (*Stopping and staring off.*) Yes . . . he sure would. (*Sighing.*) We got enough to do with that money, all right. (*She halts then, and turns and looks at her daughter-in-law hard;* RUTH *avoids her eyes and* MAMA *wipes her hands with finality and starts to speak firmly to* RUTH.) Where did you go today, girl?

RUTH. To the doctor.

MAMA. (*Impatiently.*) Now, Ruth . . . you know better than that. Old Doctor Jones is strange enough in his way but there ain't nothing 'bout him make somebody slip and call him "she"—like you done this morning.

RUTH. Well, that's what happened—my tongue slipped.

MAMA. You went to see that woman, didn't you?

RUTH. (*Defensively, giving herself away.*) What woman you talking about?

MAMA. (*Angrily.*) That woman who—

(WALTER *enters in great excitement.*)

WALTER. Did it come?

MAMA. (*Quietly.*) Can't you give people a Christian greeting before you start asking about money?

WALTER. (*To* RUTH.) Did it come?

(RUTH *unfolds the check and lays it quietly before him, watching him intently with thoughts of her own.*)

(WALTER *sits down and grasps it close and counts off the zeros.*) Ten thousand dollars. (*He turns suddenly, frantically to his mother and draws some papers out of his breast pocket.)* Mama—look. Old Willy Harris put everything on paper—

MAMA. Son—I think you ought to talk to your wife . . . I'll go on out and leave you alone if you want—

WALTER. I can talk to her later—Mama, look—

MAMA. Son—

WALTER. WILL SOMEBODY PLEASE LISTEN TO ME TODAY?

MAMA. *(Quietly.)* I don't 'low no yellin' in this house, Walter Lee, and you know it—

(WALTER stares at them in frustration and starts to speak several times.)

—and there ain't going to be no investing in no liquor stores. I don't aim to have to speak on that again.

(A long pause.)

WALTER. Oh—so you don't aim to have to speak on that again? So *you* have decided. . . . *(Crumpling his papers.)* Well, *you* tell that to my boy tonight when you put him to sleep on the living-room couch . . . *(Turning to MAMA and speaking directly to her.)* yeah—and tell ti to my wife, Mama, tomorrow when she has to go out of here to look after somebody else's kids. And tell it to *me*, Mama, every time we need a new pair of curtains and I have to watch *you* go out and work in somebody's kitchen. Yeah, you tell me then! *(WALTER starts out.)*

RUTH. Where you going?

WALTER. I'm going out!

RUTH. Where?

WALTER. Just out of this house somewhere—

RUTH. *(Getting her coat.)* I'll come too.

WALTER. I don't want you to come!

RUTH. I got something to talk to you about, Walter.

WALTER. That's too bad.

MAMA. *(Still quietly.)* Walter Lee— *(She waits and he finally turns and looks at her)*—sit down.

WALTER. I'm a grown man, Mama.

MAMA. Ain't nobody said you wasn't grown. But you still in my house and my presence. And as long as you are—you'll talk to your wife civil. Now sit down.

RUTH. *(Suddenly.)* Oh, let him go on out and drink himself to death! He makes me sick to my stomach! *(She flings her coat against him.)*

WALTER. *(Violently.)* And you turn mine too, baby!

(RUTH goes into their bedroom and slams the door behind her.)

That was my greatest mistake—

MAMA. *(Still quietly.)* Walter, what is the matter with you?

WALTER. Matter with me? Ain't nothing the matter with *me!*

MAMA. Yes there is. Something eating you up like a crazy man. Something more than me not giving you this money. The past few years I been watching it happen to you. You get all nervous acting and kind of wild in the eyes—

(WALTER jumps up impatiently at her words.)

I said sit there now, I'm talking to you!—

WALTER. Mama—I don't need no nagging at me today.

MAMA. Seem like you getting to a place where you always tied up in some kind of knot about something. But if anybody ask you 'bout it you just yell at 'em and bust out the house and go out and drink somewheres. Walter Lee, people can't live with that. Ruth's a good, patient girl in her way—but you getting to be too much. Boy, don't make the mistake of driving that girl away from you.

WALTER. Why—what she do for me?

MAMA. She loves you.

WALTER. Mama—I'm going out. I want to go off somewhere and be by myself for a while.

MAMA. I'm sorry 'bout your liquor store, son. It just wasn't the thing for us to do. That's what I want to tell you about—

WALTER. I got to go out, Mama—*(He rises.)*

MAMA. It's dangerous, son.

WALTER. What's dangerous?

MAMA. When a man goes outside his home to look for peace.

WALTER. *(Beseechingly.)* Then why can't there never be no peace in this house then?

MAMA. You done found it in some other house?

WALTER. No—there ain't no woman! Why do women always think there's a woman somewhere when a man gets restless. *(Coming to her.)* Mama—Mama—I want so many things . . .

MAMA. Yes, son—

WALTER. I want so many things that they are driving me kind of crazy . . . Mama—look at me.

MAMA. I'm looking at you. You a good-looking boy. You got a job, a nice wife, a fine boy and—

WALTER. A job. *(Looks at her.)* Mama, a job? I open and close car doors all day long. I drive a man around in his limousine and I say, "Yes, sir; no, sir; very good, sir; shall I take the Drive, sir?" Mama, that ain't no kind of job . . . that ain't nothing at all. *(Very quietly.)* Mama, I don't know if I can make you understand.

MAMA. Understand what, baby?

WALTER. *(Quietly.)* Sometimes it's like I can see the future stretched out in front of me—just plain as day. The future, Mama. Hanging over there at the edge of my days. Just waiting for me—a big, looming blank space—full of *nothing.* Just waiting for *me.* *(Pause.)* Mama—sometimes when I'm downtown and I pass them cool, quiet-looking restaurants where them white boys are sitting back and talking 'bout things . . . sitting there turning deals worth millions of dollars

. . . sometimes I see guys don't look much older than me—

MAMA. Son—how come you talk so much 'bout money?

WALTER. *(With immense passion.)* Because it is life, Mama!

MAMA. *(Quietly.)* Oh—*(Very quietly.)* —so now it's life. Money is life. Once upon a time freedom used to be life—now it's money. I guess the world really do change . . .

WALTER. No—it was always money, Mama. We just didn't know about it.

MAMA. No . . . something has changed. *(She looks at him.)* You something new, boy. In my time we was worried about not being lynched and getting to the North if we could and how to stay alive and still have a pinch of dignity too. . . . Now here come you and Beneatha—talking 'bout things we ain't never even thought about hardly, me and your daddy. You ain't satisfied or proud of nothing we done. I mean that you had a home; that we kept you out of trouble till you was grown; that you don't have to ride to work on the back of nobody's streetcar —you my children—but how different we done become.

WALTER. You just don't understand, Mama, you just don't understand.

MAMA. Son—do you know your wife is expecting another baby?

(WALTER stands, stunned, and absorbs what his mother has said.)

That's what she wanted to talk to you about.

(WALTER sinks down into a chair.)

This ain't for me to be telling—but you ought to know. *(She waits.)* I think Ruth is thinking 'bout getting rid of that child.

WALTER. *(Slowly understanding.)* No— no—Ruth wouldn't do that.

MAMA. When the world gets ugly enough—a woman will do anything for her family. *The part that's already living.*

WALTER. You don't know Ruth, Mama, if you think she would do that.

(RUTH *opens the bedroom door and stands there a little limp.*)

RUTH. *(Beaten.)* Yes I would too, Walter. *(Pause.)* I gave her a five-dollar down payment.

(There is total silence as the man stares at his wife and the mother stares at her son.)

MAMA. *(Presently.)* Well—*(Tightly.)*—well—son, I'm waiting to hear you say something . . . I waiting to hear how you be your father's son. Be the man he was. . . . *(Pause.)* Your wife say she going to destroy your child. And I'm waiting to hear you talk like him and say we a people who give children life, not who destroys them—*(She rises.)*—I'm waiting to see you stand up and look like your daddy and say we done give up one baby to poverty and that we ain't going to give up nary another one. . . . I'm waiting.

WALTER. Ruth—

MAMA. If you a son of mine, tell her!

(WALTER turns, looks at her and can say nothing.)

(She continues, bitterly.) You . . . you are a disgrace to your father's memory. Somebody get me my hat.

CURTAIN

ACT TWO

SCENE 1

TIME:

Later the same day.

AT RISE:

RUTH *is ironing again. She has the RADIO going. Presently* BENEATHA's *bedroom door opens and* RUTH's *mouth falls and she puts down the iron in fascination.*

RUTH. What have we got on tonight!

BENEATHA. *(Emerging grandly from the doorway so that we can see her thoroughly robed in the costume Asagai brought.)* You are looking at what a well-dressed Nigerian woman wears—*(She parades for* RUTH, *her hair completely hidden by the headdress; she is coquettishly fanning herself with an ornate oriental fan, mistakenly more like Butterfly than any Nigerian that ever was.)*—isn't it beautiful? *(She promenades to the radio and, with an arrogant flourish, turns off the good loud blues that is playing.)* Enough of this assimilationist junk! *(RUTH follows her with her eyes as she goes to the phonograph and puts on a record and turns and waits ceremoniously for the music to come up. Then, with a shout—)* OCOMOGOSIAY!

(RUTH jumps. The music comes up, a lovely Nigerian melody. BENEATHA *listens, enraptured, her eyes far away—"back to the past." She begins to dance.* RUTH *is dumbfounded.)*

RUTH. What kind of dance is that?

BENEATHA. A folk dance.

RUTH. *(Pearl Bailey.)* What kind of folks do that, honey?

BENEATHA. It's from Nigeria. It's a dance of welcome.

RUTH. Who you welcoming?

BENEATHA. The men back to the village.

RUTH. Where they been?

BENEATHA. How should I know—out hunting or something. Anyway, they are coming back now. . . .

RUTH. Well, that's good.

BENEATHA. *(With the record.)*
   Alundi, alundi
   Alundi alunya
   Jop pu a jeepua
   Ang gu sooooooooooo

   Ai yai yae . . .
   Ayehaye—alundi . . .

(WALTER *comes in during this performance; he has obviously been drinking. He leans against the door heavily and watches his sister, at first with distaste. Then his eyes look off—"back to the past"—as he lifts both his fists to the roof, screaming.*)

WALTER. YEAH . . . AND ETHIOPIA STRETCH FORTH HER HANDS AGAIN! . . .

RUTH. (*Drily, looking at him.*) Yes—and Africa sure is claiming her own tonight. (*She gives them both up and starts ironing again.*)

WALTER. (*All in a drunken, dramatic shout.*) Shut up! . . . I'm digging them drums . . . them drums move me! . . . (*He makes his weaving way to his wife's face and leans in close to her.*) In my heart of hearts—(*He thumps his chest.*) —I am much warrior!

RUTH. (*Without even looking up.*) In your heart of hearts you are much drunkard.

WALTER. (*Coming away from her and starting to wander around the room, shouting.*) Me and Jomo . . . (*Intently, in his sister's face. She has stopped dancing to watch him in this unknown mood.*) that's my man, Kenyatta. (*Shouting and thumping his chest.*) FLAMING SPEAR! HOT DAMN! (*He is suddenly in possession of an imaginary spear and actively spearing enemies all over the room.*) OCOMOGOSIAY . . . THE LION IS WAKING . . . OWIMOWEH! (*He pulls his shirt open and leaps up on a table and gestures with his spear. The bell rings. RUTH goes to answer.*)

BENEATHA. (*To encourage WALTER, thoroughly caught up with this side of him.*) OCOMOGOSIAY, FLAMING SPEAR!

WALTER. (*On the table, very far gone, his eyes pure glass sheets. He sees what we cannot, that he is a leader of his people, a great chief, a descendant of Chaka,* and that the hour to march has come.*) Listen, my black brothers—

BENEATHA. OCOMOGOSIAY!

WALTER. —Do you hear the waters rushing against the shores of the coastlands—

BENEATHA. OCOMOGOSIAY!

WALTER. —Do you hear the screeching of the cocks in yonder hills beyond where the chiefs meet in council for the coming of the mighty war—

BENEATHA. OCOMOGOSIAY!

WALTER. —Do you hear the beating of the wings of the birds flying low over the mountains and the low places of our land—

(RUTH *opens the door.* GEORGE MURCHISON *enters.*)

BENEATHA. OCOMOGOSIAY!

WALTER. —Do you hear the singing of the women, singing the war songs of our fathers to the babies in the great houses . . . singing the sweet war songs? OH, DO YOUR HEAR, MY BLACK BROTHERS!

BENEATHA. (*Completely gone.*) We hear you, Flaming Spear—

WALTER. Telling us to prepare for the greatness of the time—(*To* GEORGE.) Black Brother! (*He extends his hand for the fraternal clasp.*)

GEORGE. Black Brother, hell!

RUTH. (*Having had enough, and embarrassed for the family.*) Beneatha, you got company—what's the matter with you? Walter Lee Younger, get down off that table and stop acting like a fool . . .

(WALTER *comes down off the table suddenly and makes a quick exit to the bathroom.*)

RUTH. He's had a little to drink . . . I don't know what her excuse is.

GEORGE. (*To* BENEATHA.) Look honey, we're going *to* the theater—we're not going to be *in* it . . . so go change, huh?

RUTH. You expect this boy to go out with you looking like that?

BENEATHA. (*Looking at* GEORGE.) That's up to George. If he's ashamed of his heritage—

GEORGE. Oh, don't be so proud of yourself, Bennie—just because you look eccentric.

BENEATHA. How can something that's natural be eccentric?

GEORGE. That's what being eccentric means—being natural. Get dressed.

BENEATHA. I don't like that, George.

RUTH. Why must you and your brother make an argument out of everything people say?

BENEATHA. Because I hate assimilationist Negroes!

RUTH. Will somebody please tell me what assimila-whoever means!

GEORGE. Oh, it's just a college girl's way of calling people Uncle Toms—but that isn't what it means at all.

RUTH. Well, what does it mean?

BENEATHA. (*Cutting* GEORGE *off and staring at him as she replies to* RUTH.) It means someone who is willing to give up his own culture and submerge himself completely in the dominant, and in this case, *oppressive* culture!

GEORGE. Oh, dear, dear, dear! Here we go! A lecture on the African past! On our Great West African Heritage! In one second we will hear all about the great Ashanti empires; the great Songhay civilizations; and the great sculpture of Benin—and then some poetry in the Bantu—and the whole monologue will end with the word *heritage*! (*Nastily.*) Let's face it, baby, your heritage is nothing but a bunch of raggedy-assed spirituals and some grass huts!

BENEATHA. *Grass huts!*

(RUTH *crosses to her and forcibly pushes her toward the bedroom.*)

See there . . . you are standing there in your splendid ignorance talking about people who were the first to smelt iron on the face of the earth!

(RUTH *is pushing her through the door.*)

The Ashanti were performing surgical operations when the English—

(RUTH *pulls the door to, with* BENEATHA *on the other side, and smiles graciously at* GEORGE.)

(BENEATHA *opens the door and shouts the end of the sentence defiantly at* GEORGE.) —were still tattooing themselves with blue dragons. . . . (*She goes back inside.*)

RUTH. Have a seat, George. (*They both sit.* RUTH *folds her hands rather primly on her lap, determined to demonstrate the civilization of the family.*) Warm, ain't it? I mean for September. (*Pause.*) Just like they always say about Chicago weather: If it's too hot or cold for you, just wait a minute and it'll change. (*She smiles happily at this cliché of clichés.*) Everybody say it's got to do with them bombs and things they keep setting off. (*Pause.*) Would you like a nice cold beer?

GEORGE. No, thank you. I don't care for beer. (*He looks at his watch.*) I hope she hurries up.

RUTH. What time is the show?

GEORGE. It's an eight-thirty curtain. That's just Chicago, though. In New York standard curtain time is eight forty. (*He is rather proud of this knowledge.*)

RUTH. (*Properly appreciating it.*) You get to New York a lot?

GEORGE. (*Offhand.*) Few times a year.

RUTH. Oh—that's nice. I've never been to New York.

(WALTER *enters. We feel he has relieved himself, but the edge of unreality is still with him.*)

WALTER. New York ain't got nothing Chicago ain't. Just a bunch of hustling people all squeezed up together—being

"Eastern." (*He turns his face into a screw of displeasure.*)

GEORGE. Oh—you've been?

WALTER. *Plenty* of times.

RUTH. (*Shocked at the lie.*) Walter Lee Younger!

WALTER. (*Staring her down.*) Plenty! (*Pause.*) What we got to drink in this house? Why don't you offer this man some refreshment. (*To* GEORGE.) They don't know how to entertain people in this house, man.

GEORGE. Thank you—I don't really care for anything.

WALTER. (*Feeling his head; sobriety coming.*) Where's Mama?

RUTH. She ain't come back yet.

WALTER. (*Looking* GEORGE *over from head to toe, scrutinizing his carefully casual tweed sports jacket over cashmere V-neck sweater over soft eyelet shirt and tie, and soft slacks, finished off with white buckskin shoes.*) Why all you college boys wear them fairyish-looking white shoes?

RUTH. Walter Lee!

(GEORGE *ignores the remark.*)

WALTER. (*To* RUTH.) Well, they look crazy as hell—white shoes, cold as it is.

RUTH. (*Crushed.*) You have to excuse him—

WALTER. No he don't! Excuse me for what? What you always excusing me for! I'll excuse myself when I needs to be excused! (*A pause.*) They look as funny as them black knee socks Beneatha wears out of here all the time.

RUTH. It's the college *style*, Walter.

WALTER. Style, hell. She looks like she got burnt legs or something!

RUTH. Oh, Walter—

WALTER. (*An irritable mimic.*) Oh, Walter! Oh, Walter! (*To* MURCHISON.) How's your old man making out? I understand you all going to buy that big hotel on the Drive? (*He finds a beer in* the refrigerator, wanders over to MURCHISON, *sipping and wiping his lips with the back of his hand, and straddling a chair backwards to talk to the other man.*) Shrewd move. Your old man is all right, man. (*Tapping his head and half winking for emphasis.*) I mean he knows how to operate. I mean he thinks *big*, you know what I mean, I mean for a *home*, you know? But I think he's kind of running out of ideas now. I'd like to talk to him. Listen, man, I got some plans that could turn this city upside down. I mean I think like he does. *Big*. Invest big, gamble big, hell, lose *big* if you have to, you know what I mean. It's hard to find a man on this whole Southside who understands my kind of thinking—you dig? (*He scrutinizes* MURCHISON *again, drinks his beer, squints his eyes and leans in close, confidential, man to man.*) Me and you ought to sit down and talk sometimes, man. Man, I got me some ideas. . . .

MURCHISON. (*With boredom.*) Yeah—sometimes we'll have to do that, Walter.

WALTER. (*Understanding the indifference, and offended.*) Yeah—well, when you get the time, man. I know you a busy little boy.

RUTH. Walter, please—

WALTER. (*Bitterly, hurt.*) I know ain't nothing in this world as busy as you colored college boys with your fraternity pins and white shoes. . . .

RUTH. (*Covering her face with humiliation.*) Oh, Walter Lee—

WALTER. I see you all all the time—with the books tucked under your arms—going to your (*British A—a mimic.*) "clahsses." And for what! What the hell you learning over there? Filling up your heads—(*Counting off on his fingers.*)—with the sociology and the psychology—but they teaching you how to be a man? How to take over and run the world? They teaching you how to run a rubber plantation or a steel mill? Naw—just to talk proper and read books and wear white shoes. . . .

GEORGE. (Looking at him with distaste, a little above it all.) You're all wacked up with bitterness, man.

WALTER. (Intently, almost quietly, between the teeth, glaring at the boy.) And you—ain't you bitter, man? Ain't you just about had it yet? Don't you see no stars gleaming that you can't reach out and grab? You happy?—you contented son-of-a-bitch—you happy? You got it made? Bitter? Man, I'm a volcano. Bitter? Here I am a giant—surrounded by ants! Ants who can't even understand what it is the giant is talking about.

RUTH. (Passionately and suddenly.) Oh, Walter—ain't you with nobody!

WALTER. (Violently.) No! 'Cause ain't nobody with me! Not even my own mother!

RUTH. Walter, that's a terrible thing to say!

(BENEATHA enters, dressed for the evening in a cocktail dress and earrings.)

GEORGE. Well—hey, you look great.

BENEATHA. Let's go, George. See you all later.

RUTH. Have a nice time.

GEORGE. Thanks. Good night. (To WALTER, sarcastically.) Good night, Prometheus.

(BENEATHA and GEORGE exit.)

WALTER. (To RUTH.) Who is Prometheus?

RUTH. I don't know. Don't worry about it.

WALTER. (In fury, pointing after GEORGE.) See there—they get to a point where they can't insult you man to man —they got to go talk about something ain't nobody never heard of!

RUTH. How do you know it was an insult? (To humor him.) Maybe Prometheus is a nice fellow.

WALTER. Prometheus! I bet there ain't even no such thing! I bet that simple-minded clown—

RUTH. Walter—(She stops what she is doing and looks at him.)

WALTER. (Yelling.) Don't start!

RUTH. Start what?

WALTER. Your nagging! Where was I? Who was I with? How much money did I spend?

RUTH. (Plaintively.) Walter Lee—why don't we just try to talk about it. . . .

WALTER. (Not listening.) I been out talking with people who understand me. People who care about the things I got on my mind.

RUTH. (Wearily.) I guess that means people like Willy Harris.

WALTER. Yes, people like Willy Harris.

RUTH. (With a sudden flash of impatience.) Why don't you all just hurry up and go into the banking business and stop talking about it!

WALTER. Why? You want to know why? 'Cause we all tied up in a race of people that don't know how to do nothing but moan, pray and have babies! (The line is too bitter even for him and he looks at her and sits down.)

RUTH. Oh, Walter . . . (Softly.) honey, why can't you stop fighting me?

WALTER. (Without thinking.) Who's fighting you? Who even cares about you? (This line begins the retardation of his mood.)

RUTH. Well—(She waits a long time, and then with resignation starts to put away her things.)—I guess I might as well go on to bed . . . (More or less to herself.) I don't know where we lost it . . . but we have . . . (Then, to him.) I—I'm sorry about this new baby, Walter. I guess maybe I better go on and do what I started . . . I guess I just didn't realize how bad things was with us . . . I guess I just didn't really realize—(She starts out to the bedroom and stops.)—you want some hot milk?

WALTER. Hot milk?

RUTH. Yes—hot milk.

WALTER. Why hot milk?

RUTH. 'Cause after all that liquor you come home with you ought to have something hot in your stomach.

WALTER. I don't want no milk.

RUTH. You want some coffee then?

WALTER. No, I don't want no coffee. I don't want nothing hot to drink. (*Almost plaintively.*) Why you always trying to give me something to eat?

RUTH. (*Standing and looking at him helplessly.*) What else can I give you, Walter Lee Younger? (*She stands and looks at him and presently turns to go out again.*)

(*He lifts his head and watches her going away from him in a new mood which began to emerge when he asked her "Who cares about you?"*)

WALTER. It's been rough, ain't it, baby? (*She hears and stops but does not turn around and he continues to her back.*) I guess between two people there ain't never as much understood as folks generally thinks there is. I mean like between me and you—
(*She turns to face him.*)—how we gets to the place where we scared to talk softness to each other. (*He waits, thinking hard himself.*) Why you think it got to be like that? (*He is thoughtful, almost as a child would be.*) Ruth, what is it gets into people ought to be close?

RUTH. I don't know, honey. I think about it a lot.

WALTER. On account of you and me, you mean? The way things are with us. The way something done come down between us.

RUTH. There ain't so much between us, Walter . . . not when you come to me and try to talk to me. Try to be with me . . . a little even.

WALTER. (*Total honesty.*) Sometimes . . . sometimes . . . I don't even know how to try.

RUTH. Walter—

WALTER. Yes?

RUTH. (*Coming to him, gently and with misgiving, but coming to him.*) Honey . . . life don't have to be like this. I mean sometimes people can do things so that things are better. . . . You remember how we used to talk when Travis was born . . . about the way we were going to live . . . the kind of house. . . . (*She is stroking his head.*) Well, it's all starting to slip away from us. . . .

(MAMA *enters, and* WALTER *jumps up and shouts at her.*)

WALTER. Mama, where have you been?

MAMA. My—them steps is longer than they used to be. Whew! (*She sits down and ignores him.*) How you feeling this evening, Ruth?

(RUTH *shrugs, disturbed some at having been prematurely interrupted and watching her husband knowingly.*)

WALTER. Mama, where you been all day?

MAMA. (*Still ignoring him and leaning on the table and changing to more comfortable shoes.*) Where's Travis?

RUTH. I let him go out earlier and he ain't come back yet. Boy, is he going to get it!

WALTER. Mama!

MAMA. (*As if she has heard him for the first time.*) Yes, son?

WALTER. Where did you go this afternoon?

MAMA. I went downtown to tend to some business that I had to tend to.

WALTER. What kind of business?

MAMA. You know better than to question me like a child, Brother.

WALTER. (*Rising and bending over the table.*) Where were you, Mama? (*Bringing his fists down and shouting.*) Mama, you didn't go do something with that insurance money, something crazy?

(The front door opens slowly, interrupting him, and TRAVIS *peeks his head in, less than hopefully.)*

TRAVIS. *(To his mother.)* Mama, I—

RUTH. "Mama I" nothing! You're going to get it, boy! Get on in that bedroom and get yourself ready!

TRAVIS. But I—

MAMA. Why don't you all never let the child explain hisself.

RUTH. Keep out of it now, Lena.

*(*MAMA *clamps her lips together, and* RUTH *advances toward her son menacingly.)*

RUTH. A thousand times I have told you not to go off like that—

MAMA. *(Holding out her arms to her grandson.)* Well—at least let me tell him something. I want him to be the first one to hear. . . . Come here, Travis.

(The boy obeys, gladly.)

Travis—*(She takes him by the shoulder and looks into his face.)*—you know that money we got in the mail this morning?

TRAVIS. Yes'm—

MAMA. Well—what do you think your grandmama gone and done with that money?

TRAVIS. I don't know, Grandmama.

MAMA. *(Putting her finger on his nose for emphasis.)* She went out and she bought you a house!

(The explosion comes from WALTER *at the end of the revelation and he jumps up and turns away from all of them in a fury.)*

*(*MAMA *continues, to* TRAVIS.*)* You glad about the house? It's going to be yours when you get to be a man.

TRAVIS. Yeah—I always wanted to live in a house.

MAMA. All right, gimme some sugar then—*(*TRAVIS *puts his arms around her neck as she watches her son over the boy's shoulder. Then, to* TRAVIS, *after the embrace.)*—now when you say your prayers tonight, you thank God and your grandfather—'cause it was him who give you the house—in his way.

RUTH. *(Taking the boy from* MAMA *and pushing him toward the bedroom.)* Now you get out of here and get ready for your beating.

TRAVIS. Aw, Mama—

RUTH. Get on in there. *(Closing the door behind him and turning radiantly to her mother-in-law.)* So you went and did it!

MAMA. *(Quietly, looking at her son with pain.)* Yes, I did.

RUTH. *(Raising both arms classically.)* PRAISE GOD! *(Looks at* WALTER *a moment, who says nothing. She crosses rapidly to her husband.)* Please, honey—let me be glad . . . you be glad too. *(She has laid her hands on his shoulders, but he shakes himself free of her roughly, without turning to face her.)* Oh, Walter . . . a home . . . a home. *(She comes back to* MAMA.*)* Well—where is it? How big is it? How much it going to cost?

MAMA. Well—

RUTH. When we moving?

MAMA. *(Smiling at her.)* First of the month.

RUTH. *(Throwing back her head with jubilance.)* PRAISE GOD!

MAMA. *(Tentatively, still looking at her son's back turned against her and* RUTH.*)* It's—it's a nice house too . . . *(She cannot help speaking directly to him. An imploring quality in her voice, her manner, makes her almost like a girl now.)* Three bedrooms—nice big one for you and Ruth. . . . Me and Beneatha still have to share our room, but Travis have one of his own—and *(With difficulty.)* I figure if the—new baby—is a boy, we could get one of them double-decker outfits. . . . And there's a yard with a little patch of dirt where I could maybe get to grow me a few flowers . . . and a nice big basement . . .

RUTH. Walter honey, be glad—

MAMA. *(Still to his back, fingering things on the table.)* 'Course I don't want to make it sound fancier than it is. . . . It's just a plain little old house—but it's made good and solid—and it will be *ours*. Walter Lee—it makes a difference in a man when he can walk on floors that belong to *him*. . . .

RUTH. Where is it?

MAMA. *(Frightened at this telling.)* Well —well—it's out there in Clybourne Park—

(RUTH's radiance fades abruptly, and WALTER finally turns slowly to face his mother with incredulity and hostility.)

RUTH. Where?

MAMA. *(Matter-of-factly.)* Four o six Clybourne Street, Clybourne Park.

RUTH. Clybourne Park? Mama, there ain't no colored people living in Clybourne Park.

MAMA. *(Almost idiotically.)* Well, I guess there's going to be some now.

WALTER. *(Bitterly.)* So that's the peace and comfort you went out and bought for us today!

MAMA. *(Raising her eyes to meet his finally.)* Son—I just tried to find the nicest place for the least amount of money for my family.

RUTH. *(Trying to recover from the shock.)* Well—well—'course I ain't one never been 'fraid of no crackers, mind you—but—well, wasn't there no other houses nowhere?

MAMA. Them houses they put up for colored in them areas way out all seem to cost twice as much as other houses. I did the best I could.

RUTH. *(Struck senseless with the news, in its various degrees of goodness and trouble, she sits a moment, her fists propping her chin in thought, and then she starts to rise, bringing her fists down with vigor, the radiance spreading from cheek to cheek again.)* Well—well!—All I can say is—if this is my time in life—*my time* —to say good-bye—*(And she builds with momentum as she starts to circle the room with an exuberant, almost tearfully happy release.)*—to these Goddamned cracking walls!—(She pounds the walls.)—and these marching roaches!—(She wipes at an imaginary army of marching roaches.) —and this cramped little closet which ain't now or never was no kitchen! . . . then I say it loud and good, HALLELU-JAH! AND GOOD-BYE MISERY . . . I DON'T NEVER WANT TO SEE YOUR UGLY FACE AGAIN! (She laughs joyously, having practically destroyed the apartment, and flings her arms up and lets them come down happily, slowly, reflectively, over her abdomen, aware for the first time perhaps that the life therein pulses with happiness and not despair.) Lena?

MAMA. *(Moved, watching her happiness.)* Yes, honey?

RUTH. *(Looking off.)* Is there—is there a whole lot of sunlight?

MAMA. *(Understanding.)* Yes, child, there's a whole lot of sunlight.

(Long pause.)

RUTH. *(Collecting herself and going to the door of the room TRAVIS is in.)* Well —I guess I better see 'bout Travis. *(To MAMA.)* Lord, I sure don't feel like whipping nobody today! *(She exits.)*

(The mother and son are left alone now and the mother waits a long time, considering deeply, before she speaks.)

MAMA. Son—you—you understand what I done, don't you?

(WALTER is silent and sullen.)

I—I just seen my family falling apart today . . . just falling to pieces in front of my eyes. . . . We couldn't of gone on like we was today. We was going backwards 'stead of forwards—talking 'bout killing babies and wishing each other was dead. . . . When it gets like that in life—you just got to do something different, push on out and do something bigger. . . . *(She waits.)* I wish you say something, son . . . I wish you'd say how deep inside you you think I done the right thing—

WALTER. *(Crossing slowly to his bedroom door and finally turning there and speaking measuredly.)* What you need me to say you done right for? *You* the head of this family. You run our lives like you want to. It was your money and you did what you wanted with it. So what you need for me to say it was all right for? *(Bitterly, to hurt her as deeply as he knows is possible.)* So you butchered up a dream of mine—you—who always talking 'bout your children's dreams . . .

MAMA. Walter Lee—

(He just closes the door behind him. MAMA sits alone, thinking heavily.)

CURTAIN

ACT TWO

SCENE 2

TIME:
Friday night. A few weeks later.
AT RISE:
Packing crates mark the intention of the family to move. BENEATHA and GEORGE come in, presumably from an evening out again.

GEORGE. O.K. . . . O.K., whatever you say. . . .

(They both sit on the couch. He tries to kiss her. She moves away.)

Look, we've had a nice evening; let's not spoil it, huh? . . .

(He again turns her head and tries to nuzzle in and she turns away from him, not with distaste but with momentary lack of interest; in a mood to pursue what they were talking about.)

BENEATHA. I'm *trying* to talk to you.
GEORGE. We always talk.
BENEATHA. Yes—and I love to talk.
GEORGE. *(Exasperated; rising.)* I know it and I don't mind it sometimes . . . I want you to cut it out, see—the moody stuff, I mean. I don't like it. You're a nice-looking girl . . . all over. That's all you need, honey, forget the atmosphere. Guys aren't going to go for the atmosphere—they're going to go for what they see. Be glad for that. Drop the Garbo routine. It doesn't go with you. As for myself, I want a nice—*(Groping.)*—simple *(Thoughtfully.)*—sophisticated girl . . . not a poet—O.K.?

(She rebuffs him again and he starts to leave.)

BENEATHA. Why are you angry?
GEORGE. Because this is stupid! I don't go out with you to discuss the nature of "quiet desperation" or to hear all about your thoughts—because the world will go on thinking what it thinks regardless—
BENEATHA. Then why read books? Why go to school?
GEORGE. *(With artificial patience, counting on his fingers.)* It's simple. You read books—to learn facts—to get grades —to pass the course—to get a degree. That's all—it has nothing to do with thoughts.

(A long pause.)

BENEATHA. I see.

(A longer pause as she looks at him.)

Good night, George.

(GEORGE looks at her a little oddly, and starts to exit. He meets MAMA coming in.)

GEORGE. Oh—hello, Mrs. Younger.

MAMA. Hello, George, how you feeling?

GEORGE. Fine—fine, how are you?

MAMA. Oh, a little tired. You know them steps can get you after a day's work. You all have a nice time tonight?

GEORGE. Yes—a fine time. Well, good night.

MAMA. Good night.

(He exits.)

(MAMA closes the door behind her.) Hello, honey. What you sitting like that for?

BENEATHA. I'm just sitting.

MAMA. Didn't you have a nice time?

BENEATHA. No.

MAMA. No? What's the matter?

BENEATHA. Mama, George is a fool—honest. *(She rises.)*

MAMA. *(Hustling around unloading the packages she has entered with. She stops.)* Is he, baby?

BENEATHA. Yes. *(BENEATHA makes up TRAVIS' bed as she talks.)*

MAMA. You sure?

BENEATHA. Yes.

MAMA. Well—I guess you better not waste your time with no fools.

(BENEATHA looks up at her mother, watching her put groceries in the refrigerator. Finally she gathers up her things and starts into the bedroom. At the door she stops and looks back at her mother.)

BENEATHA. Mama—

MAMA. Yes, baby—

BENEATHA. Thank you.

MAMA. For what?

BENEATHA. For understanding me this time.

(She exits quickly and the mother stands, smiling a little, looking at the place where BENEATHA just stood. RUTH enters.)

RUTH. Now don't you fool with any of this stuff, Lena—

MAMA. Oh, I just thought I'd sort a few things out.

(The phone rings. RUTH answers.)

RUTH. *(At the phone.)* Hello—just a minute. *(Goes to the door.)* Walter, it's Mrs. Arnold. *(Waits. Goes back to the phone. Tense.)* Hello. Yes, this is his wife speaking . . . he's lying down now. Yes . . . well, he'll be in tomorrow. He's been very sick. Yes—I know we should have called, but we were so sure he'd be able to come in today. Yes—yes, I'm very sorry. Yes . . . thank you very much. *(She hangs up.)*

(WALTER is standing in the doorway of the bedroom behind her.)

That was Mrs. Arnold.

WALTER. *(Indifferently.)* Was it?

RUTH. She said if you don't come in tomorrow that they are getting a new man . . .

WALTER. Ain't that sad—ain't that crying sad.

RUTH. She said Mr. Arnold has had to take a cab for three days . . . Walter, you ain't been to work for three days! *(This is a revelation to her.)* Where you been, Walter Lee Younger?

(WALTER looks at her and starts to laugh.)

You're going to lose your job.

WALTER. That's right . . .

RUTH. Oh, Walter, and with your mother working like a dog every day—

WALTER. That's sad too—everything is sad.

MAMA. What you been doing for these three days, son?

WALTER. Mama—you don't know all the things a man what got leisure can find to do in this city. . . . What's this—Friday night? Well—Wednesday I borrowed Willy Harris' car and I went for a drive . . . just me and myself and I drove and drove . . . way out . . . way past South Chicago, and I parked the car and I sat and looked at the steel mills all day long. I just sat in the car and looked at them big black chimneys for hours. Then I drove back and I went to the Green Hat. (Pause.) And Thursday—Thursday I borrowed the car again and I got in and I pointed it the other way and I drove the other way—for hours—way, way up to Wisconsin, and I looked at the farms. I just drove and looked at the farms. Then I drove back and I went to the Green Hat. (Pause.) And today—today I didn't get the car. Today I just walked. All over the Southside. And I looked at the Negroes and they looked at me and finally I just sat down on the curb at Thirty-ninth and South Parkway and I just sat there and watched the Negroes go by. And then I went to the Green Hat. You all sad? You all depressed? And you know where I am going right now—

(RUTH *goes out quietly.*)

MAMA. Oh, Big Walter, is this the harvest of our days?

WALTER. You know what I like about the Green Hat? (*He turns the RADIO on and a steamy, deep blues pours into the room.*) I like this little cat they got there who blows a sax . . . he blows. He talks to me. He ain't but 'bout five feet tall and he's got a conked head and his eyes is always closed and he's all music—

MAMA. (*Rising and getting some papers out of her handbag.*) Walter—

WALTER. And there's this other guy who plays the piano . . . and they got a sound. I mean they can work on some music . . . they got the best little combo in the world in the Green Hat . . . you can just sit there and drink and listen to them three men play and you realize that don't nothing matter worth a damn, but just being there—

MAMA. I've helped do it to you, haven't I, son? Walter, I been wrong.

WALTER. Naw—you ain't never been wrong about nothing, Mama.

MAMA. Listen to me, now. I say I been wrong, son. That I been doing to you what the rest of the world been doing to you. (*She stops and he looks up slowly at her and she meets his eyes pleadingly.*) Walter—what you ain't never understood is that I ain't got nothing, don't own nothing, ain't never really wanted nothing that wasn't for you. There ain't nothing as precious to me. . . . There ain't nothing worth holding on to, money, dreams, nothing else—if it means—if it means it's going to destroy my boy. (*She puts her papers in front of him and he watches her without speaking or moving.*) I paid the man thirty-five hundred dollars down on the house. That leaves sixty-five hundred dollars. Monday morning I want you to take this money and take three thousand dollars and put it in a savings account for Beneatha's medical schooling. The rest you put in a checking account— with your name on it. And from now on any penny that come out of it or that go in it is for you to look after. For you to decide. (*She drops her hands a little helplessly.*) It ain't much, but it's all I got in this world and I'm putting it in your hands. I'm telling you to be the head of this family from now on like you supposed to be.

WALTER. (*Stares at the money.*) You trust me like that, Mama?

MAMA. I ain't never stop trusting you. Like I ain't never stop loving you.

(*She goes out, and* WALTER *sits looking at the money on the table as the MUSIC continues in its idiom, pulsing in the room. Finally, in a decisive gesture, he gets up, and, in mingled joy and desperation, picks up the money. At the same moment,* TRAVIS *enters for bed.*)

TRAVIS. What's the matter, Daddy? You drunk?

WALTER. (*Sweetly, more sweetly than*

we have ever known him.) No, Daddy ain't drunk. Daddy ain't going to never be drunk again . . .

TRAVIS. Well, good night, Daddy.

(The father has come from behind the couch and leans over, embracing his son.)

WALTER. Son, I feel like talking to you tonight.

TRAVIS. About what?

WALTER. Oh, about a lot of things. About you and what kind of man you going to be when you grow up. . . . Son—son, what do you want to be when you grow up?

TRAVIS. A bus driver.

WALTER. *(Laughing a little.)* A what? Man, that ain't nothing to want to be!

TRAVIS. Why not?

WALTER. 'Cause, man—it ain't big enough—you know what I mean.

TRAVIS. I don't know then. I can't make up my mind. Sometimes Mama asks me that too. And sometimes when I tell her I want to be like you—she says she don't want me to be like that and sometimes she says she does. . . .

WALTER. *(Gathering him up in his arms.)* You know what, Travis? In seven years you going to be seventeen years old. And things is going to be very different with us in seven years, Travis. . . . One day when you are seventeen I'll come home—home from my office downtown somewhere—

TRAVIS. You don't work in no office, Daddy.

WALTER. No—but after tonight. After what your daddy gonna do tonight, there's going to be offices—a whole lot of offices. . . .

TRAVIS. What you gonna do tonight, Daddy?

WALTER. You wouldn't understand yet, son, but your daddy's gonna make a transaction . . . a business transaction that's going to change our lives. . . . That's how come one day when you 'bout seventeen years old I'll come home and I'll be pretty tired, you know what I mean, after a day of conferences and secretaries getting things wrong the way they do . . . 'cause an executive's life is hell, man—*(The more he talks the farther away he gets.)* And I'll pull the car up on the driveway . . . just a plain black Chrysler, I think, with white walls—no—black tires. More elegant. Rich people don't have to be flashy . . . though I'll have to get something a little sportier for Ruth—maybe a Cadillac convertible to do her shopping in. . . . And I'll come up the steps to the house and the gardener will be clipping away at the hedges and he'll say, "Good evening, Mr. Younger." And I'll say, "Hello, Jefferson, how are you this evening?" And I'll go inside and Ruth will come downstairs and meet me at the door and we'll kiss each other and she'll take my arm and we'll go up to your room to see you sitting on the floor with the catalogues of all the great schools in America around you. . . . All the great schools in the world! And—and I'll say, all right, son—it's your seventeenth birthday, what is it you've decided? . . . Just tell me where you want to go to school and you'll go. Just tell me, what it is you want to be—and you'll *be* it. . . . Whatever you want to be—Yessir! *(He holds his arms open for* TRAVIS.*)* You just name it, son . . .

*(*TRAVIS *leaps into them.)*

and I hand you the world! *(*WALTER'*s voice has risen in pitch and hysterical promise and on the last line he lifts* TRAVIS *high.)*

BLACKOUT

ACT TWO

SCENE 3

TIME:
Saturday, moving day, one week later.

Before the Curtain rises, RUTH's *VOICE, a strident, dramatic church alto, cuts through the silence.*

It is, in the darkness, a triumphant surge, a penetrating statement of expectation: "Oh, Lord, I don't feel no ways tired! Children, oh, glory hallelujah!"

As the Curtain rises we see that RUTH *is alone in the living room, finishing up the family's packing. It is moving day. She is nailing crates and tying cartons.* BENEATHA *enters, carrying a guitar case, and watches her exuberant sister-in-law.*

RUTH. Hey!

BENEATHA. *(Putting away the case.)* Hi.

RUTH. *(Pointing at a package.)* Honey —look in that package there and see what I found on sale this morning at the South Center. *(*RUTH *gets up and moves to the package and draws out some curtains.)* Lookahere—hand-turned hems!

BENEATHA. How do you know the window size out there?

RUTH. *(Who hadn't thought of that.)* Oh—well, they bound to fit something in the whole house. Anyhow, they was too good a bargain to pass up. *(*RUTH *slaps her head, suddenly remembering something.)* Oh, Bennie—I meant to put a special note on that carton over there. That's your mama's good china and she wants 'em to be very careful with it.

BENEATHA. I'll do it. *(*BENEATHA *finds a piece of paper and starts to draw large letters on it.)*

RUTH. You know what I'm going to do soon as I get in that new house?

BENEATHA. What?

RUTH. Honey—I'm going to run me a tub of water up to here . . . *(With her fingers practically up to her nostrils.)* and I'm going to get in it—and I am going to sit . . . and sit . . . and sit in that hot water and the first person who knocks to tell *me* to hurry up and come out—

BENEATHA. Gets shot at sunrise.

RUTH. *(Laughing happily.)* You said it, sister! *(Noticing how large* BENEATHA *is absent-mindedly making the note.)* Honey, they ain't going to read that from no airplane.

BENEATHA. *(Laughing herself.)* I guess I always think things have more emphasis if they are big, somehow.

RUTH. *(Looking up at her and smiling.)* You and your brother seem to have that as a philosophy of life. Lord, that man— done changed so 'round here. You know —you know what we did last night? Me and Walter Lee?

BENEATHA. What?

RUTH. *(Smiling to herself.)* We went to the movies. *(Looking at* BENEATHA *to see if she understands.)* We went to the movies. You know the last time me and Walter went to the movies together?

BENEATHA. No.

RUTH. Me neither. That's how long it been. *(Smiling again.)* But we went last night. The picture wasn't much good, but that didn't seem to matter. We went— and we held hands.

BENEATHA. Oh, Lord!

RUTH. We held hands—and you know what?

BENEATHA. What?

RUTH. When we come out of the show it was late and dark and all the stores and things was closed up . . . and it was kind of chilly and there wasn't many people on the streets . . . and we was still holding hands, me and Walter.

BENEATHA. You're killing me.

*(*WALTER *enters with a large package. His happiness is deep in him; he cannot keep still with his new-found exuberance. He is singing and wiggling and snapping his fingers. He puts his package in a corner and puts a phonograph record, which he has brought in with him, on the record player. As the MUSIC comes up he dances over to* RUTH *and tries to get her to dance with him. She gives in at last to his raunchiness and in a fit of giggling*

allows herself to be drawn into his mood and together they deliberately burlesque an old social dance of their youth.)

BENEATHA. *(Regarding them a long time as they dance, then drawing in her breath for a deeply exaggerated comment which she does not particularly mean.)* Talk about—oldddddddddd-fashioneddd-dddd—Negroes!

WALTER. *(Stopping momentarily.)* What kind of Negroes? *(He says this in fun. He is not angry with her today, nor with anyone. He starts to dance with his wife again.)*

BENEATHA. Old-fashioned.

WALTER. *(As he dances with* RUTH.*)* You know, when these *New Negroes* have their convention—*(Pointing at his sister.)* —that is going to be the chairman of the Committee on Unending Agitation. *(He goes on dancing, then stops.)* Race, race, race! . . . Girl, I do believe you are the first person in the history of the entire human race to successfully brainwash yourself. *(BENEATHA breaks up and he goes on dancing. He stops again, enjoying his tease.)* Damn, even the N double A C P takes a holiday sometimes!

(BENEATHA and RUTH *laugh.)*

(He dances with RUTH *some more and starts to laugh and stops and pantomimes someone over an operating table.)* I can just see that chick someday looking down at some poor cat on an operating table before she starts to slice him, saying . . . *(Pulling his sleeves back maliciously.)* "By the way, what are your views on civil rights down there? . . ." *(He laughs at her again and starts to dance happily.)*

(The BELL sounds.)

BENEATHA. Sticks and stones may break my bones . . . but words will never hurt me! *(BENEATHA goes to the door and opens it as* WALTER *and* RUTH *go on with the clowning.* BENEATHA *in somewhat sur-*prised to see a quiet-looking middle-aged WHITE MAN *in a business suit holding his hat and a briefcase in his hand and consulting a small piece of paper.)*

MAN. Uh—how do you do, miss. I am looking for a Mrs.—*(He looks at the slip of paper.)* Mrs. Lena—Younger?

BENEATHA. *(Smoothing her hair with slight embarrassment.)* Oh—yes, that's my mother. Excuse me. *(She closes the door and turns to quiet the other two.)* Ruth! Brother! Somebody's here. *(Then she opens the door.)*

(The MAN *casts a curious glance at all of them.)*

Uh—come in please.

MAN. *(Coming in.)* Thank you.

BENEATHA. My mother isn't here just now. Is it business?

MAN. Yes . . . well, of a sort.

WALTER. *(Freely, the Man of the House.)* Have a seat. I'm Mrs. Younger's son. I look after most of her business matters.

*(*RUTH *and* BENEATHA *exchange amused glances.)*

MAN. *(Regarding* WALTER, *and sitting.)* Well—my name is Karl Lindner. . . .

WALTER. *(Stretching out his hand.)* Walter Younger. This is my wife—*(*RUTH *nods politely.)*—and my sister.

LINDNER. How do you do.

WALTER. *(Amiably, as he sits himself easily on a chair, leaning with interest forward on his knees and looking expectantly into the newcomer's face.)* What can we do for you, Mr. Lindner!

LINDNER. *(Some minor shuffling of the hat and briefcase on his knees.)* Well—I am a representative of the Clybourne Park Improvement Association—

WALTER. *(Pointing.)* Why don't you sit your things on the floor?

LINDNER. Oh—yes. Thank you. *(He slides the briefcase and hat under the chair.)* And as I was saying—I am from the Clybourne Park Improvement Association and we have had it brought to our attention at the last meeting that you people—or at least your mother—has bought a piece of residential property at —*(He digs for the slip of paper again.)* —four o six Clybourne Street. . . .

WALTER. That's right. Care for something to drink? Ruth, get Mr. Lindner a beer.

LINDNER. *(Upset for some reason.)* Oh —no, really. I mean thank you very much, but no thank you.

RUTH. *(Innocently.)* Some coffee?

LINDNER. Thank you, nothing at all.

(BENEATHA is watching the man carefully.)

LINDNER. Well, I don't know how much you folks know about our organization. *(He is a gentle man; thoughtful and somewhat labored in his manner.)* It is one of these community organizations set up to look after—oh, you know, things like block upkeep and special projects and we also have what we call our New Neighbors Orientation Committee. . . .

BENEATHA. *(Drily.)* Yes—and what do they do?

LINDNER. *(Turning a little to her and then returning the main force to WALTER.)* Well—it's what you might call a sort of welcoming committee, I guess. I mean they, we, I'm the chairman of the committee—go around and see the new people who move into the neighborhood and sort of give them the lowdown on the way we do things out in Clybourne Park.

BENEATHA. *(With appreciation of the two meanings, which escape RUTH and WALTER.)* Un-huh.

LINDNER. And we also have the category of what the association calls—*(He looks elsewhere.)*—uh—special community problems. . . .

BENEATHA. Yes—and what are some of those?

WALTER. Girl, let the man talk.

LINDNER. *(With understated relief.)* Thank you. I would sort of like to explain this thing in my own way. I mean I want to explain to you in a certain way.

WALTER. Go ahead.

LINDNER. Yes. Well. I'm going to try to get right to the point. I'm sure we'll all appreciate that in the long run.

BENEATHA. Yes.

WALTER. Be still now!

LINDNER. Well—

RUTH. *(Still innocently.)* Would you like another chair—you don't look comfortable.

LINDNER. *(More frustrated than annoyed.)* No, thank you very much. Please. Well—to get right to the point I—*(A great breath, and he is off at last.)*—I am sure you people must be aware of some of the incidents which have happened in various parts of the city when colored people have moved into certain areas—

(BENEATHA exhales heavily and starts tossing a piece of fruit up and down in the air.)

—well—because we have what I think is going to be a unique type of organization in American community life—not only do we deplore that kind of thing—but we are trying to do something about it.

(BENEATHA stops tossing and turns with a new and quizzical interest to the man.)

We feel—*(gaining confidence in his mission because of the interest in the faces of the people he is talking to.)*—we feel that most of the trouble in this world, when you come right down to it—*(He hits his knee for emphasis.)*—most of the trouble exists because people just don't sit down and talk to each other.

RUTH. *(Nodding as she might in church, pleased with the remark.)* You can say that again, mister.

LINDNER. *(More encouraged by such affirmation.)* That we don't try hard enough in this world to understand the other fellow's problem. The other guy's point of view.

RUTH. Now that's right.

(BENEATHA and WALTER *merely watch and listen with genuine interest.*)

LINDNER. Yes—that's the way we feel out in Clybourne Park. And that's why I was elected to come here this afternoon and talk to you people. Friendly like, you know, the way people should talk to each other and see if we couldn't find some way to work this thing out. As I say, the whole business is a matter of *caring* about the other fellow. Anybody can see that you are a nice family of folks, hard working and honest I'm sure.

(BENEATHA *frowns slightly, quizzically, her head tilted regarding him.*)

Today everybody knows what it means to be on the outside of *something.* And of course, there is always somebody who is out to take the advantage of people who don't always understand.

WALTER. What do you mean?

LINDNER. Well—you see our community is made up of people who've worked hard as the dickens for years to build up that little community. They're not rich and fancy people; just hard-working, honest people who don't really have much but those little homes and a dream of the kind of community they want to raise their children in. Now, I don't say we are perfect and there is a lot wrong in some of the things they want. But you've got to admit that a man, right or wrong, has the right to want to have the neighborhood he lives in a certain kind of way. And at the moment the overwhelming majority of our people out there feel that people get along better, take more of a common interest in the life of the community, when they share a common background. I want you to believe me when I tell you that race prejudice simply doesn't enter into it. It is a matter of the people of Clybourne Park believing, rightly or wrongly, as I say, that for the happiness of all concerned that our Negro families are happier when they live in their *own* communities.

BENEATHA. *(With a grand and bitter gesture.)* This, friends, is the Welcoming Committee!

WALTER. *(Dumbfounded, looking at LINDER.)* Is this what you came marching all the way over here to tell us?

LINDNER. Well, now we've been having a fine conversation. I hope you'll hear me all the way through.

WALTER. *(Tightly.)* Go ahead, man.

LINDNER. You see—in the face of all things I have said, we are prepared to make your family a very generous offer. . . .

BENEATHA. Thirty pieces and not a coin less!

WALTER. Yeah?

LINDNER. *(Putting on his glasses and drawing a form out of the briefcase.)* Our association is prepared, through the collective effort of our people, to buy the house from you at a financial gain to your family.

RUTH. Lord have mercy, ain't this the living gall!

WALTER. All right, you through?

LINDNER. Well, I want to give you the exact terms of the financial arrangement—

WALTER. We don't want to hear no exact terms of no arrangements. I want to know if you got any more to tell us 'bout getting together?

LINDNER. *(Taking off his glasses.)* Well —I don't suppose that you feel . . .

WALTER. Never mind how I feel—you got any more to say 'bout how people ought to sit down and talk to each other? . . . Get out of my house, man. *(He turns his back and walks to the door.)*

LINDNER. *(Looking around at the hostile faces and reaching and assembling his hat and briefcase.)* Well—I don't understand why you people are reacting this way. What do you think you are going to gain by moving into a neighborhood where you just aren't wanted and where some elements—well—people can get awful worked up when they feel that their whole way of life and everything they've ever worked for is threatened.

WALTER. Get out.

LINDNER. *(At the door, holding a small card.)* Well—I'm sorry it went like this.

WALTER. Get out.

LINDNER. *(Almost sadly regarding WALTER.)* You just can't force people to change their hearts, son. *(He turns and puts his card on the table and exits.)*

(WALTER pushes the door to with stinging hatred, and stands looking at it. RUTH just sits and BENEATHA just stands. They say nothing. MAMA and TRAVIS enter.)

MAMA. Well—this all the packing got done since I left out of here this morning. I testify before God that my children got all the energy of the dead. What time the moving men due?

BENEATHA. Four o'clock. You had a caller, Mama. *(She is smiling, teasingly.)*

MAMA. Sure enough—who?

BENEATHA. *(Her arms folded saucily.)* The Welcoming Committee.

(WALTER and RUTH giggle.)

MAMA. *(Innocently.)* Who?

BENEATHA. The Welcoming Committee. They said they're sure going to be glad to see you when you get there.

WALTER. *(Devilishly.)* Yeah, they said they can't hardly wait to see your face.

(Laughter.)

MAMA. *(Sensing their facetiousness.)* What's the matter with you all?

WALTER. Ain't nothing the matter with us. We just telling you 'bout the gentleman who came to see you this afternoon.

From the Clybourne Park Improvement Association.

MAMA. What he want?

RUTH. *(In the same mood as BENEATHA and WALTER.)* To welcome you, honey.

WALTER. He said they can't hardly wait. He said the one thing they don't have, that they just *dying* to have out there is a fine family of colored people! *(To RUTH and BENEATHA.)* Ain't that right!

RUTH and BENEATHA. *(Mockingly.)* Yeah! He left his card in case—

(They indicate the card, and MAMA picks it up and throws it on the floor—understanding and looking off as she draws her chair up to the table on which she has put her plant and some sticks and some cord.)

MAMA. Father, give us strength. *(Knowingly—and without fun.)* Did he threaten us?

BENEATHA. Oh—Mama—they don't do it like that any more. He talked Brotherhood. He said everybody ought to learn how to sit down and hate each other with good Christian fellowship.

(She and WALTER shake hands to ridicule the remark.)

MAMA. *(Sadly.)* Lord, protect us. . . .

RUTH. You should hear the money those folks raised to buy the house from us. All we paid and then some.

BENEATHA. What they think we going to do—eat 'em?

RUTH. No, honey, marry 'em.

MAMA. *(Shaking her head.)* Lord, Lord, Lord . . .

RUTH. Well—that's the way the crackers crumble. Joke.

BENEATHA. *(Laughingly noticing what her mother is doing.)* Mama, what are you doing?

MAMA. Fixing my plant so it won't get hurt none on the way. . . .

BENEATHA. Mama, are you going to take *that* to the new house?

MAMA. Un-huh—

BENEATHA. That raggedy-looking old thing?

MAMA. *(Stopping and looking at her.)* It expresses *me*.

RUTH. *(With delight, to* BENEATHA.*)* So there, Miss Thing!

*(*WALTER *comes to* MAMA *suddenly and bends down behind her and squeezes her in his arms with all his strength. She is overwhelmed by the suddenness of it and, though delighted, her manner is like that of* RUTH *with* TRAVIS.*)*

MAMA. Look out now, boy! You make me mess up my thing here!

WALTER. *(His face lit, he slips down on his knees beside her, his arms still about her.)* Mama . . . you know what it means to climb up in the chariot?

MAMA. *(Gruffly, very happy.)* Get on away from me now. . . .

RUTH. *(Near the gift-wrapped package, trying to catch* WALTER's *eye.)* Psst—

WALTER. What the old song say, Mama . . .

RUTH. Walter—now? *(She is pointing at the package.)*

WALTER. *(Speaking the lines, sweetly, playfully, in his mother's face.)*
I got wings . . . you got wings . . .
All God's Children got wings . . .

MAMA. Boy—get out of my face and do some work. . . .

WALTER.
When I get to heaven gonna put on my wings,
Gonna fly all over God's heaven . . .

BENEATHA. *(Teasingly, from across the room.)* Everybody talking 'bout heaven ain't going there!

WALTER. *(To* RUTH, *who is carrying the box across to them.)* I don't know, you think we ought to give her that. . . . Seems to me she ain't been very appreciative around here.

MAMA. *(Eyeing the box, which is obviously a gift.)* What is that?

WALTER. *(Taking it from* RUTH *and putting it on the table in front of* MAMA.*)* Well—what you all think? Should we give it to her?

RUTH. Oh—she was pretty good today.

MAMA. I'll good you—*(She turns her eyes to the box again.)*

BENEATHA. Open it, Mama.

(She stands up, looks at it, turns and looks at all of them, and then presses her hands together and does not open the package.)

WALTER. *(Sweetly.)* Open it, Mama. It's for you.

*(*MAMA *looks in his eyes. It is the first present in her life without its being Christmas. Slowly she opens her package and lifts out, one by one, a brand-new sparkling set of gardening tools.)*

*(*WALTER *continues, prodding.)* Ruth made up the note—read it. . . .

MAMA. *(Picking up the card and adjusting her glasses.)* "To our own Mrs. Miniver—Love from Brother, Ruth and Beneatha." Ain't that lovely. . . .

TRAVIS. *(Tugging at his father's sleeve.)* Daddy, can I give her mine now?

WALTER. All right, son.

*(*TRAVIS *flies to get his gift.)*

Travis didn't want to go in with the rest of us, Mama. He got his own. *(Somewhat amused.)* We don't know what it is. . . .

TRAVIS. *(Racing back in the room with a large hatbox and putting it in front of his grandmother.)* Here!

MAMA. Lord have mercy, baby. You done gone and bought your grandmother a hat?

TRAVIS. *(Very proud.)* Open it!

(She does and lifts out an elaborate, but very elaborate, wide gardening hat,

and all the adults break up at the sight of it.)

RUTH. Travis, honey, what is that?

TRAVIS. *(Who thinks it is beautiful and appropriate.)* It's a gardening hat! Like the ladies always have on in the magazines when they work in their gardens.

BENEATHA. *(Giggling fiercely.)* Travis—we were trying to make Mama Mrs. Miniver—not Scarlett O'Hara!

MAMA. *(Indignantly.)* What's the matter with you all! This here is a beautiful hat! *(Absurdly.)* I always wanted me one just like it! *(She pops it on her head to prove it to her grandson, and the hat is ludicrous and considerably oversized.)*

RUTH. Hot dog! Go, Mama!

WALTER. *(Doubled over with laughter.)* I'm sorry, Mama—but you look like you ready to go out and chop you some cotton sure enough!

(They all laugh except MAMA, out of deference to TRAVIS' feelings.)

MAMA. *(Gathering the boy up to her.)* Bless your heart—this is the prettiest hat I ever owned . . .

(WALTER, RUTH and BENEATHA chime in—noisily, festively and insincerely congratulating TRAVIS on his gift.)

What are we all standing around here for? We ain't finished packin' yet. Bennie, you ain't packed one book.

(The BELL rings.)

BENEATHA. That couldn't be the movers . . . it's not hardly two good yet—(BENEATHA goes into her room.)

(MAMA starts for door.)

WALTER. *(Turning, stiffening.)* Wait—wait—I'll get it. *(He stands and looks at the door.)*

MAMA. You expecting company, son?

WALTER. *(Just looking at the door.)* Yeah—yeah . . .

(MAMA looks at RUTH, and they exchange innocent and unfrightened glances.)

MAMA. *(Not understanding.)* Well, let them in, son.

BENEATHA. *(From her room.)* We need some more string.

MAMA. Travis—you run to the hardware and get me some string cord.

(MAMA goes out and WALTER turns and looks at RUTH. TRAVIS goes to a dish for money.)

RUTH. Why don't you answer the door, man?

WALTER. *(Suddenly bounding across the floor to her.)* 'Cause sometimes it hard to let the future begin! *(Stooping down in her face.)*
I got wings! You got wings!
All God's children got wings!

(He crosses to the door and throws it open. Standing there is a very slight little MAN in a not too prosperous business suit and with haunted frightened eyes and a hat pulled down tightly, brim up, around his forehead. TRAVIS passes between the men and exits.)

(WALTER leans deep in the man's face, still in his jubilance.)

When I get to heaven gonna put on my wings,
Gonna fly all over God's heaven . . .

(The little MAN stares at him.)

Heaven—
(Suddenly he stops and looks past the little man into the empty hallway.) Where's Willy, man?

BOBO. He ain't with me.

WALTER. *(Not disturbed.)* Oh—come on in. You know my wife.

BOBO. *(Dumbly, taking off his hat.)* Yes—h'you, Miss Ruth.

RUTH. *(Quietly, a mood apart from*

her husband already, seeing BOBO.*)* Hello, Bobo.

WALTER. You right on time today . . . Right on time. That's the way! *(He slaps* BOBO *on his back.)* Sit down . . . lemme hear.

*(*RUTH *stands stiffly and quietly in back of them, as though somehow she senses death, her eyes fixed on her husband.)*

BOBO. *(His frightened eyes on the floor, his hat in his hands.)* Could I please get a drink of water, before I tell you about it, Walter Lee?

*(*WALTER *does not take his eyes off the man.* RUTH *goes blindly to the tap and gets a glass of water and brings it to* BOBO.*)*

WALTER. There ain't nothing wrong, is there?

BOBO. Lemme tell you—

WALTER. Man—didn't nothing go wrong?

BOBO. Lemme tell you—Walter Lee. *(Looking at* RUTH *and talking to her more than to* WALTER.*)* You know how it was. I got to tell you how it was. I mean first I got to tell you how it was all the way . . . I mean about the money I put in, Walter Lee. . . .

WALTER. *(With taut agitation now.)* What about the money you put in?

BOBO. Well—it wasn't much as we told you—me and Willy—*(He stops.)*—I'm sorry, Walter. I got a bad feeling about it. I got a real bad feeling about it. . . .

WALTER. Man, what you telling me about all this for? . . . Tell me what happened in Springfield. . . .

BOBO. Springfield.

RUTH. *(Like a dead woman.)* What was supposed to happen in Springfield?

BOBO. *(To her.)* This deal that me and Walter went into with Willy—me and Willy was going to go down to Springfield and spread some money 'round so's we wouldn't have to wait so long for the liquor license . . . that's what we were going to do. Everybody said that was the way you had to do, you understand, Miss Ruth?

WALTER. Man—what happened down there?

BOBO. *(A pitiful man, near tears.)* I'm trying to tell you, Walter.

WALTER. *(Screaming at him suddenly.)* THEN TELL ME, GODDAMMIT . . . WHAT'S THE MATTER WITH YOU?

BOBO. Man . . . I didn't go to no Springfield, yesterday.

WALTER. *(Halted, life hanging in the moment.)* Why not?

BOBO. *(The long way, the hard way to tell.)* 'Cause I didn't have no reasons to. . . .

WALTER. Man, what are you talking about!

BOBO. I'm talking about the fact that when I got to the train station yesterday morning—eight o'clock like we planned . . . man—*Willy didn't never show up.*

WALTER. Why . . . where was he . . . where is he?

BOBO. That's what I'm trying to tell you . . . I don't know . . . I waited six hours . . . I called his house . . and I waited . . . six hours . . . I waited in that train station six hours. . . . *(Breaking into tears.)* That was all the extra money I had in the world. . . . *(Looking up at* WALTER *with the tears running down his face.)* Man, *Willy is gone.*

WALTER. Gone, what you mean Willy is gone? Gone where? You mean he went by himself. You mean he went off to Springfield by himself—to take care of getting the license—*(Turns and looks anxiously at* RUTH.*)* You mean maybe he didn't want too many people in on the business down there? *(Looks to* RUTH *again, as before.)* You know Willy got his own ways. *(Looks back to* BOBO.*)* Maybe you was late yesterday and he just went on down there without you. Maybe—maybe—he's been callin' you at home tryin' to tell you what happened or some-thing. Maybe—maybe—he just got sick. He's somewhere—he's got to be some-where. We just got to find him—me and you got to find him. (*Grabs* BOBO *sense-lessly by the collar and starts to shake him.*) We got to!

BOBO. (*In sudden angry, frightened agony.*) What's the matter with you, Wal-ter! WHEN A CAT TAKE OFF WITH YOUR MONEY HE DON'T LEAVE YOU NO MAPS!

WALTER. (*Turning madly, as though he is looking for* WILLY *in the very room.*) Willy! . . . Willy . . . don't do it . . . please don't do it . . . man, not with that money . . . man, please, not with that money . . . oh, God . . . don't let it be true. . . . (*He is wandering around, cry-ing out for* WILLY *and looking for him or perhaps for help from God.*) Man . . . I trusted you . . . man, I put my life in your hands. . . . (*He starts to crumple down on the floor as* RUTH *just covers her face in horror.*)

(MAMA *opens the door and comes into the room, with* BENEATHA *behind her.*)

Man . . . (*He starts to pound the floor with his fists, sobbing wildly.*) THAT MONEY IS MADE OUT OF MY FATHER'S FLESH. . . .

BOBO. (*Standing over him helplessly.*) I'm sorry, Walter . . .

(*Only* WALTER's *sobs reply.*)

(BOBO *puts on his hat.*) I had my life staked on this deal, too. . . . (*He exits.*)

MAMA. (*To* WALTER.) Son—(*She goes to him, bends down to him, talks to his bent head.*)—son . . . is it—gone? Son, I gave you sixty-five hundred dol-lars. Is it gone? All of it? Beneatha's money too?

WALTER. (*Lifting his head slowly.*) Mama . . . I never . . . went to the bank at all. . . .

MAMA (*Not wanting to believe him.*) You mean . . . your sister's school money . . . you used that too . . . Walter? . . .

WALTER. Yessss! All of it . . . It's all gone . . .

(*There is total silence.* RUTH *stands with her face covered with her hands;* BENEATHA *leans forlornly against a wall, fingering a piece of red ribbon from the mother's gift.* MAMA *stops and looks at her son without recognition and then, quite without thinking about it, starts to beat him senselessly in the face.* BE-NEATHA *goes to them and stops it.*)

BENEATHA. Mama!

(MAMA *stops and looks at both of her children and rises slowly and wanders vaguely, aimlessly away from them.*)

MAMA. I seen . . . him . . . night after night . . . come in . . . and look at that rug . . . and then look at me . . . the red showing in his eyes . . . the veins moving in his head . . . I seen him grow thin and old before he was forty . . . working and working and working like somebody's old horse . . . killing himself . . . and you—you give it all away in a day. . . .

BENEATHA. Mama—

MAMA. Oh, God . . . (*She looks up to* Him.) Look down here—and show me the strength.

BENEATHA. Mama—

MAMA. (*Folding over.*) Strength . . .

BENEATHA. (*Plaintively.*) Mama . . .

MAMA. Strength!

CURTAIN

ACT THREE

An hour later.

At Curtain there is a sullen light of gloom in the living room, gray light not unlike that which began the first scene of Act One. At Left we can see WALTER *within his room, alone with himself. He is stretched out on the bed, his shirt out and open, his arms under his head. He does not smoke, he does not cry out, he merely lies there, looking up at the ceiling, much as if he were alone in the world.*

In the living room BENEATHA *sits at the table, still surrounded by the now almost ominous packing crates. She sits looking off. We feel that this is a mood struck perhaps an hour before, and it lingers now, full of the empty sound of profound disappointment. We see on a line from her brother's bedroom the sameness of their attitudes. Presently the* BELL *rings and* BENEATHA *rises without ambition or interest in answering. It is* ASAGAI, *smiling broadly, striding into the room with energy and happy expectation and conversation.*

ASAGAI. I came over . . . I had some free time. I thought I might help with the packing. Ah, I like the look of packing crates! A household in preparation for a journey! It depresses some people . . . but for me . . . it is another feeling. Something full of the flow of life, do you understand? Movement, progress . . . it makes me think of Africa.

BENEATHA. Africa!

ASAGAI. What kind of a mood is this? Have I told you how deeply you move me?

BENEATHA. He gave away the money, Asagai. . . .

ASAGAI. Who gave away what money?

BENEATHA. The insurance money. My brother gave it away.

ASAGAI. Gave it away?

BENEATHA. He made an investment! With a man even Travis wouldn't have trusted.

ASAGAI. And it's gone?

BENEATHA. Gone!

ASAGAI. I'm very sorry . . . And you, now?

BENEATHA. Me? . . . Me? . . . Me I'm nothing . . . me. When I was very small . . . we used to take our sleds out in the wintertime and the only hills we had were the ice-covered stone steps of some houses down the street. And we used to fill them in with snow and make them smooth and slide down them all day . . . and it was very dangerous you know . . . far too steep . . . and sure enough one day a kid named Rufus came down too fast and hit the sidewalk . . . and we saw his face just split open right there in front of us . . . and I remember standing there looking at his bloody open face thinking that was the end of Rufus. But the ambulance came and they took him to the hospital and they fixed the broken bones and they sewed it all up . . . and the next time I saw Rufus he just had a little line down the middle of his face . . . I never got over that. . . .

(WALTER *sits up, listening on the bed. Throughout this scene it is important that we feel his reaction at all times, that he visibly respond to the words of his sister and* ASAGAI.)

ASAGAI. What?

BENEATHA. That that was what one person could do for another, fix him up— sew up the problem, make him all right again. That was the most marvelous thing in the world . . . I wanted to do that. I always thought it was the one concrete thing in the world that a human being could do. Fix up the sick, you know— and make them whole again. This was truly being God. . . .

ASAGAI. You wanted to be God?

BENEATHA. No—I wanted to cure. It used to be so important to me. I wanted to cure. It used to matter. I used to care. I mean about people and how their bodies hurt. . . .

ASAGAI. And you've stopped caring?

BENEATHA. Yes—I think so.

ASAGAI. Why?

(WALTER *rises, goes to the door of his room and is about to open it, then stops and stands listening, leaning on the door jamb.*)

BENEATHA. Because it doesn't seem deep enough, close enough to what ails mankind—I mean this thing of sewing up bodies or administering drugs. Don't you understand? It was a child's reaction to the world. I thought that doctors had the secret to all the hurts. . . . That's the way a child sees things—or an idealist.

ASAGAI. Children see things very well sometimes—and idealists even better.

BENEATHA. I know that's what you think. Because you are still where I left off—you still care. This is what you see for the world, for Africa. You with the dreams of the future will patch up all Africa—you are going to cure the Great Sore of colonialism with Independence—

ASAGAI. Yes!

BENEATHA. Yes—and you think that one word is the penicillin of the human spirit: "Independence!" But then what?

ASAGAI. That will be the problem for another time. First we must get there.

BENEATHA. And where does it end?

ASAGAI. End? Who even spoke of an end? To life? To living?

BENEATHA. An end to misery!

ASAGAI. (*Smiling.*) You sound like a French intellectual.

BENEATHA. No! I sound like a human being who just had her future taken right out of her hands! While I was sleeping in my bed in there, things were happening in this world that directly concerned me—and nobody asked me, consulted me —they just went out and did things—and changed my life. Don't you see there isn't any real progress, Asagai, there is only one large circle that we march in, around and around, each of us with our own little picture—in front of us—our own little mirage that we think is the future.

ASAGAI. That is the mistake.

BENEATHA. What?

ASAGAI. What you just said—about the circle. It isn't a circle—it is simply a long line—as in geometry, you know, one that reaches into infinity. And because we cannot see the end—we also cannot see how it changes. And it is very odd but those who see the changes are called "idealists"—and those who cannot, or refuse to think, they are the "realists." It is very strange, and amusing too, I think.

BENEATHA. You—you are almost religious.

ASAGAI. Yes . . . I think I have the religion of doing what is necessary in the world—and of worshipping man—because he is so marvelous, you see.

BENEATHA. Man is foul! And the human race deserves its misery!

ASAGAI. You see: *you* have become the religious one in the old sense. Already, and after such a small defeat, you are worshipping despair.

BENEATHA. From now on, I worship the truth—and the truth is that people are puny, small and selfish. . . .

ASAGAI. Truth? Why is it that you despairing ones always think that only you have the truth? I never thought to see *you* like that. You! Your brother made a stupid, childish mistake—and you are grateful to him. So that now you can give up the ailing human race on account of it. You talk about what good is struggle; what good is anything? Where are we all going? And why are we bothering?

BENEATHA. AND YOU CANNOT ANSWER IT! All your talk and dreams about Africa and Independence. Independence and then what? What about all the crooks and petty thieves and just plain idiots who will come into power to steal and plunder the same as before—only now they will be black and do it in the name of the new Independence— You cannot answer that.

ASAGAI. (*Shouting over her.*) I LIVE THE ANSWER! (*Pause.*) In my village at home it is the exceptional man who can even read a newspaper . . . or who ever *sees* a book at all. I will go home and much of what I will have to say will seem strange to the people of my village. . . . But I will teach and work and things will happen, slowly and swiftly. At times it will seem that nothing changes at all . . . and then again . . . the sudden dramatic events which make history leap into the future. And then quiet again. Retrogression even. Guns, murder, revolution. And I even will have moments when I wonder if the quiet was not better than all that death and hatred. But I will look about my village at the illiteracy and disease and ignorance and I will not wonder long. And perhaps . . . perhaps I will be a great man . . . I mean perhaps I will hold on to the substance of truth and find my way always with the right course . . . and perhaps for it I will be butchered in my bed some night by the servants of empire. . . .

BENEATHA. THE MARTYR!

ASAGAI. Or perhaps I shall live to be a very old man, respected and esteemed in my new nation . . . and perhaps I shall hold office and this is what I'm trying to tell you, Alaiyo; perhaps the things I believe now for my country will be wrong and outmoded, and I will not understand and do terrible things to have things my way or merely to keep my power. Don't you see that there will be young men and women, not British soldiers then, but my own black countrymen . . . to step out of the shadows some evening and slit my then useless throat? Don't you see they have always been there . . . that they always will be. And that such a thing as my own death will be an advance? They who might kill me even . . . actually replenish me!

BENEATHA. Oh, Asagai, I know all that.

ASAGAI. Good! Then stop moaning and groaning and tell me what you plan to do.

BENEATHA. Do?

ASAGAI. I have a bit of a suggestion.

BENEATHA. What?

ASAGAI. (*Rather quietly for him.*) That when it is all over—that you come home with me—

BENEATHA. (*Slapping herself on the forehead with exasperation born of misunderstanding.*) Oh—Asagai—at this moment you decide to be romantic!

ASAGAI. (*Quickly understanding the misunderstanding.*) My dear, young creature of the New World—I do not mean across the city—I mean across the ocean; home—to Africa.

BENEATHA. (*Slowly understanding and turning to him with murmured amazement.*) To—to Nigeria?

ASAGAI. Yes! . . . (*Smiling and lifting his arms playfully.*) Three hundred years later the African Prince rose up out of the seas and swept the maiden back across the middle passage over which her ancestors had come—

BENEATHA. (*Unable to play.*) Nigeria?

ASAGAI. Nigeria. Home. (*Coming to her with genuine romantic flippancy.*) I will show you our mountains and our stars; and give you cool drinks from gourds and teach you the old songs and the ways of our people—and, in time, we will pretend that—(*Very softly.*)—you have only been away for a day—

(*She turns her back to him, thinking. He swings her around and takes her full in his arms in a long embrace which proceeds to passion.*)

BENEATHA. (*Pulling away.*) You're getting me all mixed up—

ASAGAI. Why?

BENEATHA. Too many things—too many things have happened today. I must sit down and think. I don't know what I feel about anything right this minute. (*She promptly sits down and props her chin on her fist.*)

ASAGAI. (*Charmed.*) All right, I shall leave you. No—don't get up. (*Touching her, gently, sweetly.)* Just sit awhile and think . . . never be afraid to sit awhile and think. *(He goes to door and looks at her.)* How often I have looked at you and said, "Ah—so this is what the New World hath finally wrought . . ." *(He exits.)*

(BENEATHA sits on alone. Presently WALTER enters from his room and starts to rummage through things, feverishly looking for something. She looks up and turns in her seat.)

BENEATHA. *(Hissingly.)* Yes—just look at what the New World hath wrought! . . . Just look! *(She gestures with bitter disgust.)* There he is! *Monsieur le petit bourgeois noir*—himself! There he is! Symbol of a Rising Class! Entrepreneur! Titan of the system!

(WALTER ignores her completely and continues frantically and destructively looking for something and hurling things to floor and tearing things out of their place in his search.)

(BENEATHA ignores the eccentricity of his actions and goes on with the monologue of insult.) Did you dream of yachts on Lake Michigan, Brother? Did you see yourself on that Great Day sitting down at the Conference Table, surrounded by all the mighty bald-headed men in America? All halted, waiting, breathless, waiting for your pronouncements on industry? Waiting for you—Chairman of the Board?

(WALTER finds what he is looking for —a small piece of white paper—and pushes it in his pocket and puts on his coat and rushes out without ever having looked at her.)

(She shouts after him.) I look at you and I see the final triumph of stupidity in the world!

(The door slams and she returns to just sitting again. RUTH comes quickly out of MAMA's room.)

RUTH. Who was that?
BENEATHA. Your husband.
RUTH. Where did he go?
BENEATHA. Who knows—maybe he has an appointment at U.S. Steel.
RUTH. *(Anxiously, with frightened eyes.)* You didn't say nothing bad to him, did you?
BENEATHA. Bad? Say anything bad to him? No—I told him he was a sweet boy and full of dreams and everything is strictly peachy keen, as the ofay kids say!

(MAMA enters from her bedroom. She is lost, vague, trying to catch hold, to make some sense of her former command of the world, but it still eludes her. A sense of waste overwhelms her gait; a measure of apology rides on her shoulders. She goes to her plant, which has remained on the table, looks at it, picks it up and takes it to the window sill and sits it outside, and she stands and looks at it a long moment. Then she closes the window, straightens her body with effort and turns around to her children.)

MAMA. Well—ain't it a mess in here, though? *(A false cheerfulness, a beginning of something.)* I guess we all better stop moping around and get some work done. All this unpacking and everything we got to do.

(RUTH raises her head slowly in response to the sense of the line; and BENEATHA in similar manner turns very slowly to look at her mother.)

One of you all better call the moving people and tell 'em not to come.
RUTH. Tell 'em not to come?
MAMA. Of course, baby. Ain't no need in 'em coming all the way here and having to go back. They charges for that too. *(She sits down, fingers to her brow, thinking.)* Lord, ever since I was a little girl, I always remembers people saying, "Lena

—Lena Eggleston, you aims too high all the time. You needs to slow down and see life a little more like it is. Just slow down some." That's what they always used to say down home—"Lord, that Lena Eggleston is a high-minded thing. She'll get her due one day!"

RUTH. No, Lena . . .

MAMA. Me and Big Walter just didn't never learn right.

RUTH. Lena, no! We gotta go. Bennie —tell her—(*She rises and crosses to* BENEATHA *with her arms outstretched.*)

(BENEATHA *doesn't respond.*)

—tell her we can still move . . . the notes ain't but a hundred and twenty-five a month. We got four grown people in this house—we can work. . . .

MAMA. (*To herself.*) Just aimed too high all the time—

RUTH. (*Turning and going to* MAMA *fast—the words pouring out with urgency and desperation.*) Lena—I'll work . . . I'll work twenty hours a day in all the kitchens in Chicago . . . I'll strap my baby on my back if I have to and scrub all the floors in America and wash all the sheets in America if I have to—but we got to move . . . We got to get out of here. . . .

(MAMA *reaches out absently and pats* RUTH's *hand.*)

MAMA. No—I sees things differently now. Been thinking 'bout some of the things we could do to fix this place up some. I seen a second-hand bureau over on Maxwell Street just the other day that could fit right there. (*She points to where the new furniture might go.*)

(RUTH *wanders away from her.*)

Would need some new handles on it and then a little varnish and then lt look like something brand-new. And—we can put up them new curtains in the kitchen . . . why this place be looking fine. Cheer us all up so that we forget trouble ever came. . . . (*To* RUTH.) And you could get some nice screens to put up in your room round the baby's bassinet. . . . (*She looks at both of them, pleadingly.*) Sometimes you just got to know when to give up some things . . . and hold on to what you got.

(WALTER *enters from the outside, looking spent and leaning against the door, his coat hanging from him.*)

MAMA. Where you been, son?

WALTER. (*Breathing hard.*) Made a call.

MAMA. To who, son?

WALTER. To The Man.

MAMA. What man, baby?

WALTER. The Man, Mama. Don't you know who The Man is?

RUTH. Walter Lee?

WALTER. *The Man.* Like the guys in the streets say—The Man. Captain Boss— Mistuh Charley . . . Old Captain Please Mr. Bossman . . .

BENEATHA. (*Suddenly.*) Lindner!

WALTER. That's right! That's good. I told him to come right over.

BENEATHA. (*Fiercely, understanding.*) For what? What do you want to see him for?

WALTER. (*Looking at his sister.*) We going to do business with him.

MAMA. What you talking 'bout, son?

WALTER. Talking 'bout life, Mama. You all always telling me to see life like it is. Well—I laid in there on my back today . . . and I figured it out. Life just like it is. Who gets and who don't get. (*He sits down with his coat on and laughs.*) Mama, you know it's all divided up. Life is. Sure enough. Between the takers and the "tooken." (*He laughs.*) I've figured it out finally. (*He looks around at them.*) Yeah. Some of us always getting "tooken." (*He laughs.*) People like Willy Harris, they don't never get "tooken." And you know why the rest of us do? 'Cause we all mixed up. Mixed up bad.

We get to looking 'round for the right and the wrong; and we worry about it and cry about it and stay up nights trying to figure out 'bout the wrong and the right of things all the time . . . and all the time, man, them takers is out there operating, just taking and taking. Willy Harris? Shoot—Willy Harris don't even count. He don't even count in the big scheme of things. But I'll say one thing for old Willy Harris . . . he's taught me something. He's taught me to keep my eye on what counts in this world. Yeah —(*Shouting out a little.*)—thanks, Willy!

RUTH. What did you call that man for, Walter Lee?

WALTER. Called him to tell him to come on over to the show. Gonna put on a show for the man. Just what he wants to see. You see, Mama, the man came here today and he told us that them people out there where you want us to move—well they so upset they willing to pay us not to move out there. (*He laughs again.*) And—and oh, Mama—you would of been proud of the way me and Ruth and Bennie acted. We told him to get out. . . . Lord have mercy! We told the man to get out. Oh, we was some proud folks this afternoon, yeah. (*He lights a cigarette.*) We were still full of that old-time stuff. . . .

RUTH. (*Coming toward him slowly.*) You talking 'bout taking them people's money to keep us from moving in that house?

WALTER. I ain't just talking 'bout it, baby—I'm telling you that's what's going to happen.

BENEATHA. Oh, God! Where is the bottom! Where is the real honest-to-God bottom so he can't go any farther!

WALTER. See—that's the old stuff. You and that boy that was here today. You all want everybody to carry a flag and a spear and sing some marching songs, huh? You wanna spend your life looking into things and trying to find the right and the wrong part, huh? Yeah. You know what's going to happen to that boy someday—he'll find himself sitting in a dungeon, locked in forever—and the takers will have the key! Forget it, baby! There ain't no causes—there ain't nothing but taking in this world, and he who takes most is smartest—and it don't make a damn bit of difference *how*.

MAMA. You making something inside me cry, son. Some awful pain inside me. me.

WALTER. Don't cry, Mama. Understand. That white man is going to walk in that door able to write checks for more money than we ever had. It's important to him and I'm going to help him . . . I'm going to put on the show, Mama.

MAMA. Son—I come from five generations of people who was slaves and sharecroppers—but ain't nobody in my family never let nobody pay 'em no money that was a way of telling us we wansn' fit to walk the earth. We ain't never been that poor. (*Raising her eyes and looking at him.*) We ain't never been that dead inside.

BENEATHA. Well—we are dead now. All the talk about dreams and sunlight that goes on in this house. All dead.

WALTER. What's the matter with you all! I didn't make this world! It was give to me this way! Hell, yes, I want me some yachts someday! Yes, I want to hang some real pearls 'round my wife's neck. Ain't she supposed to wear no pearls? Somebody tell me—tell me, who decides which women is suppose to wear pearls in this world. I tell you I am a *man*— and I think my wife should wear some pearls in this world!

(*This last line hangs a good while and* WALTER *begins to move about the room. The word "Man" has penetrated his consciousness; he mumbles it to himself repeatedly between strange agitated pauses as he moves about.*)

MAMA. Baby, how you going to feel on the inside?

WALTER. Fine! . . . Going to feel fine . . . a man . . .

MAMA. You won't have nothing left then, Walter Lee.

WALTER. *(Coming to her.)* I'm going to feel fine, Mama. I'm going to look that son-of-a-bitch in the eyes and say—*(He falters.)*—and say, "All right, Mr. Lindner—*(He falters even more.)*—that's your neighborhood out there. You got the right to keep it like you want. You got the right to have it like you want. Just write the check and—the house is yours." And, and I am going to say—*(His voice almost breaks.)*—and you—you people just put the money in my hand and you won't have to live next to this bunch of stinking niggers! . . . *(He straightens up and moves away from his mother, walking around the room.)* Maybe—maybe I'll just get down on my black knees . . . *(He does so).*

(RUTH and BENNIE and MAMA watch him in frozen horror.)

Captain, Mistuh, Bossman. *(He starts crying.)* A-hee-hee-hee! *(Wringing his hands in profoundly anguished imitation.)* Yasssssuh! Great White Father, just gi' ussen de money, fo' God's sake, and we's ain't gwine come out deh and dirty up yo' white folks neighborhood. . . . *(He breaks down completely, then gets up and goes into the bedroom.)*

BENEATHA. That is not a man. That is nothing but a toothless rat.

MAMA. Yes—death done come in this here house. *(She is nodding, slowly, reflectively.)* Done come walking in my house. On the lips of my children. You what supposed to be my beginning again. You—what supposed to be my harvest. *(To BENEATHA.)* You—you mourning your brother?

BENEATHA. He's no brother of mine.

MAMA. What you say?

BENEATHA. I said that that individual in that room is no brother of mine.

MAMA. That's what I thought you said. You feeling like you better than he is today?

(BENEATHA does not answer.)

Yes? What you tell him a minute ago? That he wasn't a man? Yes? You give him up for me? You done wrote his epitaph too—like the rest of the world? Well, who give you the privilege?

BENEATHA. Be on my side for once! You saw what he just did, Mama! You saw him—down on his knees. Wasn't it you who taught me—to despise any man who would do that. Do what he's going to do.

MAMA. Yes—I taught you that. Me and your daddy. But I thought I taught you something else too . . . I thought I taught you to love him.

BENEATHA. Love him? There is nothing left to love.

MAMA. There is always something left to love. And if you ain't learned that, you ain't learned nothing. *(Looking at her.)* Have you cried for that boy today? I don't mean for yourself and for the family 'cause we lost the money. I mean for him; what he been through and what it done to him. Child, when do you think is the time to love somebody the most; when they done good and made things easy for everybody? Well then, you ain't through learning—because that ain't the time at all. It's when he's at his lowest and can't believe in hisself 'cause the world done whipped him so. When you starts measuring somebody, measure him right, child, measure him right. Make sure you done taken into account what hills and valleys he come through before he got to wherever he is.

(TRAVIS bursts into the room at the end of the speech, leaving the door open.)

TRAVIS. Grandmama—the moving men are downstairs! The truck just pulled up.

MAMA. *(Turning and looking at him.)* Are they, baby? They downstairs? *(She sighs and sits.)*

(LINDNER appears in the doorway. He peers in and knocks lightly, to gain attention, and comes in. All turn to look at him.)

LINDNER. *(Hat and briefcase in hand.)* Uh—hello. . . .

(RUTH crosses mechanically to the bedroom door and opens it and lets it swing open freely and slowly as the lights come up on WALTER within, still in his coat, sitting at the far corner of the room. He looks up and out through the room to LINDNER.)

RUTH. He's here.

(A long minute passes and WALTER slowly gets up.)

LINDNER. *(Coming to the table with efficiency, putting his briefcase on the table and starting to unfold papers and unscrew fountain pens.)* Well, I certainly was glad to hear from you people.

(WALTER has begun the trek out of the room, slowly and awkwardly, rather like a small boy, passing the back of his sleeve across his mouth from time to time.)

Life can really be so much simpler than people let it be most of the time. Well—with whom do I negotiate? You, Mrs. Younger, or your son here?

(MAMA sits with her hands folded on her lap and her eyes closed as WALTER advances. TRAVIS gets closer to LINDNER and looks at the papers curiously.)

Just some official papers, sonny.

RUTH. Travis, you go downstairs.

MAMA. *(Opening her eyes and looking into WALTER's.)* No. Travis, you stay right here. And you make him understand what you doing, Walter Lee. You teach him good. Like Willy Harris taught you. You show where our five generations done come to. Go ahead, son—

WALTER. *(Looks down into his son's eyes.)*

(TRAVIS grins at him merrily and WALTER draws him beside him with his arm lightly around his shoulders.)

Well, Mr. Lindner.

(BENEATHA turns away.)

We called you—*(There is a profound, simple groping quality in his speech.)*—because, well, me and my family—*(He looks around and shifts from one foot to the other.)*—well—we are very plain people. . . .

LINDNER. Yes—

WALTER. I mean—I have worked as a chauffeur most of my life—and my wife here, she does domestic work in people's kitchens. So does my mother. I mean—we are plain people . . .

LINDNER. Yes, Mr. Younger—

WALTER. *(Really like a small boy, looking down at his shoes and then up at the man.)* And—uh—well, my father, well, he was a laborer most of his life.

LINDNER. *(Absolutely confused.)* Uh, yes—

WALTER. *(Looking down at his toes once again.)* My father almost beat a man to death once because this man called him a bad name or something, you know what I mean?

LINDNER. No, I'm afraid I don't.

WALTER. *(Finally straightening up.)* Well, what I mean is that we come from people who had a lot of pride. I mean—we are very proud people. And that's my sister over there and she's going to be a doctor—and we are very proud—

LINDNER. Well—I am sure that is very nice, but—

WALTER. (*Starting to cry and facing the man eye to eye.*) What I am telling you is that we called you over here to tell you that we are very proud and that this is—this is my son, who makes the sixth generation of our famiy in this country, and that we have all thought about your offer and we have decided to move into our house because my father—my father—he earned it.

(MAMA *has her eyes closed and is rocking back and forth as though she were in church, with her head nodding the amen yes.*)

We don't want to make no trouble for nobody or fight no causes—but we will try to be good neighbors. That's all we got to say. (*He looks the man absolutely in the eyes.*) We don't want your money. (*He turns and walks away from the man.*)

LINDNER. (*Looking around at all of them.*) I take it then that you have decided to occupy.

BENEATHA. That's what the man said.

LINDNER. (*To* MAMA *in her reverie.*) Then I would like to appeal to you, Mrs. Younger. You are older and wiser and understand things better I am sure . . .

MAMA. (*Rising.*) I am afraid you don't understand. My son said we was going to move and there ain't nothing left for me to say. (*Shaking her head with double meaning.*) You know how these young folks is nowadays, mister. Can't do a thing with 'em. Good-bye.

LINDNER. (*Folding up his materials.*) Well—if you are that final about it . . . there is nothing left for me to say. (*He finishes. He is almost ignored by the family, who are concentrating on* WALTER LEE. *At the door* LINDNER *halts and looks around.*) I sure hope you people know what you're doing. (*He shakes his head and exits.*)

RUTH. (*Looking around and coming to life.*) Well, for God's sake—if the moving men are here—LET'S GET THE HELL OUT OF HERE!

MAMA. (*Into action.*) Ain't it the truth! Look at all this here mess. Ruth, put Travis' good jacket on him . . . Walter Lee, fix your tie and tuck your shirt in, you look just like somebody's hoodlum. Lord have mercy, where is my plant? (*She flies to get it amid the general bustling of the family, who are deliberately trying to ignore the nobility of the past moment.*) You all start on down . . . Travis child, don't go empty-handed . . . Ruth, where did I put that box with my skillets in it? I want to be in charge of it myself . . . I'm going to make us the biggest dinner we ever ate tonight . . . Beneatha, what's the matter with them stockings? Pull them things up, girl. . . .

(*The family starts to file out as* TWO MOVING MEN *appear and begin to carry out the heavier pieces of furniture, bumping into the family as they move about.*)

BENEATHA. Mama, Asagai—asked me to marry him today and go to Africa—

MAMA. (*In the middle of her getting-ready activity.*) He did? You ain't old enough to marry nobody—(*Seeing the moving men lifting one of her chairs precariously.*)—darling, that ain't no bale of cotton, please handle it so we can sit in it again. I had that chair twenty-five years. . . .

(*The MOVERS sigh with exasperation and go on with their work.*)

BENEATHA. (*Girlishly and unreasonably trying to pursue the conversation.*) To go to Africa, Mama—be a doctor in Africa. . . .

MAMA. (*Distracted.*) Yes, baby—

WALTER. Africa! What he want you to go to Africa for?

BENEATHA. To practice there. . . .

WALTER. Girl, if you don't get all them

silly ideas out your head! You better marry yourself a man with some loot. . . .

BENEATHA. (Angrily, precisely as in the first scene of the play.) What have you got to do with who I marry!

WALTER. Plenty. Now I think George Murchison—

(He and BENEATHA go out yelling at each other vigorously; BENEATHA is heard saying that she would not marry GEORGE MURCHISON if he were Adam and she were Eve, etc. The anger is loud and real till their voices diminish. RUTH stands at the door and turns to MAMA and smiles knowingly.)

MAMA. (Fixing her hat at last.) Yeah— they something all right, my children. . . .

RUTH. Yeah—they're something. Let's go, Lena.

MAMA. (Stalling, starting to look around at the house.) Yes—I'm coming. Ruth—

RUTH. Yes?

MAMA. (Quietly, woman to woman.) He finally come into his manhood today,

didn't he? Kind of like a rainbow after the rain. . . .

RUTH. (Biting her lip lest her own pride explode in front of MAMA.) Yes, Lena.

(WALTER's voice calls for them raucously.)

MAMA. (Waving RUTH out vaguely.) All right, honey—go on down. I be down directly.

(RUTH hesitates, then exits. MAMA stands, at last alone in the living room, her plant on the table before her as the LIGHTS start to come down. She looks around at all the walls and ceilings and suddenly, despite herself, while the children call below, a great heaving thing rises in her and she puts her fist to her mouth, takes a final desperate look, pulls her coat about her, pats her hat and goes out. The LIGHTS dim down. The door opens and she comes back in, grabs her plant, and goes out for the last time.)

CURTAIN

Ossie Davis

Purlie Victorious

A COMEDY IN THREE ACTS

"Our churches will say segregation is immoral because it makes perfectly wonderful people, white and black, do immoral things; . . .

Our courts will say segregation is illegal because it makes perfectly wonderful people, white and black, do illegal things; . . .

And finally our Theatre will say segregation is ridiculous because it makes perfectly wonderful people, white and black, do ridiculous things!"

—From "Purlie's I.O.U."

PURLIE VICTORIOUS

Purlie Victorious was first presented at the Cort Theater, New York City, September 28, 1961.

CHARACTERS:

(In Order of Appearance)

PURLIE VICTORIOUS JUDSON
LUTIEBELLE GUSSIE MAE JENKINS
MISSY JUDSON
GITLOW JUDSON
CHARLIE COTCHIPEE
IDELLA LANDY
OL' CAP'N COTCHIPEE
THE SHERIFF
THE DEPUTY

PLACE:
   The cotton plantation country of the Old South.
TIME:
   The recent past.

ACT ONE

SCENE 1

SCENE:
   The setting is the plain and simple interior of an antiquated, run-down farmhouse such as Negro sharecroppers still live in, in South Georgia. Threadbare but warm-hearted, shabby but clean. In the Center is a large, rough-hewn table with three homemade chairs and a small bench. This table is the center of all family activities. The main entrance is a door in the upstage Right corner, which leads in from a rickety porch which we cannot see. There is a small archway in the opposite corner, with some long strips of gunny-sacking hanging down to serve as a door, which leads off to the kitchen. In the center of the Right wall is a window that is wooden, which opens outward on hinges. Downstage Right is a small door leading off to a bedroom, and opposite, downstage Left, another door leads out into the backyard, and on into the cotton fields beyond. There is also a smaller table and a cupboard against the wall. An old dresser stands against the Right wall, between the window and the downstage door. There is a shelf on the Left wall with a pail of drinking water, and a large tin dipper. Various cooking utensils, and items like salt and pepper are scattered about in appropriate places.

AT RISE:
   The Curtain rises on a stage in semi-darkness. After a moment, when the LIGHTS have come up, the door in the Up Right corner bursts open. Enter PURLIE JUDSON. PURLIE JUDSON is tall, restless, and commanding. In his middle or late thirties, he wears a wide-brim, ministerial black hat, a string tie, and a claw hammer coat, which, though far from new, does not fit him too badly. His arms are loaded with large boxes and parcels, which must have come fresh from a department store. PURLIE is a man consumed with that divine impatience, without which nothing truly good, or truly bad, or even truly ridiculous, is ever accomplished in this world—with rhetoric and flourish to match.

PURLIE. (*Calling out loudly.*) Missy!

(*No answer.*)

Gitlow!—It's me—Purlie Victorious!

(*Still no answer.*)

(PURLIE *empties his overloaded arms, with obvious relief, on top of the big Center table. He stands, mops his brow, and blows.*) Nobody home it seems. (*This last he says to someone he assumes has come in with him. When there is no answer he hurries to the door through which he entered.*) Come on—come on in!

(*Enter* LUTIEBELLE JENKINS, *slowly, as if bemused. Young, eager, well-built: though we cannot tell it at the moment. Clearly a girl from the backwoods, she carries a suitcase tied up with a rope in one hand, and a greasy shoebox with what's left of her lunch, together with an outmoded, outsized handbag, in the other. Obviously she has traveled a great distance, but she still manages to look fresh and healthy. Her hat is a horror with feathers, but she wears it like a banner. Her shoes are flat-heeled and plain white, such as a good servant girl in the white folks' kitchen who knows her place absolutely is bound to wear. Her fall coat is dowdy, but well-intentioned with a stingy strip of rabbit fur around the neck.* LUTIEBELLE *is like thousands of Negro girls you might know. Eager, desirous—even anxious, keenly in search for life and for love, trembling on the brink of self-confident and vigorous young womanhood—but afraid to take the final leap: because no one has ever told her it is no longer necessary to be white in order to be virtuous, charming, or beautiful.*)

LUTIEBELLE. (*Looking around as if at a museum of great importance.*) Nobody home it seems.

PURLIE. (*Annoyed to find himself so exactly echoed, looks at her sharply. He takes his watch from his vest pocket, where he wears it on a chain.*) Cotton-picking time in Georgia it's against the law to be home. Come in—unload yourself. (*Crosses and looks out into the kitchen.* LUTIEBELLE *is so enthralled, she still stands with all her bags and parcels in her arm.*) Set your suitcase down.

LUTIEBELLE. What?

PURLIE. It's making you lopsided.

LUTIEBELLE. (*Snapping out of it.*) Is it? I didn't even notice. (*Sets suitcase, lunch box, and parcels down.*)

PURLIE. (*Studies her for a moment; goes and gently takes off her hat.*) Tired?

LUTIEBELLE. Not stepping high as I am!

PURLIE. (*Takes the rest of her things and sets them on the table.*) Hungry?

LUTIEBELLE. No, sir. But there's still some of my lunch left if you—

PURLIE. (*Quickly.*) No, thank you. Two ham-hock sandwiches in one day is my limit. (*Sits down and fans himself with his hat.*) Sorry I had to walk you so far so fast.

LUTIEBELLE. (*Dreamily.*) Oh, I didn't mind, sir. Walking's good for you, Miz Emmylou sez—

PURLIE. Miz Emmylou can afford to say that: Miz Emmylou got a car. While all the transportation we got in the world is tied up in second-hand shoe leather. But never mind, my sister, never-you-mind! (*Rises, almost as if to dance, exaltation glowing in his eyes.*) And toll the bell, Big Bethel—toll that big, black, fat and sassy liberty bell! Tell Freedom the bridegroom cometh; the day of her deliverance is now at hand! (PURLIE *catches sight of* MISSY *through door Down Left.*) Oh, there she is. (*Crosses to door and calls out.*) Missy!—Oh, Missy!

MISSY. (*From a distance.*) Yes-s-s-s-!

PURLIE. It's me!—Purlie!

MISSY. Purlie Victorious?

PURLIE. Yes. Put that battling stick down and come on in here!

MISSY. All right!

PURLIE. (*Crosses hurriedly back to above table at Center.*) That's Missy, my sister-in-law I was telling you about. (*Clears the table of everything but one of the large cartons, which he proceeds to open.*)

LUTIEBELLE. (*Not hearing him. Still*

awestruck to be in the very house, in perhaps the very same room that PURLIE *might have been born in.)* So this is the house where you was born and bred at.

PURLIE. Yep! Better'n being born outdoors.

LUTIEBELLE. What a lovely background for your home life.

PURLIE. I wouldn't give it to my dog to raise fleas in!

LUTIEBELLE. So clean—and nice—and warm-hearted!

PURLIE. The first chance I get I'ma burn the damn thing down!

LUTIEBELLE. But—Reb'n Purlie!—It's yours, and that's what counts. Like Miz Emmylou sez—

PURLIE. Come here! *(Pulls her across to the window, flings it open.)* You see that big white house, perched on top of that hill with them two windows looking right down at us like two eyeballs: that's where Ol' Cap'n lives.

LUTIEBELLE. Ol' Cap'n?

PURLIE. Stonewall Jackson Cotchipee. He owns this dump, not me.

LUTIEBELLE. Oh—

PURLIE. And that ain't all: hill and dale, field and farm, truck and tractor, horse and mule, bird and bee and bush and tree—and cotton!—cotton by bole and by bale—every bit o' cotton you see in this county!—Everything and everybody he owns!

LUTIEBELLE. Everybody? You mean he owns people?

PURLIE. *(Bridling his impatience.)* Well —look!—ain't a man, woman or child working in this valley that ain't in debt to that ol' bastard!—*(Catches himself.)* Bustard!—*(This still won't do.)* Buzzard!— And that includes Gitlow and Missy— everybody—except me.

LUTIEBELLE. But folks can't own people no more, Reb'n Purlie. Miss Emmylou sez that—

PURLIE. *(Verging on explosion.)* You ain't working for Miz Emmylou no more,

you're working for me—Purlie Victorious. Freedom is my business, and I say that ol' man runs this plantation on debt: the longer you work for Ol' Cap'n Cotchipee, the more you owe at the commissary; and if you don't pay up, you can't leave. And I don't give a damn what Miz Emmylou nor nobody else sez—that's slavery!

LUTIEBELLE. I'm sorry, Reb'n Purlie—

PURLIE. Don't apologize, wait!—just wait!—til I get my church;—wait til I buy Big Bethel back—*(Crosses to window and looks out.)* Wait til I stand once again in the pulpit of Grandpaw Kinkaid, and call upon my people—and talk to my people—about Ol' Cap'n, that miserable son-of-a—

LUTIEBELLE. *(Just in time to save him.)* Wait—!

PURLIE. Wait, I say! And we'll see who's gonna dominize this valley!—him or me! *(Turns and sees* MISSY *through door Down Left.)* Missy!

(Enter MISSY, *ageless, benign, and smiling. She wears a ragged old straw hat, a big house apron over her faded gingham, and low-cut, dragged-out tennis shoes on her feet. She is strong and of good cheer—of a certain shrewdness, yet full of the desire to believe. Her eyes light on* LUTIEBELLE, *and her arms go up and outward automatically.)*

MISSY. Purlie!

PURLIE. *(Thinks she is reaching for him.)* Missy!

MISSY. *(Ignoring him, clutching* LUTIE-BELLE, *laughing and crying.)* Well—well —well!

PURLIE. *(Breaking the stranglehold.)* For God's sake, Missy, don't choke her to death!

MISSY. All my life—all my life I been praying for me a daughter just like you. My prayers is been answered at last. Welcome to our home, whoever you is!

LUTIEBELLE. *(Deeply moved.)* Thank you, m'am.

MISSY. "M'am—m'am." Listen to the child, Purlie. Everybody down here calls me Aunt Missy, and I'd be much obliged if you would, too.

LUTIEBELLE. It would make me very glad to do so—Aunt Missy.

MISSY. Uhmmmmmm! Pretty as a pan of buttermilk biscuits. Where on earth did you find her, Purlie?

(PURLIE starts to answer.)

Let me take your things—now, you just make yourself at home. Are you hungry?

LUTIEBELLE. No, m'am, but cheap as water is, I sure ain't got no business being this thirsty!

MISSY. *(Starts forward.)* I'll get some for you—

PURLIE. *(Intercepts her; directs LUTIE-BELLE.)* There's the dipper. And right out yonder by the fence just this side of that great big live oak tree you'll find the well —sweetest water in Cotchipee county.

LUTIEBELLE. Thank you, Reb'n Purlie. I'm very much obliged. *(Takes dipper from water pail and exits Down Left.)*

MISSY. Reb'n who?

PURLIE. *(Looking off after LUTIE-BELLE).* Perfection—absolute Ethiopian perfect. Hah, Missy?

MISSY. *(Looking off after LUTIEBELLE.)* Oh, I don't know about that.

PURLIE. What you mean you don't know? This girl looks more like Cousin Bee than Cousin Bee ever did.

MISSY. No resemblance to me.

PURLIE. Don't be ridiculous; she's the spitting image—

MISSY. No resemblance whatsoever!

PURLIE. I ought to know how my own cousin looked—

MISSY. But I was the last one to see her alive—

PURLIE. Twins, if not closer!

MISSY. Are you crazy? Bee was more lean, loose, and leggy—

PURLIE. Maybe so, but this girl makes it up in—

MISSY. With no chin to speak of—her eyes sort of fickle one to another—

PURLIE. I know, but even so—

MISSY. *(Pointing off in LUTIEBELLE's direction.)* Look at her head—it ain't nearly as built like a rutabaga as Bee's own was!

PURLIE. *(Exasperated.)* What's the difference! White folks can't tell one of us from another by the head!

MISSY. Twenty years ago it was, Purlie, Ol' Cap'n laid bull whip to your natural behind—

PURLIE. Twenty years ago I swore I'd see his soul in hell!

MISSY. And I don't think you come full back to your senses yet—that ol' man ain't no fool!

PURLIE. That makes it one "no fool" against another.

MISSY. He's dangerous, Purlie. We could get killed if that old man was to find out what we was trying to do to get that church back.

PURLIE. How can he find out? Missy, how many times must I tell you, if it's one thing I am foolproof in it's white folks' psychology.

MISSY. That's exactly what I'm afraid of.

PURLIE. Freedom, Missy, that's what Big Bethel means. For you, me and Git-low. And we can buy it for five hundred dollars, Missy. Freedom!—you want it, or don't you?

MISSY. Of course I want it, but—after all, Purlie, that rich ol' lady didn't exactly leave that $500 to us—

PURLIE. She left it to Aunt Henrietta—

MISSY. Aunt Henrietta is dead—

PURLIE. Exactly—

MISSY. And Henrietta's daughter Cousin Bee is dead, too.

PURLIE. Which makes us next in line to inherit the money by law!

MISSY. All right, then, why don't we

just go on up that hill man-to-man and tell Ol' Cap'n we want our money?

PURLIE. Missy! You have been black as long as I have—

MISSY. *(Not above having her own little joke.)* Hell, boy, we could make him give it to us.

PURLIE. Make him—how? He's a white man, Missy. What you plan to do, sue him?

MISSY. *(Drops her teasing; thinks seriously for a moment.)* After all, it is our money. And it was our church.

PURLIE. And can you think of a better way to get it back than that girl out there?

MISSY. But you think it'll work, Purlie? You really think she can fool Ol' Cap'n?

PURLIE. He'll never know what hit him.

MISSY. Maybe—but there's still the question of Gitlow.

PURLIE. What about Gitlow?

MISSY. Gitlow has changed his mind.

PURLIE. Then you'll have to change it back.

GITLOW. *(Offstage.)* Help, Missy; help, Missy; help, Missy; help Missy!

(GITLOW runs on.)

MISSY. What the devil's the matter this time?

GITLOW. There I was, Missy, picking in the high cotton, twice as fast as the human eye could see. All of a sudden I missed a bole and it fell—it fell on the ground, Missy! I stooped as fast as I could to pick it up and—*(He stoops to illustrate. There is a loud tearing of cloth.)* ripped the seat of my britches. There I was, Missy, exposed from stem to stern.

MISSY. What's so awful about that? It's only cotton.

GITLOW. But cotton is white, Missy. We must maintain respect. Bring me my Sunday School britches.

MISSY. What!

GITLOW. Ol' Cap'n is coming down into the cotton patch today, and I know you want your Gitlow to look his level best.

(MISSY starts to answer.)

Hurry, Missy, hurry!

(GITLOW hurries her off.)

PURLIE. Gitlow—have I got the girl!
GITLOW. Is that so—what girl?
PURLIE. *(Taking him to the door.)* See? There she is! Well?
GITLOW. Well what?
PURLIE. What do you think?
GITLOW. Nope; she'll never do?
PURLIE. What you mean, she'll never do?
GITLOW. My advice to you is to take that girl back to Florida as fast as you can!
PURLIE. I can't take her back to Florida.
GITLOW. Why can't you take her back to Florida?
PURLIE. 'Cause she comes from Alabama. Gitlow, look at her: she's just the size—just the type—just the style.
GITLOW. And just the girl to get us all in jail. The answer is no! *(Crosses to the kitchen door.)* MISSY! *(Back to PURLIE.)* Girl or no girl, I ain't getting mixed up in no more of your nightmares—I got my own. Dammit, Missy, I said let's go!
MISSY. *(Entering with trousers.)* You want me to take my bat to you again?
GITLOW. No, Missy, control yourself. It's just that every second Gitlow's off the firing line-up, seven pounds of Ol' Cap'n's cotton don't git gotten. *(Snatches pants from MISSY, but is in too much of a hurry to put them on—starts off.)*
PURLIE. Wait a minute, Gitlow. . . . Wait!

(GITLOW is off in a flash.)

Missy! Stop him!
MISSY. He ain't as easy to stop as he used to be. Especially now Ol' Cap'n's made him Deputy-For-The-Colored.

PURLIE. Deputy-For-The-Colored? What the devil is that?

MISSY. Who knows? All I know is Gitlow's changed his mind.

PURLIE. But Gitlow can't change his mind!

MISSY. Oh, it's easy enough when you ain't got much to start with. I warned you. You don't know how shifty ol' Git can git. He's the hardest man to convince and keep convinced I ever seen in my life.

PURLIE. Missy, you've got to make him go up that hill, he's got to identify this girl—Ol' Cap'n won't believe nobody else.

MISSY. I know—

PURLIE. He's got to swear before Ol' Cap'n that this girl is the real Cousin Bee—

MISSY. I know.

PURLIE. Missy, you're the only person in this world ol' Git'll really listen to.

MISSY. I know.

PURLIE. And what if you do have to hit him a time or two—it's for his own good!

MISSY. I know.

PURLIE. He'll recover from it, Missy. He always does—

MISSY. I know.

PURLIE. Freedom, Missy—Big Bethel; for you; me; and Gitlow!

MISSY. Freedom—and a little something left over—that's all I ever wanted all my life. (Looks out into the yard.) She do look a little somewhat like Cousin Bee—about the feet!

PURLIE. Of course she does—

MISSY. I won't guarantee nothing, Purlie—but I'll try.

PURLIE. (Grabbing her and dancing her around.) Everytime I see you, Missy, you get prettier by the pound!

(LUTIEBELLE enters. MISSY sees her.)

MISSY. Stop it, Purlie, stop it! Stop it. Quit cutting the fool in front of company!

PURLIE. (Sees LUTIEBELLE, crosses to her, grabs her about the waist and swings her around too.)

How wondrous are the daughters of my people,

Yet knoweth not the glories of themselves!

(Spins her around for MISSY's inspection. She does look better with her coat off, in her immaculate blue-and-white maid's uniform.)

Where do you suppose I found her, Missy—

This Ibo prize—this Zulu Pearl—

This long lost lily of the black Mandingo—

Kikuyu maid, beneath whose brown embrace

Hot suns of Africa are burning still: where—where?

A drudge; a serving wench; a feudal fetch-pot:

A common scullion in the white man's kitchen.

Drowned is her youth in thankless Southern dishpans;

Her beauty spilt for Dixiecratic pigs!

This brown-skinned grape! this wine of Negro vintage—

MISSY. (Interrupting.) I know all that, Purlie, but what's her name?

(PURLIE looks at LUTIEBELLE and turns abruptly away.)

LUTIEBELLE. I don't think he likes my name so much—it's Lutiebelle, ma'am— Lutiebelle Gussiemae Jenkins!

MISSY. (Gushing with motherly reassurance.) Lutiebelle Gussiemae Jenkins! My, that's nice.

PURLIE. Nice! It's an insult to the Negro people!

MISSY. Purlie, behave yourself!

PURLIE. A previous condition of servitude, a badge of inferiority, and I refuse to have it in my organization! Change it!

MISSY. You want me to box your mouth for you!

PURLIE. Lutiebelle Gussiemae Jenkins! What does it mean in Swahili? Cheap labor!

LUTIEBELLE. Swahili?

PURLIE. One of the thirteen silver tongues of Africa: Swahili, Bushengo, Ashanti, Baganda, Herero, Yoruba, Bambora, Mpongwe, Swahili: a language of moons, of velvet drums; hot days of rivers, red-splashed, and birdsong bright; black fingers in rice white at sunset red! —ten thousand Queens of Sheba—

MISSY. (Having to interrupt.) Just where did Purlie find you, honey?

LUTIEBELLE. It was in Dothan, Alabama, last Sunday, Aunt Missy, right in the junior choir!

MISSY. The junior choir—my, my, my!

PURLIE. (Still carried away.)

Behold! I said, this dark and holy vessel,
In whom should burn that golden nut-brown joy
Which Negro womanhood was meant to be.
Ten thousand queens, ten thousand Queens of Sheba:

(Pointing at LUTIEBELLE.)

Ethiopia herself—in all her beauteous wonder,
Come to restore the ancient thrones of Cush!

MISSY. Great Gawdamighty, Purlie, I can't hear myself think!

LUTIEBELLE. That's just what I said last Sunday, Aunt Missy, when Reb'n Purlie started preaching that thing in the pulpit.

MISSY. Preaching it?

LUTIEBELLE. Lord, Aunt Missy, I shouted clear down to the Mourners' Bench.

MISSY. (To PURLIE.) But last time you was a professor of Negro Philosophy.

PURLIE. I told you, Missy: my intention is to buy Big Bethel back; to reclaim the ancient pulpit of Grandpaw Kincaid, and preach freedom in the cotton patch— I told you!

MISSY. Maybe you did, Purlie, maybe you did. You got yourself a license?

PURLIE. Naw! But—

MISSY. (Looking him over.) Purlie Victorious Judson: Self-made minister of the gospel—claw-hammer coattail, shoe-string tie and all.

PURLIE. (Quietly but firmly holding his ground.) How else can you lead the Negro people?

MISSY. Is that what you got in your mind: leading the Negro people?

PURLIE. Who else they got?

MISSY. God help the race.

LUTIEBELLE. It was a sermon, I mean, Aunt Missy, the likes of which has never been heard before.

MISSY. Oh, I bet that. Tell me about it, son. What did you preach?

PURLIE. I preached the New Baptism of Freedom for all mankind, according to the Declaration of Independence, taking as my text the Constitution of the United States of America, Amendments First through Fifteenth, which readeth as follows: "Congress shall make no law—"

MISSY. Enough—that's enough, son— I'm converted. But it is confusing, all the changes you keep going through. (To LUTIEBELLE.) Honey, every time I see Purlie he's somebody else.

PURLIE. Not any more, Missy; and if I'm lying may the good Lord put me down in the book of bad names: Purlie is put forever!

MISSY. Yes. But will he stay put forever?

PURLIE. There is in every man a finger of iron that points him what he must and must not do—

MISSY. And your finger points up the hill to that five hundred dollars with which you'll buy Big Bethel back, preach freedom in the cotton patch, and live happily ever after!

PURLIE. The soul-consuming passion of my life! (Draws out watch.) It's 2:15, Missy, and Gitlow's waiting. Missy, I suggest you get a move on.

MISSY. I already got a move on. Had it since four o'clock this morning!

PURLIE. Time, Missy—exactly what the colored man in this country ain't got, and you're wasting it!

MISSY. (*Looks at* PURLIE, *and decides not to strike him dead.*) Purlie, would you mind stepping out into the cotton patch and telling your brother Gitlow I'd like a few words with him?

(PURLIE, *overjoyed, leaps at* MISSY *as if to hug and dance her around again, but she is too fast.*)

Do like I tell you now—go on!

(PURLIE *exits singing.*)

(MISSY *turns to* LUTIEBELLE *to begin the important task of sizing her up.*) Besides, it wouldn't be hospitable not to set and visit a spell with our distinguished guest over from Dothan, Alabama.

LUTIEBELLE. (*This is the first time she has been called anything of importance by anybody.*) Thank you, ma'am.

MISSY. Now. Let's you and me just set back and enjoy a piece of my potato pie. You like potato pie, don't you?

LUTIEBELLE. Oh, yes, ma'am, I like it very much.

MISSY. And get real acquainted. (*Offers her a saucer with a slice of pie on it.*)

LUTIEBELLE. I'm ever so much obliged. My, this looks nice. Uhm, uhn, uhn!

MISSY. (*Takes a slice for herself and sits down.*) You know—ever since that ol' man—(*Indicates up the hill.*) took after Purlie so unmerciful with that bull whip twenty years ago—he fidgets! Always on the go; rattling around from place to place all over the country: one step ahead of the white folks—something about Purlie always did irritate the white folks.

LUTIEBELLE. Is that the truth!

MISSY. Oh, my, yes. Finally wound up being locked up a time or two for safe-keeping—

(LUTIEBELLE *parts with a loud, sympathetic grunt.*)

(*Changing her tack a bit.*) Always kept up his schooling, though. In fact that boy's got one of the best second-hand educations in this country.

LUTIEBELLE. (*Brightening considerably*). Is that a fact!

MISSY. Used to read everything he could get his hands on.

LUTIEBELLE. He did? Ain't that wonderful!

MISSY. Till one day he finally got tired, and throwed all his books to the hogs—not enough "Negro" in them, he said. After that he puttered around with first one thing then another. Remember that big bus boycott they had in Montgomery? Well, we don't travel by bus in the cotton patch, so Purlie boycotted mules!

LUTIEBELLE. You don't say so?

MISSY. Another time he invented a secret language, that Negroes could understand but white folks couldn't.

LUTIEBELLE. Oh, my goodness gracious!

MISSY. He sent it C.O.D. to the NAACP but they never answered his letter.

LUTIEBELLE. Oh, they will, Aunt Missy; you can just bet your life they will.

MISSY. I don't mind it so much. Great leaders are bound to pop up from time to time 'mongst our people—in fact we sort of look forward to it. But Purlie's in such a hurry I'm afraid he'll lose his mind.

LUTIEBELLE. Lose his mind—no! Oh, no!

MISSY. That is unless you and me can do something about it.

LUTIEBELLE. You and me? Do what, Aunt Missy? You tell me—I'll do anything!

MISSY. (*Having found all she needs to know.*) Well, now; ain't nothing ever all that peculiar about a man a good wife—and a family—and some steady home cooking won't cure. Don't you think so?

LUTIEBELLE. (*Immensely relieved.*) Oh, yes, Aunt Missy, yes. (*But still not get-*

ting MISSY's *intent.*) You'd be surprised how many tall, good-looking, great big, ol' handsome looking mens—just like Reb'n Purlie—walking around, starving theyselves to death! Oh, I just wish I had one to aim my pot at!

MISSY. Well, Purlie Judson is the uncrowned appetite of the age.

LUTIEBELLE. He is! What's his favorite?

MISSY. Anything! Anything a fine-looking, strong and healthy—girl like you could put on the table.

LUTIEBELLE. Like me? Like ME! Oh, Aunt Missy!

MISSY. (PURLIE's *future is settled.*) Honey, I mind once at the Sunday School picnic Purlie et a whole sack o' pullets!

LUTIEBELLE. Oh, I just knowed there was something—something—just reeks about that man. He puts me in the mind of all the good things I ever had in my life. Picnics, fish-fries, corn-shuckings, and love-feasts, and gospel-singings—picking huckleberries, roasting ground-peas, quilting-bee parties and barbecues; that certain kind of—welcome—you can't get nowhere else in all this world. Aunt Missy, life is so good to us—sometimes!

MISSY. Oh, child, being colored can be a lotta fun when ain't nobody looking.

LUTIEBELLE. Ain't it the truth! I always said I'd never pass for white, no matter how much they offered me, unless the things I love could pass, too.

MISSY. Ain't it the beautiful truth!

(PURLIE *enters again; agitated.*)

PURLIE. Missy—Gitlow says if you want him come and get him!

MISSY. (*Rises, crosses to door Down Left; looks out.*) Lawd, that man do take his cotton picking seriously. (*Comes back to* LUTIEBELLE *and takes her saucer.*) Did you get enough to eat, honey?

LUTIEBELLE. Indeed I did. And Aunt Missy, I haven't had potato pie like that since the senior choir give—

MISSY. (*Still ignoring him.*) That's

where I met Gitlow, you know. On the senior choir.

LUTIEBELLE. Aunt Missy! I didn't know you could sing!

MISSY. Like a brown-skin nightingale. Well, it was a Sunday afternoon—Big Bethel had just been—

PURLIE. Dammit, Missy! The white man is five hundred years ahead of us in this country, and we ain't gonna ever gonna catch up with him sitting around on our non-Caucasian rumps talking about the senior choir!

MISSY. (*Starts to bridle at this sudden display of passion, but changes her mind.*) Right this way, honey. (*Heads for door Down Right.*) Where Cousin Bee used to sleep at.

LUTIEBELLE. Yes, ma'am. (*Starts to follow* MISSY.)

PURLIE. (*Stopping her.*) Wait a minute —don't forget your clothes! (*Gives her a large carton.*)

MISSY. It ain't much, the roof leaks, and you can get as much September inside as you can outside any time; but I try to keep it clean.

PURLIE. Cousin Bee was known for her clothes!

MISSY. Stop nagging, Purlie—(*To* LUTIEBELLE.) There's plenty to eat in the kitchen.

LUTIEBELLE. Thank you, Aunt Missy. (*Exits Down Right.*)

PURLIE. (*Following after her.*) And hurry! We want to leave as soon as Missy gets Gitlow in from the cotton patch!

MISSY. (*Blocking his path.*) Mr. Preacher—(*She pulls him out of earshot.*) If we do pull this thing off—(*Studying him a moment.*) what do you plan to do with her after that—send her back where she came from?

PURLIE. Dothan, Alabama? Never! Missy, there a million things I can do with a girl like that, right here in Big Bethel!

MISSY. Yeah! Just make sure they're all

legitimate. Anyway, marriage is still cheap, and we can always use another cook in the family.

(PURLIE *hasn't the slightest idea what* MISSY *is talking about.*)

LUTIEBELLE. (*From offstage.*) Aunt Missy.

MISSY. Yes, honey.

LUTIEBELLE. (*Offstage.*) Whose picture is this on the dresser?

MISSY. Why, that's Cousin Bee.

LUTIEBELLE. (*A moment's silence. Then she enters hastily, carrying a large photograph in her hand.*) Cousin Bee!

MISSY. Yes, poor thing. She's the one the whole thing is all about.

LUTIEBELLE. (*The edge of panic.*) Cousin Bee—oh, my!—oh, my goodness! My goodness gracious!

MISSY. What's the matter?

LUTIEBELLE. But she's pretty—she's so pretty!

MISSY. (*Takes photograph; looks at it tenderly.*) Yes—she was pretty. I guess they took this shortly before she died.

LUTIEBELLE. And you mean—you want me to look like her?

PURLIE. That's the idea. Now go and get into your clothes. (*Starts to push her off.*)

MISSY. They sent it down to us from the college. Don't she look smart? I'll bet she was a good student when she was living.

LUTIEBELLE. (*Evading* PURLIE.) Good student!

MISSY. Yes. One more year and she'd have finished.

LUTIEBELLE. Oh, my gracious Lord have mercy upon my poor soul!

PURLIE. (*Not appreciating her distress or its causes.*) Awake, awake! Put on thy strength, O, Zion—put on thy beautiful garments. (*Hurries her offstage.*) And hurry! (*Turning to* MISSY.) Missy, Big Bethel and Gitlow is waiting. Grandpaw Kincaid gave his life. (*Gently places the*

bat into her hand.) It is a far greater thing you do now, than you've ever done before —and Gitlow ain't never got his head knocked off in a better cause.

(MISSY *nods her head in sad agreement, and accepts the bat.* PURLIE *helps her to the door Down Left, where she exits, a most reluctant executioner.* PURLIE *stands and watches her off from the depth of his satisfaction. The door Down Right eases open, and* LUTIEBELLE, *her suitcase, handbag, fall coat and lunch box firmly in hand, tries to sneak out the front door.* PURLIE *hears her, and turns just in time.*)

Where do you think you're going?

LUTIEBELLE. Did you see that, Reb'n Purlie? (*Indicating bedroom from which she just came.*) Did you see all them beautiful clothes—slips, hats, shoes, stockings? I mean nylon stockings like Miz Emmylou wears—and a dress, like even Miz Emmylou don't wear. Did you look at what was in that big box?

PURLIE. Of course I looked at what was in that big box—I bought it—all of it— for you.

LUTIEBELLE. For me!

PURLIE. Of course! I told you! And as soon as we finish you can have it!

LUTIEBELLE. Reb'n Purlie, I'm a good girl. I ain't never done nothing in all this world, white, colored or otherwise, to hurt nobody!

PURLIE. I know that.

LUTIEBELLE. I work hard; I mop, I scrub, I iron; I'm clean and polite, and I know how to get along with white folks' children better'n they do. I pay my church dues every second and fourth Sunday the Lord sends; and I can cook catfish—and hushpuppies—you like hushpuppies, don't you, Reb'n Purlie?

PURLIE. I love hushpuppies!

LUTIEBELLE. Hushpuppies—and corn dodgers; I can cook you a corn dodger would give you the swimming in the head!

PURLIE. I'm sure you can, but—

LUTIEBELLE. But I ain't never been in a mess like this in all my life!

PURLIE. Mess—what mess?

LUTIEBELLE. You mean go up that hill, in all them pretty clothes, and pretend—in front of white folks—that—that I'm your Cousin Bee—somebody I ain't never seen or heard of before in my whole life!

PURLIE. Why not? Some of the best pretending in the world is done in front of white folks.

LUTIEBELLE. But Reb'n Purlie, I didn't know your Cousin Bee was a student at the college; I thought she worked there!

PURLIE. But I told you on the train—

LUTIEBELLE. Don't do no good to tell ME nothing, Reb'n Purlie! I never listen. Ask Miz Emmylou and 'em, they'll tell you I never listen. I didn't know it was a college lady you wanted me to make like. I thought it was for a sleep-in like me. I thought all that stuff you bought in them boxes was stuff for maids and cooks and —why, I ain't never even been near a college!

PURLIE. So what? College ain't so much where you been as how you talk when you get back. Anybody can do it; look at me.

LUTIEBELLE. Nawsir, I think you better look at me like Miz Emmylou sez—

PURLIE. (Taking her by the shoulders tenderly.) Calm down—just take it easy, and calm down.

(She subsides a little, her chills banished by the warmth of him.)

Now—don't tell me, after all that big talking you done on the train about white folks, you're scared.

LUTIEBELLE. Talking big is easy—from the proper distance.

PURLIE. Why—don't you believe in yourself?

LUTIEBELLE. Some.

PURLIE. Don't you believe in your own race of people?

LUTIEBELLE. Oh, yessir—a little.

PURLIE. Don't you believe the black man is coming to power some day?

LUTIEBELLE. Almost.

PURLIE. Ten thousand Queens of Sheba! What kind of a Negro are you! Where's your race pride?

LUTIEBELLE. Oh, I'm a great one for race pride, sir, believe me—it's just that I don't need it much in my line of work! Miz Emmylou sez—

PURLIE. Damn Miz Emmylou! Does her blond hair and blue eyes make her any more of a woman in the sight of her men folks than your black hair and brown eyes in mine?

LUTIEBELLE. No, sir!

PURLIE. Is her lily-white skin any more money-under-the-mattress than your fine fair brown? And if so, why does she spend half her life at the beach trying to get a sun tan?

LUTIEBELLE. I never thought of that!

PURLIE. There's a whole lotta things about the Negro question you ain't thought of! The South is split like a fat man's underwear; and somebody beside the Supreme Court has got to make a stand for the everlasting glory of our people!

LUTIEBELLE. Yessir.

PURLIE. Snatch Freedom from the jaws of force and filibuster!

LUTIEBELLE. Amen to that!

PURLIE. Put thunder in the Senate!

LUTIEBELLE. Yes, Lord!

PURLIE. And righteous indignation back in the halls of Congress!

LUTIEBELLE. Ain't it the truth!

PURLIE. Make Civil Rights from Civil Wrongs; and bring that ol' Civil War to a fair and a just conclusion!

LUTIEBELLE. Help him, Lord!

PURLIE. Remind this white and wicked world there ain't been more'n a dime's

worth of difference twixt one man and another'n, irregardless of race, gender,
creed, or color—since God Himself Almighty set the first batch out to dry before the chimneys of Zion got hot! The
eyes and ears of the world is on Big
Bethel!

LUTIEBELLE. Amen and hallelujah!

PURLIE. And whose side are you fighting on this evening, sister?

LUTIEBELLE. Great Gawdamighty,
Reb'n Purlie, on the Lord's side! But Miss
Emmylou sez—

PURLIE. (Blowing up.) This is outrageous—this is a catastrophe! You're a disgrace to the Negro profession!

LUTIEBELLE. That's just what she said
all right—her exactly words.

PURLIE. Who's responsible for this?
Where's your Maw and Paw at?

LUTIEBELLE. I reckon I ain't rightly
got no Maw and Paw, wherever they at.

PURLIE. What!

LUTIEBELLE. And nobody else that I
knows of. You see, sir—I been on the
go from one white folks' kitchen to another since before I can remember. How
I got there in the first place—whatever
became of my Maw and Paw, and my
kinfolks—even what my real name is—
nobody is ever rightly said.

PURLIE. (Genuinely touched.) Oh. A
motherless child—

LUTIEBELLE. That's what Miz Emmylou always sez—

PURLIE. But—who cared for you—like
a mother? Who brung you up—who
raised you?

LUTIEBELLE. Nobody in particular—
just whoever happened to be in charge of
the kitchen that day.

PURLIE. That explains the whole thing
—no wonder; you've missed the most important part of being somebody.

LUTIEBELLE. I have? What part is that?

PURLIE. Love—being appreciated, and
sought out, and looked after; being
fought to the bitter end over even.

LUTIEBELLE. Oh, I have missed that,
Reb'n Purlie, I really have. Take mens—
all my life they never looked at me the
way other girls get looked at!

PURLIE. That's not so. The very first
time I saw you—right up there in the
junior choir—I give you that look!

LUTIEBELLE. (Turning to him in absolute ecstasy.) You did! Oh, I thought so!
—I prayed so. All through your sermon
I thought I would faint from hoping so
hard. Oh, Reb'n Purlie—I think that's
the finest look a person could ever give
a person— Oh, Reb'n Purlie! (She closes
her eyes and points her lips at him.)

PURLIE. (Starts to kiss her, but draws
back shyly.) Lutiebelle—

LUTIEBELLE. (Dreamily, her eyes still
closed.) Yes, Reb'n Purlie—

PURLIE. There's something I want to
ask you—something I never—in all my
life—thought I'd be asking a woman—
would you—I don't know exactly how to
say it—would you—

LUTIEBELLE. Yes, Reb'n Purlie?

PURLIE. Would you be my disciple?

LUTIEBELLE. (Rushing into his arms.)
Oh, yes, Reb'n Purlie, yes!

(They start to kiss, but are interrupted
by a NOISE coming from offstage.)

GITLOW. (Offstage; in the extremity of
death.) No, Missy. No—no!—NO!

(This last plea is choked off by the
sound of some solid object brought
smartly into sudden contact with flesh.
"CLUNK!" PURLIE and LUTIEBELLE
stand looking off Left, frozen for the moment.)

LUTIEBELLE. (Finally daring to speak.)
Oh, my Lord, Reb'n Purlie, what happened?

PURLIE. Gitlow has changed his mind.
(Grabs her and swings her around bodily.)
Toll the bell, Big Bethel!—toll that big,
fat, black, and sassy liberty bell. Tell
Freedom—

(LUTIEBELLE *suddenly leaps from the floor into his arms and plants her lips squarely on his. When finally he can come up for air.*)

Tell Freedom—tell Freedom—WOW!

CURTAIN

ACT ONE

SCENE 2

TIME:

It is a little later the same afternoon.

SCENE:

We are now in the little business office off from the commissary, where all the inhabitants of Cotchipee Valley buy food, clothing, and supplies. In the back a traveler has been drawn with just enough of an opening left to serve as the door to the main part of the store. Onstage Left and onstage Right are simulated shelves where various items of reserve stock are kept: a wash tub, an ax, sacks of peas, and flour; bolts of gingham and calico, etc. Downstage Right is a small desk, on which an ancient typewriter, and an adding machine, with various papers and necessary books and records of commerce are placed. There is a small chair at this desk. Downstage Left is a table, with a large cash register, that has a functioning drawer. Below this is an entrance from the street.

AT RISE:

As the Curtain rises, a young white MAN of 25 or 30, but still gawky, awkward, and adolescent in outlook and behavior, is sitting on a high stool downstage Right Center. His face is held in the hands of IDELLA, a Negro cook and woman of all work, who has been in the family since time immemorial. She is the only mother CHARLIE, who is very much oversized even for his age, has ever known. IDELLA is as little as she is old and

as tough as she is tiny, and is busily applying medication to CHARLIE's black eye.

CHARLIE. Ow, Idella, ow! Ow!

IDELLA. Hold still, boy.

CHARLIE. But it hurts, Idella.

IDELLA. I know it hurts. Whoever done this to you musta meant to knock your natural brains out.

CHARLIE. I already told you who done it— OW!

IDELLA. Charlie Cotchipee, if you don't hold still and let me put this hot poultice on your eye, you better!

(CHARLIE *subsides and meekly accepts her ministrations.*)

First the milking, then the breakfast, then the dishes, then the washing, then the scrubbing, then the lunch time, next the dishes, then the ironing—and now; just where the picking and plucking for supper ought to be—you!

CHARLIE. You didn't tell Paw?

IDELLA. Of course I didn't—but the sheriff did.

CHARLIE. (*Leaping up.*) The sheriff!

IDELLA. (*Pushing him back down.*) Him and the deputy come to the house less than a hour ago.

CHARLIE. (*Leaping up again.*) Are they coming over here?

IDELLA. Of course they're coming over here—sooner or later.

CHARLIE. But what will I do, Idella, what will I say?

IDELLA. (*Pushing him down.* CHARLIE *subsides.*) "He that keepeth his mouth keepeth his life—"

CHARLIE. Did they ask for me?

IDELLA. Of course they asked for you.

CHARLIE. What did they say?

IDELLA. I couldn't hear too well; your father took them into the study and locked the door behind them.

CHARLIE. Maybe it was about something else.

IDELLA. It was about YOU: that much

I could hear! Charlie—you want to get us both killed!

CHARLIE. I'm sorry, Idella, but—

IDELLA. (Overriding; finishing proverb she had begun.) "But he that openeth wide his lips shall have destruction!"

CHARLIE. But it was you who said it was the law of the land—

IDELLA. I know I did—

CHARLIE. It was you who said it's got to be obeyed—

IDELLA. I know it was me, but—

CHARLIE. It was you who said everybody had to stand up and take a stand against—

IDELLA. I know it was me, dammit! But I didn't say take a stand in no barroom!

CHARLIE. Ben started it, not me. And you always said never to take low from the likes of him!

IDELLA. Not so loud; they may be out there in the commissary! (Goes quickly to door Up Center and peers out; satisfied no one has overheard them she crosses back down to CHARLIE.) Look, boy, everybody down here don't feel as friendly towards the Supreme Court as you and me do—you big enough to know that! And don't you ever go outta here and pull a fool trick like you done last night again and not let me know about it in advance. You hear me!

CHARLIE. I'm sorry.

IDELLA. When you didn't come to breakfast this morning, and I went upstairs looking for you, and you just setting there, looking at me with your big eyes, and I seen that they had done hurt you—my, my, my! Whatever happens to you happens to me—you big enough to know that!

CHARLIE. I didn't mean to make trouble, Idella.

IDELLA. I know that, son, I know it. (Makes final adjustments to the poultice.) Now. No matter what happens when they do come I'll be right behind you. Keep your nerves calm and your mouth shut. Understand?

CHARLIE. Yes.

IDELLA. And as soon as you get a free minute come over to the house and let me put another hot poultice on that eye.

CHARLIE. Thank you, I'm very much obliged to you. Idella—

IDELLA. What is it, son?

CHARLIE. Sometimes I think I ought to run away from home.

IDELLA. I know, but you already tried that, honey.

CHARLIE. Sometimes I think I ought to run away from home—again!

(OL' CAP'N has entered from the Commissary just in time to hear this last remark.)

OL' CAP'N. Why don't you, boy—why don't you? (OL' CAP'N COTCHIPEE is aged and withered a bit, but by no means infirm. Dressed in traditional southern linen, the wide hat, the shoestring tie, the long coat, the twirling moustache of the Ol' Southern Colonel. In his left hand he carries a cane, and in his right a coiled bull whip: his last line of defense. He stops long enough to establish the fact that he means business, threatens them both with a mean cantankerous eye, then hangs his whip—the definitive answer to all who might foolishly question his Confederate power and glory—upon a peg. CHARLIE freezes at the sound of his voice. IDELLA tenses but keeps working on CHARLIE's eye. OL' CAP'N crosses down, rudely pushes her hand aside, lifts up CHARLIE's chin so that he may examine the damage, shakes his head in disgust.) You don't know, boy, what a strong stomach it takes to stomach you. Just look at you, sitting there—all slopped over like something the horses dropped; steam, stink and all!

IDELLA. Don't you dare talk like that to this child!

OL' CAP'N. (This stops him—momentarily.) When I think of his grandpaw,

God rest his Confederate soul, hero of the battle of Chicamauga—*(It's too much.)* Get outta my sight!

(CHARLIE gets up to leave.)

Not you—you! *(Indicates IDELLA.)*

(She gathers up her things in silence and starts to leave.)

Wait a minute—

(IDELLA stops.)

You been closer to this boy than I have, even before his ma died—ain't a thought ever entered his head you didn't know 'bout it first. You got anything to do with what my boy's been thinking lately?

IDELLA. I didn't know he had been thinking lately.

OL' CAP'N. Don't play with me, Idella —and you know what I mean! Who's been putting these integrationary ideas in my boy's head? Was it you—I'm asking you a question, dammit! Was it you?

IDELLA. Why don't you ask him?

OL' CAP'N. *(Snorts.)* Ask him! ASK HIM! He ain't gonna say a word unless you tell him to, and you know it. I'm asking you again, Idella Landy, have you been talking integration to my boy!?

IDELLA. I can't rightly answer you any more on that than he did.

OL' CAP'N. By God, you will answer me. I'll make you stand right there— right there!—all day and all night long, till you do answer me!

IDELLA. That's just fine.

OL' CAP'N. What's that! What's that you say?

IDELLA. I mean I ain't got nothing else to do—supper's on the stove; rice is ready, okra's fried, turnip's simmered, biscuits baked, and stew is stewed. In fact them lemon pies you wanted special for supper are in the oven right now, just getting ready to burn—

OL' CAP'N. Get outta here!

IDELLA. Oh—no hurry, Ol' Cap'n—

OL' CAP'N. Get the hell out of here!

(IDELLA deliberately takes all the time in the world to pick up her things.)

(Following her around trying to make his point.) I'm warning both of you; that little lick over the eye is a small skimption compared to what I'm gonna do.

(IDELLA pretends not to listen.)

I won't stop till I get to the bottom of this!

(IDELLA still ignores him.)

Get outta here, Idella Landy, before I take my cane an—*(He raises his cane but IDELLA insists on moving at her own pace to exit Down Left.)* And save me some buttermilk to go with them lemon pies, you hear me! *(Turns to CHARLIE; not knowing how to approach him.)* The sheriff was here this morning.

CHARLIE. Yessir.

OL' CAP'N. Is that all you got to say to me: "Yessir"?

CHARLIE. Yessir.

OL' CAP'N. You are a disgrace to the southland!

CHARLIE. Yessir.

OL' CAP'N. Shut up! I could kill you, boy, you understand that? Kill you with my own two hands!

CHARLIE. Yessir.

OL' CAP'N. Shut up! I could beat you to death with that bull whip—put my pistol to your good-for-nothing head— my own flesh and blood—and blow your blasted brains all over this valley! *(Fighting to retain his control.)* If—if you wasn't the last living drop of Cotchipee blood in Cotchipee County, I'd—I'd—

CHARLIE. Yessir.

(This is too much. OL' CAP'N snatches CHARLIE to his feet. But CHARLIE does not resist.)

OL' CAP'N. You trying to get non-violent with me, boy?

(CHARLIE *does not answer, just dangles there.*)

CHARLIE. *(Finally.)* I'm ready with the books, sir—that is—whenever you're ready.

OL' CAP'N. *(Flinging* CHARLIE *into a chair.)* Thank you—thank you! What with your Yankee propaganda, your barroom brawls, and all your other non-Confederate activities, I didn't think you had the time.

CHARLIE. *(Picks up account book; reads.)* "Cotton report. Fifteen bales picked yesterday and sent to the cotton gin; bringing our total to 357 bales to date."

OL' CAP'N. *(Impressed.)* 357—boy, that's some picking. Who's ahead?

CHARLIE. Gitlow Judson, with seventeen bales up to now.

OL' CAP'N. Gitlow Judson; well I'll be damned; did you ever see a cotton-pickinger darky in your whole life?!

CHARLIE. Commissary report—

OL' CAP'N. Did you ever look down into the valley and watch ol' Git a-picking his way through that cotton patch? Holy Saint Mother's Day! I'll bet you—

CHARLIE. Commissary report!

OL' CAP'N. All right! Commissary report.

CHARLIE. Yessir—well, first, sir, there's been some complaints: the flour is spoiled, the beans are rotten, and the meat is tainted.

OL' CAP'N. Cut the price on it.

CHARLIE. But it's also a little wormy—

OL' CAP'N. Then sell it to the Negras —is something wrong?

CHARLIE. No, sir—I mean, sir . . . we can't go on doing that, sir.

OL' CAP'N. Why not? It's traditional.

CHARLIE. Yessir, but times are changing —all this debt—*(Indicates book.)* According to this book every family in this valley owes money they'll never be able to pay back.

OL' CAP'N. Of course—it's the only way to keep 'em working. Didn't they teach you nothin' at school?

CHARLIE. We're cheating them—and they know we're cheating them. How long do you expect them to stand for it?

OL' CAP'N. As long as they're Negras—

CHARLIE. How long before they start a-rearing up on their hind legs, and saying: "Enough, white folks—now that's enough! Either you start treating me like I'm somebody in this world, or I'll blow your brains out"?

OL' CAP'N. *(Shaken to the core.)* Stop it—stop it! You're tampering with the economic foundation of the southland! Are you trying to ruin me? One more word like that and I'll kill—I'll shoot—

(CHARLIE *attempts to answer.*)

shut up! One more word and I'll—I'll fling myself on your Maw's grave and die of apoplexy. I'll—! I'll—! Shut up, do you hear me? Shut up!

(*Enter* GITLOW, *hat in hand, grin on face, more obsequious today than ever.*)

Now what the hell *you* want?

GITLOW. *(Taken aback.)* Nothing, sir, nothing! That is—Missy, my ol' 'oman— well, suh, to git to the truth of the matter, I got a little business—

OL' CAP'N. Negras ain't got no business. And if you don't get the hell back into that cotton patch you better. Git, I said!

(GITLOW *starts to beat a hasty retreat.*)

Oh, no—don't go. Uncle Gitlow—good ol' faithful ol' Gitlow. Don't go—don't go.

GITLOW. *(Not quite sure.)* Well— you're the boss, boss.

OL' CAP'N. *(Shoving a cigar into* GITLOW's *mouth.)* Just the other day, I was talking to the Senator about you—what's that great big knot on your head?

GITLOW. Missy—I mean, a mosquito!

OL' CAP'N. (*In all seriousness, examining the bump.*) Uh! Musta been wearin' brass knuck—and he was telling me, the Senator was, how hard it was—impossible, he said, to find the old-fashioned, solid, hard-earned, Uncle Tom type Negra nowadays. I laughed in his face.

GITLOW. Yassuh. By the grace of God, there's still a few of us left.

OL' CAP'N. I told him how you and me growed up together. Had the same mammy—my mammy was your mother.

GITLOW. Yessir! Bosom buddies!

OL' CAP'N. And how you used to sing that favorite ol' spiritual of mine: (*Sings.*) "I'm a-coming . . . I'm a-coming, For my head is bending low,"

(GITLOW *joins in on harmony.*)

"I hear the gentle voices calling, Ol' Black Joe. . . ."

(*This proves too much for* CHARLIE; *he starts out.*)

Where you going?

CHARLIE. Maybe they need me in the front of the store.

OL' CAP'N. Come back here!

(CHARLIE *returns.*)

Turn around—show Gitlow that eye.

(CHARLIE *reluctantly exposes his black eye to view.*)

GITLOW. Gret Gawdamighty, somebody done cold cocked this child! Who hit Mr. Charlie, tell Uncle Gitlow who hit you?

(CHARLIE *does not answer.*)

OL' CAP'N. Would you believe it? All of a sudden he can't say a word. And just last night, the boys was telling me, this son of mine made hisself a full-fledged speech.

GITLOW. You don't say.

OL' CAP'N. All about Negras—Ne-GROES he called 'em—four years of

college, and he still can't say the word right—seems he's quite a specialist on the subject.

GITLOW. Well, shut my hard-luck mouth!

OL' CAP'N. Yessireebob. Told the boys over at Ben's bar in town, that he was all for mixing the races together.

GITLOW. You go on 'way from hyeah!

OL' CAP'N. Said white children and darky children ought to go to the same schoolhouse together!

GITLOW. Tell me the truth, Ol' Cap'n!

OL' CAP'N. Got hisself so worked up some of 'em had to cool him down with a co-cola bottle!

GITLOW. Tell me the truth—again!

CHARLIE. That wasn't what I said!

OL' CAP'N. You calling me a liar, boy!

CHARLIE. No, sir, but I just said, that since it was the law of the land—

OL' CAP'N. It is not the law of the land no sucha thing!

CHARLIE. I didn't think it would do any harm if they went to school together —that's all.

OL' CAP'N. That's all—that's enough!

CHARLIE. They do it up North—

OL' CAP'N. This is down South. Down here they'll go to school together over me and Gitlow's dead body. Right, Git?!

GITLOW. Er, you the boss, boss!

CHARLIE. But this is the law of the—

OL' CAP'N. Never mind the law! Boy —look! You like Gitlow, you trust him, you always did—didn't you?

CHARLIE. Yessir.

OL' CAP'N. And Gitlow here, would cut off his right arm for you if you was to ask him. Wouldn't you, Git?

GITLOW. (*Gulping.*) You the boss, boss.

OL' CAP'N. Now Gitlow ain't nothing if he ain't a Negra!—Ain't you, Git?

GITLOW. Oh—two-three hundred percent, I calculate.

OL' CAP'N. Now, if you really want to know what the Negra thinks about this here integration and all lackathat, don't ask the Supreme Court—ask Gitlow. Go ahead—ask him!

CHARLIE. I don't need to ask him.

OL' CAP'N. Then I'll ask him. Raise your right hand, Git. You solemnly swear to tell the truth, whole truth, nothing else but, so help you God?

GITLOW. *(Raising hand.)* I do.

OL' CAP'N. Gitlow Judson, as God is your judge and maker, do you believe in your heart that God intended white folks and Negra children to go to school together?

GITLOW. Nawsuh, I do not!

OL' CAP'N. Do you, so help you God, think that white folks and black should mix and 'sociate in street cars, buses, and railroad stations, in any way, shape, form, or fashion?

GITLOW. Absolutely not!

OL' CAP'N. And is it not your considered opinion, God strike you dead if you lie, that all my Negras are happy with things in the southland just the way they are?

GITLOW. Indeed I do!

OL' CAP'N. Do you think ary single darky on my place would ever think of changing a single thing about the South, and to hell with the Supreme Court as God is your judge and maker?

GITLOW. As God is my judge and maker and you are my boss, I do not!

OL' CAP'N. *(Turning in triumph to* CHARLIE.*)* The voice of the Negra himself! What more proof do you want!

CHARLIE. I don't care whose voice it is—it's still the law of the land, and I intend to obey it!

OL' CAP'N. *(Losing control.)* Get outta my face, boy—get outta my face, before I kill you! Before I—

*(*CHARLIE *escapes into the commissary.* OL' CAP'N *collapses.)*

GITLOW. Easy, Ol' Cap'n, easy, suh, easy!

*(*OL' CAP'N *gives out a groan.)*

*(*GITLOW *goes to shelf and comes back with a small bottle and a small box.)* Some aspirins, suh . . . some asaphoetida?

*(*PURLIE *and* LUTIEBELLE *appear at door Left.)*

Not now—later—later! *(Holds bottle to* OL' CAP'N's *nose.)*

OL' CAP'N. Gitlow—Gitlow!

GITLOW. Yassuh, Ol' Cap'n—Gitlow is here, suh; right here!

OL' CAP'N. Quick, ol' friend—my heart. It's—quick! A few passels, if you please—of that ol' speritual.

GITLOW. *(Sings most tenderly.)* "Gone are the days, when my heart was young and gay . . ."

OL' CAP'N. I can't tell you, Gitlow—how much it easies the pain—*(*GITLOW *and* OL' CAP'N *sing a phrase together.)* Why can't he see what they're doing to the southland, Gitlow? Why can't he see it, like you and me? If there's one responsibility you got, boy, above all others, I said to him, it's these Negras—your Negras, boy. Good, honest, hard-working cotton choppers. If you keep after 'em.

GITLOW. Yes, Lawd! *(Continues to sing.)*

OL' CAP'N. Something between you and them no Supreme Court in the world can understand—and wasn't for me they'd starve to death. What's gonna become of 'em, boy, after I'm gone?

GITLOW. Dass a good question, Lawd —you answer him. *(Continues to sing.)*

OL' CAP'N. They belong to you, boy— to you, evah one of 'em! My ol' Confederate father told me on his deathbed: feed the Negras first—after the horses and cattle—and I've done it evah time! *(By now* OL' CAP'N *is sheltered in* GITLOW's *arms.)*

(The LIGHTS begin slowly to fade away. GITLOW *sings a little more.)*

Ah, Gitlow ol' friend—something, absolutely sacred 'bout that speritual—I live for the day you'll sing that thing over my grave.

GITLOW. Me, too, Ol' Cap'n, me, too! *(GITLOW's voice rises to a slow, gentle, yet triumphant crescendo, as our LIGHTS fade away.)*

BLACKOUT

CURTAIN

ACT TWO

SCENE 1

TIME:
A short while later.

SCENE:
The scene is the same: the little commissary office.

AT RISE:
The stage is empty. After a moment GITLOW hurries in from the commissary proper, crosses Down to the little back door and opens it.

PURLIE. *(Entering hurriedly.)* What took you so long?

GITLOW. S-sh! Not so loud! He's right out there in the commissary!

(PURLIE crosses over and looks out into the commissary, then crosses back to the little back door and holds out his hands. LUTIEBELLE enters. She is dressed in what would be collegiate style. She is still full of awe and wonder, and—this time—of fear, which she is struggling to keep under cover.)

Ain't she gonna carry no school books?

PURLIE. What are they doing out there?

GITLOW. The watermelon books don't balance.

PURLIE. What!

GITLOW. One of our melons is in shortage!

PURLIE. You tell him about Lutiebelle —I mean, about Cousin Bee?

GITLOW. I didn't have time. Besides, I wanted you to have one more chance to get out of here alive!

PURLIE. What's the matter with you? Don't five hundred dollars of your own lawful money mean nothing to you? Ain't you got no head for business?

GITLOW. No! The head I got is for safekeeping, and—besides—

(PURLIE lifts OL' CAP'N's bull whip down from its peg.)

don't touch that thing, Purlie! *(GITLOW races over, snatches it from him, replaces it, and pats it soothingly into place, while at the same time looking to see if OL' CAP'N is coming—and all in one continuous move.)*

PURLIE. Why not? It touched me!

GITLOW. *(Aghast.)* Man, ain't nothing sacred to you!?

OL' CAP'N. *(Calling from Off in the commissary.)* Gitlow, come in here!

GITLOW. *(Racing off.)* Coming, Ol' Cap'n, coming!

OL' CAP'N. *(Offstage.)* Now! We are going to cross-examine these watermelons one more time—one watermelon—

GITLOW. *(Offstage.)* One watermelon!

CHARLIE. *(Offstage.)* One watermelon!

OL' CAP'N. Two watermelons—

GITLOW. Two watermelons—

CHARLIE. Two watermelons—

(The sound of the watermelon countdown continues in the background. PURLIE, finding he's got a moment, comes over to reassure LUTIEBELLE.)

PURLIE. Whatever you do, don't panic!

LUTIEBELLE. *(Repeating after him: almost in hypnotic rote.)* Whatever you do, don't panic!

PURLIE. Just walk like I taught you to walk, and talk like I taught you to talk—

LUTIEBELLE. Taught like I walked you to—

PURLIE. *(Shaking her shoulders.)* Lutie-belle!

LUTIEBELLE. Yes, Reb'n Purlie!

PURLIE. Wake up!

LUTIEBELLE. Oh my goodness, Reb'n Purlie—was I sleep?

PURLIE. Alert!

LUTIEBELLE. Alert!—

PURLIE. Wide awake!—

LUTIEBELLE. Wide awake!—

PURLIE. Up on your toes!

LUTIEBELLE. *(Starting to rise on toes.)* Up on your—

PURLIE. No. No, that's just a figure of speech. Now! You remember what I told you?

LUTIEBELLE. No, sir. Can't say I do, sir.

PURLIE. Well—first: chit-chat—small-talk!

LUTIEBELLE. Yessir—how small?

PURLIE. Pass the time of day—you remember? The first thing I taught you on the train?

LUTIEBELLE. On the train— Oh! "Delighted to remake your acquaintance, I am sure."

PURLIE. That's it—that's it exactly! Now. Suppose he was to say to you: *(*PURLIE *imitates* OL' CAP'N.*)* "I bet you don't remember when you wasn't knee-high to a grasshopper and Ol' Cap'n took you by the hand, and led you down on your first trip to the cotton patch?"

LUTIEBELLE. Just like you told me on the train?

PURLIE. Yes!

LUTIEBELLE. "I must confess—that much of my past life is vague and hazy."

PURLIE. *(Imitating.)* Doggone my hide —you're the cutest li'l ol' piece of brown skin sugar I ever did see!

LUTIEBELLE. Oh, thank you, Reb'n Purlie!

PURLIE. I ain't exactly me, saying that —it's Ol' Cap'n. *(Continues imitation.)* And this is my land, and my cotton patch, and my commissary, and my bull whip —still here, just like you left us. And what might be your name, li'l gal?

LUTIEBELLE. *(Warming to the game.)* Beatrice Judson, sir.

PURLIE. And what is your daddy's name, li'l gal?

LUTIEBELLE. Horace Judson, sir.

PURLIE. And what did they teach you up in that college, li'l gal?

LUTIEBELLE. It was my major education, Ol' Cap'n.

PURLIE. You mean you majored in education. *(Resumes imitation.)* Well—nothing wrong with Negras getting an education, I always say—but then again, ain't nothing right with it, either. Cousin Bee— heh, heh, heh—you don't mind if I call you Cousin Bee, do you, honey?

LUTIEBELLE. Oh, sir, I'd be delighted!

PURLIE. Don't! Don't be delighted until he puts the money in your hands. *(Resumes imitation.)* And where did you say your Maw worked at?

LUTIEBELLE. In North Carolina.

PURLIE. Where is your maw at now?

LUTIEBELLE. She's at the cemetery: she died.

PURLIE. And how much is the inheritance?

LUTIEBELLE. Five hundred dollars for the next of kin.

PURLIE. *(Delighted at her progress.)* Wonderful, just—just—wonderful! *(Enjoying his own imitation now.)*

*(*OL' CAP'N *enters from the commissary, followed by* GITLOW. LUTIEBELLE *sees* OL' CAP'N, *but* PURLIE *is so wrapped up in his own performance he does not.)*

Say, maybe you could teach a old dog like me some new tricks. *(He tries to get a rise out of* LUTIEBELLE *but she is frozen in terror.)*

*(*OL' CAP'N *becomes aware of* PURLIE'S *presence, and approaches.)*

By swickety—a gal like you could dog-gone well change a joker's luck if she had a mind to—see what I mean? (PURLIE *hunches what he expects to be an invisible* GITLOW *in the ribs. His blow lands upon* OL' CAP'N *with such force, he falls onto a pile of sacks of chicken feed.*)

OL' CAP'N. (*Sputtering.*) What! What in the name of—

(GITLOW *and* PURLIE *scramble to help him to his feet.*)

PURLIE. My compliments, sir—are only exceeded by my humblest apologies. And allow me, if you please, to present my Aunt Henrietta's daughter, whom you remember so well: Beatrice Judson—or as we call her—Cousin Bee.

OL' CAP'N. (*He is so taken by what he sees he forgets his anger.*) Well I'll be switched!

PURLIE. Come, Cousin Bee. Say "howdo" to the man.

LUTIEBELLE. How do to the man. I mean—(*Takes time to correct herself, then.*) delighted to remake your acquaintance, I'm sure.

OL' CAP'N. What's that? What's that she's saying?

PURLIE. College, sir.

OL' CAP'N. College?

PURLIE. That's all she ever talks.

OL' CAP'N. You mean Henrietta's little ol' button-eyed pickaninny was in college? Well bust my eyes wide open! Just LOOK at that! (*Gets closer, but she edges away.*) You remember me, honey. I'm still the Ol' Cap'n round here.

LUTIEBELLE. Oh, sir, it would not be the same without you being the Ol' Cap'n round here.

OL' CAP'N. You don't say! Say, I'll bet you don't remember a long time ago when—

LUTIEBELLE. When I wasn't but knee-high to a hoppergrass, and you took me by the hand, and led me on my very first trip to the cotton patch.

OL' CAP'N. (*Ecstatic.*) You mean you remember that!

LUTIEBELLE. Alert, wide awake, and up on my toes—if you please, sir! (*Rises up on her toes.*)

OL' CAP'N. (*Moving in.*) Doggone my hide. You're the cutest li'l ol' piece of brown sugar I ever did see—

LUTIEBELLE. (*Escaping.*) And this is your land, and your cotton patch, and your commissary, and your bull whip—

OL' CAP'N. What's that?

LUTIEBELLE. Just a figure of speech or two—

OL' CAP'N. Well, Beatrice—you wouldn't mind if Ol' Cap'n was to call you Cousin Bee?

LUTIEBELLE. Oh, positively not, not!—since my mother's name was Henrietta Judson; my father's name was Horace Judson—

OL' CAP'N. But most of all, I remember that little ol' dog of yours—"Spicey," wasn't it?

LUTIEBELLE. Oh, we wasn't much for eating dogs, sir—

OL' CAP'N. No, no! Spicey was the name—wasn't it?

(LUTIEBELLE *looking to* PURLIE *for help, but* PURLIE *cannot help. He looks to* GITLOW, *who also cannot remember.*)

LUTIEBELLE. You, er, really think we really called him "Spicey"?

OL' CAP'N. Not him—her!

PURLIE. HER!

LUTIEBELLE. Oh, her! Her! I am most happy to recollect that I do.

OL' CAP'N. You do! You don't say you do!

LUTIEBELLE. I did, as I recall it, have a fond remembrance of you and "Spicey," since you-all went so well together—and at the same time!

OL' CAP'N. You do? Well hush my mouth, eh, Git?

GITLOW. Hush your mouth indeed, sir.

LUTIEBELLE. Cose soon it is my sworn and true confession that I disremembers so many things out of my early pastime that mostly you are haze and vaguey!

OL' CAP'N. Oh, am I now!

LUTIEBELLE. Oh, yes, and sir—indeedy.

OL' CAP'N. Doggone my hide, eh, Git?

GITLOW. Doggone your hide indeed, suh.

LUTIEBELLE. You see of coursely I have spount—

PURLIE. Spent—

LUTIEBELLE. Spunt so much of my time among the college that hardly all of my ancient maidenhead—

PURLIE. Hood.

LUTIEBELLE. Is a thing of the past!

OL' CAP'N. You don't say!

LUTIEBELLE. But yes, and most precisely.

OL' CAP'N. Tell me, Li'l Bee—what did they teach you up at that college?

LUTIEBELLE. Well, mostly they taught me an education, but in between I learned a lot, too.

OL' CAP'N. Is that a fact?

LUTIEBELLE. Reading, writing, 'rithmetic—oh, my Lord—just sitting out on the rectangular every evening after four o'clock home work and you have your regular headache—

OL' CAP'N. You know something, I been after these Negras down here for years: Go to school, I'd say, first chance you get—take a coupla courses in advanced cotton picking. But you think they'd listen to me? No sireebob. By swickery! A gal like you could doggone well change a joker's luck if she was a mind to. (Gives GITLOW a broad wink and digs him in his ribs. GITLOW almost falls.) See what I mean?

LUTIEBELLE. Oh, most indo I deed.

OL' CAP'N. Look—anything! Ask me anything! Whatever you want—name it and it's yours!

LUTIEBELLE. You mean—really, really, really?

OL' CAP'N. Ain't a man in Cotchipee County can beat my time when I see

something I want—name it! (Indicates with a sweep the contents of the commissary.) Some roasted peanuts; a bottle of soda water; a piece of pepmint candy?

LUTIEBELLE. Thank you, sir, but if it's all the same to you I'd rather have my money.

OL' CAP'N. (As if shot.) Your WHAT!

LUTIEBELLE. (Frightened but determined to forge ahead under her own steam.) Now I'm gonna tell you like it was, Your Honor: You see, Reb'n Purlie and Uncle Gitlow had one aunty between them, name of Harietta—

PURLIE. Henrietta!

LUTIEBELLE. Henrietta—who used to cook for this rich ol' white lady up in North Carolina years ago; and last year this ol' lady died—brain tumor—

PURLIE. Bright's disease!

LUTIEBELLE. Bright's disease—leaving five hundred dollars to every servant who had ever worked on her place, including Henrietta. But Henrietta had already died, herself: largely from smallpox—

PURLIE. No!

LUTIEBELLE. Smally from large pox?

PURLIE. Influenza!

LUTIEBELLE. Influenza—and since Henrietta's husband Harris—

PURLIE. Horace!

LUTIEBELLE. Horace—was already dead from heart trouble—

PURLIE. Gunshot wounds!

LUTIEBELLE. (Exploding.) His heart stopped beating, didn't it?

PURLIE. Yes, but—

LUTIEBELLE. Precisely, Reb'n Purlie, precisely! (Turning back to OL' CAP'N.) Since, therefore and where-in-as Cousin Bee, her daughter, was first-in-line-for-next-of-kinfolks, the five hundred dollars left in your care and keep by Aunt Henrietta, and which you have been saving just for me all these lonesome years—

OL' CAP'N. I ain't been saving no damn sucha thing!

PURLIE. (Stepping swiftly into the

breach.) Oh, come out from behind your modesty, sir!

OL' CAP'N. What!

PURLIE. Your kindness, sir; your thoughtfulness, sir; your unflagging consideration for the welfare of your darkies, sir; have rung like the clean clear call of the clarion from Maine to Mexico. Your constant love for them is both hallmark and high water of the true gentility of the dear old South.

OL' CAP'N. Gitlow, Gitlow—go get Charlie. I want him to hear this.

(GITLOW exits upstage Center.)

Go on, boy, go on!

PURLIE. And as for your faithful ol' darkies themselves, sir—why, down in the quarters, sir, your name stands second only to God Himself Almighty.

OL' CAP'N. You don't mean to tell me!

PURLIE. Therefore, as a humble token of their high esteem and their deep and abiding affection, especially for saving that five hundred dollar inheritance for Cousin Bee, they have asked me to present to you . . . this plaque! (PURLIE unveils a "sheepskin scroll" from his inside coat pocket.)

(OL' CAP'N reaches for it, but PURLIE draws it away. CHARLIE appears in the doorway upstage Center followed by GIT-LOW.)

Which bears the following citation to wit, and I quote: "Whereas Ol' Cap'n has kindly allowed us to remain on his land, and pick his cotton, and tend his cattle, and drive his mules, and whereas Ol' Cap'n still lets us have our hominy grits and fat back on credit and whereas Ol' Cap'n never resorts to bull whip except as a blessing and a benediction, therefore be it resolved, that Ol' Cap"n Cotchipee be cited as the best friend the Negro has ever had, and officially proclaimed Great White Father of the Year!"

OL' CAP'N. (Stunned.) I can't believe it —I can't believe it! (Sees CHARLIE.) Charlie, boy—did you hear it? Did you hear it, Charlie, my boy—GREAT WHITE FATHER OF THE YEAR!

PURLIE. (Like a professional undertaker.) Let me be the first to congratulate you, sir. (They shake hands solemnly.)

OL' CAP'N. Thank you, Purlie.

LUTIEBELLE. And me. (They shake hands solemnly.)

OL' CAP'N. Thank you, Cousin Bee.

GITLOW. And me, too, Ol' Cap'n.

OL' CAP'N. (On the verge of tears, as they shake hands.) Gitlow—Gitlow. I know this is some of your doings—my old friend. (He turns expectantly to CHARLIE.) Well, boy—(CHARLIE is trapped.) ain't you gonna congratulate your father?

CHARLIE. Yessir. (Shakes his hand.)

OL' CAP'N. This—is the happiest day of my life. My darkies—my Negras—my own—(Chokes up; unable to continue.)

PURLIE. Hear, hear!

GITLOW and LUTIEBELLE. Hear, hear!

(CHARLIE tries to sneak off again, but OL' CAP'N sees him.)

OL' CAP'N. I am just too overcome to talk. Come back here, boy.

(CHARLIE comes back and stands in intense discomfort.)

Silent—speechless—dumb, my friends. Never in all the glorious hoary and ancient annals of all Dixie—never before— (Chokes up with tears; blows nose with big red handkerchief, and pulls himself together.) My friends, in the holy scripture—and I could cite you chapter and verse if I was a mind to—"In the beginning God created white folks and He created black folks," and in the name of all that's white and holy, let's keep it that way. And to hell with Abraham Lincoln and Martin Luther King!

PURLIE. I am moved, Ol' Cap'n—

GITLOW AND LUTIEBELLE. Uhn!

PURLIE. Moved beyond my jurisdiction; as for example, I have upon my person a certificate of legal tender duly affixed and so notarized to said itemized effect—*(Hands over an official-looking document.)* a writ of Habeas Corpus.

OL' CAP'N. *(Taking the document.)* Habeas who?

PURLIE. Habeas Corpus. It means I can have the body.

OL' CAP'N. Body—what body?

PURLIE. The body of the cash—the five hundred dollars—that they sent you to hold in trust for Cousin Bee.

OL' CAP'N. *(Pauses to study the eager faces in the room; then.)* Charlie—

CHARLIE. Yessir.

OL' CAP'N. Bring me—five hundred dollars—will you?

(CHARLIE starts for safe.)

No, no, no—not that old stuff. Fresh money, clean money out of my private stock out back. Nothin's too good for my Negras.

CHARLIE. Yessir—yessir! *(Starts out, stops.)* And Paw?

OL' CAP'N. Yes, son?

CHARLIE. All I got to say is "Yessir!" *(Crosses to cash register.)*

OL' CAP'N. Just wait—wait till I tell the Senator: "Great White Father of the Year."

CHARLIE. *(Returns with roll of bills which he hands to his father.)* Here you are, Paw.

OL' CAP'N. Thank you, boy.

(Enter IDELLA, followed by the SHERIFF and the DEPUTY.)

IDELLA. Here everybody is, back in the office.

OL' CAP'N. *(Overjoyed to see them.)* Just in time, Sheriff, for the greatest day of my life. Gentlemen—something has happened here today, between me and my Negras, makes me proud to call myself a Confederate: I have just been named Great White Father of the Year. *(To PURLIE.)* Right?

PURLIE. Right. And now if you'll just—

SHERIFF AND DEPUTY. Great White Father of the Year! Congratulations! *(They shake his hands warmly.)*

OL' CAP'N. True, there are places in this world where the darky is rebellious, running hog wild, rising up and sitting down where he ain't wanted, acting sassy in jail, getting plumb out of hand, totally forgetting his place and his manners —but not in Cotchipee County! *(To PURLIE.)* Right?

PURLIE. Right! And now perhaps we could get back to the business at hand.

OL' CAP'N. *(Finishing his count.)* All right—five hundred dollars.

(PURLIE impulsively reaches for the money, but OL' CAP'N snatches it back.)

Just a moment. There's still one small formality: a receipt.

PURLIE. A receipt? All right, I'll—

OL' CAP'N. Not you— You! *(Thrusts a printed form toward LUTIEBELLE.)* . . . just for the record. *(Offers her a fountain pen.)* Sign here. Your full and legal name —right here on the dotted line.

PURLIE. *(Reaching for the pen.)* I'll do it—I have her power of attorney.

LUTIEBELLE. *(Beating PURLIE to the pen.)* It's all right, Reb'n Purlie, I can write. *(Takes pen and signs paper with a flourish.)*

OL' CAP'N. *(Takes up paper and reads the signature.)* Sheriff, I want this woman arrested!

PURLIE. Arrested?! For what?

OL' CAP'N. She came into my presence, together with him—*(Indicates PURLIE.)* and with him—*(Indicates GITLOW.)* and they all swore to me that she is Beatrice Judson.

PURLIE. She IS Beatrice Judson!

OL' CAP'N. *(Pouncing.)* Then how come she to sign her name: Lutiebelle Gussiemae Jenkins!

PURLIE. Uhn-uhn!

GITLOW. Uhn-uhn!

LUTIEBELLE. Uhn-uhn!

GITLOW. (Starting off suddenly.) Is somebody calling my name out there—

OL' CAP'N. Come back here, Gitlow—

(GITLOW halts in his tracks.)

You'll go out of that door when the Sheriff takes you out. And that goes for all of you.

(The SHERIFF starts forward.)

Just a minute, Sheriff. Before you take 'em away there's something I've got to do. (Crosses to where the whip is hung.)

GITLOW. (Horrified at the thought of the whip.) I'll make it up to you in cotton, Ol' Cap'n—

OL' CAP'N. Shut up, Gitlow. (Takes whip down, and starts to uncoil it.) Something I started twenty years ago with this bull whip—(Fastening his eyes on PURLIE). Something I intend to finish.

GITLOW. (Drops to his knees and begins to sing.) "Gone are the days—"

OL' CAP'N. (Turning to GITLOW.) Dammit! I told you to shut up! (Then back to PURLIE.) I'm gonna teach you to try to make a damn fool outta white folks; all right, boy, drop them britches.

PURLIE. The hell you preach!

OL' CAP'N. What's that you said?

LUTIEBELLE. He said, "The hell you preach!"

CHARLIE. Paw, wait, listen—!

OL' CAP'N. I thought I told you to shut up. (Back to PURLIE.) Boy, I'm gonna teach you to mind what I say!

(PURLIE doesn't move. OL' CAP'N takes a vicious cut at him with the bull whip, and PURLIE, leaping back to get out of the way, falls into the arms of the SHERIFF.)

SHERIFF. I distinctly heard that gentleman order you to drop your britches. (Spins PURLIE around, sets him up, and swings with all his might. PURLIE easily ducks and dances away.)

DEPUTY. Save a little taste for me, Sheriff!

(The SHERIFF swings again; and, again, PURLIE dances away. He swings still again, but to no avail.)

SHERIFF. (Aggravated.) Hold still, dammit! (Swings again, and once more PURLIE ducks away.) Confound it, boy! You trying to make me hurt myself?

DEPUTY. What's the matter, Sheriff—can't you find him?! (Laughs.)

SHERIFF. (Desperate.) Now, you listen to me, boy! Either you stand up like a man, so I can knock you down, or—

LUTIEBELLE. (Stepping between the SHERIFF and PURLIE.) Don't you dare!

SHERIFF. What!

LUTIEBELLE. Insultin' Reb'n Purlie, and him a man of the cloth! (Grabs his gun arm and bites it.)

SHERIFF. Owwww! (She kicks him in the shin.) Owwwwwww!

(The DEPUTY charges in to the rescue. He attempts to grab LUTIEBELLE, but she eludes him and steps down hard on his corns.)

DEPUTY. Owwwwwwwwwww!

PURLIE. (Going for the DEPUTY.) Keep your hands off her, you hypothetical baboon, keep your hands OFF her! (Grabs the DEPUTY, spins him around and knocks him across the room, starts to follow, but the SHERIFF grabs him and pins his arms behind him.)

CHARLIE. (Breaks loose from IDELLA, snatching at the SHERIFF.) You let him go, dammit, let him go!

(With one arm the SHERIFF pushes CHARLIE away.)

SHERIFF. (Still holding PURLIE's arms pinned back.) All right, Dep, he's all yours. Throw him your fast ball—high, tight and inside!

DEPUTY. Glad to oblige you, Sheriff! (*He draws back like a big league baseball pitcher.*)

CHARLIE. (*Rushing into the breach.*) Stop! Stop—stop in the name of the—

(*The* DEPUTY *swings from the floor,* PURLIE *ducks and rolls his head sharply to one side.*)

(CHARLIE *runs full into the force of the blow. Collapsing heavily.*) Idella—aaaaaaa!

OL' CAP'N. (*Rushing to him.*) Charlie! IDELLA. Charlie!

(PURLIE, *taking advantage of the confusion, snatches* LUTIEBELLE *by the arms and dashes with her out the back door.*)

OL' CAP'N. After them, you idiots, after them!

SHERIFF. (*To the* DEPUTY.) After them, you idiot! (*They both run off after* PURLIE *and* LUTIEBELLE.)

(OL' CAP'N *and* IDELLA *are kneeling beside the prostrate* CHARLIE. GITLOW, *after a moment, comes into the picture.*)

OL' CAP'N. His eyes, Idella, his eyes! Where are his eyes?

IDELLA. Gitlow, fetch me the asaphoetida, Ol' Cap'n, you rub his hands.

GITLOW. Yess'm.

IDELLA. (*Slapping his face.*) Charlie, honey, wake up—wake up! It's me, Idella.

(OL' CAP'N *is too disorganized to be of any assistance.* GITLOW *has returned with a bottle which he hands to* IDELLA. *He then kneels and starts rubbing* CHARLIE's *hands.*)

GITLOW. Mr. Charlie, wake up—

(*With* GITLOW *and* IDELLA's *help,* CHARLIE *slowly rises to his feet. Still unsteady, his eyes glazed and vacant.*)

OL' CAP'N. (*Snapping his fingers in front of his eyes.*) It's me, Charlie, me—it's your daddy, boy! Speak to me—talk to me—say something to me!

CHARLIE. (*Snaps suddenly into speech—but still out on his feet.*) Fourscore and seven years ago, our fathers brought forth—

OL' CAP'N. Shut up!

CURTAIN

ACT TWO

SCENE 2

TIME:
Two days later.

SCENE:
Back at the shack, outside in the yard area.

AT RISE:
MISSY *is discovered, busy working on some potted plants. She is preoccupied, but we feel some restlessness, some anticipation in the manner in which she works.* PURLIE *enters.*

PURLIE. (*The great prophet intones his sorrows.*) Toll the bell—Big Bethel; toll the big, black, ex-liberty bell; tell Freedom there's death in the family.

MISSY. Purlie—

PURLIE. All these wings and they still won't let me fly!

MISSY. Where you been these last two days, Purlie? We been lookin' for you. All this plotting and planning—risking your dad-blasted neck like a crazy man! And for what—FOR WHAT!

(IDELLA *enters.*)

Oh, come in, Miz Idella.

IDELLA. Is anybody here seen Charlie Cotchipee this morning?

MISSY. No, we haven't.

PURLIE. Is something wrong, Miz Idella?

IDELLA. He left home this morning right after breakfast—here it is after lunch and I ain't seen him since. I can't find Charlie—first time in forty-five years

I been working up there in that house I ever misplaced anything! You don't suppose he'd run away from home and not take me?

MISSY. Oh, no, Miz Idella! Not li'l Charlie Cotchipee.

IDELLA. Well, I guess I'd better be getting back. If you should see him—

MISSY. Miz Idella, we all want to thank you for keeping Purlie out of jail so kindly. (Hands her flowers.)

IDELLA. Oh, that was nothing; I just told that ol' man if he didn't stop all that foolishness about chain gangs and stuff, I would resign from his kitchen and take Charlie right along with me! But now I've lost Charlie. First time in forty-five years I ever misplaced anything. (She exits.)

MISSY. (Turns to PURLIE.) Don't you know there's something more important in this world than having that broken down ol' ex-church of a barn to preach in?

PURLIE. Yeah—like what?

MISSY. Like asking Lutiebelle to marry you.

PURLIE. Like asking Lutiebelle to marry me?

MISSY. She worships the ground you walk on. Talks about you all the time. You two could get married, settle down, like you ought to, and raise the cutest little ol' family you ever did see. And she's a cookin', po' child—she left you some of her special fritters.

PURLIE. Freedom, Missy, not fritters. The crying need of this Negro day and age is not grits, but greatness; not corn-bread but courage; not fat-back, but fight-back; Big Bethel is my Bethel; it belongs to me and to my people; I intend to have it back if I have to pay for it in blood!

MISSY. All right—come on in and I'll fix you some dinner.

GITLOW. (Enters front door, singing.) "I'm comin', I'm comin'—"

MISSY. (Entering house.) Not so loud, Gitlow. You want to wake up the mule?

GITLOW. Not on his day off. "For my head is bendin' low—" (GITLOW sits, unfolds comic section and reads.)

MISSY. Where's Lutiebelle, Gitlow?

GITLOW. "The history of the War Between the States will be continued next week." That sure is a good story—I wonder how that's gonna come out?

MISSY. Grown man, deacon in the church, reading the funny-paper. And your shirt. You sneaked outta here this morning in your clean white shirt, after I told you time and time again I was saving it!

GITLOW. Saving it for what?

MISSY. It's the only decent thing you got to get buried in! (Exits side door.)

GITLOW. Don't you know that arrangements for my funeral has been taken over by the white folks? (To PURLIE.) Besides, I got the money!

PURLIE. What kinda money?

GITLOW. The five hundred dollar kinda money.

PURLIE. Five hundred dollars! You mean Ol' Cap'n give the money to you?

GITLOW. "Gitlow," he said. "Ain't another man in this valley, black, white, or otherwise, I would trust to defend and protect me from the N double ACP but you."

PURLIE. Is that a fact?

GITLOW. Well, now. Whatever become of you? All them gretgawdamighty plans your mouth runneth over—all that white folks' psychology?

PURLIE. Gitlow! Er, Deacon Gitlow—Big Bethel is waiting!

GITLOW. So you're the good-for-nothing, raggedy ass high falute 'round here that goes for who-tied-the-bear!

PURLIE. Naw, Git, man—ain't nothing to me.

GITLOW. Always so high and mighty—can't nobody on earth handle white folks but you—don't pay no 'tention to Gitlow; naw—he's a Tom. Tease him—low-rate him—laugh at ol' Gitlow; he ain't nothing but a fool!

PURLIE. Aw, Git, man, you got me wrong. I didn't mean nothing like that!

GITLOW. Who's the fool now, my boy —who's the fool now?

PURLIE. Er—I'm the fool, Gitlow.

GITLOW. Aw, man, you can talk plainer than that.

PURLIE. I'm the fool, Gitlow.

GITLOW. Uh-huh! Now go over to that window, open it wide as it will go and say it so everybody in this whole damn valley can hear you! Go on! Go on, man—I ain't got all day!

PURLIE. *(Goes to window.)* I'm the fool, Gitlow!

GITLOW. Nice. Now beg me!

PURLIE. What!

GITLOW. I said if you want to see the money, beg me! Do it like you do white folks.

PURLIE. I'd rather die and go to hell in a pair of gasoline drawers—

(GITLOW starts to put money away.)

no, wait. Holy mackerel, dere, Massa Gitlow—hee, hee, hee. Hey! Boss, could I possible have a look at that there five hundred dollars dere, suh? Hyuh, hyuh, hyuh!

GITLOW. Man, you sure got style! You know together you and me could make the big time!

(PURLIE reaches for money.)

Come in and see me during office hours! As Deputy-For-The-Colored, I guess I'll just sort of step outside for a minute and let that low September sun shine down on a joker as rich as he is black!

PURLIE. Gitlow—Gitlow!

(GITLOW starts for side door.)

If slavery ever comes back I want to be your agent!

GITLOW. Now that was a snaggy-toothed, poverty-struck remark if I ever heard one.

MISSY. *(Enters side door.)* Youall wash your hands and git ready—Gitlow! Where's Lutiebelle?

GITLOW. *(Evasive.)* She didn't get back yet.

MISSY. We know she didn't get back yet.

PURLIE. Where is Lutiebelle, Gitlow?

GITLOW. What I mean is—on our way home from church, we stopped by Ol' Cap'n's awhile, and he asked me to leave her there to help with the Sunday dinner.

PURLIE. And you left her!

MISSY. With that frisky ol' man?

GITLOW. For goodness' sakes, she's only waiting on table.

PURLIE. The woman I love don't wait on table for nobody, especially Ol' Cap'n; I know that scoun'. I'm going and get her!

GITLOW. Wait a minute—you can't get her right now!

PURLIE. *(Studying him.)* What you mean, I can't get her right now?

GITLOW. Not right this minute—that'll spoil everything. Ol' Cap'n wouldn't like it.

MISSY. How low can you git, Gitlow!

GITLOW. I mean she's got to stay and bring us the five hundred dollars.

MISSY. What five hundred dollars?

PURLIE. I thought you already had the money?

GITLOW. Well, not exactly. But he promised me faithful to send it down by Lutiebelle.

PURLIE. I'm going and get Lutiebelle—

GITLOW. Wait a minute, wait a minute; you want to buy Big Bethel back or don't you?

PURLIE. *(A glimmering of truth.)* I hope I misunderstand you!

GITLOW. You said it yourself: It is meet that the daughters of Zion should sacrifice themselves for the cause.

PURLIE. *(Grabbing up MISSY's bat.)* Gitlow, I'll kill you—!

GITLOW. Wait a minute, wait a minute, wait a MINUTE!

(The door opens suddenly, and there stands LUTIEBELLE. *She, too, has on her Sunday best, but it is disheveled. She has a work apron over her dress, with her hat completely askew, the once proud feather now hanging over her face. In her hands she still clutches a rolling pin.)*

MISSY. Lutiebelle—Lutiebelle, honey!

LUTIEBELLE. I think I am going to faint. *(She starts to collapse, and they rush toward her to help; but suddenly she straightens up and waves them off.)* No, I ain't, either—I'm too mad! *(She shudders in recollection.)* I was never so insulted in all my dad-blamed life!

PURLIE. Lutiebelle!

LUTIEBELLE. Oh, excuse me, Reb'n Purlie—I know I look a mess, but—

MISSY. What happened up there?

LUTIEBELLE. *(Boiling again.)* I'm a maid first class, Aunt Missy, and I'm proud of it!

MISSY. Of course you are.

LUTIEBELLE. I ain't had no complaints to speak of since first I stepped into the white folks' kitchen. I'm clean; I'm honest, and I work hard—but one thing: I don't stand for no stuff from them white folks.

PURLIE. Of course you don't. You don't have to—

LUTIEBELLE. I mean, I KNOW my job, and I DO my job—and the next ol' sweaty, ol' grimey, ol' drunkeny man puts his hands on me—so much as touch like he got no business doing—God grant me strength to kill him! Excuse me, Reb'n Purlie.

GITLOW. Well, Ol' Cap'n do get playful at times—did he send the money?

LUTIEBELLE. Money! What money? There ain't none!

GITLOW. What! Naw, naw! He wouldn't do that to me—not to good ol', faithful ol' Gitlow, nawsir!

LUTIEBELLE. The whole thing was a trick—to get you out of the house—

GITLOW. Not to ME he didn't!

LUTIEBELLE. So he could—sneak up behind me in the pantry!

MISSY. What I tell you! What I tell you!

LUTIEBELLE. I knowed the minute I—come grabbing on me, Reb'n Purlie; come grabbing his dirty ol' hands on me!

PURLIE. He did!

LUTIEBELLE. And twisting me around, and—and pinching me, Reb'n Purlie!

PURLIE. Pinching you—where? Where?

LUTIEBELLE. Must I, Reb'n Purlie?

PURLIE. I demand to know—where did he pinch you!

*(*LUTIEBELLE *diffidently locates a spot on her left cheek. They all examine it anxiously.)*

MISSY. That's him all right!

GITLOW. Aw, Missy—

MISSY. I'd know them fingerprints anywhere!

LUTIEBELLE. Right in the pantry—and then he, he—Oh, Reb'n Purlie, I'm so ashamed!

PURLIE. What did he do? Tell me, woman, tell me: what did he do? WHAT DID HE DO?

LUTIEBELLE. He kissed me!

PURLIE AND MISSY. No!

LUTIEBELLE. He kissed me—right here.

MISSY. *(Squinting, it is a very small spot indeed.)* Right where?

*(*LUTIEBELLE *is so broken up, she can only point to her other cheek.)*

GITLOW. Aw, for Pete's sakes.

PURLIE. *(Almost out of control.)* He kissed my woman, Gitlow—he kissed the woman I love!

GITLOW. So what!

PURLIE. So what do you mean, "So what"? No man kisses the woman I love and lives!

*(*GITLOW *laughs.)*

Go ahead, laugh! Laugh. Let's have one last look at your teeth before I knock 'em down your throat!

GITLOW. Aw, man, git off my nerves.

PURLIE. I'm going up that hill, and I'm gonna call that buzzardly ol' bastard out, and I wouldn't be surprised if I didn't beat him until he died.

LUTIEBELLE. (Suddenly not so sure.) Reb'n Purlie—

GITLOW. (Also wondering about PUR-LIE.) Now looka here, Purlie—don't you be no fool, boy—you still in Georgia. If you just got to defend the honor of the woman you love, do it somewhere else.

PURLIE. Kissing my woman—kissing my woman! (Runs to window, flings it open and shouts out.) Man, I'll break your neck off!

LUTIEBELLE. (Helping GITLOW and MISSY to wrestle PURLIE away from the window.) Please, Reb'n Purlie!

PURLIE. (Breaks away and goes to window and shouts again.) I'll stomp your eyeballs in!

LUTIEBELLE. (They snatch him from the window again.) Don't, Reb'n Purlie—oh my goodness!—

PURLIE. (Breaks away still again and shouts from window.) I'll snatch your right arm outta the socket, and beat the rest of you to death!

LUTIEBELLE. (This time they get him away, and close the window.) Don't talk like that, Reb'n Purlie!

MISSY. (Standing at the window, arms widespread to block him.) Have you gone crazy?

GITLOW. (Still struggling with PURLIE.) You go up that hill tonight, boy, and they'll kill you!

PURLIE. Let 'em kill me, it won't be the first time.

LUTIEBELLE. Aunt Missy, stop him—

GITLOW. Listen, boy! This is your Dep-uty-For-The-Colored telling you you ain't gonna leave this house, and that's an order.

PURLIE. You try and stop me!

GITLOW. Good gracious a life, what's the matter with you? The man only kissed your woman.

PURLIE. Yeah! And what you suppose he'd a done to me if I'd a kissed his? (The one question too obvious to answer.) And that's exactly what I'm gonna do to him!

LUTIEBELLE. Please, Reb'n Purlie. I beg you on bended knees. (She throws her arms around him.)

PURLIE. (Holds her close.) For the glory and honor of the Negro National Anthem; for the glory and honor of brown-skin Negro womanhood; for the glory and honor of—

(LUTIEBELLE suddenly kisses him big and hard.)

—for LUTIEBELLE! (His emotions explode him out of the door which slams shut behind him.)

GITLOW. (Singing.) "I hear them gentle bloodhounds callin'—Old Black Joe." . . .

(LUTIEBELLE finds the deepest spot in MISSY's shoulder to bury her head in and cry, as—)

CURTAIN

ACT THREE

SCENE 1

SCENE:
   The shack.
TIME:
   Later that same night.
AT RISE:
   There is light only from a KEROSENE LAMP turned down low. The air of Sunday is gone from the room. The table-cloth has been changed, and things are as they were before. LUTIEBELLE enters Down Right.

LUTIEBELLE. Is it him, Aunt Missy, is it him?

MISSY. No, honey, not yet.

LUTIEBELLE. Oh, I could have sworn I thought it was him. What time is it?

MISSY. About four in the morning from the sound of the birds. Now, why ain't you sleep after all that hot toddy I give you?

LUTIEBELLE. I can't sleep. The strangest thing. I keep hearing bells—

MISSY. Bells?

LUTIEBELLE. Wedding bells. Ain't that funny? Oh, Lord, please don't let him be hurt bad, please! Where can he be, Aunt Missy?

MISSY. Now don't you worry 'bout Purlie. My! You put on your pretty pink dress!

LUTIEBELLE. Yes, ma'am. It's the only thing I got fitting to propose in.

MISSY. Oh?

LUTIEBELLE. I thought, to sort of show my gratitude, I'd offer him my hand in matrimony—it's all I've got.

MISSY. It's a nice hand, and a nice dress—just right for matrimony.

LUTIEBELLE. You really think so, Aunt Missy: really, really, really?

MISSY. I know so, and wherever Reb'n Purlie is this morning, you can bet your bottom dollar he knows it, too.

LUTIEBELLE. Ten thousand Queens of Sheba! Aunt Missy—

MISSY. Yes—

LUTIEBELLE. (Letting it out in a gush.) I wanted him to get mad; I wanted him to tear out up that hill; I wanted him to punch that sweaty ol' buzzard in his gizzard—you think I was wrong?

MISSY. I should say not!

LUTIEBELLE. Course I coulda punched him myself, I reckon.

MISSY. Why should you? Why shouldn't our men folks defend our honor with the white folks once in a while? They ain't got nothing else to do.

LUTIEBELLE. You really, really, really think so?

MISSY. (Shrugs.) Ten thousand Queens of Sheba—

LUTIEBELLE. Oh, my goodness, when he walks through that door, I'm just gonna—

(Door Down Left suddenly swings open to reveal GITLOW.)

GITLOW. (Entering.) Well, well, Lutiebelle.

LUTIEBELLE. Did you find him, Uncle Git?

MISSY. Don't depend on Gitlow for nothing, honey—(Exits to kitchen.)

LUTIEBELLE. Where can he be, Uncle Gitlow, where can he be?

GITLOW. Oh—good wind like this on his tail oughta put him somewhere above Macon long 'bout now, if his shoes hold out!

LUTIEBELLE. You mean—running!

GITLOW. What's wrong with running? It emancipated more people than Abe Lincoln ever did.

LUTIEBELLE. How dare you! The finest, bravest man—

GITLOW. The finer they come, the braver they be, the deader these white folks gonna kill 'em when they catch 'em!

MISSY. (Entering from the kitchen.) Gitlow, I'll skin you!

GITLOW. All that talk about calling that man out, and whipping him—

MISSY. A man is duty-bound to defend the honor of the woman he loves, and any woman worth her salt will tell you so.

LUTIEBELLE. Love can make you do things you really can't do—can't it, Aunt Missy?

GITLOW. Look. That man's got the president, the governor, the courthouse, and both houses of the congress—on his side!

MISSY. Purlie Judson is a man the Negro woman can depend on!

LUTIEBELLE. An honor to his race, and a credit to his people!

GITLOW. (Not to be sidetracked.) The

army, the navy, the marines; the sheriff, the judge, the jury, the police, the F.B.I. —all on his side. Not to mention a pair of brass knucks and the hungriest dogs this side of hell! Surely youall don't expect that po' boy to go up against all that caucasiatic power empty-handed!

MISSY. O, ye of little faith!

LUTIEBELLE. Didn't my Lord deliver Daniel?

GITLOW. Of course he did—but lions is one thing and white folks is another!

MISSY. Where there's a will there's a woman—

LUTIEBELLE. And where there's a woman there's a way!

GITLOW. (Exasperated.) Great Gawd-amighty! All right—go ahead and have it your way. But I'll lay you six bits 'gainst half my seat on the heavenly choir, Purlie ain't been up that hill. And the minute he walks in that door—if he ever shows up again around here—I'm gonna prove it! Oh, damn—I can make better time out there talkin' to that mule.

MISSY. Why not—it's one jackass to another.

(GITLOW exits to the kitchen. MISSY and LUTIEBELLE look at each other, both determined not to give way to the very real fright they feel. There is a long, uncomfortable pause.)

LUTIEBELLE. It sure is a lovely year— for this time of morning, I mean. (There is a pause.) I can't tell you how much all this fresh air, wine-smoke, and apple-bite reminds me of Alabama.

MISSY. Oh, yes—ol' Georgia can sure smile pretty when she's of a mind to—

PURLIE. (Bursts in.) "Arise and shine for thy light has come."

MISSY. Purlie—Purlie Victorious! (They embrace.)

LUTIEBELLE. Oh, you Reb'n Purlie you!

PURLIE. "Truth and Mercy are met together, Righteousness and Peace have kissed each other!" (They embrace.)

MISSY. Let me look at you—behold the

man!—knee-deep in shining glory. Great day the righteous marching! What happened to you?

PURLIE. Mine enemy hath been destroyed!

MISSY. What!

PURLIE. I told that ol' man twenty years ago, Missy, that over his dead body, Big Bethel would rise again!

MISSY. Purlie! You mean you done—

PURLIE. "Have I any pleasure that the wicked should die, saith the Lord, and not turn from his ways and live?" Lutiebelle, put on your hat and coat, and hurry!

LUTIEBELLE. Yessir!

PURLIE. Missy, throw us some breakfast into a paper sack, and quick!

MISSY. Yessir!

PURLIE. Gitlow, I'm calling on you and your fellow mule to write a new page in the annals of Negro History Week.

GITLOW. (Entering.) Well, if it ain't ol' little black riding hood, dere! How was the mean ol' peckerwolf tonight, dere, kingfish?

MISSY. Tell him, Purlie boy, what you told us: how you sashayed up that hill with force and fistfight!

GITLOW. Hallelujah!

MISSY. How you fit Ol' Cap'n to a halt and a standstill!

GITLOW. Talk that talk!

MISSY. And left him laying in a pool of his own Confederate blood!

GITLOW. For Pete sakes, Missy—quit lying!

MISSY. Don't you dare call Purlie Judson a liar!

LUTIEBELLE. No man calls Reb'n Purlie a liar and lives!

GITLOW. What's the matter with you people? Purlie ain't been up that hill; Purlie ain't seen Ol' Cap'n; Purlie ain't done doodley squat! And all that gabble about leaving somebody in a pool of his own Confederate blood ain't what the bull left in the barnyard!

PURLIE. Five hundred dollars says it is!

(Draws roll of bills from his pocket, for all to see.)

ALL. Five hundred dollars!

PURLIE. In cool September cash!

GITLOW. Money! *(Lunges forward, but PURLIE slaps his hand.)*

PURLIE. And that ain't all I got— *(Opens bag he has brought. They look in.)*

GITLOW. *(Almost choking in awe.)* Oh, my goodness, Missy—great day in the morning time—Missy—Missy!

MISSY. *(Also impressed.)* Gitlow, that's it!

GITLOW. That's it, Missy—that's it!

MISSY. Of course that's it!—ain't nothing in the world but it!

(PURLIE slowly pulls out OL' CAP'N's bull whip.)

GITLOW. Ain't but one way—one way in all this world—for nobody to get that bull whip off'n Ol' Cap'n!

MISSY. And that's off'n his dead body!

GITLOW. And that's the everlovin' truth, so help me.

PURLIE. Here, take it—and burn it in a public place. Lutiebelle—

LUTIEBELLE. Yes, Reb'n Purlie.

PURLIE. This money belongs to the Negro people—

GITLOW. Reb'n Purlie, my boy, I apologize from the bottom of my knees. *(Kneels and starts to sing.)* "Gone are the days—"

MISSY. *(Snatching him to his feet.)* Get up and shut up!

PURLIE. *(Deliberately continuing to LU-TIEBELLE.)* Take it, and wear it next to your heart.

LUTIEBELLE. *(Very conscious of the great charge laid upon her, turns her back to GITLOW and hides the money in her bosom.)* Until death do us part.

MISSY. *(To GITLOW.)* If I ever catch you with that song in your mouth again I'll choke you with it!

PURLIE. And go wake up the mule. We due in Waycross to buy Big Bethel.

GITLOW. I'm going, I'm going. *(Starts, but can't tear himself away.)* Cash—five hundred dollars in cash. And a bull whip, from Ol' Cap'n Cotchipee himself— Man, I'd give a pretty piece of puddin' to know how you did it!

MISSY. You go and wake up that mule! *(Turning back to PURLIE.)* Me, too! How did you do it, Purlie?

LUTIEBELLE. What happened when you first got there?

PURLIE. *(Almost laughing.)* Now wait a minute—don't rush me!

MISSY. That's what I say: don't rush him—let the man talk!

PURLIE. Talk! Missy, I told you. I haven't got time—

GITLOW. That's all right, Purlie, we'll listen in a hurry.

LUTIEBELLE. What happened when you called him out and whipped him?

PURLIE. I didn't call him out and whip him!

GITLOW. What!

MISSY. You didn't!

LUTIEBELLE. Reb'n Purlie?

PURLIE. I mean, I did call him out!

LUTIEBELLE. *(In ecstatic relief.)* Oh— you did call him out!

PURLIE. Yeah—but he didn't come.

ALL. What!

PURLIE. So—er—I went in to get him!

ALL. You did! Sure enough! What happened then?

PURLIE. *(Still seeking escape.)* Well, like I told you—

LUTIEBELLE. Tell us, Reb'n Purlie— please!

PURLIE. *(No escape.)* Well—here was me; and there was him—twisted and bent like a pretzel! Face twitchified like a pan of worms; eyes bugging out; sweat dreening down like rain; tongue plumb clove to the roof of his mouth! *(He looks to his audience, and is impelled to go on.)* Well— this thief—this murderer—this adulterer —this oppressor of all my people, just a sitting there: Stonewall Jackson Cotchipee, just a sitting there. *(Begins to respond to his own fantasy.)* "Go to, rich man, weep and howl, for your sorrows shall come upon you." And-a "Wherefore abhor yourself, and repent Ye in sackcloth and ashes!" cause ol' Purlie is done come to get you!

LUTIEBELLE. *(Swept away.)* Oh, my Lord!

MISSY. What he do, Purlie—what he do!?

PURLIE. Fell down on bended knees and cried like a baby!

MISSY. Ol' Cap'n Cotchipee on his knees!?

GITLOW. Great day in the morning time!

PURLIE. *(Warming to the task.)* Don't beg me, white folks, it's too late. "Mercy?" What do you know about mercy?! Did you have mercy on Ol' Uncle Tubb when he asked you not to cheat him out of his money so hard, and you knocked him deaf in his left ear? Did you have mercy on Lolly's boy when he sassed you back, and you took and dipped his head in a bucket of syrup! And twenty years ago when little Purlie, black and manly as he could be, stood naked before you and your bull whip and pleaded with tears in his li'l ol' eyes, did you have mercy!?

GITLOW. Naw!

PURLIE. —And I'll not have mercy now!

ALL. Amen! Help him, Lawd! Preach it, boy, preach it! *(Etc.)*

PURLIE. Vengeance is mine saith the Lord! *(Hallelujah!)* Ye serpents; ye vipers; ye low-down sons of—! *(Amen.)* How can ye escape the damnation of hell!

MISSY. Throw it at him, boy!

PURLIE. And then, bless my soul, I looked up—up from the blazing depths of my righteous indignation! And I saw tears spill over from his eyeballs; and I heard the heart be-clutching anguish of his outcry! His hands was both a-tremble; and slobber a-dribblin' down his lips!

GITLOW. Oh, my Lawd!

PURLIE. And he whined and whimp-ered like a ol' hound dog don't want you to kick him no more!

LUTIEBELLE. Great goodness a mighty!

PURLIE. And I commenced to ponder the meaning of this evil thing that groveled beneath my footstool—this no-good lump of nobody!—not fit to dwell on this earth beside the children of the blessed—an abomination to the Almighty and stench in the nostrils of his people! And yet—*(Pause for effect.)* and yet—a man! A weak man; a scared man; a pitiful man; like the whole southland bogged down in sin and segregation crawling on his knees before my judgment seat—but still a MAN!

GITLOW. A man, Lawd!

PURLIE. He, too, like all the South, was one of God's creatures—

MISSY. Yes, Lawd!

PURLIE. He, too, like all the South, could never be beyond the reach of love, hope, and redemption.

LUTIEBELLE. Amen!

PURLIE. Somewhere for him—even for him, some father's heart was broken, some mother's tears undried.

GITLOW. Dry 'em, Lawd!

PURLIE. I am my brother's keeper!

ALL. Yes, Lawd.

PURLIE. And thinking on these things, I found myself to pause, and stumble in my great resolve—and sorrow squeezed all fury from my heart—and pity plucked all hatred from my soul—and the racing feet of an avenging anger slowed down to a halt and a standstill—and the big, black, and burly fist of my strong correction—raised on high like a stroke of God's own lightning—fell useless by my side. The book say, "Love one another."

MISSY. Love one another!

PURLIE. The book say, "Comfort ye one another."

LUTIEBELLE. Comfort ye one another.

PURLIE. The book say, "Forgive ye one another."

GITLOW. Forgive Ol' Cap'n, Lord.

PURLIE. Slowly I turned away—to leave

this lump of human mess and misery to the infinite darkness of a hell for white folks only, when suddenly—

MISSY. Suddenly, Lord.

PURLIE. Suddenly I put on my brakes —Purlie Victorious Judson stopped dead in his tracks—and stood stark still, and planted his feet, and rared back, asked himself and all the powers—that—be some mighty important questions.

LUTIEBELLE. Yes, he did, Lawd.

MISSY. And that is the truth!

PURLIE. How come—I asked myself, it's always the colored folks got to do all the forgiving?

GITLOW. Man, you mighty right!

PURLIE. How come the only cheek gits turned in this country is the Negro cheek!

MISSY. Preach to me, boy!

PURLIE. What was this, this—man— Ol' Cap'n Cotchipee—that in spite of all his sins and evils, he still had dominion over me?

LUTIEBELLE. Ain't that the truth!

PURLIE. God made us all equal—God made us all brothers—

ALL. Amen, amen.

PURLIE. "And hath made of one blood all nations of men for to dwell on the face of the earth."—Who changed all that?

GITLOW. (Furious.) Who changed it, he said.

PURLIE. Who took it and twisted it around!

MISSY. (Furious.) Who was it, he said!

LUTIEBELLE. (Furious.) And where's that scoun' hiding?!

PURLIE. So that the Declarator of Independence himself might seem to be a liar?

GITLOW. Who, that's what I want to know, who?

PURLIE. That a man the color of his face—(Pointing up Cotchipee Hill.) could live by the sweat of a man the color of mine!

LUTIEBELLE. Work with him, Lawd, work with him!

PURLIE. —Could live away up there in his fine, white mansion, and us down here in a shack not fitting to house the fleas upon his dogs!

GITLOW. Nothing but fleas!

PURLIE. —Could wax hisself fat on the fat of the land; steaks, rice, chicken, roastineers, sweet potato pies, hot buttered biscuits and cane syrup anytime he felt like it and never hit a lick at a snake! And us got to every day git-up-and-git-with-it, sunup-to-sundown, on fatback and cornmeal hoecakes—and don't wind up owning enough ground to get buried standing up in!

MISSY. Do, Lord!

PURLIE. —And horses and cadillacs, bull whips and bourbon, and two for 'leven dollar seegars—and our fine young men to serve at his table; and our fine young women to serve in his bed!

LUTIEBELLE. Help him, Lawd.

PURLIE. Who made it like this—who put the white man on top?

GITLOW. That's what I wants to know!

PURLIE. Surely not the Lord God of Israel who is a just God!

MISSY. Hah, Lord!

PURLIE. And no respecter of persons! Who proved in the American Revolution that all men are created equal!

GITLOW. Man, I was there when he proved it!

PURLIE. Endowed with Civil Rights and First Class Citizenship, Ku Klux Klan, White Citizens Council notwithstanding!

MISSY. Oh, yes, he did!

PURLIE. And when my mind commenced to commemorate and to reconsider all these things—

GITLOW. Watch him, Lawd!

PURLIE. And I thought of the black mother in bondage—(Yes.) and I thought of the black father in prison—(Ha, Lawd!) And of Momma herself—Missy can tell how pretty she was—

MISSY. Indeed I can!

PURLIE. How she died outdoors on a dirty sheet cause the hospital doors said—

"For white folks only." And of Papa, God rest his soul—who brought her tender loving body back home—and laid her to sleep in the graveyard—and cried himself to death among his children!

MISSY. *(Crying.)* Purlie, Purlie—

PURLIE. *(Really carried away.)* Then did the wrath of a righteous God possess me; and the strength of the host and of ten thousand swept into my good right arm—and I arose and smote Ol' Cap'n a mighty blow! And the wind from my fist ripped the curtains from the eastern walls—and I felt the weight of his ol' bull whip nestling in my hands—and the fury of a good Gawd-almighty was within me; and I beat him—I whipped him—and I flogged him—and I cut him—I destroyed him!

(IDELLA enters.)

GITLOW. Great day and the righteous marching—Whoeeeee! Man, I ain't been stirred that deep since the tree caught fire on a possum hunt and the dogs pushed Papa in the pot.

MISSY. Idella, you shoulda heard him!

IDELLA. I did hear him—all the way across the valley. I thought he was calling hogs. Well, anyway; all hell is broke loose at the big house. Purlie, you better get outta here. Ol' Cap'n is on the phone to the sheriff.

MISSY. Ol' Cap'n Cotchipee is dead.

IDELLA. The hell you preach.

ALL. What!

IDELLA. Ol' Cap'n ain't no more dead than I am.

LUTIEBELLE. That's a mighty tacky thing to say about your ex-fellow man.

MISSY. Mighty tacky.

LUTIEBELLE. Reb'n Purlie just got through preaching 'bout it. How he marched up Cotchipee hill—

GITLOW. *(Showing the bull whip.)* And took Ol' Cap'n by the bull whip—

MISSY. And beat that ol' buzzard to death!

IDELLA. That is the biggest lie since the devil learned to talk!

LUTIEBELLE. I am not leaving this room till somebody apologizes to Reb'n Purlie V. Judson, the gentleman of my intended.

IDELLA. Purlie Judson! Are you gonna stand there sitting on your behind, and preach these people into believing you spent the night up at the big house whipping Ol' Cap'n to death when all the time you was breaking into the commissary!

MISSY. Breaking into the commissary!

GITLOW. Something is rotten in the cotton!

PURLIE. It's all right, Miz Idella—I'll take it from there—

MISSY. It is not all right!

PURLIE. While it is true that, maybe, I did not go up that hill just word for word, and call that ol' man out, and beat him to death so much on the dotted line—

MISSY. *(Snatching up the paper bag.)* I'm goin' to take back my lunch!

PURLIE. Missy! Wait a minute!

LUTIEBELLE. You know what, Aunt Missy?

MISSY. Yes, honey?

LUTIEBELLE. Sometimes I just wish I could drop dead for a while!

PURLIE. Wait, Lutiebelle, give me a chance to—

LUTIEBELLE. Here's your money! *(Puts roll into PURLIE's hand.)* And that goes for every other big ol' handsome man in the whole world!

PURLIE. What you want me to do? Go up that hill by myself and get my brains knocked out?

MISSY. It's little enough for the woman you love!

LUTIEBELLE. Why'd you have to preach all them wonderful things that wasn't so?

GITLOW. And why'd you have to go and change your mind?

PURLIE. I didn't mean for them not to be so: it was a—a parable! A prophecy! Believe me! I ain't never in all my life told a lie I didn't mean to make come true, some day! Lutiebelle!

IDELLA. Purlie: unless you want to give heartbreak a headache, you better run!

PURLIE. Run—run for what!

MISSY. You want Ol' Cap'n to catch you here!?

PURLIE. Confound Ol' Cap'n! Dadblast Ol' Cap'n! Damn, damn, damn, and double-damn Ol' Cap'n!

(The front door swings open and in walks OL' CAP'N *steaming with anger.)*

OL' CAP'N. *(Controlling himself with great difficulty.)* Somebody—I say somebody—is calling my name!

GITLOW. Ol' Cap'n, you just in time to settle a argument: is Rudolph Valentino still dead?

OL' CAP'N. Shut up!

GITLOW. *(To* MISSY.*)* See—I told you.

OL' CAP'N. One thing I have not allowed in my cotton patch since am-I-born-to-die! And that's stealin'! Somebody broke into my commissary tonight—took two cans of sardines, a box of soda crackers, my bull whip!—*(Picks up whip from table.)* and five hundred dollars in cash. And, boy—*(Walking over to* PURLIE.*)* I want it back!

LUTIEBELLE. Stealing ain't all that black and white.

MISSY. And we certainly wasn't the ones that started it!

GITLOW. Who stole me from Africa in the first place?

LUTIEBELLE. Who kept me in slavery from 1619 to 1863, working me to the bone without no social security?

PURLIE. And tonight—just because I went up that hill, and disembezzled my own inheritance that you stole from me—!

OL' CAP'N. *(Livid.)* I have had my belly full of your black African sass—!

(The door bursts open again; this time it is the SHERIFF *who comes in with pistol drawn.)*

SHERIFF. All right, everybody, drop that gun!

PURLIE. Drop what gun?

OL' CAP'N. So there you are, you idiot—what kept you so long?

SHERIFF. Like you told us to do on the phone, suh, we was taking a good, long, slow snoop 'round and 'bout the commissary looking for clues! And doggone if one didn't, just a short while ago, stumble smack into our hands!

OL' CAP'N. What!

SHERIFF. We caught the culprit redhanded—bring in the prisoner, Dep!

DEPUTY. Glad to oblige you, Sheriff.

(Enter DEPUTY, *dragging* CHARLIE, *who has his hands cuffed behind him; wears heavy leg shackles, and has a large white gag stuck into his mouth.)*

SHERIFF. Southern justice strikes again!

OL' CAP'N. Charlie!—oh, no!

IDELLA. Charlie, my baby!

OL' CAP'N. Release him, you idiots! Release him at once!

*(*EVERYBODY *pitches in to set* CHARLIE *free.)*

What have they done to you, my boy?

IDELLA. What have they done to you!

CHARLIE. *(Free from the gag.)* Hello, Paw—Idella—Purlie—

OL' CAP'N. I'll have your thick, stupid necks for this!

SHERIFF. It was you give the orders, suh!

OL' CAP'N. Not my son, you idiot!

DEPUTY. It was him broke into the commissary.

OL' CAP'N. What!

SHERIFF. It was him stole the five hundred dollars—he confessed!

OL' CAP'N. Steal? A Cotchipee? Suh, that is biologically impossible! *(To* CHARLIE.*)* Charlie, my boy. Tell them the truth—tell them who stole the money. It was Purlie, wasn't it, boy?

CHARLIE. Well, as a matter of fact, Paw

—it was mostly me that broke in and took the money, I'd say. In fact it WAS me!

OL' CAP'N. No!

CHARLIE. It was the only thing I could do to save your life, Paw.

OL' CAP'N. Save my life! Idella, he's delirious!

CHARLIE. When Purlie come up that hill after you last night, I seen him, and lucky for you I did. The look he had on his face against you was not a Christian thing to behold! It was terrible! I had to get into that commissary, right then and there, open that safe, and pay him his inheritance—even then I had to beg him to spare your life!

OL' CAP'N. *(To* PURLIE.*)* You spare my life, boy? How dare you? *(To* CHARLIE.*)* Charlie, my son, I know you never recovered from the shock of losing your mother—almost before you were born. But don't worry—it was Purlie who stole that money and I'm going to prove it. *(Starts to take out gun.* GITLOW *grabs gun.)* Gitlow, my old friend, arrest this boy, Gitlow! As Deputy-For-The-Colored —I order you to arrest this boy for stealing!

GITLOW. *(With a brand new meaning.)* "Gone are the days—" *(Still twirls pistol safely out of* OL' CAP'N'*s reach.)*

PURLIE. "Stealin," is it? Well, I'm gonna really give you something to arrest me for. *(Snatches bull whip.)*

OL' CAP'N. Have a care, boy: I'm still a white man.

PURLIE. Congratulations! Twenty years ago, I told you this bull whip was gonna change hands one of these days!

MISSY. Purlie, wait!

PURLIE. Stay out of my struggle for power!

MISSY. You can't do wrong just because it's right!

GITLOW. Never kick a man when he's down except in self-defense!

LUTIEBELLE. And no matter what you are, and always will be—the hero of Cotchipee Hill.

PURLIE. Am I?

LUTIEBELLE. Ten thousand queens!

PURLIE. I bow to the will of the Negro people. *(Throws whip away. Back to* OL' CAP'N.*)* But one thing, Ol' Cap'n, I am released of you—the entire Negro people is released of you! No more shouting hallelujah! every time you sneeze, nor jumping jackass every time you whistle "Dixie"! We gonna love you if you let us and laugh as we leave if you don't. We want our cut of the Constitution, and we want it now: and not with no teaspoon, white folks—throw it at us with a shovel!

OL' CAP'N. Charlie, my boy—my own, lily-white, Anglo-Saxon, semi-confederate son. I know you never recovered from the shock of losing your mother, almost before you were born. But don't worry: there is still time to take these insolent, messy cotton-picking ingrates down a peg —and prove by word and deed that God is still a white man. Tell 'em! Boy, tell em!

CHARLIE. Tell 'em what, Paw?

OL' CAP'N. Tell 'em what you and me have done together. Nobody here would believe me. Tell 'em how you went to Waycross, Saturday night, in my name—

CHARLIE. Yes, sir—I did.

OL' CAP'N. Tell 'em how you spoke to Ol' Man Pelham in my name—

CHARLIE. Yes, sir—I spoke to him.

OL' CAP'N. And paid him cash for that ol' barn they used to call Big Bethel!

CHARLIE. Yes, sir; that's what I did, all right.

OL' CAP'N. And to register the deed in the courthouse in my name—

CHARLIE. Yes, sir, that's exactly what you told me to do—

OL' CAP'N. Then—ain't but one thing left to do with that ramshackle dung-soaked monstrosity—that's burn the damn thing down. *(Laughs aloud in his triumph.)*

CHARLIE. But, Paw—

OL' CAP'N. First thing, though—let me see the deed: I wouldn't want to destroy nothing that didn't—legally—belong to me. *(Snatches deed from CHARLIE's hand. Begins to mumble as he reads it.)*

IDELLA. Twenty years of being more than a mother to you!

CHARLIE. Wait, Idella, wait. I did go to Waycross, like Paw said; I did buy the barn—excuse me, Purlie: the church—like he said; and I registered the deed at the courthouse like he told me—but not in Paw's name—

OL' CAP'N. *(Startled by something he sees on the deed.)* What's this?

CHARLIE. *(To IDELLA.)* I registered the deed in the name of—

OL' CAP'N. *(Reading, incredulous.)* "Purlie Victorious Judson—" No!

IDELLA. PURLIE VICTORIOUS Judson?

OL' CAP'N. *(Choking on the words.)* Purlie Victorious Judsssss—aaaarrrrggggghhhhh! *(The horror of it strikes him absolutely still.)*

CHARLIE. *(Taking the deed from OL' CAP'N's limp hand.)* It was the only thing I could do to save your life. *(Offering deed to PURLIE.)* Well, Purlie, here it is.

PURLIE. *(Counting out the five hundred dollars.)* You did a good job, Charlie—I'm much obliged!

CHARLIE. *(Refuses money; still holds out deeds to PURLIE.)* Thank you, Purlie, but—

PURLIE. Big Bethel is my Bethel, Charlie: it's my responsibility. Go on, take it.

CHARLIE. No, no! I couldn't take your money, Purlie—

IDELLA. Don't be a fool, boy—business is business. *(She takes the deed from CHARLIE and gives it to PURLIE, while at the same time taking the money from PURLIE.)*

CHARLIE. Idella—I can't do that!

IDELLA. I can! I'll keep it for you.

CHARLIE. Well—all right. But only, if —if—

IDELLA. Only if what?

CHARLIE. *(To PURLIE.)* Would you let me be a member of your church?

MISSY. You?

GITLOW. Li'l Charlie Cotchipee!

LUTIEBELLE. A member of Big Bethel?

CHARLIE. May I? That is—that is, if you don't mind—as soon as you get it started?

PURLIE. Man, we're already started: the doors of Big Bethel, Church of the New Freedom for all Mankind, are hereby declared "Open for business!"

GITLOW. Brother Pastor, I move we accept Brother Charlie Cotchipee as our first candidate for membership to Big Bethel on an integrated basis—

MISSY. I second that motion!

PURLIE. You have heard the motion. Are you ready for the question?

ALL. *(Except OL' CAP'N.)* Question!

PURLIE. Those in favor will signify by saying "Aye."

(EVERYBODY, except OL' CAP'N, crowds around CHARLIE, saying "Aye" over and over, in such a crescendo of welcome that PURLIE has to ride over the noise.)

Those opposed? *(Looks at OL' CAP'N, who is still standing, as if frozen, as we last saw him and who does not answer.)* Those opposed will signify by saying—

(He stops . . . all eyes focus on OL' CAP'N now, still standing in quiet, frozen-like immobility. There is a moment of silence, an unspoken suspicion in everybody's face. Finally, GITLOW goes over and touches OL' CAP'N, still standing rigid. Still he does not move. GITLOW feels his pulse, listens to his heart, and lifts up his eyelids. Nothing.)

GITLOW. The first man I ever seen in all this world to drop dead standing up!

BLACKOUT

ACT THREE

EPILOGUE

TIME:

Immediately following.

SCENE:

We are at Big Bethel at funeral services for OL' CAP'N.

AT RISE:

We cannot see the coffin. We hear the ringing of the CHURCH BELL as we come out of the BLACKOUT. PURLIE *is in the pulpit.*

PURLIE. And toll the bell, Big Bethel, toll the bell! Dearly beloved, recently bereaved, and friends, we welcome you to Big Bethel, Church of the New Freedom: part Baptist; part Methodist; part Catholic—with the merriness of Christmas and the happiness of Hanukkah; and to the first integrated funeral in the sovereign, segregated state of Georgia. Let there be no merriments in these buryments! Though you are dead, Ol' Cap'n, and in hell, I suspect—as post-mortal guest of honor, at our expense: it is not too late to repent. We still need togetherness; we still need each otherness—with faith in the futureness of our cause. Let us, therefore, stifle the rifle of conflict, shatter the scatter of discord, smuggle the struggle, tickle the pickle, and grapple the apple of peace!

GITLOW. This funeral has been brought to you as a public service.

PURLIE. Take up his bones. For he who was my skin's enemy, was brave enough to die standing for what he believed. . . . And it is the wish of his fam-ily—and his friends—that he be buried likewise—

(The PALLBEARERS *enter, carrying* OL' CAP'N'S *ornate coffin just as he would have wished: standing up! It is draped in a Confederate flag; and his hat, his bull whip, and his pistol, have been fastened to the lid in appropriate places.)*

Gently, gently. Put kindness in your fingers. He was a man—despite his own example. Take up his bones.

(The PALLBEARERS *slowly carry the upright coffin across the stage.)*

Tonight, my friends—I find, in being black, a thing of beauty: a joy; a strength; a secret cup of gladness; a native land in neither time nor place—a native land in every Negro face! Be loyal to yourselves: your skin; your hair; your lips, your southern speech, your laughing kindness —are Negro kingdoms, vast as any other! Accept in full the sweetness of your blackness—not wishing to be red, nor white, nor yellow: nor any other race, or face, but this. Farewell, my deep and Africanic brothers, be brave, keep freedom in the family, do what you can for the white folks, and write me in care of the post office. Now, may the Constitution of the United States go with you; the Declaration of Independence stand by you; the Bill of Rights protect you; and the State Commission Against Discrimination keep the eyes of the law upon you, henceforth, now and forever. Amen.

CURTAIN

LeRoi Jones

Dutchman

DUTCHMAN

Dutchman was first presented at the Cherry Lane Theater, New York City, on March 24, 1964.

CHARACTERS

CLAY, twenty-year-old Negro
LULA, thirty-year-old white woman
RIDERS OF COACH, white and black
YOUNG NEGRO
CONDUCTOR

In the flying underbelly of the city. Steaming hot, and summer on top, outside. Underground. The subway heaped in modern myth.

Opening scene is a MAN sitting in a subway seat, holding a magazine but looking vacantly just above its wilting pages. Occasionally he looks blankly toward the window on his right. Dim lights and darkness whistling by against the glass. (Or paste the lights, as admitted props, right on the subway windows. Have them move, even dim and flicker. But give the sense of speed. Also stations, whether the train is stopped or the glitter and activity of these stations merely flashes by the windows.)

The MAN is sitting alone. That is, only his seat is visible, though the rest of the car is outfitted as a complete subway car. But only his seat is shown. There might be, for a time, as the play begins, a loud scream of the actual train. And it can recur throughout the play, or continue on a lower key once the dialogue starts.

The train slows after a time, pulling to a brief stop at one of the stations. The MAN looks idly up, until he sees a WOMAN's face staring at him through the window; when it realizes that the man has noticed the face, it begins very premeditatedly to smile. The MAN smiles too, for a moment, without a trace of self-consciousness. Almost an instinctive though undesirable response. Then a kind of awkwardness or embarrassment sets in, and the MAN makes to look away, is further embarrassed, so he brings back his eyes to where the face was, but by now the train is moving again, and the face would seem to be left behind by the way the MAN turns his head to look back through the other windows at the slowly fading platform. He smiles then; more comfortably confident, hoping perhaps that his memory of this brief encounter will be pleasant. And then he is idle again.

SCENE 1

Train roars. Lights flash outside the windows.

LULA *enters from the rear of the car in bright, skimpy summer clothes and sandals. She carries a net bag full of paper books, fruit and other anonymous articles. She is wearing sunglasses, which she pushes up on her forehead from time to time.* LULA *is a tall, slender, beautiful woman with long red hair hanging straight down her back, wearing only loud lipstick in somebody's good taste. She is eating an apple, very daintily. Coming down the car toward* CLAY.

She stops beside CLAY's *seat and hangs languidly from the strap, still managing to eat the apple. It is apparent that she is going to sit in the seat next to* CLAY, *and that she is only waiting for him to notice her before she sits.*

CLAY *sits as before, looking just beyond his magazine, now and again pulling the magazine back and forth in front of his face in a hopeless effort to fan himself. Then he sees the woman hanging there beside him and he looks up into her face, smiling quizzically.*

LULA. Hello.

CLAY. Uh, hi're you?

LULA. I'm going to sit down. . . . O.K.?

CLAY. Sure.

LULA. *(Swings down onto the seat, pushing her legs straight out as if she is very weary.)* Oooof! Too much weight.

CLAY. Ha, doesn't look like much to me. *(Leaning back against the window, a little surprised and maybe stiff.)*

LULA. It's so anyway. *(And she moves her toes in the sandals, then pulls her right leg up on the left knee, better to inspect the bottoms of the sandals and the back of her heel. She appears for a second not to notice that CLAY is sitting next to her or that she has spoken to him just a second before.)*

(CLAY looks at the magazine, then out the black windows. As he does this, she turns very quickly toward him.)

Weren't you staring at me through the window?

CLAY. *(Wheeling around and very much stiffened.)* What?

LULA. Weren't you staring at me through the window? At the last stop?

CLAY. Staring at you? What do you mean?

LULA. Don't you know what staring means?

CLAY. I saw you through the window . . . if that's what it means. I don't know if I was staring. Seems to me you were staring through the window at me.

LULA. I was. But only after I'd turned around and saw you staring through that window down in the vicinity of my ass and legs.

CLAY. Really?

LULA. Really. I guess you were just taking those idle potshots. Nothing else to

do. Run your mind over people's flesh.

CLAY. Oh boy. Wow, now I admit I was looking in your direction. But the rest of that weight is yours.

LULA. I suppose.

CLAY. Staring through train windows is weird business. Much weirder than staring very sedately at abstract asses.

LULA. That's why I came looking through the window . . . so you'd have more than that to go on. I even smiled at you.

CLAY. That's right.

LULA. I even got into this train, going some other way than mine. Walked down the aisle . . . searching you out.

CLAY. Really? That's pretty funny.

LULA. That's pretty funny. . . . God, you're dull.

CLAY. Well, I'm sorry, lady, but I really wasn't prepared for party talk.

LULA. No, you're not. What are you prepared for? *(Wrapping the apple core in a Kleenex and dropping it on the floor.)*

CLAY. *(Takes her conversation as pure sex talk. He turns to confront her squarely with this idea.)* I'm prepared for anything. How about you?

LULA. *(Laughing loudly and cutting it off abruptly.)* What do you think you're doing?

CLAY. What?

LULA. You think I want to pick you up, get you to take me somewhere and screw me, huh?

CLAY. Is that the way I look?

LULA. You look like you been trying to grow a beard. That's exactly what you look like. You look like you live in New Jersey with your parents and are trying to grow a beard. That's what. You look like you've been reading Chinese poetry and drinking lukewarm sugarless tea. *(Laughs, uncrossing and recrossing her legs.)* You look like death eating a soda cracker.

CLAY. *(Cocking his head from one side*

to the other, embarrassed and trying to make some comeback, but also intrigued by what the woman is saying . . . even the sharp city coarseness of her voice, which is still a kind of gentle sidewalk throb.) Really? I look like all that?

LULA. Not all of it. *(She feints a seriousness to cover an actual somber tone.)* I lie a lot. *(Smiling.)* It helps me control the world.

CLAY. *(Relieved and laughing louder than the humor.)* Yeah, I bet.

LULA. But it's true, most of it, right? Jersey? Your bumpy neck?

CLAY. How'd you know all that? Huh? Really, I mean about Jersey . . . and even the beard. I met you before? You know Warren Enright?

LULA. You tried to make it with your sister when you were ten.

(CLAY leans back hard against the back of the seat, his eyes opening now, still trying to look amused.)

But I succeeded a few weeks ago. *(She starts to laugh again.)*

CLAY. What're you talking about? Warren tell you that? You're a friend of Georgia's?

LULA. I told you I lie. I don't know your sister. I don't know Warren Enright.

CLAY. You mean you're just picking these things out of the air?

LULA. Is Warren Enright a tall skinny black black boy with a phony English accent?

CLAY. I figured you knew him.

LULA. But I don't. I just figured you would know somebody like that. *(Laughs.)*

CLAY. Yeah, yeah.

LULA. You're probably on your way to his house now.

CLAY. That's right.

LULA. *(Putting her hand on CLAY's closest knee, drawing it from the knee up to the thigh's hinge, then removing it, watching his face very closely, and continuing to laugh, perhaps more gently than before.)* Dull, dull, dull. I bet you think I'm exciting.

CLAY. You're O.K.

LULA. Am I exciting you now?

CLAY. Right. That's not what's supposed to happen?

LULA. How do I know? *(She returns her hand, without moving it, then takes it away and plunges it in her bag to draw out an apple.)* You want this?

CLAY. Sure.

LULA. *(She gets one out of the bag for herself.)* Eating apples together is always the first step. Or walking up inhabited Seventh Avenue in the twenties on weekends. *(Bites and giggles, glancing at CLAY and speaking in loose sing-song.)* Can get you involved . . . boy! Get us involved. Um-huh. *(Mock seriousness.)* Would you like to get involved with me, Mister Man?

CLAY. *(Trying to be as flippant as LULA, whacking happily at the apple.)* Sure. Why not? A beautiful woman like you. Huh, I'd be a fool not to.

LULA. And I bet you're sure you know what you're talking about. *(Taking him a little roughly by the wrist, so he cannot eat the apple, then shaking the wrist.)* I bet you're sure of almost everything anybody ever asked you about . . . right? *(Shakes his wrist harder.)* Right?

CLAY. Yeah, right. . . . Wow, you're pretty strong, you know? Whatta you, a lady wrestler or something?

LULA. What's wrong with lady wrestlers? And don't answer because you never knew any. Huh. *(Cynically.)* That's for sure. They don't have any lady wrestlers in that part of Jersey. That's for sure.

CLAY. Hey, you still haven't told me how you know so much about me.

LULA. I told you I didn't know anything about *you* . . . you're a well-known type.

CLAY. Really?

LULA. Or at least I know the type very well. And your skinny English friend too.

CLAY. Anonymously?

LULA. *(Settles back in seat, single-mind-edly finishing her apple and humming snatches of rhythm and blues song.)* What?

CLAY. Without knowing us specifically?

LULA. Oh boy. *(Looking quickly at CLAY.)* What a face. You know, you could be a handsome man.

CLAY. I can't argue with you.

LULA. *(Vague, off-center response.)* What?

CLAY. *(Raising his voice, thinking the train noise has drowned part of his sentence.)* I can't argue with you.

LULA. My hair is turning gray. A gray hair for each year and type I've come through.

CLAY. Why do you want to sound so old?

LULA. But it's always gentle when it starts. *(Attention drifting.)* Hugged against tenements, day or night.

CLAY. What?

LULA. *(Refocusing.)* Hey, why don't you take me to that party you're going to?

CLAY. You must be a friend of Warren's to know about the party.

LULA. Wouldn't you like to take me to the party? *(Imitates clinging vine.)* Oh, come on, ask me to your party.

CLAY. Of course I'll ask you to come with me to the party. And I'll bet you're a friend of Warren's.

LULA. Why not be a friend of Warren's? Why not? *(Taking his arm.)* Have you asked me yet?

CLAY. How can I ask you when I don't know your name?

LULA. Are you talking to my name?

CLAY. What is it, a secret?

LULA. I'm Lena the Hyena.

CLAY. The famous woman poet?

LULA. Poetess! The same!

CLAY. Well, you know so much about me . . . what's my name?

LULA. Morris the Hyena.

CLAY. The famous woman poet?

LULA. The same. *(Laughing and going into her bag.)* You want another apple?

CLAY. Can't make it, lady. I only have to keep one doctor away a day.

LULA. I bet your name is . . . something like . . . uh, Gerald or Walter. Huh?

CLAY. God, no.

LULA. Lloyd, Norman? One of those hopeless colored names creeping out of New Jersey. Leonard? Gag. . . .

CLAY. Like Warren?

LULA. Definitely. Just exactly like Warren. Or Everett.

CLAY. Gag. . . .

LULA. Well, for sure, it's not Willie.

CLAY. It's Clay.

LULA. Clay? Really? Clay what?

CLAY. Take your pick. Jackson, Johnson, or Williams.

LULA. Oh, really? Good for you. But it's got to be Williams. You're too pretentious to be a Jackson or Johnson.

CLAY. Thass right.

LULA. But Clay's O.K.

CLAY. So's Lena.

LULA. It's Lula.

CLAY. Oh?

LULA. Lula the Hyena.

CLAY. Very good.

LULA. *(Starts laughing again.)* Now you say to me, "Lula, Lula, why don't you go to this party with me tonight?" It's your turn, and let those be your lines.

CLAY. Lula, why don't you go to this party with me tonight, huh?

LULA. Say my name twice before you ask, and no huh's.

CLAY. Lula, Lula, why don't you go to this party with me tonight?

LULA. I'd like to go, Clay, but how can you ask me to go when you barely know me?

CLAY. That is strange, isn't it?

LULA. What kind of reaction is that? You're supposed to say, "Aw, come on, we'll get to know each other better at the party."

CLAY. That's pretty corny.

LULA. What are you into anyway?

(Looking at him half sullenly but still amused.) What thing are you playing at, Mister? Mister Clay Williams? *(Grabs his thigh, up near the crotch.)* What are *you* thinking about?

CLAY. Watch it now, you're gonna excite me for real.

LULA. *(Taking her hand away and throwing her apple core through the window.)* I bet. *(She slumps in the seat and is heavily silent.)*

CLAY. I thought you knew everything about me? What happened?

(LULA looks at him, then looks slowly away, then over where the other aisle would be. NOISE of the train. She reaches in her bag and pulls out one of the paper books. She puts it on her leg and thumbs the pages listlessly. CLAY cocks his head to see the title of the book. NOISE of the train. LULA flips pages and her eyes drift. Both remain silent.)

Are you going to the party with me, Lula?

LULA. *(Bored and not even looking.)* I don't even know you.

CLAY. You said you know my type.

LULA. *(Strangely irritated.)* Don't get smart with me, Buster. I know you like the palm of my hand.

CLAY. The one you eat the apples with?

LULA. Yeh. And the one I open doors late Saturday evening with. That's my door. Up at the top of the stairs. Five flights. Above a lot of Italians and lying Americans. And scrape carrots with. Also . . . *(Looks at him.)* the same hand I unbutton my dress with, or let my skirt fall down. Same hand. Lover.

CLAY. Are you angry about something? Did I say something wrong?

LULA. Everything you say is wrong. *(Mock smile.)* That's what makes you so attractive. Ha. In that funnybook jacket with all the buttons. *(More animate, taking hold of his jacket.)* What've you got that jacket and tie on in all this heat for? And why're you wearing a jacket and tie

like that? Did your people ever burn witches or start revolutions over the price of tea? Boy, those narrow-shoulder clothes come from a tradition you ought to feel oppressed by. A three-button suit. What right do you have to be wearing a three-button suit and striped tie? Your grandfather was a slave, he didn't go to Harvard.

CLAY. My grandfather was a night watchman.

LULA. And you went to a colored college where everybody thought they were Averell Harriman.

CLAY. All except me.

LULA. And who did you think you were? Who do you think you are now?

CLAY. *(Laughs as if to make light of the whole trend of the conversation.)* Well, in college I thought I was Baudelaire. But I've slowed down since.

LULA. I bet you never once thought you were a black nigger. *(Mock serious, then she howls with laughter.)*

(CLAY is stunned, but after initial reaction, he quickly tries to appreciate the humor.)

(LULA almost shrieks.) A black Baudelaire.

CLAY. That's right.

LULA. Boy, are you corny. I take back what I said before. Everything you say is not wrong. It's perfect. You should be on television.

CLAY. You act like you're on television already.

LULA. That's because I'm an actress.

CLAY. I thought so.

LULA. Well, you're wrong. I'm no actress. I told you I always lie. I'm nothing, honey, and don't you ever forget it. *(Lighter.)* Although my mother was a Communist. The only person in my family ever to amount to anything.

CLAY. My mother was a Republican.

LULA. And your father voted for the man rather than the party.

CLAY. Right!

LULA. Yea for him. Yea, yea for him.

CLAY. Yea!

LULA. And yea for America where he is free to vote for the mediocrity of his choice! Yea!

CLAY. Yea!

LULA. And yea for both your parents who even though they differ about so crucial a matter as the body politic still forged a union of love and sacrifice that was destined to flower at the birth of the noble Clay . . . what's your middle name?

CLAY. Clay.

LULA. A union of love and sacrifice that was destined to flower at the birth of the noble Clay Clay Williams. Yea! And most of all yea yea for you, Clay Clay. The Black Baudelaire! Yes! (And with knifelike cynicism.) My Christ. My Christ.

CLAY. Thank you, ma'am.

LULA. May the people accept you as a ghost of the future. And love you, that you might not kill them when you can.

CLAY. What?

LULA. You're a murderer, Clay, and you know it. (Her voice darkening with significance.) You know goddamn well what I mean.

CLAY. I do?

LULA. So we'll pretend the air is light and full of perfume.

CLAY. (Sniffing at her blouse.) It is.

LULA. And we'll pretend the people cannot see you. That is, the citizens. And that you are free of your own history. And I am free of my history. We'll pretend that we are both anonymous beauties smashing along through the city's entrails. (She yells as loud as she can.) GROOVE!

BLACK

SCENE 2

Scene is the same as before, though now there are other seats visible in the car. And throughout the scene OTHER PEOPLE get on the subway. There are maybe one or two seated in the car as the scene opens, though neither CLAY nor LULA notices them. CLAY's tie is open. LULA is hugging his arm.

CLAY. The party!

LULA. I know it'll be something good. You can come in with me, looking casual and significant. I'll be strange, haughty, and silent, and walk with long slow strides.

CLAY. Right.

LULA. When you get drunk, pat me once, very lovingly on the flanks, and I'll look at you cryptically, licking my lips.

CLAY. It sounds like something we can do.

LULA. You'll go around talking to young men about your mind, and to old men about your plans. If you meet a very close friend who is also with someone like me, we can stand together, sipping our drinks and exchanging codes of lust. The atmosphere will be slithering in love and half-love and very open moral decision.

CLAY. Great. Great.

LULA. And everyone will pretend they don't know your name, and then . . . (She pauses heavily.) later, when they have to, they'll claim a friendship that denies your sterling character.

CLAY. (Kissing her neck and fingers.) And then what?

LULA. Then? Well, then we'll go down the street, late night, eating apples and winding very deliberately toward my house.

CLAY. Deliberately?

LULA. I mean, we'll look in all the shopwindows, and make fun of the queers. Maybe we'll meet a Jewish Buddhist and flatten his conceits over some very pretentious coffee.

CLAY. In honor of whose God?

LULA. Mine.

CLAY. Who is . . . ?

LULA. Me . . . and you?

CLAY. A corporate Godhead.

LULA. Exactly. Exactly. (Notices one of the other people entering.)

CLAY. Go on with the chronicle. Then what happens to us?

LULA. (A mild depression, but she still makes her description triumphant and increasingly direct.) To my house, of course.

CLAY. Of course.

LULA. And up the narrow steps of the tenement.

CLAY. You live in a tenement?

LULA. Wouldn't live anywhere else. Reminds me specifically of my novel form of insanity.

CLAY. Up the tenement stairs.

LULA. And with my apple-eating hand I push open the door and lead you, my tender big-eyed prey, into my . . . God, what can I call it . . . into my hovel.

CLAY. Then what happens?

LULA. After the dancing and games, after the long drinks and long walks, the real fun begins.

CLAY. Ah, the real fun. (Embarrassed, in spite of himself.) Which is . . . ?

LULA. (Laughs at him.) Real fun in the dark house. Hah! Real fun in the dark house, high up above the street and the ignorant cowboys. I lead you in, holding your wet hand gently in my hand . . .

CLAY. Which is not wet?

LULA. Which is dry as ashes.

CLAY. And cold?

LULA. Don't think you'll get out of your responsibility that way. It's not cold at all. You Fascist! Into my dark living room. Where we'll sit and talk endlessly, endlessly.

CLAY. About what?

LULA. About what? About your manhood, what do you think? What do you think we've been talking time?

CLAY. Well, I didn't know it wa That's for sure. Every other thing in world but that. (Notices ANOTHER PERSON entering, looks quickly, almost involuntarily up and down the car, seeing the OTHER PEOPLE in the car.) Hey, I didn't even notice when those people got on.

LULA. Yeah, I know.

CLAY. Man, this subway is slow.

LULA. Yeah, I know.

CLAY. Well, go on. We were talking about my manhood.

LULA. We still are. All the time.

CLAY. We were in your living room.

LULA. My dark living room. Talking endlessly.

CLAY. About my manhood.

LULA. I'll make you a map of it. Just as soon as we get to my house.

CLAY. Well, that's great.

LULA. One of the things we do while we talk. And screw.

CLAY. (Trying to make his smile broader and less shaky.) We finally got there.

LULA. And you'll call my rooms black as a grave. You'll say, "This place is like Juliet's tomb."

CLAY. (Laughs.) I might.

LULA. I know. You've probably said it before.

CLAY. And is that all? The whole grand tour?

LULA. Not all. You'll say to me very close to my face, many, many times, you'll say, even whisper, that you love me.

CLAY. Maybe I will.

LULA. And you'll be lying.

CLAY. I wouldn't lie about something like that.

LULA. Hah. It's the only kind of thing you will lie about. Especially if you think it'll keep me alive.

CLAY. Keep you alive? I don't understand.

LULA. (Bursting out laughing, but too shrilly.) Don't understand? Well, don't look at me. It's the path I take, that's all. Where both feet take me when I set them down. One in front of the other.

CLAY. Morbid. Morbid. You sure you're not an actress? All that self-aggrandizement.

LULA. Well, I told you I wasn't an actress . . . but I also told you I lie all the time. Draw your own conclusions.

CLAY. Morbid. Morbid. You sure you're not an actress? All scribed? There's no more?

LULA. I've told you all I know. Or almost all.

CLAY. There's no funny parts?

LULA. I thought it was all funny.

CLAY. But you mean peculiar, not ha-ha.

LULA. You don't know what I mean.

CLAY. Well, tell me the almost part then. You said almost all. What else? I want the whole story.

LULA. (Searching aimlessly through her bag. She begins to talk breathlessly, with a light and silly tone.) All stories are whole stories. All of 'em. Our whole story . . . nothing but change. How could things go on like that forever? Huh? (Slaps him on the shoulder, begins finding things in her bag, taking them out and throwing them over her shoulder into the aisle.) Except I do go on as I do. Apples and long walks with deathless intelligent lovers. But you mix it up. Look out the window, all the time. Turning pages. Change change change. Till, shit, I don't know you. Wouldn't, for that matter. You're too serious. I bet you're even too serious to be psychoanalyzed. Like all those Jewish poets from Yonkers, who leave their mothers looking for other mothers, or others' mothers, on whose baggy tits they lay their fumbling heads. Their poems are always funny, and all about sex.

CLAY. They sound great. Like movies.

LULA. But you change. (Blankly.) And things work on you till you hate them.

(MORE PEOPLE come into the train. They come closer to the couple, some of them not sitting, but swinging drearily on the straps, staring at the two with uncertain interest.)

CLAY. Wow. All these people, so suddenly. They must all come from the same place.

LULA. Right. That they do.

CLAY. Oh? You know about them too?

LULA. Oh yeah. About them more than I know about you. Do they frighten you?

CLAY. Frighten me? Why should they frighten me?

LULA. 'Cause you're an escaped nigger.

CLAY. Yeah?

LULA. 'Cause you crawled through the wire and made tracks to my side.

CLAY. Wire?

LULA. Don't they have wire around plantations?

CLAY. You must be Jewish. All you can think about is wire. Plantations didn't have any wire. Plantations were big open whitewashed places like heaven, and everybody on 'em was grooved to be there. Just strummin' and hummin' all day.

LULA. Yes, yes.

CLAY. And that's how the blues was born.

LULA. Yes, yes. And that's how the blues was born. (Begins to make up a song that becomes quickly hysterical. As she sings she rises from her seat, still throwing things out of her bag into the aisle, beginning a rhythmical shudder and twistlike wiggle, which she continues up and down the aisle, bumping into many of the standing people and tripping over the feet of those sitting. Each time she runs into a person she lets out a very vicious piece of profanity, wiggling and stepping all the time.) And that's how the blues was born. Yes. Yes. Son of a bitch, get out of the way. Yes. Quack. Yes. Yes.

And that's how the blues was born. Ten little niggers sitting on a limb, but none of them ever looked like him. *(Points to* CLAY, *returns toward the seat, with her hands extended for him to rise and dance with her.)* And that's how blues was born. Yes. Come on, Clay. Let's do the nasty. Rub bellies. Rub bellies.

CLAY. *(Waves his hands to refuse. He is embarrassed, but determined to get a kick out of the proceedings.)* Hey, what was in those apples? Mirror, mirror on the wall, who's the fairest one of all? Snow White, baby, and don't you forget it.

LULA. *(Grabbing for his hands, which he draws away.)* Come on, Clay. Let's rub bellies on the train. The nasty. The nasty. Do the gritty grind, like your ol' rag-head mammy. Grind till you lose your mind. Shake it, shake it, shake it, shake it! OOOOweeee! Come on, Clay. Let's do the choo-choo train shuffle, the navel scratcher.

CLAY. Hey, you coming on like the lady who smoked up her grass skirt.

LULA. *(Becoming annoyed that he will not dance, and becoming more animated as if to embarrass him still further.)* Come on, Clay . . . let's do the thing. Uhh! Uhh! Clay! Clay! You middle-class black bastard. Forget your social-working mother for a few seconds and let's knock stomachs. Clay, you liver-lipped white man. You would-be Christian. You ain't no nigger, you're just a dirty white man. Get up, Clay. Dance with me, Clay.

CLAY. Lula! Sit down, now. Be cool.

LULA. *(Mocking him, in wild dance.)* Be cool. Be cool. That's all you know . . . shaking that wildroot cream-oil on your knotty head, jackets buttoning up to your chin, so full of white man's words. Christ. God. Get up and scream at these people. Like scream meaningless shit in these hopeless faces. *(She screams at* PEOPLE *in train, still dancing.)* Red trains cough Jewish underwear for keeps! Expanding smells of silence. Gravy snot whistling like sea birds. Clay. Clay, you got to break out. Don't sit there dying the way they want you to die. Get up.

CLAY. Oh, sit the fuck down. *(He moves to restrain her.)* Sit down, goddamn it.

LULA. *(Twisting out of his reach.)* Screw yourself, Uncle Tom. Thomas Woolly-head. *(Begins to dance a kind of jig, mocking* CLAY *with loud forced humor.)* There is Uncle Tom . . . I mean, Uncle Thomas Woolly-Head. With old white matted mane. He hobbles on his wooden cane. Old Tom. Old Tom. Let the white man hump his ol' mama, and he jes' shuffle off in the woods and hide his gentle gray head. Ol' Thomas Woolly-Head.

(Some of the other riders are laughing now. A DRUNK *gets up and joins* LULA *in her dance, singing, as best he can, her "song."* CLAY *gets up out of his seat and visibly scans the faces of the other riders.)*

CLAY. Lula! Lula!

(She is dancing and turning, still shouting as loud as she can. The DRUNK *too is shouting, and waving his hands wildly.)*

Lula . . . you dumb bitch. Why don't you stop it? *(He rushes half stumbling from his seat, and grabs one of her flailing arms.)*

LULA. Let me go! You black son of a bitch. *(She struggles against him.)* Let me go! Help!

*(*CLAY *is dragging her towards her seat, and the* DRUNK *seeks to interfere. He grabs* CLAY *around the shoulders and begins wrestling with him.* CLAY *clubs the* DRUNK *to the floor without releasing* LULA, *who is still screaming.* CLAY *finally gets her to the seat and throws her into it.)*

CLAY. Now you shut the hell up. *(Grabbing her shoulders.)* Just shut up! You don't know what you're talking about. You don't know anything. So just keep your stupid mouth closed.

LULA. You're afraid of white people. And your father was. Uncle Tom Big Lip!

CLAY. *(Slaps her as hard as he can, across the mouth.* LULA's *head bangs against the back of the seat. When she raises it again,* CLAY *slaps her again.)* Now shut up and let me talk. *(He turns toward the* OTHER RIDERS, *some of whom are sitting on the edge of their seats.)*

(The DRUNK *is on one knee, rubbing his head, and singing softly the same song. He shuts up too when he sees* CLAY *watching him. The others go back to newspapers or stare out the windows.)*

Shit, you don't have any sense, Lula, nor feelings either. I could murder you now. Such a tiny ugly throat. I could squeeze it flat, and watch you turn blue, on a humble. For dull kicks. And all these weak-faced ofays squatting around here, staring over their papers at me. Murder them too. Even if they expected it. That man there . . . *(Points to well-dressed* MAN.) I could rip that *Times* right out of his hand, as skinny and middle-classed as I am, I could rip that paper out of his hand and just as easily rip out his throat. It takes no great effort. For what? To kill you soft idiots? You don't understand anything but luxury.

LULA. You fool!

CLAY. *(Pushing her against the seat.)* I'm not telling you again, Tallulah Bankhead! Luxury. In your face and your fingers. You telling me what I ought to do. *(Sudden scream frightening the whole coach.)* Well, don't! Don't you tell me anything! If I'm a middle-class fake white man . . . let me be. And let me be in the way I want. *(Through his teeth.)* I'll rip your lousy breasts off! Let me be who I feel like being. Uncle Tom. Thomas. Whoever. It's none of your business. You don't know anything except what's there

for you to see. An act. Lies. Device. Not the pure heart, the pumping black heart. You don't ever know that. And I sit here, in this buttoned-up suit, to keep myself from cutting all your throats. I mean wantonly. You great liberated whore! You fuck some black man, and right away you're an expert on black people. What a lotta shit that is. The only thing you know is that you come if he bangs you hard enough. And that's all. The belly rub? You wanted to do the belly rub? Shit, you don't even know how. You don't know how. That ol' dipty-dip shit you do, rolling your ass like an elephant. That's not my kind of belly rub. Belly rub is not Queens. Belly rub is dark places, with big hats and overcoats held up with one arm. Belly rub hates you. Old bald-headed four-eyed ofays popping their fingers . . . and don't know yet what they're doing. They say, "I love Bessie Smith." And don't even understand that Bessie Smith is saying, "Kiss my ass, kiss my black unruly ass." Before love, suffering, desire, anything you can explain, she's saying, and very plainly, "Kiss my black ass." And if you don't know that, it's you that's doing the kissing.

Charlie Parker? Charlie Parker. All the hip white boys scream for Bird. And Bird saying, "Up your ass, feeble-minded ofay! Up your ass." And they sit there talking about the tortured genius of Charlie Parker. Bird would've played not a note of music if he just walked up to East Sixty-seventh Street and killed the first ten white people he saw. Not a note! And I'm the great would-be poet. Yes. That's right! Poet. Some kind of bastard literature . . . all it needs is a simple knife thrust. Just let me bleed you, you loud whore, and one poem vanished. A whole people of neurotics, struggling to keep from being sane. And the only thing that would cure the neurosis would be your murder. Simple as that. I mean if I murdered you, then other white people would begin to understand me. You understand? No. I guess not. If Bessie Smith had killed some white people she wouldn't have needed that music. She could have talked very straight and plain about the world. No metaphors. No grunts. No wiggles in the dark of her soul. Just straight two and two are four. Money. Power. Luxury. Like that. All of them. Crazy niggers turning their backs on sanity. When all it needs is that simple act. Murder. Just murder! Would make us all sane. *(Suddenly weary.)* Ahhh. Shit. But who needs it? I'd rather be a fool. Insane. Safe with my words, and no deaths, and clean, hard thoughts, urging me to new conquests. My people's madness. Hah! That's a laugh. My people. They don't need me to claim them. They got legs and arms of their own. Personal insanities. Mirrors. They don't need all those words. They don't need any defense. But listen, though, one more thing. And you tell this to your father, who's probably the kind of man who needs to know at once. So he can plan ahead. Tell him not to preach so much rationalism and cold logic to these niggers. Let them alone. Let them sing curses at you in code and see your filth as simple lack of style. Don't make the mistake, through some irresponsible surge of Christian charity, of talking too much about the advantages of Western rationalism, or the great intellectual legacy of the white man, or maybe they'll begin to listen. And then, maybe one day, you'll find they actually do understand exactly what you are talking about, all these fantasy people. All these blues people. And on that day, as sure as shit, when you really believe you can "accept" them into your fold, as half-white trusties late of the subject peoples. With no more blues, except the very old ones, and not a watermelon in sight, the great missionary heart will have triumphed, and all of those ex-coons will be stand-up Western men, with eyes for clean hard useful lives, sober, pious and sane, and they'll murder you. They'll murder you, and have very rational explanations. Very much like your own. They'll cut your throats, and drag you out to the edge of your cities so the flesh can fall away from your bones, in sanitary isolation.

LULA. *(Her voice takes on a different, more businesslike quality.)* I've heard enough.

CLAY. *(Reaching for his books.)* I bet you have. I guess I better collect my stuff and get off this train. Looks like we won't be acting out that little pageant you outlined before.

LULA. No. We won't. You're right about that, at least. *(She turns to look quickly around the rest of the car.)* All right!

(The OTHERS respond.)

CLAY. *(Bending across the girl to retrieve his belongings.)* Sorry, baby, I don't think we could make it.

(As he is bending over her, the girl brings up a small knife and plunges it into CLAY's chest. Twice. He slumps across her knees, his mouth working stupidly.)

LULA. Sorry is right. *(Turning to the OTHERS in the car who have already gotten up from their seats.)* Sorry is the rightest thing you've said. Get this man off me! Hurry, now!

(The OTHERS come and drag CLAY's body down the aisle.)

Open the door and throw his body out.

(They throw him off.)

And all of you get off at the next stop. *(LULA busies herself straightening her things. Getting everything in order. She takes a notebook and makes a quick scribbling note. Drops it in her bag.)*

(The train apparently stops and all the others gets off, leaving her alone in the coach.)

(Very soon a young NEGRO *of about twenty comes into the coach, with a couple of books under his arms. He sits a few seats in back of* LULA. *When he is seated she turns and gives him a long slow look. He looks up from his book and drops the book on his lap. Then an old Negro* CONDUCTOR *comes into the car, doing a sort of restrained soft shoe, and half mumbling the words of some song.*

He looks at the young MAN, *briefly, with a quick greeting.)*

CONDUCTOR. Hey, brother!
YOUNG MAN. Hey.

(The CONDUCTOR *continues down the aisle with his little dance and the mumbled song.* LULA *turns to stare at him and follows his movements down the aisle. The* CONDUCTOR *tips his hat when he reaches her seat, and continues out the car).*

CURTAIN

James Baldwin

The Amen Corner

For
Nina, Ray, Miles, Bird
and
Billie

notes for

THE AMEN CORNER

Writing *The Amen Corner* I remember as a desperate and even rather irresponsible act—it was certainly considered irresponsible by my agent at that time. She did not wish to discourage me, but it was her duty to let me know that the American theater was not exactly clamoring for plays on obscure aspects of Negro life, especially one written by a virtually unknown author whose principal effort until that time had been one novel. She may sincerely have believed that I had gotten my signals mixed and earnestly explained to me that, with one novel under my belt, it was the *magazine* world that was open to me, *not* the world of the theater; I sensibly ought to be pursuing the avenue that was open, especially since I had no money at all. I couldn't explain to her or to myself why I wasted so much time on a play. I knew, for one thing, that very few novelists are able to write plays and I really had no reason to suppose that I could be an exception to this age-old, iron rule. I was perfectly aware that it would probably never be produced, and, furthermore, I didn't even have any ambition to conquer the theater. To this last point we shall return, for I was being very dishonest, or perhaps merely very cunning, with myself concerning the extent of my ambition.

I had written one novel, *Go Tell It on the Mountain,* and it had taken me a long time, nearly ten years, to do it. Those ten years had taken me from Harlem, through the horrors of being a civilian employee (unskilled) of the Army in New Jersey, to being an unskilled employee, period. There is no point in trying to describe the sheer physical terror which was my life in those days, for I was simply grotesquely

out of my setting and everyone around me knew it, and made me pay for it. I say "everyone" for the sake of convenience, for there were, indeed, exceptions, thank God, and these exceptions helped to save my life and also taught me what I then most bitterly needed to know—*i.e.,* that love and compassion, which always arrive in such unexpected packages, have nothing to do with the color of anybody's skin. For I was simply another black boy; there were millions like me at the mercy of the labor market, to say nothing of the labor unions, and it was very clear to me that in the jungle in which I found myself I had no future at all: my going under was simply a matter of time.

But, on the other hand, I had a family —a mother and eight younger brothers and sisters—and something in me knew that if I were to betray them and the love we bore each other, I would be destroying myself. Yet there was no possibility that I would ever be of any use to them, or anyone else, if I continued my life in factories. I was, unfortunately, not equipped for anything but hard labor. No one would ever look at me and offer me anything more than a menial job, and yet people very frequently hesitated to offer me the only jobs open to me because they obscurely felt that I was unreliable, probably inflammatory, and far more trouble than I could possibly be worth. Well, to tell the truth, I can't say very much about those years; I suppose I've blotted it out. What I did, finally, was allow myself to drop to the very bottom of the labor market, became a busboy and short-order cook in places like Riker's—and wrote all the time. And when I was twenty-four, I took the last of a Rosenwald Fellowship grant and bought a plane ticket to Paris. I bought a plane ticket because I was afraid I would lose my nerve if I waited for a boat. I got to Paris with forty dollars and no French. I slid downhill with impressive speed, which wasn't difficult considering the slightness of my eminence, ended up, successively, in one French hospital and one French jail, and then took stock. I was twenty-five and didn't have much to show for it. I started again. By 1952, I finished *Mountain,* borrowed money from Marlon Brando, one of the great and beautiful exceptions referred to above, and came home to try to sell it. I came home in the summertime, and it may have been the emotional climate and the events of that summer which caused me to write *The Amen Corner.*

I had been away for four years—four very crucial and definitive years. I myself have described my exile as a self-exile, but it was really far more complex and bitter than that. No one really wishes to leave his homeland. I left because I was driven out, because my homeland would not allow me to grow in the only direction in which I could grow. This is but another way of saying that all my countrymen had been able to offer me during the twenty-four years that I tried to live here was death—and death, moreover, on their terms. I had been lucky enough to defeat their intention, and, physically, I had escaped. But I had not escaped myself, I had not escaped my antecedents, not even France could compensate for some of the things I knew and felt that I was losing; no Frenchman or Frenchwoman could meet me with the speed and fire of some black boys and girls whom I remembered and whom I missed; they did not know enough about me to be able to correct me. It is true that they met me with something else—themselves, in fact —and taught me things I did not know (how to take a deep breath, for example)

and corrected me in unexpected and rather painful ways. But it was not really my home. I might live there forever and it would never be my home. No matter how immensely I might become reconciled to my condition, it was, nevertheless, the specialness of my condition which had driven me to France. And I had to know this; I could not, on pain of death, forget it—or, rather, to forget it would mean that my high pretensions were nothing but a fraud, that the anguish of my forebears meant nothing to me, and that I had never really intended to become a writer but had only been trying to be safe.

In New York that summer all this became very vivid to me—as vivid as a wound; and it was I, it seemed to me, who had become a kind of ambulating anguish. Not only had New York not changed—as far as I could see, it had become worse; and my hope of ever being able to live in New York diminished with every hour. And this distress was inconceivably aggravated by the one circumstance which would have seemed to be able to alleviate it: the fact that I was a young writer, with a small reputation and a possible future, whose first novel was about to be published. But, to tell the truth, I was really a young *Negro* writer, and the world into which I was moving quite helplessly, and quite without malice, had its own expectations of me, expectations which I was determined to defeat.

The editor assigned to me and my book asked me, when I entered his office for the first time and after the book had been accepted, "What about all that come-to-Jesus stuff? Don't you think you ought to take it out?" *Go Tell It on the Mountain* is the study of a Negro evangelist and his family. They do, indeed, talk in a "come-to-Jesus" idiom, but to "take it out" could only mean that my editor was suggesting that I burn the book.

I gagged, literally, and began to sweat, ran to the water cooler, tried to pull myself together, and returned to the office to explain the intention of my novel. I learned a great deal that afternoon; learned, to put it far too briefly, what I was up against; took the check and went back to Paris.

I went back to Paris, as I then thought, for good, and my reasons this time seemed very different from the reasons which had driven me there in the first place. My original reasons were that I had been forced, most reluctantly, to recognize that thought was also action; what one saw, the point of view from which one viewed the world, dictated what one did; and this meant, in my situation, that I was in danger, most literally, of *thinking* myself out of existence. I was not expected to know the things I knew, or to say the things I said, to make the kind of jokes I made, or to do the things I did. I knew that I was a black street-boy, and that knowledge was all I had. I could not delude myself about it. I did not even have the rather deadly temptations of being good-looking, for I knew that I was not good-looking. All I had, in a word, was me, and I was forced to insist on this *me* with all the energy I had. Naturally, I got my head broken, naturally people laughed when I said I was going to be a writer, and naturally, since I wanted to live, I finally split the scene. But when I came back to sell my first novel, I realized that I was being corraled into another trap: now I was a writer, a *Negro* writer, and I was expected to write diminishing versions of *Go Tell It on the Mountain* forever.

Which I refused to do. I had not, after all, paid all those dues for that. I had no idea whether or not I could write a play, but I was absolutely determined that I would not, not at that moment in my career, not at that moment in my life, attempt another novel. I did not

trust myself to do it. I was really terrified that I would, without even knowing that I was doing it, try to repeat my first success and begin to imitate myself. I knew that I had more to say and much, much more to discover than I had been able to indicate in *Mountain*. Poverty is not a crime in Paris; it does not mean that you are a worthless person; and so I returned and began what I told myself was a "writing exercise": by which I meant I'm still a young man, my family now knows that I really am a writer—that was very important to me—let us now see if I am equipped to go the distance, and let's try something we've never tried before. The first line written in *The Amen Corner* is now Margaret's line in the Third Act: "It's a awful thing to think about, the way love never dies!" That line, of course, says a great deal about me—the play says a great deal about me—but I was thinking not only, not merely, about the terrifying desolation of my private life but about the great burdens carried by my father. I was old enough by now, at last, to recognize the nature of the dues he had paid, old enough to wonder if I could possibly have paid them, old enough, at last, at last, to know that I had loved him and had wanted him to love me. I could see that the nature of the battle we had fought had been dictated by the fact that our temperaments were so fatally the same: neither of us could bend. And when I began to think about what had happened to him, I began to see why he was so terrified of what was surely going to happen to me.

The Amen Corner comes somewhere out of that. For to think about my father meant that I had also to think about my mother and the stratagems she was forced to use to save her children from the destruction awaiting them just outside her door. It is because I know what Sister Margaret goes through, and what her male child is menaced by, that I become so unmanageable when people ask me to confirm their hope that there has been *progress*—what a word!—in white-black relations. There has certainly not been enough progress to solve Sister Margaret's dilemma: how to treat her husband and her son as men and at the same time to protect them from the bloody consequences of trying to be a man in this society. No one yet knows, or is in the least prepared to speculate on, how high a bill we will yet have to pay for what we have done to Negro men and women. She is in the church because her society has left her no other place to go. Her sense of reality is dictated by the society's assumption, which also becomes her own, of her inferiority. Her need for human affirmation, and also for vengeance, expresses itself in her merciless piety; and her love, which is real but which is also at the mercy of her genuine and absolutely justifiable terror, turns her into a tyrannical matriarch. In all of this, of course, she loses her old self—the fiery, fast-talking little black woman whom Luke loved. Her triumph, which is also, if I may say so, the historical triumph of the Negro people in this country, is that she sees this finally and accepts it, and, although she has lost everything,

also gains the keys to the kingdom. The kingdom is love, and love is selfless, although only the self can lead one there. She gains herself.

One last thing: concerning my theatrical ambitions, and my cunning or dishonesty—I was armed, I knew, in attempting to write the play, by the fact that I was born in the church. I knew that out of the ritual of the church, historically speaking, comes the act of the theater, the *communion* which is the theater. And I knew that what I wanted to do in the theater was to recreate moments I remembered as a boy preacher, to involve the people, even against their will, to shake them up, and, hopefully, to change them. I knew that an unknown black writer could not possibly hope to achieve this forum. I did not want to enter the theater on the theater's terms, but on mine. And so I waited. And the fact that *The Amen Corner* took ten years to reach the professional stage says a great deal more about the American theater than it says about this author. The American Negro really is a part of this country, and on the day we face this fact, and not before that day, we will become a nation and possibly a great one.

The Amen Corner was first presented at the Ethel Barrymore Theater, April 15, 1965.

ACT ONE

A Sunday morning in Harlem.

ACT TWO

The following Saturday afternoon.

ACT THREE

The next morning.

All the action takes place on a unit set which is the church and home of Margaret Alexander.

CHARACTERS:

MARGARET ALEXANDER
ODESSA
IDA JACKSON
SISTER MOORE
SISTER BOXER
BROTHER BOXER
DAVID
LUKE
SISTER SALLY
SISTER DOUGLASS

SISTER RICE
BROTHER DAVIS
BROTHER WASHINGTON
WOMAN
OTHER MEMBERS OF CONGREGATION

ACT ONE

We are facing the scrim wall of the tenement which holds the home and church of SISTER MARGARET ALEXANDER.

It is a very bright Sunday morning.

Before the Curtain rises, we hear street sounds, laughter, cursing, snatches of someone's radio; and under everything, the piano, which DAVID *is playing in the church.*

When the Scrim rises we see, stage Right, the church, which is dominated by the pulpit, on a platform, upstage. On the platform, a thronelike chair. On the pulpit, an immense open Bible.

To the right of the pulpit, the piano, the top of which is cluttered with hymn-books and tambourines.

Just below the pulpit, a table, flanked by two plain chairs. On the table two collection plates, one brass, one straw, two Bibles, perhaps a vase of artificial flowers. Facing the pulpit, and running the length of the church, the camp chairs for the congregation.

To the Right, downstage, the door leading to the street.

The church is on a level above the apartment and should give the impression of dominating the family's living quarters.

The apartment is stage Left. Upstage, the door leading to the church; perhaps a glimpse of the staircase. Downstage, the kitchen, cluttered: a new Frigidaire, prominently placed, kitchen table with dishes on it, suitcase open on a chair.

Downstage, Left, LUKE's *bedroom. A small, dark room with a bed, a couple of chairs, a hassock, odds and ends thrown about in it as though it has long been used as a storage room. The room ends in a small door which leads to the rest of the house.*

Members of the congregation almost always enter the church by way of the street door, stage Right. Members of the family almost always enter the church by way of the inside staircase. The apartment door is stage Left of the kitchen.

At Rise, there is a kind of subdued roar and humming, out of which is heard the music prologue, "The Blues Is Man," which segues into a steady rollicking beat, and we see the congregation singing.

ALL.
One day I walked the lonesome road
The spirit spoke unto me
And filled my heart with love—
Yes, he filled my heart with love,
Yes, he filled my heart with love,
And he wrote my name above,
And that's why I thank God I'm in His care.

CHORUS.
Let me tell you now
Whilst I'm in His care,
I'm in my Saviour's care,
Jesus got His arms wrapped around me,
No evil thoughts can harm me
'Cause I'm so glad I'm in His care.

CONTRALTO.
I opened my Bible and began to read
About all the things He's done for me;
Read on down about Chapter One
How He made the earth then He made the sun.
Read on down about Chapter Two
How He died for me and He died for you.
Read on down about Chapter Three
How He made the blind, the blind to see.
Read on down about Chapter Four
How He healed the sick and blessed the poor.
Read on down about Chapter Five
How it rained forty days and Noah survived.

Six, seven, about the same
Just keep praising my Jesus' name.
Read on down about Chapter Eight,
The golden streets and the pearly gates.
Read on down about Chapter Nine
We all get to heaven in due time.
Read on down about Chapter Ten
My God's got the key and He'll let me in.
When I finish reading the rest
I'll go to judgment to stand my test.
He'll say come a little higher, come a
    little higher,
He'll say come a little higher and take
    your seat.

ALL.
Let me tell you now
Whilst I'm in His care,
I'm in my Saviour's care,
Jesus got His arm wrapped around me,
No evil thoughts can harm me
'Cause I'm so glad I'm in His care.

MARGARET. Amen! Let the church say amen!

ALL. Amen! Hallelujah! Amen!

MARGARET. And let us say amen again!

ALL. Amen! Amen!

MARGARET. Because the Lord God Almighty—the King of *Kings,* amen!—had sent out the word, "Set thine house in order, for thou shalt die and not live." And King Hezekiah turned his face to the wall.

ODESSA. Amen!

SISTER MOORE. Preach it, daughter! Preach it this morning!

MARGARET. Now, when the king got the message, amen, he didn't do like some of us do today. He didn't go running to no spiritualists, no, he didn't. He didn't spend a lot of money on no fancy doctors, he didn't break his neck trying to commit himself to Bellevue Hospital. He sent for the prophet, Isaiah. Amen. He sent for a saint of God.

SISTER BOXER. Well, amen!

MARGARET. Now, children, you know this king had a mighty kingdom. There were many souls in that kingdom. He had rich and poor, high and low, amen! And I believe he had a lot of preachers around, puffed up and riding around in chariots—just like they is today, bless God—and stealing from the poor.

ALL. Amen!

MARGARET. But the king didn't call on none of them. No. He called on Isaiah. He called on Isaiah, children, because Isaiah lived a holy life. He wasn't one of them always running in and out of the king's palace. When the king gave a party, I doubt that he even thought of inviting him. You know how people do, amen: Well, let's not have him. Let's not have her. They too sanctified. They too holy. Amen! They don't drink, they don't smoke, they don't go to the movies, they don't curse, they don't play cards, they don't covet their neighbor's husband or their neighbor's wife—well, amen! They just holy. If we invite that sanctified fool they just going to make everybody else feel uncomfortable!

ALL. Well, bless the Lord! Amen!

MARGARET. But let the trouble come. Oh, let the trouble come. They don't go to none of them they sees all the time, amen. No, they don't go running to the people they was playing cards with all night long. When the trouble comes, look like they just can't stand none of their former ways—and they go a-digging back in their minds, in their memories, looking for a saint of God. Oh, yes! I've seen it happen time and time again and I know some of you out there this morning, you've seen it happen too. Sometimes, bless the Lord, you be in the woman's kitchen, washing up her cocktail glasses, amen, and maybe singing praises to the Lord. And pretty soon, here she come, this woman who maybe ain't said two words to you all the time you been working there. She draw up a chair and she say, "Can I talk to you, sister?" She got a houseful of people but she ain't gone to them. She in the kitchen, amen, talking to a saint of God. Because the world is watching you, children, even when you think the whole world's asleep!

ALL. Amen! Amen!

MARGARET. But, dearly beloved, she can't come to you—the world can't come to you—if you don't live holy. This way of holiness is a hard way. I know some of you think Sister Margaret's too hard on you. She don't want you to do this and she won't let you do that. Some of you say, "Ain't no harm in reading the funny papers." But children, *yes,* there's harm in it. While you reading them funny papers, your mind ain't on the Lord. And if your mind ain't stayed on Him, every hour of the day, Satan's going to cause you to fall. Amen! Some of you say, "Ain't no harm in me working for a liquor company. I ain't going to be drinking the liquor, I'm just going to be driving the *truck!*" But a saint of God ain't got no business delivering liquor to folks all day—how you going to spend all day helping folks into hell and then think you going to come here in the evening and help folks into heaven? It can't be done. The Word tells me, No man can serve two masters!

ALL. Well, the Word *do* say it! Bless the Lord!

MARGARET. Let us think about the Word this morning, children. Let it take root in your hearts: "Set thine house in order, for thou shalt die and not live."

(MARGARET *begins to sing and instantly* DAVID *strikes up another "shout" song and the* CONGREGATION *sings—loud, violent, clapping of hands, tambourines, etc.* MARGARET *rises and sits.*)

MARGARET.
I got the holy spirit
To help me run this race.
I got the holy spirit,
It appointed my soul a place.
My faith looks up to heaven,

I know up there I'll see
The Father, the Son, the Holy Spirit
Watching over me.

BARITONE.
Once I was a sinner
Treading a sinful path;
Never thought about Jesus
Or the fate of His wrath.
Then I met the Saviour
And ever since that day
I been walking my faith,
Praying with love,
Looking up above.
With His arms around me,
I'm just leaning on Him.
For there is no other
On Him I can depend.
When my life is ended
And I lay these burdens down
I'm gonna walk with faith,
Pray with love,
Looking from above.

ALL.
I got the holy spirit
To help me run this race.
I got the holy spirit,
It appointed my soul a place.
My faith looks up to heaven,
I know up there I'll see
The Father, the Son, the Holy Spirit
Watching over me.

(SISTER MOORE *comes forward. The excitement begins to subside.*)

SISTER MOORE. Well, I know our souls is praising God this morning!

ALL. Amen!

SISTER MOORE. It ain't every flock blessed to have a shepherd like Sister Margaret. Let's praise God for her!

ALL. Amen! Amen!

SISTER MOORE. Now, I ain't here to take up a lot of your time, amen. Sister Margaret's got to go off from us this afternoon to visit our sister church in Philadelphia. There's many sick up there, amen! Old Mother Phillips is sick in the body and some of her congregation is sick in the soul. And our pastor done give her word that she'd go up there and try to strengthen the feeble knees. Bless God!

(MUSIC begins and underlines her speech.)

Before we close out this order of service, I'd like to say, I praise the Lord for being here, I thank Him for my life, health and strength. I want to thank Him for the way He's worked with me these many long years and I want to thank Him for keeping me *humble!* I want to thank Him for keeping me pure and set apart from the lusts of the flesh, for protecting me—hallelujah!—from all carnal temptation. When I come before my Maker, I'm going to come before Him *pure.* I'm going to say "Bless your name, Jesus, no man has ever touched me!" Hallelujah!

(Congregation begins to sing.)

ALL.
Come to Jesus, come to Jesus,
Come to Jesus, just now.
Come to Jesus, come to Jesus just now.
He will save you, He will save you,
He will save you, just now.
He will save you, He will save you just now.

SISTER MOORE. Now before we raise the sacrifice offering, the Lord has led *me,* amen, to ask if there's a soul in this congregation who wants to ask the Lord's especial attention to them this morning? Any sinners, amen, any backsliders? Don't you be ashamed, you just come right on up here to the altar.

(Tentative MUSIC on the piano.)

Don't hold back, dear ones. Is there any sick in the building? The Lord's hand is outstretched.

(Silence.)

Come, dear hearts, don't hold back.

(Toward the back of the church, a YOUNG WOMAN, *not dressed in white, rises. She holds a baby in her arms.)*

Yes, honey, come on up here. Don't be ashamed.

(The congregation turns to look at the YOUNG WOMAN. *She hesitates.* MARGARET *rises and steps forward.)*

MARGARET. Come on, daughter!

(The YOUNG WOMAN *comes up the aisle. Approving murmurs come from the* CONGREGATION. SISTER MOORE *steps a little aside.)*

That's right, daughter. The Word say, If you make one step, He'll make two. Just step out on the promise. What's your name, daughter?

YOUNG WOMAN. Jackson. Mrs. Ida Jackson.

SISTER MOORE. *(To the* CONGREGATION.*)* Sister Ida Jackson. Bless the Lord!

ALL. Bless her!

MARGARET. And what's the name of that little one?

MRS. JACKSON. His name is Daniel. He been sick. I want you to pray for him. *(She begins to weep.)*

MARGARET. Dear heart, don't you weep this morning. I know what that emptiness feel like. What been ailing this baby?

MRS. JACKSON. I don't know. Done took him to the doctor and the doctor, he don't know. He can't keep nothing on his little stomach and he cry all night, every night, and he done got real puny. Sister, I done lost one child already, please pray the Lord to make this baby well!

MARGARET. *(Steps down and touches* MRS. JACKSON.*)* Don't fret, little sister. Don't you fret this morning. The Lord is mighty to save. This here's a Holy Ghost station. *(To the* CONGREGATION.*)* Ain't that so, dear ones?

ALL. Amen!

MARGARET. He a right fine little boy.

Why ain't your husband here with you this morning?

MRS. JACKSON. I guess he at the house. He done got so evil and bitter, looks like he don't never want to hear me mention the Lord's name. He don't know I'm here this morning.

(Sympathetic murmurs from the CON-GREGATION. MARGARET *watches* MRS. JACKSON.)

MARGARET. You poor little thing. You ain't much more than a baby yourself, is you? Sister, is you ever confessed the Lord as your personal Saviour? Is you trying to lead a life that's pleasing to Him?

MRS. JACKSON. Yes, ma'am. I'm trying every day.

MARGARET. Is your husband trying as hard as you?

MRS. JACKSON. I ain't got no fault to find with him.

MARGARET. Maybe the Lord wants you to leave that man.

MRS. JACKSON. No! He don't want that!

(Smothered giggles among the WOMEN.)

MARGARET. No, children, don't you be laughing this morning. This is serious business. The Lord, He got a road for each and every one of us to travel and we is got to be saying amen to Him, no matter what sorrow He cause us to bear. *(To* MRS. JACKSON.) Don't let the Lord have to take another baby from you before you ready to do His will. Hand that child to me. *(Takes the child from* MRS. JACK-SON'S *arms.)*

SISTER MOORE. Kneel down, daughter. Kneel down there in front of the altar.

*(*MRS. JACKSON *kneels.)*

MARGARET. I want every soul under the sound of my voice to bow his head and pray silently with me as I pray.

(They bow their heads. MARGARET *stands, the child in her arms, head uplifted, and* CONGREGATION *begins to hum "Deep River.")*

Dear Lord, we come before you this morning to ask you to look down and bless this woman and her baby. Touch his little body, Lord, and heal him and drive out them tormenting demons. Raise him up, Lord, and make him a good man and a comfort to his mother. Yes, we know you can do it, Lord. You told us if we'd just call, trusting in your promise, you'd be sure to answer. And all these blessings we ask in the name of the Father—

ALL. In the name of the Father—

MARGARET. And in the name of the Son—

ALL. And in the name of the Son—

MARGARET. And in the name of the blessed Holy Ghost—

ALL. And in the name of the blessed Holy Ghost—

MARGARET. Amen.

ALL. Amen.

MARGARET. *(Returning the child.)* God bless you, daughter. You go your way and trust the Lord. That child's going to be all right.

MRS. JACKSON. Thank you, sister. I can't tell you how much I thank you.

MARGARET. You ain't got me to thank. You come by here and let us know that child's all right, that's what'll please the Lord.

MRS. JACKSON. Yes. I sure will do that.

MARGARET. And bring your husband with you. You bring your *husband* with you.

MRS. JACKSON. Yes, sister. I'll bring him.

MARGARET. Amen!

*(*MRS. JACKSON *returns to her seat.* MARGARET *looks at her watch, motions to* ODESSA, *who rises and leaves. In a moment, we see her in the apartment.*

She exits through LUKE's *room, returns a moment later without her robe, puts coffee on the stove, begins working.* SISTER MOORE *comes forward.)*

SISTER MOORE. Well now, children, without no more ado, we's going to raise the sacrifice offering. And when I say sacrifice, I *mean* sacrifice. Boxer, hand me that basket.

(BROTHER BOXER *does so.)*

(Holds a dollar up before the CONGREGATION *and drops it in the plate.)* I know you don't intend to see our pastor walk to Philadelphia. I want every soul in this congregation to drop just as much money in the plate as I just dropped, or *more,* to help with the cost of this trip. Go on, Brother Boxer, they going to give it to you, I know they is.

(The CONGREGATION, *which has been humming throughout all this, begins singing slightly more strongly as* BROTHER BOXER *passes around the plate, beginning at the back of the church.)*

ALL.
Glory, glory, hallelujah, since I laid my
    burdens down,
Glory, glory, hallelujah, since I laid my
    burdens down,
I feel better, so much better, since I laid
    my burdens down,
I feel better, so much better, since I laid
    my burdens down,
Glory, glory, hallelujah, since I laid my
    burdens down.

*(*MARGARET *leaves the pulpit and comes downstairs. The LIGHTS dim in the church; the MUSIC continues, but lower, and the offering is raised in pantomime.)*

ODESSA. Well! My sister sure walked around Zion this morning!

*(*MARGARET *sits at the table.* ODESSA *pours coffee, begins preparing something for* MARGARET *to eat.)*

MARGARET. It ain't me, sister, it's the Holy Ghost. Odessa—? I been thinking I might take David with me to Philadelphia.
ODESSA. What you want to take him up there for? Who's going to play for the service down here?
MARGARET. Well, old Sister Price, she can sort of stand by—
ODESSA. She *been* standing by—but she sure can't play no piano, not for me she can't. She just ain't got no *juices,* somehow. When that woman is on the piano, the service just gets so dead you'd think you was in a Baptist church.
MARGARET. I'd like Mother Phillips to see what a fine, saved young man he turned out to be. It'll make her feel good. She told me I was going to have a hard time raising him—by myself.

(Service is over, PEOPLE *are standing about chattting and slowly drifting out of the church.)*

ODESSA. Well, if he want to go—
MARGARET. David's got his first time to disobey me. The Word say, Bring up a child in the way he should go, and when he is old he will not depart from it. Now. That's the Word. *(At the suitcase.)* Oh Lord, I sure don't feel like wasting no more time on Brother Boxer. He's a right sorry figure of a man, you know that?
ODESSA. I hope the Lord will forgive me, but, declare, I just can't help wondering sometimes who's on top in that holy marriage bed.
MARGARET. *(Laughs.)* Odessa!
ODESSA. Don't waste no time on him. He knows he ain't got no right to be driving a liquor truck.
MARGARET. Now, what do you suppose is happened to David? He should be here.
ODESSA. He's probably been cornered by some of the sisters. They's always pulling on him.
MARGARET. I praise my Redeemer that I got him raised right—even though I

didn't have no man—you think David missed Luke?

(DAVID *enters the apartment.*)

Ah, there you are.

DAVID. Morning, Aunt Odessa. Morning, Mama. My! You two look—almost like two young girls this morning.

ODESSA. That's just exactly the way he comes on with the sisters. I reckon you know what you doing, taking him to Philadelphia.

DAVID. No, I mean it—just for a minute there. You both looked—different. Somehow—what about Philadelphia?

MARGARET. I was just asking your Aunt Odessa if she'd mind me taking you with me.

DAVID. Mama, I don't want to go to Philadelphia. Anyway—who's going to play for the service down here?

ODESSA. Sister Price can play for us.

DAVID. That woman can't play no piano.

MARGARET. Be careful how you speak about the saints, honey. God don't love us to speak no evil.

DAVID. Well, I'm sure she's sanctified and all that, but she *still* can't play piano. Not for *me*, she can't. She just makes me want to get up and leave the service.

MARGARET. Mother Phillips would just love to see you—

DAVID. I don't hardly remember Mother Phillips at all.

MARGARET. You don't remember Mother Phillips? The way you used to follow her around? Why, she used to spoil you something awful—you was always up in that woman's face—when we—when we first come north—when Odessa was still working down home and we was living in Mother Phillips' house in Philadelphia. Don't you remember?

DAVID. Yeah. Sort of. But, Mama, I don't want to take a week off from music school.

MARGARET. Is the world going to fall down because you don't go to music school for a week?

DAVID. Well, Mama, music is just like everything else, you got to keep at it.

MARGARET. Well, you keeping at it. You playing in service all the time. I don't know what they can teach you in that school. You got a *natural* gift for music, David—

(*A pause. They stare at each other.*)

the Lord give it to you, you didn't learn it in no school.

DAVID. The Lord give me eyes, too, Mama, but I still had to go to school to learn how to read.

MARGARET. I don't know what's got into you lately, David.

DAVID. Well, Mama, I'm getting older. I'm not a little boy anymore.

MARGARET. I know you is getting older. But I hope you still got a mind stayed on the Lord.

DAVID. Sure. Sure, I have.

MARGARET. Where was you last night? You wasn't out to tarry service and don't nobody know what time you come in.

DAVID. I had to go—downtown. We—having exams next week in music school and—I was studying with some guys I go to school with.

MARGARET. Till way late in the morning?

DAVID. Well—it's a pretty tough school.

MARGARET. I don't know why you couldn't have had them boys come up here to *your* house to study. Your friends is always welcome, David, you know that.

DAVID. Well, this guy's got a piano in his house—it was more convenient.

(BROTHER *and* SISTER BOXER *and* SISTER MOORE *leave the church and start downstairs. The church dims out.*)

MARGARET. And what's wrong with that piano upstairs?

DAVID. Mama, I can't practice on that piano—

MARGARET. You can use that piano anytime you want to—

DAVID. Well, I couldn't have used it last night!

(The BOXERS and SISTER MOORE enter. DAVID turns away.)

SISTER MOORE. I come down here to tell Sister Margaret myself how she blessed my soul this morning! Praise the Lord, Brother David. How do you feel this morning?

DAVID. Praise the Lord.

SISTER BOXER. Your mother sure preached a sermon this morning.

BROTHER BOXER. Did my heart good, amen. Did my heart *good*. Sister Odessa, what you got cool to drink in that fine new Frigidaire? (Opens the Frigidaire.) You got any Kool-aid?

SISTER BOXER. You know you ain't supposed to be rummaging around in folks' iceboxes, Joel.

BROTHER BOXER. This ain't no icebox, this is a *Frigidaire*. Westinghouse. Amen! You don't mind my making myself at home, do you, Sister Odessa?

MARGARET. Just make yourself at home, Brother Boxer. I got to get ready to go. David, you better start packing—don't you make me late. He got any clean shirts, Odessa?

ODESSA. I believe so—I ironed a couple last night—he uses them up so fast.

SISTER MOORE. Why, is you going to Philadelphia with your mother, son? Why, that's just lovely!

DAVID. Mama—I got something else to do—this week—

MARGARET. You better hurry.

(DAVID goes into LUKE's bedroom, pulls a suitcase from under the bed.)

BROTHER BOXER. I believe David's sweet on one of them young sisters in Philadelphia, that's why he's so anxious to go.

(DAVID re-enters from the kitchen.)

How about it, boy? You got your eye on one of them Philadelphia saints? One of them young ones?

MARGARET. David's just coming up with me because I asked him to come and help me.

SISTER MOORE. Praise the Lord. That's sweet. The Lord's going to bless you, you hear me, David?

BROTHER BOXER. Ain't many young men in the Lord like David. I got to hand it to you, boy. I been keeping my eye on you and you is—all right! (He claps DAVID on the shoulder.)

SISTER BOXER. How long you figure on being gone, Sister Margaret?

MARGARET. I ain't going to be gone no longer than I have to—this is a mighty sad journey. I don't believe poor Mother Phillips is long for this world. And the way her congregation's behaving—it's just enough to make you weep.

ODESSA. I don't know what's got into them folks up there, cutting up like they is, and talking about the Lord's anointed. I guess I *do* know what's got into them, too—ain't nothing but the Devil. You know, we is really got to watch and pray.

SISTER MOORE. They got more nerve than I got. You ain't never going to hear me say nothing against them the Lord is set above me. No sir. That's just asking for the wrath.

ODESSA. It'll fall *on* you, too. You all is seen the way the Lord is worked with Sister Margaret right here in this little tabernacle. You remember all those people tried to set themselves up against her—? Where is they now? The Lord is just let every one of them be dispersed.

SISTER BOXER. Even poor little Elder King is in his grave.

BROTHER BOXER. I sort of liked old Elder King. The Lord moved him right out just the same.

SISTER MOORE. He'd done got too *high*. He was too set in his ways. All that talk about not wanting women to preach. He didn't want women to do nothing but just sit quiet.

MARGARET. But I remember, Sister Moore, you wasn't so much on women preachers, neither, when I first come around.

SISTER MOORE. The Lord opened my eyes, honey. He opened my eyes the first time I heard you preach. Of course, I ain't saying that Elder King couldn't preach a sermon when the power was on him. And it *was* under Elder King that I come into the church.

BROTHER BOXER. You weren't sweet on Elder King, were you, Sister Moore?

SISTER MOORE. I ain't never been sweet on no man but the Lord Jesus Christ.

SISTER BOXER. You remember Elder King, son? You weren't nothing but a little bundle in them days.

DAVID. I was reading and writing already. I was even playing the piano already. It was him had this church then and we was living down the block.

BROTHER BOXER. I reckon you must have missed your daddy sometimes, didn't you, son?

SISTER MOORE. If he'd stayed around his daddy, I guarantee you David wouldn't be the fine, saved young man he is today, playing piano in church, would you, boy?

DAVID. No'm, I reckon I wouldn't. Mama, if I'm going to be gone a whole week, there is something I've got to—

BROTHER BOXER. He better off without the kind of daddy who'd just run off and leave his wife and kid to get along the best they could. That ain't right. I believe in a man doing *right,* amen!

MARGARET. You hear him, don't you? *He* know—miss his daddy? The Lord, He give me strength to be mother and daddy both. Odessa, you want to help me with my hair?

(*They start out.*)

DAVID. Mama—!

MARGARET. What is it, son?

DAVID. There is something I got to get down the block. I got to run down the block for a minute.

MARGARET. Can't it wait till you come back?

DAVID. No. I want to—borrow a music score from somebody. I can study it while I'm away.

MARGARET. Well, you hurry. We ain't got much time. You put something on. You act like you catching cold.

(ODESSA *and* MARGARET *exit through* LUKE's *room.*)

BROTHER BOXER. You got to say good-bye to some little girl down the block?

DAVID. I'll be right back. (*He rushes into the street, vanishes in the alley.*)

BROTHER BOXER. Hmmph! I wonder what kind of business he got down the block. I guarantee you one thing—it ain't sanctified business.

SISTER BOXER. The Word say we ain't supposed to think no evil, Joel.

BROTHER BOXER. I got news for you folks. You know what I heard last night?

SISTER BOXER. Don't you come on with no more foolishness, Joel. I'm too upset. I can't stand it this morning.

SISTER MOORE. Don't you be upset, sugar. Everything's going to turn out all right—what did you hear, Brother Boxer?

BROTHER BOXER. That boy's daddy is back in New York. He's working in a jazz club downtown.

SISTER MOORE. A *jazz* club?

SISTER BOXER. How come you know all this?

BROTHER BOXER. Heard it on the job, honey. God don't want us to be ignorant. He want us to know what's going on around us.

SISTER MOORE. Do Sister Margaret know this?

BROTHER BOXER. I bet you David, *he* know it—he been keeping bad company. Some young white boy, didn't have nothing better to do, went down yonder and drug his daddy up to New York—for a comeback. Last time anybody heard about him, he was real sick with TB. Everybody thought he was dead.

SISTER MOORE. Poor Sister Margaret! A jazz club!

SISTER BOXER. Poor Sister Margaret! She ain't as poor as I am.

BROTHER BOXER. You ain't poor, sugar. You got me. And I ain't going to stay poor forever.

SISTER MOORE. I'm going to talk to her about that job business now. She reasonable. She'll listen.

SISTER BOXER. She ain't going to listen.

SISTER MOORE. Of course she's going to listen. Folks is got a right to make a living.

BROTHER BOXER. Uh-huh. Folks like us ain't got nothing and ain't never supposed to have nothing. We's supposed to live on the joy of the Lord.

SISTER MOORE. It ain't like Brother Boxer was going to become a drunkard or something like that—he won't even *see* the liquor—

SISTER BOXER. He won't even be selling it.

SISTER MOORE. He just going to be driving a truck around the city, doing hard work. I declare, I don't see nothing wrong with that.

SISTER BOXER. Sister Moore, you know that woman I work for, sometime she give a party and I got to serve them people cocktails. I *got* to. Now, I don't believe the Lord's going to punish me just because I'm working by the sweat of my brow the only way I *can*. He say, "Be in the world but not of it." But you got to be *in* it, don't care how holy you get, you got to *eat*.

BROTHER BOXER. I'm glad Sister Boxer mentioned it to you, Sister Moore. I wasn't going to mention it to you myself because I was sure you'd just take Sister Margaret's side against us.

SISTER MOORE. Ain't no taking of sides in the Lord, Brother Boxer. I'm on the Lord's side. We is all sinners, saved by grace. Hallelujah!

(MARGARET *and* ODESSA *re-enter. The* BOXERS *and* SISTER MOORE *begin to sing.*)

SISTER MOORE.
What a mighty God we serve!
SISTER *and* BROTHER BOXER.
What a mighty God we serve!
TOGETHER.
Angels around the throne,
'Round the throne of God,
Crying, what a mighty God we serve!

MARGARET. Bless your hearts, children, that sure done my spirit good. You all ain't like them wayward children up in Philadelphia. It sure is nice to be here with my real faithful children.

(DAVID *enters the alley, slowly, looking back; enters the apartment.*)

BROTHER BOXER. Oh, we's faithful, Sister Margaret.

(*Jazz version of "Luke's Theme" begins.*)

SISTER MOORE. Yes, I'm mighty glad you said that, Sister Margaret. I'm mighty glad you *knows* that. Because the Lord's done laid something on my heart to say to you, right here and now, and you going to take it in the proper spirit, I know you is. I know you know I ain't trying to find fault. Old Sister Moore don't mean no wrong.

MARGARET. What is it, Sister Moore?

DAVID. Mama, can I see you for a minute?

MARGARET. In a minute, son.

SISTER MOORE. Why, Brother and Sister Boxer here, they just happened to mention to me something about this job you don't think Brother Boxer ought to take. I don't mean no wrong, Sister Margaret, and I know you the pastor and is set above me, but I'm an older woman than you are and, I declare, I don't see no harm in it.

MARGARET. You don't see no harm in it, Sister Moore, because the Lord ain't placed you where he's placed me. Ain't no age in the Lord, Sister Moore—older or younger ain't got a thing to do with it. You just remember that I'm your pastor.

SISTER MOORE. But, Sister Margaret, can't be no harm in a man trying to do his best for his family.

MARGARET. The Lord comes before all things, Sister Moore. All things. Brother Boxer's supposed to do his best for the Lord.

SISTER MOORE. But, Sister Margaret—

MARGARET. I don't want to hear no more about it.

(SISTERS MOORE and BOXER exchange a bitter look and they begin singing a church tune. ODESSA closes MARGARET's suitcase and puts it on the floor. LUKE appears in the alley, walking very slowly.)

SISTERS MOORE and BOXER.
'Bye and 'bye when the morning comes
All the saints of God are gathering home,
We will tell the story how we overcome,
And we'll understand it better 'bye and
   'bye.

(LUKE climbs the stairs into the church, walks through it slowly; finally enters the apartment as they finish the song.)

LUKE. Good morning, folks.

(Silence. Everyone stares, first at LUKE, then at MARGARET. MARGARET stands perfectly still.)

Maggie, you ain't hardly changed a bit. You *still* the prettiest woman I ever laid eyes on.

MARGARET. Luke.

LUKE. Don't look at me like that. I changed that much? Well, sure, I might of lost a little weight. But you gained some. You ever notice how men, they tend to lose weight in later life, while the

women, they gain? You look good, Maggie. It's good to see you.

MARGARET. Luke—

LUKE. (To ODESSA.) Hey, you look good too. It's mighty good to see you again. You didn't think I'd come to New York and not find you? Ain't you going to say nothing, neither?

ODESSA. Ah. You bad boy.

LUKE. I bet my son is in this room somewhere. He's got to be in this room somewhere—(To BROTHER BOXER.)—but I reckon it can't be you. I know it ain't been that long. (To DAVID.) You come downtown last night to hear me play, didn't you?

DAVID. Yes. Yes, sir. I did.

LUKE. Why didn't you come up and say hello? I saw you, sitting way in the back, way at the end of the bar. I knew right away it was you. And, time I was finished, you was gone.

(A pause.)

Cat got your tongue, Maggie? (To DAVID.) I never knowed that to happen to your mama before.

MARGARET. I never knowed my son to lie to me, neither. God don't like liars.

DAVID. I was going to tell you.

MARGARET. Luke, how'd you find us?

LUKE. I had to find you. I didn't come to cause you no trouble. I just come by to say hello.

ODESSA. Luke, sit down! I can't get over seeing you, right here in this room. I can't get over it. I didn't reckon on never seeing you no more—

LUKE. In life. I didn't neither. But here I am—

ODESSA. With your big, black no-count self. You hungry?

LUKE. Odessa, you ain't never going to change. Everytime you see a man, you think you got to go digging for some pork chops. No, I ain't hungry. I'm tired, though. I believe I'll sit down.

(He sits. ODESSA *and* DAVID *glance at each other quickly.)*

MARGARET. How long you going to be in New York, Luke? When did you get here? Nobody told me—*(She looks at* DAVID.*)* nobody told me—you was here—

LUKE. A couple of weeks is all. I figured I'd find you somewhere near a church. And you a pastor now? Well, I guess it suits you. She a good pastor?

SISTER MOORE. Amen!

LUKE. What do you think, David?

*(*DAVID *is silent.)*

Well, she sure used to keep on at me about my soul. Didn't you, Maggie? Of course, that was only toward the end, when things got to be so rough. In the beginning—well, it's always different in the beginning.

MARGARET. You ain't changed, have you? You still got the same carnal grin, that same carnal mind—you ain't changed a bit.

LUKE. People don't change much, Maggie—

MARGARET. Not unless the Lord changes their hearts—

LUKE. You ain't changed much, neither—you dress a little different.

MARGARET. Why did you come here? You ain't never brought me nothing but trouble, you come to bring me more trouble? Luke—I'm glad to see you and all but—I got to be going away this afternoon. I stay busy all the time around this church. David, he stays busy too—and he's coming with me this afternoon.

LUKE. Well, honey, I'm used to your going. I done had ten years to get used to it. But, David—David, you can find a couple of minutes for your old man, can't you? Maybe you'd like to come out with me sometime—we could try to get acquainted—

DAVID. You ain't wanted to get acquainted all this time—

LUKE. Yes, I did. It ain't my fault—at least it ain't *all* my fault—that we ain't acquainted.

ODESSA. Luke!

DAVID. You run off and left us.

LUKE. Boy, your daddy's done a lot of things he's ashamed of, but I wouldn't never of run off and left you and your mother. Your mama knows that.

(A pause.)

You tell him, Maggie. Who left? Did I leave you or did you leave me?

MARGARET. It don't make no difference now.

LUKE. Who left? Tell him.

MARGARET. When we was living with you, I didn't know half the time if I had a husband or not, this boy didn't know if he had a father!

LUKE. That's a goddam lie. *You* knew you had a husband—this boy knew he had a father. Who left the house—who left?

MARGARET. You was always on the road with them no-count jazz players—

LUKE. But who *left?*

MARGARET. I ain't going to stand here arguing with you—I got to go—David—

LUKE. *Who left?*

MARGARET. *I* did! *I* left! To get away from the stink of whisky—to save my baby—to find the Lord!

LUKE. I wouldn't never of left you, son. Never. Never in this world.

MARGARET. Leave us alone, Luke. Go away and leave us alone. I'm doing the Lord's work now—

DAVID. Mama—you just said—God don't like liars.

MARGARET. Your daddy weren't hardly ever home. I was going to explain it all to you—when you got big.

LUKE. I done spent ten years wishing you'd leave the Lord's work to the Lord. *(He rises slowly.)* You know where I'm working, boy. Come on down and see me. Please come on down and see me.

MARGARET. Luke, he ain't going down there. You want to see him, you come on up here.

LUKE. He's big enough to find his way downtown.

MARGARET. I don't want him hanging around downtown.

LUKE. It ain't no worse down there than it is up here.

MARGARET. I ain't going to fight with you—not now—in front of the whole congregation. Brother Boxer, call me a taxi. David, close that suitcase and get yourself a coat. We got to go.

(BROTHER BOXER *hesitates, rises, leaves.*)

ODESSA. Maggie, he's sick.

(LUKE *sways, falls against the table.* SISTER BOXER *screams.* DAVID *and* ODESSA *struggle to raise him.*)

SISTER MOORE. Try to get him back here in this little room. Back here, in this bed, in this little room.

(DAVID *and the women struggle with* LUKE *and get him to the bed.* DAVID *loosens his father's collar and takes off his shoes.*)

LUKE. (*Moans.*) Maggie.

SISTER BOXER. We better send that man to a hospital.

MARGARET. This here's a Holy Ghost station. The Lord don't do nothing without a purpose. Maybe the Lord wants to save his soul.

SISTER MOORE. Well, amen.

MARGARET. And Luke, if he want to keep on being hardheaded against the Lord, his blood can't be required at our hands. I got to go.

DAVID. Mama, I'm going to stay here.

(*A pause.*)

Mama, couldn't you write or telephone or something and let them folks know you can't get up there right now?

SISTER BOXER. Yes, Sister Margaret, couldn't you do that? I don't believe that man is long for this world.

SISTER MOORE. Yes, Sister Margaret, everybody understands that when you got trouble in the home, the home comes first. Send a deputy up there. I'll go for you.

MARGARET. In this home, Sister Moore, the Lord comes first. The Lord made me leave that man in there a long time ago because he was a sinner. And the Lord ain't told me to stop doing my work just because he's come the way all sinners come.

DAVID. But, Mama, he's been calling you, he going to keep on calling you! What we going to do if he start calling for you again?

MARGARET. Tell him to call on the Lord! It ain't me can save him, ain't nothing but the Lord can save him!

ODESSA. But you might be able to help him, Maggie—if you was here.

DAVID. Mama, you don't know. You don't know if he be living, time you get back.

(*The taxi HORN is heard.*)

But I reckon you don't care, do you?

MARGARET. Don't talk to your mother that way, son. I don't want to go. I got to go.

SISTER BOXER. When a woman make a vow to God, she got to keep it.

MARGARET. You folks do what you can for him, pray and hold onto God for him. (*To* ODESSA.) You send me a telegram if —if anything happens. (*To the others.*) You folks got a evening service to get through. Don't you reckon you better run, get a bite to eat, so you can get back here on time?

BROTHER BOXER. (*Offstage.*) Sister Margaret!

MARGARET. Go, do like I tell you. David, see if you can find a doctor. You ain't going to do no good, standing there like that. Praise the Lord.

ODESSA. Praise the Lord.

MARGARET. (To the others, dangerously.) Praise the Lord, I say.

SISTERS MOORE and BOXER. (Dry.) Praise the Lord.

(MARGARET goes through the church into the street.)

LUKE. Maggie. Maggie. Oh, Maggie.

ODESSA. Children, let us pray.

(Slowly, all except DAVID, go to their knees. They begin singing.)

If Jesus had to pray, what about me?
If Jesus had to pray, what about me?
He had to fall down on His knees,
Crying Father, help me if you please,
If Jesus had to pray, what about me?

In the garden Jesus prayed
While night was falling fast.
He said Father, if you will,
Let this bitter cup be past
But if I am not content,
Let my will be lost in Thine.
If Jesus had to pray, what about me?

CURTAIN

END OF ACT ONE

ACT TWO

Late afternoon the following Saturday. The sun is bright red, the street is noisy. CRIES of children playing, blaring RADIOS and JUKEBOXES, etc.

LUKE's *room is dark, the shades drawn. He is still.*

ODESSA, SISTER BOXER *and* SISTER MOORE *are in the kitchen.*

SISTER MOORE. (To ODESSA.) We all loves Sister Margaret, sugar, just as much as you do. But we's supposed to bear witnes, amen, to the truth. Don't care *who* it cuts.

SISTER BOXER. She been going around all these years acting so *pure.*

SISTER MOORE. Sister Margaret ain't nothing but flesh and blood, like all the rest of us. And she is got to watch and pray—like all the rest of us.

ODESSA. Lord, honey, Sister Margaret, *she* know that.

SISTER BOXER. She don't act like she know it. She act like she way above all human trouble. She always up there on that mountain, don't you know, just a-chewing the fat with the Lord.

SISTER MOORE. That poor man!

ODESSA. Sister Moore, you ain't never had no use for men all your life long. Now, how come you sitting up here this afternoon, talking about that *poor* man and talking against your pastor?

SISTER MOORE. Don't you try to put words in my mouth, Sister Odessa, don't you do it! I ain't talking against my pastor, no, I ain't. I ain't doing a thing but talking like a Christian.

SISTER BOXER. Last Sunday she acted like she didn't think that man was good enough to touch the hem of that white robe of her'n. And, you know, that ain't no way to treat a man who knowed one *time* what you was like with no robe on.

SISTER MOORE. Sister Boxer!

SISTER BOXER. Well, it's the truth. I'm bearing witness to the truth. I reckon I always thought of Sister Margaret like she'd been born holy. Like she hadn't never been a young girl or nothing and hadn't never had no real temptations.

(BROTHER BOXER *enters.*)

ODESSA. I don't know how you could of thought that when everybody knowed she's been married—and had a son.

BROTHER BOXER. Praise the Lord, holy sisters, can a man come in?

ODESSA. Come on in the house, Brother Boxer. (To the others.) You be careful how you talk about your sister. The Lord ain't *yet* taken away His protecting arm.

BROTHER BOXER. Look like it might rain this evening.

ODESSA. Yes. The sky is getting mighty low.

SISTER BOXER. Oh, sure, I knowed she'd been married and she had this boy. But, I declare, I thought that that was just a mistake and she couldn't wait to get away from her husband. There's women like that, you know, ain't got much nature to them somehow.

SISTER MOORE. Now, you be careful, Sister Boxer, you know I ain't never been married, nor *(Proudly.)* I ain't never knowed no man.

SISTER BOXER. Well, it's different with you, Sister Moore. You give your life to the Lord right quick and you ain't got nothing like that to remember. But, you take me now, I'm a married woman and the Lord done blessed me with a real womanly nature and, I tell you, honey, you been married once, it ain't so easy to get along single. 'Course, I know the Holy Ghost is mighty and *will* keep—but, I declare, I wouldn't like to try it. No *wonder* that woman make so much noise when she get up in the pulpit.

BROTHER BOXER. She done gone too far, she done rose too *high*. She done forgot it ain't the woman supposed to lead, it's the man.

ODESSA. Is you done forgot your salvation? Don't you know if she'd followed that man, he might have led her straight on down to hell?

SISTER BOXER. That ain't by no means certain. If she'd done her duty like a wife, she might have been able to lead that man right straight to the throne of grace. I led *my* man there.

BROTHER BOXER. Well, you's a woman, sugar, and, quite natural, you want your man to come to heaven. But I believe, in Sister Margaret's heaven, ain't going to be no men allowed. When that young woman come to the altar last Sunday morning, wanted the saints to pray for her baby, the first words out of Sister Margaret's mouth was "You better leave your husband."

SISTER BOXER. Amen! The *first* words.

ODESSA. Children, you better be careful what you say about a woman ain't been doing nothing but trying to serve the Lord.

SISTER MOORE. Is she been trying to serve the Lord? Or is she just wanted to put herself up over everybody else?

BROTHER BOXER. Now, that's what I'm talking about. The Word say, You going to know a tree by its fruit. And we ain't been seeing such good fruit from Sister Margaret. I want to know, how come she think she can rule a church when she can't rule her own house? That husband of hers is in there, dying in his sins, and that half-grown, hypocrite son of hers is just running all roads to hell.

ODESSA. Little David's just been a little upset. He ain't thinking about going back into the world, he see what sin done for his daddy.

BROTHER BOXER. I got news for you, Sister Odessa. Little David ain't so little no more. I stood right in this very room last Sunday when we found out that boy had been lying to his mother. That's *right*. He been going out to *bars*. And just this very evening, not *five* minutes ago, I seen him down on 125th Street with some white horn-player—the one he say he go to *school* with—and two other boys and three girls. Yes sir. They was just getting into a car.

ODESSA. It's just natural for David to be seeing folks his own age every now and then. And they just might be fixing to drop him at this very doorstep, you don't know. He might be here in time for tarry service.

BROTHER BOXER. I don't hear no cars drawing up in front of this door—no, I don't. And I bet you prayer meeting ain't what David had on his mind. That boy had a cigarette between his lips and had his hand on one of them girls, a real common-looking, black little thing, he had his hand on her—well, like he knowed her pretty *well* and wasn't expecting her to send him off to no prayer meeting.

SISTER MOORE. The Lord sure has been causing the scales to fall from the eyes of His servant this week. Thank you, Jesus!

ODESSA. You ought to be ashamed of yourselves! You ought to be ashamed of your black, deceitful hearts. You's liars, every one of you, and the truth's not in you!

(A pause.)

Brother Boxer, Sister Boxer, Sister Moore. Let's go upstairs and pray.

SISTER MOORE. Yes, we *better* go upstairs and pray. The Lord's been working in the hearts of some other folks in this church and they's going to be along presently, asking the elders of this church to give them an accounting—amen!—of their spiritual leader.

ODESSA. What kind of accounting, Sister Moore?

SISTER MOORE. Well, I just happened to be talking to some of the saints the other day and while we was talking some of them got to wondering just how much it cost to get to Philadelphia. Well, I said I didn't know because the Lord, He keep *me* close to home. But I said it couldn't cost but *so* much, ain't like she was going on a great long trip. Well—we got to talking about other things and then we just decided we'd come to church this evening and put our minds together. Amen. And let everybody say his piece and see how the Lord, *He* wanted us to move.

ODESSA. Was you there, too, Brother Boxer?

BROTHER BOXER. Naturally I was there too. I'm one of the elders of the church.

ODESSA. I'm one of the elders, too. But *I* wasn't there—wherever it was.

SISTER MOORE. We wasn't planning to

shut you out, Sister Odessa. Some folks just happened to drop by the house and we got to talking. That's all.

ODESSA. Is folks thinking that Margaret's stealing their money?

SISTER BOXER. That ain't no way to talk, Sister Odessa. Before God, ain't nobody said a word about stealing.

SISTER MOORE. Ain't nobody accusing Margaret of *nothing*. Don't you let the Devil put that idea in your mind. Sister Margaret's been blessed with a real faithful congregation. Folks just loves Sister Margaret. Just the other day one of the saints—was it you, Sister Boxer?—one of the saints was saying to me how much trouble she have with her old refrigerator and she say it sure done her heart good to know her pastor had a nice, new Frigidaire. Amen. She said it done her heart good.

(They exit into the church. The LIGHTS GO UP slightly as they enter and sit. The church BLACKS OUT. For a moment the stage is empty. Then DAVID appears, enters the house. He is very tired and nervous. He wanders about the kitchen; goes to LUKE's room, looks in. He is about to turn away when LUKE speaks.)

LUKE. Hello, there.

DAVID. I thought you was asleep.

LUKE. I ain't sleepy. Is it nighttime yet?

DAVID. No, not yet.

LUKE. Look like it's always nighttime in this room. You want to come in, pull up the shade for me?

(DAVID does so. A faint sound of SINGING is heard from the church upstairs.)

LUKE. Ain't you going to play piano for them tonight?

DAVID. I don't much feel like playing piano right now. *(He is flustered; reaches in his pocket, takes out a pack of cigarettes, realizes his mistake too late.)*

LUKE. Didn't know you was smoking already. Let's have a cigarette.

DAVID. You ain't suppose to be smoking. The doctor don't want you smoking.

LUKE. The doctor ain't here now.

(DAVID *gives* LUKE *a cigarette, lights it, after a moment lights one for himself.*)

DAVID. Look like you'd of had enough of smoking by now.

LUKE. Sit down. We got a minute.

(DAVID *sits on the hassock at the foot of* LUKE'S *bed.*)

LUKE. Didn't I hear you playing piano one night this week?

DAVID. No.

LUKE. Boy, I'm sure I heard you playing *one* night—at the beginning of the service?

DAVID. Oh. Yes, I guess so. I didn't stay. How did you know it was me?

LUKE. You play piano like I dreamed you would.

DAVID. I been finding out lately you was pretty good. Mama never let us keep a phonograph. I just didn't never hear any of your records—until here lately. You was right up there with the best, Jellyroll Morton and Louis Armstrong and cats like that.

LUKE. You fixing to be a musician?

DAVID. No.

LUKE. Well, it ain't much of a profession for making money, that's the truth.

DAVID. There were guys who did.

LUKE. There were guys who didn't.

DAVID. You never come to look for us. Why?

LUKE. I started to. I wanted to. I thought of it lots of times.

DAVID. Why didn't you never do it? Did you think it was good riddance we was gone?

LUKE. I was hoping you wouldn't never think that, never.

DAVID. I wonder what you expected me to think. I remembered you, but couldn't never talk about you. I used to hear about you sometime, but I couldn't never say, That's my daddy. I was too ashamed. I remembered how you used to play for me sometimes. That was why I started playing the piano. I used to go to sleep dreaming about the way we'd play together one day, me with my piano and you with your trombone.

LUKE. David. David.

DAVID. You never come. You never come when you could do us some good. You come now, now when you can't do nobody any good. Every time I think about it, think about *you,* I want to break down and cry like a baby. You make me —ah! You make me feel so bad.

LUKE. Son—don't try to get away from the things that hurt you. The things that hurt you—sometimes that's all you got. You got to learn to live with those things —and—use them. I've seen people—put themselves through terrible torture—and die—because they was afraid of getting hurt. (*He wants to get rid of his cigarette.*)

(DAVID *takes it from him. They stare at each other for a moment.*)

I used to hold you on my knee when you weren't nothing but a little—you didn't have no teeth then. Now I reckon you's already started to lose them. I reckon I thought we was a-going to bring down the moon, you and me, soon as you got a little bigger. I planned all kinds of things for you—they never come to pass.

DAVID. You ain't never been saved, like Mama. Have you?

LUKE. Nope.

DAVID. How come Mama, she got saved?

LUKE. I reckon she thought she better had—being married to me. I don't know. Your mama's kind of proud, you know, proud and silent. We had us a little trouble. And she wouldn't come to me. That's when she found the Lord.

DAVID. I remember. I remember—that

was when the baby was born dead. And Mama was in the hospital—and you was drunk, going to that hospital all the time —and I used to hear you crying, late at night. *Did* she find the Lord?

LUKE. Can't nobody know but your mama, son.

DAVID. A few months ago some guys come in the church and they heard me playing piano and they kept coming back all the time. Mama said it was the Holy Ghost drawing them in. But it wasn't.

LUKE. It was your piano.

DAVID. Yes. And I didn't draw them in. They drew me out. They setting up a combo and they want me to come in with them. That's when I stopped praying. I really began to think about it hard. And, Daddy—things started happening inside me which hadn't ever happened before. It was terrible. It was wonderful. I started looking around this house, around this church—like I was seeing it for the first time. Daddy—that's when I stopped believing—it just went away. I got so I just hated going upstairs to that church. I hated coming home. I hated lying to Mama all the time—and—I knew I had to do something—and that's how—I was scared, I didn't know what to do. I didn't know how to stay here and I didn't know how to go—and—there wasn't anybody I could talk to—I couldn't do—nothing! Every time I—even when I tried to make it with a girl—something kept saying, Maybe this is a sin. I hated it! *(He is weeping.)* I made Mama let me go to music school and I started studying. I got me a little part-time job. I been studying for three months now. It gets better all the time—you know? I don't mean *me*— I got a long way to go—but *it* gets better. And I was trying to find some way of preparing Mama's mind—

LUKE. When you seen me. And you got to wondering all over again if you wanted to be like your daddy and end up like your daddy. Ain't that right?

DAVID. Yeah, I guess that's right.

LUKE. Well, son, tell you one thing. Wasn't music put me here. The most terrible time in a man's life, David, is when he's done lost everything that held him together—it's just gone and he can't find it. The whole world just get to be a great big empty basin. And it just as hollow as a basin when you strike it with your fist. Then that man start going down. If don't no hand reach out to help him, that man goes under. You know, David, it don't take much to hold a man together. A man can lose a whole lot, might look to everybody else that he done lost so much that he ought to want to be dead, but he can keep on—he can even die with his head up, hell, as long as he got that one thing. That one thing is *him*, David, who he is inside—and, son, I don't believe no man ever got to that without somebody loved him. Somebody *looked* at him, looked *way* down in him and spied him way down there and showed him to himself—and then started pulling, a-pulling of him up—so he could live. *(Exhausted.)* Hold your head up, David. You'll have a life. Tell me there's all kinds of ways for ruined men to keep on living. You hears about guys sometimes who got a bullet in their guts and keeps on running—sunning—spilling blood every inch, keeps running a long time— before they fall. I don't know what keeps them going. Faith—or something—something—something I never had.

(A pause.)

So don't you think you got to end up like your daddy just because you want to join a band.

DAVID. Daddy—weren't the music enough?

LUKE. The music. The music. Music is a moment. But life's a long time. In that moment, when it's good, when you really swinging—then you joined to everything, to everybody, to skies and stars and every living thing. But music ain't kissing. Kissing's what you want to do. Music's what you *got* to do, *if* you got to do it. Question is how long you can keep up with the music when you ain't got nobody to kiss. You know, the music don't come out of the air, baby. It comes out of the man who's blowing it.

DAVID. You must have had a time.

LUKE. I had me a time all right.

DAVID. Didn't you never call on God?

LUKE. No. I figured it was just as much His fault as mine.

DAVID. Didn't you never get scared?

LUKE. Oh yes.

DAVID. But you're not scared now?

LUKE. Oh yes.

(DAVID *goes off, stage Left. The LIGHTS COME UP in the church, DIM DOWN in the apartment.* SISTER MOORE, SISTER BOXER, BROTHER BOXER, *along with some members of the* CONGREGATION *seen in Act One, are grouped together in camp chairs.* ODESSA *sits a little away from them.* SISTER RICE, *fortyish,* SISTER SALLY, *extremely young and voluptuous,* SISTER DOUGLASS, *quite old and slow and black.*)

SISTER SALLY. Why, a couple of months ago, just after we got married? Why, Herman and I, we had to go to Philadelphia *several* times and it don't cost no forty some odd dollars to get there. Why, it don't cost *that* much round trip.

SISTER DOUGLASS. It ain't but up the road a ways, is it? I used to go up there to see my nephew, he stay too busy to be able to get to New York much. It didn't seem to me it took so long. 'Course, I don't remember how much it cost.

ODESSA. I don't know why you folks don't just call up Pennsylvania Station and just *ask* how much it costs to get to Philadelphia.

BROTHER BOXER. Most folks don't go to Philadelphia by train, Sister Odessa.

They takes the bus because the bus is cheaper.

SISTER MOORE. Now, of course ain't nothing these days what you might call really *cheap*. Brother Boxer, you remember when Sister Boxer had to go down home to bury her sister? You was going up to Philadelphia quite regular there for a while. You remember how much it cost?

SISTER BOXER. You ain't never mentioned you knew anybody in Philadelphia.

SISTER SALLY. Men don't never tell women nothing. Look like you always finding out something new.

BROTHER BOXER. Man better not tell a woman everything he know, not if he got good sense. (*To* SISTER MOORE.) It didn't cost no more'n about three or four dollars.

SISTER BOXER. That round trip or one way?

SISTER DOUGLASS. How much you folks say you raised on the offering last Sunday?

SISTER MOORE. Brother Boxer and me, we counted it, and put it in the envelope. It come to—what did it come to altogether, Brother Boxer? Give us the *exact* figure, amen.

BROTHER BOXER. It come to forty-one dollars and eighty-seven cents.

SISTER RICE. Don't seem to me we ought to be sitting here like this, worrying about the few pennies we give our pastor last Sunday. We been doing it Sunday after Sunday and ain't nobody never had nothing to say against Sister Margaret. She's our pastor, we ain't supposed to be thinking no evil about her.

SISTER MOORE. That's what I say, amen. Sister Margaret our pastor and the few pennies we scrapes together by the sweat of our brow to give her she got a right to do with as she see *fit,* amen! And I think we ought to stop discussing it right here and now and just realize that we's blessed to have a woman like Sister Margaret for our shepherd.

ODESSA. You folks sound like a church don't have to pay no rent, and don't never pay no bills and nothing in a church don't wear out. Them chairs you got your behinds on right now, they have to keep on being replaced—you folks is always breaking them during the service, when you gets happy. Those of you what wears glasses, though, I notice you don't never break them. You holds yourself together somehow until somebody comes and takes them off'n you. Rugs on the floor cost money, robes cost money—and you people is just murder on hymnbooks, tambourines and Bibles. Now, Margaret don't use hardly none of that money on herself—ain't enough money *in* this church for nobody to be able to live off it.

BROTHER BOXER. You folks got a new Frigidaire, though. I ain't saying nothing, but—

ODESSA. That Frigidaire is in *my* name, Brother Boxer—it's the first new thing I bought for that house in I don't know how many years—with money *I* made from scrubbing white folks' floors. Ain't a one of you put a penny in it. Now. You satisfied?

SISTER MOORE. How's your mother getting along, Sister Rice? I hope she feeling better. We ain't seen her for a long time.

SISTER RICE. We's holding onto God for her. But she been doing poorly, poor thing. She say she sure do miss not being able to come out to service.

SISTER MOORE. But Sister Margaret's been there, praying for her, ain't she?

SISTER RICE. No, Sister Margaret ain't got there yet. She say she was going to make it last Sunday, but then she had to go to Philadelphia—

SISTER MOORE. Poor Sister Margaret. She sure has had her hands full.

SISTER BOXER. She got her hands full right down there in her own house. Reckon she couldn't get over to pray for your mother, Sister Rice, she couldn't stay here to pray for her own husband.

SISTER DOUGLASS. The Word say we ain't supposed to think no evil, Sister Boxer. Sister Margaret have to go the way the Lord leads her.

SISTER BOXER. I ain't thinking no evil. But the Word *do* say, if you don't love your brother who you can see, how you going to love God, who you ain't seen?

SISTER SALLY. That is a *true* saying, bless the Lord.

SISTER DOUGLASS. How is that poor, sin-sick soul?

SISTER BOXER. He ain't long for this world. He lying down there, just rotten with sin. He dying in his sins.

SISTER MOORE. He real pitiful. I declare, when you see what sin can do it make you stop and think.

SISTER RICE. Do David spend much time with him, Sister Odessa? I reckon it must make him feel real bad to see his father lying there like that.

ODESSA. Luke so sick he do a lot of sleeping, so David can't really be with him so much.

SISTER DOUGLASS. Oh. We ain't seen David hardly at all this week and I just figured he was downstairs with his father.

BROTHER BOXER. Little David—I'm mighty afraid little David got other fish to fry. The Lord has allowed me to see, with my *own* eyes, how David's done started straying from the Word. I ain't going to say no more. But the brother needs prayer. Amen. Sister Moore, do you recollect how much it cost us to get that there window painted?

SISTER MOORE. Why, no, Brother Boxer, I don't. Seem to me it cost about fifty dollars.

SISTER BOXER. It cost fifty-three dollars. I remember because Sister Margaret weren't here when the work was finished and I give the man the money myself.

SISTER DOUGLASS. It a mighty pretty window. Look like it make you love Jesus even more, seeing Him there all in the light like that.

BROTHER BOXER. You remember who she got to do it?

SISTER BOXER. Why, she got one of them folks from Philadelphia to do it. That was before we was even affiliated with that church.

BROTHER BOXER. I believe we could of got it done for less, right down here among our own.

SISTER RICE. I don't know, Brother Boxer, that's fine work. You got to have *training* for that. People think you can just get up and draw a picture, but it ain't so.

SISTER DOUGLASS. That's the truth, Sister Rice. My nephew, he draws, and he all the time telling me how hard it is. I have to help him out all the time, you know, 'cause it ain't easy to make a living that way—

SISTER BOXER. I don't know why your nephew couldn't of drew it for us. I bet you he wouldn't of charged no fifty-three dollars, either.

SISTER SALLY. My mother, she go to Bishop William's church up there on 145th Street, you know, and she was saying to me just the other day she don't see why, after all these years, Sister Margaret couldn't move her congregation to a better building.

SISTER MOORE. Sister Margaret ain't worried about these buildings down here on earth, daughter. Sister Margaret's working on another building, hallelujah, in the *heavens,* not made with hands!

SISTER SALLY. Why, that's what my mother's doing, too, Sister Moore. But she say she don't see why you got to be in dirt all the time just because you a Christian.

ODESSA. If anybody in this church is in dirt, it ain't the dirt of this church they's in. I know this ain't no palace but it's the best we can do right now. Sister Margaret's been doing her best for every one of us and it ain't right for us to sit up here this evening, back-biting against her.

SISTER MOORE. Sister Odessa, I told you downstairs it ain't nothing but the Devil putting them thoughts in your head. Ain't nobody back-biting against your sister. We's just discussing things, the Lord, He gives us eyes to see and understanding to understand.

SISTER BOXER. Amen!

SISTER MOORE. I got yet to say my first word against your sister. I know the Lord is seen fit, for reasons *I* ain't trying to discover, to burden your sister with a heavy burden. I ain't sitting in judgment. I ain't questioning the ways of the Lord. I don't know what that half-grown son of hers done seen to cause him to backslide this-a-way. *I* don't know why that man of hers is down there, dying in his sins—just rotting away, amen, before her eyes. I ain't asking no questions. I'm just waiting on the Lord because He say He'll reveal all things. In His own good time.

SISTER BOXER. Amen! And I believe He's going to use us to help him reveal.

(SISTER MOORE *begins singing.*)

ODESSA. Sister Moore!
SISTER MOORE.
You can run on for a long time,
You can run on for a long time,
You can run on for a long time,
I tell you the great God Almighty gonna cut you down.

CONTRALTO.
Some people go to church just to signify
Trying to make a date with their neighbor's wife.
Brother, let me tell you just as sure as you're born
You better leave that woman, leave her alone.
One of these days, just mark my word,
You'll think your neighbor has gone to work,
You'll walk right up and knock on the door—
That's all, brother, you'll knock no more.

Go tell that long-tongued liar, go tell that midnight rider,
Go tell the gambler, rambler, backslider,
Tell him God Almighty's gonna cut you down.

(During the last line of song MARGARET enters.)

MARGARET. Praise the Lord, children. I'm happy to see you's holding the fort for Jesus.

SISTER MOORE. Praise the *Lord,* Sister Margaret! We was just wondering if you was *ever* coming back here!

SISTER BOXER. Praise the Lord, Sister Margaret, we sure is glad you's back. Did you have a good trip?

MARGARET. Praise the Lord, children. It sure is good to be back here. The Lord, He give us the victory in Philadelphia, amen! He just worked and uncovered sin and put them children on their knees!

ALL.
What a wonder, what a marvel,
And I'm glad that I can tell
That the Lord saved me and He set me free,
He endowered me with power,
And gave me the victory.

What a wonder, what a marvel,
And I'm glad that I can tell
That the Lord saved me and He set me free,
He endowered me with power,
And gave me the victory.

What a wonder, what a marvel,
And I'm glad that I can tell
That the Lord saved me and He set me free,
He endowered me with power,
And gave me the victory.

SISTER MOORE. When it come time for the Lord to uncover, He sure do a mighty uncovering!

MARGARET. *(To* ODESSA.*)* Has everything been all right, sugar?

ODESSA. Yes, Maggie. Everything's been fine.

SISTER BOXER. How did you come down, Sister Margaret? Did you take the train or the bus?

MARGARET. Honey, one of the Philadelphia saints drove me down.

SISTER BOXER. *Drove* you down! I reckon you *did* get the victory.

(Laughter.)

SISTER MOORE. Well, bless the Lord, that's real nice. I reckon they was trying to help you cut down on expenses.

MARGARET. Children, tomorrow is going to be a mighty big Sunday. The Philadelphia church is coming down here, all of them, for the evening service. Even Mother Phillips might be coming, she say she's feeling so much better. You know, this church is going to be packed. *(To* BROTHER BOXER.*)* Brother Boxer, you going to have to clear a little space around that piano because they bringing their drums down here. *(To the others.)* They got drums up there, children, and it help the service a whole lot, I wouldn't have believed it.

(The merest pause.)

They even got a man up there making a joyful noise to the Lord on a trumpet?

BROTHER BOXER. He coming down here, too?

MARGARET. Oh, yes, he'll be here. Children, I want you all to turn out in full force tomorrow and show them Philadelphia saints how to praise the Lord.

SISTER DOUGLASS. Look like they going to be able to teach us something, they got them drums and trumpets and all—

SISTER MOORE. That don't make no difference. We been praising the Lord without that all this time, we ain't going to let them show us up.

MARGARET. You better *not* let them show you up. You supposed to be an example to the *Philadelphia* church.

SISTER RICE. But, Sister Margaret, you think it's right to let them come down here with all that—with drums and trumpets? Don't that seem kind of worldly?

MARGARET. Well, the evil ain't in the drum, Sister Rice, nor yet in the trumpet. The evil is in what folks do with it and what it leads them to. Ain't no harm in praising the Lord with anything you get in your hands.

BROTHER BOXER. It'll bring Brother David out to church again, I guarantee you that. That boy loves music.

MARGARET. I hope you don't mean he loves music more than he loves the Lord.

BROTHER BOXER. Oh, we all know how much he loves the Lord. But he got trumpets or *some* kind of horn in his *blood.*

ODESSA. I reckon you going to have to speak to David, Maggie. He upset about his daddy and he ain't been out to service much this week.

SISTER MOORE. When you upset, that's the time to come to the Lord. If you believe He loves you, you got to trust His love.

MARGARET. Poor David. He don't talk much, but he feel a whole lot.

SISTER BOXER. How is his daddy, Sister Margaret? You been down stairs to look at him yet?

ODESSA. We ain't allowed to break his rest.

MARGARET. I pray the Lord will save his soul.

SISTER MOORE. Amen. And, church, we got to pray that the Lord will draw our David back to Him, so he won't end up like his daddy. Our pastor, she got a lot to bear.

MARGARET. David ain't foolish, Sister Moore, and he done been well raised. He ain't going back into the world.

SISTER MOORE. I hope and pray you's right, from the bottom of my soul I do. But every living soul needs prayer, Sister Margaret, every living soul. And we's just trying to hold up your hand in this time of trouble.

SISTER BOXER. Sister Margaret, I ain't trying to dig up things what buried. But you told Joel and me he couldn't take that job driving that truck. And now you bringing down drums and trumpets from Philadelphia because you say the evil ain't in the thing, it's in what you do with the thing. Well, ain't that truck a *thing?* And if it's all right to blow a trumpet in church, why ain't it all right for Joel to drive that truck, so he can contribute a little more to the house of God? This church is *poor,* Sister Margaret, we ain't go no cars to ride you around in, like them folks in Philadelphia. But do that mean we got to *stay* poor?

MARGARET. Sister Boxer, you know as well as me that there's many a piano out in them night clubs. But that ain't stopped us from using a piano in this church. And there's all the difference in the world between a saint of God playing music in a church and helping to draw people in and a saint of God spending the whole day driving a liquor truck around. Now I know you got good sense and I know you see that, and I done already told you I don't want to talk no more about it.

SISTER BOXER. It don't seem to me you's being fair, Sister Margaret.

MARGARET. When is I ain't been fair? I been doing my best, as the Lord led me, for all of you, for all these years. How come you to say I ain't been fair? You sound like you done forget your salvation, Sister Boxer.

(DAVID *reappears, carrying a phonograph and a record. He enters* LUKE's *bedroom.* LUKE's *eyes are closed. He goes to the bed and touches him lightly and* LUKE *opens his eyes.*)

LUKE. What you got there?

DAVID. You going to recognize it. Be

quiet, listen. *(He plugs in the phonograph.)*

SISTER MOORE. Now the Word say Blessed is the peacemaker, so let me make peace. This ain't no way to be behaving.

MARGARET. Sister Moore, I'm the pastor of this church and I don't appreciate you acting as though we was both in the wrong.

SISTER MOORE. Ain't nobody infallible, Sister Margaret. Ain't a soul been born infallible.

ODESSA. We better all fall on our knees and pray.

MARGARET. Amen.

(DAVID has turned on the record, watching LUKE. The SOUND of LUKE's trombone fills the air.)

SISTER MOORE. Where's that music coming from?

ODESSA. It must be coming from down the street.

MARGARET. *(Recognition.)* Oh, my God.

SISTER MOORE. It's coming from your house, Sister Margaret.

MARGARET. Kneel down.

(They watch her.)

Kneel down, I say!

(LUKE takes his mouthpiece from his pajama pocket and pantomimes a phrase, then stops, his mouthpiece in his hand, staring at his son. In the church, slowly, they kneel.)

MARGARET. Pray. Every single one of you. Pray that God will give you a clean heart and a clean mind and teach you to obey. *(She turns and leaves the pulpit.)*

(Upstairs, they turn and look at each other and slowly rise from their knees. The church DIMS OUT. MARGARET stands for a moment in the door of LUKE's bedroom.)

MARGARET. David!

DAVID. Mama—I didn't hear you come in!

MARGARET. I reckon you didn't hear me come in. The way that box is going, you wouldn't of hear the Holy *Ghost* come in. Turn it off! Turn it off!

(DAVID does so.)

MARGARET. You ain't supposed to let your daddy come here and lead you away from the Word. You's supposed to lead your daddy to the Lord. *(To LUKE.)* It seems to me by this time the very sound of a horn would make you to weep or pray.

DAVID. It's one of Daddy's old records. That you never let me play.

MARGARET. Where'd that box come from? What's it doing in this house?

DAVID. I borrowed it.

MARGARET. Where'd you get that record?

DAVID. It's mine.

LUKE. That's right. It's his—now.

(A pause.)

MARGARET. I ain't trying to be hard on you, son. But we's got to watch and pray. We's got to watch and pray.

DAVID. Yes, Mama. Mama, I got to go now.

MARGARET. Where you going, son?

LUKE. Maggie, he ain't five years old, he's eighteen. Let him alone.

MARGARET. You be quiet. You ain't got nothing to say in all this.

LUKE. That's a lie. I got a lot to say in all this. That's my son. Go on, boy. You remember what I told you.

DAVID. I'm taking the record player back where I got it. *(At the door.)* So long—Daddy—

LUKE. Go on, boy. You all right?

MARGARET. David—

DAVID. I'm all right, Daddy. *(DAVID goes.)*

LUKE. So long, son.

MARGARET. Luke, ain't you never going to learn to do right? Ain't you learned nothing out all these years, all this trouble?

LUKE. I done learned a few things. They might not be the same things you wanted me to learn. Hell, I don't know if they are the same things *I* wanted me to learn.

MARGARET. I ain't never wanted you to learn but one thing, the love of Jesus.

LUKE. You done changed your tune a whole lot. That ain't what we was trying to learn in the beginning.

MARGARET. The beginning is a long time ago. And weren't nothing but foolishness. Ain't nothing but the love of God can save your soul.

LUKE. Maggie, don't fight with me. I don't want to fight no more. We didn't get married because we loved God. We loved each other. Ain't that right?

MARGARET. I sure can't save your soul, Luke.

LUKE. There was a time when I believed you could.

MARGARET. Luke. That's all past. *(She sits on the edge of the bed.)* Luke, it been a long time we ain't seen each other, ten long years. Look how the Lord done let you fall. Ain't you ready to give up to Him and ask Him to save you from your sins and bring peace to your soul?

LUKE. Is you got peace in your soul, Maggie?

MARGARET. Yes! He done calmed the waters, He done beat back the powers of darkness, He done made me a new woman!

LUKE. Then that other woman—that funny, fast-talking, fiery little thing I used to hold in my arms—He done done away with her?

MARGARET. *(Rises.)* All that's—been burned out of me by the power of the Holy Ghost.

LUKE. Maggie, I remember you when you didn't hardly know if the Holy Ghost was something to drink or something to put on your hair. I know we can't go back, Maggie. But you mean that whole time we was together, even with all our trouble, you mean it don't mean nothing to you now? You mean—you don't remember? I was your *man,* Maggie, we was everything to each other, like that Bible of yours say, we was one flesh—we used to get on each other's nerves something *awful*—you mean that's all dead and gone?

MARGARET. You is still got that old, sinful Adam in you. You's thinking with Adam's mind. You don't understand that when the Lord changes you He makes you a new person and He gives you a new mind.

LUKE. Don't talk at me like I was a congregation. I ain't no congregation. I'm your husband, even if I ain't much good to you no more.

MARGARET. Well, if it's all dead and gone—you killed it! Don't you lay there and try to make me feel accused. If it's all dead and gone, you did it, you did it!

LUKE. Ah. Now we coming. At least it wasn't the Holy Ghost. Just how did I do it, Maggie? How did I kill it?

MARGARET. I never knew why you couldn't be like other men.

LUKE. I was the man you married, Maggie. I weren't supposed to be like other men. When we didn't have nothing, I made it my business to find something, didn't I? Little David always had shoes to his feet when I was there and you wasn't never dressed in rags. And anyway—you want me to repent so you can get me into heaven, or you want me to repent so you can keep David home?

MARGARET. Is David talking about leaving home?

LUKE. Don't you reckon he going to be leaving home one day?

MARGARET. David going to work with me in these here churches and he going to be a pastor when he get old enough.

LUKE. He got the call?

MARGARET. He'll *get* the call.

LUKE. You sure got a lot of influence with the Holy Ghost.

MARGARET. I didn't come in here to listen to you blaspheme. I just come in here to try to get you to think about your soul.

LUKE. Margaret, once you told me you loved me and then you jumped up and ran off from me like you couldn't stand the smell of me. What you think *that* done to my soul?

MARGARET. I had to go. The Lord told me to go. We'd been living like—like two animals, like two children, never thought of nothing but their own pleasure. In my heart, I always knew we couldn't go on like that—we was too happy—

LUKE. Ah!

MARGARET. And that winter—them was terrible days, Luke. When I'd almost done gone under, I heard a voice. The voice said, Maggie, you got to find you a hiding place. I knowed weren't no hiding place to be found in you—not in no man. And you—you cared more about that trombone than you ever cared about me!

LUKE. You ought to of tried me, Maggie. If you had trusted me till then, you ought to have trusted me a little further.

MARGARET. When they laid my baby in the churchyard, that poor little baby girl what hadn't never drawn breath, I knowed if we kept on a-going the way we'd been going, He weren't going to have no mercy on neither one of us. And that's when I swore to my God I was going to change my way of living.

LUKE. Then that God you found—He just curse the poor? But He don't bother nobody else? Them big boys, them with all the money and all the manners, what let you drop dead in the streets, watch your blood run all over the gutters, just so they can make a lousy dime—He get along fine with them? What the hell had we done to be cursed, Maggie?

MARGARET. We hadn't never thought of nothing but ourself. We hadn't never thought on God!

LUKE. All we'd done to be cursed was to be *poor,* that's all. That's why little Margaret was laid in the churchyard. It was just because you hadn't never in your whole life had enough to eat and you was sick that winter and you didn't have no strength. Don't you come on with me about no judgment, Maggie. That was my baby, too.

MARGARET. *Your* baby, yours! I was the one who carried it in my belly, *I* was the one who felt it starving to death inside me. *I* was the one who had it, in the cold and dark alone! You wasn't nowhere to be found, you was out drunk.

LUKE. I was *there*. I was *there*. Yes, I was drunk, but I was sitting at your bedside every day. Every time you come to yourself you looked at me and started screaming about how I'd killed our baby. Like I'd taken little Margaret and strangled her with my own two hands. *Yes,* I was drunk but I was waiting for you to call me. You never did. You never did.

MARGARET. I reckon the Lord was working with me, even then.

LUKE. I reckon so.

MARGARET. Luke. Luke, it don't do to question God.

LUKE. No, it don't. It sure as hell don't.

MARGARET. Don't let your heart be bitter. You'd come way down, Luke, bitterness ain't going to help you now. Let Him break your heart, let the tears come, ask Him to forgive you for your sins, call on Him, call on Him!

LUKE. Call on Him for what, Maggie?

MARGARET. To save your soul. To keep you from the fires of hell. So we can be together in glory.

LUKE. I want to be together with you now.

MARGARET. Luke. You ain't fighting with men no more. You's fighting with God. You got to humble yourself, you got to bow your head.

LUKE. It ain't going to be like that, Maggie. I ain't going to come crawling to the Lord now, making out like I'd do better if I had it all to do over. I ain't going to go out, screaming against hell-fire. It would make *you* right. It would prove to David you was right. It would make me nothing but a dirty, drunk old man didn't do nothing but blow music and chase the women all his life. I ain't going to let it be like that. That ain't all there was to it. You know that ain't all there was to it.

MARGARET. Stubborn, stubborn, stubborn Luke! You like a little boy. You think this is a game? You think it don't hurt me to my heart to see you the way you is now? You think my heart ain't black with sorrow to see your soul go under?

LUKE. Stop talking about my soul. It's me, Maggie—*me!* Don't you remember *me?* Don't you care nothing about *me?* You ain't never stopped loving me. Have you, Maggie? Can't you tell me the truth?

MARGARET. Luke—we ain't young no more. It don't matter no more about us. But what about our boy? You want him to live the life you've lived? You want him to end up—old and empty-handed?

LUKE. I don't care what kind of life he lives—as long as it's *his* life—not mine, not his mama's, but his own. I ain't going to let you make him safe.

MARGARET. I can't do no more. Before God, I done my best. Your blood can't be required at my hands.

LUKE. I guess I could have told you—it weren't *my* soul we been trying to save.

(Low, syncopated SINGING from the church begins.)

MARGARET. Luke. You's going to die. I hope the Lord have mercy on you.

LUKE. I ain't asking for no goddam mercy. *(He turns his face to the wall.)* Go away.

MARGARET. You's going to die, Luke.

(She moves slowly from the bedroom into the kitchen.)

(ODESSA enters from the church, goes to MARGARET.)

ODESSA. Honey—they's going to have a business meeting upstairs. You hear me? You know what that means? If you want to hold onto this church, Maggie—if you do—you better get on upstairs.

(MARGARET is silent.)

Where's David? He ought to be here when you need him.

MARGARET. I don't know.

ODESSA. I'll go and see if I can find him. You all right?

MARGARET. It looks like rain out there. Put something on.

(After a moment, ODESSA goes. MARGARET walks up and down the kitchen. Her tears begin.)

Lord, help us to stand. Help us to stand. Lord, give me strength! Give me strength!

CURTAIN

ACT THREE

MUSIC is heard offstage, a slow, quiet sound.

Early the following morning. A bright quiet day. Except for LUKE, the stage is empty. His room is dark. He is sleeping.

The LIGHT comes up very slowly in the church. After a moment, MRS. JACKSON enters. She is wearing a house dress and slippers. She puts her hands to her face, moaning slightly, then falls heavily before the altar.

MARGARET enters through LUKE's bedroom. She pauses a moment at the foot of LUKE's bed, then enters the kitchen, then slowly mounts to the church.

As she enters, MRS. JACKSON stirs. They stare at each other for a moment. MRS. JACKSON is weeping.

MRS. JACKSON. Sister Margaret, you's a woman of the Lord—you say you in communion with the Lord. Why He take my baby from me? Tell me why He do it? Why He make my baby suffer so? Tell me why He do it!

MARGARET. Sister—we got to trust God —somehow. We got to bow our heads.

MRS. JACKSON. My head is bowed. My head been bowed since I been born. His daddy's head is bowed. The Lord ain't got no right to make a baby suffer so, just to make me bow my head!

MARGARET. Be careful what you say, daughter. Be careful what you say. We can't penetrate the mysteries of the Lord's will.

MRS. JACKSON. (Moves away.) Why I got to be careful what I say? You think the Lord going to do me something else? I ain't got to be careful what I say no more. I sit on the bench in the hospital all night long, me and my husband, and we waited and we prayed and we wept. I said, Lord, if you spare my baby, I won't never take another drink, I won't do nothing, nothing to displease you, if you only give me back my baby, safe and well. He was such a nice baby and just like his daddy, he liked to laugh already. But I ain't going to have no more. Such a nice baby, I don't see why he had to get all twisted and curled up with pain and scream his little head off. And couldn't nobody help him. He hadn't never done nothing to nobody. Ain't nobody never done nothing bad enough to suffer like that baby suffered.

MARGARET. Daughter, pray with me. Come, pray with me.

MRS. JACKSON. I been trying to pray. Everytime I kneel down, I see my baby again—and—I can't pray. I can't get it out of my head, it ain't right, even if He's God, it ain't right.

MARGARET. Sister—once I lost a baby, too. I know what that emptiness feels like, I declare to my Saviour I do. That was when I come to the Lord. I wouldn't come before. Maybe the Lord is working with you now. Open your heart and listen. Maybe, out of all this sorrow. He's calling you to do His work.

MRS. JACKSON. I ain't like you, Sister Margaret. I don't want all this, all these people looking to me. I'm just a young woman, I just want my man and my home and my children.

MARGARET. But that's all I wanted. That's what I wanted! Sometimes—what we want—and what we ought to have— ain't the same. Sometime, the Lord, He take away what we want and give us what we need.

MRS. JACKSON. And do I need—that man sitting home with a busted heart? Do I need—two children in the graveyard?

MARGARET. I don't know, I ain't the Lord, I don't know what you need. You need to pray.

MRS. JACKSON. No, I'm going home to my husband. He be getting worried. He don't know where I am. (She starts out.)

MARGARET. Sister Jackson!

(MRS. JACKSON turns.)

Why did you say you ain't going to have no more babies? You still a very young woman.

MRS. JACKSON. I'm scared to go through it again. I can't go through it again.

MARGARET. That ain't right. That ain't right. You ought to have another baby. You ought to have another baby right away.

(A pause.)

Honey—is there anything you want me to do for you now, in your time of trouble?

MRS. JACKSON. No, Sister Margaret, ain't nothing you can do. (She goes.)

(MARGARET stands alone in the church.)

MARGARET. Get on home to your husband. Go on home, to your man.

(*Downstairs*, ODESSA *enters through* LUKE's *room; pauses briefly at* LUKE's *bed, enters the kitchen. She goes to the stove, puts a match under the coffeepot.* MARGARET *stares at the altar; starts downstairs.*)

ODESSA. (*Sings, under her breath.*)
Some say the rose of Sharon, some say the Prince of Peace.
But I call Jesus my rock!

(MARGARET *enters.*)

ODESSA. How long you been up, Maggie?

MARGARET. I don't know. Look like I couldn't sleep.

ODESSA. You got a heavy day ahead of you.

MARGARET. I know it. David ain't come in yet?

ODESSA. No, but don't you fret. He's all right. He'll be along. It's just natural for young boys to go a little wild every now and again. Soon this'll be over, Maggie, and when you look back on it, it won't be nothing more than like you had a bad dream.

MARGARET. A bad dream!

ODESSA. They ain't going to turn you out, Maggie. They ain't crazy. They know it take a *long* time before they going to find another pastor of this church like you.

MARGARET. It won't take them so long if Sister Moore have her way. She going to be the next pastor of this church. Lord, you sure can't tell what's going on in a person's heart.

ODESSA. The Bible say the heart is deceitful above all things. And desperately wicked.

MARGARET. Who can know it? I guess whoever wrote that wasn't just thinking about the hearts of other people.

ODESSA. Maggie, you better go on in the front and lie down awhile. You got time. Sunday school ain't even started yet. I'll call you in time for you to get dressed for service.

MARGARET. I reckon I better. (*She starts out, stops.*) They talk about me letting my own house perish in sin. The Word say if you put father or mother or brother or sister or husband—or *anybody*—ahead of Him, He ain't going to have nothing to do with you on the last day.

ODESSA. Yes. The Word do say so.

MARGARET. I married that man when I weren't hardly nothing but a girl. I used to know that man, look like, just inside *out,* sometime I knowed what he was going to do before he knowed it himself. Sometime I could just look up, look up at that face, and just—*know.* Ain't no man never made me laugh the way Luke could. No, nor cry neither. I ain't never held no man until I felt his pain coming into me like little drops of acid. Odessa, I bore that man his only son. Now, you know there's still something left in my heart for that man.

ODESSA. Don't think on it, honey. Don't think on it so. Go on in front and lie down.

MARGARET. Yes. (*She starts out, stops.*) Odessa—you know what amen means?

ODESSA. Amen means—*amen.*

MARGARET. Amen means Thy will be done. Amen means So be it. I been up all morning, praying—and—I couldn't say amen. (*She goes.*)

ODESSA. Lord, have mercy. Have mercy, Lord, this morning. (*Sings, under her breath.*) Some say the Rose of Sharon, some say the Prince of Peace. But I call Jesus my rock! (*She goes to the door of* LUKE's *room.*)

(BROTHER *and* SISTER BOXER *and* SISTER MOORE *enter the church. The two women are all in white.*)

Yes, Lord. Everytime a woman don't know if she coming or going, every*time* her heart get all swelled up with grief, there's a man sleeping somewhere close by.

(SISTER BOXER *crosses the church and comes down the stairs.*)

SISTER BOXER. Praise the Lord, Sister Odessa. You all alone this morning?

ODESSA. I didn't know you folks was upstairs. How long you been there?

SISTER BOXER. We just this minute come in.

ODESSA. You all mighty early, seems to me.

SISTER BOXER. Well, Sister Moore, she thought if we got here early we might be able to see Sister Margaret before anybody else come in.

ODESSA. Sister Margaret ain't ready to see nobody yet.

SISTER BOXER. It almost time for Sunday school.

ODESSA. Sister Boxer, you know right well that Sister Margaret don't hardly never come to Sunday school. She got to save her strength for the morning service. You know that.

SISTER BOXER. Well, Sister Moore thought—maybe *this* morning—

ODESSA. Sister Boxer—don't you think enough harm's been done with all them terrible things was said last night?

SISTER BOXER. Ain't nobody said nothing last night that wasn't the gospel truth.

ODESSA. I done heard enough truth these last couple of days to last me the rest of my life.

SISTER BOXER. The truth is a two-edged sword, Sister Odessa.

ODESSA. It ain't never going to cut you down. You ain't never going to come that close to it.

SISTER BOXER. Well—do Jesus! Soon as something happens to that sister of yours you forgets all about your salvation, don't you? You better ask the Lord to watch your tongue. The tongue is a *unruly* member.

ODESSA. It ain't as unruly as it's going to get.

(*A pause.*)

Sister Boxer, this ain't no way for us to be talking. We used to be *friends.* We used to have right *good* times together. How come we got all this bad feeling all of a sudden? Look like it come out of nowhere, overnight.

SISTER BOXER. I ain't got no bad feeling toward *you,* Sister Odessa. (*After a moment,* SISTER BOXER *turns and mounts to the church.*)

(ODESSA *follows.*)

SISTER MOORE. Praise the Lord, Sister Odessa. How you this Lord's day morning?

ODESSA. I'm leaning on the Lord, Sister Moore. How you feeling?

BROTHER BOXER. Praise the Lord, Sister Odessa. I'm mighty glad to hear you say that. We needs the Lord this morning. We needs to hear Him speak peace to our souls.

ODESSA. How come you folks want to see Sister Margaret so early in the morning?

SISTER BOXER. Well, we ain't really got to see Sister Margaret, not now that you're here, Sister Odessa. You is still one of the elders of this church.

SISTER MOORE. We want to do everything we got to do in front, amen. Don't want nobody saying we went around and done it in the dark.

ODESSA. You's doing it in front, all right. You's supposed to do it in front of the whole congregation this afternoon.

BROTHER BOXER. Well, the Lord's done led us to do a little different from the way we was going to do last night.

ODESSA. How's that, Brother Boxer?

(*A pause.*)

Well, now, the way I understood it last night—you folks say that Margaret ain't got no right to call herself a spiritual leader. *You* folks say that Margaret done let her own household perish in sin and —you folks say—that all these things is a sign from the Lord that He ain't pleased with Margaret and you was going to put all that in front of this and the church from Philadelphia and see what *they* thought. Ain't that right?

SISTER BOXER. We done already spoken to the members of this church. Margaret's as good as read out of this church already, ain't hardly no need for her to come to service.

SISTER MOORE. I spoke to them myself. I been up since early this morning, bless the Lord, just ringing doorbells and stirring up the people against sin.

ODESSA. You must of got up mighty early.

SISTER MOORE. When the Lord's work is to be done, I gets up out of my bed. God don't love the slothful. And, look like the more I do, the more He gives me strength to do.

BROTHER BOXER. We thought it might be easier on Sister Margaret if we done it this way. Ain't no need for folks to know all of Sister Margaret's personal business. So we ain't said nothing about Brother Luke. Folks is bound to try and put two and two together—but *we* ain't said nothing. We ain't said nothing about Brother David. We is just told the congregation that the Lord's done revealed to the elders of this church that Sister Margaret ain't been leading the life of a holy woman, especially a holy woman in *her* position, is supposed to lead. That's all. And we said we weren't sitting in *judgment* on Sister Margaret. We was leaving it up to her conscience, amen, and the Lord.

SISTER BOXER. But we did say—since we're the elders of the church and we got a responsibility to the congregation, too—that the Lord ain't pleased at Margaret sitting in the seat of authority.

SISTER MOORE. It's time for her to come down.

ODESSA. And how did folks take it when you told them all this?

BROTHER BOXER. Well, folks ain't in this church to worship Sister Margaret. They's here to worship the Lord.

ODESSA. Folks thought Margaret was good enough to be their pastor all these years, they ain't going to stop wanting her for pastor overnight.

BROTHER BOXER. She rose overnight. She can fall overnight.

SISTER BOXER. I tell you, Sister Odessa, like the song says: "You may run on a great, long time but great God Almighty going to cut you down." Yes, indeed, He going to let the truth be known one *day*. And on that day, it's just too bad *for* you. Sister Margaret done had a lot of people fooled a long time, but now, bless God forever, the truth is out.

ODESSA. What truth? What is that woman done to make you hate her so? Weren't but only yesterday you was all saying how wonderful she was, and how blessed we was to have her. And now you can't find nothing bad enough to say about her. Don't give me that stuff about her letting her household perish in sin. Ain't a one of you but ain't got a brother or a sister or somebody on the road to hell right now. I want to know what is she *done?* What is she done to you, Sister Moore?

SISTER BOXER. *I* ain't got no brothers or sisters on the road to hell. Only sister I *had* is waiting for me in glory. And every *soul* I come in contact with is saved —except of course for them people I work for. And I got no trombone-playing husband dying in my house and I ain't got no half-grown son out fornicating in the wilderness.

SISTER MOORE. Don't you come up here and act like you thought we was just acting out of spite and meanness. Your sister ain't done nothing to me; she *can't* do nothing to me because the Lord holds me in His hands. All we's trying to do is the Lord's will—you ought to be trying to do it, too. If we want to reign with him in glory, we ain't supposed to put nobody before Him. Amen! We ain't supposed to have no other love but Him.

SISTER BOXER. I looked at that man and I says to myself, How in the *world* did Sister Margaret ever get herself mixed up with a man like that?

ODESSA. Ain't no mystery how a woman gets mixed up with a man, Sister Boxer, and you sure ought to know that, even if poor Sister Moore here *don't*.

SISTER MOORE. Don't you poor-Sister-Moore me. That man put a demon inside your sister and that demon's walking up and down inside her still. You can see it in her eyes, they done got all sleepy with lust.

ODESSA. Sister Moore, I sure would like to know just how come *you* know so much about it.

SISTER BOXER. Sister Odessa, ain't no sense to you trying to put everybody in the wrong because Sister Margaret is falling. That ain't going to raise her back up. It's the Lord's *will* she should come down.

ODESSA. I don't understand how you can take her part against my sister. *You* ought to know how much Sister Margaret's suffered all these years by herself. *You* know it ain't no easy thing for a woman to go it alone. She done spent more'n ten years to build this up for herself and her little boy. How you going to throw her out now? What's she going to do, where's she going to go?

BROTHER BOXER. She didn't worry about Elder King when she took over this church from him.

SISTER MOORE. I think you think I hates your sister because she been married. And I ain't never been married. I ain't questioning the Lord's ways. He done kept me pure to Himself for a purpose, and that purpose is working itself

out right here in this room this morning —right here in this room, this upper room. It make your sister look double-minded, I do declare it do, if she done tried, one time, to bring peace to one man, and failed, and then she jump up and think she going to bring peace to a whole lot of people.

ODESSA. Sister Margaret done give good service all those years. She ain't been acting like she was double-minded.

BROTHER BOXER. But I bet you—she is double-minded *now*.

(DAVID *enters the apartment. He is suffering from a hangover, is still a little drunk. He goes to the sink and splashes cold water on his face. He moves with both bravado and fear and there is a kind of heartbreaking humor in his actions.*)

SISTER BOXER. Odessa, a church can't have no woman for pastor who done been married once and then decided it didn't suit her and then jump up and run off from her husband and take a seat in the pulpit and act like she ain't no woman no more. That ain't no kind of example to the young. The Word say the marriage bed is holy.

ODESSA. I can't believe—I can't *believe* you really going to do it. We been friends so long.

(DAVID *dries his face. He goes to the door of* LUKE's *room, stands for a moment looking at his father. He turns back into the kitchen. At this moment,* MARGARET *enters, dressed in white. She and* DAVID *stare at each other.*)

SISTER BOXER. You the one I'm sorry for, Sister Odessa. You done spent your life, look like, protecting that sister of yours. And now you can't protect her no more.

ODESSA. It ain't been me protecting Sister Margaret. It been the Lord. And He ain't yet withdrawed His hand. He ain't never left none of His children alone.

(She starts for the rear door of the church.)

SISTER BOXER. How come you ain't never been married, Sister Odessa?

ODESSA. Suppose we just say, Sister Boxer, that I never had the time.

SISTER BOXER. It might have been better for you if you'd taken the time.

ODESSA. I ain't got no regrets. No, I ain't. I ain't claiming I'm pure, like Sister Moore here. I ain't claiming that the Lord had such special plans for me that I couldn't have nothing to do with men. Brothers and sisters, if you knew just a little bit about folks' lives, what folks go through, and the low, black places they finds their feet—you *would* have a meeting here this afternoon. Maybe I don't know the Lord like you do, but I know something else. I know how men and women can come together and change each other and make each other suffer, and make each other glad. If you putting my sister out of this church, you putting me out, too. *(She goes out through the street door.)*

(The church DIMS OUT.)

MARGARET. Where you been until this time in the morning, son?

DAVID. I was out visiting some people I know. And it got to be later than I realized and I stayed there overnight.

MARGARET. How come it got to be so late before you realized it?

DAVID. I don't know. We just got to talking.

MARGARET. Talking? *(She moves closer to him.)* What was you talking about, son? You stink of whiskey! *(She slaps him.)*

(DAVID sits at the table.)

DAVID. That ain't going to do no good, Ma.

(She slaps him again. DAVID slumps on the table, his head in his arms.)

MARGARET. Is that what I been slaving for all these long, hard years? Is I carried slops and scrubbed floors and ate leftovers and swallowed bitterness by the gallon jugful—for this? So you could walk in here this Lord's-day morning stinking from whiskey and some no-count, dirty, black girl's sweat? Declare, I wish you'd died in my belly, too, if I been slaving all these years for this!

DAVID. Mama. Mama. Please.

MARGARET. Sit up and look at me. Is you too drunk to hold up your head? Or is you too ashamed? Lord knows you ought to be ashamed.

DAVID. Mama, I wouldn't of had this to happen this way for nothing in the world.

MARGARET. Was they holding a pistol to your head last evening? Or did they tie you down and pour the whiskey down your throat?

DAVID. No. No. Didn't nobody have no pistol. Didn't nobody have no rope. Some fellows said, Let's pick up some whiskey. And I said, Sure. And we all put in some money and I went down to the liquor store and bought it. And then we drank it.

(MARGARET turns away.)

MARGARET. David, I ain't so old. I know the world is wicked. I know young people have terrible temptations. Did you do it because you was afraid them boys would make fun of you?

DAVID. No.

MARGARET. Was it on account of some girl?

DAVID. No.

MARGARET. Was it—your daddy put you up to it? Was it your daddy made you think it was manly to get drunk?

DAVID. Daddy—I don't think you can blame it on Daddy, Mama.

MARGARET. Why'd you do it, David? When I done tried so hard to raise you right? Why'd you want to hurt me this way?

DAVID. I didn't want to hurt you, Mama. But this day has been coming a long time. Mama, I can't play piano in church no more.

MARGARET. Is it on account of your daddy? Is it your daddy put all this foolishness in your head?

DAVID. Daddy ain't been around for a long time, Mama. I ain't talked to him but one time since he been here.

MARGARET. And that one time—he told you all about the wonderful time he had all them years, blowing out his guts on that trombone.

DAVID. No. That ain't exactly what he said. That ain't exactly what we talked about.

MARGARET. What *did* you talk about?

(A SOUND OF CHILDREN singing "Jesus Loves Me" comes from the church.)

DAVID. Well—he must have been talking about you. About how he missed you, and all.

MARGARET. Sunday school done started. David, why don't you go upstairs and play for them, just this one last morning?

DAVID. Mama, I told you. I can't play piano in church no more.

MARGARET. David, why don't you feel it no more, what you felt once? Where's it gone? Where's the Holy Ghost gone?

DAVID. I don't know, Mama. It's empty. *(He indicates his chest.)* It's empty here.

MARGARET. Can't you pray? Why don't you pray? If you pray, pray hard, He'll come back. The Holy Ghost will come back. He'll come down on heavenly wings, David, and *(She touches his chest.)* fill that empty space, He'll start your heart to singing—singing again. He'll fill you, David, with a mighty burning fire and burn out *(She takes his head roughly between her palms.)* all that foolishness, all them foolish dreams you carries around up there. Oh, David, David, pray that the Holy Ghost will come back, that the gift of God will come back!

DAVID. Mama, if a person don't feel it, he just don't feel it.

MARGARET. David, I'm older than you. I done been down the line. I know ain't no safety nowhere in this world if you don't stay close to God. What you think the world's got out there for you but a broken heart?

(ODESSA, unnoticed, enters.)

ODESSA. You better listen to her, David.

MARGARET. I remember boys like you down home, David, many years ago—fine young men, proud as horses, and I seen what happened to them. I seen them go down, David, until they was among the lowest of the low. There's boys like you down there, today, breaking rock and building roads, they ain't never going to hold their heads up on this earth no more. There's boys like you all over this city, filling up the gin mills and standing on the corners, running down alleys, tearing themselves to pieces with knives and whiskey and dope and sin! You think I done lived this long and I don't know what's happening? Fine young men and they're lost—they don't know what's happened to their life. Fine young men, and some of them dead and some of them dead while they living. You think I want to see this happen to you? You think I want you one day lying where your daddy lies today?

ODESSA. You better listen to her David. You better listen.

MARGARET. He ain't going to listen. Young folks don't never listen. They just go on, headlong, and they think ain't nothing ever going to be too big for them. And, time they find out, it's too late then.

DAVID. And if I listened—what would happen? What do you think would happen if I listened? You want me to stay here, getting older, getting sicker—hating you? You think I want to hate you,

Mama? You think it don't tear me to pieces to have to lie to you all the time. Yes, because I been lying to you, Mama, for a long time now! I don't want to tell no more lies. I don't want to keep on feeling so bad inside that I have to go running down them alleys you was talking about—that alley right outside this door! —to find something to help me hide—to hide—from what I'm feeling. Mama, I want to be a man. It's time you let me be a man. You got to let me go.

(A pause.)

If I stayed here—I'd end up worse than Daddy—because I wouldn't be doing what I know I got to do—I *got* to do! I've seen your life—and now I see Daddy —and I love you, I love you both!—but I've got my work to do, something's happening in the world out there, I got to go! I know you think I don't know what's happening, but I'm beginning to see—something. Every time I play, every time I listen, I see Daddy's face and yours, and so many faces—who's going to speak for all that, Mama? Who's going to speak for all of us? I can't stay home. Maybe I can say something—one day— maybe I can say something in music that's never been said before. Mama—*you* knew this day was coming.

MARGARET. I reckon I thought I was Joshua and could make the sun stand still.

DAVID. Mama, I'm leaving this house tonight. I'm going on the road with some other guys. I got a lot of things to do today and I ain't going to be hanging around the house. I'll see you before I go. *(He starts for the door.)*

MARGARET. David—?

DAVID. Yes, Mama?

MARGARET. Don't you want to eat something?

DAVID. No, Mama. I ain't hungry now. *(He goes.)*

MARGARET. Well. There he go. Who'd ever want to love a man and raise a child!

Odessa—you think I'm a hard woman?

ODESSA. No. I don't think you a hard woman. But I think you's in a hard place.

MARGARET. I done something, somewhere, wrong.

ODESSA. Remember this morning. You got a awful thing ahead of you this morning. You got to go upstairs and win them folks back to you this morning.

MARGARET. My man is in there, dying, and my baby's in the world—how'm I going to preach, Odessa? How'm I going to preach when I can't even pray?

ODESSA. You got to face them. You got to think. You got to pray.

MARGARET. Sister, I can't. I can't. I can't.

ODESSA. Maggie. It was you had the vision. It weren't me. You got to think back to the vision. If the vision was for anything, it was for just this day.

MARGARET. The vision. Ah, it weren't yesterday, that vision. I was in a cold, dark place and I thought it was the grave. And I listened to hear my little baby cry and didn't no cry come. I heard a voice say, Maggie. Maggie. You got to find you a hiding place. I wanted Luke. *(She begins to weep.)* Oh, sister, I don't remember no vision. I just remember that it was dark and I was scared and my baby was dead and I wanted Luke, I wanted Luke, I wanted Luke!

ODESSA. Oh, honey. Oh, my honey. What we going to do with you this morning?

(MARGARET cannot stop weeping.)

Come on, honey, come on. You got them folks to face.

MARGARET. All these years I prayed as hard as I knowed how. I tried to put my treasure in heaven where couldn't nothing get at it and take it away from me and leave me alone. I asked the Lord to hold my hand. I didn't expect that none of this would ever rise to hurt me no more. And all these years it just been waiting for me, waiting for me to turn a corner. And there it stand, my whole life, just like I hadn't never gone nowhere. It's a awful thing to think about, the way love never dies!

ODESSA. You's got to pull yourself together and think how you can *win*. You always been the winner. Ain't no time to be a woman *now*. You can't let them throw you out of this church. What we going to do then? I'm getting old, I can't help you. And you ain't young no more, either.

MARGARET. Maybe we could go—someplace else.

ODESSA. We ain't got no money to go no place. We ain't paid the rent for this month. We ain't even finished paying for this Frigidaire.

MARGARET. I remember in the old days whenever Luke wanted to spend some money on foolishness, that is exactly what I would have to say to him: "Man, ain't you got good sense? Do you know we ain't even paid the rent for this month?"

ODESSA. Margaret. You got to think.

MARGARET. Odessa, you remember when we was little there was a old blind woman lived down the road from us. She used to live in this house all by herself and you used to take me by the hand when we walked past her house because I was scared of her. I can see her, just as plain somehow, sitting on the porch, rocking in that chair, just looking out over them roads like she could see something. And she used to hear us coming, I guess, and she'd shout out, "How you this Lord's-day morning?" Don't care what day it was, or what time of day it was, it was always the Lord's-day morning for her. Daddy used to joke about her, he used to say, "Ain't no man in that house. It's a mighty sad house." I reckon this going to be a mighty sad house before long.

ODESSA. Margaret. You got to think.

MARGARET. I'm thinking. I'm thinking. I'm thinking how I throwed away my life.

ODESSA. You can't think about it like that. You got to remember—you gave your life to the Lord.

MARGARET. I'm thinking now—maybe Luke needed it more. Maybe David could of used it better. I know. I got to go upstairs and face them people. Ain't nothing left for me to do. I'd like to talk to Luke.

ODESSA. I'll go on up there.

MARGARET. The only thing my mother should have told me is that being a woman ain't nothing but one long fight with men. And even the Lord, look like, ain't nothing but the most impossible kind of man there is. Go upstairs, sister. Be there—when I get there.

(After a moment, ODESSA *goes. Again, we hear the sound of singing: "God be with you till we meet again."* MARGARET *walks into* LUKE's *bedroom, stands there a moment, watching him.* BROTHER BOXER *enters the kitchen, goes to the Frigidaire, pours himself a Kool-aid.)*

MARGARET. *(Turns.)* What are you doing down here, Brother Boxer? Why ain't you upstairs in the service?

BROTHER BOXER. Why ain't *you* upstairs in the service, Sister Margaret? We's waiting for you upstairs.

MARGARET. I'm coming upstairs! Can't you go on back up there now and ask them folks to be—a little quiet? He's sick, Brother Boxer. He's sick!

BROTHER BOXER. You just finding that out? He *been* sick, Sister Margaret. How come it ain't never upset you until now? And how you expect me to go upstairs and ask them folks to be quiet when you been telling us all these years to praise the Lord with fervor? Listen! They got fervor. Where's all your fervor done gone to, Sister Margaret?

MARGARET. Brother Boxer, even if you don't want me for your pastor no more, please remember I'm a woman. Don't talk to me this way.

BROTHER BOXER. A woman? Is *that* where all your fervor done gone to? You trying to get back into that man's arms, Sister Margaret? What you want him to do for you—you want him to take off that long white robe?

MARGARET. Be careful, Brother Boxer. It ain't over yet. It ain't over yet.

BROTHER BOXER. Oh, yes it is, Sister Margaret. It's over. You just don't know it's over. Come on upstairs. Maybe you can make those folks keep quiet.

(The MUSIC has stopped.)

They's quiet now. They's waiting for you.

MARGARET. You hate me. How long have you hated me? What have I ever done to make you hate me?

BROTHER BOXER. All these years you been talking about how the Lord done called you. Well, you sure come running but I ain't so sure you was called. I seen you in there, staring at that man. You ain't no better than the rest of them. You done sweated and cried in the nighttime, too, and you'd like to be doing it again. You had me fooled with that long white robe but you ain't no better. You ain't as good. You been sashaying around here acting like weren't nobody good enough to touch the hem of your garment. You was always so pure, Sister Margaret, you made the rest of us feel like dirt.

MARGARET. I was trying to please the Lord.

BROTHER BOXER. And you reckon you did? Declare, I never thought I'd see you so quiet. All these years I been running errands for you, saying, Praise the Lord, Sister Margaret. That's *right,* Sister Margaret! Amen, Sister Margaret! I didn't know if you even knew what a man was. I never thought I'd live long enough to find out that Sister Margaret weren't nothing but a woman who run off from her husband and then started ruling other people's lives because she didn't have no man to control her. I sure hope you make it into heaven, girl. You's too late to catch any other train.

MARGARET. It's not over yet. It's not over.

BROTHER BOXER. You coming upstairs?

MARGARET. I'm coming.

BROTHER BOXER. Well. We be waiting. *(He goes.)*

(MARGARET stands alone in the kitchen. As BROTHER BOXER enters, the LIGHTS in the church go up. The church is packed. Far in the back SISTER ODESSA sits. SISTER MOORE is in the pulpit, and baritone soloist is singing.)

BARITONE.

Soon I'll be done with the troubles of the world,
Troubles of the world, troubles of the world,
Soon I'll be done with the troubles of the world,
Going home to live with my Lord.

Soon I'll be done with the troubles of the world,
Troubles of the world, troubles of the world,
Soon I'll be done with the troubles of the world,
Going home to live with my Lord.

Soon I'll be done with the troubles of the world,
Troubles of the world, troubles of the world,
Soon I'll be done with the troubles of the world,
Going home to live with my Lord.

SISTER MOORE. *(Reads.)* For if after they have escaped the pollution of the world through the knowledge of the Lord and Saviour Jesus Christ they are again entangled therein and overcome, the latter end is worse with them than the beginning.

ALL. Amen!

SISTER MOORE. (Reads.) For it had been better for them not to have known the way of righteousness than after they had known it to turn away from the holy commandment delivered unto them. Amen! Sister Boxer, would you read the last verse for us? Bless our God!

SISTER BOXER. (Reads.) But it is happened unto them according to the true proverb, the dog is turned to his own vomit again and the sow that was washed to her wallowing in the mire.

(The church DIMS OUT. MARGARET walks into the bedroom.)

MARGARET. Luke?

LUKE. Maggie. Where's my son?

MARGARET. He's gone, Luke. I couldn't hold him. He's gone off into the world.

LUKE. He's gone?

MARGARET. He's gone.

LUKE. He's gone into the world. He's into the world!

MARGARET. Luke, you won't never see your son no more.

LUKE. But I seen him one last time. He's in the world, he's living.

MARGARET. He's gone. Away from you and away from me.

LUKE. He's living. He's living. Is you got to see your God to know he's living.

MARGARET. Everything—is dark this morning.

LUKE. You all in white. Like you was the day we got married. You mighty pretty.

MARGARET. It were a sunny day. Like today.

LUKE. Yeah. They used to say, "Happy is the bride the sun shines on."

MARGARET. Yes. That's what they used to say.

LUKE. Was you happy that day, Maggie?

MARGARET. Yes.

LUKE. I loved you, Maggie.

MARGARET. I know you did.

LUKE. I love you still.

MARGARET. I know you do.

(They embrace and SINGING is heard from the darkened church: "The Old Ship of Zion.")

Maybe it's not possible to stop loving anybody you ever really loved. I never stopped loving you, Luke. I tried. But I never stopped loving you.

LUKE. I'm glad you's come back to me, Maggie. When your arms was around me I was always safe and happy.

MARGARET. Oh, Luke! If we could only start again!

(His mouthpiece falls from his hand to the floor.)

Luke?

(He does not answer.)

My baby. You done joined hands with the darkness. (She rises, moving to the foot of the bed, her eyes on LUKE. She sees the mouthpiece, picks it up, looks at it.) My Lord! If I could only start again! If I could only start again!

(The LIGHT COMES UP in the church. All, except ODESSA, are singing, "I'm Gonna Sit at the Welcome Table," clapping, etc. SISTER MOORE leads the service from the pulpit. Still holding LUKE's mouthpiece clenched against her breast, MARGARET mounts into the church. As she enters, the MUSIC DIES.)

MARGARET. Praise the Lord!

SISTER MOORE. You be careful, Sister Margaret. Be careful what you say. You been uncovered.

MARGARET. I come up here to put you children on your knees! Don't you know the Lord is displeased with every one of you? Have every one of you forgot your salvation? Don't you know that it is forbidden—amen!—to talk against the Lord's anointed? Ain't a soul under the sound of my voice—bless God!—who has the right to sit in judgment of my life! Sister Margaret, this woman you see before you, has given her life to the Lord—and you say the Lord is displeased with me because ain't a one of you willing to endure what I've endured. Ain't a one of you willing to go—the road I've walked. This way of holiness ain't no joke. You can't love the Lord and flirt with the Devil. The Word of God is right and the Word of God is plain—and you can't love God unless you's willing to give up everything for Him. Everything. I want you folks to pray. I want every one of you to go down on your knees. We going to have a tarry service here tonight. Oh, yes! David, you play something on that piano—*(She stops, stares at the piano, where one of the saints from Philadelphia is sitting.)* David—David—*(She looks down at her fist.)* Oh, my God.

SISTER BOXER. Look at her! *Look* at her! The gift of God has left her!

MARGARET. Children. I'm just now finding out what it means to love the Lord. It ain't all in the singing and the shouting. It ain't all in the reading of the Bible.

(She unclenches her fist a little.) It ain't even—it ain't even—in running all over everybody trying to get to heaven. To love the Lord is to love all His children—all of them, everyone!—and suffer with them and rejoice with them and never count the cost!

(Silence. She turns and leaves the pulpit.)

SISTER MOORE. Bless our God! He give us the victory! I'm gonna feast on milk and honey.

(She is joined by the entire CONGREGATION in this final song of jubilation. MARGARET comes down the stairs. She stands in the kitchen. ODESSA comes downstairs. Without a word to MARGARET, she goes through LUKE's room, taking off her robe as she goes. The LIGHTS DIM DOWN in the church, DIM UP on MARGARET, as MARGARET starts toward the bedroom, and falls beside LUKE's bed.

The Scrim comes down. One or two people pass in the street.)

CURTAIN

Ed Bullins

In the Wine Time

to Janice

IN THE WINE TIME

In the Wine Time was first produced at the New Lafayette Theatre on December 10, 1968.

CHARACTERS:

CLIFF DAWSON
LOU DAWSON, Cliff's wife
RAY, Lou's nephew
MISS MINNY GARRISON
BUNNY GILLETTE
MRS. KRUMP
EDDIE KRUMP
BEATRICE
TINY
SILLY WILLY CLARK
RED
BAMA
DORIS
A POLICEMAN

THE PROLOGUE

She passed the corner every evening during my last wine time, wearing a light summer dress with big pockets, in small ballerina slippers, swinging her head back and to the side all special-like, hearing a private melody singing in her head. I waited for her each dusk, and for this she granted me a smile, but on some days her selfish tune would drift out to me in a hum; we shared the smile and sad tune and met for a moment each day but one of that long-ago summer.

The times I would be late she lingered, in the sweating twilight, at the corner in the barber shop doorway, ignoring the leers and coughs from within, until she saw me hurrying along the tenement fronts. On these days her yellows and pinks and whites would flash out from the smoked walls, beckoning me to hurry hurry to see the lights in her eyes before they fleeted away above the single smile, which would turn about and then down the street, hidden by the little pretty head. Then, afterwards, I would stand before the shop refusing to believe the slander from within.

"Ray . . . why do you act so stupid?" Lou asked each day I arose to await the rendezvous.

"I don't know . . . just do, that's all," I always explained.

"Well, if you know you're bein' a fool, why do you go on moonin' out there in the streets for *that?* . . ."

"She's a friend of mine, Lou . . . she's a friend."

August dragged in the wake of July in steaming sequence of sun and then hell and finally sweltering night. The nights found me awake with Cliff and Lou and our bottles of port, all waiting for the sun to rise again and then to sleep in dozes during the miserable hours. And then for me to wake hustling my liquor money and then to wait on the corner for my friend to pass.

"What'd the hell you say to her, Ray?" Cliff asked.

"Nothin'."

"Nothing?"

"Nawh . . . nothin'."

"Do you ever try?"

"Nawh," I said.

"Why? She's probably just waiting for you to . . ."

"Nawh, she's not. We don't need to say anything to each other. We know all we want to find out."

And we would go on like that until we were so loaded our voices would crack and break as fragile as eggs and the subject would escape us, flapping off over the roofs like a fat pigeon.

Summer and Cliff and Lou and me together—all poured from the same brew, all hating each other and loving, and consuming and never forgiving—but not letting go of the circle until the earth swung again into winter, bringing me closer to manhood and the freedom to do all the things that I had done for the past three summers.

We were the group, the gang. Cliff and Lou entangled within their union, soon to have Baby Man, and Henrietta, and Stinky, and Debra, and maybe who knows who by now. Summer and me wrapped in our embrace like lovers, accepting each as an inferior, continually finding faults and my weaknesses, pretending to forgive though never forgetting, always at each other's vitals. . . . My coterie and my friend . . .

She with the swinging head and flat-footed stance and the single smile and private song for me. She was missing for a day in the last week of summer.

I waited on the corner until the night boiled up from the pavements and the wine time approached too uncomfortably.

Cliff didn't laugh when learning of my loss; Lou stole a half a glass more than I should have received. The night stewed us as we blocked the stoop fighting for air and more than our shares of the port, while the bandit patrol cruised by as sinister as gods.

She was there waiting next day, not smiling nor humming but waving me near. I approached and saw my very own smile.

"I love you, little boy," she said.

I nodded, trying to comprehend.

"You're my little boy, aren't you?" She took my hand. "I have to go away but I wanted to tell you this before I left." She looked into my eyes and over my shaggy uncut hair. "I must be years older than you, but you look so much older than I. In two more years you won't be able to

stop with only wine," she said. "Do you have to do it?"

"I don't know . . . just do, that's all," I explained.

"I'm sorry, my dear," she said. "I must go now."

"Why?"

"I just must."

"Can I go with you?"

She let go of my hand and smiled for the last time.

"No, not now, but you can come find me when you're ready."

"But where?" I asked.

"Out in the world, little boy, out in the world. Remember, when you're ready, all you have to do is leave this place and come to me, I'll be waiting. All you'll need to do is search?"

Her eyes lighted for the last time before hiding behind the pretty head, swinging then away from me, carrying our sorrowful, secret tune.

I stood listening to the barber shop taunts follow her into the darkness, watching her until the wicked city night captured her; then I turned back to meet autumn and Cliff and Lou in our last wine time, meeting the years which had to hurry hurry so I could begin the search that I have not completed.

ACT ONE

The people in this play are black except for the KRUMPS and the POLICEMAN.

SCENE:

Derby Street. A small side street of a large northern American industrial city, in the early 1950's.

At left, the houses stand together on one side of the street in unbroken relief, except for a tunnel-like alley which opens between the Krumps' and the Garrisons' houses, forming a low, two-storied canyon, the smoke-stained chimneys the pin-

nacles of the ridges. *Four-letter words, arrow-pierced hearts and slangy street-talk, scrawled in haste, smear a wooden fence, painted green, across the narrow street. Tattered posters of political candidates wearing scribbled, smudged mustaches, circuses of seasons passed and fading, golden and orange snuff containers decorate the enclosure. Each building's front is dull red, not brick colored, but a gray- and violet-tinged red, the shade the paint becomes after successive seasons of assault by the city's smoke- and grit-ladened atmosphere. Precise white lines, the older ones yellowing, outline each brick of the walls, and every house has a squat stoop of five white stone steps.*

A raised level, upstage Right, between the fence and the houses, represents "The Avenue."

From within the DAWSONS' *house black MUSIC of the period—called rhythm 'n blues by disc jockeys at that time—is heard not too loudly, and continues throughout the play, interrupted only seldom by amusing, jive-talking commercials for used cars, televisions, appliances, hair straighteners and skin lighteners. Some of the recording stars of this season are King Pleasure, Johnnie Otis, Fats Domino, Little Esther, Ray Charles and "The Queen," Miss Dinah Washington. When* MISS MINNY GARRISON *raises her window GOSPEL MUSIC can be heard.*

AT RISE:

It is a sultry evening in late August. All the steps are occupied by members of the various Derby Street households.

At the end of the street, downstage, is a corner lighted by a streetlamp, the gas-burning variety found still then in some sections of Philadelphia, Baltimore, New York and Boston.

ALL LIGHTS ARE DOWN but the corner streetlamp, though dim shadows of the people on the stoops can be seen carrying on their evening activities: talk-ing, gossiping, playing checkers and cards, drinking sodas, wine and beer.

MR. KRUMP *enters and stands at the streetlamp. He is very drunk.*

LIGHTS on the Krumps' doorstoop, the nearer to the corner.

The Krumps' front door opens and MRS. KRUMP *leans out.*

THE RADIO. And here we are folks . . . on a black, juicy, jammin' 'n' groovin' hot August night . . . yeah . . . one of them nights fo' bein' wit' tha one ya loves. . . .

MRS. KRUMP. *(Strident, over the RADIO.)* Krumpy! What cha doin' on da corner? Hey, Krumpy! Hey, Krumpy! . . . *Krumpy . . . Get the hell on over here!*

(LIGHT on third doorstoop.)

CLIFF. Heee . . . heee . . . look 'a ole man Krump work out.

*(*BUNNY GILLETTE *and* DORIS *enter Derby Street at the corner and see* MR. KRUMP.*)*

LOU. Hush up, Cliff.

CLIFF. Sheeet.

BUNNY GILLETTE. Look 'a there, Doris!

LOU. Be quiet, Cliff. Will ya, huh?

DORIS. Awww, shit, girl. That's nothin' . . . it just that goddamn Mr. Krump again . . . drunk out of his fucken' mind.

THE RADIO. It's eighty-two degrees . . . maaan, that's hot-oh-rooney . . . yeah, burnin' up this evenin' . . . red hot! . . . Ouch! . . . But we're cool on the Hep Harrison red-hot, up-tight, out-a-sight weather lookout indicator. That's eighty-two degrees . . . that's eight two out there. . . . And here's a cool number that will hit you right where you're at . . . for your listenin' pleasure . . .

*(*MRS. KRUMP *has stepped to the Center of Derby Street and calls up to her second-floor window as the MUSIC begins.)*

MRS. KRUMP. *(Raspy, urban voice.)* *Hey, Edward . . . Hey, Edward! Hey, Edward . . .* come on down here and get your fa'tha! Hey, Edward . . .

DORIS. Hey, lissen ta that cow yell.

BUNNY. Ain't it a shame, girl? *(BUNNY starts off.)*

CLIFF. *(Disgust.)* God dammit . . . Lou. You always tellin' me to be quiet . . . I don't even make half the noise that some of our *good* neighbors do.

DORIS. *(To BUNNY.)* Where ya goin', broad?

LOU. *(Sitting beside CLIFF.)* Awww . . . she should leave Mr. Krump alone. All he's doin' is peein' aside the pole . . . and then he's goin' in and go ta bed.

BUNNY. Up on "The Avenue."

DORIS. Where?

(EDDIE KRUMP sticks his head from his upstairs window. He has dirty blond hair and a sharp, red nose. He is about eleven.)

EDDIE. Ohhh, Christ, Ma . . . what'cha want?

BUNNY. "The Avenue," Doris.

MRS. KRUMP. *(Furious.)* Don't you Christ me, Edward . . . come down here right away, young man!

CLIFF. *(To LOU.)* I bet he ain't gonna do it.

DORIS. Ain't you gonna see Ray? That's what you come down this way for.

LOU. He might, Cliff. Besides . . . you the one that's always sayin' everybody here on Derby Street only does what they want to do most of the time, anyway.

BUNNY. He's up there on the step . . . he could see me if he wanted. . . . C'mon, girl . . . let's split.

(They exit.)

CLIFF. 'Specially mindin' other people's business.

(RAY sits between CLIFF and LOU, one step below them.)

LOU. Wasn't that Bunny, Ray?

RAY. Think I should go and help Mr. Krump out, Cliff?

CLIFF. Nawh.

(Pause.)

LOU. Why, Cliff?

CLIFF. You stay yo' ass here where ya belong, Ray.

LOU. Don't you talk like that, Cliff.

MRS. KRUMP. *(To EDDIE in window.)* Eddie . . . are you comin' down here?

EDDIE. Nawh.

CLIFF. *(Incredulous.)* Did you hear that?

LOU. Remember . . . we mind our own business.

(From the upstairs window of the Garrisons' house, MISS MINNY GARRISON pushes her head; she has a bandana tied about her head, and she is a huge black woman.)

MRS. KRUMP. *(Starting for her door.)* I'm going to come up there and beat the hell out of you, Edward.

(EDDIE ducks his head in the window as his mother enters the door below. Sounds of MRS. KRUMP's screams, the shouts of EDDIE KRUMP and of running feet. Silence. RHYTHM 'N BLUES and GOSPEL MUSIC mingle softly. RED and BAMA enter at the corner. They see MR. KRUMP and nod to each other, then slowly, stiff-leggedly, stalk about the streetlamp, tightening the circle about MR. KRUMP on each full swing around.)

MISS MINNY. Ray . . . wha don't you help Mr. Krump git home?

(RAY stands and looks up at her.)

RAY. Yas'sum.

CLIFF. *(To RAY.)* Wha' . . . you gonna go down there and help? . . .

(RAY hesitates.)

LOU. Awww, Cliff . . . there ain't no harm in it.

CLIFF. No harm?

LOU. Ray always does it.

CLIFF. Well, it's about time he stopped.

MISS MINNY. Go on, Ray. Go on and git Mr. Krump.

RAY. Yas'sum. (He trots to the corner.)

CLIFF. (Mimics RAY in high falsetto.) Yas'sum.

LOU. (Angry.) Stop that, Cliff!

CLIFF. Sheeet!

RED. Hey . . . Ray . . . is this lump ah shit a friend of yours? . . .

RAY. Nawh.

LOU. Why don't you stop that stuff, Cliff? Ain't nothin' bein' hurt because Ray's helpin' out Mr. Krump.

BAMA. Maybe they're related.

RED. (Chuckling.) Hey, man, cool it. I know Ray don't play that. Do you, Ray?

RAY. (Trying to support MR. KRUMP.) Nawh, Red. Nawh.

RED. (To BAMA.) See, Bama, Ray don't play the dozens. You better be careful.

BAMA. Shit.

(RAY and BAMA exchange stares. BAMA is several years older than RAY.)

RED. You seen Bunny and Doris, Ray?

RAY. Yeah . . . they headed for "The Avenue."

CLIFF. Nothin' bein' hurt? Just look at that. Look at that, Lou!

(RAY has slung MR. KRUMP across his shoulder. He is husky and carries his load well.)

(Standing, shouting.) Hey, Ray! Make sure his pants fly is zipped up or you'll be a victim of a horrible calamity!

LOU. You think you so smart, Cliff.

BAMA. (To RAY.) Tote dat bar', boy . . . lift dat bale.

RED. (Booting RAY in the seat of the pants.) Git along, little doggie.

(CLIFF is pleased with himself but starts as RED kicks RAY and stands, but LOU tugs at his trouser leg and he sits back

down, chuckling over his wit, though scowling at RED and BAMA who turn laughing and exit. RAY carries his load to the Krumps' door. CLIFF lights a cigarette and takes a drink. LOU tries to ignore him.)

MRS. KRUMP. (Wearing a perpetual worried expression, at her door.) Why, thank you, Ray. Just bring him in here and put him on the couch. Thank you, Ray. That Edward is just . . .

(They go in, MRS. KRUMP at the rear, peering at MR. KRUMP's head that dangles down RAY's back.)

CLIFF. That goddamn Miss Minny's always startin' some shit!

LOU. Shusss . . . Cliff. She'll hear you.

CLIFF. (Bitter.) I don't care if the big sow does. Always pretendin' her ears are filled with nothin' but holy holy gospel music . . . when they're nothin' but brimmin' with Derby Street dirt. (Mutters.) Ole bitch!

LOU. (Uneasy.) Cliff!

CLIFF. (Looks up at MISS MINNY.) Always startin' some trouble.

(MISS MINNY closes her window. Her light goes off.)

LOU. See, she did hear you!

CLIFF. I don't give a damn . . . who she thinks she is anyway?

LOU. Cliff, you just tryin' to start some trouble with Mr. Garrison. You wouldn't say those things if Homer were home.

CLIFF. (Challenging.) Wouldn't I?

LOU. No, you wouldn't!

CLIFF. I would do anything I do now if ole four-eyed Homer was sittin' right over there on that step pickin' his big nose.

LOU. He don't pick his nose no more.

CLIFF. How do you know? Is that what Miss Minny told you?

LOU. No, Miss Minny didn't tell me a thing. His sister, Marigold, showed me a picture of him in his sergeant's uniform

. . . and I know nobody in the United States Army who makes sergeant still picks their nose.

CLIFF. Sheeet!

(Silence.)

LOU. Cliff?

CLIFF. *(Angry.)* Look what you've done to that boy, Lou. Look what you and his mother . . .

LOU. *(Angry.)* Now don't you start in talkin' 'bout my dead sister!

CLIFF. *(Angrier.)* Shut up!

(Pause and stare.)

Don't you see what all of you are tryin' to do . . . Miss Minny . . .

LOU. Who's tryin' to do what, Cliff?

CLIFF. *(Continues.)* Miss Minny . . . you . . . all the so-called high-falutin' pussy on this block . . .

LOU. *(Indignant.)* Now, you watch your mouth . . .

CLIFF. Pussy! Cunt! Bitches! Always startin' some trouble.

LOU. *(Apologetic.)* That was no trouble, Cliff.

CLIFF. It was so. . . . Who the hell Miss Minny thinks she is anyway tellin' Ray to go down there an' get ole man Krump? And gettin' kicked by that punk Red . . . Ray's nearly a man . . . he shouldn't . . .

LOU. *(Cutting.)* She didn't mean nothin' by it.

CLIFF. Just like she didn't mean nothin' the time she passed around that petition to have us run off 'a Derby Street when we first moved here.

LOU. She didn't know us then . . . we was strangers. Why don't you forget it?

CLIFF. *(Raising voice.)* What's so strange about us, huh? What was so strange about us back then when we moved in? What was so strange? Was we strange because I was goin' ta school on the G.I. Bill and not tot'in a lunch pail like all these other asses? . . .

LOU. Shusss . . . Cliff.

CLIFF. I will not shusss . . . that's what they are, aren't they? Asses! Mules! Donkeys!

LOU. I'm goin' in if you keep that up, Cliff.

THE RADIO. . . . and Fat Abe . . . your local honest used-car dealer is now offering a custom bargain fo' one of you real swingers out there . . .

(CLIFF reaches up and pulls the door shut with a slam, muffling the RADIO.)

CLIFF. You ain't goin' nowhere just because you don't want to hear the truth.

(Silence. LOU sulks.)

Well, they are asses . . . *(Ridicule.)* Derby Street Donkeys!

LOU. *(Apologetic.)* Well, I was workin', Cliff. And . . .

CLIFF. *(Cutting.)* And they made a hell of a noise about that, too. Always whisperin' how you work so hard all day in a laundry for no count me who goes around carryin' books. And gets home in the middle of the afternoon and jest lays around like a playboy . . .

LOU. They did see you with them girls all the time, Cliff.

CLIFF. I ain't been with no bitches.

LOU. Cliff . . .

CLIFF. They're lies! That's all . . . every one a lie . . . and don't you let me hear you tell me them lies again.

(Silence.)

LOU. Never?

CLIFF. Never!

LOU. What should I say when I find lipstick on your shirt . . . shades I don't use.

(Silence.)

What should I say when I see you flirtin' with the young girls on the street and with my friends?

(Silence.)

CLIFF. (Tired.) Light me a cigarette, will ya?

(She does.)

LOU. This street ain't so bad now.

CLIFF. Was we so strange because your nephew Ray stays with us . . . and don't have to work (Bitter.) like an ass or mule or fool . . . like a Derby Street Donkey!

LOU. Cliff!

CLIFF. Why was we so strange?

LOU. Nawh, we wasn't . . .

CLIFF. Who wasn't?

LOU. We wasn't!

CLIFF. Yes, we was!

LOU. Nawh . . . we seemed strange because we always drinkin' this . . . (Raising her glass.)

CLIFF. Everybody else drinks somethin' around here . . . ole man Garrison puts at least a pint of white lightnin' away a night . . . pure'dee cooked corn whisky!

LOU. But their ignorant oil don't make them yell and hollar half the night like this wine makes us.

CLIFF. (Yells.) Who yells!

LOU. (Amused.) . . . and we sing and laugh and you cuss like a sailor.

CLIFF. Who sings and laughs? . . .

LOU. We do.

CLIFF. You a liar!

LOU. Nawh, I'm not, Cliff.

(He grabs her arm and twists it behind her back.)

CLIFF. Say you a liar.

LOU. Nawh, Cliff . . . don't do that.

CLIFF. (Twists it more.) Who's a liar?

LOU. I am, Cliff.

CLIFF. (A slight jerk.) Who?

LOU. I am, Cliff. I am!

(He releases her.)

CLIFF. That's right . . . sing out when I want you to. Ha ha ha . . . (He tries to caress her.)

LOU. (Rubs arm and shoves him.) Leave me alone.

CLIFF. (Kisses her.) I'm glad you finally confessed. . . . It'll do your soul some good.

LOU. (Sulking.) You shouldn't do that, Cliff.

CLIFF. Do what?

LOU. You know what.

CLIFF. Give you spiritual comfort? . . . Apply some soul ointment?

LOU. (Disgusted.) Awwww . . .

CLIFF. I don't know if you never tell me, hon.

LOU. You know all right.

CLIFF. That I cuss like a salior?

LOU. (Remembering.) That's right . . . and . . .

CLIFF. (Cutting.) Well, you didn't say that.

LOU. I didn't?

(Pause.)

I did too, Cliff.

CLIFF. What?

LOU. Say that we yell and hollar and sing and laugh and cuss like sailors half the night.

CLIFF. (Toasts her.) Ohhh, Lou. To Lou Lou, my Hottentot queen.

LOU. I'm not!

CLIFF. My queen?

LOU. Hottentot! . . . My features are more northern . . . more Ethiopian.

CLIFF. (Ridicule.) Haaaah!

(Pause.)

Haaaaah! More northern . . . more Ethiopian! That beak nose of yours comes from that shanty Irishman who screwed your grandmammy down on the plantation.

LOU. Watch your mouth, Cliff.

CLIFF. Watch my mouth?

LOU. Yeah, watch your mouth. Some things I just won't allow you to say.

CLIFF. (Mocking.) "Some things I just won't allow you to say." (Offended.)

Watch my mouth? Well, take a look at yours. Yours comes from that Ubangi great granddaddy on your father's side. . . . Your "northern" nose, well, we've gone through its . . .

LOU. *(Warning.)* Stop it, Cliff!

CLIFF. . . . but your build is pure Hottentot, darling . . . and that's why I shall forever love you . . . however the Derby Street Donkeys bray about me being with other girls . . . younger, prettier girls, mind you. . . . But Lou, baby, you are married to an "A" number one ass man . . . and *yours* is one of the Hottentot greats of northern America.

LOU. *(Indignant.)* Fuck you!

CLIFF. *(Fake dialect.)* Wahl, hon-nee chile . . . I just wanted ta tell yawhl dat yo' husband is one ob dem connoisseurs of dem fleshy Hottentot parts which'n yous is so wonderfully invested wit'.

LOU. Fuck you, Cliff! . . . Ohhh, just listen to that. You make me say bad things, man. You think you so smart and know all them big words since you been goin' to school. You still ain't nothin' but a lowdown bastard at heart as far as I'm concerned.

(Silence. CLIFF takes a drink. LOU is wary but defiant.)

CLIFF. *(Smiles.)* We do cuss too much, don't we?

LOU. *(Smiles.)* And we drink too much.

(He pulls her over and fondles her; she kisses him but pushes him away.)

CLIFF. Like sailors?

LOU. Yes!

CLIFF. *(Amused.)* I thought we cussed like sailors.

LOU. We do.

CLIFF. *(Raises voice.)* Make up yo' mind, broad. Now what is it . . . do we cuss and drink like sailors or cuss like sailors and drink like . . . like . . . like . . . what?

LOU. Like niggers.

(At the last word LIGHTS GO UP on other stoops, revealing the occupants looking at CLIFF and LOU. Then LIGHTS DIM and COME UP on "The Avenue." The figures of RED, BAMA, DORIS and BUNNY GILLETTE are seen.)

BUNNY GILLETTE. Go on now, Red . . . stop messin' with me.

RED. Awww . . . woman . . . stop all your bullshit. You know you like me to feel your little ass . . . c'mere.

DORIS. Stop fucken with that girl, Red.

RED. What's wrong, Doris? You jealous or somethin'?

DORIS. Man . . . if you melted and turned to water and ran down the gutter I wouldn't even step over you.

RED. Why . . . scared I'd look up your dress and see your tonsils?

BUNNY GILLETTE. *(Giggling.)* Ohhh . . . girl, ain't he bad.

BAMA. C'mere, Doris. I wanna talk to you.

DORIS. You ain't never wanted to talk to me before, Bama.

(RED has his arm about BUNNY GILLETTE's waist. BAMA takes DORIS's hand.)

RED. C'mon, Bunny . . . I'll buy you a fish sandwich. *(To BAMA.)* Hey, Bam ah lam . . . do you think these broads deserve a fish sandwich?

BAMA. Nawh, man, they don't deserve shit.

DORIS. Hey, Bunny, we really hooked us some sports . . . you better make it back to Ray, girl.

(LIGHTS DOWN on "The Avenue." LIGHTS UP on Derby Street. CLIFF and LOU laugh as RAY comes out of the Krumps'. The RADIO is muffled in the background.)

MRS. KRUMP. *(Off.)* You sure you don't want another slice of cake and a glass of milk, Raymond?

RAY. Nawh, thank you, Mrs. Krump.

(EDDIE KRUMP sticks his head out of his window.)

EDDIE. Thanks ah lot, Ray.

RAY. That's okay; why don't you come on down for a while?

EDDIE. Nawh . . . I can't . . . I gotta headache.

CLIFF. *(To RAY.)* Little white Eddie don't want to come down after you carry his pissy pukey drunk daddy in for him, huh?

LOU. Cliff!

RAY. *(Embarrassed.)* Nawh.

LOU. Cliff . . . no wonder they sent around that petition. Just look how you act.

CLIFF. *(Angry.)* Yeah, just look how I act . . . fuck how I act!

LOU. You got the dirtiest mouth, Cliff.

CLIFF. *(Angrier.)* Fuck how I act . . . fuck it! *(CLIFF stands and glares about at his neighbors, who turn their heads and resume their activities.)*

LOU. Just like a sailor.

CLIFF. *(Satisfied.)* Yup . . . just like I always said . . . folks on Derby Street sure know how to mind their own business.

LOU. Just like the no-'count sailor I met and married.

CLIFF. Well, I am a mathafukken shit-ass sailor. The same you met and married, Lou.

LOU. Not any more.

CLIFF. Still! I still am. Once a sailor . . . always a sailor.

LOU. Not any more. Besides . . . you stayed most of your time in the guardhouse.

CLIFF. *(To RAY.)* Listen to that . . . listen to that, Ray. Guardhouse.

LOU. That was the reason I married you. Felt sorry for you and knew your commanding officer would go light on you if he knew you had been married when you deserted and not put you in the guardhouse for so long.

CLIFF. Yeah?

LOU. Yeah!

CLIFF. Don't think you did me any favors, baby.

LOU. Well, who else did? I went to your ship and testified . . . I kept you from gettin' a bad discharge. In fact, I'm the one who made a man out of you even though your mother and the whole entire United States Navy failed.

CLIFF. *(Mutters.)* Bitch!

LOU. Do you hear that? Failed . . . to make a man or a sailor of ya.

CLIFF. *(Ridicule.)* Ray. This broad, pardon the expression, this woman named Lou . . . Lou Ellen Margarita Crawford Dawson . . . who calls herself your aunt, by the way . . .

LOU. I am his aunt!

CLIFF. This bitch don't know what a sailor is.

LOU. I don't? . . . I don't? Then I guess you know even though you spent most of your navy time in the guardhouse.

RAY. Brig, Lou . . .

CLIFF. Thank you son. Thank you.

LOU. What? . . .

RAY. Brig, Lou . . . not guardhouse.

CLIFF. That's right . . . that's fucken "A" right. . . .

LOU. *(Mutters and takes a drink.)* Dirtiest mouth I ever heard.

CLIFF. That's a lie . . . your sister has the dirtiest mouth in north, south, west and all of this town. *(To RAY.)* That's your play-aunt Doris I'm talking' about, Ray, not your dear dead mother . . . may she rest in peace. . . .

LOU. You two-faced bastard. Listen to you soundin' like one of them white missionaries . . . "May she rest in peace . . ." Dirty-mouthed liar!

CLIFF. Liar? About what? My not being in the guardhouse?

RAY. Brig.

LOU. You know that's not what I mean.

CLIFF. Pour yourself a drink, Ray. Put

some hair on your . . . ding-a-ling. (*Begins humming.*)

LOU. I pity the day you talked me into allowing Ray to take a drink.

CLIFF. Whatta ya mean? He was a lush when he came here. His mother and him both almost drank themselves to death.

LOU. Cliff!

CLIFF. (*Defensive.*) Ain't that right, Ray?

RAY. Sort'a. I did kinda drink along with Mamma for a while until they put her away.

CLIFF. Sort'a? Stop jivin'. . . . For a youngblood you can really hide some port.

RAY. (*Flattered.*) Yeah . . . I do my share.

LOU. Now, Ray, I want you to . . .

CLIFF. (*Loud.*) Quiet! You heard him . . . he does his share. Here's a toast to you, youngblood. (*Lifts his glass.*) To Ray who does his share.

(*They drink, except for* LOU.)

RAY. Thanks, Cliff.

CLIFF. Don't mention it, Ray. Just don't mention it at all. It's your world, son. It's really your world. (*To* LOU.) Well, isn't it?

(*Silence.*)

You don't feel like toasting Ray?

(*Silence.*)

Ray . . . you know, Lou is a lot like your mother used to be. Quiet, except that your mother usually had a glass up to her mouth instead of her mouth clamped tight.

LOU. You shouldn't of said that, Cliff. You're goin'a pay for that.

CLIFF. Pay? Ray, it's your world . . . does your ole Uncle Cliff have to pay?

RAY. Well, I don't . . .

LOU. (*Cutting.*) Stop it, Cliff. Ray, I'm sorry. Cliff gets too much to drink in him . . .

CLIFF. (*Loud, cutting.*) Nice night we havin' out here on our white well-scrubbed steps . . .

(*Both together.*)

LOU.

. . . and he runs off at the mouth some-thin' terrible. I know you wasn't much past twelve when I came an' got you and kept them from puttin' you in a home. And you had already started in drinkin' 'n smokin' and foolin' around with girls . . . and I knew you drank too much for a growin' boy, much less a man. But I couldn't see you in a home—it would have messed you up . . . or sent down South to Cousin Frank's. I don't mean you so young you don't know what you want to do, Ray. I'm only six years older than you . . . but Cliff still shouldn't be givin' you so much wine and teachin' you bad habits. It ain't good for none of us, not even me. I hardly know where I'm at some of the times when I start in drinkin' after I come home from work . . . but it

CLIFF.

. . . with all of God's white stars shinin' above your black heads. Ain't that right, Lord? You old shyster. You pour white heat on these nig-gers, these Derby Street Donkeys, in the daytime and roast and fry them while they shovel shit for nex' to nothin', and steam them at night like big black lobsters . . . ha ha . . . the Krumps are little red lobsters of Yourn . . . and they just drink, an' screw in the dark and listen to jive talks an' jive music an' jive *holy* music . . . but they still think they have to face You in the mornin'. That's right, face You, You jive-ass sucker! They don't know they got to face Your jive-hot, blazin' face . . . simple niggers . . . but they do 'cause they believe in You and Your lies. Stupid donkeys! They only got to look my god in the sho' do relaxes me. And your mother is gonna call me to account for it when we meet up in heaven . . . I really know that. The devil's in Cliff, I know that, to do what he's doin' to us . . . and I ain't helpin' things much. Listen to what I say, Ray, and not to the devil. Listen to me, Ray.

Lou. *Stop it, Cliff! You're drunk 'n' crazy 'n' drivin' me out of my head!*

(Silence. Cliff stares at her.)

Ray. *(To both.)* It's all right. It's all right.

Lou. Ray, when I get to heaven your mother's gonna have a lot to say to me.

Cliff. *(Laughs.)* Heaven?

Lou. Yeah, heaven. And you better get some of the fear of the Lord in you, Cliff.

Cliff. *(Disgust.)* Every night. Every goddamn night when you start in feelin' your juice.

Lou. 'Cause I know better, that's why.

Cliff. Is that why when I get you in bed every night you hollar: *(Whining falsetto.)* "Yes, Lord. Yes, Lord. Ohhh . . . Jesus . . . one more time."

(Ray giggles.)

Lou. You're bad, Cliff. You're bad. Bad!

Cliff. Sho' I'm bad, hon-nee chile. *(Singing.)* I'm forty hands across mah chest . . . don't fear nothin' . . . not God nor death . . . I got a tombstone mind an' a graveyard disposition . . . I'm a bad mathafukker an' I don't mind . . . dyin'.

Lou. *(Cutting.)* You're just a dirty-mouthed . . .

face once and forget about You, You jive-time sucker . . . *(Remembering an old joke.)* . . . ha ha . . . she's black as night and as cool and slick as a king snake . . . *(Singing.)* . . . Yes, Lord, yes, Lord, yes, Lord, yes, Lord . . .

Cliff. *(Cutting.)* Yeah, I know . . . and I'll have you know that just because I spent one third of my navy time in various brigs, not just one, understand, baby girl, but at least an even dozen between here and Istanbul, that I was still one of the saltiest salt water sailors in the fleet . . . on dry land, in the fleet or in some fucken marine brig!

Lou. You wasn't shit, Cliff. . . . You know that, don't you?

Cliff. Sticks 'n' stones, Lou . . . sticks 'n' stones.

Lou. Pour me a drink, Ray . . . and give your no-'count step-uncle one too.

(Ray pours drinks for the three of them.)

Cliff. Step-uncle? Now how in Jesus' name did I get demoted from uncle to step?

Lou. You just did . . . suddenly you just stepped down.

Ray. Do you think I can get into the navy, Cliff?

Cliff. *(Grabs Lou's arm.)* Sometimes, Lou . . .

Ray. Huh, Cliff?

Cliff. *(Recovering.)* Navy? . . . Why sure . . . sure, Ray. When you come of age I'll sign the papers myself.

Lou. Steps can't, Cliff. But I can.

Cliff. I can, Lou . . . I should know. *(Proudly.)* I joined on my sixteenth birthday.

Lou. Steps can't.

Cliff. *(Pinches her shoulder.)* Bitch!

Lou. *(Feigning.)* Owww, Cliff. Owww.

Ray. If I'm of age then you won't have to sign, will ya?

Cliff. No, I won't. Not if you're of age, Ray.

Lou. He can't sign anyway.

Cliff. I can too, Ray. You just watch me when the time comes.

Ray. I'll be sixteen next week, Cliff

Cliff. You will?

Ray. Yeah.

CLIFF. Already?

RAY. Yeah.

CLIFF. *(To* LOU.*)* He will?

LOU. If that's what he says.

CLIFF. Damn . . . so soon.

LOU. Sixteen ain't old enough. You have to be seventeen before they'll even let me sign for you, Ray.

CLIFF. I went when I was sixteen . . . my sixteenth birthday.

LOU. *(Peeved.)* That's because you were down in Virginia in the woods . . . fool! They don't even have birth certificates down there . . . you could of went when you were thirteen if your mother had'a sworn you was old enough.

CLIFF. I was too old enough!

LOU. No, you wasn't. And Ray ain't either. He's got to wait until he's seventeen. And then I might sign for him.

RAY. I got to wait? But Uncle Cliff said I could go.

CLIFF. Yeah, you can go, Ray. I'll sign the papers myself. You're goin' to the navy and see how real men live.

LOU. *(Angry.)* He's not goin' . . . he's not old enough . . . and you ain't signin' no papers for him, Cliff. His mother wouldn't . . .

CLIFF. I'll sign anything I want fo' him. I'm his guardian. . . .

LOU. *(Ridicule.)* Guardian? How? With what? You ain't never had a job in your life over six months. What you raise him with . . . the few lousy bucks you don't drink up from your government check? You somebody's guardian . . . I . . .

*(*CLIFF *slaps her violently.)*

CLIFF. *(Low, menacing.)* You talk too much, Lou.

LOU. *(Defiant.)* It's my responsibility, Cliff. Mine. Mine. My responsibility. I'm not going to sign or let you sign. His mother . . .

CLIFF. Damn that! Damn it! I don't care what his dead mother wants. Who the hell cares what the dead want? It's

what Ray wants that counts. He's got to get out of here . . . don't you, Ray? . . . off'a Derby Street and away from here so he can grow up to be his own man.

LOU. *(Crying.)* Like you?

CLIFF. No, not like me . . . not tied down to a half-grown, scared, childish bitch!

LOU. You don't have to be.

CLIFF. But I love you.

(LIGHTS DOWN, UP on "The Avenue." RED *slaps* BUNNY GILLETTE.*)*

DORIS. *Red . . . you mathafukker . . . Stop that!*

BUNNY GILLETTE. *(Crying.)* Go on now, Red. Leave me alone . . .

RED. Bitch! Who you think you tellin' to kiss your ass? You want me to kiss your nasty ass?

BAMA. *(Reaching for him.)* Hey, lighten up, Red.

DORIS. Leave her alone!

RED. *(Being held by* BAMA.*)* You want me to kiss your . . .

BUNNY GILLETTE. Nawh, Red. Nawh.

DORIS. *(A short knife in her hand.)* You better not touch her again . . . you better not. You goin'a be sorry for this.

(LIGHTS DOWN on "The Avenue" and UP on Derby Street.)

RAY. I'm sorry, Lou.

LOU. It's all right, Ray. We've fought before . . . I'm just sorry you have to see us act like this.

CLIFF. Awww, honey . . . I'll forget it if you do.

LOU. You beat on me and I'm supposed to forget it? In my condition.

CLIFF. You got nearly six months before the baby. He can't get hurt by just a little . . .

LOU. You know the doctor told you not to be hittin' on me no mo.' You did it on purpose 'cause you don't want it.

CLIFF. I'm sorry, Lou.

LOU. It's a wonder you didn't hit me in the stomach.

CLIFF. Well, it's a wonder I didn't.

LOU. See there. You don't want it.

CLIFF. Nawh, I don't want a baby I can't take care of . . . do you?

LOU. You can get a job.

CLIFF. At a dollar an hour? Dollar-an-hour Dawson, that's me. Nawh, I don't want any kids until I can afford them. That's why I'm goin' ta school.

LOU. You studying business so you can take care of me an' your kids? What kind of job can you get in business? You got money to open you a business?

CLIFF. Lou, we've gone over this before. I'll manage.

LOU. Like you have gettin' a job?

CLIFF. Well, you want me to get a job in the laundry? Like all your cousins?

LOU. And me!

CLIFF. Startin' at a buck an hour. Hell no, I won't work!

LOU. (Scared.) But what are we goin'a do when your checks run out, Cliff?

CLIFF. Me? I'll do the best I can. Maybe ship out again.

LOU. No, Cliff!

CLIFF. If I can't turn up anything . . . well, you and the kid can get on relief.

(Silence.)

LOU. Where's your pride? A big strong man like . . .

CLIFF. A dollar an hour don't buy that much pride, Lou. There's a big rich world out there . . . I'm goin'a get me part of it or not at all.

(Both together.)

LOU.	CLIFF.
You ain't no man. My daddy he worked twenty years with his hands . . . his poor hands are hard and rough with corns	I'm goin' ta get me part of that world or stare your God in the eye and scream *why*. I am not a beast . . . an animal to be used

and callouses. He was a man . . . he worked and brought us up to take pride in ourselves and to fear God. What did I marry? I thought you was a man, Cliff. I thought because you was loud and was always fightin' and drinkin' and was so big and strong that you was a man . . . but you ain't nothin' but a lowdown and less than nothin'!

for the plows of the world. But if I am then I'll act like one, I'll be one and turn this fucken world of dreams lies and fairy tales into a jungle or a desert. And I don't give much of a happy fuck which. There's a world out there, woman. Just beyond that lamppost . . . just across "The Avenue" and it'll be mine and Ray's.

LOU. (Screams.) You're nothin'!

CLIFF. In the navy Ray can travel and see things and learn and meet lots of different . . .

LOU. No ! ! !

CLIFF . . . girls and make somethin' . . .

LOU. Is that what it did for you?

CLIFF. Yeah, that's what it did for me!

LOU. Well, I don't want him to be like you.

CLIFF. How would you want him to be like . . . one of the Derby Street Donkeys? Or one of the ditty boppers or an avenue hype . . . or . . . a drug addict . . . or what?

LOU. (Standing.) He ain't turned out so bad so far. (Determined.) He's not goin', Cliff.

(Pause.)

Ray, just get it out of your mind. I'm not signin' no navy papers . . . you're too young. (She enters the house as the LIGHTS FADE to blackness.)

CURTAIN

ACT TWO

Mythic BLUES plays. LIGHTS UP on
"The Avenue."
The couples are in embrace.

BUNNY GILLETTE. *(To* RED.) I like you
a lot . . . really I do . . . but what will
Ray say?

RED. Fuck that little punk!

DORIS. *(To* RED.) What you say 'bout
my nephew?

BAMA. He wasn't talkin' to you, Doris.

BUNNY GILLETTE. You ain't gonna
fight me anymo' . . . are ya, Red?

DORIS. I'd cut that nigger's nut off if
he had'a hit me like that, Bunny!

BAMA. You wouldn'a do nothin', Doris
. . . you just . . .

DORIS. Yeah, I would . . . and that
goes double for any jive nigger who lays
a finger on me or mine!

RED. *(Places his hands on* BUNNY'S
rear.) Why don't all you mathafukkers
shut up! Can't you see I'm concentratin'?

(LIGHTS DOWN, UP on Derby
Street. CLIFF *and* RAY *sit upon their*
stoop. The remainder of the street is in
shadow. Silence. From the last stoop up
the street BEATRICE *detaches herself from*
the shadows and walks toward the cor-
ner. She is a buxom, brown girl and car-
ries herself proudly. She speaks as she
passes each shadowy group of forms upon
the stoops.)

THE RADIO. It's seventy-eight degrees
. . . that's seven . . . eight . . .

BEATRICE. *(Passing.)* Hello, Mr.
Cooper. Miz Cooper.

SHADOWS. Hello, Beatrice. How you
doin' tonight?

BEATRICE. *(Passing.)* Hello, Miss Francis.

SHADOWS. Why hello, Bea. How ya
doin', girl?

BEATRICE. *(Passing.)* Hello, Mr. Roy.

SHADOWS. Howdy, Beatrice. How's
your folks?

BEATRICE. Just fine. *(She passes on.*
MISS MINNY *puts her head out her win-*
dow. BEATRICE *passes* CLIFF *and* RAY
without speaking, her pug nose up, her
head sighting on something upon the
Derby Street fence, on the far side of the
street. BEATRICE *comes abreast the Gar-*
risons' house and looks up.) Hello, Miss
Minny.

MISS MINNY. Hello, Beatrice . . . how
y'all?

BEATRICE. *(Stops.)* Just fine, Miss
Minny. How's Marigold and Ruth?

MISS MINNY. Awww . . . they're fine,
Beatrice. They off visitin' mah sister this
week.

BEATRICE. That's nice, Miss Minny.
Tell them I asked about them, will ya?

MISS MINNY. All right, dear. Did you
know that Homer asked about you in his
last letter?

BEATRICE. No, I didn't. Is he still in
Korea?

MISS MINNY. Yeah, he's still over there.
They done made him a sergeant.

BEATRICE. Yes, I know. Marigold told
me. He's doing okay, isn't he?

MISS MINNY. Oh, yes, he's just doin'
fine and everything. Says he likes it over
there.

BEATRICE. Tell him I asked about him,
will you?

MISS MINNY. All right, Beatrice.

*(*BEATRICE *continues, and reaching the*
corner, she exits. MISS MINNY *withdraws*
and shuts her window.)

THE RADIO. . . . . And now the genius
of the great . . .

(MUSIC plays, softly.)

CLIFF. Sheet.

RAY. What'cha say, Cliff?

(Silence. Both together.)

CLIFF.	RAY.
I said that . . .	I wonder if . . .

(Silence. Both together.)

(Annoyed.)   *(Embarrassed.)*
Go on!   Excuse me.

(Lengthy silence. Both take drinks and drag upon their cigarettes.)

CLIFF. *(Hurriedly.)* How old's that broad?
RAY. How old? . . .
CLIFF. Yeah.
RAY. Oh, Bea? . . . About my age, I guess.
CLIFF. She's certainly a snotty little stuckup heifer, ain't she?
RAY. Yeah, I guess so.

(Silence. Both together.)

CLIFF. *(Almost*   RAY. *(Explain-*
leering.)   *ing.)*
I wonder what . . .   She's always . . .

(Both halt. CLIFF *stubs out his cigarette.)*

CLIFF. *(Yells over his shoulder.)* Hey, Lou!

(No answer.)

(To RAY.*)* Guess she's out back in the kitchen or the john.
RAY. Yeah.
CLIFF. Ray?
RAY. Huh?
CLIFF. Did you ever get any ah that?
RAY. Beatrice?
CLIFF. Yeah.
RAY. Nawh.
CLIFF. What she doin', savin' it for Homer?
RAY. Homer? *(Laughing.)* She can't stand Homer. Calls him "Ole Country."
CLIFF. What'cha waitin' on, boy?
RAY. Nothin'.
CLIFF. When I was yo' age I'd ah had every little pussy on Derby Street all to myself.
RAY. You'd have them all sewed up, huh?

CLIFF. *(Not perceiving* RAY's *humor.)* Yeah, sho' would.
RAY. Ahhhuh.
CLIFF. How 'bout Marigold and Ruth?
RAY. What about them?
CLIFF. You ain't gettin' none of that either?
RAY. Nawh.
CLIFF. Why not, boy? What's the matter with you?
RAY. Nothin'.
CLIFF. Nothing?
RAY. Nawh, nothin'.
CLIFF. With all this good stuff runnin' 'round here you lettin' the chance of a lifetime slip by . . .
RAY. Yeah, I guess I am.
CLIFF. . . . always over there on Thirteenth Street messin' 'round with li'l Bunny when you should be takin' care of business back home.
RAY. I don't like any of the girls round here.
CLIFF. What's wrong with them? A girl's a girl . . . well, most of them are anyway.
RAY. *(Embarrassed.)* Well, I like Bunny. Me and her's in love.
CLIFF. In love? In love? *(Cracking the door and over the music.)* Hey, Lou Ellen . . . your nephew's in love!

(No answer.)

(Muttering.) Must'a fell in. *(Looking at* RAY.*)* Boy . . . you got a lot to learn.
RAY. I can't help it, Cliff. And she loves me too.
CLIFF. Ohhh, yeah . . . you really got a lot to learn.
RAY. Cliff . . . I . . .
CLIFF. Just because she comes down here with you on the nights that me and Lou are out don't make you be in love. You didn't think I knew, huh? Well, who the hell you think been turnin' those pillows on the couch over an' wipin' them off? Not your Aunt Lou . . . nawh nawh,

she'd damn near die if she knew you were doin' what comes naturally.

RAY. I'm sorry, Cliff.

CLIFF. Forget it. Oh yeah, now that reminds me. Clean up your own mess from now on. You're big enough.

RAY. Okay.

CLIFF. Bunny's the first girl you've had?

RAY. Nawh.

CLIFF. How many?

RAY. 'Bout half a dozen.

(Silence.)

CLIFF. Well . . . you ain't exactly backward . . . but still when I was your age . . . but let's forget about that.

RAY. Okay.

CLIFF. Now what about Marigold and Ruth, don't they like you?

RAY. All the girls on the street like me, I guess . . . 'cept'n Beatrice 'n' she used to let me kiss her . . .

CLIFF. She did, huh? Well, what happened?

RAY. I don't know.

CLIFF. Well, why don't you get one of the girls next door. Screw one of Homer's sisters. *(Chuckling.)* Get some of his stuff while he's away.

RAY. Yeah . . . yeah, Marigold likes me a lot. Homer even wants me to get Marigold so I might have to marry her and he'd have a brother-in-law he'd like, but she don't want it, not like that, and I don't see the sense of goin' with a girl if I can't do it to her.

CLIFF. You showin' some sense there, Ray. An' forget about that marriage stuff too.

RAY. Yeah, and Ruth wants to get married too bad. I'm scared as hell of her.

(Silence.)

CLIFF. Yeah, you better stick with fast little Bunny. Gettin' you in the service is gonna be hard enough. . . . If your aunt knew that anyone was thinkin' about you and marriage . . . we'd really have a case on our hands. She'd probably lock you up in the cellar.

RAY. *(Contemplating.)* And Beatrice thinks she's better than anybody else.

CLIFF. Yeah. I guess you do know what you're doin' stickin' with Bunny. But you'll be gone in a month anyway.

RAY. In a week.

CLIFF. Yeah, that's right . . . in a week . . . and things will be different then for you.

(Pause.)

Hey, do you know what, Ray?

RAY. *(Slowly.)* I met a girl the other day.

CLIFF. Do you know what, Ray?

RAY. I met a girl the other day, Cliff.

CLIFF. You did?

RAY. *(More sure.)* Yeah, I met her the other day . . . she's almost a woman.

CLIFF. She is?

RAY. A pretty girl.

CLIFF. You met her where, Ray?

(LIGHTS DOWN and UP on "The Avenue." The GIRL appears and stands under soft light. She has huge eyes and her skin is a soft black. The couples are fixed in tableau but RED and BAMA pull away from BUNNY GILLETTE and DORIS and dance about the GIRL in a seduction dance, until the two girls break their position and dance against the attraction of the girl, in a symbolic castration of the boys. LIGHTS DOWN to fantasy hues on "The Avenue" and UP on CLIFF and RAY.)

RAY. I met her over on "The Avenue."

CLIFF. Yeah, and she was pretty?

RAY. Yeah.

CLIFF. That's good. But you better not get stuck on her.

RAY. Why? Why, Cliff?

CLIFF. 'Cause you goin' away in a month. You goin' to the navy, remember?

RAY. But she can wait for me.

CLIFF. Well . . . most women are

funny. They don't wait around too long. They get anxious . . . you know, nervous that they won't get something that they think belongs to them. Never could understand what that somethin' was, but most of them are on the lookout for it, whinin' for it all the time, demandin' it. And I guess some of them even get it.

RAY. She'll wait.

CLIFF. Don't be too sure, son. Most of them don't.

RAY. Lou waited for you, didn't she?

(Silence.)

Didn't she?

(Silence.)

CLIFF. Yeah . . . but that was a little different.

RAY. How?

CLIFF. It was just different . . . that's all.

RAY. But how would it be different for you and Lou and not for me and my girl?

CLIFF. Well, for one, I don't know your girl so I can't say positively just how she'd act . . . And, two, and you better not breathe a word of this to your aunt . . . you hear?

(Pause.)

Well, Lou Ellen is different because . . . well, because she's got character.

RAY. My girl . . .

CLIFF. *(Cutting.)* And your aunt's got principle and conviction and you have to be awfully special for that.

RAY. But, Cliff . . .

CLIFF. *(Continuing.)* Now don't tell her, your aunt, I said these things, but she's special in that way.

RAY. I won't tell her.

CLIFF. For someone to have all of them qualities in these times is close to bein' insane. She's either got to be hopelessly ignorant or have the faith of an angel . . . and she's neither.

RAY. Nawh, I don't guess she is.

CLIFF. I don't deserve her, I know.

RAY. You two pretty happy together, aren't you?

CLIFF. Ray?

RAY. Yeah.

CLIFF. Don't think about her too much.

RAY. Lou?

CLIFF. Nawh . . . you know. Your girl.

RAY. Oh.

CLIFF. Yeah.

RAY. *(Distant.)* Yeah, I guess so.

CLIFF. Why do you say it like that?

RAY. Awww, I was just thinkin'. Lou says I can't go . . . and . . . and this girl . . . she . . . well, I see her every day now and . . .

CLIFF. Have you . . .

RAY. *(Upset, cutting.)* Nawh! We don't . . . we don't need to do anything. We just look at each other and smile . . . that's all.

CLIFF. Smile?

RAY. Yeah.

CLIFF. What else?

RAY. That's all. I just wait on the corner for her every afternoon and she comes dancing along with her little funny walk and sometimes she hums or sings to me a while . . . then smiles some more and goes away. . . .

(LIGHTS DOWN on "The Avenue" and the dancers.)

CLIFF. Boy, you better git yourself another drink.

RAY. I won't see her no more if I go to the navy, Cliff.

CLIFF. There's other things to see. Get her out of your head, Ray. There's a lot more fish in the ocean . . . ha ha . . . and a lot more girls where she came from. Girls all sizes and shapes . . .

RAY. *(Protesting.)* You don't know where she came from!

CLIFF. Why don't I? I just need to take one look at any girl and I know all about her. And with yours . . . well, your just tellin' me about her makes me know. I know all about her, Ray. And let me give you some advice . . . now you trust me, don't you?

(Pause.)

Good. I want you to stay away from her. There's all kinds of girls on this stinkin' planet . . . speakin' all kinds of tongues you never would think of, comin' in all kinds of shades and colors and everything. When you become a swabby, the world will open up to you.

Say, maybe you'll go to France . . . to Nice or Marseilles . . . the Riviera. Lie out in the hot sun . . . you won't need a suntan but you can lie out there anyway so those tourists and Frenchmen can see you and envy you. And you'll see all those sexy French broads in their handkerchief bathin' suits. Yeah, I can see you now, Ray, out there in your bright red trunks with sunglasses on peekin' at those girls. Or maybe you'll go to Italy and git you some of that dago stuff. Ha ha ha . . . best damn poon tang in the world, boy. *(He ruffles RAY's woolly head and takes a good-sized drink.)* Ha ha ha . . . put hair on your tonsils.

(Pause. Laughing.)

Yeah, there's nothin' like walkin' down a street in your navy blues. You know . . . you know . . . you should get tailor-made, skin tights, Ray, with buttons up both sides, and have your wallet slung around back of your pants . . . . I can see you now. Your wallet will be fat as a Bible. And . . . and the pretty little broads will be callin' out to you. "Hey, Yankee! Hey, sailor! Hey, Joe! Fucky fucky . . . two American dollah!" Ha ha ha ha . . . yeah! Yeah, that's livin', Ray. That's livin'.

RAY. *(Enthused.)* Is it, Cliff? Is it?

CLIFF. In some ports you can get a quart of the best imported whiskey for two bucks and in some ports you can get the best brandy for only a buck or so.

And the nights . . . ahhh . . . the nights at sea, boy. Ain't nothin' like it. To be on watch on a summer night in the South Atlantic or the Mediterranean when the moon is full is enough to give a year of your life for, Ray. The moon comes from away off and is all silvery, slidin' across the rollin' ocean like a path of cold, wet white fire, straight into your eye. Nothin' like it. Nothin' like it to be at sea . . . unless it's to be in port with a good broad and some mellow booze.

RAY. Do you think I can get in, Cliff?

CLIFF. Sure you can. Sure. Don't worry none about what your Aunt Lou says . . . I've got her number. I'll fix it up.

RAY. I sure hope you can.

CLIFF. Sure I can. As long as I tell your aunt I'm fixin' to ship out she'll sell you, herself, and probably her soul to keep me with her.

RAY. *(Frowning.)* You goin'a ship out, Cliff?

CLIFF. Nawh . . . nawh . . . I had my crack at the world . . . and I've made it worse, if anything . . . you young-bloods own the future . . . remember that . . . I had my chance. All I can do now is sit back and raise fat babies. It's your world now, boy.

(TINY rounds the corner.)

Well, here comes Tiny. *(Knocks on door behind him with his elbow.)* Lou. Lou. Here comes little Tiny.

(It has gotten darker and the shadowy figures have disappeared from the other stoops, into the doors of the houses, one after another.)

LOU. *(Off.)* What'cha want, Cliff. I just washed my hair.

CLIFF. It's Tiny . . . she's comin' down the street.

(TINY is a small, attractive girl in her late teens. As she comes abreast of the alley a large man in wide-brimmed hat jumps out at her and shouts.)

CLARK. *Boo!*

TINY. *Aaaaaiieeeeeee ! ! !*

(After the scream there is recognition between the two and CLARK *laughs, nearly hysterically, and begins trotting first in a circle about* TINY, *who looks furious enough to cry, then across the street to the fence where he leans and laughs, pounding the boards with his fists. Windows go up.)*

MRS. KRUMP. Is anything wrong?

MISS MINNY. What's all dat noise out dere?

LOU. *(At door, her hair disheveled.)* Clark, you shouldn't go 'round scarin' people like that!

(The POLICEMAN *passes the corner and stops and looks over the scene.)*

TINY. *(Regains breath.)* You ole stupid mathafukker!

MRS. KRUMP. Is anyone hurt?

CLIFF. *(Stands, his arm around* TINY'S *shoulder.)* Nawh, Krumpy . . . the goddamn natives are restless, that's all.

MRS. KRUMP. Ohhhh . . . I'm sorry . . . I just wanted to help.

(Her window closes.)

MISS MINNY. You and your friends shouldn't all the time be usin' that kinda language, Cliff . . . gives the street a bad name. We got enough bad streets and boys around here without you makin' it worse.

CLIFF. If you kept your head in where it belongs you wouldn't hear so much, Miss Minny. Now would you?

MISS MINNY. I'm gonna talk to somebody 'bout you, Cliff. Somethin' should be done about you.

(Her window closes.)

THE POLICEMAN. Is everything okay, Cliff?

CLIFF. Yeah, Officer Murphy. Everything's great.

THE POLICEMAN. Well keep it that way. I want it quiet around here, Cliff. *(The* POLICEMAN *turns the corner.)*

RAY. His name's not Murphy, Cliff.

CLIFF. To me it is. . . . If he doesn't know to call my right name I don't know his.

RAY. He said Cliff.

CLIFF. Yeah, he said Cliff like he was sayin' boy. He didn't say Mr. Dawson.

LOU. *(Ridicule.)* Mr. Dawson . . . and his mob.

TINY. I'm sorry, Cliff. I didn't mean to make all that noise . . . but that stupid ole Clarkie over there . . .

CLIFF. That's okay, Tiny. It's not your fault. Old nose for news up there has been after us as long as I can remember. *(To* CLARK.) Hey, Silly Willy . . . come the hell on over here and stop tryin' to tear down those people's fence . . . besides, it wasn't that funny anyway.

RAY. You sho' can holler, Tiny.

TINY. I was afraid, man. Some big old stupid thing like that jumps out at you. Damn, man . . . I'm just a little thing . . . he makes two of me.

LOU. From the way you holler, sister, I know they'll have to want you really bad to get you.

TINY. Fucken "A," baby. If they want mah little ass they gonna have to bring ass.

CLIFF. With Clark's big bad feet he couldn't catch a cold.

TINY. I should'a known better than to be walkin' along beside some alley, anyway. If I hadn't seen you folks up here on the steps I would'a been out in the middle of the street with runnin' 'n' hollarin' room all around.

RAY. You still didn't do so bad.

(CLARK comes over, snuffling and wheezing. He has a large moon face and is in his early thirties.)

CLARK. *(Giggles.)* I'm sorry, Tiny . . . ha ha ha . . . but I couldn't help myself when I saw you over on Ninth Street turn the corner.

TINY. (*Peeved.*) You been following me that long, man?

CLARK. (*Nearly convulsed.*) Heee heee . . . yeah, I ran through the alley and waited . . . and . . . heee heee . . . and when . . . heee heee . . . I heard your walk I jumped out.

LOU. (*Angry.*) Somebody's goin'a shoot you, you old dumb nut.

RAY. Wow, Tiny, you almost scared me. You sure can hollar.

TINY. Yeah, man, I really can when somethin's after me.

LOU. C'mon girl. C'mon in while I fix my hair. (*Lou's hair is long and bushy, just having been washed. It covers her head like a gigantic crown.*)

TINY. (*Steps across* RAY.) Okay, girl. Hey, Ray, don't cha look up my dress.

RAY. (*Jest.*) Why not, Tiny?

TINY. You must think you're gettin' big, boy.

RAY. (*Drawl.*) I is.

LOU. Not that big, boy.

CLIFF. Why do you keep pesterin' the boy, Lou? If he didn't try and look I'd be wonderin' what's wrong with him.

LOU. Is that what you do, look?

CLIFF. What do you think?

(*Silence.* CLARK *begins snuffling.*)

LOU. The only thing that's wrong with Ray is you, Cliff. I know some of those nasty things you been tellin' him.

(*Silence.* LOU *and* CLIFF *stare at each other.*)

TINY. I saw Doris and Bunny, Lou. (*Pause.*) They said they'd be over. Said they had some business to take care of.

(*Pause.*)

CLARK. Doris comin' over?

TINY. (*To* CLARK.) Yeah . . . yeah, stupid ass. She said she'd be down. And Ray, Bunny said you'd better keep yo' ass

home too. She wants to ask you some questions about that girl you been seein' out on "The Avenue."

RAY. What did she say?

CLIFF. (*Grinning.*) So it's finally got back home.

LOU. (*Hostile.*) Yeah, it's gotten back. You don't like it?

TINY. She said you'd better keep yo' black ass home, Ray. That's what she said.

CLIFF. (*Weary.*) Awww . . . Lou . . . please.

LOU. Followin' after you the way he does it's a wonder he ain't always in some trouble.

CLIFF. (*Caressing her leg.*) But, baby . . .

(*She pulls her leg back.*)

RAY. (*Angry.*) What she mean I better keep mah black ass home? I'll go where I want . . . with who I want. She better watch it . . . or I won't be lettin' her come down here.

CLARK. Hey, listen to Tiger.

LOU. I ain't gonna let you start anything with little Bunny, you hear, Ray? Don't be hittin' on that little girl.

RAY. Awwww . . . sheeet.

LOU. What'd you say?

CLIFF. What'd it sound like he said?

LOU. Now you keep out of this, Cliff.

CLARK. You women folks are sho somethin' else.

TINY. You shut your mouth and mind your business, Clark.

LOU. Now listen here, Ray. Don't you talk to me like that, frownin' up your face an' rollin' yo' eyes. You gittin' too mannish 'round here. You hear?

(RAY *doesn't answer, but gives a deep sigh.*)

Don't you bother that girl.

CLIFF. Ray?

RAY. Yeah?

CLIFF. If Bunny fucks with you . . . you knock her on her ass, ya hear?

RAY. Yeah, that's what I'm aimin' ta do, Cliff. Right on her ass.

(LOU and TINY go in.)

CLARK. Hey, how 'bout pourin' me some of that wine you hidin' down there?

RAY. We ain't hidin' no wine.

CLIFF. Pour your own troubles, garbage gut.

CLARK. Why, hell, you ain't got nothin' here 'cept enough for maybe Ray here.

CLIFF. Ray, here? What do you mean "Ray here?" Why this youngblood nephew of mine will drink you underneath the table and into the middle of nex' week, ole Silly Willy Clark.

CLARK. Sheeet.

CLIFF. Can't you, Ray?

RAY. (Proudly.) Sure as hell can.

CLARK. Well, we'll see . . . come on, let's go on up to the store and get us a big man.

RAY. A big man?

CLARK. That's right . . . a whole gallon.

(CLIFF stands and beckons RAY.)

CLIFF. Never stand in the way of a man who wants to part with some coins . . . and buy ya a drink at the same time, I say.

CLARK. Yeah, c'mon . . . (As an afterthought.) . . . I'm buyin'.

CLIFF. (Humming.) Hummmm hummm hummm . . . don't mind if I do get a little refreshing night air . . . c'mon, Ray, let's take a stroll.

CLARK. Well, which liquor store we goin' to? The one up on "The Avenue" or the one down by the bridge?

CLIFF. Let's go up on "The Avenue." (Pause.) That's okay with you, Ray?

RAY. Yeah, fine with me.

CLARK. Boy, we gonna get pissy pukey fallin' down drunk tonight.

CLIFF. If you see your girl up on "The Avenue" you'll point her out to me, Ray, won'tcha?

RAY. Yeah, Cliff. Yeah.

(They exit. The street is clear. MUSIC plays, then a COMMERCIAL begins. And LIGHTS DOWN.)

CURTAIN

ACT THREE

TIME:

Forty-five minutes later.

SCENE:

Derby Street. LOU, TINY, DORIS, BUNNY GILLETTE, RED, and BAMA sit upon the Dawsons' stoop.

A gallon jug of red wine is on the pavement beside the steps, and everyone except RED and LOU has a paper cup in hand.

DORIS is a small girl, not as small as TINY, and has a full figure. RED looks like a hungry wolf and BAMA seems to be mostly elbows and knees.

LOU. I don't see how you folks drink that nasty ole muscatel wine.

DORIS. (Demonstrating.) There's nothin' to it, baby sis.

RED. That's about the only goddamn thing we got in common, Lou. I don't drink that fucken hawg wash neither.

LOU. (Primly.) If you must sit on my steps this late at night, Red, I wish you'd respect me and the other girls here by not bein' so foul mouthed.

RED. (Indignant.) Shit, woman, talk to your ole man, Cliff . . . I'm usin' Mr. Dawson's rule book.

LOU. Don't blame Cliff!

BAMA. (To RED.) Forget it, huh?

RED. You sometimes forget who your husband is, don't you, woman?

TINY. Yeah . . . knock it off, you guys.

RED. (To TINY.) Fuck you, bitch!

LOU. *(To* RED.*)* I got a good memory, little red nigger.

RED. So use it . . . and don't bug me.

BUNNY GILLETTE. If you fools gonna keep this up all night I'm goin'a go home!

BAMA. Bye!

LOU. But I got to live with Cliff, Red . . . not you . . . hear?

DORIS. *(In high voice, nearly drunk.)* Do y'all want a hot dog? Do y'all want a hot dog?

TINY. Why don't we all stop arguing? I knew this would happen if you bought more wine, Bama.

BUNNY. You been drinkin' much as anybody.

BAMA. Ahhh, don't blame me. If I didn't get it somebody else would.

BUNNY. They up on "The Avenue" gettin' some more now.

LOU. Cliff and Ray's probably out lookin' for some ole funky bitches.

TINY. That's the way those punk-ass men are, girl.

BUNNY. Sho' is!

LOU. Who you callin' punk-ass?

TINY. Not anybody . . . well, I don't mean punk . . . it's just that all men are messed up.

BAMA. What chou' talkin' 'bout, broad?

RED. Hey, Bama, you better straighten your ole lady out before I have to do it.

DORIS. Do y'all want a hot dog?

BUNNY. Yeah, who's this girl Ray's been seein', Lou?

LOU. Don't ask me, chile. Don't even let him know I said anything.

RED. Tell Ray I want to meet her, Bunny.

(BUNNY threatens to pour her wine on him.)

TINY. When will Cliff be back?

DORIS. I said do y'all want a hot dog?

LOU. You waitin' for Cliff now, Tiny?

TINY. Yeah . . . Doris, I want one . . . but give them time to cook, will . . .

LOU. I asked you a question, Tiny.

TINY. Nawh . . . nawh . . . can't you see I'm with Bama. Ain't I, Bama?

RED. *(Mutters.)* Goddamn what a collection of cop-outs.

BAMA. Hey, get me a hot dog too.

DORIS. The mathafukkers should be done by now.

TINY. *(Nervous laugh.)* Woman, stop usin' all that bad language. You know Lou don't like it.

DORIS. Shit on you and Lou both, it's my mouth.

LOU. Now I ain't gonna warn none of you no longer. . . . Next one says one bad word has got to go home.

BAMA. Will you listen to this now?

RED. Hey, Doris, get me one of those fucken hot dogs, will ya?

LOU. That did it, Red. . . . Go home!

RED. Okay.

TINY. Doris, you can't say two words without cussin'. Don't you know any better?

RED. *(Stands.)* But before I go, Lou, tell me what did I say that was so bad?

LOU. I don't have to repeat it.

DORIS. I wouldn't be talkin' 'bout people so fucken much if I was you, Tiny. Remember I know somethin' . . . now don't I?

LOU. That goes for you too, Doris.

TINY. *(Frightened.)* Whatta ya mean, Doris?

BUNNY. Uuuhhh uhhh . . .y'all sure do act funny when you start in drinkin' this mess.

BAMA. Yeah . . . whatta ya mean, Doris?

DORIS. I ain't talkin' ta you, Bama.

BAMA. I'm talkin' ta you. *(To* TINY.*)* What she got on you, Mamma?

TINY. Whatta ya mean?

DORIS. *(Drunk.)* Whattaya think I mean?

BAMA. That's what I'm tryin' to find out . . . what ya mean.

RED. Shall we go . . . children?

TINY. That's what I'm askin' ya . . . whatta ya mean?

LOU. Now look. You broads can take that business back where you got it.

BAMA. *(Amused.)* That's tellin' them, Lou.

TINY. Don't you be callin' me a broad!

BUNNY. *(To RED.)* Red . . . don't you think . . .

RED. Shut up, woman!

LOU. *(Amazed.)* Wha' . . . I didn't . . .

BAMA. *(Joking.)* Yeah, you did. I hear you.

DORIS. *(Jest.)* Don't be talkin' to mah baby sister like that.

TINY. *(Scared and belligerent.)* What you gonna do 'bout it, bitch! You gonna tell her bout Cliff and me?

BAMA. Hey, cool it, baby.

LOU. What did you say?

BUNNY. Now Lou . . . don't get mad . . .

LOU. *(Disgust.)* Okay, let's forget about it. You guys don't have to go home . . . I want you to wait on Cliff.

RED. *(Sitting.)* Wasn't plannin' on goin', anyway.

LOU. Now looka hare, Red.

RED. *(Angry.)* Goddammit! Make up your mind!

DORIS. *(To TINY.)* You tryin' to be bad, ain't you, you li'l sawed-off heifer?

TINY. *(Rising.)* Little heifer!

(CLIFF, RAY and SILLY WILLY CLARK *turn the corner. They have a gallon jug of wine, half-emptied, which they pass between themselves and take large draughts. They visibly feel their drinks and stop under the streetlamp and drink and talk.)*

CLIFF. Ray . . . just learn this one thing in life . . . When the time comes . . . be a man . . however you've lived up till then . . . throw it out of your mind . . . Just do what you have to do as a man.

RAY. *(Not sober.)* Sure, Cliff . . . sure.

CLARK. *(Still drunker.)* That sho is right, Dawson . . . that's right . . . but why can't we be men all the time, Dawson?

CLIFF. *(Annoyed.)* You don't know what I'm talkin' 'bout, silly ass, do you . . . do you now?

BUNNY. Here comes Cliff, Ray, and Silly Willy Clark.

DORIS. *(Moving toward TINY.)* I'm tired of your little ass jumpin' bad around here, Tiny.

TINY. *(Scared but standing her ground.)* You are?

BAMA. *(Between them.)* Hey, knock off the bullshit . . . ya hear?

RED. Nawh, Bama . . . let them get it on and see who's the best.

TINY. *(Crying.)* Bama, why you always takin' somebody's side against me?

LOU. Shut up, all of you!

BAMA. I'm not takin' nobody's side against you, baby.

DORIS. You ain't takin' my side, Bama? And what you callin' her baby fo'?

TINY. *(To BAMA.)* Y'are!

BAMA. I ain't. We all just out to have a good time . . . that's all . . . a good time, huh? *(He pulls DORIS down beside him and puts his arm about her.)*

TINY. *(Scratching at his face.)* You bastard . . . I thought you was comin' down here to see me.

(DORIS *pulls her small knife.)*

LOU. *Doris, stop!*

DORIS. What the fuck's wrong with you, bitch!

(CLIFF *comes up and sees* DORIS's *knife but doesn't appear to notice; she puts it away.)*

I'm goin' in an' get a hot dog. *(Same high voice.)* Y'all want a hot dog?

(No answer. She enters the house. BAMA, TINY, *and* LOU *glare at each other.* RED *and* BUNNY *sit together.)*

RED. Well, if it ain't Mr. Dawson and nephew . . . the Derby Street killjoys. And hello, Mr. Silly Willy Clark . . . you simple mathafukker.

CLARK. Hey, everybody . . . *(Passing*

them the bottle.) . . . knock yourselves out.

BAMA. We got ours.

*(*LOU *silently stands, looks at* CLIFF *and the drunken* RAY *and enters the house.)*

RED. *(Hugs* BUNNY, *looks at* RAY.*)* Hey, what'cha mathafukkers doin'? Why don't you all have a sit down?

CLARK. Don't mind if I do, Red. . . . Hey, Cliff, is it okay if I sit down on your steps?

CLIFF. Be my guest . . . you know me, don't you?

BUNNY. *(Pulls away from* RED.*)* C'mon now, Red . . . stop all that stuff, man.

RED. You like it. *(He feels her breasts as they break.)*

LOU. *(Looking out the door.)* I don't want to hear any more of that nasty shit from your mouth tonight, Red. And watch how you act!

RED. Watch how I act?

CLIFF. Yeah, that's what she said . . . watch how you act.

LOU. Yeah, you keep your hands to yourself. I saw that.

RED. Hey, what's wrong with you goddamn people tonight? Is there a full moon or somethin'?

BAMA. Hey, Red, let's split.

RED. Mr. and Mrs. Dawson . . . and nephew . . . I'm sorry. Forgive me. Will you please accept my humble-ass apology, huh? Will you Dawsons do that? *(*RED *places his hand upon* LOU's *leg; she pulls away.)* Now what have I done?

BUNNY. What's wrong with you, Ray?

DORIS. *(Sticks head out of door.)* Do y'all want a hot dog?

TINY. Ray's gone off somewhere behind that wine . . . look at him slobber spit . . . probably with his . . .

BUNNY. With his what?

TINY. Nothin', hon . . . I was just kiddin' . . . *(Shakes* RAY.*)* Wasn't I, Ray?

RAY. Yeah . . . yeah.

BAMA. *(Mimics* DORIS.*)* "Do yawhl wants a hot dawg?"

TINY. Don't be so mean, Bama.

DORIS. Y'all can kiss mah ass.

LOU. *(Caricature.)* Don't be so mean, Bama.

BAMA. *(Furious.) Who you tellin' to kiss your ass, woman? I thought you saw what Bunny got tonight up on "The Avenue" for . . .*

*(*MISS MINNY's *window goes up.)*

TINY. Don't be so noisy, baby.

RED. I thought you was gonna get me one ah those mathafukkin' hot dogs, woman.

MISS MINNY. Cliff . . . Cliff . . . I see you out there . . . I'm callin' the police right now about all this disturbance!

(Her window goes down.)

DORIS. You better watch your little self, Tiny.

LOU. I told you about your mouth, Red.

TINY. Watch myself?

RED. My mouth . . . awww . . . Lou. You can't be serious.

CLIFF. Well, children, it's time that Daddy got to bed . . . I suggest that everyone goes home to bed or just home. Good night, all.

LOU. Ain't you gonna stay out here and wait for the cops, Cliff?

CLIFF. Good night, my love. Don't be too long . . . I think your hair's sexy.

*(*LOU *has her hair in curlers. He goes in, followed by* DORIS.*)*

DORIS. *(Off.)* Do y'all wants a hot dog, Cliff?

RED. If I hadn't seen Cliff beat so many bad niggers' asses I would think he's a chicken-hearted punk.

LOU. There's more than one way to be a coward.

BAMA. You better not let him hear you say that, lady.

CLARK. It's been a hard night, heh, Bunny?

BUNNY. Honey, these wine times is somethin' else.

RAY. *(Mumbling.)* Sho is, baby. Sho is.

DORIS. *(Back again, peering bleary-eyed at each one.)* Do y'all want a hot dog? Do y'all want a hot dog? If y'all don't, speak up . . . dese hare hot dogs gonna be all gone cause I'm eatin' them fast as I can.

RED. Shove 'em up your ass . . . you silly bitch.

LOU. Okay, you all have to go now!

(RED rises and is followed by the rest, except RAY, who snores on the step. LOU goes back into the house and her fussing with CLIFF about RAY's condition, his friends, and TINY can be more sensed than heard.)

BUNNY. Ray . . . Ray?

RAY. Yeah?

BUNNY. I gotta tell you somethin' . . . Ray? . . . Ray? . . . I got somethin' to tell ya.

BAMA. Leave him alone, Bunny.

TINY. Yeah, let him sleep. He'll find out.

RAY. Yeah . . . what is it?

BUNNY. I'm Red's girl now.

(SILLY WILLY CLARK gets up and enters the house.)

Did you hear me, Ray? Did you hear me?

(RED faces the building, and urinates in one of the wine bottles.)

RAY. *(Groggy.)* Yeah . . . I heard you, Bunny. You're Red's girl now.

BAMA. *(Giggling.)* I guess Ray's really got himself a new girl, Bunny.

(RED hands RAY the wine bottle he has just finished with.)

RED. Let's toast to that, Ray.

(Blindly, RAY lifts the jug to his lips, as BAMA and TINY gasp.)

BUNNY. *No! . . . No, Raayyy ! ! !* *(She knocks the jug out of his grasp, smashing it upon the pavement.)*

(RAY wakes instantly, perceives her action, and lashes out at her face. He lands a solid punch that knocks her sprawling in the street. RED rushes RAY and hits him with a haymaker aside the head. RAY grabs him for support and the two fall to the pavement, grappling. TINY screams. And MISS MINNY's window goes up. There are SHOUTS and NOISE of running feet. The fighters roll about the pavement and BAMA reaches down and pulls RAY off RED and holds him as the older boy smashes him in the face. SILLY WILLY CLARK rushes from the house and grabs BAMA from behind. Upon his release from BAMA, RAY butts RED in the midriff and staggers him to the entrance of the alley. RED pulls a bone-handled switch-blade; RAY grabs his arm and they fight their way into the alley. DORIS comes out of the house holding her small knife.)

DORIS. *(To BUNNY.) Where's Ray . . . Where's Ray!*

(BUNNY, dazed, points to the alley. DORIS enters the alley as CLIFF runs out of the door in only pants in time to see her disappear in the tunnel. The street is lit; the Krumps' upper windows are open.)

EDDIE. *Kill 'em . . . Kill 'em!*

MRS. KRUMP. Keep back, Edward . . . there may be stray bullets!

(SILLY WILLY CLARK has choked BAMA into surrender.)

RED. *(From the alley, muffled.)* All right . . . all right . . .

(As CLIFF runs into the alley there is a sharp sigh, then noise of more struggle and a groan. LOU, TINY, BUNNY, and Derby Street residents crowd around the alley entrance.)

MISS MINNY. Oh Lord . . . what's happened . . . what's happened?

MRS. KRUMP. Close the window, Edward . . . Close the window!

(The Krumps' window closes. The PO-LICEMAN turns the corner at a run.)

RESIDENT. *(To another* RESIDENT.*)* Did you see what happen, Mr. Roy?

MR. ROY. Nawh, Miz Cooper . . . but I knew somethin' had to happen with all this goin' on down here.

*(*RAY *emerges from the alley, blood on his shirt.* DORIS *follows him, her dress splotched with blood.)*

THE POLICEMAN. *(Running up with hand on pistol.)* What's happened here?

*(*CLIFF *steps out of the alley, holding* RED's *knife.)*

CLIFF. *(Hands knife to* POLICEMAN *and points in alley.)* I killed him.

LOU. *(Incredulous.)* You killed him . . .

*(*CLIFF *nods.)*

RESIDENT. Did you hear that?

MISS MINNY. What happened? What happened, Miss Francis?

RESIDENT. Cliff Dawson's done killed a boy.

MISS MINNY. Ohhh . . . my Lord.

TINY. *(Disbelief.)* You killed him?

THE POLICEMAN. *(Leads* CLIFF *to stoop.)* Okay, everybody . . . get back and don't nobody leave. By the looks of most of you . . . we'll want to talk to you. Get back. . . . Will somebody call an ambulance and wagon?

MISS MINNY. I already did.

*(*BAMA *has revived; he looks sick and sits beside the alley entrance.* BUNNY, CLARK *and* DORIS *support* RAY, *who looks to be in shock.)*

LOU. Cliff . . . Cliff . . . don't do it . . . don't leave me! Tell the truth.

*(*CLIFF *caresses her.)*

CLIFF. It won't be for long . . . I was protectin' my family . . . our family.

*(*LOU *cries, joining* TINY, BUNNY *and one of the neighbors.* DORIS *appears resigned to the situation.)*

RAY. She's gone . . . she's gone . . .

(A SIREN is heard.)

DORIS. Who's gone, Ray? Who?

RAY. She is . . . my girl . . . my girl on "The Avenue."

DORIS. She'll be back.

RAY. No, she's not. She won't be back.

THE POLICEMAN. I have to warn you, Mr. Dawson, that anything you say can be used against you.

CLIFF. *(Genuine.)* Yes, sir.

*(*BEATRICE *turns the corner.)*

RAY. Never . . . she'll never be back.

CLIFF. Lou . . . Lou, I want one thing from you . . .

*(*LOU *looks at him, then at* RAY.*)*

LOU. He's all I got left, Cliff. . . . He's all the family I got left.

(He looks at her until she places her head upon his chest and sobs uncontrollably.)

BEATRICE. *(Walking up to* MISS MINNY *in her window.)* What's the trouble, Miss Minny?

MISS MINNY. Ohhh, somethin' terrible, girl . . . I can't tell you now.

CLIFF. *(Handcuffed to the* POLICEMAN.*)* It's your world, Ray . . . It's yours, boy. . . . Go on out there and claim it.

(SIRENS nearer, LIGHTS DOWN and MUSIC rises.)

MISS MINNY. Come down tomorrow for tea, Beatrice, dear, and I'll tell you all about it.

BEATRICE. All right, Miss Minny. The Lord bless you tonight.

MISS MINNY. He will, dear . . . 'cause he works in mysterious ways.

BEATRICE. *(Starting off.)* Amen!

(LIGHTS DOWN to blackness and a COMMERCIAL begins.)

CURTAIN

Charles Gordone

No Place to be Somebody

A BLACK BLACK COMEDY
IN THREE ACTS

To the memory of Sidney Bernstein, producer of "The Blacks"

NO PLACE TO BE SOMEBODY

No Place to be Somebody was first produced on May 2, 1969, at the New York Shakespeare Festival Public Theater, New York City.

CHARACTERS:

GABE GABRIEL, a young fair-skinned Negro
SHANTY MULLIGAN, a young white man
JOHNNY WILLIAMS, a young Negro
DEE JACOBSON, a young white woman
EVIE AMES, a young Negro woman
CORA BEASLEY, a young Negro woman
MELVIN SMELTZ, a young Negro man
MARY LOU BOLTON, a white girl
ELLEN, a white girl
SWEETS CRANE, an elderly Negro
MIKE MAFFUCCI, a young white man
TRUCK DRIVER, a young white man
JUDGE BOLTON, a middle-aged white man, father of Mary Lou
MACHINE DOG, a young Negro (in Johnny's imagination)
SERGEANT CAPPALETTI, a young white man
HARRY, a Negro detective
LOUIE, a young white man

The production was directed by Ted Cornell; sets and lighting were designed by Michael Davidson.

ACT ONE

SCENE 1

TIME:
The past fifteen years.
PLACE:
New York City.
SETTING:
Johnny's Bar
AT RISE:
GABE *sits near jukebox, typing. Rips page from typewriter. Balls it up, flings it angrily at audience.*

GABE. Excuse me. Forgot you were out there. My name is Gabe. Gabe Gabriel, to be exact. I'm a writer. Didn't mean to lose my temper. Something I've been working on all my life. Not losing my temper. (*Takes out marihuana cigarette. Lights it. Inhales it. Holds smoke in.*) Right now I'm working on a play. They say if you wanna be a writer you gotta go out an' live. I don't believe that no more. Take my play for instance. Might not believe it but I'm gonna make it all up in my head as I go along. Before I prove it to you, wanna warn you not to be thinkin' I'm tellin' you a bunch'a barefaced lies. An' no matter how far out I git, don't want you goin' out'a here with the idea what you see happenin' is all a figment of my grassy imagination. 'Cause it ain't! (*He picks up Bible from table. Raises it above his head. Without looking turns pages.*) "And I heard a Voice between the banks of the U'Lai. And it called, Gabriel! Gabriel! Make this man understand the vision! So He came near where I stood! And when He came, I was frightened and fell upon my face!"

(*He closes Bible. As he exits, LIGHTS DIM OUT, then come up on* SHANTY, *at* JUKEBOX. *Jazz is playing.* SHANTY *takes out his drumsticks. Begins to rap on bar.* JOHNNY *enters. Hangs up raincoat and umbrella.*)

JOHNNY. Cool it, Shanty.
SHANTY. Man, I'm practicing.
JOHNNY. Damned if that bar's anyplace for it. Git on that floor there.
SHANTY. (*Puts drumsticks away. Takes broom.*) Ever tell you 'bout the time I

went to this jam session? Max Roach was there. Lemme sit in for him.

JOHNNY. Said you played jus' like a spade.

SHANTY. What's wrong with that? Ol' Red Taylor said wasn't nobody could hold a beat an' steady cook it like me. Said I had "the thing"! Member one time we played "Saints." For three hours, we played it.

JOHNNY. Had to git a bucket'a col' water an' throw it on you to git you to quit.

SHANTY. One these days I'm gonna have me a boss set'a skins for my comeback. Me an' Cora was diggin' a set up on "Four-Six Street." Sump'm else ag'in. Bass drum, dis'pearin' spurs, snares, tom-toms . . .

JOHNNY. Gon' steal 'em?

SHANTY. I been savin' up. Gonna git me them drums. Know what I'm gonna do then? I'm gonna quit you flat. Go for that. Sheee! I ain't no lifetime apron. That's for damned sure.

JOHNNY. Yeah, well meantime how 'bout finishin' up on that floor? Time to open the store.

(DEE and EVIE enter. Hang coats up.)

You broads let them two ripe apples git away from you, huh?

DEE. Don't look at me.

EVIE. Aw, later for you an' your rich Texas trade.

DEE. Just gettin' too damned sensitive.

EVIE. Sensitive my black behin'! Excuse me, I mean black ass. (Goes to juke-box. Punches up number.)

DEE. Last night we bring those two johns up to her pad. An' like, Jack? One with the cowboy hat? Stoned? Like out of his skull. And like out of nowhere he starts cryin'.

EVIE. All weekend it was "Nigger this an' Nigger that."

DEE. Never bothered you before. I didn't like it when he started sayin' things like "The black sons a'bitches are gettin' to be untouchables! Takin' over the coun-try!"

EVIE. Bet he'll think twice before he says sump'm like that ag'in.

DEE. That lamp I gave her? One the senator brought me back from Russia? Evie goes an' breaks it over his head.

JOHNNY. What the hell'd you do that for?

EVIE. Sure hated to lose that lamp.

JOHNNY. Wouldn't care if they b'longed to the Ku Klux Klan long's they gimme the bread. (He goes into DEE's purse.)

SHANTY. Sure had plenty of it too! When they was in here, they kept buyin' me drinks. Thought I was the boss.

JOHNNY. Crackers cain't 'magine Nig-gers runnin' nothin' but elevators an' toilets.

DEE. Leave me somethin', please.

EVIE. Ain't gon' do nothin' with it nohow.

JOHNNY. (Finds pair of baby shoes in DEE's purse.) Thought I tole you to git rid'a these?

DEE. I forgot.

JOHNNY. Save you the trouble. (He starts to throw them away.)

DEE. Don't you do that, you black bas-tard. So help me, Johnny.

EVIE. Aw, let 'er have them things, Nigger! Wha's the big deal?

JOHNNY. Tend to your own business, bitch. Ain't a minute off your ass for messin' it up las' night.

EVIE. Excuse me. Didn't know you was starvin' to death.

JOHNNY. (Goes for EVIE but quickly checks himself when she reaches for her purse. He turns back to DEE.) Look'a here, girl. I ain't gon' have no harness bulls knockin' down yo' door.

DEE. All of a sudden you worried about me.

JOHNNY. Jus' git rid'a that crap. Wor-rin' over sump'm pass, over an' done with.

(CORA *enters. A wet newspaper covers her head.*)

CORA. Lawd'a mercy! Now I gotta do this un'form all over ag'in. Bad as I hate to iron.

JOHNNY. Ironin' for them crackers. Cain't see why you cain't iron for yourself.

CORA. This ain't no maid's un'form as any fool kin see. I makes my livin' as a pract'cal nurse. I ain't nobody's maid.

JOHNNY. Somebody tole me they seen you wheelin' a snotty nose, blue-eyed baby th'ough Washin'ton Square the other day.

CORA. They was a Wash'ton Square lie. Onlies' baby I wheel aroun' gon' be my own.

JOHNNY. Hell! By the time you an' Shanty git aroun' to somethin' like that . . . you ain't gon' wheel nothin' roun' but a tray'a black-ass coffee.

(DEE *and* EVIE *laugh.*)

CORA. You cheap husslers don't hit the street, you gon' be sellin' yo' wares in'a home for the cripple an' infirm.

EVIE. Gon' have to bring ass to git ass.

(CORA *comes off her stool. Jerks off shoe.* EVIE *comes up with a switchblade.*)

JOHNNY. Hey! Hey! Git under the bed with that shit! (*He races around bar. Comes between them.*) What the hell's the matter with you, Cora? Cain't you take a little joke?

CORA. Don't know why every time I come in here, I gotta be insulted by you an' these here Harlows.

(EVIE *still has her knife out.*)

EVIE. Bet if that heifer messes with me, I'll carve her up like'a fat piece'a barbecue.

JOHNNY. Naw you won't neither. Not in here, you won't. Put it away! I said put it away.

(EVIE *reluctantly puts knife away.*)

DEE. Let's get out of here, Evie. She's always pickin' her nose about somethin'.

EVIE. She don't scare me none. Jus' smells bad, tha's all.

DEE. (*Looks at her watch.*) Well, I gotta date, and you gotta see your headshrinker, don't you?

JOHNNY. Headshrinker? Damned if Evie ain't gone an' got herself a pimp.

EVIE. He don't come as expensive as some pimps I know.

DEE. (*Goes for the coats.*) Now, don't you two start up again.

(*The* TWO WOMEN *start for the street doors.*)

JOHNNY. Make money, baby. Make that money.

DEE. That's all you ever think about. Can't you just dig me for my soul?

JOHNNY. Wrong color be talkin' 'bout soul.

DEE. Negroes. Think you gotta corner on soul.

EVIE. Us has suffahd, das why.

(DEE *and* EVIE *exit.*)

CORA. Gimme a martini, Shangy. Gotta bad taste in my mouth.

JOHNNY. Make sure she pays for that drink.

CORA. I works an' I pays. I don't ask a livin' ass for nothin'.

JOHNNY. 'Member when you did.

CORA. I was broke. Couldn't fin' no work. 'Sides I had you to take care of! Like I p'omised yo' mama I would. 'Fore she died. Till you had to go git in trouble with that Eye-tralian boy.

JOHNNY. Maybe I jus' got tired'a all them col'-cuts an' fuck-ups.

CORA. When you got out'a that 'form school, I was ready to take care you ag'in! But that bad Nigger Sweets Crane got holt you an' ruint ya.

JOHNNY. Fixed it so's I didn't have to

go to that orphan-house, didn't he? Took me in, treated me like I was his own son, didn't he? Damned sight more'n you or that drunken bitch of a mama'a mine did.

CORA. Jay Cee? Might God strike you dead. Maybe I ain't yo' flesh an' blood. But yo' mama? She couldn't he'p none'a the things she did.

JOHNNY. Do me a favor, bitch. Leave my mama on the outside. 'Nother thing, if you cain't say nothin' boss 'bout Sweets Crane, you don't have to come in here yo' dam-self. (He slaps her on the behind and exits to the kitchen.)

CORA. Well, fan me with a brick! Tha's one Nigro you jus' cain't be civil with. (She sips her drink as SHANTY finishes sweeping floor.) Eb'm as a chile—give him a piece'a candy, wudn't the kin' he wanted, he'd rare back an' th'ow it at you. An' he'd stan' there lookin' all slang-eyed darin' you to touch him. (She watches SHANTY beat on the bar.) Never had no papa. 'Less you call that ol' dog Sweets Crane a father. His mama was always sickly an' she did drink. Never would give it out though, who it was did it to her. Carried that to her grave! (She downs her drink.) I knowed her ever since I was a li'l gal down South. You know, they was always sump'm funny 'bout her. Swore Jay Cee was born with a veil over his face.

SHANTY. A what?

CORA. A veil over his face. Ev'body knows babies born with veils over they faces is s'pose to see ghostes an' raise forty-one kin's'a hell.

SHANTY. Johnny? Sheee.

CORA. If I'm lyin', I'm flyin'!

SHANTY. Cora, you're superstishus as hell.

CORA. Cain't he'p but be, li'l bit. My people's all had fogey-isms. Where I come from ev'body had 'em. One kin' or 'nother.

(MELVIN enters, hangs up knapsack and rain jacket, takes cap off. Knocks the wet from his pants. His head is almost clean-shaven.)

Chile! you sho' don't have to worry 'bout yo' head goin' back home!

MELVIN. My home, sweety, is in Saint Albans. You don't have to inform me as to where yours is. (He goes into a soft-shoe dance and sings.)

"Where the people beat they feet on the Mississippi mud."

CORA. Now, ain't that jus' like you ig'orint Nigroes. If they cain't think'a nothin' to say, they start slippin' you into the dozens.

JOHNNY. (Enters from kitchen.) You late, Mel.

MELVIN. Today was my dance class, remember? Anyway, who can get a cab in this weather?

JOHNNY. White folks, baby. Wheeeet folks!

MELVIN. Objectively speaking, plenty of them were passed up too. (He begins to stretch his leg muscles.)

JOHNNY. Dig? One of these days we gon' see this on tee vee.

MELVIN. You got your people mixed. The dances they do on television is ster-ictly commercial.

JOHNNY. What hell's wrong with that? If you gon' run 'roun' wigglin' yo' tukus, mights well git paid for it.

MELVIN. I study with a great artist! He deplores that sort of thing.

JOHNNY. Whozis great artist you study with?

MELVIN. Victor Weiner! He teaches the Chenier method.

JOHNNY. This Shimmy-yay method you don't wiggle the tukus?

MELVIN. Why?

JOHNNY. Them turkeys on tee vee mus' make a whole lotta coins jus' for wigglin' they tukeruseys.

MELVIN. Prostitutes. All of them.

JOHNNY. Pros'tutes, huh? (He goes to jukebox. Punches up number.)

(CLASSICAL MUSIC comes on.)

Go with a little sample what you jokers is puttin' down.

MELVIN. Nothing doing. To appreciate true art, one must first be familiar with it.

CORA. Talk that talk, Mel. What do Jay Cee know 'bout bein' artistic?

JOHNNY. (Rejects the music.) This Wineberg you study with? He's a Jew, ain't he?

MELVIN. So what?

JOHNNY. Gotta give it to him. Connin' spades into thinkin' they gotta be taught how to dance.

MELVIN. You're just prejudiced, Johnny. That's why you have no appreciation.

JOHNNY. When you start teachin' him, maybe I'll git me some pre-she-a-shun.

(A loud voice is heard offstage.)

VOICE. Inn keeper!

GABE. (Bursts in clad in army raincoat and sou'wester. He brandishes an umbrella and briefcase.) Cock-a-doodle-doo!

(JOHNNY paws the floor with his feet.)

"I am a ringtailed squeeler. I am that very infant that refused his milk before his eyes was opened an' called out for a bottle of old rye."

(They circle each other.)

JOHNNY. "This is me! Johnny Earthquake. I rassle with light'nin', put a cap on thunder. Set every mammy-jammer in the graveyard on a wonder."

GABE. "I grapple with lions! Put knots in they tails! Sleep on broken glass an' for breakfast, eat nails. I'm a ba-a-a-d mother-for-ya."

(JOHNNY goes behind the bar and takes down a bottle of whisky as GABE spies CORA.)

Eeeeeow! I feel like swallowin' a nappy-headed woman whole!

CORA. (Pushes him away playfully.) Better stay out'a my face, fool.

(JOHNNY moves around bar to Center. Theatrically pours a waterglass half-full of whisky. Sets glass before GABE on table. GABE removes coat and hat. Hands them to CORA. He eyes the whisky. Sniffs. Picks up the glass.)

A-Lawd! Gabe, you ain't . . .

(GABE puts glass to his lips and begins to drink.)

Ooooo!

(GABE is emptying the glass.)

Ooooo!

(He finishes. Eyes crossed. Sets the glass down. Grimaces. Shakes his head. JOHNNY and SHANTY laugh.)

I swear! Y'all is sho' crazy. Ain't neither one'a ya got good sense.

GABE. Needed that. Needed that one bad. Gimme another one.

(SHANTY reaches for the bottle.)

CORA. Don't you do it, Shangy. Let that fool kill hisse'f. Ain't no call for you to he'p him.

JOHNNY. Dam, Gabe! You ain't done gone an' got alcoholic on us?

GABE. Don't you worry yo' li'l happy head 'bout me, sir. Matter fact, I'm cuttin' myself right out'a the herd.

JOHNNY. Tell me sump'm, baby? Is this herd pink? An' got snoots an' grea' big ears?

GABE. No they ain't. In color, they're black with big, thick, lip-pussys.

JOHNNY. Man! Them ain't elephants you been hangin' out with, them's hippo-bottom'a-the-pot'a-muses!

(JOHNNY and GABE give each other some skin.)

CORA. Lawd! What in the devil an' Tom Walker you Nigros talkin' 'bout now?

JOHNNY. Keep her in the dark, Gabe. Keep that mulyan in the black.

MELVIN. They're talking about Gabe's audition, Cora. Gabe had an audition today.

GABE. I said it was a herd call, Melvino Rex!

MELVIN. Lots of actors there, huh?

GABE. Actors? Actors did you say? Well, yes! Every damned black actor in town.

CORA. Well, why didn't you say so in the first place? Lawd, chile! You ought'a lean up off this stuff.

(GABE *tries to put his arm around her.*)

An' take yo' arm out from 'roun' my neck.

MELVIN. How'd you make out at that audition, Gabe?

GABE. Dig this. It was a musical! A musical about slavery.

MELVIN. Slavery? Well! It's about time.

JOHNNY. Gabe's gon' play'a ha'f-white house Nigger! An' they ain't no whiter, ha'f-white house Nigger in New Yawk than Gabe is, I'll bet'a fat man.

GABE. You jus'a-got-dat-wrong, John. Stage manager calls me over. Whispers they're auditionin' the white actors tomorrow. Baby! I refuse to see anything musical at all about slavery.

(EVERYONE *breaks up laughing.*)

CORA. Say, Gabe? How about doin' one o' them crazy po'ms'a your'n? Ain't heard none in a long time.

SHANTY. Yeah, Gabe! How 'bout it?

MELVIN. Might make you feel better.

JOHNNY. Git under the bed with that shit! Ain't runnin' no cabaret. Fixin' to git me a summons!

GABE. What you wanna hear?

CORA. Anythin'.

JOHNNY. If you jus' gotta. Knowin' you, you always jus' gotta. Make it sump'm you know.

GABE. Dig this one.

(*All except* JOHNNY *eagerly take seats.*)

They met on the banks of the Potomac, the rich, the great and the small!

It's impossible to tell you, should'a been there an' seen it all!

They came by train, by plane, by bus an' by car!

Bicycle an' tricycle from near an' very far!

On mule an' on horseback!

With greasy bag an' kroker sack!

Buckboard an' clapboard an' goats pullin' wagons!

Tin lizzies an' buggies an' trucks so weighted down with people, you could see the backends saggin'!

Carts with motors, an' trams!

Wheelchairs an' wheelbarrels an' women pushin' prams!

Little boys on scooters! Little girls on skates!

Beatnicks, hippies an' hoboes, most of them had come by freights!

We had walked in light-footed an' barefooted, had walked all out'a our shoes! Some hopped it on crutches for days!

An' then we got the news, some black power agitators was arrested along the way!

'Course they was a lotta Cadillacs an' Buicks, rich people showin' off! I didn't pay that no min',

I jus' took comfort in the thought we needed people of every kin'!

An' if all America had been there or seen it on tee vee,

They would'a knowed we all meant business in gittin' our e-kwa-le-tee!

Well, we moved to the square with the pool in the middle!

While we waited, some strange young folk from New Yawk played a flute an' a fiddle!

Then somebody pro-nounced that reb'm somebody would pray!

An' by the settin' sun, we knelt in the dust'a that day!

Somebody else got up with a great loud voice!

Said they had on han' the speaker of our
    choice!
Said this black man was a black man of
    black deeds an' black fame!
(I'll be damned to hell, I disremember his
    name!)
Then a hush fell on all them people that
    night,
'Cause we was there for one thing, our
    civil right!
This black man, he rizzed up an' walked
    to the stan'! I could tell at a glance that
    he was the man!
An' he boomed out over that mickey-
    phone an' called for all black folks to
    unite an' not roam to other orguzashuns
    who jus' wanted to fight white people
    an' git what they can in a country that
    would soon give liberty an' 'quality to
    every man!
If we worked long an' hard, he admitted
    it'd be rough!
But he said, black unity an' solidarity
    would be enough!
Then he rizzed up his arms an' bobbled
    his head!
Best as I kin I'll try to remember what he
    said!

(GABE *pretends he is skinning a team
of mules.*)

Hya!
You, Afro-Americans!
Hya!
You, American Afros!
Hya!
You Muslims an' nay-cee-pees!
Hya!
You so-called Negroes!
Tan liberals!
Black radicals!
Hya!
You respec-rabble black boorwahzeees!
Hya!
Black Demos an' 'Publicans,
Git back on the track!
You Nash-na-lissys and Marx-a-sissies
Who all been pin-pointin' black!

Hya!
You half-white pro-fesh-nals!
Hya!
Civil rights pro-sesh-nals!
Hya!
You cursed sons-a-ham!
Don't rock no boat!
Don't cut ne'r th'oat!
Be a beacon for some black magazeen!
Come doctor!
Come lawyer!
Come teacher!
Black employer!
An' keepers of white latrines!
On Donner!
On Blitzen!
You black nick-surd-rich-ins!
On! On! With the soul kweezeen!
You inter-urbans!
Satisfied suburbans!
To you, I gotta say whoa!
What's needed to save us
Is not Some-a-Davus!
Or even Benjammer O.!
Giddy-up! Yippeee-ay! Or Kidney Po-
    teeay!
They already got they dough!
Now, here are the bare facks,
Grab yo' selves by the bootblacks!
Leave Heroin Manderson on the side!
An' all you take notice,
You'll all git yo' lettuce!
You'll own the post office yet!
Off-springs off mixed couples
Who're more than a han'fu,
You'll make the cover of *Jet!*
We'll have invented a machine that
    delivers
A cream to make crackers pay the debt!
Now junkies don't dilly
You husslers don't dally!
Don't waste yo' time smokin' pot
In some park or some alley,
'Cause Cholly is watchin' you!"

Well, he would a'went that'a way
To this very day but his th'oat
It got too hoarse!

When he sat down wasn't a clap ner a
   soun',
Couldn't tell if he'd got to the end!
A cracker preacher there, then said a
   prayer!
Said civil rights you could not fo'ce!
By this time I was so confused my head
   was in a spin!
Somebody else got up with a grinnin'
   face!
Said to leave that place like we found it!
Tha's when I reached in my pocket an'
   pulled out my packet an' before every-
   body took a sip'a my wine!
Then we lef' that place without ne'r trace!
An' we didn't leave ner' chit'lin' behin'!

(EVERYONE *laughs and claps his hands.*)

JOHNNY. If you ask me, it's all a big-ass
waste'a time an' energy. Jus' how long
you gon' keep this up? Ought'a be in some
office makin'a white man's pay.

GABE. Sheee! Think I'd rather be hawk-
in' neckbones on a Hundred an' Twenty-
Fifth Street.

CORA. Uh-aw! Better git out'a here 'fore
you two start goin' at it agin. (*She gets
newspaper and peers out of window.*) An'
'fore it starts up rainin' ag'in! Lawd knows
I ain't prepared for neither one. (*She
moves to* MELVIN *who is stirring something in a skillet. She sniffs.*) Shangy! If
you want sump'm 'sides Mel's warmed-
over chili better see you for supper.

GABE. Better watch it, Shanty. She's
thinkin' the way to a man's heart is
through his stomach.

CORA. (*Moves to street doors.*) Sho'
ain't no way to stay there. (*She exits.*)

(MELVIN *exits to kitchen.* SHANTY
busies himself. GABE *sits. Looks thoughtful.* JOHNNY *tosses him some bills.*)

GABE. What's this?
JOHNNY. Aw, take the bread, nigger.

(GABE *does not pick up the money.*)

Look'a here, Gabe. I know you think I'm

all up 'side the wall. You hip to the books
an' all like'a that. But ser-us-ly! Why ain't
they doin' you no good?

GABE. Let's jus' say I ain't in no big
rush.

JOHNNY. It's Charlie, ain't it?

GABE. What about Charlie?

JOHNNY. It's wrote all over you! Might
be foolin' some people. Cock-a-doodle-
dooin' an' comin' on with yo' funky po'-
try . . .

GABE. When you git some answers
other than the one's you been handin'
me, I'll git in the bed with you.

JOHNNY. One thing Sweets says to me,
'fore he got his time. He says . . .

GABE. Screw it, John. When you start
bringin' Sweets into the picture, I know
exactly what's comin' next. The answer is
still negative.

JOHNNY. Still wanna believe you kin
sell papers an' become President, huh?
Snowballs in Egypt.

GABE. I ain't lookin' to break no law.

JOHNNY. They ain't no law. They kill
you an' me in the name'a the law. You
an' me wouldn't be where we at, if it
wasn't for the law. Even the laws they
write for us makes us worse off.

GABE. From the git-go, they don't operate like Sweets anymore. Harlem's all
caught up.

JOHNNY. Who's operatin' in Harlem?

GABE. You can't be thinkin' about
down here! It was branchin' out'a Harlem
got Sweets where he's at right now.

JOHNNY. Man, what you think I been
doin' the ten years Sweets been in the
joint? I tell you the scheme is together.
Me an' him gon' git us a piece'a this
town.

GABE. An' end up on the bottom'a the
East River with it tied aroun' your necks.

JOHNNY. Bet we'll have us a box'a
crackers under each armpit if we do!

GABE. Well, I don't dig crackers that
much.

JOHNNY. Okay, Hollywood! Keep

knockin' on doors with yo' jeans at half-mast. Sellin' yo'self like some cheap-ass whore. If I know one thing about you, you ain't that good'a actor. Whitey knows right away you cain't even stan' to look at him.

(GABE *grins, picks money up. Pockets it.*)

BLACKOUT

ACT ONE

SCENE 2

TIME:
A week later.
PLACE:
The same.
SETTING:
The same.
AT RISE:
GABE *stands at Center.*

GABE. When I'm by myself like this, for days, weeks, even months at a time, it sort'a gets to me! I mean deep down inside things begin to happen. Lemme confess, sometimes I git to feelin'—like I get so vicious, I wanna go out an' commit mass murder. But don't misunderstand me. Because I call myself a black playwright, don't git the impression I'm hung up on crap like persecution an' hatred. 'Cause I ain't! I'm gonna leave that violence jazz to them cats who are better at it than me. I ain't been out of the house in over two months. Not because I been that busy, I just been too damned scared. I been imaginin' all kind'a things happenin' out there. An' they're waitin' just for me. All manner of treachery an' harm. But don't think because of it my play is about Negro self-pity. Or even that ol' "You-owe-me-whitey party line." 'Cause it ain't. In spite of what I learned in college, it did not give me that introduction to success, equality an'

wealth, that to my parents were the most logical alternatives to heaven. Anyway, like I say, I'm gonna leave that social protest jive to them cats who are better equipped than me.

(LIGHTS DIM OUT on GABE *and COME UP on* JOHNNY, *who is asleep on the floor. One shoe is off and an empty bottle and glass lie nearby. A telegram is pushed under the door.* JOHNNY *rouses himself. Puts on his shoe and goes to the door. Picks up the telegram and studies it. Someone is heard trying the street doors. He hides the telegram and opens the door.* DEE *enters. Goes behind the bar. Makes a Bromo.* JOHNNY *takes out the telegram. Peers at it again.)*

DEE. What is it?
JOHNNY. Looks like a telegram from Sweets. *(He gives her the telegram.)* Read it.

(DEE downs her Bromo.)

Read it, I said.

(She picks up the telegram.)

DEE. It's from Sweets all right.
JOHNNY. Well, what does it say?
DEE. Says he's going to be released in three weeks.

(JOHNNY snatches telegram.)

Makes you pretty happy, doesn't it?
JOHNNY. Babeee! Happy ain't the word! I am dee-ler-russ! Yeeeeoweee!
DEE. *(Grabs her head.)* Hold it down, will ya?
JOHNNY. S'matter? Rough night?
DEE. What else?
JOHNNY. Go home! Cop some zees!
DEE. Just sit here for a while! If you don't mind.
JOHNNY. Dam'dest thing. Las' night I stayed here. Burnt one on. Fell asleep right here. Had this dream. 'Bout Sweets gittin' out. Man' tha's weird! Tha's damned weird.

DEE. Today's my birthday.

JOHNNY. Dam! Forgot all about it.

DEE. Wish to hell I could.

JOHNNY. Anybody'd think you was a wrinkled up ol' mulyan. (He takes money from her purse. Tosses her a few bills, stuffs the rest into his pocket.) Here. Go out an' buy yourself sump'm real nice.

DEE. (Flinging the bills back at him.) I don't want anything for my birthday.

JOHNNY. Now, lissen. Don't you start no shit this mornin'. I'm in too good'a humor.

DEE. Johnny. Let's you and me just take off for somewhere! For a couple of weeks.

JOHNNY. You off your wood, girl? With Sweets gittin' out?

DEE. I gotta bad feelin'.

JOHNNY. I don't give'a dam what kind'a feelin' you got. Sweets was like a father to me.

DEE. So you told me. A thousand times you told me.

JOHNNY. I know. That bitch Evie's been puttin' ideas into your head.

DEE. That's not true. You lay off her, Johnny.

JOHNNY. Lissen to her, she'll have you husslin' tables at Howard Johnson's.

DEE. Might be better off.

JOHNNY. (Slaps her.) Kiss me an' tell me you sorry.

DEE. (She kisses him.) Sorry. (She moves to street doors.)

JOHNNY. Hey, girl. Gotta celebrate your birthday some way. Tomorrow mornin'. Bring over the Sunday papers an' a bottle my bes' wampole. "All day, all night, Mary Ann."

(DEE exits. JOHNNY peers at telegram. Goes to jukebox. Punches up number. Presently CORA and SHANTY enter.)

CORA. Jay Cee? I know it ain't none'a my business, but that woman'a yours? She's out there in the car. Jus'a cryin' her eyeballs out.

JOHNNY. (Getting his jacket, moving to street doors.) Hol' down the store, Shanty. Be back in'a couple'a hours. (He exits.)

(SHANTY goes to door. Locks it. Punches up number on jukebox.)

CORA. Shangy? I been doin' some thinkin'. You heard anything from Gloria?

SHANTY. Heard what?

CORA. 'Bout yo' divorce! Tha's what.

SHANTY. Gloria ain't gonna give me no die-vo'ce.

CORA. Well, if she ain't that don't stop us from livin' together, do it?

SHANTY. What made you change your mind?

CORA. 'Nother thing. Ever since I knowed you, you been belly-achin' 'bout gittin' you some drums.

SHANTY. Gonna git 'em too!

CORA. Well, I'm willin' to do everything I kin to help you.

SHANTY. You mean—you mean, you'd help me git 'em? No jive?

CORA. Then you could quit ol' Jay Cee an' go back to playin' in them nightclubs like you said you used to.

SHANTY. You really mean it? You'd help me git my drums?

CORA. Ain't talkin' jus' to hear myse'f rattle.

SHANTY. Mama, you are the greatest. (He hugs her.)

CORA. Honey, hush.

SHANTY. Know what I'm gonna do, Cora? Soon's I git them drums I'm gonna bring 'em in here. Set 'em up an' play "the thing" for Johnny.

CORA. Lawd, Shangy! I wouldn't miss that for nothin' in this worl'.

(SHANTY takes out marihuana cigarette. Wets, lights it. Smokes.)

Lawd, Shangy! I done tole you 'bout smokin' them ol' nasty things.

(He passes the cigarette to her.)

(She grins.) Guess it won't hurt none once in a while. (She inhales. Coughs.)

NO PLACE TO BE SOMEBODY : 419

SHANTY. I was just thinkin' about ol' Gloria. How much she hated jazz. Nigger music, she called it. Man, every time I'd set up my skins to practice, she'd take the kids an' go over to her mother's.

(They begin to pass the cigarette back and forth.)

Dig? One night after a gig, brought some cats over for a little game. Some spade cat grabs her between the legs when I wasn't lookin'.

CORA. Spent the bes' part'a my life on Nigros that won't no good. Had to baby an' take care all of 'em.

SHANTY. Never heard the last of it. You'd think he raped her or somethin'.

CORA. Cain't hol' no job! Take yo' money and spen' it all on likker.

SHANTY. Got this job playin' the Borsh-Belt. My skins was shot! Had to borrow a set from Champ Jones.

CORA. Cain't make up their min's! Jus' be a man, I says.

SHANTY. Gone about a week. Come home. Shades all down. Key won't fit in the door.

CORA. Git evil. Nex' thing you know they goin' up 'side yo' head.

SHANTY. She's over at her mother's. Says she gonna sue me for desershun.

CORA. I thought you was a dif'rent kind'a Nigger. I'm gon' git me a white man, one that'll take care me. Or he'p me take care myse'f.

SHANTY. I never did nothin' to her.

CORA. Tha's when he went up 'side my head with the ash tray!

SHANTY. Said she needed some bread. Went to the bank. Cashed my check. Come back. Skins the cat loaned me are gone.

CORA. I loved him so much.

SHANTY. Grabbed a broom out'a the closet. Went to work on the bitch.

CORA. Them awful things he said to me.

SHANTY. Bitch never made a soun' or dropped a tear.

CORA. I cried sump'm ter'ble.

SHANTY. Says I'd never see my kids ag'in or the drums neither.

CORA. Wanted children so bad! Doctor said I couldn't have none.

SHANTY. Started chokin' her. Would'a killed her, if my kid hadn't jumped on my back.

CORA. Ain't hard to satisfy me. 'Cause Lawd knows I ain't never asked for much.

SHANTY. One thing I learned. Stay away from bitches like that. Just ain't got no soul. *(He gets can of spray deodorant. Opens street doors and sprays the bar.)*

CORA. *(Rouses herself. Wipes tears.)* Shangy! I sho' wanna see Jay Cee's face when he sees you play them drums.

BLACKOUT

ACT ONE

SCENE 3

TIME:
 Three weeks later.
PLACE:
 The same.
SETTING:
 The same.
AT RISE:
 MELVIN *is doing his dance exercises.* JOHNNY *enters with white tablecloth and slip of paper.* SHANTY *busies himself behind the bar.*

JOHNNY. Sure we need all this, Mel?

MELVIN. You hired me to be a short order cook around here. That's exactly what that list is too. A short order.

JOHNNY. Jus' checkin'. Don't want you slippin' none'a that what-wuzzit over on me ag'in.

MELVIN. Po-tahge par-mun-teeay. Everybody else liked it.

JOHNNY. Been some chit'lin's, you'da been sayin' sump'm.

MELVIN. Chit'lin's? Sometimes I think you have the taste-buds of a slave. *(He snatches the slip of paper out of JOHNNY's hands and exits as MARY LOU BOLTON enters and goes to a table.)*

JOHNNY. Sump'm I kin do for you?

MARY LOU. I'd like a daiquiri, please. . . .

JOHNNY. Got any identification?

MARY LOU. Really!

JOHNNY. Mary Lou Bo—

MARY LOU. Mary Lou Bolton.

JOHNNY. This the school you go to?

MARY LOU. Just graduated.

JOHNNY. *(Goes behind the bar to mix drink.)* Buddy'a mine come out'a there. . . .

MARY LOU. Elmira is an all-woman's school.

JOHNNY. I mean the slammers up there.

MARY LOU. Beg your pardon?

JOHNNY. *(Sets drink before her.)* Prison.

MARY LOU. Oh, yes! My father spent a lot of time up there.

JOHNNY. You kiddin'? Your father did?

MARY LOU. *(She laughs.)* He was a criminal lawyer.

JOHNNY. He ain't no lawyer no more?

MARY LOU. He's a judge now.

JOHNNY. Must'a been a hell of a lawyer.

MARY LOU. Oh, I suppose so. . . .

JOHNNY. What you mean, you s'pose so?

MARY LOU. I'd rather not discuss it.

JOHNNY. Sorry.

(ELLEN enters. Carries a civil rights placard.)

ELLEN. C'mon, Mary! Everyone's waitin' on you.

MARY LOU. Be there in a second, Ellen. *(She looks into her purse.)*

(ELLEN exits.)

What do I owe you for the drink?

JOHNNY. Ain't you gonna finish it?

MARY LOU. I really shouldn't. But this is my first time out! Kind of nervous, you know?

JOHNNY. First time out?

MARY LOU. We're picketing the construction work up the street. The new hospital they're building.

JOHNNY. What for?

MARY LOU. Haven't you heard? The unions won't accept qualified Negroes.

JOHNNY. Why don't them qualified Nigroes do they own pickitin'?

MARY LOU. It's everyone's responsibility.

JOHNNNY. You only git in the way.

MARY LOU. I'm glad all Negroes don't feel the way you do.

JOHNNY. You don't know how I feel.

MARY LOU. *(Puts a bill on the table and prepares to leave.)* I don't think I care to find out.

JOHNNY. Jus' happen to think somebody invented this civil rights jive to git a whole lotta people runnin' in the wrong direction.

MARY LOU. *(Starts to move to street doors.)*

(JOHNNY catches her by the arm.)

Would you mind?

JOHNNY. Know what's in that daiquiri, baby?

MARY LOU. Let me go, please.

JOHNNY. Jizzum juice. A triple dose of jizmistic juice. Any minute you gonna turn into a depraved sex maniac! A teenage Jeckle an' Hide. Yo' head is gon' sprout fuzzy like somebody from the Fee-gee Eye-lan's. Yo' hot tongue'll roll out'a your mouth like a fat snake. You'll pant like'a go-rilla in heat. Yo' buzzooms will blow up like gas balloons an' the nipples will swell an' hang like ripe purple plums. Yo' behin' will begin to work like the ol' gray mare an' you'll strut aroun' flappin' yo' wings like'a raped duck. Then you'll suck me up with one mighty slurp an' fly out'a here a screamin' vampire. They'll finally subdue an' slay you on top'a the Empire State Buildin', with ray guns where you'll be attemptin' to empale yo'self astride that giant antenna. An' nobody will ever know that you, li'l Mary Lou Bolton, who jus' graduated from Elmira College, was lookin' to lay down in front of a big, black bulldozer, to keep America safe for democracy.

MARY LOU. I think I get your point.

(ELLEN *enters.*)

ELLEN. Mary Lou! Are you coming or not? Everyone's leaving.

(MARY LOU *and* ELLEN *exit,* ELLEN *scolding.* CORA *enters.*)

CORA. Shangy! Movin' man's waitin'.

(SHANTY *takes off his apron.*)

JOHNNY. Where you think you goin'?

SHANTY. Movin' in with Cora today.

JOHNNY. Not on my time, you ain't! An' me 'spectin' Sweets any minute.

CORA. What's so 'portant 'bout that Crane Nigro Shangy's just gotta be here? Or maybe you 'spectin' standin' room for the 'casion?

JOHNNY. Ain't lettin' him off an' tha's it.

CORA. Jay Cee, why is you so bent'n boun' on breakin' up our li'l club?

JOHNNY. Somebody's gotta look out for Shangy if he don't.

CORA. What is you talkin' about? Shangy's free, white an' long pass twenty-one! It ain't none'a yo' business what he does outside this bucket'a blood.

JOHNNY. Well, bitch, I got news for you. I put him in here when none'a these other hunkies 'roun' here would hire him. Talkin' his up 'side the wall talk an' beatin' up they benches.

CORA. Wha's that gotta do with me?

JOHNNY. Ain't lettin' you or nobody else turn his head but so far. Jus' per-teckin' my interest.

CORA. Ain't gon' let you stan' in my way, Jay Cee. Me an' Shangy took a likin' for one 'nother from the day I walked in here an' foun' you runnin' this

place. Up to now they ain't been much happiness in this worl' for neither one of us. But what li'l we got comin', figger we bes' jump on it with all fo' feet.

JOHNNY. That the way you feel 'bout it, Shanty?

SHANTY. Man, she's gonna help me git my drums.

JOHNNY. She ain't gon' do nothin' but turn you into sump'm you don't wanna be.

CORA. What is you talkin' 'bout, fool?

JOHNNY. This black bitch is gon' turn you into a real white man, Shanty.

SHANTY. What??

CORA. You kin quit this nigger today, honey. We'll manage.

JOHNNY. You wanna be a white man, Shanty?

SHANTY. Knock that stuff off, Johnny! I don't go for it.

JOHNNY. You think if you git with somebody like Cora, it'll make the whole thing complete, huh?

CORA. Hush up, Jay Cee.

JOHNNY. Well, it won't. She'll make you so damn white you won't be able to bang two spoons together.

CORA. I'm warnin' you, Jay Cee.

JOHNNY. An' play the drums? You'll never play no drums.

(CORA *rushes at* JOHNNY. *He catches her arm and throws her to the floor.* SHANTY *is shocked by* JOHNNY's *cruelty. He makes a move to* JOHNNY.)

SHANTY. Why you—you—you mother fucker!

(JOHNNY *stands ready to throw a punch.* SHANTY *checks himself. Turns away.* CORA *gets to her feet and goes to him. Puts her arm around him. He shuns her. Exits, slowly.*)

CORA. Tha's alright, Jay Cee honey. Tha's all right! That day ain't long off, 'fore you gon' git yours. Honey, you gon' git a hurtin' put on you. You gon' git a hurtin' put on you in the place where you do wrong.

JOHNNY. Better wish all that hurtin' on all them Niggers that messed up yo' min'.

(CORA *exits as* GABE *enters.*)

GABE. Dam! What was all that smoke about?

JOHNNY. Them two ain't got sense nuff to pour piss out'a a boot if the directions was wrote on the heel.

GABE. You just don't wanna see anybody git any enjoyment out'a life.

JOHNNY. Bastard's movin' in with her. You dig that?

GABE. An' you tried to stop 'em, huh?

(JOHNNY *doesn't answer. Takes bottle of champagne and bucket. Sets it on a table.*)

Well, I see you're gittin' ready for the big homecomin', huh?

JOHNNY. That's right. An' I don't want you goin' into none'a yo' high'n mighty when Sweets git here. Tell you right now he don't go for none of that giddy-up-yippee-yaye shit!

GABE. Didn't come to stay. Lemme hold some coins! Lan'lord's on my tail.

JOHNNY. Good. (JOHNNY *grins. Spreads bills over the table.*)

(GABE *picks them up.*)

GABE. You'll git it all back soon's I git me a show.

JOHNNY. You keepin' a record?

(*A* BLACK MAN *enters.*)

On yo' way, wine.

SWEETS. S'matter, Sonny Boy? Don't you know me?

JOHNNY. Sweets? Is it really you?

SWEETS. It's me, all right. (SWEETS *coughs.*)

(JOHNNY *rushes forward. Embraces* SWEETS.)

JOHNNY. Lock the doors, Gabe. Don't want no innerrupshuns.

(GABE *locks the street doors.* JOHNNY *and* SWEETS *box playfully.*)

SWEETS. Minute there, was 'bout to go out an' come back in again.

JOHNNY. Reason I didn't rec'nize you at firs' was, well, I always remember you bein' 'bout as sharp as a skeeter's peter in the dead'a winter. Three hundred suits he had, Gabe. Nothin' but the fines' vines. Never seen so many kicks in one closet. Wasn't a cat in Harlem. . . .

(SWEETS *coughs violently.*)

Dam! What you doin' 'bout that cough, Sweets?

SWEETS. Little souvenir I picked up at the jute mill.

JOHNNY. Jute mill?

SWEETS. Where they make burlap bags at.

JOHNNY. Pretty rough in Fedsville, huh?

(SWEETS *coughs again.*)

Meet my man, Gabe.

(GABE *and* SWEETS *shake hands.*)

GABE. Pleased to meet you, Mister Crane.

SWEETS. Jus' call me Sweets.

JOHNNY. (*Brings bottle and two glasses.*) Sweets, some'a Pete Zerroni's bes'.

SWEETS. Zerroni? You don't mean ol' big fat Pete from up there in the Bronx?

JOHNNY. Yeah. He's runnin' everything down here from soup to nuts! But we gon' change all that, ain't we, Sweets?

(JOHNNY *struggles with cork.*)

SWEETS. Sonny Boy, we wasn't much on sendin' kites. Wha's been happenin' since I been in the joint?

JOHNNY. Jews, Irish an' the Ginees still runnin' things as usual.

SWEETS. No. I mean with you, Sonny Boy.

JOHNNY. Like you know I had a tough gaff gittin' my divorce. Whole thing started when I wanted her to do a little merchandizin' for me. Real Magdaleen, she was! One thing led to 'nother. Boom! Back to mama she went. Had a helluva time gittin' her to sign this joint over to me. Went into my act. Fell down on my deuce'a benders. Gave her the ol' routine. Like how the worl' been treatin' us black folk an' everything . . . *(He pops cork. Pours. Holds his glass up. The two men clink their glasses.)* Well, look here, Sweets, here's to our li'l piece'a this town.

SWEETS. *(Looks into his glass as* JOHNNY *sips.)* Speakin'a husslers, Sonny Boy. *(He coughs.)*

*(*GABE *goes to bar. Gets large glass and fills it with champagne.)*

You runnin' any kind'a stable?

JOHNNY. You kiddin', Sweets? *(Gives* GABE *a dirty look.)*

SWEETS. Pushin' or bookin'?

JOHNNY. Nay, that ain't my stick.

SWEETS. Sonny Boy, when I was yo' age, I was into some'a ev'thing.

JOHNNY. Wish you wouldn't call me that, Sweets! I ain't that little boy runnin' up an' down Saint Nicklas Avenue for you no more.

SWEETS. Jus' habit, Johnny. But I sort'a was hopin' you was into sump'm on yo' own, like.

JOHNNY. Hell! I been tryin' to stay clean. Waitin' on you, man! Like we planned.

SWEETS. Well, now! Tha's—tha's what I wanna talk to you 'bout, Sonny Boy.

JOHNNY. Yes, sir! You still the boss, Sweets. Didn't think you wanted to git into it jus' yet. Figgered we'd have us a few drinks. Talk 'bout ol' times . . .

SWEETS. Sonny Boy!

JOHNNY. Sir?

SWEETS. Firs' off! I gotta tell you I'm th'ough. . . .

JOHNNY. Whatchu say?

SWEETS. Wrappin' it all up for good . . .

JOHNNY. Wrappin' what up?

SWEETS. The rackets.

JOHNNY. You gotta be jokin'.

SWEETS. Never been more ser'us in all my life. . . .

JOHNNY. Sweets, you jus' tired.

SWEETS. Don't need no res'. . . .

JOHNNY. Git yo'self together. . . .

SWEETS. My min's made up.

JOHNNY. Waitin' on you this long, little more ain't gon' kill me.

SWEETS. Look, Sonny Boy, it's like this. . . .

JOHNNY. Shut up with that Sonny Boy, shit! *(He tries to control himself.)*

*(*GABE *laughs.)*

Look, man. You ain't let the slammers psyche you out? That ain't like you. That ain't like you, at all. *(He reaches out to touch* SWEETS, *who jerks away.* JOHNNY *grabs* SWEETS *by the throat violently.)* Mother fucker! I been waitin' on you for ten long-ass years. You ain't gon' cop out on me like this.

GABE. *(Moves to contain* JOHNNY.*)* Cut it out, John! Let him alone. Cain't you see the man's sick?

*(*JOHNNY *hits* GABE *in the stomach.* GABE *doubles over. Goes to the floor.)*

JOHNNY. *(To* SWEETS.*)* What the hell they do to you, huh?

SWEETS. What'd who do to me?

JOHNNY. In the bastille. They did sump'm to you.

SWEETS. Nothin' that wasn't already done to me. *(*SWEETS *moves to* GABE.*)* You all right, young fella?

GABE. Yeah—yeah, I—I'm okay.

SWEETS. *(Takes wallet from* GABE's *back pocket. Puts it into his own pocket.)* Shouldn'a mixed in. *(He turns back to*

JOHNNY.) You got the Charlie fever, Johnny. Tha's what you got. I gave it to you. Took yo' chile's min' an' filled it with the Charlie fever. Givin' you a eduction or teachin' you to dinner-pail, didn't seem to me to be no way for you to grow up an' be respected like'a man. Way we was raised, husslin' an' usin' yo' biscuit to pull quickies was the only way we could feel like we was men. Couldn't copy Charlie's good points an' live like men. So we copied his bad points. That was the way it was with my daddy an' his daddy before him. We just pissed away our lives tryin' to be like bad Charlie. With all our fine clothes an' big cars. All it did was make us hate him all the more an' ourselves too. Then I tried to go horse-to-horse with 'em up there in the Bronx. An' ended up with a ten. All because'a the Charlie fever. I gave you the Charlie fever, Johnny. An' I'm sorry! Seems to me, the worse sickness'a man kin have is the Charlie fever.

JOHNNY. *(Glares at* SWEETS.) Git out'a here, Sweets. Goddam you! Git out'a here! 'Fore I kill you.

*(*SWEETS *coughs and exits to the street.* JOHNNY *looks after him.)*

They did sump'm to him. White sons'a bitches. They did sump'm to him. Sweets don't give up that easy. Charlie fever. Sheeee!

GABE. Ten years is a long time. An' the man's sick. Anyone kin see that.

JOHNNY. He could be fakin'. He's into sump'm! Don't want me in on it. He used to do that to me all the time. He better be fakin'. *(Brings his arm up to look at his watch.)*

GABE. What? What the hell . . . *(He searches frantically in his pockets.)* I'll be goddam.

JOHNNY. Hell's matter with you?

GABE. My watch! It's gone.

JOHNNY. Hell with your watch!

GABE. It's gone! An' my wallet! The bread you loaned me! It's gone, too.

*(*JOHNNY *begins to laugh hysterically.)*

What the hell's so goddamn funny?

JOHNNY. It's Sweets! The bastard is fakin'. He snatched it!

BLACKOUT

ACT TWO

SCENE 1

TIME:
   Two days later.
PLACE:
   The same.
SETTING:
   The same.
AT RISE:
   GABE *sits at table. Whisky bottle before him. He is obviously drunk. He begins to sing an old Protestant hymn.*

GABE.
"Whiter than snow, yes!
Whiter than snow!
Now, wash me, and I shall be
Whiter than snow!"
   (He chants.)
We moved out of that dirty-black slum!
Away from those dirty-black people!
Who live in those dirty-black hovels,
Amidst all of that garbage and filth!
Away from those dirty-black people,
Who in every way,
Prove daily
They are what they are!
Just dirty-black people!

We moved to a house with a fenced-in yard!
To a clean-white neighborhood!
It had clean-white sidewalks
And clean-white sheets
That hang from clean-white clotheslines to dry!

They were clean-white people!
Who in every way
Prove daily
They are what they are!
Just clean-white people!

Now those clean-white people thought we were
Dirty-black people!
And they treated us like we were
Dirty-black people!
But we stuck it out!
We weathered the storm!
We cleansed and bathed
And tried to be and probably were
Cleaner than most of those clean-white people!
(He sings.)
"Break down every idol, cast out every foe!
Oh, wash me and I shall be whiter than snow!"
(He speaks again.)
We went to schools that had clean-white
Rooms with clean-white teachers
Who taught us and all of the clean-white
Children how to be clean and white!
(He laughs.)
Now, those dirty-black people across
The tracks became angry, jealous and mean!
When they saw us running or skipping or
Hopping or learning with all of those
Clean-white children!

They would catch us alone
When the clean-white children weren't there!
And kick us or slap us and spit
On our clean-white clothes!
Call us dirty-black names
And say that we wanted to be like our clean-white
Neighbors!

But in spite of the kicking, the slapping
The spitting, we were exceedingly glad!
For we knew we weren't trying to be like

Our clean-white neighbors! Most of all,
We were certain we weren't like those
Dirty-black Niggers,
Who live in hovels, far away across the tracks!
(He sings.)
"Whiter than snow! Oh, whiter than snow!
Please wash me, and I shall be whiter than snow!"
(He speaks again.)
So we grew up clean and keen!
And all of our clean-white neighbors
Said we had earned the right to go
Out into the clean-white world
And be accepted as clean-white people!
But we soon learned,
The world was not clean and white!
With all of its powders and soaps!
And we learned too that no matter how
Much the world scrubbed,
The world was getting no cleaner!

Most of all!
We saw that no matter how much or how
Hard we scrubbed,
It was only making us blacker!
So back we came to that dirty-black slum!
To the hovels, the filth and the garbage!
Came back to those dirty-black people!
Away from those clean-white people!
That clean, white anti-septic world!
That scrubs and scrubs and scrubs!

But those dirty-black people!
Those dirty-black people!
Were still angry, jealous and mean!
They kicked us and slapped us and spit again
On our clothes!
Denied us!
Disowned us
And cast us out!
And we still were exceedingly glad!

For at last they knew
We were not like our clean-white neighbors!
Most of all! We were safe!

Assured at last!
We could never more be
Like those dirty-black Niggers!
Those filthy, dirty-black Niggers!
Who live far away!
Far away, in hovels across the tracks!
(*He bursts into song.*)
"Whiter than snow! Yes! Whiter than
snow!"
Oh, wash me and I shall be whiter than
snow!"
(GABE *is on his knees, hands stretched
up to heaven.*)

(*LIGHTS SLOWLY DIM OUT on
him, and come up on bar.* SHANTY *is behind the bar.* MIKE MAFFUCCI *stands at
Center, throwing darts into a dartboard.*
SWEETS CRANE *enters.*)

SHANTY. Hit the wind, Mac. This ain't
the place.
SWEETS. Johnny here?
SHANTY. What you want with Johnny?
SWEETS. I'm a frien'a has.
SHANTY. Yeah? Well, he ain't here.
SWEETS. Where's me a broom an' a
drop pan?
SHANTY. What for?
SWEETS. Need me a bucket an' some
rags too.
SHANTY. What do you want all that
shit for?
SWEETS. The floor, they don't look too
good an' the windas, it could stan' . . .
SHANTY. Eighty-six, ol' timer! We ain't
hirin'.
SWEETS. Ain't askin' f'no pay.
SHANTY. What'a ya? Some kind'a nut?
C'mon! Out you go. Eighty-six.
SWEETS. Think you better wait till
Johnny gets here. Let him put me out.
(SWEETS *pushes* SHANTY *roughly aside
and moves to kitchen.*) Think I'll fin' what
I need back here.

SHANTY. (*Looks incredulous. Scratches
his head and follows* SWEETS *to kitchen.*)

(JOHNNY *enters.* SHANTY *rushes in from
kitchen.*)

Hel, Johnny! Some ol' timer just came
in an' . . .
MAFFUCCI. How you doin', Johnny
Cake?
JOHNNY. (*Stops short.*) Only one cat
usta call me that.
MAFFUCCI. Gettin' warm, Johnny Cake.
JOHNNY. (*Moves behind bar.*) Little
snotty-nose wop kid, name Mike Maf-
fucci.
MAFFUCCI. On the nose. (*Sends a dart
in* JOHNNY'S *direction.*)

(JOHNNY *ducks. The dart buries into
the wood of the back bar. Both men
laugh. They shake hands.*)

Long time no see, eh, Johnny Cake?
JOHNNY. What you drinkin'?
MAFFUCCI. Little dago red. Gotta take
it easy on my stomach with the hard stuff.

(JOHNNY *snaps his fingers.* SHANTY
brings bottle.)

SHANTY. Dig, Johnny! Some ol'
goat . . .
JOHNNY. Cool it, Shanty. Can't you see
I'm busy? How's your ol' man, Footch?
MAFFUCCI. (*Makes the sign of the
cross*). My ol' man chalked out, Johnny.
Heart attack. Right after you went to the
nursery. You ain't still sore 'bout what
happened, are you, Johnny Cake?
JOHNNY. Bygones is bygones, Footch!
MAFFUCCI. Glad'a hear ya say that,
Johnny. Didn't know what happened to
you after that. When they tole me you
was runnin' this joint, had'a come over
an' see ya. (*He looks around.*)

(SWEETS *enters with broom and rags.
Proceeds to sweep the floor.* JOHNNY *reg-
isters surprise and anger.* SHANTY *starts
to say something but* JOHNNY *puts his
finger to his lips.*)

How ya doin' with the place, Johnny?

JOHNNY. Stabbin' horses to steal blankets. Jay Cee ag'inst the worl'.

MAFFUCCI. Joe Carneri used to say that. You ain't never forgot that huh, Johnny?

(JOHNNY *glances angrily at* SWEETS.)

Remember the first time they busted him? There was this pitchure on the front page. Joe's standin' on the courthouse steps. Cops an' reporters all aroun'. Joe's yellin' "Jay Cee ag'inst the worl'! Jay Cee ag'inst the worl'!"

JOHNNY. He sho' was your hero all right.

MAFFUCCI. Too bad he had'a go an' git hit like that. Sittin' in a barber chair!

JOHNNY. Better'n the electric chair.

(SWEETS *is now dusting the chairs.*)

MAFFUCCI. You know, Johnny Cake, that was a groovy idea for a kid! Coppin' all that scrapiron from ol' Julio an' then sellin' it back to him. (*He breaks up laughing.*)

JOHNNY. Wasn't so pretty when I tried to tell the fuzz you was in on it with me.

MAFFUCCI. Awful sorry 'bout that, Johnny Cake. (MAFFUCCI *puts his hand on* JOHNNY'S *shoulder.*)

(JOHNNY *knocks his hand off.* MAFFUCCI *comes down on* JOHNNY'S *shoulder with a karate chop.* JOHNNY *punches* MAFFUCCI *in the stomach and shoves him away. Comes toward* MAFFUCCI *menacingly.* SWEETS *keeps sweeping.*)

JOHNNY. One thing I gotta give you Ginees credit for. Sho' know how to stick together when you wanna.

MAFFUCCI. (*Backs away.*) He was my father, Johnny. Any father would'a done the same thing. If he had the connections.

JOHNNY. Who tole you I was runnin' this joint, Footch?

MAFFUCCI. To give you the works, Johnny, I'm one'a Pete Zerroni's local boys now.

(SWEETS *dusts near* MAFFUCCI.)

JOHNNY. No jive! Battin' in the big leagues, ain't you? Your ol' man was aroun', bet he'd be pretty proud'a you.

MAFFUCCI. Would you believe, my ol' man had ideas 'bout me bein' a lawyer or a doctor?

JOHNNY. What you doin' for Pete?

MAFFUCCI. Sort'a community relations like, Johnny.

JOHNNY. (*Laughs.*) I'm one'a Pete's customers! What kind'a community relashuns you got for me?

MAFFUCCI. Glad you opened that, Johnny Cake. Pete says you got him a little concerned.

JOHNNY. What is he, crazy? Ain't he got more 'portant things on his min'?

MAFFUCCI. Way we got it, first thing ol' Sweets Crane did when he got out was come see you.

JOHNNY. So what? Sweets was like'a father to me.

MAFFUCCI. So I hear. But before they shut the gate on him, he let some things drop. Like, he made a few threats. What I hear 'bout him, might be crazy enough to give 'em a try.

(JOHNNY *laughs.*)

What, am I throwin' zingers or sump'm? What's the joke?

JOHNNY. Sweets came 'roun' to tell me he's all caught up.

MAFFUCCI. Wouldn't promote me, would you, Johnny Cake? For ol' time's sake, let's not you an' me go horse-to-horse 'bout nothin'.

JOHNNY. On the up an' up, Footch. Sweets has wrapped it all up for good. Matter'a fack, right now he's doin' odd gigs an' singin' the straight an' narrow.

MAFFUCCI. Wanna believe you, Johnny. But just in case you an' this Sweets are thinkin' 'bout makin' a little noise, Pete wants me to give you the six-to-five!

(SWEETS *bumps into* MAFFUCCI, *spill-*

ing the wine down the front of MAF-FUCCI's *suit.)*

Hey! Watch it there, pops!

SWEETS. Awful sorry 'bout that, mister! *(Attempts to wipe* MAFFUCCI's *suit with the rag.* MAFFUCCI *pushes him aside.)*

MAFFUCCI. That's okay, pops!

*(*SWEETS *continues to wipe* MAFFUCCI's *vest.)*

Okay, okay, I said!

*(*SWEETS *stops, and continues with his work.)*

Well, Johnny Cake. Like to stay an' rap with ya a little bit but you know how it is. Community relations.

JOHNNY. Sho' preshiate you lookin' out for me, Footch!

MAFFUCCI. Think nothin' of it, Johnny Cake. It's Pete. He don't like jigs. Says the minute they git a little somethin', they start actin' cute. You an' me, we was like brothers. Way I see it, was like you took a dive for me once. Figger I owe ya.

JOHNNY. You don't owe me a dam thing, Footch.

MAFFUCCI. *(Heads for the street doors. Turns back.)* You know, Johnny Cake, some reason I never been able to git you off my mind. After all these years. I think if you'da been a wop, you'da been a big man in the rackets. *(Exits.)*

*(*SWEETS *holds watch to ear.)*

JOHNNY. All right now, Sweets. Goddamit, wha's this game you playin'?

SHANTY. Sweets??? That's Sweets Crane?

JOHNNY. Shut up, Shanty. *(Snatches the rag out of* SWEETS' *hand. Gets broom. Gives both to* SHANTY.*)* Take this crap back to the kitchen.

*(*SHANTY *takes them to kitchen.)*

Man, you either gotta be stir-buggy or you puttin' on one helluva ack.

SWEETS. *(Checks the watch.)* Jus' tryin' to be helpful, Sonny Boy.

JOHNNY. Don't you be kickin' no more farts at me, man. Wha's with this pil'fin stuff off'a people an' makin' like'a dam lackey? You mus' be plumb kinky.

SWEETS. Cain't see no point in watchin' George Raff on tee vee ev'a night. All my life I been into things. Always active.

JOHNNY. This what you call bein' active? An' look at you! Look like you jus' come off the Bow'ry! Ain't they no pride lef' in you?

SWEETS. Pride? Sheee. Pride, Sonny Boy, is sump'm I ain't got no mo' use for.

JOHNNY. For the las' time, ol' man. You better tell me wha's happenin' with you. Don't you make me have to kill you.

SWEETS. *(Produces an envelope.)* I'm as good as dead right now! *(He hands* JOHNNY *the envelope.)*

JOHNNY. What the hell is it?

SWEETS. Guess you could call it my will.

JOHNNY. *(Turns it over.)* Yo' will??

SWEETS. Open it up.

JOHNNY. Shanty!

SHANTY. *(Enters.)* How ya doin', Sweets?

JOHNNY. Check this out, Shanty. I don't read this jive so good.

SHANTY. *(Reads will.)* It's legal stuff. Says here you're gonna inherit interest in barbershops, meat markets, stores an' a whole lotta Harlem real estate. Dam!

JOHNNY. *(Snatches the papers out of* SHANTY's *hands.)* You gotta be jokin'.

SWEETS. I'm leavin' it all to you, Sonny Boy. My lawyers will take care ev'thing.

JOHNNY. How come you ain't tole me nothin' 'bout this before?

SWEETS. Couldn't take no chance it gittin' out. Might'a strung me out on a tax rap too.

JOHNNY. You lookin' to take some kind'a back gate commute? Suicide?

SWEETS. (Coughs.) Doctors ain't gimme but six months to ride. Didn't wanna lay it on you till they made sho'.

JOHNNY. Six months, huh?

SWEETS. Mo' or less.

JOHNNY. Goddamit, Sweets. What the hell kin I say? I sho' been a real bastard. Guess it don't help none for me to say I'm sorry.

SWEETS. Might he'p some if you was to turn all this into sump'm worth while an' good. Maybe the Lawd will f'give me f'the way I got it. (Bursts into laughter and coughs.)

JOHNNY. Git off it, Sweets. Jus' 'cause you s'pose to chalk out on us don't mean you gotta go an' 'brace relijun.

SWEETS. Figure it won't hurt none if I do.

JOHNNY. Shit. That good Lawd you talkin' 'bout is jus' as white as that judge who sent yo' black ass to Fedsville.

SWEETS. How you know? You ever seen him? When I was down there in that prison. I reads a lot. Mos'ly the Bible. Bible tells me, the Lawd was hard to look upon. Fack is, he was so hard to look upon that nobody eva looked at him an' lived. Well, I got to figgerin' on that. An' reasons that was so, 'cause he was so black. (Goes into loud laughter and coughs again.) Lawd knows! White's easy nuff to look at!

(JOHNNY throws the will on the floor. SWEETS goes to his knees and clutches the will.)

What you doin', Sonny Boy? My life is in them papers! (Hits JOHNNY with hat.)

(JOHNNY reaches under the bar and comes up with a revolver. Levels it at SWEETS.)

JOHNNY. See this, Sweets? My firs' an' only pistol. You gave it to me long time ago when I was a lookout for you when you was pullin' them owl jobs in Queens. I worshipped the groun' you walked on. I thought the sun rose an' set in yo' ass. You showed me how to make thirteen straight passes without givin' up the dice. Stood behin' me an' nudged me when to play my ace. Hipped me how to make a gapers cut. How to handle myself in a pill joint. Taught me to trust no woman over six or under sixty. Turned me on to the best horse players an' number runners. Showed me how to keep my asspocket full'a coins without goin' to jail. Said the wors' crime I ever committed was comin' out'a my mama screamin' black. Tole me all about white folks an' what to expect from the best of 'em. You said as long as there was a single white man on this earth, the black man only had one free choice. That was the way he died. When you went to jail for shootin' Cholly you said, "Sonny Boy, git us a plan." Well, I got us a plan. Now, you come back here nutty an' half dead, dancin' all over me about me goin' through a change'a life. An' how you want me to help you git ready to meet yo' Lawd. Well, git ready, mother fucker. Tha's exactly what I'm gon' do. Help you to meet him. (JOHNNY pulls back the hammer of the gun.)

(SWEETS coughs and looks at the barrel of the gun.)

SWEETS. You ain't gon' shoot me, Johnny. You cain't shoot me. They's a whole lotta you I ain't even touched. (SWEETS exits.)

BLACKOUT

ACT TWO

SCENE 2

TIME:
Two weeks later.

PLACE:
The same.

SETTING:

The same.

AT RISE:

GABE *sits at a table, glass of red wine before him, strumming a guitar.* MELVIN *stands next to him thumbing through a playscript.* SHANTY *is behind the bar as usual.*

MELVIN. "The Tooth of a Red Tiger"? What part will you play, Gabe?

GABE. What you tryin' to do, Mel? Jinx me? I ain't got the part yet.

MELVIN. They gave you this script, didn't they?

GABE. The part calls for a guitar player. Cain't you hear these clinkers?

(MELVIN *puts script on table.*)

How was your recital?

MELVIN. Ugh! Don't remind me, Gabe. I have this solo in "variations and diversions." I have to do three tour jêtés? Well, ol' Mel fell! Would you believe it? I stumbled and fell! Victor, my teacher, he was there shaking! He was actually shaking.

GABE. What the hell, Mel. Always another recital.

MELVIN. I suppose you could look at it that way! Anyway, I was simply heartbroken. Gabe, do you like Carl Sandburg?

GABE. Ain't exactly in love with him.

MEL. I was thinking, since you do write poetry, maybe you'd like to go with me to hear some of his works. Peter Demeter is reading tomorrow night. . . .

GABE. Got somethin' I gotta do.

MELVIN. Well, maybe you'd like to hear some chamber music at the Brooklyn Academy over the weekend.

GABE. Don't dig chamber music, Mel.

MELVIN. I believe an artist should learn all he can about the other forms too. (*Slaps* GABE *on his back and exits to kitchen.*)

DEE. (*Enters and goes to the bar.*) Squeeze the bar rag out, Shanty. (*She glances at* GABE.) Full of little surprises, aren't you?

GABE. Jus' fakin'.

(SHANTY *pours her drink. She takes bottle and glass to a table. Suddenly she catches* GABE *staring at her.*)

DEE. What's with the fish eyes? I gotta new wrinkle or sump'm?

GABE. Sorry! Just thinkin'!

DEE. (*Downs drink.*) You think too much. Give it a rest!

GABE. Tell me somethin', Dee . . .

DEE. What'a ya? Writin' a book or sump'm?

GABE. How'd you meet up with John in the first place?

DEE. (*Doesn't answer. Pours another drink. Presently gets to her feet. Goes to window. Peers out.*) Got Evie to thank for that. She used to come in here a lot when the joint was really jumpin'. She'll never admit it but I think she had it for Johnny. She's never been much of a drinker but one night she got too looped to drive. Johnny brought her home. When they came in, I was in the process of having my face lifted by a boy friend. Johnny pulled him off.

GABE. Stop me if I'm bein' a little too personal.

DEE. Oh, you be as personal as you like, Gabe.

GABE. How do chicks like you an' Evie . . .

DEE. Get into the life? Is that what you're askin'? For me it was easy! Got a job as a sales girl! Rich Johns would come in propositioning the girls! One day I took one up on it, and here I am.

GABE. Was it for the money?

DEE. What cheap paperbacks you been readin', Gabe?

GABE. I get it! You hate your father.

DEE. That poor miserable bastard? That bum? He ain't worth hating.

GABE. You love John?

DEE. Johnny? Johnny's not the kind of man you love. I think I pity Johnny. Don't get me wrong. I don't mean the kind of pity you'd give to my father or some bum on the street. Somebody blindfolded him. Turned him around. Somewhere inside Johnny's got something. It just come out crooked! Comes out the wrong way. *(She takes drink and becomes theatrical.)* In a way, Johnny reminds me of a classmate of mine in high school.

GABE. Boyhood sweetheart, huh?

DEE. Got me pregnant. Nice decent boy. Only, he was black. Went to my folks. Said, "I'll marry her." The crazy bastard. They made his life miserable. I don't have to tell you.

GABE. Did you love this boy?

DEE. You mean, why didn't we run away together? We were too young and stupid.

GABE. And the baby?

DEE. Oh, they got rid of it for me. *(She almost appears to be improvising.)* Word got out somehow. My mother fled to Puerto Rico for a well needed vacation. I stayed around the house. *(She lapses into theatrical Southern dialect à la Tennessee Williams.)* For weeks I just read, listened to the radio or watched television. One night late my father came in dead drunk. Staggered into my room and got into bed with me. Week later, I came to New York. *(She giggles.)* Funny thing. When I first got into the life, I was always thinkin' about my father. He was always comin' into my mind. Like it was him I was screwin' over and over again. Like I was takin' him away from my mother and punishin' him for lettin' her rule his life.

GABE. You know? Just the way you're standin' there, you remind me of somebody?

DEE. Dame May Whitty?

GABE. Maxine.

DEE. Who?

GABE. Maxine.

DEE. Who's Maxine?

GABE. Probably every woman I've ever known.

DEE. I don't usually think of you with a woman.

GABE. Come on, Dee!

DEE. I didn't mean it like that, Gabe. I always think of you—well, sort'a like the intellectual type! For some reason people kind'a think intellectual types don't even use the toilet! So who's Maxine?

GABE. My mother.

DEE. Talking to you is like eatin' cotton candy.

GABE. She was the little girl who sat across from me.

DEE. In grade school?

GABE. I stole a quarter from her. It was in her inkwell. Teacher lined us up. Searched us. The quarter rolled out of the pocket of my hightop boots. I kin still hear them kids yellin' "Our theeefer!"

DEE. Pretty humiliatin', huh?

GABE. We sang duets together in the high school choir. Neck an' rub stomachs in dark alleys an' doorways. They kicked her out'a school when she got pregnant. Sent her away. They was sure I did it. Her mama was wild an' crazy. Turned tricks for a cat who owned a Cadillac. Didn't want me messin' aroun' with Maxine. Said I was a dirty Nigger an' jus' wanted Maxine's ass. When Maxine didn't make her period, her mama got drunk an' come lookin' for me with a razor. I hid out for a couple days. Heard later she slashed all the upholsterin' in her pimp's Cadillac. Ha! She was smart, Maxine was. An' Jewish too. Taught me social consciousness. Said I was a good lover. Said white boys got their virility in how much money they made an' the kind'a car they drove. Said I related better 'cause I was black an' had nothin' to offer but myself. So I quit my job. Used to hide in the closet when her folks came in from Connecticut. Listened to 'em de-gradin' her for livin' with an' supportin' a Nigger. Maxine got herself an Afro hair-do an' joined the Black Nationalists when I couldn't afford to get her hair straight-ened at Rose Meta's! Didn't really wanna marry me. Jus' wanted my baby so she could go on welfare. She is out there somewhere. Maxine is. She's out there, waitin' on me to come back to her, Maxine is.

DEE. *(Laughs.)* Gabe? Gabe, are you sure you're all right?

(He grins.)

You really loved Maxine, didn't you? *(She puts her arms around his neck.)*

GABE. I sure wanted to . . .

JOHNNY. *(Enters.)* What the hell's goin' on here?

GABE. You jealous?

JOHNNY. Depen's on yo' intenshuns.

(GABE puts guitar into case. Picks up script. Prepares to leave.)

JOHNNY. What, you done gone an' got yo'self a job an' ain't tole nobody?

GABE. It's only an audition.

DEE. Good luck, Gabe.

JOHNNY. Yeah. I'm lookin' forward to gettin' a few payments back on all them loans.

(GABE gives a razz-berry and exits.)

You know, Dee? I been thinking. Maybe we ought'a take that trip after all.

DEE. Well now, you don't say? Sweets Crane wouldn't have anything to do with this sudden change of mind, would he? *(She starts to pour another drink.)*

JOHNNY. *(Snatches bottle out of her hands.)* Take it easy on that stuff, girl! Still wanna go, don't you?

DEE. Right now I got somethin' more important on my mind.

JOHNNY. Dump it on me.

DEE. I want out of the life, Johnny.

JOHNNY. Dam! You are stoned, ain't you?

DEE. I mean it, Johnny.

JOHNNY. Thought you an' me had a understandin'.

DEE. There's a hell of a lot more room for a better one.

JOHNNY. Like what, for instance?

DEE. I need some permanence.

JOHNNY. You mean git married?

DEE. Maybe.

JOHNNY. Thought you was down on all that housewife jazz.

DEE. I don't take tee vee commercials very seriously if that's what you mean.

JOHNNY. I gotta business here! Tough nuff time keepin' it perm'nant! Wasn't for the coins you bring in, I'd go under 'fore the week was out.

DEE. Let's build it back up, Johnny. Together. Together, Johnny.

JOHNNY. What the hell you know 'bout this business?

DEE. Teach me, Johnny! You could teach me.

JOHNNY. No good. Ain't no woman'a mine gon' be workin'. She b'long at home.

(She laughs.)

Look'a here, go on home. Git yo'self together. We'll talk 'bout it later.

DEE. I'll tie a string around my finger. *(She gathers her things. Weaves to the street door.)*

JOHNNY. Hey, girl! You still ain't said where you wanna go.

DEE. *(Whirls.)* I don't know. I hear the North Pole's pretty swingin' these days.

JOHNNY. Keep it up. I'll break yo' damn chops yet.

DEE. Where thou goest, I will follow, Johnny baby.

JOHNNY. Thinkin' 'bout makin' the Bim'ni scene. Won't have to worry 'bout crackers doin' the bird with the long red neck. Split this weekend. You make res'-vashuns.

DEE. *(Blows him a kiss. Bows theatrically.)* Yah suh, Boss! *(She exits.)*

JOHNNY. Bitches. Cain't please none of 'em.

BLACKOUT

ACT TWO

SCENE 3

TIME:

A day later.

PLACE:

The same.

SETTING:

The same.

AT RISE:

MELVIN *is arranging chairs and straightening tablecloths.* GABE *enters.*

MELVIN. What happened, Gabe? Did you get the part?

GABE. Nah! Wasn't the right type after all.

MELVIN. What type did they want?

GABE. Whatever it was I wasn't it.

JOHNNY. *(Enters from kitchen. He is munching a sandwich.)* Nigra type.

MELVIN. What type is that?

JOHNNY. Whatever it is, tha's what he ain't.

MELVIN. Doesn't talent have anything to do with it?

JOHNNY. Prop'ganda, Mel! When whitey pick one'a y'all you gotta either be a clown, a freak or a Nigra type.

GABE. They do the same thing among themselves too.

JOHNNY. 'Mongst themselves, they ain't so damn choosey.

GABE. Should'a seen the cat they did pick. Hell, I'm as black as he is.

JOHNNY. Gabe, ain't they no mirrors in yo' house?

GABE. I mean black in here!

MELVIN. You people are more preoccupied with color than white people are.

JOHNNY. They won't let us be porcupined with nothin' else.

GABE. Don't make no difference what color I am. I'm still black.

JOHNNY. Yeah! But you ain't gon' git no chance to prove it. Not on no stage, you ain't. You remin' whitey'a too many things he don't wanna take'a look at. Figgers he's got nuff problems dealin' with Niggers who jus' look black, like me.

GABE. Aw, shut the fuck up, John.

JOHNNY. Who you talkin' to?

GABE. You, you bastard. I'm tellin' you to shut the fuck up. Jus' cool it with yo' shit.

JOHNNY. Jus' tryin' to tell you like it is, Gabe! You jus' don't b'lieve a hard head makes a sof' ass!

MELVIN. *(Pats* GABE *on the back.)* Like you told me, Gabe. Always another recital. (MELVIN *exits to kitchen.)*

(JOHNNY *tosses* GABE *some bills.)*

GABE. No more handouts, baby.

JOHNNY. This ain't no handout! Want you to do me a favor.

GABE. Yeah?

JOHNNY. Me an' Dee goin' on a little vacation. Want you to help Shanty an' Mel with the store while we gone.

GABE. When you leavin'?

JOHNNY. End'a the week. Makin' it to Bim'ni.

(CORA *and* SHANTY *enter. Carry black drum cases.)*

CORA. Give us a han' here, Gabe? They's more out there in the cab.

(GABE *exits to the street.)*

JOHNNY. What you bringin' this junk in here for?

CORA. We bringin' this junk in here as you call it on a purpose.

JOHNNY. Be damned if tha's so. Git out'a here, an' Shanty, let's git to work.

(GABE *returns with another case.)*

CORA. Look'a here, Jay Cee. Me an' Shangy swore when we got these here drums, we was gon' bring 'em in here for you to look at an' lissen to with yo' own eyes and ears.

JOHNNY. All of a sudden I done gone deaf an' blin'. Now, git this hazarae out'a here.

CORA. Ain't gon do ner such thing. Not till me an' Shangy has got som'a what we's set out to do.

GABE. Sure got a pretty good start.

CORA. Shangy! What is you doin' with the broom?

(JOHNNY *reaches for one of the drum cases.*)

Take yo' nasty, stinkin', filthy black han's off them drums!

(JOHNNY *recoils.*)

MELVIN. (*Comes out of the kitchen.*) What on earth is happening?

CORA. It ain't happenin' yet.

MELVIN. Well, I just never would have believed it. Isn't it wonderful?

CORA. 'Fore Shangy gits on these drums, they's sump'm you oughta know, Jay Cee.

JOHNNY. You runnin' the show.

CORA. Shangy is quittin' you today. Right now.

JOHNNY. Why the hell didn't you say that in the first place?

CORA. 'Cause you was so busy gittin' these drums out'a here. Tha's why.

MELVIN. You're really going to play for us, Shanty?

CORA. Tha's his intenchun, thank you. Shangy! Will you come on over here? Gabe don't know nothin' 'bout what he's doin'.

(SHANTY *hands* JOHNNY *the broom. Approaches the drums reluctantly.*)

JOHNNY. Some reason, Shangy, you don't look so happy. Now I want you to jump up there an' give ol' Jay Cee a little

wham-bam-thank-ya-ma'm. Piece'a the funky nitty-gritty. Like the time they said you played like'a spade. Guess I kin risk gettin' a summons on that.

CORA. Ne' min', Jay Cee. Go 'head, honey! Git yo'se'f together. Take all the time you need.

GABE. Wail, baby.

(SHANTY *sits on the stool. Fumbles. Accidentally puts foot on pedal. Strikes pose. Taps cymbals. Moves to snares. Mixes. Pumps. Works. Gets loud.* CORA *fidgets. Anxious.* SHANTY *fakes. Can't cover up. Becomes frustrated. Louder. Stands. Begins to beat wildly. Moves around the drums banging for all he's worth.* CORA *is ashamed.* GABE *frowns.* CORA *grabs* SHANTY's *arm. He pushes her away. Becomes a windmill.*)

CORA. Stop it, Shangy! Stop it, I said!

(SHANTY *beats as if possessed.* CORA *is helpless.* JOHNNY *calmly reaches behind the bar. Gets pitcher of water. Pours it over* SHANTY's *head.*)

SHANTY. Ya-hoooo! (*Leaps into the air.*) I had it! I was on it! I was into it, babee! (*He moves around doing the pimp walk.*) Ol' Red Taylor said I had the thing. Said, "Shanty man! You got the thing!" (*Goes to* MEL.) Gimme some skin, mother fucker.

(MEL *gives him some skin. Goes to* GABE.)

Gimme some skin.

(GABE *doesn't put his hand out.*)

Ah, fuck you, man. Didn't I hip you to my happenin's, Johnny? Didn't I show you where it's at?

JOHNNY. You burned, baby, you burned.

(SHANTY *gives* JOHNNY *some skin.*)

CORA. Shangy! I—think you better start packin' up now.

SHANTY. Git away from me, you funky black bitch.

CORA. Shangy!

SHANTY. Just stay away from me—you evil piece'a chunky.

CORA. You ain't got no call to say nothin' like that to me.

SHANTY. Oh, no? You ain't jive timin' me, you just like Gloria.

CORA. What you sayin', Shangy?

SHANTY. You don't want me to play no drums.

CORA. You wrong, Shangy.

SHANTY. Thought you'd make a fool out'a me, did you? Gittin' me to bring these drums in here. You thought I'd mess it up. Well, I showed you where it was at. I showed all'a you.

CORA. Shangy, you crazy! You the one suggestid that!

SHANTY. Bitch, call the man. Have him come git these drums.

CORA. Come git the drums? Why, Shangy? Why?

SHANTY. I don't need you to help me get my drums. I get my own drums. Dig it?

CORA. This chile done clean los' his min'.

SHANTY. You an' me are through! Dig it? We are through. We've had it. Splitsville.

(CORA is numb.)

Now you believe me, huh, Johnny? A bucket'a cold water an' throw it on me, huh?

JOHNNY. To git you to quit. Come on, baby. Let's git some dry clothes on you. (JOHNNY leads SHANTY to the kitchen.)

SHANTY. A bucket'a cold water like the night we played "Saints" . . .

(JOHNNY and SHANTY exit to kitchen. For a moment CORA looks up at the clock.)

CORA. What time is it, Gabe?

GABE. My watch was stolen. . . .

CORA. (Points to clock above cash register.) What time do that clock say?

GABE. Quarter after three . . .

CORA. Know sump'm, Gabe? I ain't never learned how to tell time. Thirty years ol' an' I don't even know the time'a day. But when I gits up in the mornin', tha's the very firs' thing I'm gon' do. I'm gonna learn how to tell me some time. (She exits.)

JOHNNY. (Enters from kitchen.) Go back there an' help Shanty, Mel! He don't feel so good.

(MELVIN goes to kitchen.)

Help me tear down this thing, Gabe. (JOHNNY begins to dismantle drums.)

GABE. Do it your damned-self. I ain't feelin' so hot either. (Exits hurriedly.)

JOHNNY. Now, what in hell's matter with you? (Busies himself with the drums.)

(MARY LOU BOLTON enters.)

MARY LOU. Hello . . .

JOHNNY. (His attention is still with the drums.) Sump'm I kin do for you?

MARY LOU. (Moves to table. Sits.) I'd like a daiquiri, please.

JOHNNY. (Looks up.) Tha's one drink I ain't never been able to make right.

MARY LOU. Simple! Just go easy with the sugar.

JOHNNY. (Goes behind bar. Begins to mix drink. Dumps in a lot of sugar.) Never 'spected to see you back here ag'in.

MARY LOU. Let's just say, I don't scare so easy. By the way, what were you trying to prove anyway?

JOHNNY. (Comes to her table and sets the drink before her.) I was waitin' for you to ask sump'm like that.

MARY LOU. Really?

JOHNNY. You sho' didn't come back here for no drink.

MARY LOU. Pretty conceited, aren't you?

JOHNNY. Jus' hipt to yo' kin', tha's all.

MARY LOU. "My kind," huh?

JOHNNY. You don't like to be kept in the dark 'bout nothin'.

MARY LOU. That's the difference between man and beast.

JOHNNY. I kin see you aint' learned a damned thing in that college, neither.

MAFFUCCI. (*Enters with* TRUCK DRIVER *who carries case of whisky to kitchen.*) How you doin', Johnny Cake?

JOHNNY. Okay, Gumba. What'd Pete do? Demote you? Got you ridin' the truck.

MAFFUCCI. New kind'a community relations, Johnny Cake. Ride aroun' with the boys, see if the customers are happy. You happy, Johnny Cake?

(TRUCK DRIVER *comes out of kitchen, exits.*)

JOHNNY. Dee-leer-iuss.

MAFFUCCI. (*Spies* MARY LOU.) Good, good. Makes me happy too. (*He moves to* MARY LOU.) Say! Ain't you Judge Bolton's kid?

MARY LOU. Why, yes. Yes I am.

MAFFUCCI. (*Takes her in his arms. Handles her. She resists, to no avail.*) Never forget a face. Turned out to be a real nice tomata, huh? Don't mind me, kid. (*He releases her.*) Next time you see your ol' man, tell him Mike Maffucci says "Hello!" (*He pats her on the behind.*) See you aroun', Johnny Cake! (*Looks at drums. Taps them.*) Didn't know you was rhythmical.

JOHNNY. (JOHNNY *reacts playfully by toying with the drum sticks.*) Chow, Footch.

(MAFFUCCI *exits.*)

Okay. How does he know yo' ol' man?

MARY LOU. (*Visibly shaken.*) They were clients of his.

JOHNNY. They? They who? You mean Footch?

MARY LOU. (*Nods.*) Something about

bribing a city official. And someone was murdered.

JOHNNY. Mary. Does the name Pete Zerroni ring a bell?

MARY LOU. Yes! He was one of the defendants. My father won the case.

JOHNNY. I don't care what nobody say. Your father was a damn good lawyer.

MARY LOU. What's your interest? You know this Pete Zerroni?

JOHNNY. Not personal.

MARY LOU. He's not a very good person to know.

JOHNNY. With Pete, sometimes you ain't got no choice.

(*She prepares to leave.*)

Here! Lemme freshen up yo' drink.

MARY LOU. No thanks. I'm getting— I'm getting a headache. (*She moves to the street doors.*) Goodbye, mister . . .

JOHNNY. Johnny. Johnny Williams.

MARY LOU. Goodbye, Johnny. . . . (*She exits, leaving her purse.*)

JOHNNY. (*Picks her purse up. Thinks for a moment. Goes to phone, dials.*) Hey, Dee? Cancel them reservashuns. Sump'm important jus' came up. Won't be able to after all. Now don't hand me no crap. Just cancel.

BLACKOUT

ACT THREE

SCENE 1

TIME:
Two weeks later.
PLACE:
The same.
SETTING:
The same.
AT RISE:
Table at Center has a folded newspaper leaning against a large Molotov cocktail. Its headline reads: "Negroes Riot!" A banner resembling the American flag

dangles from a flagstand. Next to the Molotov cocktail is a plate, on which rests a large black automatic pistol. Beside the plate is a knife and fork. A toilet is heard flushing. GABE *comes on stage zipping his pants. His attitude is ceremonial.*

GABE.
"They's mo' to bein' black than meets
the Eye!
Bein' black, is like the way ya walk an'
Talk!
It's a way'a lookin' at life!
Bein' black, is like sayin', "Wha's hap-
penin', Babeee!"
An' bein' understood!
Bein' black has a way'a makin' ya call
some-
Body a mu-tha-fuc-kah, an' really meanin'
it!
An' namin' eva'body broh-thah, even if
you don't!
Bein' black, is eatin' chit'lins an' wah-tah-
Melon, an' to hell with anybody, if they
don't
Like it!
Bein' black has a way'a makin' ya wear
bright
Colors an' knowin' what a fine hat or a
good
Pair'a shoes look like an' then—an'
then—
It has a way'a makin' ya finger pop!
Invent a
New dance! Sing the blues! Drink good
Scotch!
Smoke a big seegar while pushin' a black
Cadil-Lac with white sidewall tires! It's
conkin' yo'
Head! Wearin' a black rag to keep the
wave!
Carryin' a razor! Smokin' boo an' lis-
tenin' to
Gut-bucket jazz!
Yes! They's mo' to bein' black than meets
the eye!
Bein' black is gittin' down loud an'
wrong! Uh-huh!

It's makin' love without no hangups!
Uh-huh! Or
Gittin' sanctified an' holy an' grabbin' a
han'ful'a
The sistah nex' to ya when she starts
speakin' in
Tongues!
Bein' black is havin' yo' palm read!
Hittin' the
Numbers! Workin' long an' hard an'
gittin' the
Short end'a the stick an' no glory! It's
Knowin' they ain't no dif'rence 'tween
White trash an' white quality! Uh-huh!
Bein' black is huggin' a fat mama an'
Havin' her smell like ham-fat, hot biscuits
An' black-eyed peas!
Yes! They's mo' to bein' black than meets
The eye!
Bein' black has a way'a makin' ya mad
mos'
Of the time, hurt all the time an' havin'
So many hangups, the problem'a soo-side
Don't even enter yo' min'! It's buyin'
What you don't want, beggin' what you
don't
Need! An' stealin' what is yo's by rights!
Yes! They's mo' to bein' black than meets
The eye!
It's all the stuff that nobody wants but
Cain't live without!
It's the body that keeps us standin'! The
Soul that keeps us goin'! An' the spirit
That'll take us thooo!
Yes! They's mo' to bein' black than meets
The eye!"

(GABE *sits at table. Cuts into gun with knife and fork. Finally picks gun up. Bites into it. Chews and swallows. Takes drink from Molotov cocktail. Wipes mouth.*) Bru-thas an' sistahs! Will ya jine me!

(BLACKOUT on GABE. *LIGHTS COME UP on* DEE *and* SHANTY. *She sits at table, bottle of whisky in front of her.* SHANTY *sits on stool reading copy of* Downbeat.)

DEE. Ain't like him to stay away from the joint like this. Can't reach him at his apartment either.

SHANTY. He don't come in but about once a day. Just to check things out—

DEE. It's a woman he's with, isn't it?

SHANTY. Huh?

DEE. Hello?

SHANTY. What you say? Eh, *que pasa?*

DEE. He's with a woman—it's a woman he's with. . . .

SHANTY. Uh—it's uh—Mel's day off, Dee—gotta go clean up the kitchen . . .

DEE. Shanty, come here a second. . . . *(He comes to her reluctantly.)* Thanks, huh? *(She stuffs a bill into the pocket of his apron.)* For nothing!

(He shrugs. Exits to kitchen. She goes back to drinking.)

EVIE. *(Enters. Spies* DEE. *Moves to jukebox.)* Hey.

DEE. Hey, yourself!

(MUSIC comes on.)

How does it feel to be on your way to good citizenship?

EVIE. Yeah, huh? Imagine me doin' it to an IBM machine.

DEE. It ain't hard.

EVIE. That bottle ain't doin' you a damn bit'a good.

DEE. Tha's debatable.

EVIE. How 'bout a nice hot cup'a black coffee?

DEE. Uh-uh! Gotta stay here an' wait for Johnny.

EVIE. Pretty soon you'll be waitin' for him flat on the floor.

DEE. Drunk or sober, it doesn't matter anyway.

EVIE. Why you doin' this? Sheee! He ain't worth the powder it'd take to blow him up.

DEE. Tha's mah business.

EVIE. It's my business you was up at Jack's last night.

DEE. Where'd you hear that?

EVIE. Jack. He called me. Now, if you wanna kill yourself, or git killed—go right ahead! But I wanna warn you 'bout one thing. Stay out'a Jack's, you hear me? A lotta Niggers in there, jus' waitin' for somebody like you! 'Nother thing! Jack's my uncle—don't want'a see him lose his license—on account'a some bitch like you!

DEE. Okay, so I was up at Jack's!

EVIE. What was you lookin' for anyway? Way off yo' beat! Ain't nobody up there got your price!

DEE. I wasn't sellin'—I was buyin'.

EVIE. You was what?

DEE. The biggest blackest cat you ever saw picked me up.

EVIE. You just lookin' to git yourself hurt, girl.

DEE. Oh, he was polite. Too polite. Took me to his room. Smelled like that greasy pomade an' hair straightener you smell sometimes on those pretties in the subway. An' when he put on his silk stocking-cap—I just about cracked. Kept the light on so he could watch.

EVIE. Git yourself together, girl. Drunk as you are—you liable to tell Johnny 'bout this an' he'd have to kill you.

DEE. When it got good to him he started singin', "Black an' white together —black an' white together!" And the toilet down the hall was flushing over and over again.

EVIE. Bitch, did you hear what I said?

DEE. No! I ain't goin' anyplace! I'm stayin' right here. . . . *(She sits at table. Goes into purse. Takes out can of shoe polish.)* If I have to stage a sit-in to do it. *(She puts mirror before her. Begins to apply polish to her face.)*

EVIE. Girl, what are you doin' . . .

DEE. *(Knocks* EVIE's *hand away.)* Take your hands off me, you stinkin' cunt! Dirty black sow!

EVIE. *(Slaps* DEE *viciously.)* All right, you crazy, uptight, drunken whore! Sure as shit you gon' end up in Bellvue or git your ass sliced up an' thrown to the rats in some alley. . . .

(JOHNNY *enters.* DEE *sing-songs him.*)

DEE. Where you been keepin' yo'se'f, Johnneee, babeee!

JOHNNY. Git that crap off your face an' git the hell out'a here!

DEE. (*Snaps her fingers.*) I's black an' I's proud!

EVIE. Listen here, Johnny! This girl is in trouble!

JOHNNY. She's free, white an' always right!

(DEE *laughs. He goes to her, wipes the black from her face, forcing her to relent.* DEE *begins to weep. He is almost tender with her.*)

EVIE. She ain't free a'you—Dee, if you got an ounce a sense left in yo' head you'll git on up and come on out with me now.

DEE. Hit the wind, sugar! Git on back to your stupid analyst an' your fuckin' IBM machine! Hit da win', sugar.

(EVIE *shakes her head, moves quickly to the door.*)

JOHNNY. Hey! Pussy!

(*She turns angrily.*)

I know what's eatin' yo' ass. You don't like it 'cause I went for her an' not you! Tha's it, ain't it?

(EVIE *moves quickly to the two of them. Takes* DEE *by the shoulders. Pulls her up and draws her to her roughly. Plants a hard kiss upon* DEE's *mouth. She shoves* DEE *into the arms of* JOHNNY *who quickly puts* DEE *aside. He faces* EVIE *furiously.* SHANTY *enters.*)

EVIE. Darlin', you way off base. I've known Niggers like you all my life! Think everything's a game. I wouldn't piss on you if yo' ass was on fire. Lef' to me, I'd give you a needle—let you sit in a cor-

ner like little Jackie Horner, jerkin' off all by yourself!

(JOHNNY *raises his hand.* EVIE *beats him to the punch, clubs him with her forefinger between the legs. He winces and doubles over.* EVIE *exits quickly.* DEE *laughs hysterically.* MARY LOU BOLTON *enters.* DEE *is lying on the floor.*)

MARY LOU. Johnny, I . . .

JOHNNY. Stay where you at, Mary.

MARY LOU. Johnny, maybe I'd better . . .

DEE. Well, well, well. And just might who you be, Miss Baby Cakes?

MARY LOU. Johnny!

JOHNNY. I said stay where you at!

DEE. (*Struggles to her feet. Gathers her belongings.*) Baby Cakes, let me give you the best advice you ever had in your whole little life. Run away from here fast. Run for your life. (*She goes into her purse. Comes up with baby shoes. Drops them on the floor. Exits.*)

MARY LOU. Who is she, Johnny?

JOHNNY. Some chick with a problem.

MARY LOU. She—she looked . . .

JOHNNY. She was wiped out.

MARY LOU. (*Picks up the baby shoes.*) Who do these belong to . . .

JOHNNY. (*Snatches them out of her hands and throws them into the waste basket.*) Don't ask me! Never had no kid'a mine if tha's what you're thinkin'!

MARY LOU. I don't think you'll be seeing me anymore, Johnny.

JOHNNY. Why the hell not, Mary?

MARY LOU. Are you in any trouble, Johnny?

JOHNNY. Trouble? What kind'a trouble?

MARY LOU. My father! Someone called him about us!

JOHNNY. What about?

MARY LOU. Whoever it was said if he didn't stop me from seeing you, they would.

(*He grins.*)

Are you in some kind of trouble?

JOHNNY. That depen's, Mary. Take off, Shanty!

SHANTY. Man, I still got . . .

JOHNNY. I said, take off!

(SHANTY takes off apron. Gets hat. Exits. JOHNNY locks doors behind him.)

'Member when we was talkin' 'bout Pete Zerroni?

MARY LOU. Yes . . .

JOHNNY. Pete don't like it if a Nigger's got a place'a business in his ter'tory.

MARY LOU. You gotta be kidding.

JOHNNY. Ain't you learned nothin' from all that civil rights?

MARY LOU. What proof do you have?

JOHNNY. Baby, this ain't no ord'nary type 'scrimunashun. They give you the signal. You ignore it. Place burns down.

MARY LOU. But why don't they want me to see you?

JOHNNY. Your ol' man was Zerroni's lawyer. Think maybe I might try to work you. . . .

MARY LOU. Work me?

JOHNNY. Yo' ol' man might have somethin' on Zerroni an' his boys in his records or files.

MARY LOU. That's silly! It could never be used as any real evidence.

JOHNNY. Sho' could make it hot for a whole lotta people if the D.A. happened to get a few tips.

MARY LOU. What are you getting at?

JOHNNY. Nothin'. You wanted to know why they didn't want you to see me, didn't you? 'Les yo' ol man's prege'dice.

MARY LOU. He knows I've dated Negroes before. *(She thinks for a moment.)* You really believe if you got this information it would keep Zerroni off your back?

JOHNNY. Well, they still don't know who killed Rep'senative Mahoney. . . .

MARY LOU. Well, you know I couldn't do anything like that. I mean take that information. My father would never forgive me.

JOHNNY. Like I say. Tha's the only reason I kin figger why they don't want you to be seein' me.

MARY LOU. Anyway, he keeps that sort of thing locked in a safe! In his office.

JOHNNY. *(Comes to her. Takes her by the hand and pulls her to him. He kisses her gently.)*

(She responds.)

Queer, ain't it? Yo' ol' man's a judge. Sworn to uphol' justice. We cain't even go to him for help.

MARY LOU. I'll speak to him about it, Johnny.

JOHNNY. Don't you do that, Mary. Don't you do nothin' like that.

MARY LOU. But why, Johnny? He could probably help you.

JOHNNY. For all we know, he might be in with Zerroni.

MARY LOU. Don't you say that.

JOHNNY. Funny, after that rotten bunch'a Ginees got off he got to be judge right away.

MARY LOU. I think I'd better leave now.

JOHNNY. Why'd you come back here, Mary? Make like you wanted a daiquiri. Think I'd be a sucker for some white missionary pussy?

MARY LOU. That is a terrible thing to say.

JOHNNY. You don't give a dam about civil rights. What about my civil rights? Don't I git any?

MARY LOU. There are ways to stop Zerroni. There are people we can go to for help.

JOHNNY. Yeah? An' they'll go over to Zerroni's an' picket!

MARY LOU. That's not funny.

JOHNNY. You liberal-ass white people kill me! All the time know more 'bout wha's bes' for Niggers'n Niggers do.

MARY LOU. You don't have to make the world any worse.

JOHNNY. Never had no chance to make it no better neither.

(There is pounding on street doors. JOHNNY unlocks them. MARY LOU rushes out as GABE hurries in.)

GABE. Git your coat, John. Quick!

JOHNNY. What the hell for?

GABE. It's Dee! She's dead.

JOHNNY. Dead?

GABE. Can't figger how they got my number. She slit her wrists. Why'd they call me?

JOHNNY. Where is she?

GABE. The ladies' room. Hotel Theresa.

BLACKOUT

ACT THREE

SCENE 2

TIME:
Three days later.
PLACE:
The same.
SETTING:
The same.
AT RISE:
MUSIC from jukebox is going full blast. SHANTY is seated on a barstool. Beats on the next stool with drumsticks.

SHANTY. Aw, blow it, baby! Workout! Yeah! I hear ya! Swing it! Work yo' show!

(JOHNNY and GABE enter dressed in suits. GABE as usual carries briefcase.)

JOHNNY. Goddamit, Shanty! Git under the bed with that shit. Ain't you got no respect for the dead? *(Pulls cord out of socket.)*

(SHANTY puts sticks away. MELVIN comes out of kitchen.)

MELVIN. How was the funeral?

GABE. How is any funeral, Mel?

JOHNNY. *(Goes behind bar. Mixes drinks.)* Every damned whore in town showed up! Think they'd have a little respeck an' stay home!

MELVIN. Was her people there?

GABE. Only us!

SHANTY. *(Picks up newspaper.)* Paper sure gave you hell, Johnny!

JOHNNY. Who the hell asked ya? *(He comes around bar.)* Comin' on like some bitch in a cheap-ass movie! Writin' all that jive on the shithouse wall with lipstick!

SHANTY. I always liked Dee! Good tipper.

JOHNNY. *(Bangs on bar.)* Anybody'd think I killed her! Blamin' me for everything! Hell, I never did nothin' to her!

GABE. Nothin' for her neither!

CORA. *(Enters. Dressed to kill. Wears white rose corsage.)* Hello, ev'body.

GABE. Hello, Cora. . . .

CORA. Wha's ev'body lookin' so down in the mouth about? Like you jus' come from a funeral.

JOHNNY. Is that yo' idea of some kind'a damn joke?

MELVIN. Ain't you heard, Cora?

CORA. Heard what?

MELVIN. It's been in all the papers! Johnny's friend, Dee. She committed suicide a couple of days ago.

CORA. Lawd have mercy! I'm so sorry! I—I haven't exactly been keepin' up with the news lately! You see I—I jus' got married this morning.

MELVIN. Married? I hope you'll be very happy, Cora.

GABE. Congratulations, Cora.

CORA. Oh, thank you! Thank you so much.

JOHNNY. Must'a been a whirlwin' co't-ship.

CORA. Ack-shully, I been knowin' him f'quite some time! He's a heart spesh-lis' I met at the hospital.

JOHNNY. From the looks of you, he mus' be a pretty good'n.

CORA. He's jus' aroun' the corner gittin' the car checked over! It's a good distance to Kwee-beck.

GABE. Quebec?

CORA. Our honeymoon! Wants me to meet his peoples! 'Cause they's French, you know. Jay Cee? *(She goes to* JOHNNY.*)*

JOHNNY. What?

CORA. Awfully sorry 'bout what happened.

JOHNNY. Yeah! Sure, Cora!

CORA. Sump'm ter'ble must'a happen to drive her to do a thing like that!

JOHNNY. Good luck with the married bag, huh?

CORA. Why, thank you, Jay Cee! Thank you. You know me an' you knowed each other a lotta years. Some reason, I could never do nothin' to suit you. No matter how hard I tried. Sometimes you make me so mad I ha'f wanna kill you! But I was fool 'nuff to care sump'm 'bout you anyway. 'Cause to me you always been that li'l bad boy who was lef' all alone in the worl' with nobody to take care of him!

JOHNNY. Guess it'll always be "Jay Cee ag'inst the worl'!"

CORA. *(Tries to touch him.)*

(He jerks away. She looks at SHANTY.*)*

Ain't you gon' wish me good luck too, Shangy Mulligans?

*(*SHANTY *remains silent. Stares out of the window. She shrugs. Moves to street doors.)*

Well, o-re-vo-ree, ev'body! O-re-vo-ree! *(She giggles.)* Tha's French, you know! That means, "Bye, y'all!" *(She exits happily.)*

SHANTY. Se-la-goddam-vee.

MELVIN. She sure was happy!

GABE. Different too.

JOHNNY. Married a doctor! Ain't that

a bitch? Say one thing for her! That number don't give up! She . . .

SHANTY. Shut up, man!

JOHNNY. What you say?

SHANTY. I said shut up, nigger.

JOHNNY. Now, look. I know you upset 'bout Cora, but . . .

SHANTY. Will you cool it! Big man! Mister hot daddy! Think you know everything in the whole goddam world, don't you? Well, lemme tell you somethin', man. You don't know a mu-thah-fuc-kun thing.) *(He rips off his apron and flings it into* JOHNNY's *face.)* Here! Do your own dirty Nigger work! I've done all I'm gonna do! Took all I'm gonna take! *(He pulls out his drumsticks, boldly beats on the bar.)* Stood behind this bar! Let you put me down for the last time 'cause my skin is white. *(He beats harder on the bar.)* Yeah, baby. I'm white. An' I'm proud of it. Pretty an' white. Dynamite. Eh, mothah fuckah. Know what else I got that you ain't got? I got soul. You ain't got no soul. Mothah-fuckah's black an' ain't got no soul. If you're an example of what the white race is ag'inst, then baby, I'm gittin' with 'em. They are gonna need a cat like me. Somebody that really knows where you black sons-a-bitches are at. *(He picks up the butcher knife. Plunges it into the top of the bar.)* That's what I think of this ol' piece'a kindlin'! Take it an' stick it up you black, rusty, dusty! *(He moves quickly to the street doors. Turns. Gives* JOHNNY *the finger and exits quickly.)*

JOHNNY. Well, looks like ol' Cora-belle Beasley done turned Shanty into a real white man, after all. Now, what about you, Mel?

MELVIN. Huh?

JOHNNY. Don't you wanna cuss me out an' split too?

MELVIN. I ain't got nothin' against you, Johnny.

JOHNNY. Tha's too damn bad. *(Tosses* MELVIN *some bills.)*

MELVIN. What's this for, Johnny?

JOHNNY. Cain't afford to keep the kitchen open no more. Business all aroun' ain't worth lickin' the lead on a pencil.

MELVIN. Let me stay on, Johnny, please? Shanty's gone. I can tend bar and still do whatever short orders there are. Please, Johnny, don't let me go.

JOHNNY. Dam, Mel. Didn't know you liked it aroun' here that much.

GABE. What about your dancin', Mel? You wanna work in a bar the rest of your life?

MELVIN. I—I quit my dancin', Gabe. . . .

GABE. Why'd you do that?

MELVIN. Well, I—I went to this party Victor gave at his penthouse. A lot of celebrities were there. And Gabe, you just wouldn't have believed it.

GABE. What happened?

MELVIN. I'm ashamed to tell you!

JOHNNY. Aw, go on, Mel. We big boys.

MELVIN. Well, they all got plastered! They were smoking marihuana, too! Even the women! Can you imagine? And then they started taking off their clothes.

JOHNNY. Didn't you know where these turkeys was at before you went?

MELVIN. I don't go to parties much. I don't drink. You know that.

JOHNNY. Did you take your clothes off too?

MELVIN. Are you kidding?

GABE. So you left.

MELVIN. They wouldn't let me leave. So I ran into that bathroom and locked that door. But they jimmied the door open.

JOHNNY. An' then what happened?

MELVIN. They—they held me down and took all my clothes off. It was awful. I said if that's what you gotta do to be a dancer then . . .

JOHNNY. Mel, yo' mama must'a gave you too many hot baths when you was a baby.

MARY LOU. (Enters. She carries a pa-per bag.) Helped my father at the office yesterday. Must have watched him dial the combination to that safe at least twenty times.

(JOHNNY snatches bag. Locks doors. Comes behind bar. MARY LOU follows.)

Didn't get a chance to hear the tapes. Glanced through some of the other stuff, though. Looks pretty explosive.

JOHNNY. Don't read so good, Mary. What's this stuff say?

MARY LOU. Zerroni admits that he had Joseph Mahoney killed! Maffucci did it. And here it says that he was in on several bribes. . . .

JOHNNY. Mary, this is it. This is the stuff I need!

MARY LOU. I—I thought about it a long time. There just wasn't any other solution.

(JOHNNY stuffs papers back into bag.)

Johnny, I—I . . . (She peers at GABE and MELVIN.)

JOHNNY. Go 'head! You kin say anything in front'a them.

MARY LOU. Well, it's not the kind of thing you would say in front of . . .

JOHNNY. Mary, I don't think it's wise for you to be seen aroun' here. I want you to lay low for a while.

MARY LOU. I can't go home, Johnny. Daddy will know I . . .

JOHNNY. Ain't they some girlfri'n you kin stay with?

MARY LOU. I—I suppose so. But I thought we . . .

GABE. What's this all about, John?

MARY LOU. It's to keep Pete Zerroni from forcing Johnny out of business. Don't you know about it?

MELVIN. First time I've heard about it.

GABE. What's your father got to do with it?

MARY LOU. He was Zerroni's lawyer.

GABE. And you stole that material from your father?

MARY LOU. Yes, I stole that material from my father. There was nothing else we could do.

GABE. Why, you stupid, naive little bitch. Don't you know what he wants that stuff for?

MARY LOU. To keep Zerroni from forcing him out of business.

GABE. That's a lie! He wants it so he kin blackmail his way into his own dirty racket.

MARY LOU. That's not true! Tell him, Johnny.

GABE. A black Mafia. That's what he wants. (GABE laughs.)

MARY LOU. You're crazy. Johnny, are you going to stand there and . . .

JOHNNY. I gotta right to my own game. Just like they do.

MARY LOU. What?

JOHNNY. My own game!

MARY LOU. Johnny!

GABE. What did you do it for, Mary? For love? Sheee! He hates you, you bitch. Hates everything you stand for. Nice little suffering white girl.

(MARY LOU slaps GABE. *He throws her into a chair. She begins to weep.*)

Lemme tell you something. Before he kin lay one hot hand on you, you gonna have to git out there on that street an' hussle your ass off. (GABE *moves to* JOHNNY.) Gimme that file, John.

(JOHNNY *reaches under bar. Comes up with revolver. Levels it at* GABE. MELVIN *gasps. Falls to floor.*)

JOHNNY. I don't wanna kill you, Gabe. This is the one break I been waitin' on. It ain't much but it's gon' have to do.

GABE. You kill me that file ain't gonna do you no good anyway. I'm tellin' you. Gimme that file.

(JOHNNY *finally lowers gun.* GABE *puts bag into briefcase. Starts to move to street doors.* MAFFUCCI *and* JUDGE BOLTON *enter.*)

BOLTON. Get in the car, Mary Lou.

MARY LOU. Daddy, I . . .

BOLTON. I said get in the car!

(MARY LOU *rushes out, followed by* MAFFUCCI.)

You know what I'm here for, Williams.

JOHNNY. Just like that, huh?

BOLTON. Just like that.

(MAFFUCCI *re-enters.*)

JOHNNY. I wanna talk to Pete Zerroni.

MAFFUCCI. Pete ain't got nothin' to say to you, Johnny Cake.

BOLTON. Those notes belong to me. Not to Zerroni.

JOHNNY. I ain't budgin' till I see Pete, personal. He's got to come here an' go horse-to-horse with me. Ain't gon' wait too long neither. 'Lection's comin' up. Li'l phone call to the D.A. could make him very happy 'bout his future.

(MAFFUCCI *suddenly pulls gun on* JOHNNY.)

BOLTON. Put that away, you fool!

(MAFFUCCI *returns gun to shoulder holster.*)

JOHNNY. Footch, don't think Pete or the Judge here wanna see me git hit jus' yet.

BOLTON. What is it, Williams? Money? (*Produces an envelope.*)

JOHNNY. You ofays sho' think money's the root'a all evil, don't you, judge?

MAFFUCCI. Let's go, Frank. We're just wastin' time.

BOLTON. Williams, you'd better listen to me and listen good. You're in dangerous trouble. If you don't hand over that material, I'm not going to be responsible for what happens to you.

JOHNNY. An' I sho' ain't gon' be responsible for what happens to you neither, Judge.

(*Both* JOHNNY *and the* JUDGE *laugh.* BOLTON *starts to exit.*)

Judge?

(BOLTON turns. JOHNNY tosses him MARY LOU's purse. BOLTON exits.)

MAFFUCCI. Johnny Cake?

JOHNNY. What?

MAFFUCCI. Right now, your life ain't worth a plug nickel.

JOHNNY. Footch? *(Puts his thumbnail under his upper teeth and flicks it at MAFFUCCI.)*

(MAFFUCCI exits.)

JOHNNY. Gabe-ree-el. How come you didn't hand over the file?

GABE. I couldn't! When I saw those two bastards together, I just couldn't bring myself to do it! *(GABE removes bag from briefcase. Hands it to JOHNNY.)*

JOHNNY. Mel, take this over to the drugstore. Get copies made, quick! Move!

(MELVIN exits quickly.)

GABE. You know they're gonna git you.

JOHNNY. Gabe, we was got the day we was born! Where you been? Jus' bein' black ain't never been no real reason for livin'.

GABE. If I thought that I'd probably go crazy or commit suicide.

BLACKOUT

ACT THREE

SCENE 3

TIME:
   A day later.
PLACE:
   The same.
SETTING:
   The same.
AT RISE:
   JOHNNY *is seated on a barstool, checking his gun.* GABE *exits to kitchen.* MACHINE DOG *appears wearing a shabby military uniform.*

MACHINE DOG. I don't work at the garage no more, brother.

JOHNNY. You jive. You don't know nothin' else.

MACHINE DOG. They's other work to be done. They's other mo' important things to be worked on and fixed. Like my black brothers. They needs fixin' bad. Tha's when I got to thinkin'a you, Brother Williams.

JOHNNY. Yea, well you can just kick them farts at somebody else.

MACHINE DOG. On yo' feet, mothah fuckah!

(JOHNNY comes to his feet militarily.)

(MACHINE DOG presents a Nazi-like salute.) By the powers invested in me by the brothers I hereby deliver to you the edick!

(JOHNNY and MACHINE DOG give each other some skin. MACHINE DOG goes back to his salute.)

Brother Williams. The brothers have jus' sennunced an' condemned you to death. Now, repeat after me. I have been chosen to be the nex' brother to live on in the hearts an' min's'a the enemy host.

JOHNNY. I have been chosen to be the nex' brother to live on in the hearts an' min's'a the enemy host.

MACHINE DOG. My duty will be to ha'nt they cripple an' sore min's.

JOHNNY. My duty will be to haunt they cripple an' sore min's.

MACHINE DOG. I will cling to the innermos' closets'a they brains an' agonize them.

JOHNNY. I will cling to the innermos' closets'a they brains an' agonize them.

MACHINE DOG. *(Breaks his salute and gives an aside.)* Maniacks though they is already! *(He goes back into his salute.)* The more they will try to cas' me out, the mo' they torment will be.

JOHNNY. The more they will try to cast me out, the more they torment will be!

MACHINE DOG. Se la an' ayman! (MA-CHINE DOG *shakes* JOHNNY's *hand.)* You will have plen'y'a he'p, Brother Williams. All them brothers that went before you an' all them tha's comin' after you.

JOHNNY. I gladly accept the condem-nashun, Gen'ral Sheen. Tell the brothers I won't let 'em down. Tell 'em I look forward to meetin' 'em all in par'dise.

MACHINE DOG. Se la an' ay-man!

(They salute each other.)

JOHNNY. Se la an' ay-man!

(MACHINE DOG goes into kitchen as JUDGE BOLTON and two plainclothesmen, CAPPALETTI and HARRY, enter.)

BOLTON. This is the man, Al!

(CAPPALETTI flashes his badge.)

CAPPALETTI. Capalleti. Vice squad.
JOHNNY. Big deal!
CAPPALETTI. Judge Bolton, here. His daughter was picked up this afternoon.
JOHNNY. So what?
CAPPALETTI. She tried to solicit this officer here.
JOHNNY. What's that got to do with me?
CAPPALETTI. Said she was workin' for you.
JOHNNY. Tha's a lie. Tha's a goddam lie. Lemme hear her say that to my face.
CAPPALETTI. Plenty of time for that.
JOHNNY. What the hell you tryin' to pull, Bolton?
CAPPALETTI. Now, why would the Judge wanna pull anything on you, Johnny?
JOHNNY. He—he don't want his daugh-ter seein' me. 'Cause I'm a Nigger. I'll lay odds she don't know nothin' about this.
CAPPALETTI. Go get Miss Bolton, Harry.

(HARRY moves to street doors.)

JOHNNY. Hurry, Harry!

(HARRY grins. Exits.)

CAPPALETTI. By the way. Ain't you the guy this girl killed herself about a few days ago. She was a call girl?
JOHNNY. Tell you like I tole them other fuzzys. What she did was her own busi-ness.
CAPPALETTI. Just the same you kin see how we kin believe Miss Bolton's story.

(HARRY leads MARY LOU into bar. CAPPALETTI seats her.)

Now, Miss Bolton. We'll ask you again. Who did you say you was workin' for when you was picked up?
MARY LOU. I—I . . .
CAPPALETTI. Speak up, Miss Bolton. We can't hear you.
MARY LOU. Daddy, I . . .
BOLTON. All you have to do is identify him. Is he the man?

(CAPPALETTI puts his hand on MARY LOU's head.)

Take your hands off her!

(HARRY laughs.)

Mary Lou! Is he or isn't he?
MARY LOU. *(Forces herself to face* JOHNNY.) Yes! This is the man! Johnny Williams! I was working for him! (MARY LOU *rushes from bar followed by* HARRY.)
JOHNNY. Dirty lyin' bitch.
BOLTON. Now, see here, Williams!
CAPPALETTI. You're gonna have to come with me, Johnny.
JOHNNY. What is this, a pinch? You gonna book me? I'm gonna call my law-yer!
CAPPALETTI. Shut up! You're not call-in' nobody right now. Let's go.
BOLTON. Just a minute, Al. I want a few words with him before you take him down.
CAPPALETTI. Okay, Frank, but make it snappy.
BOLTON. Williams, I've worked too

long and too hard to get where I am. I'm giving you one last chance to give back those notes and tape. If you don't, it's on the bottom of the woodpile for you. Even if I have to sacrifice my own daughter to do it. I want that file.

JOHNNY. Okay, Judge. Okay. You win. (JOHNNY *goes behind bar. Brings out paper bag.*)

(JUDGE *checks it. Nods to* CAPPALETTI *and exits.*)

CAPPALETTI. All right, Johnny. All of a sudden the Judge wants me to forget the whole thing. Lucky we didn't get you down to the precinct. Would have busted you up on general principles. (CAPPALETTI *exits.*)

(*Quickly* JOHNNY *puts his revolver into his back pocket. Goes behind the bar.*)

JOHNNY. Better split, Gabe. While the gittin's good.

GABE. Don't think so, John. I'm gonna stick aroun'.

JOHNNY. Suit yo'self!

(*Doors open.* JOHNNY *goes for his gun.* SWEETS CRANE *enters. He is practically in tatters. He carries a shopping bag. Goes to table and begins to take out various articles of food. He coughs and rubs his hands together.*)

SWEETS. I got fried chicken! Ham! Candied yams! Got me some hot chit'lin's! Blackeyed peas an' rice! Cornbread! Mustard greens an' macaroni salit! (*Coughs.*) Top ev'thing off I got me'a thermos full'a —full'a—lemme see now. How'd my gran'daddy used to call it? Chassy San'-burg coffee. (*Laughs.*) An' a big chunk'a pee-kan pie. Y'all fellas is welcomed to join me.

JOHNNY. Wouldn't touch it if it was blessed by the pope!

SWEETS. Well, now tha's a dam shame. 'Member when I couldn't pull you away from my cookin'.

GABE. You don't mind if I join him, do you, John?

JOHNNY. Be my guest.

SWEETS. He'p yo'se'f, young fella. They's plen'y here. Have some'a these here chit'lin's!

GABE. Ain't never had none before.

SWEETS. Then let this be the day you start.

(GABE *takes a sniff.*)

Go 'head! Go 'head! You don't eat the smell.

GABE. Lemme ask you sump'm, Sweets.

SWEETS. Hope I kin answer it.

GABE. How come you took my watch an' wallet?

SWEETS. Son, all my life I been one kind'a thief or 'nother. It's jus' in me. 'Course I don't have to steal. But I steals for the pure enjoyment of it. Jus' the other day I stole a rat'la from a baby. (*Laughs.*) When you steals for fun it don't matter who you steals from! (*Goes into his pocket. Comes up with* GABE's *watch and wallet.*)

GABE. It's all here!

SWEETS. 'Co'se it is! Gave the baby back his rat'la too.

JOHNNY. You ain't gon' make the white man's heaven this way.

SWEETS. The Lawd died 'tween two thieves.

MAFFUCCI. (*Enters with* LOUIE.) Wouldn't listen to me, would you, Johnny Cake?

JOHNNY. What Pete say? Give a jig a half'a chance. . . .

SWEETS. This the fella work for big fat Pete, Sonny Boy?

MAFFUCCI. What's it to ya, Pops? You an' this other joker better get the hell out'a here before you catch cold.

SWEETS. I ain't never got up from a meal in my life 'fore I was finished . . .

MAFFUCCI. Look, Pops! Don't make me have to . . . (*Glances at food.*) What's that? Macaroni salad you got there?

SWEETS. Matter fack it is!

MAFFUCCI. *(Dips into it.)* Ummm! Not bad. Who made it?

SWEETS. I did.

MAFFUCCI. No kiddin'? Knew it didn't taste like dela-ga-tes. Mama used to make macaroni salad.

SWEETS. Have a piece'a my fried chicken to go with it.

JOHNNY. If Zerroni could see you now, Footch.

MAFFUCCI. How's that, Johnny Cake?

JOHNNY. Tha's the great Sweets Crane you eatin' with.

MAFFUCCI. Pops, here? He's Sweets Crane?

SWEETS. Wha's lef' of me.

MAFFUCCI. You'd made out better as a cook, Pops. Mama couldn't beat that macaroni salad!

SWEETS. *(Produces MAFFUCCI's watch.)* I think this b'longs to you.

MAFFUCCI. My watch! I been lookin' all over for it. Pops, you copped my watch? *(Laughs.)* How come you're givin' it back? This watch is worth a lotta bread.

SWEETS. Figger you need it wors'n I do.

MAFFUCCI. Say, Johnny Cake, you sure Pops here is Sweets Crane?

JOHNNY. You don't know how much I wish he wasn't.

MAFFUCCI. Too bad Johnny didn't learn a lesson after what happened to you, Pops. Gotta give him credit though. Takes a lotta balls to try to put the bleed on Pete Zerroni.

SWEETS. You was tryin' to blackmail ol' big fat Pete, Sonny Boy?

JOHNNY. What the hell. Couldn't pull it off. Don't matter much now.

MAFFUCCI. That's where you're wrong, Johnny Cake. Matters a helluva lot to me. Pete now, he's willin' to forget the whole thing. Says the trick is not to take you jigs too serious. I can't do nothin'

like that, Johnny. Don't look good on my record.

JOHNNY. What you gonna do about it, Footch?

(MAFFUCCI quickly pulls his gun. Levels it at JOHNNY. Backs to street doors. Locks them. Pulls shades. Takes a large sign from his pocket. It reads, "CLOSED." He puts it on the bar in front of JOHNNY.)

MAFFUCCI. The sign in both hands, Johnny Cake.

(JOHNNY slowly picks up sign.)

Pops, you an' that other joker stay put! *(MAFFUCCI nods to LOUIE who moves behind SWEETS and GABE.)*

(JOHNNY starts to tear sign.)

Ah-ah! I want you to lick that sign an' paste it right up there on the door. Start lickin', Johnny Cake!

(JOHNNY begins to wet sign with his tongue.)

That's it! Wet it up a little more! That's enough! Now start walkin' real careful like!

(JOHNNY moves to street door with sign.)

Now, paste it up there!

(JOHNNY does so.)

Now, back up! Real slow!

(JOHNNY backs up.)

(MAFFUCCI seats JOHNNY on a barstool.)

SWEETS. You don't have to do that, Sonny Boy. *(Goes to the door with knife he has been eating with.)* You don't have to do nothin' like that. *(He pulls the sign from the window and tears it up.)*

MAFFUCCI. What are you doin', Pops? Look, if you don't want hi-call-it to get hit . . .

JOHNNY. Keep out'a this, Sweets. This is my game.

SWEETS. Not any more, it ain't. You don't have to do nothin' like that. *(Advances to* MAFFUCCI.*)*

MAFFUCCI. What'a ya, crazy, Pops? Put that ax away.

JOHNNY. Lay out of it, Sweets. Lay out of it, I said!

MAFFUCCI. I'm warnin' you, Pops! Take another step an' . . .

*(*SWEETS *lunges at* MAFFUCCI *as* MAFFUCCI *fires. Knife penetrates* MAFFUCCI's *heart.* JOHNNY *kills* LOUIE. *Whirls and fires three shots into* MAFFUCCI. *Rushes to* SWEETS.*)*

JOHNNY. Goddamit, Sweets! I tole you I could handle it!

GABE. I'll call a doctor!

SWEETS. Fuck a doctor! Cain't you see I'm dead? *(Coughs. Winces in pain.)* Lissen to me, Sonny Boy! You—you gotta promise me one thing. . . .

JOHNNY. What is it, Sweets?

SWEETS. The—the will! It's here in— in my pocket.

*(*JOHNNY *finds will.)*

If—if you git out'a this. Promise you'll git straightened out. *(He grabs* JOHNNY's *arm.)* Promise!

JOHNNY. I—I promise.

SWEETS. Swear!

JOHNNY. Yeah! Yeah! I swear, Sweets!

SWEETS. Git—git rid'a the—the Ch-Cholly fever— *(*SWEETS *goes limp.)*

GABE. He did it for you, John. . . .

JOHNNY. Look, Gabe. We gotta git our story together. When the fuzz gits here we gotta have us a story.

GABE. We tell 'em the truth, John. . . .

JOHNNY. What you say?

GABE. We tell the police the truth!

JOHNNY. Shit. The truth is I'm alive! I got a copy'a that file an' Sweets' will.

GABE. But you tole Sweets you was gonna throw them ideas out'a your head.

JOHNNY. Come on, man, you didn't think I meant that shit, did you?

GABE. With his last dyin' breath, you gave that ol' man your word. You swore.

JOHNNY. What good is anybody's word to that ol' bastard? He's dead an' cain't remember.

GABE. You are mad.

JOHNNY. I'm goin' ahead with my plans. *(He holds up will.)* An' he's gon' help me do it.

GABE. Naw, naw! That ain't the way it's s'pose to be!

JOHNNY. You in this as deep as I am. It's our word ag'inst these dead turkeys. You gave me back that file, remember?

GABE. That's where I got off. I ain't got no stomach for this personal war you got ag'inst the white man.

JOHNNY. It's your war too, Nigger. Why can't you see that? You wanna go on believin' in the lie? We at war, Gabe! Black ag'inst white.

GABE. You're wrong, John. You're so goddam wrong.

*(*JOHNNY *picks up gun. Puts it into* GABE's *hand.)*

JOHNNY. Take this gun in yo' han'. Feel that col' hard steel. Bet you ain't never held a heater in yo' han' like that in yo' life. Well, you gon' have to, Gabe. They gon' make you do it. 'Cause we at war, Gabe. Black ag'inst white.

GABE. I—I don't wanna—kill— you. . . .

JOHNNY. You ain't got the guts! You wanna believe you kin sell papers an' become President! You're a coward, Gabe! A lousy, yellow, screamin' faggot coward!

(Enraged, GABE *fires at* JOHNNY. JOHNNY *tumbles backward and then forward into* GABE's *arms.* GABE *eases* JOHNNY *to the floor.* JOHNNY *goes limp.* MACHINE DOG *enters.)*

GABE. *(Startled.)* Who're you? Where did you come from?

MACHINE DOG. The Brothers call me Machine Dog! It is written: "He that slays a true brother, he hisse'f shall howsomever be perished!"

GABE. He made me kill him! He . . . *(During* MACHINE DOG's *speech,* GABE *takes gun. Wipes it off. Places it in* JOHNNY's *hand. Covers* JOHNNY *with tablecloth. Exits.)*

MACHINE DOG. Hush yo' lyin', traitious tongue! Ver'ly, ver'ly, I says into you! You has kilt all them li'l innusunt cherbs'a the ghetto! Them li'l rams who been hatin' 'thorty eb'm from the cradle! All them holy de-lin-cunts who been the true creators'a unsolver thef's an' kill-in's! You has slewn an' slaughtered them young goateed billygoats who been dedcated to that sanctified an' precious art'a lootin' the destruction'a private public poverty! You has hung an' lynched the black angels'a color who went by that high code'a rooftops an' been baptized in the stink of urine-scented hallways! You has burnt an' melted down a million switchblade knives an' razors an' broke preshus bottles'a communion upon the empty white-paved streets'a the enemy host! An' lef' the brothers thirsty an' col' to bang the doors'a the guilty white Samaritan! You has crushed the very life fum black an' profane souls! Hordes'a un-re-gen-rants! An' smashed the spirit an' holy ghost fum rollers an' dancers who founded they faith on black, human sufferin'! Burnt an' tortured souls who knew th'ough the power of love that they trials an' trib'lashuns could not be leg'-slated away by no co't, no congruss, not eb'm God Hisse'f! You has scorched an' scalded them black Moheekans an' stuffed them in the very stoves they cooked on! Se la! An' ay-man!

BLACKOUT

EPILOGUE

*(*GABE *enters dressed as a woman in mourning. A black shawl is draped over his head.)*

GABE. Like my costume? You like it? You don't like it! I know what I am by what I see in your faces. You are my mirrors. But unlike a metallic reflection, you will not hold my image for very long. Your capacity for attention is very short. Therefore, I must try to provoke you. Provoke your attention. Change my part over and over again. I am rehearsing at the moment. For tomorrow, I will go out amongst you, "The Black Lady in Mourning." I will weep, I will wail, and I will mourn. But my cries will not be heard. No one will wipe away my bitter tears. My black anguish will fall upon deaf ears. I will mourn a passing! Yes. The passing and the ending of a people dying. Of a people dying into that new life. A people whose identity could only be measured by the struggle, the dehumanization, the degredation they suffered. Or allowed themselves to suffer perhaps. I will mourn the ending of those years. I will mourn the death of a people dying. Of a people dying into that new life.

BLACKOUT

THE END

Lonne Elder III

Ceremonies in Dark Old Men

This play is dedicated to
  My son, David Dubois Elder
  My wife, Judith Ann
  To the memory of my life's teacher,
    Dr. William E. B. Dubois
  To the memory of Dr. Martin Luther King
  To the Negro Ensemble Company

CEREMONIES IN DARK OLD MEN

The Negro Ensemble Company production of *Ceremonies in Dark Old Men* opened at the St. Marks Playhouse, New York City, on February 4, 1969.

CHARACTERS:

MR. RUSSELL B. PARKER
MR. WILLIAM JENKINS
THEOPOLIS PARKER
BOBBY PARKER
ADELE ELOISE PARKER
BLUE HAVEN
YOUNG GIRL

Early spring, about 4:30 in the afternoon, now.

A small, poverty-stricken barbershop on 126th Street between Seventh and Lenox avenues, Harlem, U.S.A.

There is only one barber's throne in this barbershop. There is a not too lengthy mirror along the wall, and a high, broad shelf in the immediate area of the throne. There are two decks of shelves of equal width projecting just below the main shelf. These shelves are covered by small, sliding panels. On the far left corner of the shop is the street door, and on the far right corner is a door leading to a back room. Just to the right of the door, flush against the wall, is a card table and two chairs. Farther right is a clothes rack. Against the wall to the far left of the shop, near the door, are four chairs lined up uniformly.

The back room is like any back room in a poverty-stricken barbershop. It has an old refrigerator, an even older antique-type desk, and a medium-size bed. On the far right is a short flight of stairs leading up. A unique thing about this room: a door to stairs coming up from a small basement.

The action of the play takes place in the barbershop and the back room.

ACT ONE

SCENE 1

As the Curtain rises, MR. RUSSELL B. PARKER *is seated in the single barber's throne, reading the* Daily News. *He is in his early or middle fifties. He rises nervously, moves to the window, and peers out, his right hand over his eyebrows. He returns to the chair and continues to read. After checking his watch, he rises again and moves to the window for another look. Finally he sees the right person coming and moves to the door to open it.* MR. WILLIAM JENKINS *enters: early fifties, well dressed in a complete suit of clothes, and carrying a newspaper under his arm.*

MR. PARKER. Where have you been?

MR. JENKINS. Whatcha mean? You know where I was.

MR. PARKER. You want to play the game or not?

MR. JENKINS. That's what I came here for.

MR. PARKER. (*Slides open a panel in the counter.*) I wanted to get in at least three games before Adele got home, but this way we'll be lucky if we get in one.

MR. JENKINS. Stop complaining and get the board out—I'll beat you, and that will be that.

MR. PARKER. I can do without your bragging. (*Pulls out a checkerboard and a small can, quickly places them on the table, then shakes up the can.)* Close your eyes and take a man.

MR. JENKINS. *(Closing his eyes.)* You never learn. *(Reaches into the can and pulls out a checker.)* It's red.

MR. PARKER. All right, I get the black. *(Sits at the table and rushes to set up his men.)* Get your men down, Jenkins!

MR. JENKINS. *(Sits.)* Aw, man, take it easy, the checkers ain't gon' run away! *(Setting his men up.)* If you could play the game I wouldn't mind it—but you can't play! —Your move.

MR. PARKER. I'll start here—I just don't want Adele to catch us here playing checkers. She gave me and the boys a notice last week that we had to get jobs or get out of the house.

MR. JENKINS. Don't you think it's about time you got a job? In the five years I've been knowing you, I can count the heads of hair you done cut in this shop on one hand.

MR. PARKER. This shop is gon' work yet; I know it can. Just give me one more year and you'll see. . . . Going out to get a job ain't gon' solve nothing—all it's gon' do is create a lot of bad feelings with everybody. I can't work! I don't know how to! *(Moves checker.)*

MR. JENKINS. I bet if all your children were living far from you like mine, you'd know how to. That's one thing I don't understand about you, Parker. How long do you expect your daughter to go on supporting you and those two boys?

MR. PARKER. I don't expect that! I just want some time until I can straighten things out. My dear Doris understood that. She understood me like a book. *(Makes another move.)*

MR. JENKINS. You mean to tell me your wife enjoyed working for you?

MR. PARKER. Of course she didn't, but she never worried me. You been married, Jenkins: you know what happens to a man when a woman worries him all the time, and that's what Adele been doing, worrying my head off! *(Makes another move.)*

MR. JENKINS. Whatcha gon' do about it?

MR. PARKER. I'm gon' get tough, evil and bad. That's the only sign a woman gets from a man. *(Makes move.)*

(THEOPOLIS PARKER enters briskly from the street. He is in his twenties, of medium height, and has a lean, solid physique. His younger brother BOBBY follows, carrying a huge paper bag whose contents are heavy and fragile.)

THEO. That's the way I like to hear you talk, Pop, but she's gon' be walking through that door soon, and I wants to see how tough you gon' be.

MR. PARKER. Leave me alone, boy.

THEO. Pop, we got six more days. You got to do something!

MR. PARKER. I'll do it when the time comes.

THEO. Pop, the time is *now.*

MR. PARKER. And right now I am playing a game of checkers with Mr. Jenkins, so leave me alone!

THEO. All right—don't say I didn't warn you when she locks us out of the house!

(THEO and BOBBY rush through the back room. BOBBY places the brown bag in the old refrigerator as they dart up the stairs leading to the apartment. PARKER makes another move.)

MR. PARKER. *You're trapped, Jenkins!*

(Pause.)

MR. JENKINS. *(Pondering.)* Hmmm-mmm . . . It looks that way, don't it?

MR. PARKER. *(Moves to the door.)* While you're moaning over the board, I'll just make a little check to see if Adele is coming . . . Don't cheat now! *(He backs toward the window, watching that his adversary does not cheat. He quickly looks out the window.)* Uh-uh! It's Adele! She's in the middle of the block, talking to Miss Thomas! *(Rushes to take out a towel and spreads it over the checkerboard.)* Come on, man! *(Drags* MR. JENKINS *by the arm toward the back room.)*

MR. JENKINS. *What are you doing, Parker!*

MR. PARKER. You gon' have to hide out in the back room, 'cause if Adele comes in here and sees you, she'll think that we been playing checkers all day!

MR. JENKINS. I don't care about that!

MR. PARKER. You want to finish the game, don't you?

MR. JENKINS. Yeah, but—

MR. PARKER. All you have to do, Jenks, is lay low for a minute, that's all. She'll stop in and ask me something about getting a job, I'll tell her I got a good line on one, and then she'll go on upstairs. There won't be nobody left here but you and me. Whatcha say, Jenks?

(Pause.)

MR. JENKINS. All right, I'll do it. I don't like it, but I'll do it, and you better not mention this to nobody, you hear!

MR. PARKER. Not a single soul in this world will know but you and me.

MR. JENKINS. *(Moves just inside the room and stands.)* This is the most ridiculous thing I ever heard of, hiding in somebody's back room just to finish up a checker game.

MR. PARKER. Stop fighting it, man!

MR. JENKINS. All right!

MR. PARKER. Not there!

MR. JENKINS. What in the hell is it now!

MR. PARKER. *You've got to get under the bed!*

MR. JENKINS. No, I'm not gettin' under nobody's bed!

MR. PARKER. Now look . . . Adele never goes through the front way. She comes through the shop and the back room, up the basement stairs to the apartment. Now you want her to catch you hiding in there, looking like a fool?

MR. JENKINS. No, I can take myself out of here and go home!

MR. PARKER. *(Pushes* JENKINS *over to the table and uncovers the checkerboard.)* Look at this! Now you just take a good look at this board! *(Releases him.)*

MR. JENKINS. I'm looking, so what?

MR. PARKER. So what? I got you and you know it! There ain't no way in the world you'll ever get out of that little trap I got you in. *And it's your move.* How many years we been playing against each other?

MR. JENKINS. Three.

MR. PARKER. Never won a game from you in all that time, have I?

MR. JENKINS. That ain't the half of it. You ain't gon' win one either.

MR. PARKER. Now that I finally got you, that's easy talk, comin' from a running man. All right, go on. Run. *(Moves away.)*

MR. JENKINS. Go on, hell! All I gotta do is put my king here, give you this jump here, move this man over there, and you're dead!

MR. PARKER. *(Turns to him.)* Try me then. Try me, or are you scared at last I'm gon' beat you?

MR. JENKINS. I can't do it now, there ain't enough time!

MR. PARKER. *(Strutting like a sport.)* Run, rabbit, run . . .

MR. JENKINS. All right! I'll get under the bed. But I swear, Parker, I'm gon' beat you silly! *(They move into the back room.)*

MR. PARKER. Hurry it up then. We ain't got much time.

(As MR. PARKER *struggles to help* MR. JENKINS *get under the bed in the back room,* ADELE *comes in from the street. She is in her late twenties, well dressed in conventional New York office attire.*

She is carrying a smart-looking handbag and a manila envelope. She stops near the table on which checkerboard is hidden under towel. MR. PARKER enters from the back room.)

MR. PARKER. Hi, honey.

(She doesn't answer, instead busies herself putting minor things in order.)

ADELE. You looked for work today?
MR. PARKER. All morning . . .

(Pause.)

ADELE. No luck in the morning, and so you played checkers all afternoon.
MR. PARKER. No, I've been working on a few ideas of mine. My birthday comes up the tenth of the month, and I plan to celebrate it with an idea to shake up this whole neighborhood, and then I'm gon' really go to the country!
ADELE. Don't go to the country—go to work, huh? *(Moves toward back room.)* Oh, God, I'm tired!
MR. PARKER. *(Rushing to get her away from bed.)* Come on and let me take you upstairs. I know you must've had yourself a real tough day at the office . . . and you can forget about cooking supper and all of that stuff.
ADELE. *(Breaks away, moves back into shop toward counter.)* Thank you, but I've already given myself the privilege of not cooking your supper tonight.
MR. PARKER. You did?
ADELE. The way I figure it, you should have my dinner waiting for me.
MR. PARKER. But I don't know how to cook.
ADELE. *(Turns sharply.)* You can learn.
MR. PARKER. Now look, Adele, if you got something on your mind, say it, 'cause you know damn well I ain't doin' no cooking.
(Pause.)

ADELE. All right, I will. A thought came to me today as it does every day, and I'm damn tired of thinking about it—
MR. PARKER. What?
ADELE. —and that is, I've been down at that license-bureau so long, sometimes I forget the reasons I ever took the job in the first place.
MR. PARKER. Now look, everybody knows you quit college and came home to help your mama out. Everybody knows it! What you want me to do? Write some prayers to you?

(The two boys enter the back room from upstairs.)

ADELE. I just want you to get a job!

(The boys step into shop and stand apart from each other.)

BOBBY. Hey, Adele.
ADELE. Well! From what cave did you fellows crawl out of? I didn't know you hung around barbershops. . . . Want a haircut, boys?
THEO. For your information, this is the first time we been in this barbershop today. We been upstairs thinking.
ADELE. With what?
THEO. With our *minds,* baby!
ADELE. If the two of you found that house upstairs so attractive to keep you in it all day, then I can think of only three things: the telephone, the bed, and the kitchen.
BOBBY. The kitchen, that's it: we been washing dishes all day!
ADELE. I don't like that, Bobby!
BOBBY. And I don't like your attitude!
ADELE. Do you like it when I go out of here every morning to work?
THEO. There you go again with that same old tired talk: work! Mama understood about us, I don't know why you gotta give everybody a hard time . . .
ADELE. That was one of Mama's troubles: understanding everybody.

THEO. Now don't start that junk with me!

ADELE. I have got to start that, *Mr. Theopolis Parker!*

MR. PARKER. Hold on now, there's no need for all this. . . . Can't we settle this later on, Adele. . . .

ADELE. We settle it now. You got six days left, so you gotta do something, and quick. I got a man coming here tomorrow to change the locks on the door. So for the little time you have left, you'll have to come by me to enter this house.

THEO. Who gives you the right to do that?

ADELE. Me, Adele Eloise Parker, black, over twenty-one, and the only working person in this house!

(Pause.)

I am not going to let the three of you drive me into the grave the way you did Mama. And if you really want to know how I feel about that, I'll tell you: Mama killed herself because there was no kind of order in this house. There was nothing but her old-fashion love for a bum like you, Theo—and this one *(Points to* BOBBY.) who's got nothing better to do with his time but to shoplift every time he walks into a department store. And you, Daddy, you and those fanciful stories you're always ready to tell, and all the talk of the good old days when you were the big vaudeville star, of hitting the numbers big. How? How, Daddy? The money you spent on the numbers you got from Mama. . . . In a way, you let Mama make a bum out of you—you let her kill herself!

MR. PARKER. That's a terrible thing to say, Adele, and I'm not going to let you put that off on me!

ADELE. But the fact remains that in the seven years you've been in this barbershop you haven't earned enough money to buy two hot dogs! Most of your time is spent playing checkers with that damn Mr. Jenkins.

THEO. *(Breaks in.)* Why don't you get married or something! We don't need you —Pop is here, it's HIS HOUSE!

ADELE. You're lucky I don't get married and—

THEO. Nobody wants you, baby!

ADELE. (THEO's *remark stops her for a moment. She resettles herself.)* All right, you just let someone ask me, and I'll leave you with *Pop,* to starve with Pop. Or, there's another way: why don't the three of you just leave right now and try making it on your own? Why don't we try that!

MR. PARKER. What about my shop?

ADELE. Since I'm the one that has to pay the extra forty dollars a month for you to keep this place, there's going to be no more shop. It was a bad investment and the whole of Harlem knows it!

MR. PARKER. *(Grabbing her by the arm, in desperation.)* I'm fifty-four years old!

ADELE. *(Pulling away.)* Don't touch me!

MR. PARKER. You go ahead and do what you want, but I'm not leaving this shop! *(Crosses away from her.)*

ADELE. Can't you understand, Father? I can't go on forever supporting three grown men! *That ain't right!*

(Long pause.)

MR. PARKER. *(Shaken by her remarks.)* No, it's not right—it's not right at all.

ADELE. —It's going to be *you* or *me.*

BOBBY. *(After a pause.)* I'll do what I can, Adele.

ADELE. You'll do *more* than you can.

BOBBY. I'll do more than I can.

ADELE. Is that all right by you, Mr. Theopolis?

THEO. Yes.

(Pause.)

ADELE. That's fine. Out of this house

tomorrow morning—before I leave here, or with me—suit your choice. And don't look so mournful *(Gathers up her belongings at the shelf.)*, smile. You're going to be happier than you think, earning a living for a change. *(Moves briskly through the back room and up the stairs.)*

BOBBY. You do look pretty bad, Theo. A job might be just the thing for you.

(MR. JENKINS comes rushing from the bed into the shop.)

MR. PARKER. Jenkins! I plumb forgot—

MR. JENKINS. I let you make a fool out of me, Parker!

MR. PARKER. We can still play!

MR. JENKINS. *(Gathering his jacket and coat.)* We can't play nothing, I'm going home where I belong!

MR. PARKER. Okay, okay, I'll come over to your place tonight.

MR. JENKINS. That's the only way. I ain't gon' have my feelings hurt by that daughter of yours.

MR. PARKER. I'll see you tonight—about eight.

MR. JENKINS. *(At the door.)* And, Parker, tell me something?

MR. PARKER. Yeah, what, Jenks?

MR. JENKINS. Are you positively sure Adele is your daughter?

MR. PARKER. Get out of here!

(MR. JENKINS rushes out.)

Now what made him ask a silly question like that?

THEO. I think he was trying to tell you that you ain't supposed to be taking all that stuff from Adele.

BOBBY. Yeah, Pop, he's right.

(MR. PARKER starts putting his checker set together.)

THEO. *(To BOBBY.)* I don't know what you talking about—you had your chance a few minutes ago, but all you did was poke your eyes at me and nod your head like a fool.

BOBBY. I don't see why you gotta make such a big thing out of her taking charge. Somebody's gotta do it. I think she's right!

THEO. I know what she's up to. She wants us to get jobs so she can fix up the house like she always wanted it, and then it's gon' happen.

BOBBY. What's that?

THEO. She gon' get married to some konkhead out on the Avenue, and then she gon' throw us out the door.

BOBBY. She wouldn't do that.

THEO. She wouldn't, huh? Put yourself in her place. She's busting thirty wide open. *Thirty years old*—that's a lot of years for a broad that's not married.

BOBBY. I never thought of it that way . . .

THEO. *(In half confidence.)* And you know something else, Pop? I sneaked and peeped at her bank book, and you know what she got saved?

MR. PARKER and BOBBY. *(Simultaneously, turning their heads.)* How much?

THEO. Two thousand two hundred and sixty-five dollars!

BOBBY. WHAT!!!

MR. PARKER. I don't believe it!

THEO. You better—and don't let her hand you that stuff about how she been sacrificing all these years for the house. The only way she could've saved up that kind of money was by staying right here!

MR. PARKER. Well, I'll be damned—two thousand dollars!

THEO. She better watch out is all I gotta say, 'cause I know some guys out there on that Avenue who don't do nothing but sit around all day figuring out ways to beat working girls out of their savings.

MR. PARKER. You oughta know, 'cause you're one of them yourself. The way I figure it, Theo, anybody that can handle you the way she did a few minutes ago can very well take care of themselves.

(He occupies himself putting checkers and board away and cleaning up.)

THEO. That's mighty big talk coming from you, after the way she treated you.

MR. PARKER. Lay off me, boy.

THEO. You going out to look for a job?

MR. PARKER. I'm giving it some serious thought.

THEO. Well, I'm not. I ain't wasting myself on no low, dirty, dead-end job. I got my paintings to think about.

BOBBY. Do you really think you're some kind of painter or something?

THEO. You've seen them.

BOBBY. Yeah, but how would I know?

THEO. *(Rushes into the back room, takes paintings from behind the refrigerator.)* All right, look at 'em.

BOBBY. Don't bring that stuff in here to me—show it to Pop!

(THEO holds up two ghastly, inept paintings to his brother. MR. PARKER, sweeping the floor, pays no attention.)

THEO. Look at it! Now tell me what you see.

BOBBY. Nothing.

THEO. You've got to see something— even an idiot has impressions.

BOBBY. I ain't no idiot.

THEO. All right, fool then.

BOBBY. Now look, you better stop throwing them words "fool" and "idiot" at me any time you feel like it. I'm gon' be one more fool, and then my fist is gonna land right upside your head!

THEO. Take it easy now—I tell you what: try to see something.

BOBBY. Try?

THEO. Yeah, close your eyes and really try.

BOBBY. *(Closes his eyes.)* Okay, I'm trying, but I don't know how I'm gon' see anything with my eyes closed!

THEO. Well, open them!

BOBBY. They open.

THEO. Now tell me what you see.

BOBBY. I see paint.

THEO. I know you see paint, stupid.

BOBBY. *(Slaps him ferociously across the face.)* Now I told you about that! Every time you call me out of my name, you get hit!

THEO. You'll never understand!

BOBBY. All I know is that a picture is supposed to be pretty, but I'm sorry, that mess you got there is downright ugly!

THEO. You're hopeless.—You understand this, don't you, Pop? *(Holding the painting for him to see.)*

MR. PARKER. *(Not looking at the painting.)* Don't ask me—I don't know nothing about no painting.

THEO. You were an artist once.

MR. PARKER. That was a different kind.

THEO. Didn't you ever go out on the stage with a new thing inside of you? One of them nights when you just didn't want to do that ol' soft-shoe routine? You knew you had to do it—after all, it was your job—but when you did it, you gave it a little bite here, a little acid there, and still, with all that, they laughed at you anyway. Didn't that ever happen to you?

MR. PARKER. More than once. . . . But you're BSn', boy, and you know it. You been something new every year since you quit school. First you was going to be a racing-car driver, then a airplane pilot, then a office big shot, and now it's a painter. As smart a boy as you is, you should've stayed in school, but who do you think you're fooling with them pictures?—It all boils down to one thing: you don't want to work. But I'll tell you something, Theo: time done run out on you. Adele's not playing, so you might as well put all that junk and paint away.

THEO. Who the hell is Adele? You're my father, you're the man of the house.

MR. PARKER. True, and that's what I intend to be, but until I get a job, I'm gon' play it cool.

THEO. You're going to let her push you

out into the streets to hustle up a job. You're an old man. You ain't used to working, it might kill you.

MR. PARKER. Yeah, but what kind of leg do I have to stand on if she puts me out in the street?

THEO. She's bluffing!

MR. PARKER. A buddy of mine who was in this same kind of fix told me exactly what you just said. Well, the last time I saw him, he was standing on the corner of Eighth Avenue and 125th Street at four o'clock in the morning, twenty-degree weather, in nothing but his drawers, mumbling to himself, "I could've sworn she was bluffing!"

THEO. Hey, Pop! Let me put it to you this way: if none of us come up with anything in that two-week deadline she gave us—none of us, you hear me?

MR. PARKER. I hear you and that's just about all.

THEO. Don't you get the point? That's three of us—you, me, and Bobby. What she gon' do? Throw the three of us out in the street? I tell you, she ain't gon' do that!

MR. PARKER. If you want to take that chance, that's your business, but don't try to make me take it with you. Anyway, it ain't right that she has to work for three grown men. It just ain't right.

THEO. Mama did it for you.

MR. PARKER. (Sharply.) That was different. She was my wife. She knew things about me you will never know. We oughtn' talk about her at all.

THEO. I'm sorry, Pop, but ever since Mama's funeral I've been thinking. Mama was the hardest-working person I ever knew, and it killed her! Is that what I'm supposed to do? No, that's not it, I know it's not. You know what I've been doing? I've been talking to some people, to a very important person right here in Harlem, and I told him about this big idea of mine—

MR. PARKER. You're loaded with ideas, boy—bad ideas! (Puts broom away.)

THEO. WHY DON'T YOU LISTEN TO WHAT I HAVE TO SAY!

MR. PARKER. Listen to you for what? Another con game you got up your sleeve because your sister's got fed up with you lying around this house all day while she's knocking herself out. You're pulling the same damn thing on me you did with those ugly paintings of yours a few minutes ago.

THEO. Okay, I can't paint. So I was jiving, but now I got something I really want to do—something I got to do!

MR. PARKER. If you're making a point, Theo, you've gotta be smarter than you're doing to get it through to me.

THEO. (Goes to back room, opens refrigerator, and takes out brown-paper bag, then comes back into the shop.) Pop, I got something here to show how smart I really am. (Lifts an old jug out of the bag.) Check this out, Pop! Check it out!

MR. PARKER. What is it?

THEO. Whiskey—corn whiskey—you want some?

MR. PARKER. (Hovers.) Well, I'll try a little bit of it out, but we better not let Adele see us.

THEO. (Starts unscrewing cork from jug.) That girl sure puts a scare in you, Pop, and I remember when you wouldn't take no stuff off Mama, Adele, or anybody.

MR. PARKER. God is the only person I fear.

THEO. (Stops unscrewing the jug.) God! Damn, you're all alike!

MR. PARKER. What are you talking about, boy?

THEO. You, the way Mama was—ask you any question you can't answer, and you throw that Bible stuff at us.

MR. PARKER. I don't get you.

THEO. For instance, let me ask you about the black man's oppressions, and you'll tell me about some small nation in the East rising one day to rule the world. Ask you about pain and dying, and you say, "God wills it." . . . Fear?—and you'll tell me about Daniel, and how Daniel wasn't scared of them lions. Am I right or wrong?

MR. PARKER. It's all in the book and you can't dispute it.

THEO. You wanta bet? If that nation in the East ever do rise, how can I be sure they won't be worse than the jokers we got running things now?—Nobody but nobody wills me to pain and dying, not if I can do something about it. That goes for John, Peter, Mary, J.C., the whole bunch of 'em! And as for ol' Daniel: sure, Daniel didn't care nothing about them lions—*but them lions didn't give a damn about him either! They tore him into a million pieces!*

MR. PARKER. That's a lie! That's an ungodly, unholy lie! *(Takes his Bible from the shelf.)* And I'll prove it!

THEO. What lie?

MR. PARKER. *(Moving from the counter, thumbing through Bible.)* You and those bastard ideas of yours. Here, here it is! *(Reading from Bible.)* "And when he came near unto the den to Daniel, he cried with a pained voice; The King spoke and said to Daniel: 'O Daniel, servant of the living God, is thy God, whom thou servest continually, able to deliver thee from the lions?' Then said Daniel unto the King: 'O King, live forever! My God hath sent his angel, and hath shut the lions' mouths, and they have not hurt me; for as much as before him innocence was found in me, and also before thee, O King, have I done no hurt.' Then was the King exceeding glad, and commanded that they should take Daniel up out of the den. So Daniel was taken up out of the den, and no manner of hurt was found upon him, because he trusted his God!!!" *(Slams the book closed, triumphant.)*

THEO. Hollywood, Pop, Hollywood!

MR. PARKER. Damn you! How I ever brought something like you into this world, I'll never know! You're no damn good! Sin! That's who your belief is! Sin and corruption! With you, it's nothing but women! Whiskey! Women! Whiskey! *(While he is carrying on, THEO pours out a glass of corn and puts it in MR. PARKER's hand.)* Women! Whiskey! *(Takes a taste.)* Whisk—where did you get this from? *(Sits on throne.)*

THEO. *(Slapping BOBBY's hand.)* I knew you'd get the message, Pop—I just knew it!

MR. PARKER. Why, boy, this is the greatest corn I ever tasted!

BOBBY. And Theo puts that stuff together like he was born to be a whiskey maker!

MR. PARKER. Where did you learn to make corn like this?

THEO. Don't you remember? You taught me.

MR. PARKER. By George, I did! Why, you weren't no more'n nine years old—

THEO. Eight. Let's have another one. *(Pours another for PARKER.)* Drink up. Here's to ol' Daniel. You got to admit one thing—he had a whole lot of heart!

MR. PARKER. *(Drinks up and puts his hand out again.)* Another one, please . . .

THEO. *(Pouring.)* Anything you say, Pop! *You're the boss of this house!*

MR. PARKER. Now that's the truth if you ever spoke it. *(Drinks up.)* Whew! This is good! *(Putting his glass out again, slightly tipsy.)*

THEO. About this idea of mine, Pop: well, it's got something to do with this corn.

MR. PARKER. *(Drinks up.)* Wow! Boy, people oughta pay you to make this stuff.

THEO. Well, that's what I kinda had in mind. I tested some of it out the other day, and I was told this corn liquor could start a revolution—that is, if I wanted to start one. I let a preacher taste some, and he asked me to make him a whole keg for him.

MR. PARKER. *(Pauses. Then, in a sudden change of mood.)* God! Damnit!

BOBBY. What's wrong, Pop?

MR. PARKER. I miss her, boy, I tell you, I miss her! Was it really God's will?

THEO. Don't you believe that—*don't you ever believe that!*

MR. PARKER. But I think, boy—I think hard!

THEO. That's all right. We think hard too. We got it from you. Ain't that right, Bobby?

BOBBY. Yeah.

(Pause.)

MR. PARKER. You know something? That woman was the first woman I ever got close to—your mama . . .

BOBBY. *How old were you?*

MR. PARKER. Twenty.

BOBBY. Aw, come on, Pop!

MR. PARKER. May God wipe me away from this earth . . .

THEO. Twenty years old and you had never touched a woman? You must've been in bad shape.

MR. PARKER. I'll tell you about it.

THEO. Here he goes with another one of his famous stories!

MR. PARKER. I can always go on upstairs, you know.

THEO. No, Pop, we want to hear it.

MR. PARKER. Well, I was working in this circus in Tampa, Florida—your mother's hometown. You remember Bob Shepard—well, we had this little dance routine of ours we used to do a sample of outside the tent. One day we was out there doing one of our numbers, when right in the middle of the number I spied this fine, foxy-looking thing, blinking her eyes at me. 'Course ol' Bob kept saying it was him she was looking at, but I knew it was *me*—'cause if there was one thing that was my specialty, it was a fine-looking woman.

THEO. You live twenty years of life not getting anywhere near a woman, and all of a sudden they become *your specialty?*

MR. PARKER. Yeah, being that—

THEO. Being that you had never had a woman for all them terrible years, naturally it was on your mind all the time.

MR. PARKER. That's right.

THEO. And it being on your mind so much, you sorta became a specialist on women?

MR. PARKER. Right again.

THEO. *(Laughs.)* I don't know. But I guess you got a point there!

MR. PARKER. You want to hear this or not!

BOBBY. Yeah, go on, Pop. *I'm* listening.

MR. PARKER. Well, while I was standing on the back of the platform, I motions to her with my hand to kinda move around to the side of the stand, so I could talk to 'er. She strolled 'round to the side, stood there for a while, and you know what? Ol' Bob wouldn't let me get a word in edgewise. But you know what she told him; she said Mister, you talk like a fool!

(All laugh.)

BOBBY. That was Mama, all right.

MR. PARKER. So I asked her if she would like to meet me after the circus closed down. When I got off that night, sure enough, she was waiting for me. We walked up to the main section of town, off to the side of the road, 'cause we had a hard rain that day and the road was full of muddy little ponds. I got to talking to her and telling her funny stories and she would laugh—boy, I'm telling you that woman could laugh!

THEO. That was your technique, huh? Keep 'em laughing!

MR. PARKER. Believe it or not, it worked—'cause she let me kiss her. I kissed her under this big ol' pecan tree. She could kiss too. When that woman kissed me, somethin' grabbed me so hard and shook me so, I fell flat on my back into a big puddle of water! *And that woman killed herself laughing!*

(Pause.)

I married her two weeks later.

THEO. And then you started making up for lost time. I'm glad you did, Pop—'cause if you hadn't, I wouldn't be here today.

MR. PARKER. If I know you, you'd have made some kind of arrangement.

BOBBY. What happened after that?

MR. PARKER. We just lived and had fun—and chlidren too, that part you know about. We lived bad and we lived good—and then my legs got wobbly, and my feet got heavy, I lost my feeling, and everything just stayed as it was.

(Pause.)

I only wish I had been as good a hair-cutter as I was a dancer. Maybe she wouldn't have had to work so hard. She might be living today.

THEO. Forget it, Pop—it's all in the gone by. Come on, you need another drink. *(Pouring.)*

MR. PARKER. Get me to talking about them old days. It hurts, I tell you, it—

THEO. Pop, you have got to stop thinking about those things. We've got work to do!

MR. PARKER. You said you had an idea . . .

THEO. Yes—you see, Pop, this idea has to do with Harlem. It has to do with the preservation of Harlem. That's what it's all about. So I went to see this leader, and I spoke to him about it. He thought it was great and said he would pay me to use it!

MR. PARKER. Who wants to preserve this dump? Tear it down, is what I say!

THEO. But this is a different kind of preserving. Preserve it for black men—

preserve it for men like you, me, and Bobby. That's what it's all about.

MR. PARKER. That sounds good.

THEO. Of course I told this leader, I couldn't promise to do anything until I had spoken to my father. I said, after straightening everything out with you I would make arrangements for the two of you to meet.

MR. PARKER. Meet him for what?

THEO. For making money! For business! *This man knows how to put people in business!*

MR. PARKER. All right, I'll meet him. What's his name?

THEO. —But first you gotta have a showdown with Adele and put her in her place once and for all.

MR. PARKER. Now wait just a minute. You didn't say Adele would have anything to do with this.

THEO. Pop, this man can't be dealing with men who let women rule them. Pop, you've got to tell that girl off or we can't call ourselves men!

(Pause.)

MR. PARKER. All right. If she don't like it, that's too bad. Whatever you have in mind for us to do with this leader of yours, we'll do it.

THEO. Now that's the way I like to hear my old man talk! Take a drink, Pop! *(Starts popping his fingers and moves dancing about the room.)*

> We're gonna show 'em now
> We're gonna show 'em how
> All over
> This ol' Harlem Town!

(THEO and BOBBY start making rhythmic scat sounds with their lips as they dance around the floor.)

Come on, Pop, show us how you used to cut one of them things!

BOBBY. *(Dancing.)* This is how he did it!

THEO. Nawwww, that's not it. He did it like this!

MR. PARKER. (Rising.) No, no! Neither one of you got it! Speed up that riff a little bit . . .

(The two boys speed up the riff, singing, stomping their feet, clapping their hands. Humped over, MR. PARKER looks down on the floor concentrating.)

Faster!

(They speed it up more.)

THEO. Come on now, Pop—let 'er loose!

MR. PARKER. Give me time . . .

BOBBY. Let that man have some time!

(MR. PARKER breaks into his dance.)

THEO. Come on, Pop, take it with you!

BOBBY. Work, Pop!

THEO. DOWNTOWN!

(MR. PARKER does a coasting "camel walk.")

BOBBY. NOW BRING IT ON BACK UPTOWN!

(MR. PARKER really breaks loose: a rapid series of complicated dance steps.)

THEO. YEAHHHHHHHH!

BOBBY. That's what I'm talkin' about!

(ADELE enters, stops at the entrance to the shop, observes the scene, bemused. PARKER, glimpsing her first, in one motion abruptly stops dancing and reaches for the broom. BOBBY looks for something to busy himself with. THEO just stares.)

ADELE. Supper's ready, fellows!

CURTAIN

ACT ONE

SCENE 2

Six days later. Late afternoon.
BOBBY *is seated in the barber's throne,*

munching on a sandwich. THEO *enters from the front of the shop.*

THEO. Did Pop get back yet?

(BOBBY *shrugs shoulders.*)

THEO. You eating again? Damn. (Calling upstairs.) Pop!

(No answer. THEO checks his watch, steps back into shop, looks through window, then crosses to BOBBY and snatches the sandwich from his mouth.)

You eat too damn much!

BOBBY. What the fuck you do that for?

THEO. (Handing the sandwich back.) 'Cause you always got a mouth full of peanut butter and jelly!

BOBBY. I'm hungry! And let me tell you something: don't you *ever* snatch any food from my mouth again.

THEO. You'll hit me—you don't care nothing about your brother. One of these days, I'm gon' hit back.

BOBBY. *Nigger!* The day you swing your hand at me, you'll draw back a nub.

THEO. You see! That's exactly what I mean. Now when Blue gets here tonight, I don't want you talking like that, or else you gon' blow the whole deal.

BOBBY. I know how to act. I don't need no lessons from you.

THEO. Good. I got a job for you.

BOBBY. A job? Shit!

THEO. Don't get knocked out now—it ain't no real job. I just want you to jump over to Smith's on 125th Street and pick me up a portable typewriter.

BOBBY. Typewriter—for what?

THEO. Don't ask questions, just go and get it.

BOBBY. Them typewriters cost a lotta money.

THEO. You ain't gon' use money.

BOBBY. You mean—

THEO. —I mean you walk in there and take one.

BOBBY. Naw, you don't mean I walk into nowhere and take nothing!

THEO. Now, Bobby.

BOBBY. No!

THEO. Aw, come on, Bobby. You the one been bragging about how good you are, how you can walk into any store and get anything you wanted, provided it was not too heavy to carry out.

BOBBY. I ain't gon' do it!

THEO. You know what day it is?

BOBBY. Thursday.

THEO. That's right. Thursday, May 10th.

BOBBY. What's that suppose to mean, Thieves' Convention on 125th Street?

THEO. It's Pop's birthday!

BOBBY. I didn't know he was still having them.

THEO. Well, let me tell you something: Adele remembered it and she's planning on busting into this shop tonight with a birthday cake to surprise him.

BOBBY. She suppose to be throwing us out today. That don't make no sense with her buying him a birthday cake.

THEO. He's been looking for work, I guess she changed her mind about him. Maybe it's gon' be just me and you that goes.

(Pause.)

BOBBY. What's he gon' type?

THEO. Them lies he's always telling—like the one about how he met Mama. Pop can tell some of the greatest lies you ever heard of and you know how he's always talking about writing them down.

BOBBY. Pop don't know nothing 'bout writing—specially no typewriting!

THEO. *(Takes out his father's notebook.)* Oh no? take a look at this. *(Hands book to* BOBBY.*)* All he has to do is put it down on paper the way he tells it. Who knows, somebody might get interested in it for television or movies, and we can make ourselves some money, and besides, I kinda think he would get a real charge out of you thinking about him that way—don't you?

(Pause.)

BOBBY. Well, ain't no use in lettin' you go over there, gettin' yourself in jail with them old clumsy fingers of yours.

THEO. Good boy, Bobby!

(MR. PARKER enters the shop.)

Hey, Pop! Did you get that thing straightened out with Adele yet?

MR. PARKER. What?

THEO. *Adele?*

MR. PARKER. Oh, yeah, I'm gon' take care of that right away. *(Shoves* BOBBY *out of throne and sits.)*

THEO. Where you been all day?

(BOBBY moves into back room.)

MR. PARKER. Downtown, seeing about some jobs.

THEO. You sure don't care much about yourself.

MR. PARKER. I can agree with you on that, because lookin' for a job can really hurt a man. I was interviewed five times today, and I could've shot every last one of them interviewers—the white ones and the colored ones too. I don't know if I can take any more of this.

THEO. Yeah, looking for a job can be very low-grading to a man, and it gets worse after you get the job. Anyway, I'm glad you got back here on time, or you would've missed your appointment.

(No response from PARKER.*)*

Now don't tell me you don't remember! The man, the man that's suppose to come here and tell you how life in Harlem can be profitable.

MR. PARKER. *(Steps out of throne, edging toward back room.)* Oh, that.

THEO. *(Following him.)* Oh, that—my foot! Today is the day we're suppose to come up with those jobs, and you ain't said one word to Adele about it—not one single word! All you do is waste your time looking for work! Now that don't make no sense at all, Pop, and you know it.

MR. PARKER. Look, son. Let me go upstairs now and tell her about all the disappointments I suffered today, soften her up a bit, and then I'll come on back down here to meet your man. I promise, you won't have to worry about me going downtown any more—not after what I went through today. And I certainly ain't giving up my shop for nobody! *(Exits upstairs.)*

THEO. *(Turns to* BOBBY, *who's at the mirror.)* Now that's the way I like to hear my old man talk! Hey, baby, don't forget that thing. It's late, we ain't got much time.

BOBBY. All right!

(A jet-black-complexioned young man comes in. He is dressed all in blue and wears sunglasses. He carries a gold-top cane and a large salesman's valise. He stops just inside the door.)

THEO. Blue, baby!
BLUE. Am I late?

THEO. No, my father just walked in the door. He's upstairs now, but he'll be right back down in a few minutes. Let me take your things. *(Takes* BLUE's *cane and valise.)* Sit down, man, while I fix you a drink. *(Places* BLUE's *things on the table and moves into back room.)*

*(*BOBBY *enters shop.)*

BLUE. Hey, Bobby. How's the stores been treating you?
BOBBY. I'm planning on retiring next year. *(Laughs.)*
THEO. *(Returning with jug and two glasses. Moves to the table and pours.)* I was thinking, Blue—we can't let my old man know about our "piano brigade." I know he ain't going for that, but we can fix it where he will never know a thing.
BLUE. You know your father better than I do. *(Takes a drink.)*

BOBBY. What's the "piano brigade"?
THEO. Blue here has the best thieves and store burglars in this part of town, and we plan to work on those businesses over on 125th Street until they run the insurance companies out of business.
BOBBY. You mean breaking into people's stores at night and taking their stuff?
THEO. That's right, but not the way you do it. We'll be organized, we'll be revolutionary.
BOBBY. If the police catch you, they ain't gon' care what you is, and if Pop ever finds out, the police gon' seem like church girls! *(Slips out the front door.)*
THEO. *(After him.)* You just remember that the only crime you'll ever commit is the one you get caught at!

(Pause.)

Which reminds me, Blue—I don't want Bobby to be a part of that "piano brigade."
BLUE. If that's the way you want it, that's the way it shall be, Theo. How's your sister?
THEO. You mean Adele?
BLUE. You got a sister named Mary or something?
THEO. What this with Adele?
BLUE. I want to know, how are you going to get along with her, selling bootleg whiskey in this place?
THEO. This is not her place, it's my father's. And once he puts his okay on the deal, that's it. What kind of house do you think we're living in, where we gon' let some woman tell us what to do? Come here, let me show you something. *(Moves into back room.* BLUE *follows.)* How you like it—ain't it something?
BLUE. *(Standing in doorway.)* It's a back room.
THEO. Yeah, I know. But I have some great plans for reshaping it by knocking down this wall, and putting—
BLUE. Like I said, it's a back room. All I wanta know is, will it do the job?

It's a good room. You'll do great with that good-tasting corn of yours. You're going to be so busy here, you're going to grow to hate this place—you might not have any time for your love life, Theopolis!

THEO. *(Laughing.)* Don't you worry about that—I can manage my sex life!

BLUE. Sex! Who's talking about sex? You surprise me, Theo. Everyone's been telling me about how you got so much heart, how you so deep. I sit and talk to you about life, and you don't know the difference between sex and love.

THEO. Is it that important?

BLUE. Yes, it is, ol' buddy, if you want to hang out with me, and you do want to hang out with me, don't you?

THEO. That depends—

BLUE. It depends upon you knowing that sex's got nothing to do with anything but you and some woman laying up in some funky bed, pumping and sweating your life away all for one glad moment— you hear that, *one moment!*

THEO. I'll take that moment!

BLUE. With every woman you've had?

THEO. One out of a hundred!

BLUE. *(Laughing, and moving back into shop.)* One out of a hundred! All that sweat! All that pumping and grinding for the sake of one little dead minute out of a hundred hours!

(MR. PARKER comes in from upstairs.)

(Pause.)

THEO. *(Stopping PARKER.)* Pop, you know who this is?

MR. PARKER. I can't see him.

THEO. This is Blue!

MR. PARKER. Blue who?

THEO. The man I was telling you about . . . *Mr. Blue Haven.*

MR. PARKER. *(Extends his hand to shake BLUE's.)* Please to make your acquaintance, Mr. Haven.

BLUE. *(Shaking MR. PARKER's hand.)* Same to you, Mr. Parker.

THEO. You sure you don't know who Blue Haven is, Pop?

MR. PARKER. I'm sorry, but I truly don't know you, Mr. Haven. If you're a celebrity, you must accept my apology. You see, since I got out of the business, I don't read *Variety* any more.

THEO. I'm not talking about a celebrity.

MR. PARKER. Oh, no?

THEO. He's the leader!

MR. PARKER. Ohhhhh!

THEO. Right here in Harlem.

MR. PARKER. Where else he gon' be but in Harlem? We got more leaders within ten square blocks of this barbershop than they got liars down in City Hall. That's why you dressed up that way, huh, boy? So people can pick you out of a crowded room?

THEO. Pop, this is serious!

MR. PARKER. All right, go on, don't get carried away—there are some things I don't catch on to right away, Mr. Blue.

THEO. Well, get to this: I got to thinking the other day when Adele busted in here shoving everybody around—I was thinking about this barbershop, and I said to myself: Pop's gon' lose this shop if he don't start making himself some money.

MR. PARKER. Now tell me something I don't know. *(Sits on throne.)*

THEO. Here I go. What would you say if I were to tell you that Blue here can make it possible for you to have a thriving business going on, right here in this shop, for twenty-four hours a day?

MR. PARKER. What is he—some kind of hair grower!

THEO. Even if you don't cut but one head of hair a week!

MR. PARKER. Do I look like a fool to you?

THEO. *(Holds up his jug.)* Selling this!

(Pause.)

MR. PARKER. Well, well, well. I knew it was something like that. I didn't exactly know what it was, but I knew it was something. And I don't want to hear it!

THEO. Pop, you've always been a man to listen—even when you didn't agree, even when I was wrong, you listened! That's the kind of man you are! You—

MR. PARKER. Okay, okay, I'm listening!

(Pause.)

THEO. Tell him who you are, Blue.

BLUE. I am the Prime Minister of the Harlem De-Colonization Association.

(Pause.)

MR. PARKER. Some kind of organization?

BLUE. Yes.

MR. PARKER *(As an aside, almost under his breath.)* They got all kinds of committees in Harlem. What was that name again, "De"?

THEO. De-Colo-ni-zation! Which means that Harlem is owned and operated by Mr. You-Know-Who. Let me get this stuff—we gon' show you something. . . . *(Moves to the table and opens* BLUE's *valise.)*

BLUE. We're dead serious about this project, Mr. Parker. I'd like you to look at this chart.

THEO. And you'll see, we're not fooling. *(Hurriedly pins charts taken from* BLUE's *valise on wall out in the shop.)*

MR. PARKER. *(Reading from center chart.)* The Harlem De-Colonization Association, with Future Perspective for Bedford Stuyvesant. *(Turns to* BLUE.*)* All right, so you got an organization. What do you do? I've never heard of you.

BLUE. The only reason you've never heard of us is because we don't believe in picketing, demonstrating, rioting, and all that stuff. We always look like we're doing something that we ain't doing, but we are doing something—and in that way nobody gets hurt. Now you may think

we're passive. To the contrary, we believe in direct action. We are doers, enterprisers, thinkers—and most of all, we're businessmen! Our aim is to drive Mr. You-Know-Who out of Harlem.

MR. PARKER. Who's this Mr. You-Know-Who?

THEO. Damn, Pop! The white man!

MR. PARKER. Oh, himmm!

BLUE. We like to use that name for our members in order to get away from the bad feelings we have whenever we use the word "white." We want our members to always be objective and in this way we shall move forward. Before we get through, there won't be a single Mr. You-Know-Who left in this part of town. We're going to capture the imagination of the people of Harlem. And that's never been done before, you know.

MR. PARKER. Now, tell me how?

BLUE. *(Standing before the charts, pointing with his cane.)* You see this here. This is what we call a "brigade." And you see this yellow circle?

MR. PARKER. What's that for?

BLUE. My new and entertaining system for playing the numbers. You do play the numbers, Mr. Parker?

MR. PARKER. I do.

BLUE. You see, I have a lot of colors in this system and these colors are mixed up with a whole lot of numbers, and the idea is to catch the right number with the right color. The right number can be anything from one to a hundred, but in order to win, the color must always be black. The name of this game is called "Black Heaven." It's the color part that gives everybody all the fun in playing this game of mine.

MR. PARKER. Anybody ever catch it?

BLUE. Sure, but not until every number and every color has paid itself off. The one thing you'll find out about my whole operation: you can't lose. *(Pause for effect.)*

MR. PARKER. Keep talking.

BLUE. Now over here is the Red Square Circle Brigade, and this thing here is at the heart of my dream to create here in Harlem a symbolic life-force in the heart of the people.

MR. PARKER. You don't say. . . .

BLUE. Put up that target, Theo.

(THEO *hurriedly pins on wall a dart target with the face of a beefy, Southern-looking white man as bull's-eye.*)

MR. PARKER. Why, that's that ol' dirty sheriff from that little town in Mississippi!

BLUE. (*Taking a dart from* THEO.) That's right—we got a face on a target for every need. We got governors, mayors, backwood crackers, city crackers, Southern crackers, and Northern crackers. We got all kinds of faces on these targets that any good Harlemite would be willing to buy for the sake of slinging one of these darts in that bastard's throat! (*Throws dart, puncturing face on board.*)

MR. PARKER. Let me try it one time. (*Rising, takes dart from* BLUE *and slings it into the face on the target.*) Got him! (*A big laugh.*)

BLUE. It's like I said, Mr. Parker: the idea is to capture the imagination of the people!

MR. PARKER. You got more? Let me see more!

BLUE. Now this is our green circle— That's Theo and his corn liquor—for retail purposes will be called "Black Lightning." This whiskey of Theo's can make an everlasting contribution to this life-force I've been telling you about. I've tested this whiskey out in every neighborhood in Harlem, and everybody claimed it was the best they ever tasted this side of Washington, D.C. You see, we plan to supply every after-hours joint in this area, and this will run Mr. You-Know-Who and his bonded product out of Harlem.

THEO. You see, Pop, this all depends on the barbershop being open night and day so the people can come and go as they please, to pick up their play for the day, to get a bottle of corn, and to take one of them targets home to the kiddies. They can walk in just as if they were getting a haircut. In fact, I told Blue that we can give a haircut as a bonus for anyone who buys two quarts.

MR. PARKER. What am I suppose to say now?

THEO. You're suppose to be daring. You're suppose to wake up to the times, Pop! These are urgent days—a man has to stand up and be counted!

MR. PARKER. The police might have some counting of their own to do.

THEO. Do you think I would bring you into something that was going to get us in trouble? Blue has an organization! Just like Mr. You-Know-Who. He's got members on the police force! In the city government, the state government.

BLUE. Mr. Parker, if you have any reservations concerning the operation of my association, I'd be only too happy to have you come to my summer home, and I'll let you in on everything—especially our protective system against being caught doing this thing.

THEO. Did you hear him, Pop, *he's got a summer home!*

MR. PARKER. Aw, shut up, boy! Let me think! (*Turns to* BLUE.) So you want to use my place as a headquarters for Theo's corn, the colored numbers, and them targets?

BLUE. Servicing the area of 125th to 145th, between the East and West rivers.

(*Pause.*)

MR. PARKER. I'm sorry, fellows, but I can't do it. (*Moves into back room.*)

THEO. (*Following* MR. PARKER.) Why?

MR. PARKER. It's not right.

THEO. Not right! What are you talking about? Is it right that all that's out there for us is to go downtown and push one of them carts? I have done that, and I ain't gon' do it no more!

MR. PARKER. That still don't make it right.

THEO. I don't buy it! I'm going into this thing with Blue, with or without you!

MR. PARKER. Go on, I don't care! You quit school, I couldn't stop you! I asked you to get a job, you wouldn't work! You have never paid any attention to any of my advice, and I don't expect you to start heeding me now!

THEO. Remember what you said to me about them paintings, and being what I am—well, this is me! At last I've found what I can do, and it'll work—I know it will. Please, Pop, just—

MR. PARKER. Stop begging, Theo. (Crosses back into shop, looks at BLUE.) Why?

BLUE. I don't get you.

MR. PARKER. What kind of boy are you that you went through so much pain to dream up this cockeyed, ridiculous, plan of yours?

BLUE. Mr. Parker, I was born about six blocks from here, and before I was ten I had the feeling I had been living for a hundred years. I got so old and tired I didn't know how to cry. Now you just think about that. But now I own a piece of this neighborhood. I don't have to worry about some bastard landlord or those credit crooks on 125th Street. Beautiful, black Blue—they have to worry about me! (Reaches into his pocket and pulls out a stack of bills. Places them in PARKER's hands.) Can't you see, man— I'm here to put you in business!

(MR. PARKER runs his fingers through the money.)

Money, Mr. Parker—brand-new money.
. . .

(After concentrated attention, MR. PARKER drops money on tables and moves into back room. THEO hurriedly follows. MR. PARKER sits on bed, in deep thought.)

THEO. That's just to get us started. And if we can make a dent into Mr. You-Know-Who's goings-on in Harlem, nobody's going to think of us as crooks. We'll be heroes from 110th Street to Sugar Hill. And just think, Pop, you won't have to worry about jobs and all that. You'll have so much time for you and Mr. Jenkins to play checkers, your arms will drop off. You'll be able to sit as long as you want, and tell enough stories and lies to fit between the cover of a 500-page book. That's right! Remember you said you wanted to write all them stories down! Now you'll have time for it! You can dress up the way you used to. And the girls—remember how you used to be so tough with the girls before you got married? All that can come back to you, and some of that you never had. It's so easy! All you have to do is call Adele down those stairs and let her know that you're going into business and if she don't like it she can pack up and move out, because you're not going to let her drive you down because you're a man, and—

MR. PARKER. All right! (Moves back into shop, where BLUE is putting away his paraphernalia.) I'll do it!

(Pause.)

I'll do it under one condition—

BLUE. And that is?

MR. PARKER. If my buddy Jenkins wants to buy into this deal, you'll let him.

BLUE. Theo?

THEO. It's all right.

MR. PARKER. (Extending his hand to BLUE.) Then you got yourself some partners, Mr. Haven!

BLUE. Welcome into the association, Mr. Parker.

MR. PARKER. Welcome into my barbershop!

THEO. (Jubilantly.) Yehhhhhhhhhh!

(BLUE checks his watch. ADELE comes into the back room.)

BLUE. Well, I have to check out now, but I'll stop over tomorrow and we will set the whole thing up just as you want it, Mr. Parker. See you later, Theo.

MR, PARKER. *(To* BLUE *as he is walking out the front door.)* You should stick around awhile and watch my polish!

THEO. Pop, don't you think it would be better if you would let me give the word to Adele?

MR. PARKER. No. If I'm going to run a crooked house, *I'm* going to run it, and that goes for you as well as her.

THEO. But, Pop, sometimes she kinda gets by you.

MR. PARKER. Boy, I have never done anything like this in my life, but since I've made up my mind to it, you have nothing to say—not a word. You have been moaning about me never making it so you can have a chance. Well, this time you can say I'm with you. But let me tell you something: I don't want no more lies from you, and no more conning me about painting, airplane piloting, or nothing. If being a crook is what you want to be, you're going to be the best crook in the world—even if you have to drink mud to prove it.

(Pause.)

THEO. Okay, Pop.

MR. PARKER. *(Moves toward back room.)* Well, here goes nothing. Adele! *(Just as he calls,* ADELE *steps out of the back room, stopping him in his tracks.)*

ADELE. Yes, Father.

MR. PARKER. Oh, you're here already. Well, I want to talk to—well, I, er—

ADELE. What is it?

(Pause.)

MR. PARKER. Nothing. I'll talk to you later. *(He spots* BOBBY *entering from the outside with a package wrapped in newspaper.)* What you got there?

BOBBY. Uh . . . uh . . . —fish!

MR. PARKER. Well, you better get them in the refrigerator before they stink on you.

THEO. *(Going over to* BOBBY *and taking package from him.)* No, no. Now, Bobby, I promised Pop we would never lie to him again. It ain't fish, Pop. We've got something for you. *(Puts the package on the table and starts unwrapping it. The two boys stand over the table, and as the typewriter is revealed, both turn to him.)*

THEO and BOBBY. Happy Birthday!

MR. PARKER. Birthday? Birthday?

THEO *and* BOBBY. Yes, Happy Birthday!

MR. PARKER. Now hold on just a minute!

BOBBY. What are we holding on for, Pop?

(Pause.)

MR. PARKER. That's a good question, son. We're—we're holding on for a celebration! *(Laughs loudly.)* Thanks, fellows! But what am I going to do with a typewriter! I don't know nothing about no typing!

ADELE. I would like to know where they got the money to buy one!

THEO. *(Ignoring her.)* You know what you told me about writing down your stories—now you can write them down three times as fast!

MR. PARKER. But I don't know how to type!

THEO. With the money we're gonna be having, I can hire somebody to teach you!

ADELE. What money you going to have?

THEO. We're going into business, baby —right here in this barbershop!

MR. PARKER. Theo—

THEO. *(Paying no attention.)* We're going to sell bootleg whiskey, numbers, and—

ADELE. You're what!?

MR. PARKER. Theo—

THEO. You heard me, and if you don't like it you can pack your bags and leave!

ADELE. Leave? I pay the rent here!

THEO. No more! I pay it now!

MR. PARKER. Shut up, Theo!

THEO. We're going to show you something, girl. You think—

MR. PARKER. *I said shut up!*

ADELE. Is he telling the truth?

MR. PARKER. Yes, he is telling the truth.

ADELE. You mean to tell me you're going to turn this shop into a bootleg joint?

MR. PARKER. I'll turn it into anything I want to!

ADELE. Not while I'm still here!

MR. PARKER. The lease on this house has my signature, not yours!

ADELE. I'm not going to let you do this!

MR. PARKER. You got no choice, Adele. *You don't have a damn thing to say!*

ADELE. *(Turns sharply to* THEO.*)* You put him up to this!

MR. PARKER. Nobody puts me up to anything I don't want to do! These two boys have made it up in their minds they're not going to work for nobody but themselves, and the thought in my mind is *why should they!* I did like you said, I went downtown, and it's been a long time since I did that, but *you're* down there every day, and you oughta know by now that I am too old a man to ever dream I . . . could overcome the dirt and filth they got waiting for me down there. I'm surprised at you, that you would have so little care in you to shove me into the middle of that mob.

ADELE. You can talk about caring? What about Mama? She *died* working for you! Did you ever stop to think about that! In fact, *did you ever love her?* No!!!

MR. PARKER. That's a lie!

ADELE. I hope that one day you'll be able to do one good thing to drive that doubt out of my mind. *But this is not it!* You've let this hoodlum sell you his twisted ideas of making a short cut through life. But let me tell you something—this bastard is going to ruin you!

THEO. *(Into her face.)* Start packing, baby!

ADELE. *(Strikes him across the face.)* Don't you talk to me like that!

(He raises his hand to strike her back.)

MR. PARKER. Drop your hand, boy!

*(*THEO *does not respond.)*

I said, drop your goddamn hand!

THEO. She hit me!

MR. PARKER. I don't care if she had broken your jaw. If you ever draw your hand back to hit this girl again—*as long as you* live! You better not be in my hand reach when you do, 'cause *I'll split your back in two!* *(To* ADELE.*)* We're going into business, Adele. I have come to that and I have come to it on my own. I am going to stop worrying once and for all whether I live naked in the cold or whether I die like an animal, unless I can live the best way I know how to. I am getting old and I oughta have some fun. I'm going to get me some money, and I'm going to spend it! I'm going to get drunk! I'm going to dance some more! *I'm getting old! I'm going to fall in love one more time before I die!* So get to that, girl, and if it's too much for you to bear, I wouldn't hold it against you if you walked away from here this very minute—

ADELE. *(Opens the door to the back room to show him the birthday surprise she has for him.)* Happy birthday!

MR. PARKER. *(Goes into the room and stands over table where birthday cake is.)* I guess I fooled all of you. Today is not my birthday. It never was. *(Moves up the stairs.)*

ADELE. It's not going to work! You're going to cut your throat—you hear me! You're going to rip yourself into little pieces! *(Turns to* THEO.*)* It's not going to be the way you want it—because I know Mr. Blue Haven, and he is not a person to put your trust in.

*(*THEO *turns his back on her, heads for the shop door.)*

. . . I am talking to you!

THEO. *(Stops and turns.)* Why don't you leave us alone. You're the one who said we had to go out and do something. Well, we did, but we're doing it our way. Me and Bobby, we're men—if we lived the way you wanted us to, we wouldn't have nothing but big fat veins popping out of our heads.

ADELE. I'll see what kind of men you are every time a cop walks through that door, every time a stranger steps into this back room and you can't be too sure about him, and the day they drag your own father off and throw him into a jail cell.

THEO. But, tell me, what else is there left for us to do. You tell me and I'll do it. You show me where I can go to spin the world around before it gets too late for somebody like Mama living fifty years just to die on 126th Street! *You tell me of a place where there are no old crippled vaudeville men!*

ADELE. There is no such place.

(Pause.)

But you don't get so hung up about it you have to plunge a knife into your own body. You don't bury yourself here in this place; you climb up out of it! Now that's something for you to wonder about, boy.

THEO. I wonder all the time—how you have lived here all your whole life on this street, and you haven't seen, heard, learned, or felt a thing in all those years. I wonder how you ever got to be such a damn fool!

CURTAIN

ACT TWO

SCENE 1

Two months later. It is about 9 P.M.

As the Curtain rises, the LIGHTS *come up in the back room.* BOBBY *is there, listening to a record of James Brown's "Money Won't Change You, But Time Will Take You On." As he is dancing out to the shop,* THEO *appears from the cellar, which has been enlarged by taking out a panel in the lower section of the wall and houses the whiskey-making operation.* THEO *brings in two boxes filled with bottles of corn whiskey and shoves them under the bed.*

BOBBY *moves past* THEO *into the shop, carrying a target rolled up in his hand, and two darts. He is wearing a fancy sports shirt, new trousers, new keen-toed shoes, and a stingy, diddy-bop hat. He pins the target up on the wall of the shop. In the center of the target is the face of a well-known American racist.*

BOBBY. *(Moves away from the target, aims and hurls the dart.)* That's for Pop! Huh! *(Throws another.)* And this is for me! Huh! *(Moves to the target to pull darts out.)*

*(*THEO *cuts record off abruptly. A knock at the door.)*

THEO. *(Calling out to* BOBBY *from the back room.)* Lock that door!

BOBBY. Lock it yourself!

THEO. *(With quick but measured steps moves toward front door.)* I'm not selling another bottle, target, or anything, till I get some help! *(Locks door in spite of persistent knocking.)* We're closed!

BOBBY. I don't think Blue is gon' like

you turning customers away. *(Sits in barber chair, lighting up cigar.)*

THEO. You can tell Blue I don't like standing over that stove all day, that I don't like him promising me helpers that done show up. There are a lot of things I don't go for, like Pop taking off and not showing up for two days. I make this whiskey, I sell it, I keep the books, I peddle numbers and those damn targets. *And I don't like you standing around here all day not lifting a finger to help me!*

BOBBY. *(Taking a big puff on his cigar.)* I don't hear you.

THEO. Look at you—all decked out in your new togs. Look at me: I haven't been out of these dungarees since we opened this place up.

BOBBY. *(Jumps out of chair.)* I don't wanta hear nothing! You do what you wanta do, and leave me alone!

THEO. What am I supposed to be, a work mule or something?

BOBBY. You're the one that's so smart —you can't answer your own stupid questions?

THEO. You done let Blue turn you against me, huh?

BOBBY. You ask the questions, and you gon' answer them—but for now, stop blowing your breath in my face!

THEO. You make me sick. *(Moves into back room. Sits on bed.)*

ADELE. *(Enters from upstairs, dressed in smart Saks Fifth Avenue outfit.)* Getting tired already, Theo?

THEO. No, just once in a while I'd like to have some time to see one of my women!

ADELE. You being the big industrialist and all that, I thought you had put girls off for a year or two!

THEO. Get away from me. *(Crosses to desk and sits.)*

ADELE. I must say, however—it is sure a good sight to see you so wrapped up in work. I never thought I'd live to see the day, but—

THEO. Don't you ever have anything good to say?

ADELE. I say what I think and feel. I'm honest.

THEO. Honest? You're just hot because Pop decided to do something my way for a change.

ADELE. That's a joke, when you haven't seen him for two whole days. Or, *do* you know where he has gone to practically every night since you opened up this little store.

THEO. He's out having a little sport for himself. What's wrong with that? He hasn't had any fun in a long time.

ADELE. Is fun all you can think of? When *my* father doesn't show up for two days, I worry.

THEO. You're not worried about nobody but yourself—I'm on to your game. You'd give anything in the world to go back just the way we were, because you liked the idea of us being dependent on you. Well, that's all done with, baby. We're on our own. So don't worry yourself about Pop. When Blue gets here tonight with our money, he'll be here!

ADELE. If my eyes and ears are clear, then I would say that Father isn't having the kind of money troubles these days that he must rush home for your pay day.

THEO. What do you mean by that?

ADELE. I mean that he has been dipping his hands into that little drawer of yours at least two or three times a week.

THEO. You ain't telling nothing I don't know.

ADELE. What about your friend Blue?

THEO. I can handle him.

ADELE. I hope so, since it is a known fact that he can be pretty evil when he thinks someone has done him wrong— and it happened once, in a bar uptown, he actually killed a man.

THEO. You're lying. *(He moves quickly*

to shop entrance.) Bobby, have you heard anything about Blue killing a man?

(BOBBY, seated in the barber's chair, looks at him, then turns away, not answering. THEO returns to the back room.)

ADELE. Asking him about it is not going to help you. Ask yourself a few questions and you will know that you are no better than Blue—because it is you two who are the leaders of those mysterious store raids on 125th Street, and your ace boy on those robberies is no one other than your brother, Bobby Parker!

THEO. Bobby!

ADELE. I don't know why that should surprise you, since he is known as the swiftest and coolest young thief in Harlem.

THEO. I didn't know about Bobby— *who told you!*

ADELE. As you well know by now, I've been getting around lately, and I meet people, and people like to have something to talk about, and you know something: this place is becoming the talk along every corner and bar on the Avenue!

THEO. You're just trying to scare me.

ADELE. I wish to God I was. *(Starts out.)*

THEO. Where are you going?

ADELE. *(Stops, turns abruptly.)* Out. Do you mind?

THEO. *That's all you ever do!*

ADELE. Yes, you're right.

THEO. They tell me you're going with Wilmer Robinson?

ADELE. Yes, that's true. *(Moving through shop toward door.)*

(BOBBY doesn't move from the barber's throne and buries his nose in a comic book.)

THEO *(Following behind her.)* He's a snake.

ADELE. No better or worse than someone like you or Blue.

THEO. He'll bleed you for every dime you've got!

ADELE. So what. He treats me like a woman, and that's more than I can say for any man in this house!

THEO. He'll treat you like a woman until he's gotten everything he wants, and then he's gon' split your ass wide open!

ADELE. *(Turns sharply at door.)* Theooooooooooooo!

(Pause.)

You talk like that to me because you don't know how to care for the fact that I am your sister.

THEO. But why are you trying to break us up? Why?

ADELE. I don't have to waste that kind of good time. I can wait for you to bust it up yourself. Good night! *(Slams the door behind herself.)*

(THEO stands with a long, deep look in his eyes, then goes down cellar. MR. PARKER steps into the shop, all dapper, dressed up to a fare-thee-well, holding a gold-top cane in one hand and a book in the other. BOBBY stares at him, bewildered.)

BOBBY. What's that you got on?

MR. PARKER. What does it look like?

BOBBY. Nothing.

MR. PARKER. You call this nothing!

BOBBY. Nothing—I mean, I didn't mean nothing when I asked you that question.

MR. PARKER. Where's Theo?

BOBBY. In the back, working.

MR. PARKER. Good! Shows he's got his mind stretched out for good and great things. *(Hangs up hat and puts away cane.)*

BOBBY. He's been stretching his mind out to find out where you been.

MR. PARKER. Where I been is none of his business, Blue is the man to think about. It's pay day, and I wanta know, where the hell is he! *(Checks his watch,* taps BOBBY, *indicating he should step down from chair.*)

BOBBY. *(Hops down from chair. PARKER sits.)* Whatcha reading?

MR. PARKER. A book I picked up yesterday. I figured since I'm in business I might as well read a businessman's book.

BOBBY. Let me see it. *(Takes the book in his hand.) The Thief's Journal,* by Jean Gin-nett. *(Fingering through pages.)* Is it a good story?

MR. PARKER. So far—

BOBBY. *(Hands it back.)* What's it all about?

MR. PARKER. A Frenchman who was a thief.

BOBBY. Steal things?

MR. PARKER. Uh-huh.

BOBBY. Where did he get all that time to write a book?

MR. PARKER. Oh, he had the time all right, 'cause he spent most of it in jail.

BOBBY. Some thief!

MR. PARKER. The trouble with this bird is that he became a thief and then he became a thinker.

BOBBY. No shucking!

MR. PARKER. No shucking. But it is my logicalism that you've got to become a thinker and then you become a crook! Or else, why is it when you read up on some of these politicians' backgrounds you find they all went to one of them big law colleges? That's where you get your start!

BOBBY. Well, I be damned!

MR. PARKER. *(Jumps down out of the chair, moves briskly toward door.)* Now where is Blue! He said he would be here nine thirty on the nose! *(Opens the door and JENKINS comes in.)* Hey, Jenkins! What's up!

MR. JENKINS. That Blue fellow show up yet?

MR. PARKER. No, he didn't, and I'm gon' call him down about that too.

MR. JENKINS. It don't matter. I just want whatever money I got coming, and then I'm getting out of this racket.

MR. PARKER. Don't call it that, it's a committee!

MR. JENKINS. This committee ain't no committee. It ain't nothing but a racket, and I'm getting out of it!

MR. PARKER. You put your money into this thing, man. It ain't good business to walk out on an investment like that.

MR. JENKINS. I can, and that's what I'm doing before I find myself in jail! Man, this thing you got going here is the talk in every bar in this neighborhood.

MR. PARKER. There ain't nothing for you to be scared of, Jenkins. Blue guaranteed me against ever being caught by the police. Now that's all right by me, but I've got some plans of my own. When he gets here tonight, I'm gon' force him to make me one of the leaders in this group, and if he don't watch out, I just might take the whole operation over from him. I'll make you my right-hand man, and not only will you be getting more money, and I won't just guarantee you against getting caught, but I'll guarantee you against being scared!

MR. JENKINS. There's nothing you can say to make me change my mind. I shouldn't've let you talk me into this mess in the first place. I'm getting out, and that's it! *(Starts for the door.)* And if he gets back before I do, you hold my money for me! *(Exiting.)*

MR. PARKER. *(Pursuing him to door.)* Suit yourself, but you're cutting your own throat. This little set-up is the biggest thing to hit this neighborhood since the day I started dancing! *(Slams door.)* Fool! *(Takes off coat, hangs it up. Goes to mirror to primp.)*

BOBBY. Going somewhere again?

MR. PARKER. Got myself a little date to get to if Blue ever gets here with our money—*and he better get here with our money!*

BOBBY. You been dating a lot lately—

nighttime dates, and day ones too—and Theo's not happy about it. He says you don't stay here long enough to cut Yul Brynner's hair.

MR. PARKER. He can complain all he wants to. I'm the boss here, and he better not forget it. He's the one that's got some explaining to do: don't talk to nobody no more, don't go nowhere, looking like he's mad all the time. . . . I've also noticed that he don't get along with you any more.

BOBBY. Well, Pop, that's another story.

MR. PARKER. Come on, boy, there's something on his mind, and you know what it is.

BOBBY. (Moving away.) Nothing, except he wants to tell me what to do all the time. But I've got some ideas of my own. I ain't no dumbbell; I just don't talk as much as he do. If I did, the people I talk to would know just as much as I do. I just want him to go his way, and I'll go mine.

MR. PARKER. There's more to it than that, and I wanta know what it is.

BOBBY. There's nothing.

MR. PARKER. Come on now, boy.

BOBBY. That's all, Pop!

MR. PARKER. (Grabs him.) It's not, and you better say something!

BOBBY. He—I don't know what to tell you, Pop. He just don't like the way things are going—with you, me—Adele. He got in a fight with her today and she told him about Blue killing a man.

MR. PARKER. Is it true?

BOBBY. Yeah. Blue killed this man one time for saying something about his woman, and this woman got a child by Blue but Blue never married her and so this man started signifying about it. Blue hit him, the man reached for a gun in his pocket, Blue took the gun from him, and the—man started running, but by that time Blue had fire in his eyes, and he shot the man three times.

MR. PARKER. Well . . .

BOBBY. Blue got only two years for it!

MR. PARKER. Two years, hunh? That's another thing I'm gon' throw in his face tonight if he tries to get smart with me. Ain't that something. Going around bumping people off, and getting away with it too! What do he think he is, white or something!

(THEO comes in and sits at desk. MR. PARKER checks his watch.)

I'm getting tired of this! (Moves into back room.) Where's that friend of yours? I don't have to wait around this barbershop all night for him. It's been two months now, and I want my money! When I say be here at nine thirty, I mean be here!

THEO. (Rising from desk.) Where have you been, Pop?

MR. PARKER. That's none of your business! Now where is that man with my money!

THEO. Money is not your problem— you've been spending it all over town! And you've been taking it out of this desk!

MR. PARKER. So? I borrowed a little.

THEO. You call four hundred dollars a little! Now I've tried to fix these books so it don't show too big, and you better hope Blue don't notice it when he starts fingering through these pages tonight.

MR. PARKER. To hell with Blue! It's been two months now, and he ain't shown us a dime!

THEO. What are you doing with all that money, Pop?

MR. PARKER. I don't have to answer to you! I'm the boss here. And another thing, there's a lot about Blue and this association I want to know about. I want a position! I don't have to sit around here every month or so, waiting for somebody to bring me my money.

THEO. Money! Money! That's all you can think about!

MR. PARKER. Well, look who's talking.

You forget this was all your idea. Remember what I told you about starting something and sticking with it. What is it now, boy? The next thing you'll tell me is that you've decided to become a priest or something. What's the new plan, Theo?

THEO. No new plans, Pop. I just don't want us to mess up. Don't you understand—things must be done right, or else we're going to get ourselves in jail. We have to be careful, we have to think about each other all the time. I didn't go into this business just for myself, I wasn't out to prove how wrong Adele was. I just thought the time had come for us to do something about all them years we laid around here letting Mama kill herself!

MR. PARKER. I have told you a thousand times I don't wanta hear any talk about your mama. She's dead, damnit! So let it stay that way! (Moves toward shop.)

THEO. All right, let's talk about Adele then.

MR. PARKER. (Stopping at steps.) What about her?

THEO. She's out of this house every night.

MR. PARKER. Boy, you surprise me. What do you think she should do, work like a dog all day and then come to this house and bite her fingernails all night?

THEO. She's got herself a boy friend too, and—

MR. PARKER. (Crossing to counter.) Good! I got myself a girl friend, now that makes two of us!

THEO. (Following him.) But he's—aw, what's the use. But I wish you'd stay in the shop more!

MR. PARKER. That's too bad. I have things to do. I don't worry about where you're going when you leave here.

THEO. I don't go anywhere and you know it. If I did, we wouldn't do an hour's business. But we have been doing great business! And you wanta know why? They love it! Everybody loves the way ol' Theo brews corn! Every after-hours joint is burning with it! And for us to do that kind of business, I've had to sweat myself down in this hole for something like sixteen hours a day for two whole months!

MR. PARKER. What do you want from me?

THEO. I just want you here in the shop with me, so at least we can pretend that this is a barbershop. A cop walked through that door today while I had three customers in here, and I had to put one of them in that chair and cut his hair.!

MR. PARKER. How did you make out?

THEO. Pop, I don't need your jokes!

MR. PARKER. All right, don't get carried away. (Goes to THEO and puts his arm around the boy's shoulders.) I'll make it my business to stay here in the shop with you more.

THEO. And make Blue guarantee me some help.

MR. PARKER. You'll get that too. But you've got to admit one thing, though— you've always been a lazy boy. I didn't expect you to jump and all of a sudden act like John Henry!

THEO. I have never been lazy. I just didn't wanta break my back for the man!

MR. PARKER. Well, I can't blame you for that. I know, because I did it. I did it when they didn't pay me a single dime!

BOBBY. When was that?

MR. PARKER. When I was on the chain gang!

BOBBY. Now you know you ain't never been on no chain gang!

MR. PARKER. (Holds up two fingers.) Two months, that's all it was. Just two months.

BOBBY. Two months, my foot!

MR. PARKER. I swear to heaven I was. It was in 19-something, I was living in

Jersey City, New Jersey. . . . (*Crosses to throne and sits.*)

BOBBY. Here we go with another story!

MR. PARKER. That was just before I started working as a vaudeville man, and there was this ol' cousin of mine we used to call "Dub," and he had this job driving a trailer truck from Jersey City to Jacksonville, Florida. One day he asked me to come along with him for company. I weren't doing nothing at the time, and—

BOBBY. As usual.

MR. PARKER. I didn't say that! Anyway, we drove along. Everything was fine till we hit Macon, Georgia. We weren't doing a thing, but before we knew it this cracker police stopped us, claiming we'd ran through a red light. He was yelling and hollering and, boyyy, did I get mad—I was ready to get a hold of that cracker and work on his head until . . .

BOBBY. Until what?

MR. PARKER. Until they put us on the chain gang, and the chain gang they put us on was a chain gang and a half! I busted some rocks John Wayne couldn't've busted! I was a rock-busting fool! (*Rises and demonstrates how he swung the hammer.*) I would do it like this! I would hit the rock, and the hammer would bounce—bounce so hard it would take my hand up in the air with it—but I'd grab it with my left hand and bring it down like this: Hunh! (*Carried away by the rhythm of his story, he starts twisting his body to the swing of it.*) It would get so good to me, I'd say: Hunh! Yeah! Hunh! I'd say, Ooooooooooooweeeee! I'm wide open now! (*Swinging and twisting.*) Yeah, baby, I say, Hunh! Sooner or later that rock would crack! Old Dub ran into a rock one day that was hard as Theo's head. He couldn't bust that rock for nothing. He pumped and swung, but that rock would not move. So finally he said to the captain: "I'm sorry, Cap, but a elephant couldn't break this rock." Cap didn't wanna hear nothing. He said, "Well, Dub, I wanna tell you something—your lunch and your supper is in the middle of that rock." On the next swing of the hammer, Dub busted that rock into a thousand pieces! (*Laughs.*) I'm telling you, them crackers is mean. Don't let nobody tell you about no Communists, Chinese, or anything: there ain't nothing on this earth meaner and dirtier than an American-born cracker! We used to sleep in them long squad tents on the ground, and we was all hooked up to this one big long chain: the guards had orders to shoot at random in the dark if ever one of them chains would rattle. You couldn't even turn over in your sleep! (*Sits on throne.*)

BOBBY. A man can't help but turn over in his sleep!

MR. PARKER. Not on this chain gang you didn't. You turn over on this chain gang in your sleep and your behind was shot! But if you had to, you would have to wake up, announce that you was turning over, and then you go back to sleep!

BOBBY. What!

MR. PARKER. Just like this. (*Illustrating physically.*) "Number 4 turning over!" But that made all the chains on the other convicts rattle, so they had to turn over too and shout: "Number 5 turning over! Number 6 turning over! Number 7!"

THEO. Why don't you stop it!

MR. PARKER. I ain't lying!

BOBBY. Is that all?

MR. PARKER. Yeah, and I'm gon' get Adele to type that up on my typewriter! (*Goes to the window.*) Now where the hell is that Blue Haven!

MR. JENKINS. (*Rushing in.*) Did he show up yet?

MR. PARKER. Naw, and when he does, I'm—

MR. JENKINS. I told you I didn't trust that boy—who knows where he is! Well,

I'm going out there and get him! (*Starts back out.*)

MR. PARKER. (*Grabs him by the arm.*) Now don't go out there messing with Blue, Jenkins! If there's anybody got a reason for being mad with him, it's me. Now take it easy. When he gets here, we'll all straighten him out. Come on, sit down and let me beat you a game one time. (*Takes board out quickly.*)

BOBBY. Tear him up, Pop!

(*Pause.*)

MR. JENKINS. Okay, you're on. (*Moves toward* MR. PARKER *and the table.*) It's hopeless. I been playing your father for three solid years, and he has yet to beat me one game!

MR. PARKER. Yeah! But his luck done come to past!

MR. JENKINS. My luck ain't come to past, 'cause my luck is skill. (*Spelling the word out.*) S-K-I-L-L.

MR. PARKER. (*Shakes up the can.*) Come on now, Jenkins, let's play the game. Take one.

(MR. JENKINS *pulls out a checker.*)

You see there, you get the first move.

MR. JENKINS. You take me for a fool, Parker, and just for that I ain't gon' let you get a king.

MR. PARKER. Put your money where your lips is. I say I'm gon' win this game!

MR. JENKINS. I don't want your money, I'm just gon' beat you!

MR. PARKER. I got twenty dollars here to make a liar out of you! (*Slams down a twenty-dollar bill on the table.*) Now you doing all the bragging about how I never beat you, but I'm valiant enough to say that, from here on in, you can't win air, and I got twenty dollars up on the table to back it up.

MR. JENKINS. Oh, well, he ain't satisfied with me beating him all the time for sport. He wants me to take his money too.

MR. PARKER. But that's the difference.

MR. JENKINS. What kind of difference?

MR. PARKER. We're playing for money, and I don't think you can play under that kind of pressure. You do have twenty dollars, don't you?

MR. JENKINS. I don't know what you're laughing about, I always keep some money on me. (*Pulls out change purse and puts twenty dollars on the table.*) You get a little money in your pocket and you get carried away.

MR. PARKER. It's your move.

MR. JENKINS. Start you off over here in this corner.

MR. PARKER. Give you that little ol' fellow there.

MR. JENKINS. I'll take him.

MR. PARKER. I'll take this one.

MR. JENKINS. I'll give you this man here.

MR. PARKER. I'll jump him—so that you can have this one.

MR. JENKINS. I'll take him.

MR. PARKER. Give you this man here.

MR. JENKINS. All right. (*He moves.*)

MR. PARKER. I'll take this one.

(*Series of grunts and groans as they exchange men.*)

And I'll take these three. (*Jumping* MR. JENKINS' *men and laughing loud.*) Boom! Boom! Boom!

(*The game is now definitely in favor of* MR. PARKER. MR. JENKINS *is pondering over his situation.*)

(*Relishing* MR. JENKINS' *predicament.*) Study long, you study wrong. I'm afraid that's you, ol' buddy . . . I knew it, I knew it all the time—I used to ask myself: I wonder how ol' Jenks would play if he really had some pressure on him? You remember how the Dodgers used to raise hell every year until they met the Yankees in the World Series, and how under all that pressure they would crack up? (*Laughs.*) That pressure got him!

MR. JENKINS. Hush up, man. I'm trying to think!

MR. PARKER. I don't know what you could be thinking about, 'cause the rooster done came and wrote, skiddy biddy!

MR. JENKINS. *(Finally makes a move.)* There!

MR. PARKER. *(In sing-song.)* That's all —that's all . . . *(Makes another jump.)* Boom! Just like you say, Bobby—"tear him up!" *(Rears his head back in ecstatic laughter.)*

MR. JENKINS. *(Makes a move.)* It's your move.

MR. PARKER. *(His laughter trails off sickly as he realizes that the game is now going his opponent's way.)* Well, I see. I guess that kinda changes the color of the game. . . . Let me see now. . . .

MR. JENKINS. *(Getting his revenge.)* Why don't you laugh some more? I like the way you laugh, Parker.

MR. PARKER. Shut up, Jenkins. I'm thinking!

MR. JENKINS. Thinking? Thinking for what? The game is over! *(Now he is laughing hard.)*

(MR. PARKER ruefully makes his move.)

Uh-uh! Lights out! *(Still laughing, answers PARKER's move.)* Game time, and you know it! Take your jump!

(MR. PARKER is forced to take his jump. JENKINS takes his opponent's last three men.)

I told you about laughing and bragging in my game! Boom! Boom! Boom!

MR. PARKER. *(Rises abruptly from the table and dashes to coat rack.)* DAMNIT!!!

MR. JENKINS. Where you going—ain't we gon' play some more?

MR. PARKER. *(Putting on coat.)* I don't wanta play you no more. You too damn lucky!

MR. JENKINS. Aw, come on, Parker. I don't want your money, I just want to play!

MR. PARKER. You won it, you keep it —I can *afford* it! But one of these days you're going to leave that voodoo root of yours home, and that's gonna be the day —you hear me, you sonofabitch!

BOBBY. Pop!

MR. PARKER. I don't want to hear nothing from you!

MR. JENKINS. *(Realizing that PARKER is really upset.)* It's only a game—and it don't have nothing to do with luck. . . . But you keep trying, Parker, and one of these days you're going to beat me. And when you do, it won't have nothing to do with luck—it just might be the unluckiest and worst day of your life. You'll be champion checker player of the world. Meanwhile, I'm the champ, *and you're gonna have to live with it.*

MR. PARKER. *(Smiling, grudgingly moves toward him with his hand extended.)* All right, Jenkins! You win this time, but I'm gon' beat you yet. I'm gon' whip your behind until it turns white!

BOBBY. That's gon' be some strong whipping!

(There's a tap at the door.)

That must be Blue. *(Rushes to the door and opens it.)*

MR. PARKER. About time.

(BLUE enters.)

Hey, boy, where have you been?

BLUE. *(Moves in, carrying an attaché case.)* I got stuck with an emergency council meeting.

MR. PARKER. What kind of council?

BLUE. The council of the Association. I see you're sporting some new clothes there, Mr. P. You must be rolling in extra dough these days.

MR. PARKER. Just a little something I picked up the other day. All right, where is the money, Blue?

BLUE. You'll get your money, but

first I want to see those books. *(Moves to the desk in the back room and starts going over the books.)*

(In the shop an uneasy silence prevails. JENKINS, *out of nervousness, sets up the checkers for another game.)*

BLUE. I see. *(Takes out pencil and pad and starts scribbling on a sheet of paper.)* Uh-huh. Uh-huh . . . *(Re-enters shop.)*

MR. PARKER. Well?

BLUE. Everything seems to be okay.

MR. PARKER. Of course everything is all right. What did you expect? *(Angry, impatient.)* Now come on and give me my money.

BLUE. Take it easy, Mr. Parker. *(Takes a white envelope from his case and passes it on to* PARKER.) Here's your money.

MR. PARKER. Now this is what I like to see!

BLUE. *(Passes some bills to* MR. JEN-KINS.) And you, Mr. Jenkins.

MR. JENKINS. Thank you, young man. But from here on in, you can count me out of your operation.

BLUE. What's the trouble?

MR. JENKINS. No trouble at all. I just want to be out of it.

BLUE. People and headaches—that's all I ever get from all the Mr. Jenkinses in this world!

MR. JENKINS. Why don't you be quiet sometime, boy.

MR. PARKER. I'm afraid he's telling you right, Blue.

BLUE. *He's telling me that he is a damn idiot, who can get himself hurt!*

THEO. Who's going to hurt him?

(They all stare at BLUE.)

BLUE. *(Calming down.)* I'm sorry. I guess I'm working too hard these days. I got a call today from one of them "black committees" here in Harlem . . .

THEO. What did they want?

BLUE. They wanted to know what we

did. They said they had heard of us, but they never see us—meaning they never see us picketing, demonstrating, and demanding something all the time.

MR. PARKER. So?

BLUE. They want us to demonstrate with them next Saturday, and I have decided to set up a demonstrating committee, with you in charge, Mr. Parker.

MR. PARKER. You what!

BLUE. You'd be looking good!

MR. PARKER. You hear that! *(Cynical laughter.)* I'd be looking good! Count me out! When I demonstrate, it's for real!

BLUE. You demonstrate in front of any store out there on that street, and you'll have a good sound reason for being there!

MR. PARKER. I thought you said we was suppose to be different, and we was to drive out that Mr. You-Know-Somebody—well, ain't that what we doing? Two stores already done put up "going out of business" signs.

BLUE. That's what we started this whole thing for, and that's what we're doing.

MR. PARKER. I got some questions about that, too. I don't see nothing that we're doing that would cause a liquor store, a clothing store, and a radio store to just all of a sudden close down like that, unless we've been raiding and looting them at night or something like that.

*(*BOBBY *quickly moves out of the shop into the back room and exits upstairs.)*

BLUE. It's the psychological thing that's doing it, man!

MR. PARKER. Psychological? Boy, you ain't telling me everything, and anyway I wanta know who made this decision about picketing.

BLUE. The council!

MR. PARKER. Who is on this council?

BLUE. You know we don't throw names around like that!

MR. PARKER. I don't get all the mystery, Blue. This is my house, and you know everything about it from top to bottom. I got my whole family in this racket!

BLUE. You're getting a good share of the money—ain't that enough?

MR. PARKER. Not when I'm dealing with you in the dark.

BLUE. You're asking for something, so stop beating around corners and tell me what it is you want!

MR. PARKER. All right! You been promising my boy some help for two months now, and he's still waiting. Now I want you to give him that help starting tomorrow, and I want you to put somebody in this shop who can cut hair to relieve me when I'm not here. And from here on in, I want to know everything that's to be known about this "de-colonization committee"—how it works, who's in it, who's running it—*and I want to be on that council you was talking about!*

BLUE. NO!

MR. PARKER. Then I can't cooperate with you any more!

BLUE. What does that mean?

MR. PARKER. It means that we can call our little deal off, and you can take your junk out of here!

BLUE. Just like that?

MR. PARKER. Just any ol' way you want it. I take too many risks in this place, not to know where I stand.

BLUE. Mr. Parker—

MR. PARKER. All right, let me hear it and let me hear it quick!

BLUE. There is an opening on our council. It's a—

MR. PARKER. Just tell me what position is it!

BLUE. President.

MR. PARKER. President?

BLUE. The highest office on our council.

MR. PARKER. Boy, you're gonna have to get up real early to get by an old fox like me. A few minutes ago you offered me nothing, and now you say I can be president—that should even sound strange to *you!*

BLUE. There's nothing strange. A few minutes ago you weren't ready to throw me out of your place, but now *I've got no other choice!*

MR. PARKER. (*Pointing his finger at him and laughing.*) That's true! You don't! All right, I'll give you a break—I accept! Just let me know when the next meeting is. (*Checks watch and grabs his hat.*) Come on, Jenkins, let's get out of here! (*Starts out with* MR. JENKINS.)

THEO. Hey, Pop—you're going out there with all that money in your pocket.

MR. PARKER. Don't worry about it. I'm a grown man, I can take care of myself.

THEO. But what about our part of it?

MR. PARKER. Look, son, he held me up—I'm late already. You'll get yours when I get back.

THEO. But, Pop—

MR. PARKER. Good night, Theo! (*Bolts out the door, with* MR. JENKINS *following*).

THEO. (*Rushes to the door.*) Pop, you better be careful! I'll be waiting for you! I don't care if it's till dawn!

BLUE. You're becoming a worrier, Theo!

(*Pause.*)

But that's the nature of all things . . . I'm forever soothing and pacifying someone. Sometimes I have to pacify myself. You don't think that president stuff is going to mean anything, do you? He had me up-tight, so what I did was to bring him closer to me so I would be definitely sure of letting him know less and having more control over him—and over you, too.

THEO. What do you mean by that?

BLUE. It didn't take me more than one glance into those books to know that he's been spending money out of the box. And to think—you didn't bother to tell me about it.

THEO. Why should I? I trust your intelligence.

BLUE. Please don't let him do it any more.

THEO. Why don't you hire your own cashier and bookkeeper? *(He goes into back room.)*

BLUE. *(Following him.)* That's an idea! What about Adele! Now that was a thought in the back of my mind, but I'm putting that away real quick. Seems this sweet, nice-girl sister of yours has took to partying with the good-time set and keeping company with a simple ass clown like Wilmer Robinson. No, that wouldn't work, would it? I'd have more trouble with her than I'm having with you. When a girl as intelligent as your sister, who all of a sudden gets into things, and hooked up to people who just don't go with her personality, that could mean trouble. To be honest with you, I didn't think this thing was going to work, but *it is working,* Theo! I've got three places just like this one, and another on the way. A man has to care about what he does. Don't you want to get out of this place?

THEO. Yes, but lately I've been getting the feeling that I'm gonna have to hurt someone.

BLUE. I see.

THEO. You think the old man was asking you those questions about stores closing down as a joke or something?

BLUE. He asks because he thinks, but he is still in the dark!

THEO. He was playing with you! And when my father holds something inside of him and plays with a man, he's getting meaner and more dangerous by the minute.

BLUE. I don't care what he was doing —he is messing with my work! He has gotten himself into a "thing" with one of the rottenest bitches on the Avenue, who happens to be tight with a nigger who is trying to fuck up my business. Now that's something you had better get

straight: it's your turn to soothe and pacify!

THEO. Why should I do anything for you when you lied to me and sent my brother out with that band of thieves of yours?

BLUE. He said he needed the money, and I couldn't stop him.

THEO. But I told you I didn't want that!

BLUE. Let's face it, baby! Bobby's the greatest thief in the world! He's been prancing around stores and stealing all of his life! And I think that's something to bow down to—because he's black and in trouble, just like you and me. So don't ride me so hard, Theo! *(They cross back into shop. He picks up attaché case, preparing to leave.)*

THEO. Blue! Now I don't care what kind of protection you got, but I say those store raids are dangerous and I don't want my brother on them, and I mean it!

BLUE. When we first made our plans, you went along with it—you knew somebody had to do it. What makes you and your brother so special?

THEO. Well, you better—

BLUE. *To hell with you, Theo!* I could take this hand and make you dead! You are nothing but what I make you be!

(Pause.)

THEO. That just might be. But what if tomorrow this whole operation were to bust wide open in your face because of some goof-up by my father or sister— something that would be just too much for you to clean up. What would you do? Kill them?

BLUE. *(Pause. Then calmly and deliberately.)* The other day I went up on the hill to see my little boy. I took him out for a ride and as we were moving along the streets he asked me where all the people were coming from. I said from work, going home, going to the store, and coming back from the store. Then we went out to watch the river and then he asked me about the water, the ships, the weeds—everything. That kid threw so many questions at me, I got dizzy—I wanted to hit him once to shut him up. He was just a little dark boy discovering for the first time that there are things in the world like stones and trees. . . . It got late and dark, so I took him home and watched him fall asleep. Then I took his mother into my arms and put her into bed. I just laid there for a while, listening to her call me all kinds of dirty mother-fuckers. After she got that out of her system, I put my hands on her and before long our arms were locked at each other's shoulders and then my thighs moved slowly down between her thighs and then we started that sweet rolling until the both of us were screaming as if the last piece of love was dying forever. After that, we just laid there, talking soft up into the air. I would tell her she was the loveliest bitch that ever lived, and all of a sudden she was no longer calling me a dirty mother-fucker, she was calling me a sweet mother-fucker. It got quiet. I sat up on the edge of the bed with my head hanging long and deep, trying to push myself out of the room and back into it at one and the same time. She looked up at me and I got that same question all over again. Will you marry me and be the father of your son! I tried to move away from her, but she dug her fingernails into my shoulders. I struck her once, twice, and again and again—with this hand! And her face was a bloody mess! And I felt real bad about that. I said, I'll marry you, *Yes! Yes! Yes!*

(Pause.)

I put my clothes on and I walked out into the streets, trembling with the knowledge that now I have a little boy who I must walk through the park with every Sunday, who one day just may blow my head off—and an abiding wife who on a given evening may get herself caught in the bed of some other man, and I could be sealed in a dungeon until dead! I was found lying in a well of blood on the day I was born! But I have been kind! I have kissed babies for the simple reason they were babies! I'm going to get married to some bitch and that gets me to shaking all over! *(He moves close to* THEO.) The last time I trembled this way *I killed a man! (Quickly and rhythmically takes out a long, shiny switchblade knife. It pops open just at* THEO's *neck.* BLUE *holds it there for a moment, then withdraws and closes it. Puts it away. Then he collects his belongings, then calmly addresses* THEO.) Things are tight and cool on my end, Theo, and that's how you should keep it here. If not, everything gets messy and I find myself acting like a policeman, keeping order. I don't have the time for that kind of trick. (BLUE *exits.)*

THEO. *(After a moment of silent thought, moves decisively to the back-room stairs and calls.)* Bobby!

*(*BOBBY *comes downstairs.)*

THEO. I want you to stay away from those store raids, Bobby.

BOBBY. Not as long as I can get myself some extra money. *(Moving close to him.)* You didn't say nothing to me before, when I was stealing every other day and giving you half of everything I stole. You didn't think nothing that day you sent me for that typewriter!

THEO. I don't know what you're going to do from here on in, because I'm calling the whole affair off with Blue.

BOBBY. That won't stop me, and you know it!

THEO. What is it, Bobby—we used to be so close! Bobby! don't get too far away from me!

BOBBY. *(Heatedly.)* What do you want me to do? Stick around you all the time?

Hell, I'm tired of you! I stick by you and I don't know what to do! I steal and that puts clothes on my back and money in my pockets! *That's* something to do! But I sit here with you all day just thinking about the next word I'm going to say —I'm not stupid! I sit here all day thinking about what I'm going to say to you. I stuck by you and I hoped for you because whatever you became, I was gonna become. I thought about that, and that ain't shit! *(He leaves the shop.)*

(THEO is alone with his troubled thoughts. Suddenly he rushes into back room, gets hat and shirt, puts them on, and goes out into the street.)

MR. PARKER. *(Stepping down into the back room from the apartment upstairs.)* Come on, girl!

(A very attractive, well-dressed, YOUNG GIRL in her early twenties follows him into the shop.)

MR. PARKER. You wanted to see it. Well, here it is.

GIBL. *(Looking about the place.)* So this is where you do your business. Like I keep asking you, Russell, what kind of business is it for you to make all that money you got?

MR. PARKER. *(Heading toward the refrigerator in the back room.)* Come on in here, sweetheart. I'll fix us a drink!

GIRL. *(Moves briskly after him.)* I asked you a question, Russell.

MR. PARKER. *(Still ignoring her question, he takes a jug out of refrigerator and grabs two glasses.)* I'm going to make you a special drink, made from my own hands. It's called "Black Lightning."

GIRL. *(Surveys the room as PARKER pours drink.)* That should be exciting.

MR. PARKER. Here you go. *(Hands her the drink.)* Toujours l'amour!

GIRL. *(Gasping from the drink.)* What the fuck is this! What *is* this, Russell?

MR. PARKER. *(Patting her on the back.)*

Knocks the tail off of you, don't it! But it gets smoother after the second swallow. . . . Go on, drink up!

GIRL. Okay. *(Tries it again and scowls. Moves away as he sits on bed.)*

MR. PARKER. Now, did you think about what I asked you last night?

GIRL. About getting married?

MR. PARKER. Yes.

GIRL. Why do you want to marry me, Russell?

MR. PARKER. Because I love you, and I think you could make me happy.

GIRL. Well, I don't believe you. When I asked you a question about your business, you deliberately ignored me. It was like you didn't trust me, and I thought that love and trust went together.

MR. PARKER. I'm not so sure about that. My son Theo, I'm wild about him, but I wouldn't trust him no farther 'n I could throw a building.

GIRL. I'm not your son!

MR. PARKER. What is it you wanta know?

GIRL. Where you gettin' all that money from?

MR. PARKER. Oh, that. That's not for a girl to know, baby doll.

GIRL. Then it's time for me to go. I'm not gettin' myself hooked up with no mystery man! *(Moves as if to leave. PARKER stops her, then pauses for a moment.)*

MR. PARKER. All right, I'll tell you. I'm partners in a big business, which I'm the president of.

GIRL. Partners with who, Russell?

MR. PARKER. That's not important, baby.

GIRL. Partners with who, Russell.

MR. PARKER. Mr. Blue Haven.

GIRL. *Blue Haven!* Then it's crooked business.

MR. PARKER. Oh no, baby, it's nothing like that. It's real straight.

GIRL. What does that mean?

MR. PARKER. That what we're doing is right!

GIRL. Tell me about it, then.

MR. PARKER. I've said enough. Now let's leave it at that! *(Tries to embrace her.)*

GIRL. *(Wards him off, sits on bed.)* All you take me for is something to play with.

MR. PARKER. That's not true, I wanna marry you. *(Sits beside her.)*

GIRL. You say you want to marry me, but how do you expect me to think about marrying somebody who won't confide in me about what they're doing. How do I know I'm not letting myself in for trouble.

MR. PARKER. *(Ponders for a moment, then rises.)* All right, I'll tell you! We peddle a variety of products to the community and we sell things to people at a price they can't get nowhere else in this city. Yes, according to the law it's illegal, but we help our people, our own people. We take care of business and at the same time we make everybody happy. We take care of our people. Just like I been taking care of you.

GIBL. You take care of me? How? You've never given me more than ten dollars in cash since I've known you.

MR. PARKER. Well, I've got a big present for you coming right out of this pocket and I'm gon' take you downtown tomorrow and let you spend till the store runs out.

GIRL. Taking me to a store and giving me spending change makes me feel like a child and I don't like it and I'm not gonna stand for it any more.

MR. PARKER. Then take this and you do whatever you want with it.

GIRL. *(Taking the money and putting it away.)* Now don't get the idea I'm just in love with your money.

MR. PARKER. Now I want you to stop talking to me about money. I've got *plenty* of it! You've got to understand— I'm the most different man you ever met. I've been around this world, I danced

before the King and Queen of England. I've seen and heard many a thing in my lifetime—and you know what: I'm putting it all down on paper—my story!

GIRL. Your story!

(MR. PARKER moves into shop, gets notebook from behind one of the sliding panels. During his absence GIRL checks under the bed.)

MR. PARKER. *(Re-enters.)* Here it is, right here. *(Sits next to her on the bed, giving her the notebook.)*

GIRL. *(Thumbing through the pages.)* You write things too?

MR. PARKER. I certainly do—and I've been thinking about writing a poem about you.

GIRL. A poem about me!

MR. PARKER. *(Taking book from her and dropping it on floor.)* I'm gon' do it tonight before I go to sleep. *(He kisses her neck and reaches for the hem of her dress.)*

GIRL. *(Breaking out of his embrace.)* No, Russell, not here!

MR. PARKER. Why not?

GIRL. Just because there's a bed wherever we go don't mean that we have to jump into it. You don't understand, Russell! You've got to start treating me the same as if I was your wife.

MR. PARKER. *That's exactly what I'm trying to do!*

GIRL. *(Rising.)* Don't yell at me!

MR. PARKER. All right. I tell you what: I'm kinda tired, let's just lie down for a while and talk. I ain't gon' try nothing.

GIRL. Russell—

MR. PARKER. May the Lord smack me down this minute into hell—I swear I won't do nothing.

GIRL. What are the three biggest lies men tell to women, Russell?

MR. PARKER. I ain't just any man— I'm the man you gon' spend your life with.

GIRL. Okay, Russell, we'll lie down,

but you've got to keep your word. If I'm the girl you want to marry, you've got to learn to keep your word.

(They lie on bed. To her surprise, PARKER is motionless, seemingly drifting off to sleep. After a moment she takes the initiative and begins love-making. He responds, and once his passion has reached an aggressive peak she breaks off abruptly.)

Where do you get these things you sell to people?

MR. PARKER. What are you talking about?

GIRL. You know what I'm saying. I overheard you tell Mr. Jenkins you suspected your son was robbing stores.

MR. PARKER. You heard no such thing!

GIRL. *(Desperately.)* Where do they keep the stuff?

MR. PARKER. Now, baby, you've got to relax and stop worrying about things like that! *(Pulls her by the shoulders. She does not resist.)* Come here. *(He pulls her down to the bed, takes her into his arms and kisses her, reaching again for the hem of her dress.)*

GIRL. *(Struggling, but weakening to his ardor.)* Russell, you said you wouldn't do nothing!

MR. PARKER. I ain't! I just want to get a little closer to you!

GIRL. Russell, not here!

MR. PARKER. Just let me feel it a little bit!

GIRL. You swore to God, Russell!

(THEO comes in the front door and heads toward back room.)

MR. PARKER. I ain't gon' do nothing!

GIRL. *(Hears THEO.)* Russell! Russell! Somebody is out there!

MR. PARKER. *(Jumps up quickly.)*

(THEO stands before him.)

What are you doing here?

THEO. The question is, *what are you doing!*

MR. PARKER. I have been having a private talk with a good friend of mine. Now get out of here!

(GIRL jumps up, moving past MR. PARKER.)

MR. PARKER. *(Stopping her.)* Where are you going?

GIRL. Home!

MR. PARKER. Hold it now, honey!

GIRL. I never should have come here in the first place!

MR. PARKER. No, you're not going anywhere. This is my place and you don't have to run off because of this Peeping Tom!

THEO. Pop, it's time to give us our money.

MR. PARKER. You'll get your share tomorrow and not before!

THEO. I want it now before you give it all to that girl. Pop, cut that broad loose!

MR. PARKER. What was that?

THEO. I said, cut her loose! She don't need an old man like you, she's just pumping you for information. That bitch is a hustler!

MR. PARKER. *(Slaps THEO with the back of his hand.)* Bite your tongue!

GIRL. I think I better go, Russell. *(Heads for the front door.)*

MR. PARKER. *(Following her.)* Okay, but I'll be right with you as soon as I get things straight here. You will be waiting for me, won't you?

GIRL. Sure!

MR. PARKER. You run along now and I'll be right over there.

(GIRL exits.)

(PARKER whirls back into shop.) What do you think you're doing, boy?

THEO. Just be careful, Pop. Please be careful.

MR. PARKER. If there's anybody I got

to be careful of, it's you! You lying selfish sonofabitch! You think I don't know about you and Blue running that gang of thieves—about you sending your own brother out there with them?

THEO. I didn't do that!

MR. PARKER. If Bobby gets hurt out on them streets, I'm gonna kill you, boy! I'm gonna kill you. *(Hurriedly collects hat and coat.)*

THEO. You're not worried about Bobby! All you can think of is the money you're rolling in. The clothes. And that stupid outfit you've got on.

(ADELE comes in from the street, obviously distraught.)

MR. PARKER. What's wrong with you? Are you drunk? *(Moves in. ADELE doesn't answer, so he moves off.)*

THEO. Of course she's drunk. What did you expect—did you think everything would stop and stand still while you were being reborn again!

MR. PARKER. What do you want from me? Call this whole thing off? It was your idea, not mine! But now that I've got myself something—I'm not going to throw it away for nobody!

THEO. But can't you see what's happening here?

MR. PARKER. If she wants to be a drunken wench, let her! I'm not going to take the blame. And as for you— *(Fumbles in his coat pocket.)* If you want this money, you can take it from me—I can throw every dollar of it into the ocean if I want to! You can call me a fool too, but I'm a *burning fool!* I'm going to marry that little girl. She is not a whore! She is a woman! And I'm going to marry her! And if the two of you don't like it, you can kiss my ass! *(Bolts out into the street.)*

THEO. You're not drunk. What happened?

ADELE. *(Heading for the back room.)*

What does it look like. Wilmer hit me.

THEO. *(Following.)* Why?

ADELE. *(Sits on bed.)* He caught me in Morgan's with a friend of his after I had lied about going bowling with the girls. He just walked in and started hitting me, over and over again. His friend just stood there pleading with him not to hit me, but he never did anything to stop him. I guess he figured, "Why should I risk getting myself killed over just another piece of ass?" I thought he was going to kill me but then Blue came in with some of his friends and they just grabbed him by the arms and took him away.

THEO. Was Bobby with them?

ADELE. I couldn't tell.

THEO. Damnit. Everything gets fucked up!

ADELE. It had to, because you don't think. If you're going to be a crook, you don't read a comic book for research, you don't recruit an old black man that's about to die!

THEO. No matter what you do, he's gon' die anyway. This whole place was built for him to die in—so you bite, you scratch, you kick: you do anything to stay alive!

ADELE. Yes, you bite! You scratch, you steal, you kick, and you get killed anyway! Just as I was doing, coming back here to help Momma.

THEO. Adele, I'm sick and tired of your talk about sacrifices. You were here because you had no other place to go. You just got scared too young and too soon.

ADELE. You're right. All I was doing was waiting for her to die so I could get on with what I thought I wanted to do with myself. But, God, *she took so long to die!* But then I found myself doing the same things she had done, taking care of three men, trying to shield them from the danger beyond that door, *but who the hell ever told every black woman she was some kind of goddamn savior!* Sure, this place was built for us to die in, but if we aren't very careful, Theo—that can actually happen. Good night. *(Heads for the stairs.)*

THEO. Adele—

(She stops in her tracks and turns.)

I've decided that there's going to be no more of Blue's business here. It's over. We're geting out.

(After a long pause.)

ADELE. Theo, do you really mean it?

(THEO nods yes.)

ADELE. What about Daddy?
THEO. He will have to live with it. This set-up can't move without me.
ADELE. And Bobby?
THEO. I'll take care of him.
ADELE. That's fine, Theo. We'll throw the old things into the river—and we'll try something new: I won't push and you won't call me a bitch! *(Goes upstairs.)*

(THEO picks up his father's notebook from the floor beside the bed. A knock at the door.)

THEO. We're closed!

(The knocking continues.)

THEO. WE'RE CLOSED!

(The knocking turns to banging and a voice calls out to THEO. He rushes to the door and opens.)

THEO. I SAID WE'RE CLOSED! Oh, I'm sorry, Mr. Jenkins, I didn't know that it was you. . . . What are you doing here this time of night?
MR. JENKINS. I want to speak to Parker.
THEO. You know him—he's been keeping late hours lately. . . .
MR. JENKINS. I'll wait for him.

THEO. Suit yourself, but don't you have to work tomorrow?
MR. JENKINS. I have something to tell him, and I'll wait if it takes all night
THEO. In that case, you can tell me about it.

(ADELE comes downstairs and stops on steps leading to shop, looking about confusedly. She has a deadly, almost blank look on her face.)

THEO. What's wrong with you?

(Pause.)

ADELE. Some—somebody just called me.
THEO. What did they call you about?

(She does not answer. JENKINS rises and sets her gently on bed.)

Didn't you hear me—what about?

(She still does not respond.)

WHAT IS IT, ADELE!!!
MR. JENKINS. THEO!!!

(THEO turns to MR. JENKINS.)

I think she probably just heard that your brother Bobby has been killed in a robbery by a night watchman.
THEO. Uh-uh, nawww, nawww, that's not true.
MR. JENKINS. Yes, it is, son.
ADELE. Yes.
THEO. No.
MR. JENKINS. Yes! *(Moves toward the shop door.)*
THEO. *I don't believe you!*
MR. JENKINS. I saw him, boy, I saw him.

(Dead silence as MR. JENKINS slowly moves toward the street exit.)

THEO. You should've seen this dude I caught the other day on Thirty-second Street. He had on a bright purple suit, gray shirt, yellow tie, and his hair was processed with bright purple color. What a sight he was! But I have to say one thing for him—he was clean.

(The lights are slowly dimming.)

Used to be a time when a dude like that came in numbers, but you don't see too many of them nowadays. I have to say one thing for him—he was clean. You don't see too many like—he was clean. He was—he was clean—

BLACKOUT

ACT TWO

SCENE 2

About two hours later, in the shop.
MR. PARKER *and* MR. JENKINS *enter the shop.* MR. PARKER *is drunk, and* MR. JENKINS *helps him walk and finally seats him on the barber's throne.*

MR. PARKER. Thank you, Jenkins. You are the greatest friend a man can have. They don't make 'em like you any more. You are one of the last of the great friends, Jenkins. Pardon me, Mister Jenkins. No more will I ever call you Jenks or Jenkins. From now on, it's Mister Jenkins!

MR. JENKINS. Thank you, but when I ran into Theo and Adele tonight, they said they had something important to say to you, and I think you oughta see them.

MR. PARKER. I know what they want. They want to tell me what an old fool I am.

MR. JENKINS. I don't think that's it, and you should go on upstairs and—

MR. PARKER. Never! Upstairs is for the people upstairs!

MR. JENKINS. Russell, I—

MR. PARKER. I am downstairs people! You ever hear of downstairs people?

(Pause.)

MR. JENKINS. No.

MR. PARKER. Well, they're the people to watch in this world.

MR. JENKINS. If you say so.

MR. PARKER. *Put your money on 'em!*

MR. JENKINS. Come on, Mister Parker: why don't you lie down in the back room and—

MR. PARKER. Oh! No—you don't think I'd have come all the way over here just for me to go to bed, do you? I wouldn't do a thing like that to you, Jenkins. I'm busy—Mister Jenkins. Just stay with me for a little while . . . *(His tone changes.)* Why did that girl lock me out? She said she would be waiting for me, but she locked me out. Why did she do a thing like that? I give her everything—money, clothes, pay her rent. I even love her!

MR. JENKINS. Russell—

MR. PARKER. *(Rising precariously.)* Tell me something, Mister Jenkins—since you are my friend—why do you think she locked me out?

MR. JENKINS. *(Steadying him.)* I don't know.

MR. PARKER. I'll tell you why. I'm an old man, and all I've got is a few dollars in my pocket. Ain't that it?

MR. JENKINS. I don't know . . . Good night, Parker. *(Starts out.)*

MR. PARKER. *(Grabs his arm.)* You think a man was in that room with my girl?

MR. JENKINS. *Yes!*

MR. PARKER. *Goddamnit! Goddamnit!*

MR. JENKINS. Russell—

MR. PARKER. I don't believe it! When I love 'em, they stay loved!

MR. JENKINS. Nobody's got that much love, man!

(Pause.)

MR. PARKER. No, no—you're wrong. My wife—my dear Doris had more love in her than life should've allowed. A hundred men couldn't have taken all that love.

MR. JENKINS. We ain't talking about Doris, Russell.

MR. PARKER. Aw, forget it! *(Crossing toward table.) Goddamnit!* You stumble around like an old black cow and you never get up again . . .

> I have had my fun!
> If I don't get well no more!
> I have had my fun!
> If I—

(PARKER falls down.) Get up, old bastard! Get up! *(Rises to his feet, aided by JEN-KINS.)* Get up and fall back down again. Come on, Mister Jenkins, let's play ourselves a game of checkers.

MR. JENKINS. I don't want to play no damn checkers.

MR. PARKER. Why do you curse my home, Mister Jenkins?

(Pause.)

MR. JENKINS. I apologize for that.

MR. PARKER. Come on, have a game of checkers with your good friend. *(Sits at table.)*

MR. JENKINS. *(Moves to the table.)* All right, one game and then I'm going home.

MR. PARKER. One game.

MR. PARKER. *(Pausing while JENKINS sits down.)* I said a lot of dirty things to my children tonight—the kind of things you have to live a long time to overcome.

MR. JENKINS. I know exactly what you mean.

(JENKINS sets up jumps for PARKER. PARKER seems unaware of it. They play briefly. PARKER stops.)

MR. PARKER. Theo is a good boy, and a smart one too, but he lets people push him around. That's because he's always trying to con somebody out of something —you know the kind: can't see for looking. And Bobby? He wouldn't hurt a flea.

A lot of people think that boy is dumb, but just let somebody try to trick or fool him if they dare! *(Begins a series of checker jumps.)*

(Pause.)

Got a story for you.

MR. JENKINS. No stories tonight, Parker . . .

MR. PARKER. Mr. Parker.

(The last move is made, the game is over.)

(His conquest slowly sinks in. And MR. PARKER is at long last the victor. Rising from the table.) Call me champ!

(THEO and ADELE enter shop from outside, and stand just inside the door.)

(PARKER is laughing.) You're beat! I beat you! I beat you! *(MR. PARKER throws his arm around MR. JENKIN's waist and holds him from behind.)* . . . You fall down and you never get up! *(Still laughing.)* Fall down, old man! Fall down! *(Releases JENKINS upon seeing ADELE and THEO.)* You hear that, children, I beat him! I beat him! *(His laughter subsides as he realizes they are not responding to him. Guilt-ridden, he approaches* THEO, *looks at him intently, then reaches into his inside coat pocket and pulls out the money.)* Here, Theo, here's the money, here's all of it. Take it, it's yours. Go out and try to get happy, boy.

(THEO does not move or take the money from his father's outstretched hand. He turns to ADELE. Her face is almost a blank.)

WHY DON'T SOMEBODY SAY SOMETHING!

(ADELE attempts to speak but PARKER cuts her off.)

I know you have some trouble with me. . . . *(PARKER spies the notebook in the throne, takes it in his hand, and approaches ADELE.)* You have a woman, you love her, you stop loving her, and sooner or later she ups and dies and you sit around behaving like you was a killer. I didn't have no more in me. I just didn't have no more in me!

(Pause.)

I know you don't believe I ever loved your mother, but it's here in this book—read it. . . .

(She does not respond.)

You wanta read something, boy!

(THEO turns away.)

(PARKER slowly crosses, hands the book to MR. JENKINS, and addresses his remarks to him.) I got sour the day my legs got so trembly and sore on the stage of the Strand Theater—I couldn't even walk out to take a proper bow. It was then I knew nobody would ever hire me to dance again. I just couldn't run downtown to meet the man the way she did—not after all those years of shuffling around like I was a dumb clown, with my feet hurting and aching the way they did, having my head patted as if I was some little pet animal: back of the bus, front of the train, grinning when I was bleeding to death! . . . After all of that I was going to ask for more by throwing myself into the low drag of some dusty old factory in Brooklyn. All I could do was to stay here in this shop with you, my good friend. And we acted out the ceremony of a game. And you, boy— *(Turns to THEO.)* —You and Blue with your ideas of overcoming the evil of white men. To an old man like me, it was nothing more than an ounce of time to end my dragging about this shop. All it did was to send me out into those streets to live a time—and I did live myself a time for a while. I did it amongst a bunch of murderers—all kinds of 'em —where at times it gets so bad till it seems that the only thing that's left is for you to go out there and kill somebody before they kill you. That's all—that's out there! *(Goes to ADELE.)* Adele, as for that girl that was here tonight, she's probably no good, but if at my age I was stupid enough to think that I could have stepped out of here and won that little girl, loved her, and moved through the rest of my days without killing anybody, that was a victory! *(Moves to center stage, stands silently, then does a little dance.)* Be a dancer—any kind of dancer you wanta be—but dance it! *(Tries out a difficult step, but can't quite make it.)* Uh-uhhh! Can't make that one no more. *(Continues to dance.)* Be a singer—sing any song you wanta sing, but sing! *(Stops in his tracks.)* And you've got enough trouble to take you to the graveyard!

(Pause.)

But think of all that life you had before they buried you. *(Breaks into a frantic dance, attempting steps that just cross him up. He stumbles about until he falls. Everyone in the room rushes to help him up.)* . . . I'm okay, I'm okay. . . . *(He rises from the floor, slowly.)* I'm tired, I'm going to bed and by the time tomorrow comes around, let's see if we can't all throw it into the river. *(Moves into the back room, singing.)*

> I have had my fun!
> If I don't get well no more
> I have had my fun
> If I don't get well no more—

(A thought strikes him. He turns and moves back to where JENKINS is standing at the entrance to the back room.) Jenkins, you said that the day I beat you playing checkers, you said it could be the unluckiest day of my life. But after all that's happened today—I'm straight— I feel just great! *(Moves to the stairs leading up, suddenly stops, turns and briskly moves back to the doorway leading to the shop.)* Say, where's Bobby?

CURTAIN